Introduction to
LITERATURE
pearson custom library

Pearson Learning Solutions

New York   Boston   San Francisco
London   Toronto   Sydney   Tokyo   Singapore   Madrid
Mexico City   Munich   Paris   Cape Town   Hong Kong   Montreal

Senior Vice President, Editorial and Marketing: Patrick F. Boles
Senior Sponsoring Editor: Natalie Danner
Development Editor: Mary Kate Paris
Assistant Editor: Jill Johnson
Operations Manager: Eric M. Kenney
Production Manager: Jennifer Berry
Rights Manager: Jillian Santos
Art Director and Cover Designer: Renée Sartell

Cover Art: Photography by Chris Beaudoin.

Please visit our website at *www.pearsoncustom.com*.

Attention bookstores: For permission to return any unsold stock, contact
us at *pe-uscustomreturns@pearson.com*.

Pearson Learning Solutions, 501 Boylston Street, Suite 900, Boston, MA 02116
A Pearson Education Company
www.pearsoned.com

ISBN 10: 1-256-22195-3
ISBN 13: 978-1-256-22195-1

LITERATURE

Introduction to

pearson custom library

Acknowledgements

A project as broad, far-reaching, challenging, and path-breaking as *The Pearson Custom Library: Introduction to Literature* could not be undertaken or accomplished without the support and participation of many colleagues. For their contributions, research, ideas, and suggestions, the editors particularly wish to thank David L.G. Arnold, University of Wisconsin, Stevens Point; Lydia M. Barovero, Providence College; Lisa Bickmore, Salt Lake City Community College; Claire Connolly, University of Wales–Cardiff; Allison Fernley, Salt Lake City Community College; Lisa Fluet, Boston College; Clint Gardner, Salt Lake City Community College; Curtis Gruenler, Hope College; Hilary Justice, Illinois State University; Martin Kevorkian, University of Texas, Austin; Lynn Kilpatrick, University of Utah; Susanne Liaw; Mark Lovely, Merrimack College; James J. Lu, California Baptist University; Sarah McKibben, University of Notre Dame; Cristanne Miller, University of Buffalo, The State University of New York; Jim Miracky, College of the Holy Cross; Bill Morgan, Illinois State University; Mark Morrison, Pennsylvania State University; John Mulrooney, College of the Holy Cross; Jamil Mustafa, Lewis University; Lisa Perdigao, Florida Institute of Technology; Jason Pickavance, Salt Lake City Community College; Robin Schulze, Pennsylvania State University; Mary Trotter, University of Wisconsin–Madison; Steve Vineberg, College of the Holy Cross; Helen Whall, College of the Holy Cross; Mario Pereira, Brown University; and Janice Wiggins.

Your *Introduction to Literature* purchase includes access to online resources designed to complement your readings. This Companion Website is located at the following URL:

http://www.pearsoncustom.com/dbintrolit/introlit/student

When prompted, enter the User Name: **ilstudent** and Password: **illearn**

(*Note:* The User Name and Password are case-sensitive, so be sure to use upper and lower case characters exactly as shown above.)

Once logged in, you will have access to the following resources:

> *Link Library.* A collection of vetted web links organized by key terms and literary figures which offer you background and context for many of the selections you'll be reading.

> *The Writing Process.* Advice that can aid you during the writing process. Included are guidelines and suggestions for each phase of writing, from start to finish.

> *Plagiarism.* Suggestions to help you maintain academic honesty, with illustrative examples.

> *Grammar Guide.* Spells out some of the rules and conventions of standard written English.

> *MLA Style.* A brief guide to help you follow MLA style in citing your sources. The Modern Language Association style is widely used for papers in English composition, literature, and foreign languages.

We invite you to explore!

Contents

Why Read Literature

LOOK INTO ANY GYM these days and you'll inevitably see people walking and running on treadmills, riding stationary bicycles, or climbing on Stairmasters, all the while reading—reading books, magazines, and newspapers. The image of a person working out while reading can seem strange, awkward, or even distressing—the sign of a frenetically busy society that forces us to "multi-task." But this picture also serves to capture a basic truth about human experience, for both reading and physical exercise are fundamental aspects of our daily life. In a real sense, reading is no more a choice than physical exertion. All peoples and cultures engage in the practice of reading and writing, if in radically different forms and contexts. There is no such thing as a group of people that does not somehow tell stories, whether through poetry, folktales, mythology, or the written word proper. By the same token, we would be hard-pressed to imagine a truly "illiterate" person, if we understand literacy as an engagement with narrative—experience or imagination expressed through story. As "narrative" beings, we find deep satisfaction in giving and receiving stories, which mythologist Joseph Campbell describes as "the characteristic pleasure of the human mind." Everyone likes a good story, whether it's found in movies, television, newspapers, sporting events, or everyday conversation. Reading literature "proper"—prose fiction, literary essays, drama, and poetry—is perhaps the most challenging and rewarding way to experience stories of all kinds. Just as there are excellent reasons to keep fit, it's imperative that we "work out" our minds and imaginations through the exercise of reading. For many of us, literary reading, like physical exercise, might be something of an acquired habit that initially requires discipline and perseverance. Once integrated into our lives, however, reading becomes a deeply fulfilling pastime—a true form of "re-creation."

We perhaps most often regard literature as an educational medium—an external force that acts on our intellect in a beneficial way. This is what Elizabethan poet Sir Philip Sidney had in mind when he characterized poetry as "a speaking picture, with this end: to teach and delight." The primary revolution of the printing press—independently developed in China (1041) and Europe (1436)—is that it made possible the widespread dissemination of written texts, which no longer had to be laboriously inscribed by hand, but could be inexpensively mass produced and distributed. This invention made education itself a possibility in even the unlikeliest of circumstances. Consider the example of the late African-American activist Malcolm X. Imprisoned in 1944 for burglary, Malcolm became discouraged at his inability to write letters. In his famous *Autobiography of Malcolm X* (1965), he writes "in the street I had been the most articulate hustler out there . . . But now, trying to write simple English, I not only wasn't articulate, I wasn't even functional." Malcolm ultimately resorted to copying every entry in the prison library's dictionary, an almost unimaginable task that dramatically improved his vocabulary and whetted his appetite for literature that ranged from Aesop's Fables to W. E. B. Du Bois's *The Souls of Black Folk*. Long after "lights out," Malcolm continued to read by the faint light available through his cell door. Recalling the "homemade education" that he achieved in prison, Malcolm declares that "ten guards and the warden couldn't have torn me out of those books . . . I have often reflected upon the new vistas that reading opened to me. I knew right there in prison that reading had changed forever the course of my life." Malcolm X's dramatic encounter with the written word illustrates the liberative potential of reading—"the ability to read," he affirms would "awake inside me some long dormant craving to be mentally alive."

The experience of Malcolm X exemplifies the ways in which reading involves more than intellectual development, inspiring a profound spiritual, psychological, and political "awakening." This is precisely the vision of reading asserted by the transcendentalist philosopher Ralph Waldo Emerson. Writing over a century before Malcolm X, Emerson argues in his address "The American Scholar" (1837) that colleges should not simply drill students through rote memorization, but should rather seek to "gather from far every ray of various genius to their hospitable halls, and, by the concentrated fires, set the hearts of their youth on flame." Although he hardly could have imagined it, Emerson theorized what Malcolm X put into practice: "One must be an inventor to read well . . . There is then creative reading as well as creative writing. When the mind is braced by labor and invention, the page of whatever book we read becomes luminous with manifold allusion." For Emerson the text "lights up" only when a particular reader finds in it something interesting, significant, or personally relevant. We are not mere empty receptacles ready to be filled with information, but living beings who are inspired by literary encounters to explore and transform ourselves. We might at first immerse ourselves in those narratives that we find interesting and pleasurable—many of us begin by reading "popular" literatures such as detective and adventure stories, historical romance novels, westerns, or horror and science fiction. You might have been warned against the deleterious effects of "junk fiction" (to use Thomas J. Roberts's phrase); for the last few centuries, cultural authorities have pronounced such materials textual narcotics that will become "addictive" and "rot your brain." In a sense, however, the matter doesn't matter, because the point is to make reading habitual and to examine our responses to the books that we enjoy. Literary critic and novelist C. S. Lewis assures us that a youngster reading *Treasure Island* with a flashlight under the blanket enjoys a more authentic literary experience than the adults pretentiously discussing the latest literary trends in the living room. But we all eventually come upon books that seem boring, unsettling, or even downright shocking. Indeed, most canonical and experimental (i.e., "good" and "serious") writers work within the conventions of popular genres in order to creatively frustrate their readers' expectations. These more arduous reading experiences prove at times to be difficult; but even painful or tedious textual encounters help us to better understand our deepest desires, aspirations, and anxieties.

Literary encounters can be pivotal—as Lewis suggests, "The first reading of some literary work is often, for the literary, an experience so momentous that only experiences of love, religion or bereavement can furnish a standard of comparison." For this very reason, committed readers crave the peace and quiet to pursue their passion. The experience of literature is therefore most often a solitary one; those reading amidst a crowd—on a bus, at a coffee shop, or in the gym—seem lost in another world. A few hundred years ago, some critics actually feared that the solitary experience of reading a novel could become a form of autoerotic gratification. This is perhaps why, in one of the most famous moments in his 1797 autobiography, Benjamin Franklin confides, "In order to secure my credit and character as a tradesman, I took care not only to be in *reality* industrious and frugal, but to avoid the appearances to the contrary. I dressed plain, and was seen at no places of idle diversion. I never went out afishing or shooting; a book indeed sometimes debauched me from my work, but that was seldom, was private, and gave no scandal." It is interesting to note that Franklin, a great lover of books, includes reading in his catalog of idle diversions as a kind of "debauchery" that might distract one from more pressing concerns of business and public life. Under the neoclassical Enlightenment ideals of democracy and public service, an overindulgence in anything, including the personally enriching practice of reading, could appear unduly self-involved (indeed, the word "idiot" derives from the Greek work for "private person"). But there is another very real sense in which reading provides a sense of connection with the human community at large. Literature allows us to "get over ourselves" and for a moment, at least, enter into another's vision and perspective. Although, as Lewis writes, "Each of us by nature sees the whole world from one point of view, . . . We want to see with other eyes, to imagine with other imaginations, to feel with other hearts, as well as with our own." And the personal "enlargement" afforded by reading literature has immediate consequences for society at large. A 2004 study conducted by the National Endowment for the Arts concludes that those who read are more likely to visit museums, attend performing arts events, and serve their communities through volunteer or charity work. Franklin himself believed that universal literacy, supported by a system of public libraries, played a central role in the life of a democratic society: "These libraries have improved the general conversation of the Americans, made the common tradesmen and farmers as intelligent as most gentlemen from other countries, and perhaps have contributed in some degree to the stand so generally made throughout the colonies in defense of their privileges."

The NEA survey also found that readers are more apt to participate in sports, along with intellectual and social activities. And so we return to our introductory "conceit," or analogy. Exercise and reading parallel each other and, finally, intersect. In reading, as in athletics, we submit ourselves to an external influence, and the result is on one hand the acquisition of knowledge. More than this, however, we struggle with and against literary texts, much in the way that a weight lifter builds muscle through resistance training. Interacting with a poem, story, or play, we open ourselves to a profound and even life-changing encounter. Athletes and readers alike assure us that their pursuits go beyond getting strong or getting smart to engender deep psychological, emotional, sometimes even spiritual transformations. Reading is therefore intensely personal; to read is to place oneself into another's perspective. But the total experience of literature—in all its various dimensions—is also vital to the well-being of our community. Reflecting on the general decline of reading in the United States, NEA Chairman Dana Gioia argues, "America can no longer take active and engaged literacy for granted. As more Americans lose this capability, our nation becomes less informed, active, and independent minded. These are not qualities that a free, innovative, or productive society can afford to lose." Whether you enjoy a book for a few minutes each day (say, while you're riding an exercise bike) or become a scholar of literature, know that reading is a fundamentally human activity that is deeply important to the development of the individual psyche and to the health of the "body politic" as a whole.

Active Reading of Literature

DOES THE FOLLOWING SCENARIO sound familiar to you?

> Sitting in your Introduction to Literature course, you wonder what you might possibly be able to say about the story assigned for today's class. Another student, in response to a question by your instructor, offers an interpretation of the main character's behavior. "How did she *come up* with that?" you wonder. "I read the same story and *nothing* like that even occurred to me. I guess some people just have it and some don't."

Don't be too sure of that. Many people share a relatively common misperception about understanding literature—that some people can read a story, a novel, a play, or a poem once and understand all of its subtle nuances. Not so. In fact, critics, instructors, and experienced students of literature formulate insightful observations not because of some genetic literary superiority but because of the *way they read* a literary work. Those critics, instructors, and students engage in what is called **active reading**, an activity in which they engage with the work rather than simply passively taking in what the author has written. Most of us do a good deal of **passive reading** every day: We scan newspaper or magazine articles; we read letters, notes, e-mails; we browse Web sites. But there is a significant difference between this type of reading and the type necessary to appreciate fully a work of literature. Perhaps an analogy to listening would help explain the difference. Although people are surrounded by music much of the time, they don't always *listen* to it. When the radio is on in the background—in the cafeteria, in the car, at the gym, at home—people rarely really pay attention to the music. They are aware of it, but they don't appreciate it fully. Even when people are dancing, they focus on little more than the rhythm of the music. But when you have just bought your favorite artist's new CD, or when a friend has burned an exciting new mix for you, or when you are settling in at a live concert, you pay attention. You hear the melodies; you listen to the lyrics; you distinguish between instruments and voices. It is at times such as these that you truly appreciate the music. The same holds true for reading: There is a time to treat reading as a chore, or as a type of background music, and there is a time to truly pay attention to it. In order to appreciate what literature can reveal about humanity, its history, and its prospects, it is necessary to take the time to explore or analyze works of literature.

"Easy for you to say," you may be thinking. Actually, it *is* easy for experienced readers of literature to say—after all, they have developed an aptitude for analysis. But this appreciation is not something reserved for the literary scholar. Active reading can be learned, and it can benefit even the most skeptical reader.

Reading Actively

What happens when you read actively? Put simply, you become engaged in a conversation with the author—a conversation that expands when you discuss the literary work in class, read articles about the work, and eventually write a paper about it. These larger conversations, however, begin privately, between the reader and the writer. Since you, the reader, are just feeling your way around the material, you cannot expect to take much meaning from it at first. You and the author do not know each other yet. You might consider the analogy of a couple's first meeting on a blind date, or of college roommates meeting for the first time. You converse, and you understand each other's words, but you do not yet know that your roommate is a very reticent, low-key person whose "It's all right" is the equivalent of your "Wow, this is fabulous!" You only get to know those things after paying close attention to the other person's way of speaking, to his or her "style." You do much the same thing with the literature you read. Some writers are like the first roommate—their prose is clipped, sparse, and seemingly not very demonstrative. Consider, for example, this passage from Bobbie Ann Mason's story "Shiloh":

> Leroy is a truckdriver. He injured his leg in a highway accident four months ago, and his physical therapy, which involves weights and a pulley, prompted Norma Jean to try building herself up. Now she is attending a body-building class. Leroy has been collecting temporary disability since his tractor-trailer jackknifed in Missouri, badly twisting his left leg in its socket. He has a steel pin in his hip. He will probably not be able to drive his rig again.

Others write with an abundant, complex, and rich style, as in this passage from William Faulkner's "A Rose for Emily":

> They rose when she entered—a small, fat woman in black, with a thin old chain descending to her waist and vanishing into her belt, leaning on an ebony cane with a tarnished gold head. Her skeleton was small and spare; perhaps that was why what would have been merely plumpness in another was obesity in her. She looked bloated, like a body long submerged in motionless water, and of that pallid hue. Her eyes, lost in the fatty ridges of her face, looked like two small pieces of coal pressed into a lump of dough as they moved from one face to another while the visitors stated their errand.

You are not always aware of such differences when you first encounter an author. And even if you have already read something by a given author, you cannot know his or her characters, the situation of a story or play, or the theme of a poem until you have lived with them for a while. That roommate whom you were sure you would never understand may well become your best friend by the end of the semester; the blind dates who seemed completely inscrutable to each other may end up spending the rest of their lives together. In both cases, continuing the conversation makes it possible for the parties to understand each other better. So the moral of *this* story is: Look at the mystery of a literary work as a challenge, an adventure of sorts. Getting to know a story, a play, or a poem can be enjoyable in much the same way that getting to know another person is—if you take the time and put in the effort.

The first thing to do when you set out to read a literary work actively is to leave yourself enough time to truly engage with the work. Consider Kate Chopin's "The Story of an Hour" (reproduced at the end of this chapter), for example. This brief story would not take more than ten or fifteen minutes to read passively. But such a reading would at best clue you in to the basic plot of the story. If you are to get a sense of the flavor of Chopin's language, the significance of her imagery, or the inner workings of Mrs. Mallard's mind, you have to slow down and become engaged with the story. This chapter will introduce you to some of the strategies that will help you to enter into a conversation of sorts with a writer, focusing on you and the literary work. There are two stages involved in active reading: **preliminary reading** and **annotating the text**. The following outline provides a glimpse of what will be covered in the remainder of the chapter.

Preliminary Reading
>   Reviewing Prior Knowledge
>   Asking Questions

Annotating the Text
>   Commenting on Language
>   Making Note of Familiar Passages
>   Commenting on Imagery and Theme
>   Making Note of Difficult Passages

Preliminary Reading

Even before you begin reading, you can prepare yourself to get the most out of a work of literature. The first steps to take in active reading might be more accurately called **preliminary reading: reviewing prior knowledge** and **asking questions**.

Reviewing Prior Knowledge

What is prior knowledge? Quite simply, it refers to what you may already know that is relevant to the literary work you are reading. Perhaps you have read something before by this author, or heard the author's name in another class. Perhaps you are familiar with the *genre* (play, poem, short story, novel, essay) or with the setting of the work. In addition to considering what you already know, you may also want to begin thinking about any relevance a literary work may have to your own experience. Often in an introductory literature class, the instructor will briefly lecture about the writer and the context in which a literary work was produced; in an anthology such as this, headnotes provide biographical and other contextual information on the writer; an instructor might also provide a link to an electronic source such as *Dictionary of Literary Biography*. Such resources can be invaluable in helping you enter into conversation with the writer. Consider, for example, the headnote for Kate Chopin (at the end of this chapter). In it you learn that Kate Chopin wrote at the turn of the twentieth century, that she grew up in a household dominated by strong women, and that her best work, *The Awakening*, caused a scandal that all but ended her publishing career. Perhaps you recall a history class in which you learned about American cultural values during that period, perhaps you too come from a home in which women played a dominant role, or perhaps you have read *The Awakening* in another course. When your instructor introduces the story by talking about the sense of freedom that creeps up on Mrs. Mallard after she is told of her husband's death, perhaps you think about what you have come to know about rigidly prescribed sex roles in the late nineteenth century. All of these pieces of information constitute *prior knowledge*, and taken together, they can help you to navigate your way through the story. No matter how marginally relevant prior knowledge seems at first, it can come in handy by making the material you are about to read more familiar to you. Your recollections from the history class and your knowledge of turn-of-the-twentieth-century sex roles, for example can help you understand Mrs. Mallard's sense of married life as a sort of prison. Your own experience with strong women might prepare you for Chopin's characterization of Mrs. Mallard. And your familiarity with *The Awakening* can prepare you for Mrs. Mallard's rather shocking response to the news of her husband's death. Regardless of the extent of your general knowledge or the nature of your personal experience, drawing on prior knowledge offers you a unique perspective from which to consider the story.

Asking Questions

Many students have been afraid, at one time or another, that their questions might sound stupid to others—especially to an instructor. Granted, it is sometimes difficult to ask a question in front of an entire class, but when you are in the privacy of your own reading space, who cares how stupid the question seems to be? Nobody is there to hear it but you, and most "stupid" questions are not stupid at all. In fact, you should be asking questions throughout your reading process, and beyond it in your discussions of a literary work. However, the initial questions you ask can help you make sense of what you are reading. One of the first and most common questions readers have about literary works is, "Why this title?" (In fact, that question is particularly relevant with regard to Chopin's story, since a well-received film version of it was retitled "The Joy that Kills.") When you think about the original title, "The Story of an Hour," you might ask yourself why the time frame of an hour is so significant. With this question in mind, you will be more likely to appreciate the profound significance of this one hour in Mrs. Mallard's life—in one sense, she lives her entire life in that hour. This single question at the beginning of your reading can lead you to a clearer understanding of an apparently significant theme in the story.

More academically oriented questions can lead you to do a little research even before reading a literary work. Often research is considered an activity that occurs well after reading, writing responses, and discussing a work—an expansion, if you will, of the initial conversation between reader and writer. Occasionally, however, you might find yourself interested enough to do a little preliminary research. For example, say you want to learn more about the author before reading the work. Although it is not necessary to have biographical information before reading a text, it is often interesting to get an idea of the mind behind the material. That is why this anthology includes headnotes on each writer. If you consider engaging with a text as a conversation between you and the writer, then it might seem natural to explore the writer's world more closely before reading. Often two parties engaged in conversation try to find out something about one another; in this case, as a reader you might want to know more about the writer with whom you are engaged in this form of conversation. The headnotes provided are obviously a starting point, but you can also explore Web sites such as the *Dictionary of Literary Biography* to discover more about the author. Biographical information will not necessarily unlock all of the mysteries found in a literary work. However, in much the same way that people discussing any subject sometimes like to know a little about their partners in conversation, readers sometimes feel more comfortable if they know something about the author before they begin to read. Learning about the strong female role models in Chopin's life, for example, will probably make Mrs. Mallard's brief experience with freedom more understandable, while the knowledge that Chopin herself was very happy in her marriage will strike a discordant note. Taken together, these two pieces of information should cause you to look more closely at Chopin's characterization of Mrs. Mallard. Thus preliminary questions not only provide you with an interesting perspective from which to read, but encourage you to pay keener attention to the text as well.

Annotating the Text

Whether you have made extensive prereading notes or simply jotted down a few questions, the next steps in active reading will truly be active, engaging you in that conversation with the author that has been promised throughout the first part of this chapter. As you begin to read more closely, you will begin **annotating** the text: underlining significant words, phrases, and passages, as well as writing observations and questions in the margins. Sometimes you will find yourself underlining brief passages that simply grab you. If a passage is compelling enough for you to underline it, then it is probably worth remembering, and it can help you to understand the work better. You might also find your pen drawn to sections that make you think, perhaps a segment in which the writer seems to present in excessive detail a scene that at first appears irrelevant. For example, in "The Story of an Hour" Chopin provides the following lengthy description of what Mrs. Mallard sees from her window as she takes in the news of her husband's death.

> She could see in the open square before her house the tops of trees that were all aquiver with the new spring life. The delicious breath of rain was in the air. In the street below a peddler was crying his wares. The notes of a distant song which some one was singing reached her faintly, and countless sparrows were twittering in the eaves.
> There were patches of blue sky showing here and there through the clouds that had met and piled one above the other in the west facing her window.

You might wonder why Chopin takes such care with a description of a scene wholly unrelated to the train accident, the news that Mrs. Mallard has received, and her response to that news. You might underline a few of the more vivid images in the description and write in the margin something like "significance of scene?" Later, when you have finished your close reading of the story, you will be able to put that annotation together with others to get a sense of how they fit and contribute to an understanding of the story.

As you read you will find other reasons for underlining passages or making notes in the margins. Perhaps a description in a play reminds you of a religious image, for example, or a name in a novel sounds like it comes from a famous Greek myth. Perhaps a certain phrase recurs several times in a poem, or a character in a story has a distinctive way of speaking. Or perhaps you come across a passage that intrigues you—you are not quite sure of what it means or what to make of it. When you encounter such references or uses of language, it is well worth making note of them. At first you might be uncertain about what to annotate, but rest assured, the more you engage in active reading, the more comfortable you will become with how and when to annotate a text. As you discuss your annotations with fellow students, you will also discover that each reader responds differently to a text.

A word of caution: Underlining significant passages is fine so long as you do not overdo it. When you begin to discuss the literary work, and especially when you begin to write a formal paper about it, you do not want to look at pages and pages filled from top to bottom with underlined passages. If you underline too much, you defeat the purpose of the exercise. Remember, underlining should be reserved for *selected* important words and passages.

Now that you are familiar with the how-to, what are some of the things to look for when annotating a selection? Again, what you choose to annotate depends on your experience, your familiarity with the author or the genre, and your personal response to the literature. If you pursue the study of literature further, your critical perspective will also influence the nature of your annotations. What follows is a discussion of some common types of annotation that you might find helpful as you become accustomed to reading actively. The following outline lists the areas that will be covered:

Commenting on Language
  Images
  Descriptions
  Repetition
  Similes and Metaphors

Making Note of Familiar Passages
  Cross-References
  Reminders of Your Own Experience
  References to Myths, Religion, or Classical Figures

Commenting on Characterizations
  Personalities of Characters
  Dialogue

Making Note of Difficult Passages
Intriguing Passages

In the following discussion you will encounter examples from a number of different literary works that might not appear in your anthology. Do not be concerned if you are not familiar with many of them; it is not necessary to understand the entire work in order to appreciate, for example, an author's use of language. In fact, it is only through careful attention to language, dialogue, and references *as you read* that you can come to a fuller understanding of a literary work. (At the end of the chapter you will find a few sample annotations of "The Story of an Hour" for you to compare with your own annotations.)

Commenting on Language

Frequently, when readers are engrossed in a literary work, they pay little conscious attention to the language used by the writer. But in fact, it is precisely that language that makes the work so engrossing. Think for a moment: Do you know people who always tell a great story, or others who can bore and confuse you with even the most exciting material? Anyone who has heard the same story from two different sources understands how important language is to the tale. Naturally, then, one of the first things you will find yourself looking at as you annotate a text is how the author presents the material. The following examples illustrate various uses of language and should give you an idea of what to look for as you make note of significant passages.

Images

You might be familiar with F. Scott Fitzgerald's *The Great Gatsby*. The last line of that book creates a very powerful image: "And so we beat on, boats against the current, borne back ceaselessly into the past." Some of you might also be familiar with William Butler Yeats's poem "The Second Coming," which ends with the question "And what rough beast, its hour come round at last, / Slouches toward Bethlehem to be born?"

Each of these passages focuses on an *image*, a picture created by the writer to help the reader understand what he is saying. Some readers find that Fitzgerald's image suggests a world-weary frustration with life. Even without having read the novel, someone who thinks about these lines can feel the drag of the current (the past) on the boats (people trying desperately to move beyond the past). Similarly, reading Yeats's last lines creates a picture in some readers' minds: A "rough beast" is surely something to fear, especially since the poet tells us that its time (to rule the world?) has come "at last." Even without considering the cryptic reference to Bethlehem, the town of Jesus of

Nazareth's birth, the image is disquieting. It is through an understanding of images like these—an understanding that arises not from the intellect but from the emotions—that readers begin to make sense of the larger work.

Descriptions

One of the most powerful tools a writer has at her or his disposal is *description*; the mark of a skilled writer is the ability to convey a sense of place so that the reader can fully experience it. In *Incidents in the Life of a Slave Girl*, Harriet Jacobs describes the tiny attic space in which she hid from her master for almost seven years.

> The garret was only nine feet long and seven wide. The highest part was three feet high, and sloped down abruptly to the loose board floor. There was no admission for either light or air. . . . To this hole I was conveyed as soon as I entered the house. The air was stifling; the darkness total. A bed had been spread on the floor. I could sleep quite comfortably on one side; but the slope was so sudden that I could not turn on the other without hitting the roof. The rats and mice ran over my bed; but I was wary, and I slept such sleep as the wretched may, when a tempest has passed over them.

Note that there is no flowery language used in this description; the garret is described in the simplest and most ordinary terms. But that is precisely what makes the scene so compelling—to think that this hole, as Jacobs calls it, was her dwelling place for almost seven years. No amount of inflated prose extracted from the pages of a thesaurus could come close to this matter-of-fact, photographic account of Jacobs's prison.

Sometimes, however, it is appropriate to use more lavish language to describe a scene. Consider Elizabeth Barrett Browning's apocalyptic vision in "The Cry of the Human."

> The plague runs festering through the town,
>   And never a bell is tolling,
> And corpses, jostled 'neath the moon,
>   Nod to the dead-cart's rolling;
> The young child calleth for the cup,
>   The strong man brings it weeping,
> The mother from her babe looks up,
>   And shrieks away its sleeping.
>   Be pitiful, O God!

Barrett Browning's language is certainly less ordinary than Jacobs's. Each writer is describing a fearsome place, but the approach is quite different in the poem. The fact that Barrett Browning chooses language that cries out with emotion tells the reader that her purpose is different from Jacobs's. There has to be a *reason* why Jacobs does not choose to use the kind of language Barrett Browning uses; as readers continue to annotate, write about, and discuss the two works, these reasons will become clearer. But the first step toward understanding is simply making note of the fact that the writer has used a particular type of description—an underlined passage, with the marginal note "vivid language," is enough to remind the reader that the description is worth remembering.

Repetition

The importance of repetition in verse is indisputable. From the song-games children play to the music adults listen to, the refrain plays an important role in conveying meaning. In speeches, repetition is particularly effective. Many of you are probably familiar with one of the most famous phrases in modern American history, the "I have a dream" refrain from Martin Luther King, Jr.'s speech at the 1963 March on Washington.

Even in fiction, repetition can take on the role of a refrain. Consider, for example, the first paragraphs of Leslie Marmon Silko's short story "Yellow Woman." At the opening of the story the narrator, having awakened on a riverbank before her lover, mounts a horse, observing that the animal "felt warm underneath me." Then as she talks to her mysterious lover, she remembers the previous night and "his warmth around me." Later, as they embrace, she reflects on the way he feels, "warm, damp, his body beside me." At the end of the section, when the lover finally brings the narrator to his house, he asks her to "come inside where it's warm." If you read this section of the short story closely, you cannot help but make a mental note of the repetition of the word "warm." Clearly, that sensation is important to the narrator. Simply making note of this refrain, either by underlining the repeated words or by writing a margin note, will inform your reading of the rest of the story.

Similes and Metaphors

Perhaps the most powerful tools of language that the writer can use are similes and metaphors. Sometimes referred to as *figurative language*, similes and metaphors allow the writer to use a familiar image to help explain something that might not be familiar to the reader, or to convey a particular impression. In Nadine Gordimer's novel *A Sport of Nature*, for example, the following simile appears: "He talked about 'his book' as a companion and a leg-iron by which he had been shackled a long time, dragging it around the world with him." Comparing a book that a person is writing to the image of a companion is something most of us can understand. But comparing the book to a leg-iron is something else again. Some readers will sense that the task of writing serves to imprison this character.

Metaphors, unlike similes, actually present an equation without using the words "like" or "as." The main character in James Joyce's "The Dead" uses a metaphor to convey how he responds to the sound of a song. "To follow the voice, without looking at the singer's face, was to feel and share the excitement of swift and secure flight." Clearly the song in this instance has a profound effect on Gabriel; he feels himself take wing as he listens.

Both metaphors and similes help readers understand what writers and their characters want to convey. As readers make note of these figures of speech, they can begin to put the figures together with other elements of the literary work to make its meaning clearer.

Making Note of Familiar Passages

One of the reasons why literature provides pleasure for so many readers is the sense of familiarity it offers. As readers enter the world created by the writer, they become familiar with language, settings, characters, and action. Sometimes they find material that relates to their own lives, and sometimes they discover references to other works they have read—particularly classics, myths, or religious texts. This familiarity not only provides pleasure, but it also helps readers make meaning of literary works.

Cross-References

Dictionaries, encyclopedias, and other reference books make frequent use of **cross-references**, references in one part of the book to related material in another part. For example, in an encyclopedia entry on "World Series" you might find the cross-reference "See also 'Baseball.' " In a literary work, the writer frequently makes reference to other parts of the work. The reference might be in the form of dialogue, with different characters saying almost the same thing at different times. Or a writer might use similar terms or images to describe different settings or characters. It is up to the reader to make note of those cross-references. As you read a literary work, you will become aware gradually of references to other parts of the selection. In August Wilson's *Joe Turner's Come and Gone*, for example, characters continually make reference to travel and roads: In the first scene a character talks of men "working on the road gang with the sweat glistening on them." Later in that same scene a new-comer tells where he has come from: "Come from all over. Which ever way the road take us that's the way we go." Toward the end of the scene a woman tells of her lost love, who "was born in Alabama then . . . come to West Texas and find me and we come here . . . [Then] he started walking down the road and ain't never come back." This story is followed closely by a young man's asking her to be his companion: "You wanna go along the road a little ways with me?" When considered together, these and numerous other references to roads, wandering, and travel lead some readers to discover a *theme* of instability and searching in the play. A reader who has underlined such references and made margin notes of pages where cross-references appear will be able to recognize the pattern that emerges.

Reminders of Your Own Experience

Often readers find themselves drawn to works that reflect their own experience. Literature is an exploration of the human condition; therefore it is only natural that readers find characters, settings, or concepts that remind them of their own experience. For example, someone reading John Donne's "The Good Morrow" might recall that feeling brought on by first deep love:

> I wonder, by my troth, what thou and I
> Did till we loved?
>
>   . . .
>
> If ever any beauty I did see,
> Which I desired, and got, 'twas but a dream of thee.

Many people reading this poem will have experienced deep love at least once, and many will sympathize with Donne's wondering what he and his lover did all their lives until they met, as well as sharing his belief that all other beauty is "but a dream of" the only true beauty, his love.

References to Myths, Religion, or Classical Figures

At times readers recognize references to myths, religion, or classical figures in literature. Since most writers are themselves avid readers, such references abound in poetry, drama, and fiction. Consider, for example, Thomas Pynchon's novel *The Crying of Lot 49*. Pynchon's main character, Mrs. Oedipa Maas, must solve the riddle of the estate left by real estate mogul Pierce Inverarity. The names in the novel call attention to themselves; would any reader know real people by those names? This is a fairly clear indication that the names are significant. Many readers will recognize that "Oedipa" is the feminine form of "Oedipus." The fact that Oedipa must solve a riddle of sorts recalls *Oedipus Rex*, the ancient Greek play by Sophocles in which Oedipus must solve the riddle of the sphinx. A reader familiar with the Oedipus story will be able to make use of the reference in coming to terms with the novel.

References to religion also abound in literature. Regardless of the writer's affiliation, he or she can draw on religious images familiar in the culture. In her poem "I dreaded that first Robin," for example, Emily Dickinson calls the bird "The Queen of Calvary." Many readers will recognize the reference to the hill on which Jesus of Nazareth was executed. That reference underscores the dread the speaker feels in the first line, calling up a vivid image of pain, suffering, and death.

In Robert Bolt's play *A Man for All Seasons* a particular reference to a classical figure is found. The "man for all seasons" is Thomas More, the great humanist and Chancellor of England under King Henry VIII. When Henry insists that More sign an oath declaring the king to be the head of the Church of England, More cannot bring himself to comply—even though his refusal means certain death. When told that he has been dubbed "the English Socrates," More replies, "Socrates! I've no taste for hemlock, Your Excellency, if that's what you require." This scene calls to mind quite specifically the ancient Greek philosopher's suicide after being condemned for his teachings. The reference not only emphasizes Thomas More's intense desire to avoid martyrdom, but it also reinforces the greatness of his character. After all, few people in history are as widely known and respected as Socrates.

Perhaps a reader is not familiar with all of the references cited here. They assume some knowledge of the concept of romantic love, of classical mythology, of the New Testament of the Bible, and of ancient Greek philosophers. Every reader encounters unfamiliar references on occasion. Sometimes a literary work is grounded in a culture unfamiliar to you, or sometimes you find references to classic works of your own culture that you have yet to read. Most literary works, however, can be understood without a thorough knowledge of all references; furthermore, many college texts (such as this one) provide annotations to acquaint readers with unfamiliar references. And as you continue your education, you will become better acquainted with your own and other cultures. Regardless, you will always find many references to some familiar material in your reading, and paying close attention to those references can enhance your appreciation of a literary work.

Commenting on Characterizations

Readers come to know characters in literary works in much the same way that they come to know others in real life. The character's own words and actions are often revealing, as is what others (in literature, narrators and/or authors) say about the character.

Descriptions of Characters

In Margaret Atwood's *Cat's Eye*, the young girl narrating the story describes her only friend in school, Carol. The passage reads like one half of a conversation in which one person is describing to another her initial impressions of a third person.

> She tells me her hair is honey-blond, that her haircut is called a pageboy, that she has to go to the hairdresser's every two months to get it done. . . . Carol and her younger sister have matching outfits for Sundays: fitted brown tweed coats with velvet collars, round brown velvet hats with an elastic under the chin to hold them on. They have brown gloves and little brown purses. She tells me all this.

This description reveals to readers a little girl caught up in appearance, probably well-to-do, and perhaps a bit of a snob. (Of course, the narrator also reveals something about herself as she describes Carol: There is more than a touch of envy in the lines.) A reader might underline or bracket this passage and make a margin note referring to both Carol's character and the narrator's envy.

Dialogue

Often a character is best understood through his or her own words. In real life, initial impressions are often formed to a great extent through conversation. It is possible to tell where a person comes from, her social class, education, likes, and dislikes simply by listening to her in conversation. Characters in literature provide readers with the same opportunity. In drama readers expect to become acquainted with characters through their words, since plays are almost exclusively dialogue. But fiction writers also use dialogue to allow their characters' personalities to emerge. Eudora Welty does precisely this in her story "Petrified Man." In the following conversation, the beautician Leota and her customer Mrs. Fletcher are discussing how they met their husbands. Mrs. Fletcher says, "I met Mr. Fletcher, or rather he met me, in a rental library." Leota responds, "Honey, me an' Fred, we met in a rumble seat eight months ago and we was practically on what you might call the way to the altar inside of half an hour."

Mrs. Fletcher's reference to her husband as "Mr. Fletcher" (implying that it is not ladylike for a woman to introduce herself to a man), and her reference to the rental library reveal a woman who prides herself on propriety. Leota, on the other hand, calls Mrs. Fletcher "honey," calls her husband by his first name, uses nonstandard English ("me an' Fred," "we was"), and jokingly intimates that she and Fred engaged in sex in the back seat of a car on their first date. Leota is clearly not one to worry about proper behavior; in fact she seems to revel in her earthiness. Each of these women is characterized without the author's ever having commented on her; the women themselves reveal their personalities. Noting these personality characteristics in the margins of the text allows readers to recall the basis on which they have made judgments about the two women.

You should be aware that characterization is not confined to fiction and drama. Often a poem reveals character as well. In Countee Cullen's "Incident," for example, the narrator relates the story of his first visit to Baltimore as a child. Smiling at a white child, he is shocked when the other child responds by sticking his tongue out and saying, "Nigger." The poem ends with the narrator's lament that of everything that happened during his six-month stay in the city, "That's all that I remember." The innocence of the narrator and the ignorant hatred of the white child contribute significantly to the meaning of the poem.

Making Note of Difficult Passages

At one time or another every reader encounters confusing or intriguing passages in a literary work. Sometimes it is only after several readings and a good deal of conversation that readers can make meaning of such passages. Simply making note of them by underlining and perhaps putting a question mark in the margin is all you need to do initially. Often you will come to a clearer understanding of the passage as you continue to read. If not, you can address the issue as you write about the work and discuss your responses to it with classmates.

Intriguing Passages

Poetry often presents readers with intriguing passages. Because of the need to say so much in so little space, and the need to pay close attention to rhythms as well as to meaning, poetry can be difficult to understand on first reading. But it is precisely that difficulty that makes reading poetry so rewarding—in poetry, perhaps more so than in any other genre, the reader is aware of the interaction, the conversation, between writer and audience. A case in point is Gerard Manley Hopkins's "I wake and feel the fell of dark." The last two stanzas of this poem read as follows:

> I am gall, I am heartburn. God's most deep decree
> Bitter would have me taste: my taste was me;
> Bones built in me, flesh filled, blood brimmed the curse.

> Selfyeast of spirit a dull dough sours. I see
> The lost are like this, and their scourge to be
> As I am mine, their sweating selves; but worse.

Why would the speaker describe himself as "gall" and "heartburn"? Is he tasting something or is he talking about what he tastes like? What is "selfyeast" and why does the "dull dough" sour? And what does sweating have to do with anything else in these lines? All of these questions seem unanswerable at first, but in fact, if you began to address them, you would begin to make meaning of the poem. Simply making note of the lines as you annotate will call your attention to them later as you write about the poem and discuss it in class.

Conclusions

When you begin doing prereading activities and reading actively, perhaps all that you will do is follow the steps outlined in this chapter. That's all right; frequently it is only later, after reflection, that you begin to put some of these annotations together to make meaning of the literary work. You will also develop your own style of making notes and annotating, using symbols and code words that have evolved as you feel more and more comfortable reading literature. In fact, once you become accustomed to reading actively, you might find yourself unable to pick up a literary work without a pen in your hand. You can also find yourself willingly—sometimes eagerly—rereading lines, passages, and even entire sections of a work. When that happens, you will know that you have taken your place in the initial conversation that leads to making meaning of a text.

Sample Annotations

Kate Chopin
[1851–1904]

Awakening feminist

Born in St. Louis to an Irish immigrant father and a French Creole mother, KATE CHOPIN *enjoyed a life of wealth and privilege. During her early years she* <ins>*was influenced heavily by a number of strong women;*</ins> *after her father's death in 1855, Kate was reared by her mother, grandmother, and great-grandmother. Although her upbringing was conventional according to genteel Southern standards, she exhibited an* <ins>*independent spirit*</ins> *at an early age, preferring her books and writing tablet to dancing with shallow young men. Regardless of her tastes, at nineteen she wed a Louisiana businessman, Oscar Chopin, to whom she was* <ins>*happily married*</ins> *for twelve years before his untimely death. A young widow with six children, Chopin returned to St. Louis and began writing. Her first stories were published in 1889, followed by a novel,* At Fault, *in 1890.*

like me!

not like Edna in Awakening!

Chopin gained national attention with the publication in 1894 of Bayou Folk, *a collection of stories that featured settings and characters culled from her years in Louisiana among French Creoles. Soon she was being compared to other* <ins>*"local color" writers*</ins>—*writers who focus on the cultures and customs of specific areas of the country—such as Sarah Orne Jewett and Hamlin Garland. Critics also recognized the influence of French writer Guy de Maupassant, as well as Americans Nathaniel Hawthorne and Walt Whitman, in Chopin's work. In 1897 a second collection,* A Night in Acadie, *was greeted with equal enthusiasm by readers and critics alike. Both turned on the author in 1899, however, when her novel* The Awakening *was published. Exploring the sexual and social rebellion of protagonist Edna Pointelleir, a young wife and mother,* <ins>*the novel challenged existing moral standards*</ins> *and shocked the public. Chopin was accused of fostering immoral behavior with her uncritical depiction of Edna, who chooses suicide rather than succumb to the rigid requirements of marriage and motherhood in turn-of-the-century New Orleans. Reception of the novel was so harsh that Chopin's publisher cancelled publication of her next volume of short stories,* A Voice and a Vocation, *in 1899.*

1890s— rigid morality

Chopin was devastated by the negative response to The Awakening, *which she considered (as do many contemporary critics) her best work. Although she had published twenty poems, almost a hundred short stories—including children's stories, two novels, a play, and several critical essays—in a ten-year period, she wrote very little after 1900. When she died of a brain hemorrhage at age 53, her contributions to American literature were almost forgotten. Her reputation was revived in 1969 with the publication of* The Complete Works of Kate Chopin, *edited by Per Seyersted. Late twentieth-century critics recognized the* <ins>*existential quality of Chopin's work,*</ins> *as well as her courageous* <ins>*social criticism,*</ins> *particularly with regard to women's lives.* <ins>*Chopin's women,*</ins> *from the peasant Calixta in "The Storm" to the middle-class Mrs. Mallard in "The Story of an Hour,"* <ins>*exhibit an independence and vitality rarely found in late-nineteenth-century female characters.*</ins> *Chopin's prose is considered as vividly poetic as that of Hawthorne, and her characters as complex as those of Henry James. In the past several decades she has been recognized as one of the most significant writers in the American canon.*

Edna

🔖 🔖 🔖

one hour?

The Story of <u>an Hour</u>

KATE CHOPIN

KNOWING THAT MRS. MALLARD was afflicted with a heart trouble, great care was taken to break to her as gently as possible the news of her husband's death.

It was her sister Josephine who told her, in broken sentences, veiled hints that revealed in half concealing. Her husband's friend Richards was there, too, near her. It was he who had been in the newspaper office when intelligence of the railroad disaster was received, with Brently Mallard's name leading the list of "killed." He had only taken the time to assure himself of its truth by a second telegram, and had hastened to forestall any less careful, less tender friend in bearing the sad message.

She did not hear the story as many women have heard the same, with a paralyzed inability to accept its significance. She wept at once, with sudden, wild abandonment, in her sister's arms. When the storm of grief had spent itself she went away to her room alone. She would have no one follow her.

There stood, facing the open window, a comfortable, roomy armchair. Into this she sank, pressed down by a physical exhaustion that haunted her body and seemed to reach into her soul.

detailed description of nature -significance of scene?

She could see in the open square before her house the <u>tops of trees</u> that were all <u>aquiver with the new spring life.</u> The delicious <u>breath of rain</u> was in the air. In the street below a peddler was crying his wares. The notes of a distant song which someone was singing reached her faintly, and <u>countless sparrows</u> were twittering in the eaves.

"elixir of life"

There were <u>patches of blue sky</u> showing here and there <u>through the clouds</u> that had met and piled above the other <u>in the west</u> facing her window.

She sat with her head thrown back upon the cushion of the chair, quite motionless, except when a sob came up into her throat and shook her, as a child who has cried itself to sleep continues to sob in its dreams.

strong woman

She was <u>young,</u> with a fair, calm face, whose lines bespoke <u>repression and</u> even a certain <u>strength.</u> But now there was a dull stare in her eyes, whose gaze was fixed away off yonder on one of those patches of blue sky. It was not a glance of reflection, but rather indicated a suspension of intelligent thought.

There was something coming to her and she was waiting for it, fearfully. What was it? She did not know; it was too subtle and elusive to name. But she felt it, <u>creeping out of the sky, reaching toward</u> her through the sounds, the scents, the color that filled the air.

image — animal?

Now her bosom rose and fell tumultuously. She was beginning to recognize this thing that was approaching to possess her, and she was striving to beat it back with her will—as powerless as her two white slender hands would have been.

When she abandoned herself a little whispered word escaped her slightly parted lips. She said it over and over under her breath: "Free, free, free!" The vacant stare and the look of terror that had followed it went from her eyes. They stayed keen and bright. Her pulses beat fast, and the coursing blood warmed and relaxed every inch of her body.

She did not stop to ask if it were or were not a <u>monstrous joy</u> that held her. A clear and exalted perception enabled her to dismiss the suggestion as trivial.

dissonance:
monstrous
|
joy
"joy that kills"

She knew that she would weep again when she saw the kind, tender hands folded in death; the face that had never looked save with love upon her, fixed and gray and dead. But she saw beyond that bitter moment a long procession of years to come that would belong to her absolutely. And she opened and spread her arms out to them in welcome.

There would be no one to live for her during those coming years; she would live for herself. There would be <u>no powerful will bending her</u> in that blind persistence with which men and women believe they have a right to impose a private will upon a fellow-creature. A <u>kind intention or a cruel intention made the act seem no less a crime as</u> she looked upon it in that brief moment of illumination.

And yet <u>she had loved him</u>—sometimes. Often she had not. What did it matter! What could love, the unsolved mystery, count for in face of this possession of self-assertion which she suddenly recognized as the strongest impulse of her being!

important —
loved him

"Free! Body and soul free!" she kept whispering.

Josephine was kneeling before the closed door with her lips to the keyhole, imploring for admission. "Louise, open the door! I beg; open the door—you will make yourself ill. What are you doing, Louise? For heaven's sake open the door."

description
of nature
¶ 5,6

"Go away. I am not making myself ill." No; <u>she was drinking in a very elixir of life through that open window.</u>

Her fancy was running riot along those days ahead of her. <u>Spring days, and summer days,</u> and <u>all sorts of days</u> that would be her own. She breathed a quick prayer that <u>life might be long.</u> It was only yesterday she had thought with a shudder that <u>life might be long.</u>

days...
days...
days

She arose at length and opened the door to her sister's importunities. There was a feverish triumph in her eyes, and she carried herself unwittingly <u>like a goddess of Victory.</u> She clasped her sister's waist, and together they descended the stairs. Richards stood waiting for them at the bottom.

classical
image

Someone was opening the front door with a latchkey. It was Brently Mallard who entered, a little travel-stained, composedly carrying his gripsack and umbrella. He had been far from the scene of accident, and did not even know there had been one. He stood amazed at Josephine's piercing cry; at Richards' quick motion to screen him from the view of his wife.

But Richards was <u>too late.</u>

When the doctors came they said she had died of heart disease—<u>of joy that kills.</u>

dissonance:
"joy that kills"
|
"monstrous
joy"

On Writing About Literature

Literature: Reading, Responding, Writing

LITERATURE EVOKES MANY KINDS of responses, prompting readers to write about their reactions, their insights, and their theories. These responses fall into a variety of categories, but all responses give readers an opportunity to think critically about the text and its situation in the world. Responses to literature also give readers an opportunity to discover ideas and attitudes that can come as a surprise. In fact, good writing assignments often aim to evoke those discoveries and surprises. Responses also cover a wide range of styles and purposes. As a reader, you will have had a variety of experiences in reacting to literature. Think about the following suggestions, noting which kinds of writing you have done and which are new to you. Your teacher will choose among these differing ways of writing when giving you your writing assignments.

Journals and logs, immediate responses

At the beginning, your teacher might ask you to jot down your experience of the text immediately after you have finished reading it or even while you are reading it. These initial responses can be simply your impressions and reactions, or they can be more explicitly guided by either your teacher's questions or the questions provided by this textbook. You will want to ask yourself about the nature of the literary text you are reading. Remember that you are not writing a review of the piece (unless that is the assignment), so you will want to think more critically than about your own preferences and likes and dislikes. What does the work remind you of in your past reading? What other authors tackle these themes? What imagery is familiar, or surprising? What social issues does the work evoke? What do you have to know about history or society to understand the work? These kinds of questions will help you to read more deeply and to ask yourself better questions as well. For short fiction, ask yourself about the characters, the setting, the time period, the action, the climax or major turning point of the story. You will also want to ask yourself what you think of the ideas in the story. Do they speak to you and your life issues? Do you identify with the characters? Have you learned anything about other people by reading the story? Did anything make you mad? Sad? Sorry? Shocked? Pleased? Were you surprised? Annoyed? Disappointed? Confused? Where does the story fit in history? Does it address social issues that are still relevant? How does the story address issues of gender, class, and power? Will you remember the story and tell it to others? Note all these reactions and any others that strike you as important. You will also want to note how the story is told. What is the point of view of the story? Who is the narrator? Do you trust the person telling the story? Do you have the same worldview? If not, what reaction do you have to the author's voice?

For poetry, pay attention to the sound and feel of the language. Read the poem aloud. Ask someone else to read it aloud to you. Listen to the voice of the poem. Try singing it if you feel so inclined. Then write about your reactions to the sound and rhythm of the poem. What did you see as you read or heard the poem? How did the form affect your reading? Did you notice anything particular about that form? What about the words themselves? How do the words work for you? Are they familiar words in new patterns or new words? Where were you in time and place? Do you trust the narrator of the poem? Why or why not? What imagery came to mind? Would any of the lines be worth remembering in the way that you remember your favorite song lyrics? Note your reactions to the poem both as you read it for the first time and when you have read or heard the poem several times.

For drama, you will be responding in a variety of ways because drama asks for involvement that goes beyond the printed page. A play asks the reader to live the life of the drama for the time it takes to read or watch the work. Whose world are you in when you begin to experience the play? What kinds of characters do you meet? Are they characters you recognize, or are they strange to you? Do they have your values and attitudes, or do they challenge your assumptions about the world? How do they relate to one another? Are they trapped in a closed setting such as a house, a castle, a building, or are they in the elements? Where are they in time: within the last twenty years, the last century, before that? Are they in the future? What happens to them, in any case? Are they afraid of life, or are they bold and even a little flashy? Do they act in ways that you approve of and understand, or are they breaking moral and ethical rules you hold dear? What happens to them as a result of their actions? Do you think the results appropriate, natural, and/or shocking? How would you end the play if you were the playwright? Is the story of the play worth your own time and energy? Why or why not?

Analytical papers

Your teacher might ask you to write an essay about the text you have read. Such essays often run around eight hundred to a thousand words, but the specifications can vary from task to task. If you have been keeping a reading log or journal in which you have taken notes and jotted down ideas, you will have many resources for writing. This text also includes writing activities for each of the works that you will read. The most important thing to remember is that no essay exists in a vacuum.

All writing grows from a rhetorical situation. That means you have a role to play as the writer of the essay and that you are stepping into a conversation about the work, even if you are only imagining the conversation at this point. You have to make several assumptions about the reader of your paper, in order to get started on a paper about a literary text. The first, and most obvious, assumption is that your reader cares about what you have to say. Thus you should do some discovery writing. What do you have to say that is evocative and worth a conversation with someone else? What new ideas do you bring to the table? Remember that you will not need to summarize the literary work because the convention in writing about literature is to assume that the reader has read the text and is ready to talk with you about it. Also, you will want to explain and analyze your reactions in detail. Because your reader will also have ideas about the text, you must give clearly thought-out reasons for the argument you make about the text.

Group Discussion

At this point, take some time to talk to friends and class members who have also read the work or works you will be investigating. What have they seen as they read? What do you and they know about the work? Where is it situated historically? What kinds of social issues surround the work? Current conversations about literature tend to form around questions of power, gender, race, and class. Are any of these issues important to this work? How do they come into play? How is the work situated in relationship to the big issues of life: falling in love; finding an identity (over and over in life); social status; facing loss and death; conflict among people and nations? Talk over these issues with one another to see what others think and say. Then you can begin to formulate a paper that will be of interest in the conversation about the work. You will not fall into the trap of saying what everyone else thinks or, on the other hand, of ignoring new and interesting readings of the work. You can begin with these conversations in mind.

Wider Reading

Depending on the time you have available and the expectations of your assignment, you might also want to read what others have written on your topic. Your teacher can direct you to interesting essays that will help your thinking, or you can ask a librarian to help you investigate possible sources you could read. A word of caution: If you do read other sources, you are obligating yourself to cite them carefully and to give the author credit when you use ideas other than your own. Given this consideration about citing other sources, you may find that other writings work exactly like conversations with your classmates. Outside sources can be "conversations" that you initiate. For example, you might want to write about the Southern writer Flannery O'Connor. In a "dialogue" with the author you would find that she herself wrote many essays about both her own attitudes and beliefs and about the subject of writing itself. You might find that her own perspectives enrich your reading of a story or that her perspectives confirm ideas that you discovered as you read, thought about, and discussed the text.

Beginning to Write: Discovery

The first draft you write will help you discover what you think about your topic. Take the example of a Flannery O'Connor story. Perhaps you are from the South and find her characters strange and even insulting. A discovery draft will help you to ask why these characters are so sharply and even cruelly drawn. What effect do the characters have on readers? Analyze your reaction to the text. Why do you think that she draws the characters the way that she does? Why do you react the way that you do? Why does the humor insult you rather than amuse you? What social or cultural facts do you know that will help you in your analysis? Why is your experience different from O'Connor's? All these questions help in your discovery of the analysis you want to do in your paper. During the drafting process, you should try to keep writing, even if you seem to hit roadblocks in your thinking. Work to get the draft on paper.

Reflecting and Regrouping

Once you have a draft, you should look back at the issues that are raised concerning journals. What questions can you ask yourself about your draft? Have you taken into consideration the issues that are important to the conversations you investigated? Have you written a draft that you think is worth going back and rereading? Get together with others from your class either in class in small groups or in other contexts and read one another's papers. What is similar? What is different? How can others help you to be more insightful and communicative in your paper? What have you said that is new and challenging? What have you said that others already thought or knew? Ask your teacher to take a look at your draft and make suggestions. Consultation might be a required part of your class, but even if it is not, most teachers are glad to talk with you about your ideas and your discovery draft.

Adding, Subtracting, and Reorganizing

Nothing is harder than taking something away from a finished draft, but your first task is to remove anything from your discovery draft that your peer readers have found to be obvious or anything that you found in other people's ideas. If it was obvious to them, then it does not add to the strength of your own ideas. Next, add new ideas that you have discovered. This does not mean to add a sentence here or there. It can mean starting nearly at the end, (often we do not really get going until we have written several hundred words), and beginning again. At the very least, it means adding the ideas that have struck you as important as you reconsidered the questions in the journal you have kept. Keep looking for fresh perspectives, and keep in mind the current conversations in literary circles: historical context, social issues, economic pressures, feminist issues, psychological perspectives.

Would it help to know that O'Connor was a cartoonist in college? Would it help to know that she was ill with a fatal disease? Would it help to know that she was an intellectual forced to live with her very down-to-earth mother in a small town far from the friends and entertainments she loved? Could any of this information or these new perspectives strengthen what you have written? Answer these questions and continue writing. Then take a long look at your organization. At this point, if you are not a natural outliner, you should construct an outline of what you have written. Then force yourself to rethink the ways in which you have ordered the paper. What would happen if you took your favorite paragraph or idea and put it first or last? Writers in the twenty-first century are privileged to have computer technology at their fingertips. Use that technology to play with the order and structure of your paper.

Go Back to The Well

Once again ask others to read your next draft. Ask your readers to notice the changes you find most important. It is important to guide a reader's responses to your text. Tell the reader what you have done to the paper and what your intentions were. Ask how well you have met your own goals. Ask for further suggestions, and pay attention. Then consider carefully what you will use and when you will say "enough."

Final Touches

It is true that no paper is ever finished, only abandoned, but you will want to take considerable time at the end of your writing to proofread carefully. That means read each line backwards; ask others to read for clarity and surface issues. Then read again looking for spots where you can be more clear and/or more graceful.

Conclusion

Why write about literature? Why do we go to movies and plays with friends? We want to have conversations with others about what we have seen and heard. It is not enough to experience a poem, play, or story; inevitably we want to think about what we have experienced. We want to analyze our responses, and to analyze the text and its influence on us, and we want to do this in the presence of others. We read literary criticism because we want to know what others make of the texts that are important to us. And we write, so that we can more deeply understand and investigate our own responses, and so that we can show others our thinking. We write to learn and to communicate what we have learned.

Critical Approaches to Literature

Introduction: Why Study Critical Methodologies?

NUMEROUS NEW APPROACHES TO the study of literature have arisen since World War I in response to the formalization of the study of English and American literature. These theories have foregrounded a shifting understanding of the relationship between author, text, and reader. Scholars have moved, since the early twentieth century, from a sense of the literary work as a stable and eternal artifact—and of the author as the controlling figure in the production of that work's meaning—to a sense that the meaning of any literary text is produced by its interaction with its readers, and thus the text's meaning is determined in large part by the social context of both the writing and the reading of it. Embedded in this changing notion of literary meaning is an equally important change in terminology, from thinking about a literary "work" to thinking about a literary "text." Such a change brings to the forefront the impermanence of a text's meaning, as well as its openness to a reader's critical interpretation. Given this, the study of literary theory and critical approaches to literature is driven by an interest in understanding how readers and texts interact, as well as in learning how the culture in which author, text, and reader all participate affects the production and reception of any literary text.

The critical approaches briefly sketched here are listed in a semi-chronological order to reflect when the approach came to prominence, as well as the kinds of influence that they had on one another.

Formalisms

Formalism is a blanket term covering a number of different approaches to the study of literature, all of which are interested in the *form* a literary text takes, rather than its content. The term refers to a cluster of ideas that arose in schools of Russian literary thought during the period surrounding the Russian Revolution. Key figures in Russian formalism include Viktor Shklovsky, Roman Jakobson, and Vladimir Propp. Russian formalism is most notable for having introduced principles derived from linguistics into the study of literature, suggesting that the work of literary critics is best focused not on interpreting the meaning of any given literary text, but rather on studying *how* literary texts work—particularly how they are organized—and whether there are common systems of symbols and rules of narrative devices that can be discovered among many texts. Such formalist criticism relies on a kind of empiricism; the formalist critic understands the text primarily as a structure, a type of machine, that can be studied objectively. Because formalism bears such a close relationship to linguistics, formalist critics often view literature first and foremost as a specialized use of language. The literary text, in this view, brings forward the language used in a text rather than the content of that language. The "literariness" of a work often manifests itself in a dizzying set of deviations from so-called ordinary language. The effect of such literary language on the reader is one of estrangement or defamiliarization, resulting in an invigorated reading experience as well as an awakened sensitivity to daily life.

While few critics today practice the same kind of linguistic formalism as was practiced by critics such as Shklovsky or Propp, certain formalist concepts maintain great significance today. The most lasting aspects of Russian formalism in contemporary literary study are in the analysis of the metrical structure of poems, as well as the use of rhyme, alliteration, and other devices within poetic language. Formalist studies of narrative structure also continue within the branch of criticism known as narratology.

New Criticism

The New Criticism, simultaneously the most influential and the most repudiated of the twentieth-century critical approaches to the study of literature, arose out of the work of post–World War I British scholars such as F. R. Leavis and Q. D. Leavis—editors of the highly influential journal *Scrutiny*—as well as I. A. Richards, author of *Practical Criticism* (1929). These British critics, in many ways founders of the field of English as we now know it, worked in express opposition to the stiff philological tradition of the study of classical texts that dominated the academy to that point. It is no coincidence that these scholars, all working at the University of Cambridge, were of middle-class origins; their challenge was not to simplify the dominant methods of the academic study of literature, but to delve into the very core of composition itself, and the study of it. As many historians of the field of English have pointed out, the movement led by Richards and the Leavises was revolutionary, transforming the academic opinion of English literature in ten short years from one of condescension (i.e., literature was fine for leisure reading, but not for serious study) to one of respect. By the early 1930s, the study of English literature had become central to the humanities. This transformation was made possible, in part, by the fact that these scholars stressed rigorous criticisms of literature, and by the analysis of the elitism that literary studies spawned. English literature was thereby added to university curricula through a mere shift in the boundary between "high culture" and "mass culture"—not by eliminating that boundary.

New Criticism has its origins in the work of Richards and the Leavises, but is largely an American phenomenon. This mode of critical analysis—most closely associated with scholars including John Crowe Ransom, Cleanth Brooks, Robert Penn Warren, W. K. Wimsatt, Allen Tate, and others—arose in the American South as a reaction to the perceived scientism and industrialization of the North. The new criticism stressed, as the cornerstone of its methodology, "close reading," a practice that has become so central to literary studies that we no longer think of it as a theory at all. The method focuses on taking a text apart in a sustained and detailed fashion, then analyzing and interpreting the words on the page with great rigor. Close readings bear a particular interest in tensions and ambiguities suggested within the language, figures of speech, and symbols contained within the text, but also focus on the resolution or reconciliation of those tensions and ambiguities within the "internal unity" of the text.

New Criticism's most radical intervention into literary criticism was the naming of what has been called the "intentional fallacy"; by positing the reliance on authorial intention in literary criticism as a mistake, the New Critics argued that the meaning of a text is not determined by its author, but rather by the text itself. In this fashion, the poem—and it was overwhelmingly poetry with which the New Critics were concerned—becomes a self-contained entity, and the critic is led to restrict his or her attention to that which exists within its boundaries, with no concern for external forces such as cultural and historical context. These critical readings, despite their tendency to empower the critic over the author in the interpretive process, nonetheless foster the illusion that a text can be understood in isolation, and that its meaning is somehow eternal, separated from the interventions of both author and reader.

New Criticism came to prominence at a moment when the study of English literature in the United States was first becoming "professionalized" within academia. The resulting irony is that this mode of criticism, which was founded in the rejection of a culture that was perceived as being increasingly technocratic, itself became a kind of technocracy. The techniques of close reading, once understood as a methodology, were by the 1950s so much a part of English department curricula that they seemed inseparable from reading itself. A number of further interventions into critical methodologies beginning in that decade, however, began to call scholars' attention not simply to the text but to the act of reading itself.

Semiotics and Structuralism

Semiotics, or the study of signs, takes its origins from the field of linguistics, and particularly from the work of American linguist C. S. Peirce and French linguist Ferdinand de Saussure. Peirce noted that signs fall into one of three categories: the iconic, in which the sign resembles the referent (e.g., an image); the indexical, in which the sign is somehow related to the referent (footprints as a sign that someone was there, for instance, or smoke as a sign of fire); and the symbolic, in which the sign is arbitrary, connected to the referent only by social convention (as in the case of language). Saussure added to this understanding in his *Course in General Linguistics* (1915), when he argued that the sign has two parts: a signifier (the material image, or sound, or marks on a page) and a signified (the concept or idea). Saussure also contributed to semiotics the notion that the meanings of signs within a language are determined by their differences from one another (in other words, *cat* obtains its particular meaning by virtue of its distinctions from *cap* or *mat*). Saussure also introduced into linguistics the distinction between *parole*, or any particular utterance in a language, and *langue*, the entirety of the language as it exists at any moment in time, asserting that the goal of semiotics should be to study the *parole* only as a means of aiding in the ultimate understanding of the *langue*.

The principles of semiotics came in later years to be applied to numerous fields other than linguistics itself. Claude Lévi-Strauss, for instance, imported the concepts of semiotics into the study of anthropology; Jacques Lacan introduced ideas from semiotics into Freudian psychoanalysis; and Roland Barthes applied notions from semiotics to the study of literature and other forms of cultural expression, just to name a few. Structuralism, the critical approach that links these three scholars, is thus not equivalent to semiotics, but it similarly develops out of the work of Saussure, such that the fields bear a deep critical relationship. Structuralism developed primarily around the work of a number of French scholars in the 1950s, first and foremost Lévi-Strauss, who brought the principles of Saussurean linguistics to the study of mythologies, kinship relations, and other aspects of cultural anthropology. Structuralism numbers among its aims the objective, scientific study of social and cultural phenomena, understanding the basis of the underlying structure of a culture. The deep structure these critics are interested in is composed of what have been called "relational entities," within which signs have meaning through their differences from—and particularly their binary opposition to—other signs.

In structuralism, literature itself comes to be understood as a system, and the objective of the literary critic comes to be seen as developing in a scientific fashion the rules of this system. Northrop Frye's *Anatomy of Criticism* (1957), for instance, argues that literature is a system governed by laws that structure the various modes, genres, and archetypes underlying all texts. For the structuralist, the author of the text is no longer an autonomous individual in control of the text's meaning, but rather a "subject" governed by (and indeed constructed through) the rules of the system within which he or she writes. In this sense, the author is "written" by the system as much as is the text, a notion that gives rise to the concept of the "decentered" subject. While many ideas arising from structuralist criticism, including that of the decentered subject, remain influential today, by the 1960s critics began to take issue with the purported scientism of the structuralist enterprise, and particularly with the rigidity and exclusions of the system of binary oppositions on which the structuralists were focused. Moreover, many critics began to dispute structuralism's ahistoricity and its failures to deal with the problem of ideology; in these critiques, a new, poststructuralist critical mode gained ascendancy.

Psychoanalysis

Psychoanalytic literary criticism first arose in the 1920s out of the work of Sigmund Freud, who developed the mechanisms of psychoanalysis as a means of investigating and curing neuroses. In his later work, he began to apply the principles of psychoanalysis to a broader range of historical and cultural phenomena. In this sense, Freudian psychoanalytic criticism considers the literary text as a phenomenon akin to the neurotic symptom or the dream, a highly symbolic manifestation of the repressed desires of the subject. The work of the psychoanalytic literary critic is to interpret the manifest content of the literary text—and particularly its revealingly *symptomatic* moments of distortion, ambiguousness, or elision—in order to uncover its latent meaning, in such a way that similarly uncovers the effects of the literary text on its reader. Freudian-based psychoanalytic literary critics include Simon Lesser (*Fiction and the Unconscious*, 1957); Norman Holland (*The Dynamics of Literary Response*, 1968); and Harold Bloom (*The Anxiety of Influence*, 1975).

Jacques Lacan transformed psychoanalytic criticism by bringing together the lessons of structuralism with those of psychoanalysis, arguing that "the unconscious is structured like a language." Lacan further revised Freud's theories of psychosexual development, (which were primarily focused on principles of the Oedipus complex), to explore the initiation of the child into the dominant systems of representation. Lacan posits a pre-linguistic stage of development that he names the imaginary, in which the distinctions between subject and object, between self and other, have not yet taken shape. Once the child develops linguistic skills, he or she becomes a part of the symbolic order, which manifests through the law of the father and the phallus (a symbolic manifestation thereof) is given a privileged position as the primary signifier, from which all other signifiers draw meaning. The entry into language is, for Lacan, a process of being severed from the "real," which is in his formulation an inaccessible realm—one that exists outside and is only inadequately described by the symbolic order. This is not to say that nothing exists outside of language according to Lacan, but rather he posits that language provides our only point of access to reality, and because of the unstable and arbitrary nature of the sign, that point of access is inadequate at best. Lacan, moreover, draws from the structuralist idea of subjectivity as a construction of the social order by reformulating the ego as a narcissistic and fictive projection of a unified self.

The result of all this, for psychoanalytic literary criticism, is a continued displacement of the figure of the author from the point of analysis, and an interest in the effects of the slipperiness of meaning on the text and on the reading subject. Lacanian psychoanalysis in particular has had a significant influence on feminist literary theory, through the work of figures such as Julia Kristeva, Helene Cixous, and Luce Irigaray, all of whom investigate the "phallocentrism" of linguistic representation.

Reader-Response Theory

Reader-response criticism refers to a range of critical practices that grow out of the branch of philosophy known as phenomenology, which is most closely identified with the work of German philosopher Edmund Husserl. Phenomenology argues that, because all we know of the objects in the word is how they appear to us, it is impossible to study objects directly, and that we must instead study perception and consciousness. Reader-response criticism thus turns from a focus on how the text structures meaning, to an investigation of how meaning is created within an active process of engagement by a reader. Reader-response criticism suggests that there is no one correct interpretation of any text, given the individual reading processes and subjectivities that each reader brings to the reading experience, but different critics take different positions on the degree to which a text *prefers* certain meanings over others, constraining a reader's potential range of responses. Most reader-response critics are clear that it is possible to label certain readings as misreadings, even if we cannot settle on any one correct interpretation.

The work of Wolfgang Iser is exemplary in the field of reader-response criticism. Iser, in *The Act of Reading* (1976), understands the literary text as guiding the reader's responses, but argues that there are gaps or indeterminacies that enable—indeed, require—the reader to participate creatively in the production of the text's meaning, making connections and filling in gaps in order to make sense of the text as a whole. Iser focuses on the "implied reader," the subject position that the text constructs and promotes as the ideal position from which it can be understood. For Iser, the best literary texts are those that require the reader to become conscious of the codes that he or she uses to interpret the text. Stanley Fish brought to reader-response criticism the idea of "interpretive communities," which seeks to explain how individuals do not produce wholly idiosyncratic readings of texts, but rather develop relatively common interpretations; readers draw on knowledge that has been read into them by the society in which they live.

Some recent reader-response criticism focuses on the historical and cultural circumstances that produce particular readings or understandings of literary texts; in particular, reception theory—a branch of reader-response criticism—focuses on the changing reading values and strategies of the general reading public over time. Its primary proponent, Hans Robert Jauss, posited the notion of a reader's "horizon of expectations," with which any text interacts. As that horizon of expectations changes, the interpretation and valuation of the text changes as well.

Marxism

One of the criticisms that has been leveled at the critical methodologies covered so far is that they all fail, to varying degrees, to account for the politics of representation. Among the first theories of literary criticism that dealt with political aspects of literature was Marxism. Marxism, an extremely diverse and often contentious set of ideas founded on the work of nineteenth-century German thinkers Karl Marx and Friedrich Engels, argues that the social and cultural development of any society, its institutions, and its ideas are determined in the last instance by its mode of production, that is, its economic system. Marx and Engels argued that the ruling ideas of any age would of necessity be the ideas of the ruling class. Later developments in the theory of ideology complicated that relationship, focusing on the multiple ways in which systems of power manifest themselves in society and structure the consciousnesses of those living in that society.

Marxist literary theory and criticism has been through several phases of development since its inception. Much of early Marxist criticism would now be described as "vulgar" Marxism, in which a narrow correlation is drawn between the economic, and particularly the bourgeois, aspects of a literary text and its role in the ongoing class struggle. Recent Marxist literary criticism, however, displays a more nuanced sense of the relationship between cultural production, ideology, and economics. Hungarian theorist Georg Lukács, for instance, has explored the ways that the nineteenth-century realist fiction created recognizable portraits of the capitalist world in which its readers lived. Walter Benjamin's influential essay, "The Work of Art in the Age of Mechanical Reproduction," (1935) focuses on the ways that twentieth-century technologies have affected the relationships between the work of art, its creator, and its consumer, suggesting that by demystifying the cult of originality and authenticity surrounding the unique art work, mechanical reproduction allows for the possibility of a revolutionary political art. Louis Althusser brought Marxism into conversation with structuralism, exploring the systems through which ideology operates in society, and through which individuals are unconsciously called into being as subjects of ideology. In the Althusserian model, readers and writers alike are all products of the social structure in which we live—and thus so are our texts and our interpretations of them.

Significant recent Marxist literary critics include Raymond Williams and Fredric Jameson. Williams introduced into Marxist literary thought the notion that multiple competing ideologies circulate throughout a culture at any given moment, including not only the dominant ideology but also residual and emergent ideologies; ideology is by this view not fixed but dynamic, responding to shifts and changes in a culture. Fredric Jameson's early work brought avenues of analysis from structuralism, psychoanalysis, semiotics, and deconstruction together with Marxist theory to develop a complex understanding of the role of the political unconscious at work in literary texts. Jameson was even more influential later in his career in the development of the concept of postmodernism.

Poststructuralism

Poststructuralism, as its name suggests, arose in conscious relation and response to the ideas previously circulated under the rubric of structuralism. Poststructuralism has come to serve as an umbrella under which many different critical perspectives are brought together. Poststructuralism begins in the work of theorists such as Jacques Derrida, as they attack both the claims to scientificness on the part of the structuralists, as well as the exclusions and oversimplifications that structuralist analysis often produced. Derrida's "Structure, Sign, and Play in the Discourse of the Humanities," first delivered as a lecture in 1966, announced a radical change in approach. In this essay, Derrida argues that when scholars begin to study what he calls "the structurality of structure"—taking such structures not as givens but rather as themselves the objects of analysis—it is discovered that each such structure presupposes a "center," one that serves as the foundation of the structure, organizes the structure and yet is not subject to it. When that center is recognized to be absent from the structure—when the structure itself is decentered—the result is a kind of "play" in the system, whereby the relationships between the signifier and the signified, and among the many signs governed by a structure, become slippery and unstable. Deconstruction is Derrida's name for the critical operation of taking apart the binary oppositions and other structures of meaning on which foundational principles rely. The process of deconstruction demonstrates that these structures of meaning are always riven with internal contradictions, such that the logic of any text is always in some sense self-undermining. Deconstruction is thus one aspect of poststructuralist theory, though it is by no means identical to it.

All poststructuralist thought, however, begins from a moment of antifoundationalism similar to that contained in Derrida's essay. The other two key figures that undergird most poststructuralist criticism are French psychoanalyst Jacques Lacan and French historian Michel Foucault. In poststructuralism, one often finds an intensive focus on theory in criticism, suggesting that the critic must foreground the theories and methodologies with which he or she is working. Poststructuralist thought takes as a basis the work begun in structuralism toward decentering the subject; poststructuralism is in many of its manifestations an explicit critique of humanism. This critique distinguishes the unique, coherent, discrete, purposeful individual of humanist thought from the fragmented, socially constructed, contradictory subject whose actions are less the result of will than of the unconscious workings of language and ideology.

This decentering of the subject has primarily focused on the figure of the author, as Roland Barthes wrote in an extremely influential article, "The Death of the Author" (1968); and Michel Foucault further argued the next year in his essay "What Is an Author?" for the replacement of the author by what he termed the "author function"—a figure constructed entirely through discourse. In both cases, the author is replaced by the reader as the key figure in the process of literary interpretation. Foucault further argues that the sum of the verbal exchanges that take place in all modes of communication, (which he puts under the blanket term "discourse") functions less to describe a reality than to create it, by creating the rules within which power disciplines knowledge, separating the thinkable from the unthinkable, controlling what can be known.

Many of the modes of critical thought described in what remains of this essay—particularly postmodernist theory, contemporary feminist and gender theory, and critical race theory—partake significantly of the ideas put forward by poststructuralism, inflecting those ideas with the notion that particular political concerns rest at the heart of both the literary and the critical enterprise.

Postmodernism

Postmodernist cultural theory arises out of a debate between German philosopher Jurgen Habermas, French philosopher Jean-François Lyotard, and American theorist Fredric Jameson, each of whom puts forward the notion that the period thought of as the modern has been supplanted by a radically new mode known as the "postmodern." Though in literary circles, modernism is generally used to refer to the art and literature of the first half of the twentieth century, the modern against which the postmodern is defined is a bit more expansive than that; it is instead the Western world as it has developed since the Renaissance, a world characterized by its belief in rationality and progress. In this sense, the postmodern refers to a world in which faith in rationality and progress appear to have broken down.

The term postmodernism originated among artists and critics in New York in the 1950s and '60s as a way of talking about style. However, the term was picked up by European theorists in the 1970s; the opening statement in what came to be known as "the postmodern debate" was a lecture by Jurgen Habermas delivered in 1980, titled "Modernity—An Incomplete Project." In this lecture, Habermas characterizes modernity as based in the Enlightenment impulse to provide for the rational organization of the social world; an impulse with a socially progressive background. This rational organization of the world depends on effective communication between what Habermas sees as the three differentiated spheres of modern life: science, morality, and art. By the mid-twentieth century, however, these spheres had not merely separated, claims Habermas, but have become autonomous, cutting off communication between them and thus rendering them ineffectual in the promotion of social progress. For Habermas, then, the notion of the fragmented and decentered society that typifies postmodernism is a fundamentally conservative, if not reactionary phenomenon, that must be resisted.

Jean-François Lyotard, in *The Postmodern Condition* (1979), and particularly in that volume's concluding essay, "Answering the Question: What is Postmodernism?", rejects Habermas's notion that communication among these differentiated spheres is a good thing, pointing out that it is based on a concept of *consensus* that often leads to oppression in the social order. In fact, Lyotard rejects any kind of totalization in terms of what he calls "grand narratives," the legitimizing myths of the modern age. Among these myths are the progressive liberation of humanity through science—the idea that philosophy can lead to truth. Instead, Lyotard looks to the modernist phenomenon of avant-garde art, which he claims effectively disrupts the "solace of good forms," keeping its viewers from any complacent acceptance of their social condition. But Lyotard also points out how quickly modernist invention gets subsumed into corporate culture. The art he terms postmodern is the art that continually renews that modernist "shock of the new," and thus, ironically, any contemporary art must *first* be postmodern *before* it can be thought of as modern.

The third major player to enter the postmodern debate is Fredric Jameson. In Jameson's model, postmodernism is neither Habermas's reactionary social-philosophical attitude, nor Lyotard's avant-garde cultural-aesthetic strategy, but is rather a fundamental principle of our existence—the cultural dominant—under late capitalism. While Jameson's model is problematic in ignoring its own tendency toward totalization, in which everything becomes a factor of existence under multinational capitalism, the qualities Jameson points to as the constitutive elements of postmodernism are worth a closer look, as they recur in most later conceptions of the theory. First, Jameson points out in postmodernism the appearance of "a new depthlessness, which finds its prolongation both in contemporary 'theory' and in a whole new culture of the image or simulacrum" (6). This depthlessness is, in Jameson's view, a destruction of the depth models or master narratives that had previously informed our cultural and intellectual existence, including such grand ideas as Marxism, Freudianism, existentialism, structuralism, and so on. The end of these depth models has also produced for Jameson the effacement of the high-modernist frontier between high culture and mass or commercial culture. Second, Jameson links postmodernism to a "weakening of historicity, both in our relationship to public History and in the new forms of our private temporality" (6). This weakening of historicity—and when Jameson says History, one should hear his Marxist background speaking through—has produced a series of shifts in our culture that has led to the replacement of history by nostalgia and parody by pastiche. The connected weakening of private temporality and subsequent schizophrenia of the contemporary era has also produced the much-touted fragmentation and decentering of the self. Jameson also lists among the features of postmodernism "the deep constitutive relationships of all this to a whole new technology, which is itself a figure for a whole new world economic system" (6).

Later critics of postmodernist theory, including Terry Eagleton, have described postmodernism as an academic construct invented to explain a world in which Marxism is dead, suggesting that the founding error of this discourse is that Marxism is not really dead at all, and thus postmodernism is a socially regressive phenomenon that has given up on revolution. Whether it is considered progressive or conservative in nature, postmodernist theory has been criticized for existing within a self-reflexive hall of mirrors, in which every discussion of the postmodern devolves into an argument about whether postmodernism is in fact a good thing or a bad thing. Postmodernism has also been taken to task by critics, including Phillip Brian Harper, who argue that the so-called postmodern condition is in fact a spread to the dominant sector of the population the experiences long held by marginalized groups; the suggestion is that postmodernist theory is a means for a group of predominantly white male critics to co-opt the language and experiences of marginalization written about by women and people of color.

Feminist, Gender, and Sexuality Studies

To introduce feminist literary criticism—much less the interrelated fields of gender and sexuality studies—in such a compressed space is to do the field a kind of violence; feminism as a term is already a significant reduction of what is a multiplicity of political, ideological, social, and critical positions. Feminist criticism focuses on the historical, social, and cultural means by which the binary opposition of male/female has been perpetuated, and particularly the ways in which the qualities associated with the male have been affirmed and given power at the expense of the female. These social networks of power and privilege that structure gender relations are often referred to collectively as patriarchy.

Feminist critiques of patriarchal culture have a long history, dating back as far as Mary Wollstonecraft's *A Vindication of the Rights of Woman* (1792). Other significant literary voices in early phases of the feminist movement include Margaret Fuller (*Woman in the Nineteenth Century*, 1845); Virginia Woolf (*A Room of One's Own*, 1919); and Simone de Beauvoir (*The Second Sex*, 1949). In the late 1960s, feminist literary scholars began to focus squarely on the ideological role of literature in promoting and enforcing patriarchal power, beginning most notably with Kate Millett's *Sexual Politics* (1969). On the heels of these critical interventions, many feminist literary scholars, such as Elaine Showalter in *A Literature of Their Own* (1977), began to write about a previously suppressed women's literary tradition.

Feminism, however, represents a multiplicity of political positions, with widely varying goals. These feminisms include liberal or bourgeois feminism; Marxist feminism; radical feminism; and poststructuralist feminism, among others. One basic distinction that can be drawn among these distinctions is that between essentialist feminism on the one hand, which assumes there is a basic "truth" about woman that patriarchal society has kept hidden, (whether this truth is biological in origin or socially constructed), and antiessentialist feminism, on the other hand, which attempts to understand the processes through which female subjectivity is constituted in patriarchal culture—but without a notion of "essential" femininity behind the socially constructed subject. Antiessentialist feminism, which has gained critical ascendancy through its connections with poststructuralist theory, is concerned with links between a given sex identity and the patriarchal order, studying also the processes through which sexuality and subjectivity are constructed together.

To consider just two of the different feminisms and their relationships to literary criticism: First, liberal feminist criticism is heavily dependent on content analysis, exploring recurrent images of women in patriarchal literature; this mode of criticism has been extremely important in documenting what we have come to understand as a prevalent way of understanding women in literature and popular culture, but it unfortunately does not tell us much about how those images are produced or how they mean. Second, poststructuralist feminist criticism rejects the dichotomy between masculine and feminine as metaphysical or biological and aims at a recognition of the categories' fundamental cultural construction. Poststructuralist feminism analyzes the symbolic systems through which we communicate and organize our lives in an attempt to understand how it is that we learn through language to become what our culture calls "women" as opposed to what it calls "men." Much poststructuralist feminist criticism arises from the work of the French feminists, including Helene Cixous, Luce Irigaray, and Julia Kristeva.

More recent work in gender and sexuality studies has attempted to further disrupt the categories of binary gender by exploring the means through which the social order disciplines subjects not only into patriarchy but also into a given sexual identity, declaring any other subjectivity unthinkable. The work of Judith Butler (*Gender Trouble*, 1990) has been particularly influential in thinking about the relationship between gender, sexuality, and discourse.

New Historicism

New Historicism as a school of literary criticism arose in reaction to the new criticism's rigorously maintained exclusion of all materials that lie outside the boundaries of the text, including that text's historical and social context. The new historicists are primarily interested in exploring the complex relationships between the literature of a period and its surrounding culture. In fact, most critics prior to the rise of the new criticism viewed literature within its historical context. What makes the new historicism "new" is its interactions with Marxist, poststructuralist, and feminist theory, and particularly with the work of French historian Michel Foucault. Foucault, by confronting the historical through the lens of discourse, explored history not as a coherent set of dates and events but rather as the multiple conflicting movements of power through which contemporary epistemologies (or ways of knowing) have been created.

The New Historicism is most closely associated with the work of Stephen Greenblatt, a scholar of Renaissance literature, who announced in a 1982 special issue of the journal *Genre* that a "new historicism" had arisen in literary criticism. This criticism takes into consideration the institutions that promoted a complex set of ideologies and practices in Elizabethan and Jacobean society—and particularly the effects of these institutions, ideologies, and practices as manifested in literary texts of the period. In this statement, Greenblatt argues that those scholars who wish to understand the writing of a historical period must understand the relationships between texts and the society as a whole. Accordingly, New Historicists often place canonical literary texts alongside other, marginal, nonliterary historical documents, drawing on fields such as economics, politics, and anthropology as source material for their critical study. In fact, new historicists suggest that any remnants of historical cultural activity can provide equally important material for analysis; this refusal to distinguish between literary and nonliterary texts has at times made the New Historicism a controversial approach within literary studies. For his part, Greenblatt argues that given literature's situated-ness within a historically specific culture, his work and the work of other new historicists functions to describe a poetics of power that must exist alongside literary poetics.

In recent years, New Historicism has come to be considered problematic by many literary scholars, because it appears to present a formulaic methodology for the understanding of historical cultures and texts. Most scholars working in the field, however, understand New Historicism not to be an overarching theory of culture or an interpretive method, but rather a set of reading practices organized around a common cluster of questions about power, individual agency, and literature.

Ethnic, Critical, and Postcolonial Studies

In ways that are related to the interests of Marxist and feminist forms of literary criticism, the fields of ethnic studies, critical race studies, and postcolonial studies have all brought to the interpretation of literature an interest in the relationship between the literary and the movement of ideology through a culture. Like feminism, these approaches to literary study are multiplicitous in nature, and bring with them a wide variety of goals. Ethnic studies of literature, for instance, encompass both the study of literature produced by groups still treated as marginal in the United States, (e.g., Asian Americans, Latinos,

Chicanos, and Native Americans), as well as the study of literature produced by earlier ethnic immigrant groups who have fully or partially been accepted as white (e.g., Irish, Italian, and Jewish Americans). What these various modes of ethnic studies share in common is an interest in the histories and cultures of ethnic minority groups in the United States and their varying relationships both to one another and to the dominant American culture.

Much African-American criticism stems from the work of W. E. B. Du Bois, who argued in *The Souls of Black Folk* (1903) that the problem of the new century would be the problem of "the color line." He introduced to critical thought the notion of the double-consciousness of African-American literature—works that are seen through African and American eyes, and through the eyes of the white majority. Stemming from these concerns, early African-American literary criticism focused primarily on the relationship between the literary subject matter and African-American culture more generally. That early direction was largely set by Du Bois who, as editor of the NAACP–sponsored journal *Crisis*, worked toward the goals of racial uplift and social development for African Americans. African-American criticism developed through several periods in the twentieth century, including the Harlem Renaissance of the first decades of the century and the Black Arts Movement of 1960s and '70s. Throughout, as in early feminist literary criticism, a primary goal of the critique was the revaluation of a specifically black literary culture as one part of a project of political resistance. This goal required, however, that race be considered an intrinsic part of identity, an assumption that, in the wake of poststructuralist theory, came to be seen as problematic. The primary distinction between what is now thought of as "critical race theory" and earlier models of African-American criticism is the shift from an essentialist model of race—in which there is posited some core black identity—to an antiessentialist model, in which race is instead studied as a cultural construct, a way of thinking created and maintained through discourse. Key figures in this later critical work include Henry Louis Gates, Jr. (*The Signifying Monkey*, 1988) and bell hooks (*Black Looks*, 1992).

Postcolonialism, like poststructuralism and postmodernism, is founded on an antiessentialist notion of identity and cultural meaning, and shares with these theories a critique of cultural hierarchies. But postcolonialism has altogether different political objectives; postcolonialism is the study of the ideological and cultural impact of Western colonialism and its aftermath. Postcolonialism is interested both in continuing colonialist (or neocolonialist) situations, and in the emergence of new national and individual identities after the fall of colonial power. The experience of the postcolonial subject is not an either/or situation (either British or Indian, for instance), but rather both/and (both a British subject and an Indian national). Theories of postcolonialism thus reveal a double, divided, conflicted, and often transitory subject—much like Du Bois's concept of the double consciousness of the African American. Postcolonialism is interested in undermining essentialist notions of selfhood (by which one can *know* that someone belongs to a particular racial or ethnic group through a definite set of characteristics), by introducing the notion of hybridity, the ways in which the postcolonial subject lives both within the dominant culture and within the subaltern. The key figures in the origin of postcolonial theory include Frantz Fanon, a Martinique-born doctor and Marxist revolutionary whose books *Black Skin, White Masks* (1952) and *The Wretched of the Earth* (1961) explore the structures of colonial power; Edward Said, whose *Orientalism* (1978) argues that all Western scholarship on the East proceeds from a eurocentric perspective and ultimately succumbs to describing the "Oriental" as the "Other"; and more recently, a range of critics including Homi Bhabha and Gayatri Spivak.

Conclusion

The story of the development of critical approaches to literature will hardly end here. Each year, critics put forward new ideas about how literature can be read and understood. What has happened throughout the twentieth century, however, and into the twenty-first, has been a progressive foregrounding of the critic's assumptions and methods in approaching literary study. Accordingly, it serves the beginning student of literature well to think about these different approaches when formulating his or her ideas about the meaning of any text and what it is to read.

Formal Writing Assignments in Literature Classes

IN A LITERATURE CLASS you can expect to spend a good deal of time discussing various features of literary works; you may also be asked to write informal responses to the works in order to help you interpret their meaning. Almost certainly, however, you will be evaluated on your ability to compose formal essays that explore some feature of a literary work. Such essays are normally divided into two categories: *explication* and *analysis*. *Explication* refers to explaining how the meaning of the literary work emerges; *analysis* refers to examining how different parts of the work contribute to its meaning. Those parts include *character, setting, symbols, point of view (narrative perspective), language,* and *theme*. Whether you are asked to explicate or to analyze, it is essential that you make specific reference to the literary work in order to support your interpretation. This chapter provides a brief overview of formal writing assignments, with examples of explication and analysis of Robert Frost's poem "Mending Wall" and Kate Chopin's short story "The Story of an Hour." (The complete poem and story can be found at the end of the chapter.)

Explication

When you *explicate*, you demonstrate how the pieces of a literary work come together to make meaning of the whole. Explication is more than mere summary: The emphasis in explication is not on what happens in the work but rather on how each piece contributes to your sense of the work as a whole. Because of this emphasis, explication requires careful, close reading of the literary work. Although it can be helpful to explicate fiction and drama, explication is most often associated with writing about poetry. Consider the following explication of the first eleven lines of Robert Frost's poem "Mending Wall":

> The speaker in this poem feels rebellious toward the tradition of maintaining walls between neighbors. The very first line of the poem, "Something there is that doesn't love a wall," suggests that some force greater than humans or nature is at work in damaging the wall each winter. The speaker recognizes the gaps resulting from nature's "frozen-ground-swell" and from hunters who "have left not one stone on a stone." But he is at a loss to explain all of the damage: "The gaps I mean,/ No one has seen them made or heard them made,/ But at spring mending-time we find them there." The speaker implies that this "something," this mysterious force, conspires each winter to undo what he and his neighbor accomplish each spring when they mend the wall.

Notice how the explication goes beyond simply summarizing the passage to explore its relationship to the overall meaning of the poem.

Analysis of Character

One of the most common writing assignments for fiction and drama (as well as for some forms of narrative poetry) is analysis of *character*, largely because it is through identification with or recognition of characters that readers come to understand a literary work. Just as you observe and draw conclusions about people whom you meet in real life, you observe and draw conclusions about fictional characters as well; however, unlike real people, fictional characters exist in a world carefully constructed by the writer, and thus understanding those characters helps readers to make meaning of that world. In constructing a character analysis, you may focus on personality traits, on behavior, on development, on motivation, or on interactions with other characters. Your analysis will also be informed by the character's physical description and his or her language.

Kate Chopin's "The Story of an Hour" provides only brief glimpses of Mrs. Mallard, but those glimpses provide a powerful characterization of the woman who has just been informed that her husband is dead. Here is a paragraph in which Mrs. Mallard's character is analyzed:

> *Through the course of this hour, Mrs. Mallard undergoes a transformation from a typical subservient housewife into a powerful independent woman. Chopin presents these changes in physical terms, describing Mrs. Mallard first as a woman "afflicted with a heart trouble" who is "pressed down by a physical exhaustion" when she retires to her room after hearing the news of her husband's death. But gradually, as she stares out her window, a metamorphosis begins: "There was something coming to her and she was waiting for it, fearfully." She attempts to fight off the feeling, but her will is "as powerless as her two white slender hands would have been." When Mrs. Mallard finally succumbs to the feeling and utters the words "free, free, free," the image of fragile woman "afflicted with a heart trouble" is replaced by one of a strong woman whose eyes are "keen and bright" and whose "pulses beat fast" with "coursing blood." When she finally leaves her room, it is with "a feverish triumph in her eyes." These physical descriptions reflect a far more substantial transformation within Mrs. Mallard, one that reaches into her soul.*

Notice how this analysis focuses on the physical descriptions of Mrs. Mallard and her reaction to her husband's death in order to underscore the profound change that her character undergoes in the story.

Analysis of Setting

The fictional world inhabited by these characters constitutes *setting*, which includes not just place (e.g., geographical location, nature, buildings, and weather), but also time (e.g., era, season, and time of day) and cultural environment (e.g., social, political, and religious contexts). When analyzing setting, you may focus on its influence on the behavior of characters, its impact on the action, or its contribution to the tone of the work.

In "The Story of an Hour," setting contributes significantly to the transformation of Mrs. Mallard, as the following analysis demonstrates:

> *The contrast between the house and the world outside illustrates the emergence of Mrs. Mallard from the conformity of nineteenth-century views of women into the freedom of the wider world. The house is a place of confinement, with doors to keep the world outside at bay. Within that house Mrs. Mallard is subject to her husband's will, as was considered appropriate for a middle-class housewife of that period. But her room also has a window through which she can see "the tops of trees that were aquiver with the new spring of life" and smell the "delicious breath of rain . . . in the air"; through the window she can hear the "notes of a distant song which some one was singing" and the "twittering" of "countless sparrows." It is through that window that the "something" comes to Mrs. Mallard, causing her to embrace the freedom represented by the sights, smells, and sounds of the natural world outside.*

Notice that the analysis makes note not only of the house and nature, but also of the time period in which the story is set, with particular focus on the expectations for married women during that era.

Analysis of Symbol

In poetry as well as fiction and drama, *symbols* contribute significantly to meaning. A symbol can be an object, a place, or a character whose meaning extends beyond the literal. The concrete nature of symbols makes them readily visible to readers in much the same way that characters are visible. Analysis of symbols leads to a richer understanding of the meaning of the literary work.

In "The Story of an Hour," nature performs a symbolic role, representing the freedom that beckons to Mrs. Mallard. Consider the following analysis of the symbolic role played by nature in the story:

> *If the house in this story represents the restrictions placed upon women in the late nineteenth century, then the scene outside Mrs. Mallard's window represents freedom. It is springtime, a time of rebirth, and Mrs. Mallard looks out to "the tops of trees" reaching toward the sky. While Mrs. Mallard is still in the grip of her conventional life, she can only see "patches of blue sky." The thing that reaches out to her, however, comes "creeping out of the sky, reaching toward her through the sounds, the scents, and color that filled the air." Those sounds, scents, and colors of nature come together to symbolize the freedom that she feels once she realizes how confining her marriage has been.*

Notice that the same material used in the previous analysis of setting is used here to analyze symbols. The same feature can serve many different purposes in a literary work; indeed, this richness is what makes a literary work so memorable.

Analysis of Point of View (Narrative Perspective)

In fiction and narrative poetry, the *point of view* (or *narrative perspective*) from which the story is told has a significant impact on the reader's perception of the story. Analysis of point of view may focus on the credibility of the narrator, the narrator's prejudices or beliefs, or other relevant features of the narrator's character.

The speaker in "Mending Wall" exhibits not only specific personality traits, but also a firmly held belief in the wrong-ness of building and maintaining walls. The following paragraph analyzes the narrative perspective of the poem:

> *The speaker in Frost's "Mending Wall" approaches his subject from a whimsical perspective at first, speculating on what that "something" is "that doesn't love a wall." He muses over whether nature actually "sends the frozen-ground-swell" up to tumble the rocks, and envisions hunters who "would have the rabbit out of hiding,/ To please the yelping dogs." The speaker also teases his neighbor, asking why they need the wall: "He is all pine and I am all apple orchard/ My apple trees will never get across/ And eat the cones under his pines, I tell him." This whimsy, however, leads to a more serious objection to the notion of walls, when the speaker says, "Before I built a wall I'd ask to know/ What I was walling in or walling out,/ And to whom I was like to give offense." By the end of the poem he describes his neighbor, who insists on rebuilding the wall each year, as "an old-stone savage armed" who "moves in darkness," this final image establishing firmly the speaker's heartfelt belief that "Something there is that doesn't love a wall."*

Notice that analysis of point of view often overlaps with character analysis. Again, this overlap is evidence of the richness of the literary work itself.

Analysis of Language

The effect of a literary work on readers is influenced heavily by the language a writer uses. The writer's *tone*, or attitude toward characters and subject, can affect how readers make meaning of the work. *Style*—sentence or line length, relative complexity of sentences, relative formality of diction, and use of figurative language—also affects readers' perceptions. More often than not, assignments focusing on analysis of language refer to the writer's use of figurative language: *metaphors* (implied comparisons) and *similes* (stated comparisons). A writer's use of figurative language reflects his or her perspective on the subject or character.

An analysis of figurative language in "Mending Wall" reveals the subtle shift in tone as the poem progresses, as seen in the following paragraph:

The language of "Mending Wall" reflects the change in the speaker's attitude toward the annual ritual of repairing the wall. Early in the poem he refers to the boulders that have fallen from the wall as "loaves" and "nearly balls" that play games with him and his neighbor, who "have to use a spell to make them balance." The game image is made explicit when he refers to mending the wall as "just another kind of outdoor game,/ One on a side." As the speaker becomes more serious, however, the images change. His neighbor is no longer a participant in a game, but rather an enemy, "Bringing a stone grasped firmly by the top/ In each hand, like an old-stone savage armed." This savage, far removed from the speaker who identifies with the "mischief" of spring, "moves in darkness . . ./ Not of woods only and the shade of trees." The images at the end of the poem are themselves dark, illustrating the shift in tone from playfulness to sorrow, even fear.

Notice that in this paragraph the writer refers to a number of features, including tone, metaphor, and simile in examining the language of the poem.

Analysis of Theme

A *theme* is a central unifying idea of a story, a play, or a narrative poem. Although similar to the moral of a fairy tale or a parable, theme is more complex, reflecting an understanding of what it means to be human. Character, setting, symbol, point of view, and language all contribute to theme in a literary work.

Readers of "The Story of an Hour" have articulated a number of themes related to love, marriage, freedom, and gender roles. The following analysis examines the story as a commentary on women's experience of marriage in the late nineteenth century:

"The Story of an Hour" can be read as Kate Chopin's commentary on the oppressive nature of marriage in the late nineteenth century. As Mrs. Mallard slowly becomes aware that the "something coming to her" through her bedroom window is freedom, she first resists it, "striving to beat it back with her will." The reader recognizes at this point that Mrs. Mallard has been unaware of how oppressive her marriage has been; she has never before sought freedom from her husband. In fact, she knows that "she would weep again when she saw the kind, tender hands folded in death; the face that had never looked save with love upon her, fixed and gray and dead." Her husband was never abusive; it is the institution itself that has abused her. In surrendering herself to that freedom "creeping out of the sky" she revels in the thought that she will no longer be subject to her husband's "powerful will bending hers," and instead can look forward to "a long procession of years to come that would belong to her absolutely." She realizes that it does not matter whether she has loved her husband or not; what matters is the "self-assertion which she suddenly recognized as the strongest impulse of her being." So powerful is

Mrs. Mallard's embrace of liberation that when her husband appears alive at the end of the story, she drops dead. According to Chopin, death is preferable to a continuing life of oppression.

Notice that the writer does not simply claim that the story is about oppression within marriage, but instead articulates the statement that the story makes about that oppression. The analysis also demonstrates how different features of the story contribute to the theme.

Supporting Evidence for Analysis

Each of the paragraphs above explores literary works in different ways, but all share one common feature: *supporting evidence*. If an explication or an analysis is to be credible, the writer must do more than simply assert his or her opinion. For opinion to become legitimate interpretation, reference to the literary work must be offered in support of that interpretation. The characterization of Mrs. Mallard above, for example, focuses on the contrast between the descriptions of her as "pressed down by a physical exhaustion" and as exultant, with "keen and bright" eyes and "pulses [that] beat fast" with "coursing blood." Similarly, the analysis of point of view in "Mending Wall" contrasts lines such as the playful "My apple trees will never get across/ And eat the cones under his pines" with the more serious "Before I built a wall I'd ask to know/ What I was walling in or walling out,/ And to whom I was like to give offense." In each case, specific reference to the story and the poem lend credibility to the writer's interpretation of the works.

There is no such thing as a single correct interpretation of a literary work. However, no interpretation can be considered valid without supporting evidence from the work itself. When responding to writing assignments in literature classes, it is essential to demonstrate that you have read the work closely and that there is ample evidence within the work to support your interpretation.

Mending Wall

ROBERT FROST

Something there is that doesn't love a wall,
That sends the frozen-ground-swell under it,
And spills the upper boulders in the sun;
And makes gaps even two can pass abreast.
The work of hunters is another thing: *5*
I have come after them and made repair
Where they have left not one stone on a stone,
But they would have the rabbit out of hiding,
To please the yelping dogs. The gaps I mean,
No one has seen them made or heard them made,   *10*
But at spring mending-time we find them there.
I let my neighbor know beyond the hill;
And on a day we meet to walk the line.
And set the wall between us once again.
We keep the wall between us as we go.   *15*
To each the boulders that have fallen to each.
And some are loaves and some so nearly balls
We have to use a spell to make them balance:
"Stay where you are until our backs are turned!"
We wear our fingers rough with handling them.   *20*
Oh, just another kind of outdoor game,
One on a side. It comes to little more:
There where it is we do not need the wall:
He is all pine and I am apple orchard.
My apple trees will never get across   *25*
And eat the cones under his pines, I tell him.
He only says, "Good fences make good neighbors."
Spring is the mischief in me, and I wonder
If I could put a notion in his head:
"*Why* do they make good neighbors? Isn't it   *30*
Where there are cows? But here there are no cows.

First appeared in Frost's second book of poems, *North of Boston,* in 1914.

Before I built a wall I'd ask to know
What I was walling in or walling out,
And to whom I was like to give offense.
Something there is that doesn't love a wall,   35
That wants it down," I could say "Elves" to him,
But it's not elves exactly, and I'd rather
He said it for himself. I see him there
Bringing a stone grasped firmly by the top
In each hand, like an old-stone savage armed.   40
He moves in darkness as it seems to me,
Not of woods only and the shade of trees.
He will not go behind his father's saying,
And he likes having thought of it so well
He says again, "Good fences make good neighbors."   45

[1914]

The Story of an Hour

KATE CHOPIN

KNOWING THAT MRS. MALLARD was afflicted with a heart trouble, great care was taken to break to her as gently as possible the news of her husband's death.

It was her sister Josephine who told her, in broken sentences, veiled hints that revealed in half concealing. Her husband's friend Richards was there, too, near her. It was he who had been in the newspaper office when intelligence of the railroad disaster was received, with Brently Mallard's name leading the list of "killed." He had only taken the time to assure himself of its truth by a second telegram, and had hastened to forestall any less careful, less tender friend in bearing the sad message.

She did not hear the story as many women have heard the same, with a paralyzed inability to accept its significance. She wept at once, with sudden, wild abandonment, in her sister's arms. When the storm of grief had spent itself she went away to her room alone. She would have no one follow her.

There stood, facing the open window, a comfortable, roomy armchair. Into this she sank, pressed down by a physical exhaustion that haunted her body and seemed to reach into her soul.

She could see in the open square before her house the tops of trees that were all aquiver with the new spring life. The delicious breath of rain was in the air. In the street below a peddler was crying his wares. The notes of a distant song which someone was singing reached her faintly, and countless sparrows were twittering in the eaves.

There were patches of blue sky showing here and there through the clouds that had met and piled above the other in the west facing her window.

She sat with her head thrown back upon the cushion of the chair, quite motionless, except when a sob came up into her throat and shook her, as a child who has cried itself to sleep continues to sob in its dreams.

She was young, with a fair, calm face, whose lines bespoke repression and even a certain strength. But now there was a dull stare in her eyes, whose gaze was fixed away off yonder on one of those patches of blue sky. It was not a glance of reflection, but rather indicated a suspension of intelligent thought.

First published in 1894.

There was something coming to her and she was waiting for it, fearfully. What was it? She did not know; it was too subtle and elusive to name. But she felt it, creeping out of the sky, reaching toward her through the sounds, the scents, the color that filled the air.

Now her bosom rose and fell tumultuously. She was beginning to recognize this thing that was approaching to possess her, and she was striving to beat it back with her will—as powerless as her two white slender hands would have been.

When she abandoned herself a little whispered word escaped her slightly parted lips. She said it over and over under her breath: "Free, free, free!" The vacant stare and the look of terror that had followed it went from her eyes. They stayed keen and bright. Her pulses beat fast, and the coursing blood warmed and relaxed every inch of her body.

She did not stop to ask if it were or were not a monstrous joy that held her. A clear and exalted perception enabled her to dismiss the suggestion as trivial.

She knew that she would weep again when she saw the kind, tender hands folded in death; the face that had never looked save with love upon her, fixed and gray and dead. But she saw beyond that bitter moment a long procession of years to come that would belong to her absolutely. And she opened and spread her arms out to them in welcome.

There would be no one to live for her during those coming years; she would live for herself. There would be no powerful will bending her in that blind persistence with which men and women believe they have a right to impose a private will upon a fellow-creature. A kind intention or a cruel intention made the act seem no less a crime as she looked upon it in that brief moment of illumination.

And yet she had loved him—sometimes. Often she had not. What did it matter! What could love, the unsolved mystery, count for in face of this possession of self-assertion which she suddenly recognized as the strongest impulse of her being!

"Free! Body and soul free!" she kept whispering.

Josephine was kneeling before the closed door with her lips to the keyhole, imploring for admission. "Louise, open the door! I beg; open the door—you will make yourself ill. What are you doing, Louise? For heaven's sake open the door."

"Go away. I am not making myself ill." No; she was drinking in a very elixir of life through that open window.

Her fancy was running riot along those days ahead of her. Spring days, and summer days, and all sorts of days that would be her own. She breathed a quick prayer that life might be long. It was only yesterday she had thought with a shudder that life might be long.

She arose at length and opened the door to her sister's importunities. There was a feverish triumph in her eyes, and she carried herself unwittingly like a goddess of Victory. She clasped her sister's waist, and together they descended the stairs. Richards stood waiting for them at the bottom.

Someone was opening the front door with a latchkey. It was Brently Mallard who entered, a little travel-stained, composedly carrying his grip-sack and umbrella. He had been far from the scene of accident, and did not even know there had been one. He stood amazed at Josephine's piercing cry; at Richards' quick motion to screen him from the view of his wife.

But Richards was too late.

When the doctors came they said she had died of heart disease—of joy that kills.

[1894]

A Brief Introduction to Literary Research

Why Do Literary Research?

Different kinds of writing assignments in literature classes ask the student to conduct different kinds of inquiry. Some, for instance, will ask you to focus closely on your own interpretation of a literary text, drawing evidence to support the claims made in the course of your paper solely from that text. Others will require that you perform extensive research into what are often called "secondary sources," texts that are not themselves the object of analysis, but instead provide a cultural, historical, theoretical, or critical lens through which a piece of literature might be understood. Included among such secondary sources are critical texts about the object of analysis, containing other scholars' interpretations and understandings of the text in question. This essay focuses on research into such critical writing about literature, as used to support your own writing and analysis.

Your research will have different purposes depending upon the assignment you have been given. You may be asked, for instance, to analyze the critical interpretations of a particular literary text as they have emerged over time; such a project will require you to uncover the debates among a number of scholars, how they agree and disagree with one another, and what the stakes of their various points of contention might be. Other assignments will ask you to write a research paper that is primarily focused on your own original argument about the literary text, but with attention to the responses of other scholars. In conducting this kind of research, you must guard against simply "trolling for quotes" and against an over-reliance on "authoritative" voices. The purpose of literary research is generally to enable you to enter into a field of critical discourse that is already in progress, to participate in an ongoing conversation about a literary text, and to stake out the significance of your way of approaching the text by acknowledging the approaches of other scholars and suggesting what questions have thus far been left unanswered.

Literary research, however, requires a particular set of skills, both in terms of finding appropriate sources and in reading, evaluating, and incorporating those sources into your own thinking. Your instructor will likely have some specific requirements for your research; what follows should be taken as general advice, a good set of strategies for beginning your work, and not as a replacement for any methods preferred by your instructor.

Step 1: Go to the Library

This step is not suggested facetiously: in fact, the first and most important piece of advice that you can receive is to get to know the research or reference librarians at your school's library. These librarians are specialists in information retrieval, and they will therefore have the best insights into the databases and bibliographies subscribed to by your library, as well as the other engines through which the material in your library may be found. They will also be of help in tracking down sources that may be difficult to obtain, whether through a consortial lending arrangement that your library participates in or through a broader interlibrary loan program. Your school's reference librarians may have areas of specialization within the curriculum, so you should consult your library's website to find out whether there are one or more librarians focused on research in literature. These librarians will be your best resource for finding the right material within the sea of possible information sources, so you should talk with them early and often.

Formulate Your Research Question

Though they are experts in information retrieval, your librarians will likely not be able to help you unless you have a sense of *what* information you are looking for. The first task you must undertake, then, is to figure out the basic parameters of your search. You must thus begin by formulating a basic research question. This question may, and in fact should, change as you progress in your research, as the arguments presented by other scholars will affect the way that you frame your own ideas; because of that, your initial research question will likely not be a fully elaborated thesis, but rather a general area of interest. This focus should not be too broad, however; beginning your research with an area of interest like "Hemingway" will result in more secondary sources than you can reasonably manage. Be as specific as you can: "representations of bullfighting in Hemingway" as a starting point will produce better results.

Consult a Wide Variety of Sources

The next task in front of you will be to find out what published texts will be of interest in your research. The most important sources for the kinds of research that you are undertaking will be scholarly books and journals. It's important to ensure that you consult a broad range of such sources: using only books as sources for your research may cause you to inadvertently exclude some of the most recent and significant analyses of the texts you are studying (because books generally take a lot longer to get into print than do journal articles), but using only journal articles may likewise cause you to inadvertently over-look some of the most important sustained arguments about your primary text. Your paper may wind up only citing one or the other form of publica-tion, but you should be certain that your research involves both forms.

Use the Right Database

These searches should be conducted primarily through scholarly databases, accessible either in your school's library or, often, through your library's web-site. Google is generally not a good site through which to conduct serious research, both because of the overwhelming number of results that the search engine can produce for any given search terms and because of the often unre-liable nature of the documents that such searches turn up. And while Wikipedia can often be a good source for general (or even very specific or arcane) infor-mation about a particular subject, it is not usually considered an acceptable source to cite in a college-level research paper, for the same reasons that citing any encyclopedia would be considered inappropriate: encyclopedias do not contain the results of original research, but rather condensations and sum-maries of the ideas and arguments made elsewhere. Google and Wikipedia might be useful as you begin to formulate your research question, but the actual research you do should be conducted using scholarly sources.

A brief note here on Google Scholar: While the material that this engine catalogs and searches is, indeed, scholarly in origin, the cataloging method that Google Scholar uses isn't considered terribly reliable, and the material that is cataloged is overwhelmingly weighted toward the sciences and social sciences. A search of Google Scholar cannot hurt, but it should by no means be the only database you consult. Furthermore, there are many online repositories containing electronic versions of scholarly journals, including Project Muse, JSTOR, and so forth, all of which provide the ability to search their holdings. These will be excellent sources for articles that you'll want to consult, but you shouldn't begin your search from these sites, as they index a limited number of journals.

Evaluate Sources Critically

Whatever their provenance, however—whether in print or online, whether books or articles—all of the sources that you uncover in the process of your research will require careful evaluation as to their reliability and credibility. You should consider, for instance, with each source you consult, whether the pub-lisher or publication is an appropriate one. A university press will generally be considered more authoritative as a source of scholarly books than a "vanity" press. Similarly, a scholarly journal will often be considered more reliable than a popular magazine. However, different kinds of arguments will require different kinds of source material, so you will need to use your own judgment. You should also evaluate the credibility of your sources' authors: are the writers authorities on the subject? Have they done thorough research? Finally, you must evaluate the arguments themselves: are the claims made by the source warranted and supported by the evidence? In the end, you should only use sources that your careful evaluation suggests are reliable.

Search the MLA Bibliography

The best way to begin finding authoritative sources, again, will be by searching scholarly databases. In literary studies, the primary database that you will want to search is the MLA Bibliography, published by the Modern Languages Association of America (though there are of course other databases to which your library might subscribe as well, and you shouldn't overlook your library's catalog; consult your librarian for information about them). The vast majority of journals in literature and language studies are indexed in the MLA Bibliography, as are many books in the field. There are many different search engines that provide access to the MLA Bibliography, each with slightly different characteristics, so you may want to consult with your librarian for specific instructions on searching the database. Generally, however, the database will provide the ability to search by Keyword, by Title, and by Author, among other parameters. Note, however, that "Title" and "Author" here refer to the sources indexed in the database, and not the primary text about which you are researching; to find sources *about* Hemingway, you should search for "Hemingway" as a keyword.

However, as I write, a keyword search for "Hemingway" in the MLA database produces 3969 results, which suggests that the search is too broad. Your database's search engine will provide some means of what is called Boolean searching, which allows you to use connectors like AND and OR to further refine your searches. AND as a Boolean term narrows a search, as both terms connected by the AND must be present for the record to be included; OR, by contrast, broadens a search, as a record will be included if it contains either term. A search, for instance, for "Hemingway AND bullfight" produces 11 results, which might seem reasonable. However, using "bullfight" as a term doesn't necessarily give access to results that use terms like "bullfights" or "bullfighting." Your search engine should give you the ability to use wildcards in your search terms, which instruct the engine to return related words; "bullfight*" as a search term would thus return any term that begins with "bullfight," no matter what characters complete the word (thus including bullfights, bullfighting, bullfighter, and so forth). A search for "Hemingway AND bull-fight*" produces 41 results, which is a very good place to begin.

Evaluate Your Search Results

Your job is now to sort through these citations and see which ones appear to be most relevant to your research question. A number of the article citations that result from the "Hemingway AND bullfight*" search, for instance, focus on the novel *The Sun Also Rises*, though you may be writing about the short story "The Capital of the World." It is up to you to determine whether those articles' arguments about the novel are applicable to your own analysis of the short story. Sometimes the database records will include an abstract, or a short précis of the article's argument, which may help you make a decision. Other times there will be no abstract included, but you can get more information about the article by examining the record closely, as it will contain certain descriptors designed to facilitate searches. The record for Kathy G. Willingham's article, "The Sun Hasn't Set Yet: Brett Ashley and the Code Hero Debate," includes the descriptors "characterization," "Ashley, Lady Brett," and "hero-ine," which suggests that the article might be applicable to research into the relationship between the representation of bullfighting in Hemingway's writing and questions about gender.

If your initial search turns up either too many or too few results, or results that don't provide the kinds of sources that you're really looking for, you should think about how to refine your search terms. Examine the kinds of descriptors that the database's records include, and think about how you might use those terms to find better results. For instance, if you are thinking about Hemingway's representations of women, rather than searching for "Hemingway AND women," you might try a search for "Hemingway AND female characters." A reference librarian may be of particular help as you refine your search. Throughout the search process, you should keep good records for yourself of the searches you've conducted and the results they've produced.

Go to the Source

Once you've accumulated a number of citations that appear to be applicable to your research question, the next stage is to obtain the sources themselves. Some libraries' database configurations will provide information about whether the source is contained in the library's holdings; my institution's MLA database, for instance, includes a "Get This Item" link on each record, which leads the user to a page with more information about how to obtain the article or book. Some such sources will be very easily obtainable, as the journals may be archived online; others may require you to track down print copies of the journal or book in the library's stacks, and still others may not be in the library's holdings at all, requiring you to use an interlibrary loan program to obtain them. *You must not restrict your research to digitally available sources.* Because many journals have only been digitized since the early 1990s, and because very few books are available digitally, many of the most important sources for your research will require you to leave the computer behind, and venture into the library's stacks. There's a great benefit to doing so, however, which is a kind of serendipity that no digital search has yet been able to mirror: when you are flipping through the print back issues of a journal, or scanning the spines of books on a shelf, looking for the source that your search uncovered, you are very likely to run into something promising that for whatever reason didn't turn up in your search. These accidental encounters are a key element of the research process; don't miss out on them by sticking too closely to what's electronically available.

Reading and Notetaking

Once you've gotten your first round of sources, the next step is, unsurprisingly, to read them. You might skim them quickly at first, to see whether they in fact seem as applicable to your research question as their citations made them appear, and then read them more closely in order to uncover the finer points of their reasoning, which will be helpful to you in constructing your own argument. You should be certain to take thorough, accurate notes as you read, particularly keeping detailed records of the bibliographic information from each source, which you'll need when you construct your "works cited" list, as well as scrupulously ensuring that any direct quotations or paraphrases that you draw from these sources are properly attributed to their authors. Failure to do so constitutes plagiarism, whether the failure is intentional or inadvertent, and plagiarism may carry quite severe consequences, including failure or, in some cases, expulsion. Be very careful in your notetaking to indicate clearly to yourself which notes are drawn from the texts you're reading, whether quotations or paraphrases, and which constitute your own thinking. Don't rely on your memory for this purpose, as memory can deceive you.

Repeat

It is important also to note that your research process should be recursive; after reading a couple of sources on your initial research question, you might discover that your question has shifted directions slightly, requiring a return to the database to see if there are sources that more closely approximate your new idea. Moreover, you might find as you read an article that its author cites a further source that sounds like it might be useful to you; explore the bibliographies included with the secondary texts that you read to see whether there are previous sources that you should consult.

Remember throughout the process, however, what the purpose of the research you're conducting is; a report on the critical interpretations of a particular text will require very different uses of the material that you uncover than will a research paper that is intended to be focused on your own original argument. For the former, you'll want to keep track of the debates among the critics that you read; what seem to be the key points about which they agree, and over which they disagree, and why? For the latter, you should think not just about ways that the critical texts support the argument you want to make, but also about your points of entry into the critical conversation; how does your own interpretation of the text differ from those of the critics you are reading, and why? What questions do the critical interpretations to this point raise? What gaps do you find in the critical conversation? What would your perspective add to a reader's understanding of the text you're studying?

Literary research, like any other form of research, requires a set of skills that can only be developed through practice. Your instructor and your librarian may have further advice to help you as you work, but the best way to learn how to conduct this kind of research is simply to plunge in, poke around in the databases, explore the sources, and see what turns up. With a flexible sense of how your search terms work, with careful attention to the credibility of the sources you uncover, and with conscientious notetaking, you should be able to find your way quickly into the critical conversation about your topic.

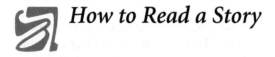 *How to Read a Story*

THROUGHOUT HUMAN HISTORY the story has been an essential element in every culture. Children have been taught lessons about behavior from stories; nations have celebrated their heroes in stories; even religions have promulgated their moral lessons through stories. In classical Greece and Rome, epic narratives such as *The Iliad* (c. 850 B.C.E.) and Virgil's *The Aeneid* (c. 15 B.C.E.) recounted heroic adventures in verse; tragedies such as Sophocles's *Oedipus Rex* (c. 430 B.C.E.) were presented in dramatic form. Prose narratives appeared much later, with Shikibu Marasaki's *The Tale of Genji* (c. 1000) and Miguel de Cervantes's *Don Quixote de la Mancha* (1605, 1615). It was not until the eighteenth century, however, that the form now known as the **novel** appeared, when writers such as Daniel Defoe and Henry Fielding established the novel as a legitimate literary genre in England. The new genre flourished in the following century, with writers such as Charlotte Brontë, Charles Dickens, Theodore Dostoevsky, Honore de Balzac, and Henry James. James and other writers such as Kate Chopin and Joseph Conrad also composed **novellas,** shorter works of prose fiction (usually fifty to one hundred pages long). The novel continued to be popular among readers and scholars throughout the twentieth century, with writers such as F. Scott Fitzgerald, Zora Neale Hurston, D. H. Lawrence, Virginia Woolf, Vladimir Nabokov, Nathalie Surraute, Salman Rushdie, and Edwidge Danticat.

The short story is a relatively recent phenomenon, tracing its roots to the nineteenth century, when writers such as Washington Irving and Walter Scott published self-contained short prose narratives. Since that time, the genre has flourished with writers such as Nathaniel Hawthorne, Nikolai Gogol, Kate Chopin, and Anton Chekhov in the nineteenth century; and Katherine Mansfield, James Joyce, Frank O'Connor, Nadine Gordimer, Margaret Atwood, and Alice Walker in the twentieth. Although the form and style of the short story have evolved over the past two centuries, most of the common features remain the same; an understanding of those features can enhance your reading of any story, whether it be from the early nineteenth century or the late twentieth.

Although our initial response to reading a story reflects the extent to which we simply enjoy it, more careful reading can enhance that enjoyment. Several features of the story contribute to our enjoyment: *plot, character; setting, point of view, voice, tone, and style;* and *theme.* Understanding these features will help you to become a more engaged reader and to appreciate more fully what a good story can offer.

Plot

A reader's most basic involvement with a story centers on **plot,** or the action in the story. That action can involve actual events (*external action*), but it can also focus more on changes within a character (*internal action*). In Nathaniel Hawthorne's "Rappaccini's Daughter," for example, the plot revolves around the young student Giovanni's attempt to save his love, Beatrice, from the poisons of her father's garden. The action in Mary Helen Ponce's "Enero," on the other hand, takes place primarily within the mind of the long-suffering mother Constancia. Whether external or internal, the action normally features a *conflict* between opposing forces: Giovanni struggles with Rappaccini for possession of Beatrice, while Constancia struggles with the conflicting teachings of her doctor and her religion.

Traditionally, the plot of a story progresses through several stages as the conflict is established, played out, and resolved. The *exposition* introduces characters, describes the setting, and presents the conflict. In Chinua Achebe's "Civil Peace," for example, the opening of the story introduces readers to the ever-optimistic Jonathan Iwegbu, as he and his family try to re-establish a life in their village after a bloody civil war. The *rising action* develops the conflict, in the case of "Civil Peace" by presenting the complications that face Iwegbu as he deals with such problems as devalued currency, unemployment, and a damaged house. The *climax,* or moment of crisis, arrives when thieves awaken the Iwegbu family in the middle of the night. Following the climax, most traditionally plotted stories provide a *denouement* (French for untying a knot) or *falling action,* in which the conflict is resolved. The denouement of "Civil Peace" features the Iwegbu family once again picking up the pieces of their lives, and the *conclusion* reflects Iwegbu's gratitude for his survival.

The intricacies of plotting can contribute significantly to the enjoyment of a short story. Techniques such as *foreshadowing* and *flashback* often increase suspense in a story and enrich its texture. In Katherine Anne Porter's "Maria Concepcion," for example, Maria's skill in killing chickens foreshadows her murder of Maria Rosa; in Ambrose Bierce's "An Occurrence at Owl Creek Bridge," Peyton Farquhar's flashbacks in the moments before his execution not only explain his situation but also underscore the immorality of war. Writers also employ *irony* in furthering a plot. In *situational irony,* the reader is led to expect a certain outcome, only to be surprised when the plot turns in an entirely different direction. Edith Wharton, for example, leads readers to expect a confrontation between Alice Waythorn's former husbands in "The Other Two"; when all three find themselves in the same room, however, ordinary social conventions prevail. *Dramatic irony* refers to situations in which the reader understands what a character does not, as in Herman Melville's

"Bartleby, the Scrivener," in which the narrator continues to believe that his ingenious schemes will dislodge Bartleby from his offices long after readers recognize the scrivener's intransigence.

While many contemporary short stories dispense with the traditional conventions of plot, an understanding of the features of a skillfully plotted story can help readers not only understand a story, but appreciate its artistic value as well.

Character

Regardless of the intricacies of plot, *character* is often what drives a successful story; effective *characterization* allows readers to recognize themselves and others in the characters that populate a story. The central character of a story, the *protagonist*, is more often than not sympathetic (e.g., Phoenix Jackson in Eudora Welty's "A Worn Path"), but on occasion, as with the scientist Aylmer in Hawthorne's "The Birthmark," the protagonist is decidedly unsympathetic. The central character frequently undergoes substantial change as the story progresses; such a character is called *dynamic.* In Hawthorne's "Young Goodman Brown," for example, the protagonist's adventure in the night forest changes him profoundly—and not for the better. Aylmer, however, does not learn from his unexpectedly deadly experiment, and is thus *static,* or unchanging. Neither character possesses a fully developed personality; rather, both are memorable as representatives of certain types of human frailty. Such characters are called *flat.* A *round* character, on the other hand, emerges as fully human. Calixta in Kate Chopin's "The Storm," capable of a passionate sexual encounter with a former lover even as she worries about the safety of her husband and son, is a round character.

Writers develop characters through a number of devices. Sometimes the physical description of a character is indicative of personality. In Alice Walker's "Everyday Use," for example, Dee wants to return to her African roots, calling herself Wangero and wearing traditional African garb. Dialogue can also reveal character, as in Melville's "Bartleby, the Scrivener": Bartleby's consistent response to any request, "I prefer not to," reveals his personality more vividly than any lengthy description might do. William Dean Howells's Editha, in his story of that name, goads her reluctant fiancé into enlisting in the army during the Spanish-American War; in this case, it is the character's actions that reveal her to readers. The author's own words can also bring a character to life. The final paragraph of "Young Goodman Brown" begins with Hawthorne's own description of the central character after his encounter in the forest: "A stern, a sad, a darkly meditative, a distrustful, if not a desperate man did he become from the night of that fearful dream." Of course, in most stories, characters are developed through several and sometimes all of these techniques.

Setting

In every story, the action takes place and the characters exist within a *setting*, which refers to the place, time, and social context of the story. Setting can contribute to the mood of a story, it can help to establish character, and it can further the development of plot. In Chopin's "Désirée's Baby," for example, the description of L'Abri, the house in which Desiree and Armand live, creates an oppressive atmosphere of foreboding early in the story. In Tadeusz Borowski's "This Way for the Gas, Ladies and Gentlemen," the behavior of the protagonist is understandable only within the context of the setting, a concentration camp in Nazi Europe: His total disregard for human life and dignity would be inexplicable in another setting. Setting furthers the plot in a story such as Welty's "A Worn Path," as the obstacles that Pheonix Jackson encounters in the December woods hinder her in her quest for her grandchild's life-saving medicine.

In Welty's story it is place that looms largest; the ruggedness of the landscape that Phoenix traverses is more significant than the time period or social context (even though both contribute to the meaning of the story). In Borowski, however, social context is profoundly significant. While the physical conditions in the camp are certainly important, it is the utter breakdown of human values within the culture of the camp that accounts for the despicable behavior of both guards and inmates. And Chopin's setting her story in the pre–Civil War South makes the birth of a mixed-race baby to Désirée and Armand an earth-shattering crisis. Each of these stories reflects the multiple ways in which setting contributes to the meaning of a narrative.

Point of View

In order to appreciate a story fully, it is necessary to understand the perspective, or *point of view*, from which the story is told. A story can be narrated from a *first-person* point of view, with a character (either major or minor) speaking directly in his or her own voice. When a story is told from a *third-person* point of view, the narrator is not a character in the story. An *omniscient* third-person narrator can see into the minds of all characters; a *limited omniscient* narrator sees into the mind of one character (or sometimes two); an *objective* narrator, who sees into no character's mind, can only report on the action in the story.

A first-person narrator creates an immediate bond with the reader, a bond that often leads the reader to share the narrator's perspective. In Amy Tan's "Two Kinds," for example, readers are drawn into Jing-Mei's world, sympathizing with her resistance to her mother's attempts to transform her into a child prodigy. First-person narrators, however, often reveal to the reader facets of their personalities of which the narrators themselves are unaware. In Eudora Welty's "Why I Live at the P.O.," for example, readers are quite aware of Sister's emotional instability, despite Sister's conviction of her own rationality and level-headedness. Similarly, readers of "Bartleby, the Scrivener" readily perceive the narrator's self-righteousness even though he appears blissfully unaware of that trait.

Third-person narration is far more common in most literary fiction, with limited omniscient perhaps the most common form of third-person narrator. Such a narrator recounts the story of "Rappaccini's Daughter" through the consciousness of Giovanni, whose morbid fascination with Beatrice blinds him to the dangers of Rappaccini's science. Readers must be aware of the limitations of such a narrator, whose perspective is as narrow as that of the first-person narrator. Just as Jing-Mei cannot see what is in her mother's mind, neither can Hawthorne's narrator see, from within the confines of Giovanni's consciousness, what is in the minds of Beatrice or Rappaccini. What the third-person narrator can do, however, that the first-person narrator cannot, is offer relatively reliable commentary on the character from whose perspective the story is told. Readers can be more confident of the narrator's characterization of Giovanni than of Jing-Mei's attempts to characterize herself.

Unlike the narrator of "Rappaccini's Daughter," the narrator of "The Birthmark" is omniscient, seeing into the minds of both Aylmer and Georgianna. With an omniscient narrator, the reader need not worry about reliability; narration is not filtered through the consciousness of any character, and each character's mind is open to the reader. With an objective narrator, however, readers must be content to simply observe the action and the behavior of characters, and listen to their dialogue. In "The Revolt of 'Mother,' " for example, Mary E. Wilkins Freeman presents the story in much the same way as a filmmaker would, providing the audience with scenes to interpret for themselves. In stories with an objective narrator, dialogue and setting become all the more important as readers attempt to infer characters' motivation.

Voice, Tone, and Style

All narrators, whether first- or third-person, omniscient, limited omniscient, or objective, speak with distinct *voice, tone,* and *style*. A narrator's voice can be energetic, even frantic, as is Sister's in "Why I Live at the P.O.," or it can be matter-of-fact and relatively emotionless, as is the omniscient narrator's in Bobbie Ann Mason's "Shiloh." Tone conveys the author's or the narrator's attitude toward the story, as seen in the first-person narration of "This Way for the Gas, Ladies and Gentlemen." The flat narrative, devoid of any hint of true feeling, contrasts so sharply with the horrors being conveyed that the reader is moved to revulsion.

Style refers to the author's use of language—the length and simplicity or complexity of sentences, the formality or informality of diction, and the use of figurative language. The styles of Ernest Hemingway and William Faulkner, for example, differ markedly with regard to complexity, with Hemingway's spare, short, and direct sentences contrasting with Faulkner's lengthy, complex, and sometimes convoluted sentences. Edith Wharton's diction, or word choice, is quite formal, reflecting the language of New York Society in the Gilded Age, while Mark Twain's informal diction reflects the rough frontier towns of which he writes. Regardless of these distinctions, however, all writers make use of figurative language, primarily in the form of *symbols,* elements in a story that have both a concrete, literal meaning, and an abstract, figurative meaning. The toy sailboat, for example, in Toni Cade Bambara's "The Lesson" is at once a real toy and a symbol of the economic inequity that comes to trouble Sylvia. Similarly, the storm in Chopin's story of that name is quite real, but at the same time it clearly symbolizes the passion between Calixta and Alcee. When an entire story functions on a symbolic rather than a real level, it is called an *allegory.* The fantastic quality of "Young Goodman Brown," for example, suggests that it is an allegory.

The ways in which writers use language can vary dramatically, not only from writer to writer but sometimes from story to story. Paying attention to voice, tone, and style can enhance your appreciation of a story considerably.

Theme

All of the elements of a story work together to contribute to its *theme,* or the central unifying idea of the story. More complex than the moral of a fairy tale or a parable, theme reflects an understanding of some facet of the human condition. Any given story can have a number of themes, and different readers can detect different themes in the same story. One reader might consider "Everyday Use," for example, as a commentary on the value of functionality over artistic value: Mrs. Johnson's decision to give the quilt to Maggie rather than to Dee reflects her desire to see it put to "everyday use" rather than hung like a painting. Another reader, however, might focus on the superficiality of Dee's embracing her African heritage, considering the story's theme to reflect Walker's critique of those who would dismiss their real heritage in favor of some mythical ancestral heritage.

In discovering the theme of a story, readers look to plot, characterization, point of view, voice, tone, and style. Because all of these elements work together to contribute to the overall meaning of the story, readers can reach different conclusions regarding theme. Of course different readers experience stories in different ways, but even the same reader can experience the same story in different ways at different points in his or her life. Thus the possibilities for interpretation of stories are many—which is one of the reasons for the enduring popularity of the short story over the past two centuries.

Kate Chopin
[1851–1904]

Born in St. Louis to an Irish immigrant father and a French Creole mother,
KATE CHOPIN *enjoyed a life of wealth and privilege. During her early years she*
was influenced heavily by a number of strong women; after her father's death in
1855, Kate was reared by her mother, grandmother, and great-grandmother.
Although her upbringing was conventional according to genteel Southern stan-
dards, she exhibited an independent spirit at an early age, preferring her books
and writing tablet to dancing with shallow young men. Regardless of her tastes,
at nineteen she wed a Louisiana businessman, Oscar Chopin, to whom she was
happily married for twelve years before his untimely death. A young widow with
six children, Chopin returned to St. Louis and began writing. Her first stories
were published in 1889, followed by a novel, At Fault, *in 1890.*

Chopin gained national attention with the publication in 1894 of Bayou
Folk, *a collection of stories that featured settings and characters culled from her*
years in Louisiana among French Creoles. Soon she was being compared to other
"local color" writers—writers who focus on the cultures and customs of specific
areas of the country—such as Sarah Orne Jewett and Hamlin Garland. Critics
also recognized the influence of French writer Guy de Maupassant, as well as
Americans Nathaniel Hawthorne and Walt Whitman, in Chopin's work. In 1897
a second collection, A Night in Acadie, *was greeted with equal enthusiasm by*
readers and critics alike. Both turned on the author in 1899, however, when her
novel The Awakening *was published. Exploring the sexual and social rebellion of*
protagonist Edna Pointelleir, a young wife and mother, the novel challenged
existing moral standards and shocked the public. Chopin was accused of fostering
immoral behavior with her uncritical depiction of Edna, who chooses suicide
rather than succumb to the rigid requirements of marriage and motherhood in
turn-of-the-century New Orleans. Reception of the novel was so harsh that
Chopin's publisher cancelled publication of her next volume of short stories, A
Voice and a Vocation, *in 1899.*

Chopin was devastated by the negative response to The Awakening, *which*
she considered (as do many contemporary critics) her best work. Although she
had published twenty poems, almost a hundred short stories—including chil-
dren's stories, two novels, a play, and several critical essays—in a ten-year period,
she wrote very little after 1900. When she died of a brain hemorrhage at age 53,
her contributions to American literature were almost forgotten. Her reputation
was revived in 1969 with the publication of The Complete Works of Kate
Chopin, *edited by Per Seyersted. Late twentieth-century critics recognized the*
existential quality of Chopin's work, as well as her courageous social criticism,

particularly with regard to women's lives. Chopin's women, from the peasant Calixta in "The Storm" to the middle-class Mrs. Mallard in "The Story of an Hour," exhibit an independence and vitality rarely found in late nineteenth century female characters. Chopin's prose is considered as vividly poetic as that of Hawthorne, and her characters as complex as those of Henry James. In the past several decades she has been recognized as one of the most significant writers in the American canon.

William Faulkner
[1897–1962]

Born in New Albany, Mississippi, WILLIAM CUTHBERT FALKNER *(The writer added the "u" to his name as a young man) moved with his family to Oxford, Mississippi in 1902, where his father worked as a livery stable owner, a hardware store owner, and finally as a business manager at the University of Mississippi. Although the presence of the university in this otherwise small, nondescript southern town likely influenced Faulkner's decision to become a writer, it is more probable that he looked to his paternal grandfather, William Clark Falkner (1825–1889), as a source of inspiration. A writer and a figure out of antebellum mythology, the Old Colonel, as the family referred to him, lead a life of almost cartoonish violence and bravado, stories of which filled the young Faulkner with wonder. With some modifications, this larger-than-life figure made his way into Faulkner's fiction as Colonel John Sartoris, a recurrent character in Faulkner's fiction.*

Faulkner's relationships with both his parents also enhanced and compli-cated his literary aspirations. While his mother was devoted to reading and cul-ture, his father was immersed in the masculine world of horses, whisky, and physical violence. These parental influences are evident in a body of fiction that is both dizzyingly intellectual and insistently physical. Though he demonstrated early precociousness at school, he was drifting away by the eighth grade, and he never managed to take a degree at the local university. In 1918 he volunteered for and was rejected by the Army Air Corps because of his diminutive size. Not to be cheated out of the opportunity to relive the martial grandeur of his grandfather, he traveled to Toronto and enlisted in the RAF in July 1918, only to have World War I end before he could complete his training. He returned to Oxford in December of that year sporting an RAF captain's uniform, a phony limp, and a story about being shot down over enemy lines in France. Though no one in Oxford much believed him, he carried an obsession with World War I that stayed with him from his first novel, Soldier's Pay *(1926), through the late work* A Fable *(1954), both of which focus on the hollowness and hypocrisy that sometimes over-shadow the heroics of war.*

Faulkner's literary career can be considered in terms of three phases. Throughout the early 1920s, Faulkner wrote a series of unsuccessful works—a collection of poetry titled the The Marble Faun *(1924) and the early novels* Soldier's Pay, Mosquitoes *(1927), and* Flags in the Dust *(published in 1929 as* Sartoris*). This period is also marked by transience and uncertainty, as Faulkner moved to New York, New Orleans, and back to Oxford. He studied briefly at the University of Mississippi, served for a time as the university's postmaster, and* worked at odd jobs about the town of Oxford. Despite its flaws, Flags in the Dust represents Faulkner's first attempt to use the history of his family and his region as a source for his art. The novel therefore heralds the second, mature phase of his career. Faulkner gained critical acclaim with The Sound and the Fury (1929), the story of a disintegrating Southern family told through the modernist techniques of stream-of-consciousness narration and multiple, fragmented points of view. In 1930, the noteworthy Faulkner then became somewhat notorious with the publication of Sanctuary, a lurid potboiler about bootlegging, prostitution, and rape. In the same year, Faulkner completed yet another important novel, As I Lay Dying. Here again presented through the distracted comments of several narrators (including a purported lunatic, a traumatized young boy, and a delusional religious zealot), this harrowing tale treats a poor rural family who struggle to carry their dead mother to a cemetery many miles away. In this story, the language of the rural South becomes a kind of mythological poetry. This burst of creative activity launched the major period of Faulkner's career, eleven or twelve years that saw the publication of Light in August (1932), Absalom, Absalom! (1935), The Unvanquished (1938), The Wild Palms (1939), and Go Down, Moses (1942). During this time Faulkner also wrote short stories and worked in Hollywood as a screenwriter, an occupation he loathed. His near destitution would only begin to abate in 1948, when he was paid $50,000 by MGM for the film rights to his 1948 novel Intruder in the Dust and when, in 1949, he received the Nobel Prize for Literature. The third and final phase of Faulkner's career is characterized by a mellowing of his artistic vision, as is evident in his final novel, The Reivers (1962). In his later years, Faulkner assumed the role of "elder man of letters." He traveled to Japan as a kind of literary ambassador, served as a writer-in-residence at the University of Virginia, and addressed cadets at West Point, where his son-in-law had gone to school. He also weighed in on the racial controversies of the time, but his comments seemed to anger equally those on all sides of the debate. As he aged, Faulkner's health suffered from his heavy drinking and from several falls sustained while riding horses. It is suspected that one of these falls landed him in the hospital on July 5, 1962, where he died of a heart attack the next day.

Critical reception of Faulkner's work ranged from prudish dismissal to adulation, but today he is widely regarded as the best American writer of the twentieth century. During the eighties and nineties many critics began to question this status, given the apparent racism and misogyny that color Faulkner's canon. This debate is ongoing, but what remains unimpeachable, besides the explosive beauty of his experiments with language and style, and with the form of the novel itself, is his quiet confidence in the perseverance of the human soul.

—David L. G. Arnold, University of Wisconsin, Stevens Point

A Rose for Emily

WILLIAM FAULKNER

I

WHEN MISS EMILY GRIERSON DIED, our whole town went to her funeral: the men through a sort of respectful affection for a fallen monument, the women mostly out of curiosity to see the inside of her house, which no one save an old manservant—a combined gardener and cook—had seen in at least ten years.

It was a big, squarish frame house that had once been white, decorated with cupolas and spires and scrolled balconies in the heavily lightsome style of the seventies, set on what had once been our most select street. But garages and cotton gins had encroached and obliterated even the august names of that neighborhood; only Miss Emily's house was left, lifting its stubborn and coquettish decay above the cotton wagons and the gasoline pumps—an eyesore among eyesores. And now Miss Emily had gone to join the representatives of those august names where they lay in the cedar-bemused cemetery among the ranked and anonymous graves of Union and Confederate soldiers who fell at the battle of Jefferson.

Alive, Miss Emily had been a tradition, a duty, and a care; a sort of hereditary obligation upon the town, dating from that day in 1894 when Colonel Sartoris, the mayor—he who fathered the edict that no Negro woman should appear on the streets without an apron—remitted her taxes, the dispensation dating from the death of her father on into perpetuity. Not that Miss Emily would have accepted charity. Colonel Sartoris invented an involved tale to the effect that Miss Emily's father had loaned money to the town, which the town, as a matter of business, preferred this way of repaying. Only a man of Colonel Sartoris' generation and thought could have invented it, and only a woman could have believed it.

When the next generation, with its more modern ideas, became mayors and aldermen, this arrangement created some little dissatisfaction. On the first of the year they mailed her a tax notice. February came, and there was no

Reprinted from *The Collected Short Stories of William Faulkner*, by permission of Lee Caplin.

reply. They wrote her a formal letter, asking her to call at the sheriff's office at her convenience. A week later the mayor wrote her himself, offering to call or to send his car for her, and received in reply a note on paper of an archaic shape, in a thin, flowing calligraphy in faded ink, to the effect that she no longer went out at all. The tax notice was also enclosed, without comment.

They called a special meeting of the Board of Aldermen. A deputation waited upon her, knocked at the door through which no visitor had passed since she ceased giving china-painting lessons eight or ten years earlier. They were admitted by the old Negro into a dim hall from which a staircase mounted into still more shadow. It smelled of dust and disuse—a close, dank smell. The Negro led them into the parlor. It was furnished in heavy, leather-covered furniture. When the Negro opened the blinds of one window, a faint dust rose sluggishly about their thighs, spinning with slow motes in the single sun-ray. On a tarnished gilt easel before the fireplace stood a crayon portrait of Miss Emily's father.

They rose when she entered—a small, fat woman in black, with a thin gold chain descending to her waist and vanishing into her belt, leaning on an ebony cane with a tarnished gold head. Her skeleton was small and spare; perhaps that was why what would have been merely plumpness in another was obesity in her. She looked bloated, like a body long submerged in motionless water, and of that pallid hue. Her eyes, lost in the fatty ridges of her face, looked like two small pieces of coal pressed into a lump of dough as they moved from one face to another while the visitors stated their errand.

She did not ask them to sit. She just stood in the door and listened quietly until the spokesman came to a stumbling halt. Then they could hear the invisible watch ticking at the end of the gold chain.

Her voice was dry and cold. "I have no taxes in Jefferson. Colonel Sartoris explained it to me. Perhaps one of you can gain access to the city records and satisfy yourselves."

"But we have. We are the city authorities, Miss Emily. Didn't you get a notice from the sheriff, signed by him?"

"I received a paper, yes," Miss Emily said. "Perhaps he considers himself the sheriff. . . . I have no taxes in Jefferson."

"But there is nothing on the books to show that, you see. We must go by the—"

"See Colonel Sartoris. I have no taxes in Jefferson."

"But, Miss Emily—"

"See Colonel Sartoris." (Colonel Sartoris had been dead almost ten years.) "I have no taxes in Jefferson. Tobe!" The Negro appeared. "Show these gentlemen out."

II

So she vanquished them, horse and foot, just as she had vanquished their fathers thirty years before about the smell. That was two years after her father's death and a short time after her sweetheart—the one we believed would marry her—had deserted her. After her father's death she went out very little; after her sweetheart went away, people hardly saw her at all. A few of the ladies had the temerity to call, but were not received, and the only sign of life about the place was the Negro man—a young man then—going in and out with a market basket.

"Just as if a man—any man—could keep a kitchen properly," the ladies said, so they were not surprised when the smell developed. It was another link between the gross, teeming world and the high and mighty Griersons.

A neighbor, a woman, complained to the mayor, Judge Stevens, eighty years old.

"But what will you have me do about it, madam?" he said.

"Why, send her word to stop it," the woman said. "Isn't there a law?"

"I'm sure that won't be necessary," Judge Stevens said. "It's probably just a snake or a rat that nigger of hers killed in the yard. I'll speak to him about it."

The next day he received two more complaints, one from a man who came in diffident deprecation. "We really must do something about it, Judge. I'd be the last one in the world to bother Miss Emily, but we've got to do something." That night the Board of Aldermen met—three graybeards and one younger man, a member of the rising generation.

"It's simple enough," he said. "Send her word to have her place cleaned up. Give her a certain time to do it in, and if she don't . . ."

"Dammit, sir," Judge Stevens said, "will you accuse a lady to her face of smelling bad?"

So the next night, after midnight, four men crossed Miss Emily's lawn and slunk about the house like burglars, sniffing along the base of the brickwork and at the cellar openings while one of them performed a regular sowing motion with his hand out of a sack slung from his shoulder. They broke open the cellar door and sprinkled lime there, and in all the outbuildings. As they recrossed the lawn, a window that had been dark was lighted and Miss Emily sat in it, the light behind her, and her upright torso motionless as that of an idol. They crept quietly across the lawn and into the shadow of the locusts that lined the street. After a week or two the smell went away.

That was when people had begun to feel sorry for her. People in our town remembering how old lady Wyatt, her great-aunt, had gone completely crazy at last, believed that the Griersons held themselves a little too high for what they really were. None of the young men were quite good enough for Miss Emily and such. We had long thought of them as a tableau: Miss Emily a slender figure in white in the background, her father a spraddled silhouette in the foreground, his back to her and clutching a horsewhip, the two of them framed by the backflung front door. So when she got to be thirty and was still single, we were not pleased exactly, but vindicated; even with insanity in the family she wouldn't have turned down all of her chances if they had really materialized.

When her father died, it got about that the house was all that was left to her; and in a way, people were glad. At last they could pity Miss Emily. Being left alone, and a pauper, she had become humanized. Now she too would know the old thrill and the old despair of a penny more or less.

The day after his death all the ladies prepared to call at the house and offer condolence and aid, as is our custom. Miss Emily met them at the door, dressed as usual and with no trace of grief on her face. She told them that her father was not dead. She did that for three days, with the ministers calling on her, and the doctors trying to persuade her to let them dispose of the body. Just as they were about to resort to law and force, she broke down, and they buried her father quickly.

We did not say she was crazy then. We believed she had to do that. We remembered all the young men her father had driven away, and we knew that with nothing left, she would have to cling to that which had robbed her, as people will.

III

She was sick for a long time. When we saw her again, her hair was cut short, making her look like a girl, with a vague resemblance to those angels in colored church windows—sort of tragic and serene.

The town had just let the contracts for paving the sidewalks, and in the summer after her father's death they began to work. The construction company came with niggers and mules and machinery, and a foreman named Homer Barron, a Yankee—a big, dark, ready man, with a big voice and eyes lighter than his face. The little boys would follow in groups to hear him cuss the niggers, and the niggers singing in time to the rise and fall of picks. Pretty soon he knew everybody in town. Whenever you heard a lot of laughing anywhere about the square, Homer Barron would be in the center of the group. Presently we began to see him and Miss Emily on Sunday afternoons driving in the yellow-wheeled buggy and the matched team of bays from the livery stable.

At first we were glad that Miss Emily would have an interest, because the ladies all said, "Of course a Grierson would not think seriously of a Northerner, a day laborer." But there were still others, older people, who said that even grief could not cause a real lady to forget *noblesse oblige*—without calling it *noblesse oblige*. They just said, "Poor Emily. Her kinsfolk should come to her." She had some kin in Alabama; but years ago her father had fallen out with them over the estate of old lady Wyatt, the crazy woman, and there was no communication between the two families. They had not even been represented at the funeral.

And as soon as the old people said, "Poor Emily," the whispering began. "Do you suppose it's really so?" they said to one another. "Of course it is. What else could . . ." This behind their hands; rustling of craned silk and satin behind jalousies closed upon the sun of Sunday afternoon as the thin, swift clop-clop-clop of the matched team passed: "Poor Emily."

She carried her head high enough—even when we believed that she was fallen. It was as if she demanded more than ever the recognition of her dignity as the last Grierson; as if it had wanted that touch of earthliness to reaffirm her imperviousness. Like when she bought the rat poison, the arsenic. That was over a year after they had begun to say "Poor Emily," and while the two female cousins were visiting her.

"I want some poison," she said to the druggist. She was over thirty then, still a slight woman, though thinner than usual, with cold, haughty black eyes in a face the flesh of which was strained across the temples and about the eye-sockets as you imagine a lighthouse-keeper's face ought to look. "I want some poison," she said.

"Yes, Miss Emily. What kind? For rats and such? I'd recom—"

"I want the best you have. I don't care what kind."

The druggist named several. "They'll kill anything up to an elephant. But what you want is—"

"Arsenic," Miss Emily said. "Is that a good one?"

"Is . . . arsenic? Yes ma'am. But what you want—"

"I want arsenic."

The druggist looked down at her. She looked back at him, erect, her face like a strained flag. "Why, of course," the druggist said. "If that's what you want. But the law requires you to tell what you are going to use it for."

Miss Emily just stared at him, her head tilted back in order to look him eye for eye, until he looked away and went and got the arsenic and wrapped it up. The Negro delivery boy brought her the package; the druggist didn't come back. When she opened the package at home there was written on the box, under the skull and bones: "For rats."

IV

So the next day we all said, "She will kill herself"; and we said it would be the best thing. When she had first begun to be seen with Homer Barron, we had said, "She will marry him." Then we said, "She will persuade him yet," because Homer himself had remarked—he liked men, and it was known that he drank with the younger men in the Elk's Club—that he was not a marrying man. Later we said, "Poor Emily," behind the jalousies as they passed on Sunday afternoon in the glittering buggy, Miss Emily with her head high and Homer Barron with his hat cocked and a cigar in his teeth, reins and whip in a yellow glove.

Then some of the ladies began to say that it was a disgrace to the town and a bad example to the young people. The men did not want to interfere, but at last the ladies forced the Baptist minister—Miss Emily's people were Episcopal—to call upon her. He would never divulge what happened during that interview, but he refused to go back again. The next Sunday they again drove about the streets and the following day the minister's wife wrote to Miss Emily's relations in Alabama.

So she had blood-kin under her roof again and we sat back to watch developments. At first nothing happened. Then we were sure that they had to be married. We learned that Miss Emily had been to the jeweler's and ordered a man's toilet set in silver, with the letters H.B. on each piece. Two days later we learned that she had bought a complete outfit of men's clothing, including a nightshirt, and we said "They are married." We were really glad. We were glad because the two female cousins were even more Grierson than Miss Emily had ever been.

So we were surprised when Homer Barron—the streets had been finished some time since—was gone. We were a little disappointed that there was not a public blowing-off, but we believed that he had gone on to prepare for Miss Emily's coming, or to give a chance to get rid of the cousins. (By that time it was a cabal, and we were all Miss Emily's allies to help circumvent the cousins.) Sure enough, after another week they departed. And, as we had expected all along, within three days Homer Barron was back in town. A neighbor saw the Negro man admit him at the kitchen door at dusk one evening.

And that was the last we saw of Homer Barron. And of Miss Emily for some time. The Negro man went in and out with the market basket, but the front door remained closed. Now and then we would see her at a window for a moment, as the men did that night when they sprinkled the lime, but for almost six months she did not appear on the streets. Then we knew that this was to be expected too; as if that quality of her father which had thwarted her woman's life so many times had been too virulent and too furious to die.

When we next saw Miss Emily, she had grown fat and her hair was turning gray. During the next few years it grew grayer and grayer until it attained an even pepper-and-salt iron-gray, when it ceased turning. Up to the day of her death at seventy-four it was still that vigorous iron-gray, like the hair of an active man.

From that time on her front door remained closed, save for a period of six or seven years, when she was about forty, during which she gave lessons in china-painting. She fitted up a studio in one of the downstairs rooms, where the daughters and granddaughters of Colonel Sartoris' contemporaries were sent to her with the same regularity and in the same spirit that they were sent on Sundays with a twenty-five cent piece for the collection plate. Meanwhile her taxes had been remitted.

Then the newer generation became the backbone and the spirit of the town, and the painting pupils grew up and fell away and did not send their children to her with boxes of color and tedious brushes and pictures cut from the ladies' magazines. The front door closed upon the last one and remained closed for good. When the town got free postal delivery Miss Emily alone refused to let them fasten the metal numbers above her door and attach a mailbox to it. She would not listen to them.

Daily, monthly, yearly we watched the Negro grow grayer and more stooped, going in and out with the market basket. Each December we sent her a tax notice, which would be returned by the post office a week later, unclaimed. Now and then we would see her in one of the downstairs windows—she had evidently shut up the top floor of the house—like the carven torso of an idol in a niche, looking or not looking at us, we could never tell which. Thus she passed from generation to generation—dear, inescapable, impervious, tranquil, and perverse.

And so she died. Fell ill in the house filled with dust and shadows, with only a doddering Negro man to wait on her. We did not even know she was sick; we had long since given up trying to get any information from the Negro. He talked to no one, probably not even to her, for his voice had grown harsh and rusty, as if from disuse.

She died in one of the downstairs rooms, in a heavy walnut bed with a curtain, her gray head propped on a pillow yellow and moldy with age and lack of sunlight.

V

The Negro met the first of the ladies at the front door and let them in, with their hushed, sibilant voices and their quick, curious glances, and then he disappeared. He walked right through the house and out the back and was not seen again.

The two female cousins came at once. They held the funeral on the second day, with the town coming to look at Miss Emily beneath a mass of bought flowers, with the crayon face of her father musing profoundly above the bier and the ladies sibilant and macabre; and the very old men—some in their brushed Confederate uniforms—on the porch and the lawn, talking of Miss Emily as if she had been a contemporary of theirs, believing that they had danced with her and courted her perhaps, confusing time with its mathematical progression, as the old do, to whom all the past is not a diminishing road, but, instead, a huge meadow which no winter ever quite touches, divided from them now by the narrow bottleneck of the most recent decade of years.

Already we knew that there was one room in the region above the stairs which no one had seen in forty years, and which would have to be forced. They waited until Miss Emily was decently in the ground before they opened it.

The violence of breaking down the door seemed to fill this room with pervading dust. A thin, acrid pall as of the tomb seemed to lie everywhere upon this room decked and furnished as for a bridal: upon the valance curtains of faded rose color, upon the rose-shaded lights, upon the dressing table, upon the delicate array of crystal and the man's toilet things backed with tarnished silver, silver so tarnished that the monogram was obscured. Among them lay a collar and tie, as if they had just been removed, which, lifted, left upon the surface a pale crescent in the dust. Upon a chair hung the suit, carefully folded; beneath it the two mute shoes and the discarded socks.

The man himself lay in the bed.

For a long while we just stood there, looking down at the profound and fleshless grin. The body had aparently once lain in the attitude of an embrace, but now the long sleep that outlasts love, that conquers even the grimace of love, had cuckolded him. What was left of him, rotted beneath what was left of the nightshirt, had become inextricable from the bed in which he lay; and upon him and upon the pillow beside him lay that even coating of the patient and biding dust.

Then we noticed that in the second pillow was the indentation of a head. One of us lifted something from it, and leaning forward, that faint and invisible dust dry and acrid in the nostrils, we saw a long strand of iron-gray hair.

[1930]

QUESTIONS

WILLIAM FAULKNER, *A Rose for Emily*

1. Describe your experience of reading "A Rose for Emily." What portions of the story do you find intriguing, surprising, or unsettling?

2. How does Faulkner use the tactic of suspense and surprise to captivate the reader?

3. Who narrates this story? Why is this figure's perspective important in the understanding we gain of Emily Grierson?

4. Describe Emily's relationship with her father. How is this important in our attempt to understand Emily's character?

5. How does the narrator describe Emily's house and neighborhood? How is this description important in our attempt to understand Emily's character?

6. Describe Homer Barron. How does his character and the relationship he develops with Emily help us understand Emily's character?

7. In what sense does the notion that Emily has been sleeping beside a corpse suggest a critique of the South on Faulkner's part?

8. Research and compose an interpretive essay about Faulkner's participation in the literary Gothic. What are the basic conventions of Gothic literature? What are some of its cultural, philosophical, and even political implications? How does Faulkner interpret Gothic traditions in "A Rose for Emily"?

Ernest Hemingway
[1899–1961]

ERNEST HEMINGWAY *was born in Oak Park, Illinois. His father was a devoted naturalist who shared his outdoor pursuits with his family during summers spent in rural Michigan. His mother was a professional-level musician, who followed the Victorian practice of dressing all toddlers in feminine clothing. This has fueled speculation regarding Hemingway's hatred of her; their problems stemmed more directly from their similar strong, artistic personalities. Although he is often accused of misogyny, most critics now say that he was questioning gender roles, and subtly critiquing their artificiality. In his writing, Hemingway displaced his sympathy for his female characters and his awe at their innate power onto the natural world.*

Hemingway first worked as a reporter for the Kansas City Star. *At the outbreak of World War I he volunteered for the ambulance service (he never served as a combatant with any army), was stationed in Italy, and was wounded at the front. During convalescence, he fell in love with his nurse, on whom he later modeled Catherine in* A Farewell to Arms *(1929). He returned to the United States a celebrity—the first American wounded in the war. After the war, he lived briefly in Chicago, where he met his first wife, Hadley Richardson, and the writer Sherwood Anderson, on whose advice the couple moved to Paris. There he met Gertrude Stein, who strongly influenced his early style, and F. Scott Fitzgerald. Still a journalist, he strove for literary publication, but a suitcase containing almost all of his work was randomly stolen. He overcame subsequent writer's block by deliberately crafting single sentences and paragraphs. Critics cite these efforts as the formation of his concise early style. These paragraphs became the "chapters" between short stories in his first major work,* In Our Time *(1925). He achieved early critical success with* The Sun Also Rises *(1926). Critics were stymied by his 1930s work, especially* Death in the Afternoon *(1931), an allegory for the conflict between aesthetics and capitalism, but disguised as a bullfighting encyclopedia. Critics celebrated his return to a form they understood with* For Whom the Bell Tolls *(1940), his greatest mature novel, set during the Spanish Civil War, (which he had covered in the 1930s, predicting the spread of fascism and the advent of World War II). After covering the war in Europe, he began several ambitious projects that occupied the rest of his life. Dismissed as a has-been in the reviews for* Across the River and Into the Trees *(1950), he stunned the world with* The Old Man and the Sea *(1952). This novel drew on his fear instilled by two near-fatal plane crashes, and it earned the Nobel Prize in 1954. He published no more literature in his lifetime; much work appeared posthumously, including* A Moveable Feast *(1964) and* The Garden of Eden *(1986).*

In the two plane crashes, Hemingway suffered severe internal injuries and a skull fracture, but it was weeks before he received adequate medical care. He sought interim pain management through alcohol; his drinking, which had never had any impact on his writing, became a spiraling problem. He came under government scrutiny for his uncanny perception of political and ideological trends, especially in Cuba, where he had lived since 1939. Always prone to depression, and finally unable to write due to memory loss exacerbated by electro-shock therapy, Hemingway ended his life with a shotgun in Idaho on July 2, 1961.

—Hillary Justice, *Illinois State University*

🐌 🐌 🐌

Hills Like White Elephants

ERNEST HEMINGWAY

THE HILLS ACROSS THE valley of the Ebro[1] were long and white. On this side there was no shade and no trees and the station was between two lines of rails in the sun. Close against the side of the station there was the warm shadow of the building and a curtain, made of strings of bamboo beads, hung across the open door into the bar, to keep out flies. The American and the girl with him sat at a table in the shade, outside the building. It was very hot and the express from Barcelona would come in forty minutes. It stopped at this junction for two minutes and went on to Madrid.

"What should we drink?" the girl asked. She had taken off her hat and put it on the table.

"It's pretty hot," the man said.

"Let's drink beer."

"Dos cervezas," the man said into the curtain.

"Big ones?" a woman asked from the doorway.

"Yes. Two big ones."

The woman brought two glasses of beer and two felt pads. She put the felt pads and the beer glasses on the table and looked at the man and the girl. The girl was looking off at the line of hills. They were white in the sun and the country was brown and dry.

"They look like white elephants," she said.

"I've never seen one," the man drank his beer.

"No, you wouldn't have."

"I might have," the man said. "Just because you say I wouldn't have doesn't prove anything."

The girl looked at the bead curtain. "They've painted something on it," she said. "What does it say?"

"Anis del Toro. It's a drink."

"Could we try it?"

---

[1]River in northern Spain.

Reprinted from *Men Without Women,* by permission of Simon & Schuster.

The man called "Listen" through the curtain. The woman came out from the bar.

"Four reales."[2]

"We want two Anis del Toro."

"With water?"

"Do you want it with water?"

"I don't know," the girl said. "Is it good with water?"

"It's all right."

"You want them with water?" asked the woman.

"Yes, with water."

"It tastes like licorice," the girl said and put the glass down.

"That's the way with everything."

"Yes," said the girl. "Everything tastes of licorice. Especially all the things you've waited so long for, like absinthe."

"Oh, cut it out."

"You started it," the girl said. "I was being amused. I was having a fine time."

"Well, let's try and have a fine time."

"All right. I was trying. I said the mountains looked like white elephants. Wasn't that bright?"

"That was bright."

"I wanted to try this new drink. That's all we do, isn't it—look at things and try new drinks?"

"I guess so."

The girl looked across at the hills.

"They're lovely hills," she said. "They don't really look like white elephants. I just meant the coloring of their skin through the trees."

"Should we have another drink?"

"All right."

The warm wind blew the bead curtain against the table.

"The beer's nice and cool," the man said.

"It's lovely," the girl said.

"It's really an awfully simple operation, Jig," the man said. "It's not really an operation at all."

The girl looked at the ground the table legs rested on.

"I know you wouldn't mind it, Jig. It's really not anything. It's just to let the air in."

The girl did not say anything.

---

[2]Spanish coins

"I'll go with you and I'll stay with you all the time. They just let the air in and then it's all perfectly natural."

"Then what will we do afterward?"

"We'll be fine afterward. Just like we were before."

"What makes you think so?"

"That's the only thing that bothers us. It's the only thing that's made us unhappy."

The girl looked at the bead curtain, put her hand out and took hold of two of the strings of beads.

"And you think then we'll be all right and be happy."

"I know we will. You don't have to be afraid. I've known lots of people that have done it."

"So have I," said the girl. "And afterward they were all so happy."

"Well," the man said, "if you don't want to you don't have to. I wouldn't have you do it if you didn't want to. But I know it's perfectly simple."

"And you really want to?"

"I think it's the best thing to do. But I don't want you to do it if you don't really want to."

"And if I do it you'll be happy and things will be like they were and you'll love me?"

"I love you now. You know I love you."

"I know. But if I do it, then it will be nice again if I say things are like white elephants, and you'll like it?"

"I'll love it. I love it now but I just can't think about it. You know how I get when I worry."

"If I do it you won't ever worry?"

"I won't worry about that because it's perfectly simple."

"Then I'll do it. Because I don't care about me."

"What do you mean?"

"I don't care about me."

"Well, I care about you."

"Oh, yes. But I don't care about me. And I'll do it and then everything will be fine."

"I don't want you to do it if you feel that way."

The girl stood up and walked to the end of the station. Across, on the other side, were fields of grain and trees along the banks of the Ebro. Far away, beyond the river, were mountains. The shadow of a cloud moved across the field of grain and she saw the river through the trees.

"And we could have all this," she said. "And we could have everything and every day we make it more impossible."

"What did you say?"

"I said we could have everything."

"We can have everything."

"No, we can't."

"We can have the whole world."

"No, we can't."

"We can go everywhere."

"No, we can't. It isn't ours any more."

"It's ours."

"No, it isn't. And once they take it away, you never get it back."

"But they haven't taken it away."

"We'll wait and see."

"Come on back in the shade," he said. "You mustn't feel that way."

"I don't feel any way," the girl said. "I just know things."

"I don't want you to do anything that you don't want to do—"

"Nor that isn't good for me," she said. "I know. Could we have another beer?"

"All right. But you've got to realize—"

"I realize," the girl said. "Can't we maybe stop talking?"

They sat down at the table and the girl looked across at the hills on the dry side of the valley and the man looked at her and at the table.

"You've got to realize," he said, "that I don't want you to do it if you don't want to. I'm perfectly willing to go through with it if it means anything to you."

"Doesn't it mean anything to you? We could get along."

"Of course it does. But I don't want anybody but you. I don't want any one else. And I know it's perfectly simple."

"Yes, you know it's perfectly simple."

"It's all right for you to say that, but I do know it."

"Would you do something for me now?"

"I'd do anything for you."

"Would you please please please please please please please stop talking?"

He did not say anything but looked at the bags against the wall of the station.

There were labels on them from all the hotels where they had spent nights.

"But I don't want you to," he said, "I don't care anything about it."

"I'll scream," the girl said.

The woman came out through the curtains with two glasses of beer and put them down on the damp felt pads. "The train comes in five minutes," she said.

"What did she say?" asked the girl.

"That the train is coming in five minutes."

The girl smiled brightly at the woman, to thank her.

"I'd better take the bags over to the other side of the station," the man said. She smiled at him.

"All right. Then come back and we'll finish the beer."

He picked up the two heavy bags and carried them around the station to the other tracks. He looked up the tracks but could not see the train. Coming back, he walked through the barroom, where people waiting for the train were drinking. He drank an Anis at the bar and looked at the people. They were all waiting reasonably for the train. He went out through the bead curtain. She was sitting at the table and smiled at him.

"Do you feel better?" he asked.

"I feel fine," she said. "There's nothing wrong with me. I feel fine."

[1927]

QUESTIONS

ERNEST HEMINGWAY, *Hills Like White Elephants*

1. What is the couple arguing about in the story? What specific lines best illustrate their positions in this argument in the first half of the story? In the second half?

2. Toward the beginning of the story, the narrator notes that, "the express from Barcelona was coming in forty minutes." Near the end of the story, the man translates the barmaid's announcement that "the train is coming in five minutes." The couple does not have thirty-five minutes' worth of conversation between these lines. Where, specifically, in the story, does time pass in silence? What must each character be thinking, privately, during each silence in order for the next dialogue to make sense?

3. Compare the description of the Ebro valley that begins the story with the one that occurs halfway through (when Jig moves to the end of the station). Draw a map of the story's setting, including as many details as you can find. How does Hemingway use setting to symbolize the couple's problem and to illustrate possible "solutions"?

4. Consider that this story was written in the 1920s and set in Spain, a Catholic country. How do those details complicate the balance of power in this relationship, especially given the specifics of the couple's current circumstances?

5. Hemingway is often considered a misogynist—a woman hater. What evidence can you find for this in the story? What evidence can you find in the story that contradicts it?

6. If there is no character change in a story, it is not a very good story. Consider Jig's attitude toward their situation throughout the story, and her attitude toward the American man. Identify any moments of change, however subtle. Then do the same for the American man's attitudes toward their situation and toward Jig. Who changes? When? How? Why?

7. The story follows the musical pattern of a "theme and variation." Everything that happens in the first half of the story also happens in the second half, but with slight alterations. Locate where in the story the "variation" half begins, list as many points of similarity as you can, and then describe the differences.

8. Many Hemingway stories involve a sporting conflict set in an arena—a matador engaging a bull in a bullring; a fisherman's epic battle with an

enormous fish encircled by the ocean's horizon. How does this story—which has nothing to do with sport—fit this pattern? What does this say about the larger stakes in the story? Does it elevate them to a universal, epic grandeur, or diminish them to the point of triviality? Or does the story support both readings?

9. What does the couple decide, either individually or together, to do at the end of the story?

11. Research the various options that have been historically available to women and couples who find themselves in similar situations to the one discussed in the story. Discuss how these options have evolved over the last hundred years, and then assess what elements of the couple's predicament remain unchanged despite changes in culture and technology.

12. Write about gender relations as you see them in your town, school, or social groups. How do men and women communicate, and how do they miscommunicate? Decide what, if anything, has changed since the 1920s.

13. Hemingway wrote this story on his honeymoon in 1927 and dedicated the manuscript to his Catholic bride, Pauline, who had just moved across the Atlantic to live with him in France. Write about how this biographical detail contributes to your understanding of the moment at which the man moves the suitcases in the story, and about how it might affect your conclusion regarding what the couple's final decision might be.

Shirley Jackson
[1919–1965]

At once a doting mother who wrote humorous accounts of her family life and a self-described witch who penned incisive studies of psychologic aberration and unsettling tales of the supernatural, **SHIRLEY JACKSON** *explored the unstable boundary between domesticity and horror. Considered one of the finest American fiction writers of the 1950s and 1960s, Jackson is now best known for the widely anthologized short story "The Lottery" (1948).*

Jackson was born in 1919 in San Francisco, the first child of an affluent and conservative family. During childhood and adolescence and well into adulthood, this unruly and overweight daughter struggled against her mother Geraldine's firmly held standards of propriety and femininity. As she resisted the conventions of class and gender, Jackson developed her gift of seeing beneath the decorous surface of middle-class life into its vicious core. In the sunny and seemingly placid northern California suburb of Burlingame, where she attended high school and began writing poetry and short stories, Jackson discerned her neighbors' intolerance and cruelty—traits that later characterized the suburbanites of her fiction.

In 1933 Jackson's family moved to Rochester, New York. After attending the University of Rochester from 1934 to 1936, Jackson withdrew from school and spent a year at home, writing a thousand words a day. In 1937 she entered Syracuse University, where she edited the campus humor magazine, won second prize in a poetry contest, and founded the literary magazine Spectre. *She married the magazine's managing editor, Stanley Edgar Hyman, immediately after her graduation in 1940. The couple moved to New York City, where Jackson held a variety of unsatisfying jobs while continuing to write. In 1941 her experience selling books at Macy's formed the basis for "My Life with R. H. Macy," published in the* New Republic. *This success was followed by the birth of her first child and the publication of many stories in the New Yorker. Her reputation as a writer of short fiction grew, and in 1944 "Come Dance with Me in Ireland" was the first of her four stories chosen for* Best American Short Stories.

Jackson's family continued to grow, and her body of writing continued to expand after she moved to North Bennington, Vermont. She had three more children and published short stories, novels, family chronicles, a one-act play, a children's book, and a nonfictional account of witchcraft in Salem. Her works were made into plays, films, and television shows. "The Lottery" appeared as a short play, a television drama, a radio show, an opera, and a ballet. The family chronicles Life Among the Savages *(1953) and* Raising Demons *(1957) were bestsellers, and Jackson's popular success was matched by critical acclaim for her short fiction and novels alike. These latter include* The Road Through the Wall *(1948), a look at the dark side of suburban life inspired by Jackson's years in Burlingame;* Hangsaman *(1951) and* The Bird's Nest *(1954), two penetrating depictions of mental illness; and* The Sundial *(1958), a Gothic fantasy about the end of the world. Jackson's last two novels,* The Haunting of Hill House *(1959) and* We Have Always Lived in the Castle *(1962), are her best. At once chilling and tender, these haunted-house stories transcend their genre, portraying the often-strained relationship between mother and daughter with consummate sympathy and skill. Three years after* We Have Always Lived in the Castle *appeared on the bestseller list and was named one of the year's best novels by* Time *magazine, Shirley Jackson died of heart failure on August 8, 1965.*

—Jamil Musstafa, *Lewis University*

The Lottery

SHIRLEY JACKSON

THE MORNING OF JUNE 27TH was clear and sunny, with the fresh warmth of a full-summer day; the flowers were blossoming profusely and the grass was richly green. The people of the village began to gather in the square, between the post office and the bank, around ten o'clock; in some towns there were so many people that the lottery took two days and had to be started on June 26th, but in this village, where there were only about three hundred people, the whole lottery took less than two hours, so it could begin at ten o'clock in the morning and still be through in time to allow the villagers to get home for noon dinner.

The children assembled first, of course. School was recently over for the summer, and the feeling of liberty sat uneasily on most of them; they tended to gather together quietly for a while before they broke into boisterous play, and their talk was still of the classroom and the teacher, of books and reprimands. Bobby Martin had already stuffed his pockets full of stones, and the other boys soon followed his example, selecting the smoothest and roundest stones; Bobby and Harry Jones and Dickie Delacroix—the villagers pronounced this name "Dellacroy"—eventually made a great pile of stones in one corner of the square and guarded it against the raids of the other boys. The girls stood aside, talking among themselves, looking over their shoulders at the boys, and the very small children rolled in the dust or clung to the hands of their older brothers or sisters.

Soon the men began to gather, surveying their own children, speaking of planting and rain, tractors and taxes. They stood together, away from the pile of stones in the corner, and their jokes were quiet and they smiled rather than laughed. The women, wearing faded house dresses and sweaters, came shortly after their menfolk. They greeted one another and exchanged bits of gossip as they went to join their husbands. Soon the women, standing by their husbands, began to call to their children, and the children came reluctantly, having to be called four or five times. Bobby Martin ducked under his mother's grasping hand and ran, laughing, back to the pile of stones. His father spoke up sharply, and Bobby came quickly and took his place between his father and his oldest brother.

Reprinted from *The Lottery and Other Stories,* by permission of Farrar, Straus & Giroux, LLC. Copyright © 1976, 1977 by Laurence Hyman, Barry Hyman, Mrs. Sarah Webster and Mrs. Joanne Schnurer.

The lottery was conducted—as were the square dances, the teenage club, the Halloween program—by Mr. Summers, who had time and energy to devote to civic activities. He was a round-faced, jovial man and he ran the coal business, and people were sorry for him, because he had no children and his wife was a scold. When he arrived in the square, carrying the black wooden box, there was a murmur of conversation among the villagers, and he waved and called, "Little late today, folks." The postmaster, Mr. Graves, followed him, carrying a three-legged stool, and the stool was put in the center of the square and Mr. Summers set the black box down on it. The villagers kept their distance, leaving a space between themselves and the stool, and when Mr. Summers said, "Some of you fellows want to give me a hand?" there was a hesitation before two men, Mr. Martin and his oldest son, Baxter, came forward to hold the box steady on the stool while Mr. Summers stirred up the papers inside it.

The original paraphernalia for the lottery had been lost long ago, and the black box now resting on the stool had been put into use even before Old Man Warner, the oldest man in town, was born. Mr. Summers spoke frequently to the villagers about making a new box, but no one liked to upset even as much tradition as was represented by the black box. There was a story that the present box had been made with some pieces of the box that had preceded it, the one that had been constructed when the first people settled down to make a village here. Every year, after the lottery, Mr. Summers began talking again about a new box, but every year the subject was allowed to fade off without anything's being done. The black box grew shabbier each year; by now it was no longer completely black but splintered badly along one side to show the original wood color, and in some places faded or stained.

Mr. Martin and his oldest son, Baxter, held the black box securely on the stool until Mr. Summers had stirred the papers thoroughly with his hand. Because so much of the ritual had been forgotten or discarded, Mr. Summers had been successful in having slips of paper substituted for the chips of wood that had been used for generations. Chips of wood, Mr. Summers had argued, had been all very well when the village was tiny, but now that the population was more than three hundred and likely to keep on growing, it was necessary to use something that would fit more easily into the black box. The night before the lottery, Mr. Summers and Mr. Graves made up the slips of paper and put them in the box, and it was then taken to the safe of Mr. Summers' coal company and locked up until Mr. Summers was ready to take it to the square next morning. The rest of the year, the box was put away, sometimes one place, sometimes another; it had spent one year in Mr. Graves's barn and another year underfoot in the post office, and sometimes it was set on a shelf in the Martin grocery and left there.

There was a great deal of fussing to be done before Mr. Summers declared the lottery open. There were the lists to make up—of heads of families, heads of households in each family, members of each household in each family. There was the proper swearing-in of Mr. Summers by the postmaster, as the official of the lottery; at one time, some people remembered, there had been a recital of some sort, performed by the official of the lottery, a perfunctory, tuneless chant that had been rattled off duly each year; some people believed that the official of the lottery used to stand just so when he said or sang it, others believed that he was supposed to walk among the people, but years and years ago this part of the ritual had been allowed to lapse. There had been, also, a ritual salute, which the official of the lottery had had to use in addressing each person who came up to draw from the box, but this also had changed with time, until now it was felt necessary only for the official to speak to each person approaching. Mr. Summers was very good at all this; in his clean white shirt and blue jeans, with one hand resting carelessly on the black box, he seemed very proper and important as he talked interminably to Mr. Graves and the Martins.

Just as Mr. Summers finally left off talking and turned to the assembled villagers, Mrs. Hutchinson came hurriedly along the path to the square, her sweater thrown over her shoulders, and slid into place in the back of the crowd. "Clean forgot what day it was," she said to Mrs. Delacroix, who stood next to her, and they both laughed softly. "Thought my old man was out back stacking wood," Mrs. Hutchinson went on, "and then I looked out the window and the kids were gone, and then I remembered it was the twentyseventh and came a-running." She dried her hands on her apron, and Mrs. Delacroix said, "You're in time, though. They're still talking away up there."

Mrs. Hutchinson craned her neck to see through the crowd and found her husband and children standing near the front. She tapped Mrs. Delacroix on the arm as a farewell and began to make her way through the crowd. The people separated good-humoredly to let her through; two or three people said, in voices just loud enough to be heard across the crowd, "Here comes your Missus, Hutchinson," and "Bill, she made it after all." Mrs. Hutchinson reached her husband, and Mr. Summers, who had been waiting, said cheerfully, "Thought we were going to have to get on without you, Tessie." Mrs. Hutchinson said, grinning, "Wouldn't have me leave m'dishes in the sink, now, would you, Joe?" and soft laughter ran through the crowd as the people stirred back into position after Mrs. Hutchinson's arrival.

"Well, now," Mr. Summers said soberly, "guess we better get started, get this over with, so's we can go back to work. Anybody ain't here?"

"Dunbar," several people said. "Dunbar, Dunbar."

Mr. Summers consulted his list. "Clyde Dunbar," he said. "That's right. He's broke his leg, hasn't he? Who's drawing for him?"

"Me, I guess," a woman said, and Mr. Summers turned to look at her. "Wife draws for her husband," Mr. Summers said. "Don't you have a grown boy to do it for you, Janey?" Although Mr. Summers and everyone else in the village knew the answer perfectly well, it was the business of the official of the lottery to ask such questions formally. Mr. Summers waited with an expression of polite interest while Mrs. Dunbar answered.

"Horace's not but sixteen yet," Mrs. Dunbar said regretfully. "Guess I gotta fill in for the old man this year."

"Right," Mr. Summers said. He made a note on the list he was holding. Then he asked, "Watson boy drawing this year?"

A tall boy in the crowd raised his hand. "Here," he said. "I'm drawing for m'mother and me." He blinked his eyes nervously and ducked his head as several voices in the crowd said things like "Good fellow, Jack," and "Glad to see your mother's got a man to do it."

"Well," Mr. Summers said, "guess that's everyone. Old Man Warner make it?"

"Here," a voice said, and Mr. Summers nodded.

A sudden hush fell on the crowd as Mr. Summers cleared his throat and looked at the list. "All ready?" he called. "Now, I'll read the names—heads of families first—and the men come up and take a paper out of the box. Keep the paper folded in your hand without looking at it until everyone has had a turn. Everything clear?"

The people had done it so many times that they only half listened to the directions; most of them were quiet, wetting their lips, not looking around. Then Mr. Summers raised one hand high and said, "Adams." A man disengaged himself from the crowd and came forward. "Hi, Steve," Mr. Summers said, and Mr. Adams said, "Hi, Joe." They grinned at one another humorlessly and nervously. Then Mr. Adams reached into the black box and took out a folded paper. He held it firmly by one corner as he turned and went hastily back to his place in the crowd, where he stood a little apart from his family, not looking down at his hand.

"Allen," Mr. Summers said. "Anderson . . . Bentham."

"Seems like there's no time at all between lotteries any more," Mrs. Delacroix said to Mrs. Graves in the back row. "Seems like we got through with the last one only last week."

"Time sure goes fast," Mrs. Graves said.

"Clark . . . Delacroix."

"There goes my old man," Mrs. Delacroix said. She held her breath while her husband went forward.

"Dunbar," Mr. Summers said, and Mrs. Dunbar went steadily to the box while one of the women said, "Go on, Janey," and another said, "There she goes."

"We're next," Mrs. Graves said. She watched while Mr. Graves came around from the side of the box, greeted Mr. Summers gravely, and selected a slip of paper from the box. By now, all through the crowd there were men holding the small folded papers in their large hands, turning them over and over nervously. Mrs. Dunbar and her two sons stood together, Mrs. Dunbar holding the slip of paper.

"Harburt . . . Hutchinson."

"Get up there, Bill," Mrs. Hutchinson said, and the people near her laughed.

"Jones."

"They do say," Mr. Adams said to Old Man Warner, who stood next to him, "that over in the north village they're talking of giving up the lottery."

Old Man Warner snorted. "Pack of crazy fools," he said. "Listening to the young folks, nothing's good enough for *them*. Next thing you know, they'll be wanting to go back to living in caves, nobody work any more, live *that* way for a while. Used to be a saying about 'Lottery in June, corn be heavy soon.' First thing you know, we'd all be eating stewed chickweed and acorns. There's *always* been a lottery," he added petulantly. "Bad enough to see young Joe Summers up there joking with everybody."

"Some places have already quit lotteries," Mrs. Adams said.

"Nothing but trouble in *that*," Old Man Warner said stoutly. "Pack of young fools."

"Martin." And Bobby Martin watched his father go forward. "Overdyke . . . Percy."

"I wish they'd hurry," Mrs. Dunbar said to her older son. "I wish they'd hurry."

"They're almost through," her son said.

"You get ready to run tell Dad," Mrs. Dunbar said.

Mr. Summers called his own name and then stepped forward precisely and selected a slip from the box. Then he called, "Warner."

"Seventy-seventh year I been in the lottery," Old Man Warner said as he went through the crowd. "Seventy-seventh time."

"Watson." The tall boy came awkwardly through the crowd. Someone said, "Don't be nervous, Jack," and Mr. Summers said, "Take your time, son."

"Zanini."

After that, there was a long pause, a breathless pause, until Mr. Summers, holding his slip of paper in the air, said, "All right, fellows." For a minute, no one moved, and then all the slips of paper were opened. Suddenly, all the women began to speak at once, saying, "Who is it?" "Who's got it?" "Is it the Dunbars?" "Is it the Watsons?" Then the voices began to say, "It's Hutchinson. It's Bill," "Bill Hutchinson's got it."

"Go tell your father," Mrs. Dunbar said to her older son.

People began to look around to see the Hutchinsons. Bill Hutchinson was standing quiet, staring down at the paper in his hand. Suddenly, Tessie Hutchinson shouted to Mr. Summers, "You didn't give him time enough to take any paper he wanted. I saw you. It wasn't fair."

"Be a good sport, Tessie," Mrs. Delacroix called, and Mrs. Graves said, "All of us took the same chance."

"Shut up, Tessie," Bill Hutchinson said.

"Well, everyone," Mr. Summers said, "that was done pretty fast, and now we've got to be hurrying a little more to get done in time." He consulted his next list. "Bill," he said, "you draw for the Hutchinson family. You got any other households in the Hutchinsons?"

"There's Don and Eva," Mrs. Hutchinson yelled. "Make them take their chance!"

"Daughters draw with their husbands' families, Tessie," Mr. Summers said gently. "You know that as well as anyone else."

"It wasn't *fair*," Tessie said.

"I guess not, Joe," Bill Hutchinson said regretfully. "My daughter draws with her husband's family, that's only fair. And I've got no other family except the kids."

"Then, as far as drawing for families is concerned, it's you." Mr. Summers said in explanation, "and as far as drawing for households is concerned, that's you, too. Right?"

"Right," Bill Hutchinson said.

"How many kids, Bill?" Mr. Summers asked formally.

"Three," Bill Hutchinson said. "There's Bill, Jr., and Nancy, and little Dave. And Tessie and me."

"All right, then," Mr. Summers said. "Harry, you got their tickets back?"

Mr. Graves nodded and held up the slips of paper. "Put them in the box, then," Mr. Summers directed. "Take Bill's and put it in."

"I think we ought to start over," Mrs. Hutchinson said, as quietly as she could. "I tell you it wasn't *fair*. You didn't give him time enough to choose. *Every*body saw that."

Mr. Graves had selected the five slips and put them in the box, and he dropped all the papers but those onto the ground, where the breeze caught them and lifted them off.

"Listen, everybody," Mrs. Hutchinson was saying to the people around her.

"Ready, Bill?" Mr. Summers asked, and Bill Hutchinson, with one quick glance around at his wife and children, nodded.

"Remember," Mr. Summers said, "take the slips and keep them folded until each person has taken one. Harry, you help little Dave." Mr. Graves took the hand of the little boy, who came willingly with him up to the box. "Take a paper out of the box, Davy," Mr. Summers said. Davy put his hand into the box and laughed. "Take just *one* paper," Mr. Summers said. "Harry, you hold it for him." Mr. Graves took the child's hand and removed the folded paper from the tight fist and held it while little Dave stood next to him and looked up at him wonderingly.

"Nancy next," Mr. Summers said. Nancy was twelve, and her school friends breathed heavily as she went forward, switching her skirt, and took a slip daintily from the box. "Bill, Jr.," Mr. Summers said, and Billy, his face red and his feet over-large, nearly knocked the box over as he got a paper out. "Tessie," Mr. Summers said. She hesitated for a minute, looking around defiantly, and then set her lips and went up to the box. She snatched a paper out and held it behind her.

"Bill," Mr. Summers said, and Bill Hutchinson reached into the box and felt around, bringing his hand out at last with the slip of paper in it.

The crowd was quiet. A girl whispered, "I hope it's not Nancy," and the sound of the whisper reached the edges of the crowd.

"It's not the way it used to be," Old Man Warner said clearly. "People ain't the way they used to be."

"All right," Mr. Summers said. "Open the papers. Harry, you open little Dave's."

Mr. Graves opened the slip of paper and there was a general sigh through the crowd as he held it up and everyone could see that it was blank. Nancy and Bill, Jr., opened theirs at the same time, and both beamed and laughed, turning around to the crowd and holding their slips of paper above their heads.

"Tessie," Mr. Summers said. There was a pause, and then Mr. Summers looked at Bill Hutchinson, and Bill unfolded his paper and showed it. It was blank.

"It's Tessie," Mr. Summers said, and his voice was hushed. "Show us her paper, Bill."

Bill Hutchinson went over to his wife and forced the slip of paper out of her hand. It had a black spot on it, the black spot Mr. Summers had made the night before with the heavy pencil in the coal-company office. Bill Hutchinson held it up, and there was a stir in the crowd.

"All right, folks," Mr. Summers said. "Let's finish quickly."

Although the villagers had forgotten the ritual and lost the original black box, they still remembered to use stones. The pile of stones the boys had made earlier was ready; there were stones on the ground with the blowing scraps of paper that had come out of the box. Mrs. Delacroix selected a stone so large she had to pick it up with both hands and turned, to Mrs. Dunbar. "Come on," she said. "Hurry up."

Mrs. Dunbar had small stones in both hands, and she said, gasping for breath, "I can't run at all. You'll have to go ahead and I'll catch up with you."

The children had stones already, and someone gave little Davy Hutchinson a few pebbles.

Tessie Hutchinson was in the center of a cleared space by now, and she held her hands out desperately as the villagers moved in on her. "It isn't fair," she said. A stone hit her on the side of the head.

Old Man Warner was saying, "Come on, come on, everyone." Steve Adams was in the front of the crowd of villagers, with Mrs. Graves beside him.

"It isn't fair, it isn't right," Mrs. Hutchinson screamed, and then they were upon her.

[1949]

QUESTIONS

1. Where is the village located? How does the story's setting influence our response to its ending?

2. At what point do we suspect that the lottery is not what it appears to be? What is the significance of Old Man Warner's saying, "Lottery in June, corn be heavy soon"? What was the lottery's original function, and what is its current function?

3. How do characters' names reflect their personalities and roles?

4. How does irony function in the story?

5. What does the black box symbolize? What other symbols are important to the story?

6. What does the story suggest about tradition and change? about gender roles? about community?

7. Write an essay focused on Tessie Hutchinson as the story's protagonist. Identify her antagonist(s), and consider why she is late to the lottery.

Nathaniel Hawthorne
[1804–1864]

No writer's work has been more informed by the ghosts of the past than NATHANIEL HAWTHORNE'S. *He was born on Independence Day, 1804, in Salem, Massachusetts, to a family whose ancestors included a judge who persecuted Quakers, and another who played a key role in the Salem witchcraft trials. An acute awareness of his Puritan past would later lead to the complex explorations of sin and guilt found in his short stories and novels: As critic Alfred Kazin remarked, "Hawthorne's great subject was, indeed, the sense of guilt that is perhaps the most enduring theme in the moral history of the West—guilt that is the secret tie that binds us to others and to our own past."*

His position as a major literary figure was slow in coming, however. After graduating from Bowdoin College in Maine (where his classmates included poet Henry Wadsworth Longfellow and future U.S. President Franklin Pierce), he spent the next twelve years at his mother's house in Salem. During this time, he earned little income, lived in relative isolation, and immersed himself in literature and New England history. In 1828 he anonymously published the historical novel Fanshawe, *a work he would later go to great lengths to repudiate (always the harshest critic of his own work, he retrieved and destroyed as many copies of the novel as he could find). He struggled to find a publisher for a collection of his stories until 1836, when old friend Horatio Bridge helped him publish* Twice-told Tales. *Named after a line in Shakespeare's* King John, *the book featured several of Hawthorne's most enduring stories, including "The Maypole of Merry Mount" and "The Minister's Black Veil."*

Despite his success, Hawthorne still found it hard to make a living from writing. In order to support himself, and to earn money for his impending marriage (to Sophia Peabody in 1842), he spent the next couple of years working as a salt and coal measurer in the Boston Custom House. He also lived for a time at the experimental utopian community Brook Farm in West Roxbury, Massachusetts—an experience that provided the plot for his novel The Blithedale Romance *(1852). Hawthorne also published several more collections of short stories, including* Mosses from an Old Manse *in 1846. However, it was his novel* The Scarlet Letter *(1850) that secured his place in American letters. The story of Hester Prynne, a woman condemned by her community for bearing a child out of wedlock, the novel created a literary sensation in both the United States and England, and has since become one of the classics of literature.*

Hawthorne's other novels are The House of the Seven Gables *(1851), a work whose biographical elements include a family curse, and* The Marble Faun *(1860). He also penned the campaign biography* The Life of Franklin Pierce

(1852), an endeavor that his old Bowdoin classmate rewarded with a consulship at Liverpool, England. This position finally earned Hawthorne a measure of financial security for his later years in Concord, Massachusetts, when his creative abilities were on the decline. He died, most likely from a brain tumor, while visiting Pierce in Plymouth, New Hampshire, in 1864. He left behind a legacy of some of the most psychologically penetrating stories and novels in all of American fiction.

—Mark Lovely, *Merrimack College*

Young Goodman Brown

NATHANIEL HAWTHORNE

YOUNG GOODMAN BROWN CAME forth, at sunset, into the street of Salem village, but put his head back, after crossing the threshold, to exchange a parting kiss with his young wife.[1] And Faith, as the wife was aptly named, thrust her own pretty head into the street, letting the wind play with the pink ribbons of her cap, while she called to Goodman Brown.

"Dearest heart," whispered she, softly and rather sadly, when her lips were close to his ear, "pr'y thee, put off your journey until sunrise, and sleep in your own bed to-night. A lone woman is troubled with such dreams and such thoughts, that she's afeard of herself, sometimes. Pray, tarry with me this night, dear husband, of all nights in the year!"

"My love and my Faith," replied young Goodman Brown, "of all nights in the year, this one night must I tarry away from thee. My journey, as thou callest it, forth and back again, must needs be done 'twixt now and sunrise. What, my sweet, pretty wife, dost thou doubt me already, and we but three months married!"

"Then, God bless you!" said Faith, with the pink ribbons, "and may you find all well when you come back."

"Amen!" cried Goodman Brown. "Say thy prayers, dear Faith, and go to bed at dusk, and no harm will come to thee."

So they parted; and the young man pursued his way, until, being about to turn the corner by the meeting-house, he looked back, and saw the head of Faith still peeping after him, with a melancholy air, in spite of her pink ribbons.

"Poor little Faith!" thought he, for his heart smote him. "What a wretch am I, to leave her on such an errand! She talks of dreams, too. Methought, as she spoke, there was trouble in her face, as if a dream had warned her what work is to be done to-night. But, no, no! 'twould kill her to think it. Well; she's a blessed angel on earth; and after this one night, I'll cling to her skirts and follow her to Heaven."

---

[1]"Goodman" and "Goodwife" (short form "Goody") were typical forms of address for common people in colonial New England.

First published in the *New England Magazine* in April, 1835. Collected in *Mosses from an Old Manse* in 1846.

With this excellent resolve for the future, Goodman Brown felt himself justified in making more haste on his present evil purpose. He had taken a dreary road, darkened by all the gloomiest trees of the forest, which barely stood aside to let the narrow path creep through, and closed immediately behind. It was all as lonely as could be; and there is this peculiarity in such a solitude, that the traveller knows not who may be concealed by the innumerable trunks and the thick boughs overhead; so that, with lonely footsteps, he may yet be passing through an unseen multitude.

"There may be a devilish Indian behind every tree," said Goodman Brown, to himself; and he glanced fearfully behind him, as he added, "What if the devil himself should be at my very elbow!"

His head being turned back, he passed a crook of the road, and looking forward again, beheld the figure of a man, in grave and decent attire, seated at the foot of an old tree. He arose, at Goodman Brown's approach, and walked onward, side by side with him.

"You are late, Goodman Brown," said he. "The clock of the Old South[2] was striking as I came through Boston; and that is full fifteen minutes agone."

"Faith kept me back awhile," replied the young man, with a tremor in his voice, caused by the sudden appearance of his companion, though not wholly unexpected.

It was now deep dusk in the forest, and deepest in that part of it where these two were journeying. As nearly as could be discerned, the second traveller was about fifty years old, apparently in the same rank of life as Goodman Brown, and bearing a considerable resemblance to him, though perhaps more in expression than features. Still, they might have been taken for father and son. And yet, though the elder person was as simply clad as the younger, and as simple in manner too, he had an indescribable air of one who knew the world, and would not have felt abashed at the governor's dinner-table, or in King William's court, were it possible that his affairs should call him thither. But the only thing about him, that could be fixed upon as remarkable, was his staff, which bore the likeness of a great black snake, so curiously wrought, that it might almost be seen to twist and wriggle itself, like a living serpent. This, of course, must have been an ocular deception, assisted by the uncertain light.

"Come, Goodman Brown!" cried his fellow-traveller, "this is a dull pace for the beginning of a journey. Take my staff, if you are so soon weary."

"Friend," said the other, exchanging his slow pace for a full stop, "having kept covenant by meeting thee here, it is my purpose now to return whence I came. I have scruples, touching the matter thou wot'st[3] of.

---

[2]The Old South Church in Boston, near Salem village.

[3]Knowest

"Sayest thou so?" replied he of the serpent, smiling apart. "Let us walk on, nevertheless, reasoning as we go, and if I convince thee not, thou shalt turn back. We are but a little way in the forest, yet."

"Too far, too far!" exclaimed the goodman, unconsciously resuming his walk. "My father never went into the woods on such an errand, nor his father before him. We have been a race of honest men and good Christians, since the days of the martyrs.[4] And shall I be the first of the name of Brown, that ever took this path, and kept—"

"Such company, thou wouldst say," observed the elder person, interpreting his pause. "Well said, Goodman Brown! I have been as well acquainted with your family as with ever a one among the Puritans; and that's no trifle to say. I helped your grandfather, the constable, when he lashed the Quaker woman so smartly through the streets of Salem. And it was I that brought your father a pitch-pine knot, kindled at my own hearth, to set fire to an Indian village, in King Philip's war.[5] They were my good friends, both; and many a pleasant walk have we had along this path, and returned merrily after midnight. I would fain be friends with you, for their sake."

"If it be as thou sayest," replied Goodman Brown, "I marvel they never spoke of these matters. Or, verily, I marvel not, seeing that the least rumor of the sort would have driven them from New-England. We are a people of prayer, and good works, to boot, and abide no such wickedness."

"Wickedness or not," said the traveller with the twisted staff, "I have a very general acquaintance here in New-England. The deacons of many a church have drunk the communion wine with me; the selectmen, of divers towns, make me their chairman; and a majority of the Great and General Court[6] are firm supporters of my interest. The governor and I, too—but these are state-secrets."

"Can this be so!" cried Goodman Brown, with a stare of amazement at his undisturbed companion. "Howbeit, I have nothing to do with the governor and council; they have their own ways, and are no rule for a simple husbandman,[7] like me. But, were I to go on with thee, how should I meet the eye of that good old man, our minister, at Salem village? Oh, his voice would make me tremble, both Sabbath-day and lecture-day!"[8]

---

[4]Reference to the hundreds of Protestants executed between 1553 and 1558, during the reign of Roman Catholic Queen Mary I (1516–1558), who was known as Bloody Mary.

[5]Public whipping was a punishment for unrepentant Quakers, according to a 1661 Massachusetts law. Wampanoag chief Metacom, known as King Philip, led New England Indians in the King Philip's War against English colonists in 1675 and 1676,

[6]The legislative body of the Massachusetts Bay colony.

[7]Common man

[8]A mid-week day when attendance at a sermon was required.

Thus far, the elder traveller had listened with due gravity, but now burst into a fit of irrepressible mirth, shaking himself so violently, that his snake-like staff actually seemed to wriggle in sympathy.

"Ha! ha! ha!" shouted he, again and again; then composing himself, "Well, go on, Goodman Brown, go on; but pr'y thee, don't kill me with laughing!"

"Well, then, to end the matter at once," said Goodman Brown, considerably nettled, "there is my wife, Faith. It would break her dear little heart; and I'd rather break my own!"

"Nay, if that be the case," answered the other, "e'en go thy ways, Goodman Brown. I would not, for twenty old women like the one hobbling before us, that Faith should come to any harm."

As he spoke, he pointed his staff at a female figure on the path, in whom Goodman Brown recognized a very pious and exemplary dame, who had taught him his catechism, in youth, and was still his moral and spiritual adviser, jointly with the minister and Deacon Gookin.

"A marvel, truly, that Goody Cloyse[9] should be so far in the wilderness, at night-fall!" said he. "But, with your leave, friend, I shall take a cut through the woods, until we have left this Christian woman behind. Being a stranger to you, she might ask whom I was consorting with, and whither I was going."

"Be it so," said his fellow-traveller. "Betake you to the woods, and let me keep the path."

Accordingly, the young man turned aside, but took care to watch his companion, who advanced softly along the road, until he had come within a staff's length of the old dame. She, meanwhile, was making the best of her way, with singular speed for so aged a woman, and mumbling some indistinct words, a prayer, doubtless, as she went. The traveller put forth his staff, and touched her withered neck with what seemed the serpent's tail.

"The devil!" screamed the pious old lady.

"Then Goody Cloyse knows her old friend?" observed the traveller, confronting her, and leaning on his writhing stick.

"Ah, forsooth, and is it your worship, indeed?" cried the good dame. "Yea, truly is it, and in the very image of my old gossip, Goodman Brown, the grandfather of the silly fellow that now is. But—would your worship believe it?—my broomstick hath strangely disappeared, stolen, as I suspect, by that unhanged witch, Goody Cory,[10] and that, too, when I was all anointed with the juice of smallage and cinque-foil and wolf's-bane—"[11]

---

[9]Sarah Cloyse was one of the women sentence to death for witchcraft in 1692; she was not executed.

[10]Martha Corey was hanged as a witch in 1692.

[11]Plants thought to be used by witches.

"Mingled with fine wheat and the fat of a new-born babe," said the shape of old Goodman Brown.

"Ah, your worship knows the receipt," cried the old lady, cackling aloud. "So, as I was saying, being all ready for the meeting, and no horse to ride on, I made up my mind to foot it; for they tell me, there is a nice young man to be taken into communion to-night. But now your good worship will lend me your arm, and we shall be there in a twinkling."

"That can hardly be," answered her friend. "I may not spare you my arm, Goody Cloyse, but here is my staff, if you will."

So saying, he threw it down at her feet, where, perhaps, it assumed life, being one of the rods which its owner had formerly lent to the Egyptian Magi.[12] Of this fact, however, Goodman Brown could not take cognizance. He had cast up his eyes in astonishment, and looking down again, beheld neither Goody Cloyse nor the serpentine staff, but his fellow-traveller alone, who waited for him as calmly as if nothing had happened.

"That old woman taught me my catechism!" said the young man; and there was a world of meaning in this simple comment.

They continued to walk onward, while the elder traveller exhorted his companion to make good speed and persevere in the path, discoursing so aptly, that his arguments seemed rather to spring up in the bosom of his audi-tor, than to be suggested by himself. As they went, he plucked a branch of maple, to serve for a walking-stick, and began to strip it of the twigs and little boughs, which were wet with evening dew. The moment his fingers touched them, they became strangely withered and dried up, as with a week's sunshine. Thus the pair proceeded, at a good free pace, until suddenly, in a gloomy hol-low of the road, Goodman Brown sat himself down on the stump of a tree, and refused to go any farther.

"Friend," said he, stubbornly, "my mind is made up. Not another step will I budge on this errand. What if a wretched old woman do choose to go to the devil, when I thought she was going to Heaven! Is that any reason why I should quit my dear Faith, and go after her?"

"You will think better of this, by-and-by," said his acquaintance, compos-edly. "Sit here and rest yourself awhile; and when you feel like moving again, there is my staff to help you along."

Without more words, he threw his companion the maple stick, and was as speedily out of sight, as if he had vanished into the deepening gloom. The young man sat a few moments, by the road-side, applauding himself greatly, and thinking with how clear a conscience he should meet the minister, in his morning-walk, nor shrink from the eye of good old Deacon Gookin. And

---

[12]In the Book of Exodus (7:9–12), Egyptian priests transform their rods into serpents.

what calm sleep would be his, that very night, which was to have been spent so wickedly, but purely and sweetly now, in the arms of Faith! Amidst these pleasant and praiseworthy meditations, Goodman Brown heard the tramp of horses along the road, and deemed it advisable to conceal himself within the verge of the forest, conscious of the guilty purpose that had brought him thither, though now so happily turned from it.

On came the hoof-tramps and the voices of the riders, two grave old voices, conversing soberly as they drew near. These mingled sounds appeared to pass along the road, within a few yards of the young man's hiding-place; but owing, doubtless, to the depth of the gloom, at that particular spot, neither the travellers nor their steeds were visible. Though their figures brushed the small boughs by the way-side, it could not be seen that they intercepted, even for a moment, the faint gleam from the strip of bright sky, athwart which they must have passed. Goodman Brown alternately crouched and stood on tip-toe, pulling aside the branches, and thrusting forth his head as far as he durst, without discerning so much as a shadow. It vexed him the more, because he could have sworn, were such a thing possible, that he recognized the voices of the minister and Deacon Gookin, jogging along quietly, as they were wont to do, when bound to some ordination or ecclesiastical council. While yet within hearing, one of the riders stopped to pluck a switch.

"Of the two, reverend Sir," said the voice like the deacon's, "I had rather miss an ordination-dinner than to-night's meeting. They tell me that some of our community are to be here from Falmouth and beyond, and others from Connecticut and Rhode-Island; besides several of the Indian powows,[13] who, after their fashion, know almost as much deviltry as the best of us. Moreover, there is a goodly young woman to be taken into communion."

"Mighty well, Deacon Gookin!" replied the solemn old tones of the minister. "Spur up, or we shall be late. Nothing can be done, you know, until I get on the ground."

The hoofs clattered again, and the voices, talking so strangely in the empty air, passed on through the forest, where no church had ever been gathered, nor solitary Christian prayed. Whither, then, could these holy men be journeying, so deep into the heathen wilderness? Young Goodman Brown caught hold of a tree, for support, being ready to sink down on the ground, faint and over-burthened with the heavy sickness of his heart. He looked up to the sky, doubting whether there really was a Heaven above him. Yet, there was the blue arch, and the stars brightening in it.

"With Heaven above, and Faith below, I will yet stand firm against the devil!" cried Goodman Brown.

---

[13]Medicine men

While he still gazed upward, into the deep arch of the firmament, and had lifted his hands to pray, a cloud, though no wind was stirring, hurried across the zenith, and hid the brightening stars. The blue sky was still visible, except directly overhead, where this black mass of cloud was sweeping swiftly northward. Aloft in the air, as if from the depths of the cloud, came a confused and doubtful sound of voices. Once, the listener fancied that he could distinguish the accents of town's-people of his own, men and women, both pious and ungodly, many of whom he had met at the communion-table, and had seen others rioting at the tavern. The next moment, so indistinct were the sounds, he doubted whether he had heard aught but the murmur of the old forest, whispering without a wind. Then came a stronger swell of those familiar tones, heard daily in the sunshine, at Salem village, but never, until now, from a cloud of night. There was one voice, of a young woman, uttering lamentations, yet with an uncertain sorrow, and entreating for some favor, which, perhaps, it would grieve her to obtain. And all the unseen multitude, both saints and sinners, seemed to encourage her onward.

"Faith!" shouted Goodman Brown, in a voice of agony and desperation; and the echoes of the forest mocked him, crying—"Faith! Faith!" as if bewildered wretches were seeking her, all through the wilderness.

The cry of grief, rage, and terror, was yet piercing the night, when the unhappy husband held his breath for a response. There was a scream, drowned immediately in a louder murmur of voices, fading into far-off laughter, as the dark cloud swept away, leaving the clear and silent sky above Goodman Brown. But something fluttered lightly down through the air, and caught on the branch of a tree. The young man seized it, and beheld a pink ribbon.

"My Faith is gone!" cried he, after one stupefied moment. "There is no good on earth; and sin is but a name. Come, devil! for to thee is this world given."

And maddened with despair, so that he laughed loud and long, did Goodman Brown grasp his staff and set forth again, at such a rate, that he seemed to fly along the forest-path, rather than to walk or run. The road grew wilder and drearier, and more faintly traced, and vanished at length, leaving him in the heart of the dark wilderness, still rushing onward, with the instinct that guides mortal man to evil. The whole forest was peopled with frightful sounds; the creaking of the trees, the howling of wild beasts, and the yell of Indians; while, sometimes, the wind tolled like a distant church-bell, and sometimes gave a broad roar around the traveller, as if all Nature were laughing him to scorn. But he was himself the chief horror of the scene, and shrank not from its other horrors.

"Ha! ha! ha!" roared Goodman Brown, when the wind laughed at him. "Let us hear which will laugh loudest! Think not to frighten me with your deviltry! Come witch, come wizard, come Indian powow, come devil himself! and here comes Goodman Brown. You may as well fear him as he fear you!"

In truth, all through the haunted forest, there could be nothing more frightful than the figure of Goodman Brown. On he flew, among the black pines, brandishing his staff with frenzied gestures, now giving vent to an inspiration of horrid blasphemy, and now shouting forth such laughter, as set all the echoes of the forest laughing like demons around him. The fiend in his own shape is less hideous, than when he rages in the breast of man. Thus sped the demoniac on his course, until, quivering among the trees, he saw a red light before him, as when the felled trunks and branches of a clearing have been set on fire, and throw up their lurid blaze against the sky, at the hour of midnight. He paused, in a lull of the tempest that had driven him onward, and heard the swell of what seemed a hymn, rolling solemnly from a distance, with the weight of many voices. He knew the tune; it was a familiar one in the choir of the village meeting-house. The verse died heavily away, and was lengthened by a chorus, not of human voices, but of all the sounds of the benighted wilderness, pealing in awful harmony together. Goodman Brown cried out; and his cry was lost to his own ear, by its unison with the cry of the desert.

In the interval of silence, he stole forward, until the light glared full upon his eyes. At one extremity of an open space, hemmed in by the dark wall of the forest, arose a rock, bearing some rude, natural resemblance either to an altar or a pulpit, and surrounded by four blazing pines, their tops aflame, their stems untouched, like candles at an evening meeting. The mass of foliage, that had overgrown the summit of the rock, was all on fire, blazing high into the night, and fitfully illuminating the whole field. Each pendent twig and leafy festoon was in a blaze. As the red light arose and fell, a numerous congregation alternately shone forth, then disappeared in shadow, and again grew, as it were, out of the darkness, peopling the heart of the solitary woods at once.

"A grave and dark-clad company!" quoth Goodman Brown.

In truth, they were such. Among them, quivering to-and-fro, between gloom and splendor, appeared faces that would be seen, next day, at the council-board of the province, and others which, Sabbath after Sabbath, looked devoutly heavenward, and benignantly over the crowded pews, from the holiest pulpits in the land. Some affirm, that the lady of the governor was there. At least, there were high dames well known to her, and wives of honored husbands, and widows, a great multitude, and ancient maidens, all of excellent repute, and fair young girls, who trembled, lest their mothers should espy them. Either the sudden gleams of light, flashing over the obscure field, bedazzled Goodman Brown, or he recognized a score of the churchmembers of Salem village, famous for their especial sanctity. Good old Deacon Gookin had arrived, and waited at the skirts of that venerable saint, his revered pastor.

But, irreverently consorting with these grave, reputable, and pious people, these elders of the church, these chaste dames and dewy virgins, there were men of dissolute lives and women of spotted fame, wretches given over to all mean and filthy vice, and suspected even of horrid crimes. It was strange to see, that the good shrank not from the wicked, nor were the sinners abashed by the saints. Scattered, also, among their palefaced enemies, were the Indian priests, or powows, who had often scared their native forest with more hideous incantations than any known to English witchcraft.

"But, where is Faith?" thought Goodman Brown; and, as hope came into his heart, he trembled.

Another verse of the hymn arose, a slow and mournful strain, such as the pious love, but joined to words which expressed all that our nature can conceive of sin, and darkly hinted at far more. Unfathomable to mere mortals is the lore of fiends. Verse after verse was sung, and still the chorus of the desert swelled between, like the deepest tone of a mighty organ. And, with the final peal of that dreadful anthem, there came a sound, as if the roaring wind, the rushing streams, the howling beasts, and every other voice of the unconverted wilderness, were mingling and according with the voice of guilty man, in homage to the prince of all. The four blazing pines threw up a loftier flame, and obscurely discovered shapes and visages of horror on the smokewreaths, above the impious assembly. At the same moment, the fire on the rock shot redly forth, and formed a glowing arch above its base, where now appeared a figure. With reverence be it spoken, the figure bore no slight similitude, both in garb and manner, to some grave divine of the New-England churches.

"Bring forth the converts!" cried a voice, that echoed through the field and rolled into the forest.

At the word, Goodman Brown stept forth from the shadow of the trees, and approached the congregation, with whom he felt a loathful brotherhood, by the sympathy of all that was wicked in his heart. He could have well nigh sworn, that the shape of his own dead father beckoned him to advance, looking downward from a smoke-wreath, while a woman, with dim features of despair, threw out her hand to warn him back. Was it his mother? But he had no power to retreat one step, nor to resist, even in thought, when the minister and good old Deacon Gookin seized his arms, and led him to the blazing rock. Thither came also the slender form of a veiled female, led between Goody Cloyse, that pious teacher of the catechism, and Martha Carrier,[14] who had received the devil's promise to be queen of hell. A rampant hag was she! And there stood the proselytes, beneath the canopy of fire.

---

[14]Hanged as a witch in 1692.

"Welcome, my children," said the dark figure, "to the communion of your race! Ye have found, thus young, your nature and your destiny. My children, look behind you!"

They turned; and flashing forth, as it were, in a sheet of flame, the fiend-worshippers were seen; the smile of welcome gleamed darkly on every visage.

"There," resumed the sable form, "are all whom ye have reverenced from youth. Ye deemed them holier than yourselves, and shrank from your own sin, contrasting it with their lives of righteousness, and prayerful aspirations heavenward. Yet, here are they all, in my worshipping assembly! This night it shall be granted you to know their secret deeds; how hoary-bearded elders of the church have whispered wanton words to the young maids of their households; how many a woman, eager for widow's weeds, has given her husband a drink at bedtime, and let him sleep his last sleep in her bosom; how beardless youths have made haste to inherit their fathers' wealth; and how fair damsels—blush not, sweet ones!—have dug little graves in the garden, and bidden me, the sole guest, to an infant's funeral. By the sympathy of your human hearts for sin, ye shall scent out all the places—whether in church, bed-chamber, street, field, or forest—where crime has been committed, and shall exult to behold the whole earth one stain of guilt, one mighty blood-spot. Far more than this! It shall be yours to penetrate, in every bosom, the deep mystery of sin, the fountain of all wicked arts, and which inexhaustibly supplies more evil impulses than human power—than my power, at its utmost!—can make manifest in deeds. And now, my children, look upon each other."

They did so; and, by the blaze of the hell-kindled torches, the wretched man beheld his Faith, and the wife her husband, trembling before that unhallowed altar.

"Lo! there ye stand, my children," said the figure, in a deep and solemn tone, almost sad, with its despairing awfulness, as if his once angelic nature could yet mourn for our miserable race. "Depending upon one another's hearts, ye had still hoped, that virtue were not all a dream. Now are ye undeceived! Evil is the nature of mankind. Evil must be your only happiness. Welcome, again, my children, to the communion of your race!"

"Welcome!" repeated the fiend-worshippers, in one cry of despair and triumph.

And there they stood, the only pair, as it seemed, who were yet hesitating on the verge of wickedness, in this dark world. A basin was hollowed, naturally, in the rock. Did it contain water, reddened by the lurid light? or was it blood? or, perchance, a liquid flame? Herein did the Shape of Evil dip his hand, and prepare to lay the mark of baptism upon their foreheads, that they might be partakers of the mystery of sin, more conscious of the secret guilt of others, both in deed and thought, than they could now be of their own. The husband cast one look at his pale wife, and Faith at him. What polluted wretches would the next glance shew them to each other, shuddering alike at what they disclosed and what they saw!

"Faith! Faith!" cried the husband. "Look up to Heaven, and resist the Wicked One!"

Whether Faith obeyed, he knew not. Hardly had he spoken, when he found himself amid calm night and solitude, listening to a roar of the wind, which died heavily away through the forest. He staggered against the rock and felt it chill and damp, while a hanging twig, that had been all on fire, besprinkled his cheek with the coldest dew.

The next morning, young Goodman Brown came slowly into the street of Salem village, staring around him like a bewildered man. The good old minister was taking a walk along the grave-yard, to get an appetite for breakfast and meditate his sermon, and bestowed a blessing, as he passed, on Goodman Brown. He shrank from the venerable saint, as if to avoid an anathema. Old Deacon Gookin was at domestic worship, and the holy words of his prayer were heard through the open window. "What God doth the wizard pray to?" quoth Goodman Brown. Goody Cloyse, that excellent old Christian, stood in the early sunshine, at her own lattice, catechising a little girl, who had brought her a pint of morning's milk. Goodman Brown snatched away the child, as from the grasp of the fiend himself. Turning the corner by the meeting-house, he spied the head of Faith, with the pink ribbons, gazing anxiously forth, and bursting into such joy at sight of him, that she skipt along the street, and almost kissed her husband before the whole village. But, Goodman Brown looked sternly and sadly into her face, and passed on without a greeting.

Had Goodman Brown fallen asleep in the forest, and only dreamed a wild dream of a witch-meeting?

Be it so, if you will. But, alas! it was a dream of evil omen for young Goodman Brown. A stern, a sad, a darkly meditative, a distrustful, if not a desperate man, did he become, from the night of that fearful dream. On the Sabbath-day, when the congregation were singing a holy psalm, he could not listen, because an anthem of sin rushed loudly upon his ear, and drowned all the blessed strain. When the minister spoke from the pulpit, with power and fervid eloquence, and, with his hand on the open Bible, of the sacred truths of our religion, and of saint-like lives and triumphant deaths, and of future bliss or misery unutterable, then did Goodman Brown turn pale, dreading, lest the roof should thunder down upon the gray blasphemer and his hearers. Often, awakening suddenly at midnight, he shrank from the bosom of Faith, and at morning or eventide, when the family knelt down at prayer, he scowled, and muttered to himself, and gazed sternly at his wife, and turned away. And when he had lived long, and was borne to his grave, a hoary corpse, followed by Faith, an aged woman, and children and grand-children, a goodly procession, besides neighbors, not a few, they carved no hopeful verse upon his tombstone; for his dying hour was gloom.

[1835]

QUESTIONS

NATHANIEL HAWTHORNE, *Young Goodman Brown*

1. What is the significance of Faith's name? Why does Brown tell his guide that "Faith kept me back awhile?"

2. In what ways does the guide resemble Brown himself? What is the significance of the guide telling Brown of his acquaintance with the young man's family?

3. Why does Brown give up hope after the cloud passes by? How does he interpret the appearance of the pink ribbon?

4. What does the forest represent to Brown? Why is it necessary that his venture into the forest take place during the night?

5. The gathering in the forest is described as reminiscent of a church meeting, complete with altar, hymns, sacraments, and clergymen. How does this description contribute to the theme of the story?

6. How do you interpret the presence of so many reputable townspeople, along with "men of dissolute lives and women of spotted fame," in the forest? Why is it significant that, "the good shrank not from the wicked, nor were the sinners abashed by the saints"?

7. After Brown's adventure is over, the narrator asks whether or not it was no more than a dream. Would the meaning of the story be altered if this were a dream? If so, how? If not, why not?

8. The ritual in which Brown and Faith are the central figures is a combination of baptism and marriage, both of which are designed to welcome the pair into the community of evil. The ritual is also rife with sexual overtones. How might the nature of this ritual reflect Brown's ambiguous feelings about the sexual component of marriage?

9. Write an essay analyzing "Young Goodman Brown" as an exploration of the nature of sin. Consider in your response such issues as Brown's reason for entering the forest, Faith's entreating him to stay, Faith's appearance in the forest, the presence of townspeople in the forest, and Brown's lifelong despair.

10. "Young Goodman Brown" is a story filled with ambiguities. For example, the guide's staff may or may not be transformed into a serpent, the voices in the forest may simply be the wind, and the guide may be Brown's father. Identify other ambiguities and write an essay analyzing their purpose in the story.

Flannery O'Connor
[1925–1964]

Born an only child in Savannah, Georgia, FLANNERY O'CONNOR *moved with her parents to a farm near Milledgeville, Georgia, at age twelve. Her father died of lupus, a disease of the immune system, when O'Connor was fifteen; O'Connor herself succumbed to the disease at age thirty-nine. An intellectual in a rural environment, she quickly began to see the world as sometimes annoying, but often amusing. O'Connor graduated from Georgia State College of Women in 1945, where she was a cartoonist for the student newspaper. Many of her stories draw characters in cartoonish ways, a whimsical, and sometimes slightly cruel, way of seeing humanity. O'Connor went on to the University of Iowa, where she received her Masters of Fine Arts in 1947. It was at the University of Iowa where she published her first short story, "The Geranium," in* Accent *(1946). She went on to an artist's residency at Yaddo in Saratoga Springs, New York, where she developed the professional friendships that were to sustain her throughout her artistic life. Though she returned to the family farm permanently due to her health, she continued to correspond with her artistic colleagues. Her correspondence was collected and published in 1979 as* Letters of Flannery O'Connor: The Habit of Being.*

O'Connor wrote constantly throughout her short life, producing two novels and numerous short stories that have amused readers for the last forty years. Her novels, Wise Blood *(1952) and* The Violent Bear It Away *(1960), present a world where grotesque characters search for meaning, almost without awareness of their own searches. Critics found the novels somewhat perplexing and gave mixed reviews, but the critical reaction to O'Connor's short stories, collected in* A Good Man Is Hard to Find *(1955) and* Everything That Rises Must Converge *(1965), has been consistent and positive throughout the years. There are two important things to know about O'Connor, without which none of her work can be adequately understood: she was a devout Catholic and a southerner. The stories portray the southern qualities much more obviously than they do the Catholicism, but the human search for grace and forgiveness is an important theme throughout her writing. O'Connor depicted the rural south in comic strokes that sometimes bordered on cruel, such as in her description of the idiot blue-eyed cooing daughter of the old farm woman in "A Good Man Is Hard to Find," and the young Bible salesman in "Good Country People" with hair like brown gravy rolling down his head. In a later story, "Revelation," a young college-educated woman hits a pious farm woman with a large human psychology book for mouthing meaningless platitudes. The scene is one of O'Connor's best, but it also demonstrates why some readers find her offensive. Her characters may seem to be on the road to destruction, but O'Connor presents them through her own particular aesthetic, revealing their humanity, and their search for wholeness.*

ā ā ā

A Good Man Is Hard to Find

FLANNERY O'CONNOR

THE GRANDMOTHER DIDN'T WANT to go to Florida. She wanted to visit some of her connections in east Tennessee and she was seizing every chance to change Bailey's mind. Bailey was the son she lived with, her only boy. He was sitting on the edge of his chair at the table, bent over the orange sports section of the *Journal*. "Now look here, Bailey," she said, "see here, read this," and she stood with one hand on her thin hip and the other rattling the newspaper at his bald head. "Here this fellow that calls himself The Misfit is aloose from the Federal Pen and headed toward Florida and you read here what it says he did to these people. Just you read it. I wouldn't take my children in any direction with the criminal like that aloose in it. I couldn't answer to my conscience if I did."

Bailey didn't look up from his reading so she wheeled around then and faced the children's mother; a young woman in slacks, whose face was as broad and innocent as a cabbage and was tied around with a green headkerchief that had two points on the top like rabbit's ears. She was sitting on the sofa, feeding the baby his apricots out of a jar. "The children have been to Florida before," the old lady said. "You all ought to take them somewhere else for a change so they would see different parts of the world and be broad. They never have been to east Tennessee."

The children's mother didn't seem to hear her, but the eight-year-old boy, John Wesley, a stocky child with glasses, said, "If you don't want to go to Florida, why dontcha stay at home?" He and the little girl, June Star, were reading the funny papers on the floor.

"She wouldn't stay at home to be queen for a day," June Star said without raising her yellow head.

"Yes, and what would you do if this fellow, The Misfit, caught you?" the grandmother asked.

"I'd smack his face," John Wesley said.

"She wouldn't stay at home for a million bucks," June Star said. "Afraid she'd miss something. She has to go everywhere we go."

"All right, Miss," the grandmother said. "Just remember that the next time you want me to curl your hair."

June Star said her hair was naturally curly.

The next morning the grandmother was the first one in the car, ready to go. She had her big black valise that looked like the head of a hippopotamus in one corner, and underneath it she was hiding a basket with Pitty Sing, the cat, in it. She didn't intend for the cat to be left alone in the house for three days because he would miss her too much and she was afraid he might brush against one of the gas burners and accidentally asphyxiate himself. Her son Bailey didn't like to arrive at a motel with a cat.

She sat in the middle of the back seat with John Wesley and June Star on either side of her. Bailey and the children's mother and the baby sat in the front and they left Atlanta at eight forty-five with the mileage on the car at 55890. The grandmother wrote this down because she thought it would be interesting to say how many miles they had been when they got back. It took them twenty minutes to reach the outskirts of the city.

The old lady settled herself comfortably, removing her white cotton gloves and putting them up with her purse on the shelf in front of the back window. The children's mother still had on slacks and still had her head tied up in a green kerchief, but the grandmother had on a navy blue straw sailor hat with a bunch of white violets on the brim and a navy blue dress with a small white dot in the print. Her collar and cuffs were white organdy trimmed with lace and at her neckline she had pinned a purple spray of cloth violets containing a sachet. In case of an accident, anyone seeing her dead on the highway would know at once that she was a lady.

She said she thought it was going to be a good day for driving, neither too hot nor too cold, and she cautioned Bailey that the speed limit was fifty-five miles an hour and that the patrolmen hid themselves behind billboards and small clumps of trees and sped out after you before you had a chance to slow down. She pointed out interesting details of the scenery: Stone Mountain; the blue granite that in some places came up to both sides of the highway; the brilliant red clay banks slightly streaked with purple; and the various crops that made rows of green lace-work on the ground. The trees were full of silverwhite sunlights and the meanest of them sparkled. The children were reading comic magazines and their mother had gone back to sleep.

"Let's go through Georgia fast so we don't have to look at it much," John Wesley said.

"If I were a little boy," said the grandmother, "I wouldn't talk about my native state that way. Tennessee has the mountains and Georgia has the hills."

"Tennessee is just a hillbilly dumping ground," John Wesley said, "and Georgia is a lousy state too."

"You said it," June Star said.

"In my time," said the grandmother, folding her thin veined fingers, "children were more respectful of their native states and their parents and everything else. People did right then. Oh look at the cute little pickaninny!" she said and pointed to a Negro child standing in the door of a shack. "Wouldn't that make a picture now?" she asked and they all turned and looked at the little Negro out of the back window. He waved.

"He didn't have any britches on," June Star said.

"He probably didn't have any," the grandmother explained. "Little niggers in the country don't have things like we do. If I could paint, I'd paint that picture," she said.

The children exchanged comic books.

The grandmother offered to hold the baby and the children's mother passed him over the front seat to her. She set him on her knee and bounced him and told him about the things they were passing. She rolled her eyes and screwed up her mouth and stuck her leathery thin face into his smooth bland one. Occasionally he gave her a faraway smile. They passed a large cotton field with five or six graves fenced in the middle of it, like a small island. "Look at the graveyard!" the grandmother said, pointing it out. "That was the old family burying ground. That belonged to the plantation."

"Where's the plantation?" John Wesley asked.

"Gone With the Wind," said the grandmother. "Ha. Ha."

When the children finished all the comic books they had brought, they opened the lunch and ate it. The grandmother ate a peanut butter sandwich and an olive and would not let the children throw the box and the paper napkins out the window. When there was nothing else to do they played a game by choosing a cloud and making the other two guess what shape it suggested. John Wesley took one the shape of a cow and June Star guessed a cow and John Wesley said, no, an automobile, and June Star said he didn't play fair, and they began to slap each other over the grandmother.

The grandmother said she would tell them a story if they would keep quiet. When she told a story, she rolled her eyes and waved her head and was very dramatic. She said once when she was a maiden lady she had been courted by a Mr. Edgar Atkins Teagarden from Jasper, Georgia. She said he was a very good-looking man and a gentleman and that he brought her a watermelon every Saturday afternoon with his initials cut in it, E.A.T. Well, one Saturday, she said, Mr. Teagarden brought the watermelon and there was nobody at home and he left it on the front porch and returned in his buggy to Jasper, but she never got the watermelon, she said, because a nigger boy ate it when he saw the initials, E.A.T.! This story tickled John Wesley's funny bone and he giggled and giggled but June Star didn't think it was any good. She said she wouldn't marry a man that just brought her a watermelon on Saturday.

The grandmother said she would have done well to marry Mr. Teagarden because he was a gentleman and had bought Coca-Cola stock when it first came out and that he had died only a few years ago, a very wealthy man.

They stopped at The Tower for barbecued sandwiches. The Tower was a part-stucco and part-wood filling station and dance hall set in a clearing outside of Timothy. A fat man named Red Sammy Butts ran it and there were signs stuck here and there on the building and for miles up and down the highway saying, TRY RED SAMMY'S FAMOUS BARBECUE. NONE LIKE FAMOUS RED SAMMY'S! RED SAM! THE FAT BOY WITH THE HAPPY LAUGH. A VETERAN! RED SAMMY'S YOUR MAN!

Red Sammy was lying on the bare ground outside The Tower with his head under a truck while a gray monkey about a foot high, chained to a small chinaberry tree, chattered nearby. The monkey sprang back into the tree and got on the highest limb as soon as he saw the children jump out of the car and run toward him.

Inside, The Tower was a long dark room with a counter at one end and tables at the other and dancing space in the middle. They all sat down at a broad table next to the nickelodeon and Red Sam's wife, a tall burnt-brown woman with hair and eyes lighter than her skin, came and took their order. The children's mother put a dime in the machine and played "The Tennessee Waltz," and the grandmother said that tune always made her want to dance. She asked Bailey if he would like to dance but he only glared at her. He didn't have a naturally sunny disposition like she did and trips made him nervous. The grandmother's brown eyes were very bright. She swayed her head from side to side and pretended she was dancing in her chair. June Star said play something she could tap to so the children's mother put in another dime and played a fast number and June Star stepped out onto the dance floor and did her tap routine.

"Ain't she cute?" Red Sam's wife said, leaning over the counter. "Would you like to come be my little girl?"

"No, I certainly wouldn't," June Star said. "I wouldn't live in a broken-down place like this for a million bucks!" and she ran back to the table.

"Ain't she cute?" the woman repeated, stretching her mouth politely.

"Aren't you ashamed?" hissed the grandmother.

Red Sam came in and told his wife to quit lounging on the counter and hurry up with these people's order. His khaki trousers reached just to his hip bones and his stomach hung over them like a sack of meal swaying under his shirt. He came over and sat down at a table nearby and let out a combination sigh and yodel. "You can't win," he said. "You can't win," and he wiped his sweating red face off with a gray handkerchief. "These days you don't know who to trust," he said. "Ain't that the truth?"

"People are certainly not nice like they used to be," said the grandmother.

"Two fellers come in here last week," Red Sammy said, "driving a Chrysler. It was an old beat-up car but it was a good one and these boys looked all right to me. Said they worked at the mill and you know I let them fellers charge the gas they bought? Now why did I do that?"

"Because you're a good man!" the grandmother said at once.

"Yes'm, I suppose so," Red Sam said as if he were struck with this answer.

His wife brought the orders, carrying the five plates all at once without a tray, two in each hand and one balanced on her arm. "It isn't a soul in this green world of God's that you can trust," she said. "And I don't count nobody out of that, not nobody," she repeated, looking at Red Sammy.

"Did you read about that criminal, The Misfit, that's escaped?" asked the grandmother.

"I wouldn't be a bit surprised if he didn't attack this place right here," said the woman. "If he hears about it being here, I wouldn't be none surprised to see him. If he hears it's two cent in the cash register, I wouldn't be a tall surprised if he . . ."

"That'll do," Red Sam said. "Go bring these people their Co'-Colas," and the woman went off to get the rest of the order.

"A good man is hard to find," Red Sammy said. "Everything is getting terrible. I remember the day you could go off and leave your screen door unlatched. Not no more."

He and the grandmother discussed better times. The old lady said that in her opinion Europe was entirely to blame for the way things were now. She said the way Europe acted you would think we were made of money and Red Sam said it was no use talking about it, she was exactly right. The children ran outside into the white sunlight and looked at the monkey in the lacy chinaberry tree. He was busy catching fleas on himself and biting each one carefully between his teeth as if it were a delicacy.

They drove off again into the hot afternoon. The grandmother took cat naps and woke up every few minutes with her own snoring. Outside of Toombsboro she woke up and recalled an old plantation that she had visited in this neighborhood once when she was a young lady. She said the house had six white columns across the front and that there was an avenue of oaks leading up to it and two little wooden trellis arbors on either side in front where you sat down with your suitor after a stroll in the garden. She recalled exactly which road to turn off to get to it. She knew that Bailey would not be willing to lose any time looking at an old house, but the more she talked about it, the more she wanted to see it once again and find out if the little twin arbors were still standing. "There was a secret panel in this house," she said craftily, not telling the truth but wishing that she were, "and the story went that all the family silver was hidden in it when Sherman came through but it was never found. . . ."

"Hey!" John Wesley said. "Let's go see it! We'll find it! We'll poke at the wood work and find it! Who lives there? Where do you turn off at? Hey Pop, can't we turn off there?"

"We never have seen a house with a secret panel!" June Star shrieked. "Let's go to the house with the secret panel! Hey, Pop, can't we go see the house with the secret panel!"

"It's not far from here, I know," the grandmother said. "It wouldn't take over twenty minutes."

Bailey was looking straight ahead. His jaw was as rigid as a horseshoe. "No," he said.

The children began to yell and scream that they wanted to see the house with the secret panel. John Wesley kicked the back of the front seat and June Star hung over her mother's shoulder and whined desperately into her ear that they never had any fun even on their vacation, that they could never do what THEY wanted to do. The baby began to scream and John Wesley kicked the back of the seat so hard that his father could feel the blows in his kidney.

"All right!" he shouted and drew the car to a stop at the side of the road. "Will you all shut up? Will you all just shut up for one second? If you don't shut up, we won't go anywhere."

"It would be very educational for them," the grandmother murmured.

"All right," Bailey said, "but get this. This is the only time we're going to stop for anything like this. This is the one and only time."

"The dirt road that you have to turn down is about a mile back," the grandmother directed. "I marked it when we passed."

"A dirt road," Bailey groaned.

After they had turned around and were headed toward the dirt road, the grandmother recalled other points about the house, the beautiful glass over the front doorway and the candle lamp in the hall. John Wesley said that the secret panel was probably in the fireplace.

"You can't go inside the house," Bailey said. "You don't know who lives there."

"While you all talk to the people in front, I'll run around behind and get in a window," John Wesley suggested.

"We'll all stay in the car," his mother said.

They turned onto the dirt road and the car raced roughly along in a swirl of pink dust. The grandmother recalled the times when there were no paved roads and thirty miles was a day's journey. The dirt road was hilly and there were sudden washes in it and sharp curves on dangerous embankments. All at once they would be on a hill, looking down over the blue tops of trees for miles around, then the next minute, they would be in a red depression with the dust-coated trees looking down on them.

"This place had better turn up in a minute," Bailey said, "or I'm going to turn around."

The road looked as if no one had traveled on it in months.

"It's not much further," the grandmother said and just as she said it, a horrible thought came to her. The thought was so embarrassing that she turned red in the face and her eyes dilated and her feet jumped up, upsetting her valise in the corner. The instant the valise moved, the newspaper top she had over the basket under it rose with a snarl and Pitty Sing, the cat, sprang onto Bailey's shoulder.

The children were thrown to the floor and their mother, clutching the baby, was thrown out the door onto the ground; the old lady was thrown into the front seat. The car turned over once and landed right-side-up in a gulch on the side of the road. Bailey remained in the driver's seat with the cat—gray-striped with a broad white face and an orange nose—clinging to his neck like a caterpillar.

As soon as the children saw they could move their arms and legs, they scrambled out of the car shouting, "We've had an ACCIDENT!" The grandmother was curled up under the dashboard, hoping she was injured so that Bailey's wrath would not come down on her all at once. The horrible thought she had had before the accident was that the house she had remembered so vividly was not in Georgia but in Tennessee.

Bailey removed the cat from his neck with both hands and flung it out the window against the side of a pine tree. Then he got out of the car and started looking for the children's mother. She was sitting against the side of the red gutted ditch, holding the screaming baby, but she only had a cut down her face and a broken shoulder. "We've had an ACCIDENT!" the children screamed in a frenzy of delight.

"But nobody's killed," June Star said with disappointment as the grandmother limped out of the car, her hat still pinned to her head but the broken front brim standing up at a jaunty angle and the violet spray hanging off the side. They all sat down in the ditch, except the children, to recover from the shock. They were all shaking.

"Maybe a car will come along," said the children's mother hoarsely.

"I believe I have injured an organ," said the grandmother, pressing her side, but no one answered her. Bailey's teeth were clattering. He had on a yellow sport shirt with bright parrots designed in it and his face was as yellow as the shirt. The grandmother decided that she would not mention that the house was in Tennessee.

The road was about ten feet above and they could see only the tops of the trees on the other side of it. Behind the ditch they were sitting in there were more woods, tall and dark and deep. In a few minutes they saw a car some distance away on top of a hill, coming slowly as if the occupants were watching them. The grandmother stood up and waved both arms dramatically to attract their attention. The car continued to come on slowly, disappeared around a bend and appeared again, moving even slower, on top of the hill they had gone over. It was a big black battered hearselike automobile. There were three men in it.

It came to a stop just over them and for some minutes, the driver looked down with a steady expressionless gaze to where they were sitting, and didn't speak. Then he turned his head and muttered something to the other two and they got out. One was a fat boy in black trousers and a red sweat shirt with a silver stallion embossed on the front of it. He moved around on the right side of them and stood staring, his mouth partly open in a kind of loose grin. The other had on khaki pants and a blue striped coat and a gray hat pulled down very low, hiding most of his face. He came around slowly on the left side. Neither spoke.

The driver got out of the car and stood by the side of it, looking down at them. He was an older man than the other two. His hair was just beginning to gray and he wore silver-rimmed spectacles that gave him a scholarly look. He had a long creased face and didn't have on any shirt or undershirt. He had on blue jeans that were too tight for him and he was holding a black hat and a gun. The two boys also had guns.

"We've had an ACCIDENT!" the children screamed.

The grandmother had the peculiar feeling that the bespectacled man was someone she knew. His face was as familiar to her as if she had known him all her life but she could not recall who he was. He moved away from the car and began to come down the embankment, placing his feet carefully so that he wouldn't slip. He had on tan and white shoes and no socks, and his ankles were red and thin. "Good afternoon," he said, "I see you all had you a little spill."

"We turned over twice!" said the grandmother.

"Oncet," he corrected. "We see it happen. Try their car and see will it run, Hiram," he said quietly to the boy with the gray hat.

"What you got that gun for?" John Wesley asked. "Whatcha gonna do with that gun?"

"Lady," the man said to the children's mother, "would you mind calling them children to sit down by you? Children make me nervous. I want all you all to sit down right together there where you're at."

"What are you telling us what to do for?" June Star asked.

Behind them the line of woods gaped like a dark open mouth. "Come here," said their mother.

"Look here now," Bailey began suddenly, "we're in a predicament! We're in . . ."

The grandmother shrieked. She scrambled to her feet and stood staring. "You're The Misfit!" she said. "I recognized you at once!"

"Yes'm," the man said, smiling slightly as if he were pleased in spite of himself to be known. "But it would have been better for all of you, lady, if you hadn't of reckernized me."

Bailey turned his head sharply and said something to his mother that shocked the children. The old lady began to cry and The Misfit reddened.

"Lady," he said, "don't you get upset. Sometimes a man says things he don't mean. I don't reckon he meant to talk to you thataway."

"You wouldn't shoot a lady, would you?" the grandmother said and removed a clean handkerchief from her cuff and began to slap at her eyes with it.

The Misfit pointed the toe of his shoe into the ground and made a little hole and then covered it up again. "I would hate to have to," he said.

"Listen," the grandmother almost screamed, "I know you're a good man. You don't look a bit like you have common blood. I know you must come from nice people!"

"Yes mam," he said, "finest people in the world." When he smiled he showed a row of strong white teeth. "God never made a finer woman than my mother and my daddy's heart was pure gold," he said. The boy with the red sweat shirt had come around behind them and was standing with his gun at his hip. The Misfit squatted down on the ground. "Watch them children, Bobby Lee," he said. "You know they make me nervous." He looked at the six of them huddled together in front of him and he seemed to be embarrassed as if he couldn't think of anything to say. "Ain't a cloud in the sky," he remarked, looking up at it. "Don't see no sun but don't see no cloud neither."

"Yes, it's a beautiful day," said the grandmother. "Listen," she said, "you shouldn't call yourself The Misfit because I know you're a good man at heart. I can just look at you and tell."

"Hush!" Bailey yelled. "Hush! Everybody shut up and let me handle this!" He was squatting in the position of a runner about to spring forward but he didn't move.

"I pre-chate that, lady," The Misfit said and drew a little circle in the ground with the butt of his gun.

"It'll take a half a hour to fix this here car," Hiram called, looking over the raised hood of it.

"Well, first you and Bobby Lee get him and that little boy to step over yonder with you," The Misfit said, pointing to Bailey and John Wesley. "The boys want to ask you something," he said to Bailey. "Would you mind stepping back in them woods there with them?"

"Listen," Bailey began, "we're in a terrible predicament! Nobody realizes what this is," and his voice cracked. His eyes were as blue and intense as the parrots in his shirt and he remained perfectly still.

The grandmother reached up to adjust her hat brim as if she were going to the woods with him but it came off in her hand. She stood staring at it and after a second she let it fall on the ground. Hiram pulled Bailey up by the arm as if he were assisting an old man. John Wesley caught hold of his father's hand and Bobby Lee followed. They went off toward the woods and just as they reached the dark edge, Bailey turned and supporting himself against a gray naked pine trunk, he shouted, "I'll be back in a minute, Mamma, wait on me!"

"Come back this instant!" his mother shrilled but they all disappeared into the woods.

"Bailey Boy!" the grandmother called in tragic voice but she found she was looking at The Misfit squatting on the ground in front of her. "I just know you're a good man," she said desperately. "You're not a bit common!"

"Nome, I ain't a good man," The Misfit said after a second as if he had considered her statement carefully, "but I ain't the worst in the world neither. My daddy said I was a different breed of dog from my brothers and sisters. 'You know,' Daddy said, 'it's some that can live their whole life out without asking about it and it's others has to know why it is, and this boy is one of the latters. He's going to be into everything!' " He put on his black hat and looked up suddenly and then away deep into the woods as if he were embarrassed again. "I'm sorry, I don't have on a shirt before you ladies," he said, hunching his shoulders slightly. "We buried our clothes that we had on when we escaped and we're just making do until we can get better. We borrowed these from some folks we met," he explained.

"That's perfectly all right," the grandmother said. "Maybe Bailey has an extra shirt in his suitcase."

"I'll look and see terrectly," The Misfit said.

"Where are they taking him?" the children's mother screamed.

"Daddy was a card himself," The Misfit said. "You couldn't put anything over on him. He never got in trouble with the Authorities though. Just had the knack of handling them."

"You could be honest too if you'd only try," said the grandmother. "Think how wonderful it would be to settle down and live a comfortable life and not have to think about somebody chasing you all the time."

The Misfit kept scratching in the ground with the butt of his gun as if he were thinking about it. "Yes'm, somebody is always after you," he murmured.

The grandmother noticed how thin his shoulder blades were just behind his hat because she was standing up looking down on him. "Do you ever pray?" she asked.

He shook his head. All she saw was the black hat wiggle between his shoulder blades. "Nome," he said.

There was a pistol shot from the woods, followed closely by another. Then silence. The old lady's head jerked around. She could hear the wind move through the tree tops like a long satisfied insuck of breath. "Bailey Boy!," she called.

"I was a gospel singer for a while," The Misfit said. "I been most everything. Been in the arm service, both land and sea, at home and abroad, been twict married, been an undertaker, been with the railroads, plowed Mother Earth, been in a tornado, seen a man burnt alive oncet," and he looked up at the children's mother and the little girl who were sitting close together, their faces white and their eyes glassy; "I even seen a woman flogged," he said.

"Pray, pray," the grandmother began, "pray, pray . . ."

"I never was a bad boy that I remember of," The Misfit said in an almost dreamy voice, "but somewheres along the line I done something wrong and got sent to the penitentiary. I was buried alive," and he looked up and held her attention to him by a steady stare.

"That's when you should have started to pray," she said. "What did you do to get sent to the penitentiary that first time?"

"Turn to the right, it was a wall," The Misfit said, looking up again at the cloudless sky. "Turn to the left, it was a wall. Look up it was a ceiling, look down it was a floor. I forgot what I done, lady. I set there and set there, trying to remember what it was I done and I ain't recalled it to this day. Oncet in a while, I would think it was coming to me, but it never come."

"Maybe they put you in by mistake," the old lady said vaguely.

"Nome," he said. "It wasn't no mistake. They had the papers on me."

"You must have stolen something," she said.

The Misfit sneered slightly. "Nobody had nothing I wanted," he said. "It was a head-doctor at the penitentiary said what I had done was kill my daddy but I known that for a lie. My daddy died in nineteen ought nineteen of the epidemic flu and I never had a thing to do with it. He was buried in the Mount Hopewell Baptist churchyard and you can go there and see for yourself."

"If you would pray," the old lady said, "Jesus would help you."

"That's right," The Misfit said.

"Well then, why don't you pray?" she asked trembling with delight suddenly.

"I don't want no hep," he said, "I'm doing all right by myself."

Bobby Lee and Hiram came ambling back from the woods. Bobby Lee was dragging a yellow shirt with bright blue parrots in it.

"Throw me that shirt, Bobby Lee," The Misfit said. The shirt came flying at him and landed on his shoulder and he put it on. The grandmother couldn't name what the shirt reminded her of. "No, lady," The Misfit said while he was buttoning it up, "I found out the crime don't matter. You can do one thing or you can do another, kill a man or take a tire off his car, because sooner or later you're going to forget what it was you done and just be punished for it."

The children's mother had begun to make heaving noises as if she couldn't get her breath. "Lady," he asked, "would you and that little girl like to step off yonder with Bobby Lee and Hiram and join your husband?"

"Yes, thank you," the mother said faintly. Her left arm dangled helplessly and she was holding the baby, who had gone to sleep, in the other. "Hep that lady up, Hiram," The Misfit said as she struggled to climb out of the ditch, "and Bobby Lee, you hold onto that little girl's hand."

"I don't want to hold hands with him," June Star said. "He reminds me of a pig."

The fat boy blushed and laughed and caught her by the arm and pulled her off into the woods after Hiram and her mother.

Alone with The Misfit, the grandmother found that she had lost her voice. There was not a cloud in the sky nor any sun. There was nothing around her but woods. She wanted to tell him that he must pray. She opened and closed her mouth several times before anything came out. Finally she found herself saying, "Jesus. Jesus," meaning, Jesus will help you, but the way she was saying it, it sounded as if she might be cursing.

"Yes'm," The Misfit said as if he agreed. "Jesus thrown everything off balance. It was the same case with Him as with me except He hadn't committed any crime and they could prove I had committed one because they had the papers on me. Of course," he said, "they never shown me any papers. That's why I sign myself now, I said long ago, you get you a signature and sign everything you do and keep a copy of it. Then you'll know what you done and you can hold up the crime to the punishment and see do they match and in the end you'll have something to prove you ain't been treated right. I call myself The Misfit," he said, "because I can't make what all I done wrong fit with all I gone through in punishment."

There was a piercing scream from the woods, followed closely by a pistol report. "Does it seem right to you, lady, that one is punished a heap and another ain't punished at all?"

"Jesus!" the old lady cried. "You've got good blood! I know you wouldn't shoot a lady! I know you come from nice people! Pray! Jesus, you ought not to shoot a lady. I'll give you all the money I've got!"

"Lady," The Misfit said, looking beyond her far into the woods, "there was never a body that give the undertaker a tip."

There were two more pistol reports and the grandmother raised her head like a parched old turkey hen crying for water and called, "Bailey Boy, Bailey Boy!" as if her heart would break.

"Jesus was the only One that ever raised the dead," The Misfit continued, "and He shouldn't have done it. He thown everything off balance. If He did what He said, then it's nothing for you to do but thow away everything and follow Him, and if He didn't then it's nothing for you to do but enjoy the few minutes you got left the best way you can—by killing somebody or burning down his house or doing some other meanness to him. No pleasure but meanness," he said and his voice had become almost a snarl.

"Maybe He didn't raise the dead," the old lady mumbled, not knowing what she was saying and feeling so dizzy that she sank down in the ditch with her legs twisted under her.

"I wasn't there so I can't say He didn't," The Misfit said. "I wisht I had of been there," he said, hitting the ground with his fist. "It ain't right I wasn't there because if I had of been there I would of known. Listen lady," he said in a high voice, "if I had of been there I would of known and I wouldn't be like I am now." His voice seemed about to crack and the grandmother's head cleared for an instant. She saw the man's face twisted close to her own as if he were going to cry and she murmured, "Why, you're one of my babies. You're one of my own children!" She reached out and touched him on the shoulder. The Misfit sprang back as if a snake had bitten him and shot her three times through the chest. Then he put his gun down on the ground and took off his glasses and began to clean them.

Hiram and Bobby Lee returned from the woods and stood over the ditch, looking down at the grandmother who half sat and half lay in a puddle of blood with her legs crossed under her like a child's and her face smiling up at the cloudless sky.

Without his glasses, The Misfit's eyes were red-rimmed and pale and defenseless-looking. "Take her off and thow her where you thown the others," he said, picking up the cat that was rubbing itself against his leg.

"She was a talker, wasn't she?" Bobby Lee said, sliding down the ditch with a yodel.

"She would of been a good woman," The Misfit said, "if it had been somebody there to shoot her every minute of her life."

"Some fun!" Bobby Lee said.

"Shut up, Bobby Lee," The Misfit said. "It's no real pleasure in life."

[1953]

QUESTIONS

FLANNERY O'CONNOR, *A Good Man Is Hard to Find*

1. What does the grandmother do that causes the accident? What mistake about place does she make? How does her mistake fit with her personality?

2. The conversation with Red Sammy reveals many of the issues of the story. What does Red Sammy have to say about the nature of human beings?

3. The Misfit has been jailed for crimes he does not remember. How do we know that he really is a criminal? What should readers make of his claims about himself?

4. Is it true that no one can be trusted, as Red Sammy and the Grandmother say? What can be said about people who do not trust other people?

5. O'Connor took the idea of this story from a newspaper article about a criminal called The Misfit. What does society do with its misfits? How are they generally treated, and what does this treatment do to them?

6. O'Connor believed that people needed something to wake them up from their complacency. What do the grandmother's last words say about our need to recognize the needs of others?

7. O'Connor uses imagery and color to bring her ideas vividly to life. How does she use color in place, dress, and figure in this story? Note the descriptions of the monkey, the cat, Bailey's shirt.

8. The story centers around the moment of the accident. What is the irony of the children's response to the accident? What clues tell the reader that someone will, indeed, be killed?

9. Sammy uses the words "a good man is hard to find," after his wife has said that she trusts no one, including him. Why are these words put in the mouth of a man like Sammy?

10. Find a newspaper article that interests you and write a story that includes the information in the article.

11. Read about the South of the past that the grandmother remembers. Write about life in that time and place. Consider race and class issues as you write.

12. What causes cruelty? What is the mind set of people who have lost their ability to identify with others? Write about this issue, using a particular event in past or current history (World War II, The Civil war, etc.).

The King James Bible
[1611]

The Bible is the most authoritative text in the Judeo-Christian tradition, and is regarded as divinely inspired, even today, by more conservative elements within Christianity and Judaism. It is divided into two large parts: the Jewish Scriptures, known to Christians as the Old Testament; and the New Testament, containing twenty-seven books recognized as authoritative by Christians but not by Jews. In addition to the thirty-nine books of the Old Testament recognized by Protestant Christianity and by normative Judaism are another fifteen books or parts of books that were handed down with the ancient Greek version of the Jewish Scriptures, known as the Septuagint. Most of these are accepted as canonical by the Roman Catholic Church and are referred to in its tradition as the "deuterocanonical" books.

The Old Testament contains a great variety of writings including myths, legends, legal codes, chronicles, edifying stories, poetry, prophecy, and wisdom literature. The original texts were compiled at various times between the twelfth and the second centuries B.C.E. Almost all of them were written in classical Hebrew, except for a few short passages in Aramaic. The canon of the Hebrew scriptures (the so-called Massoretic text) was only established by Palestinian Jews toward the end of the first century C.E. and has remained substantially unchanged since that time. Greek Christians, however, made use of the Septuagint text, while Roman Catholic Christians in the Middle Ages used the Latin translation of St. Jerome (C. 342–420 C.E.) based on the Hebrew. Since the Reformation the customary practice in Protestant countries is to use vernacular translations based on the original Hebrew text.

In the first generations folowing the death of Christ (29/30 C.E.), Christians continued to use the Jewish Scriptures as sacred writings, interpreting them in the light of the teachings of Jesus and the apostle Paul. Gradually they assembled a body of their own writings, believed to be of apostlic origin. These were written in Greek during a seventy-five-year period between about 50 and 125 C.E. The first attested use of the expression "New Testament," however, comes in the writings of Tertullian around 200 C.E., and the first serious attempts by the Church to define the canon of the New Testament date only from the late fourth century C.E. The New Testament includes four early accounts of the life and teachings of Christ (the Gospels), a historical account of the early missions of the Church (the Acts of the Apostles); letters of various apostles; and a book for prophecies (Revelation) attributed to the apostle John. The letters of the apostle Paul are particularly significant statements of early Christian theology, and all the apostolic epistles contain instructions concerning morality and Church discipline.

Martin Luther first translated the Bible into the common language of the people in the 1500s. His German translation is still widely used. In the early 1600s King James of England commissioned an English translation that is still widely acclaimed as the most beautiful poetry and prose version of the text. The modern era has seen translations into hundreds of languages, and both scholarly and popular translations into English. Reading preferences depend on the purposes of the reader, but the King James is still the version most often used for aesthetic purposes.

The Parable of the Prodigal Son

THE KING JAMES BIBLE

AND HE SAID. A certain man had two sons: And the younger of them said to his father, Father, give me the portion of goods that falleth to me. And he divided unto them his living. And not many days after the younger son gathered all together, and took his journey into a far country, and there wasted his substance with riotous living. And when he had spent all, there arose a mighty famine in that land; and he began to be in want. And he went and joined himself to a citizen of that country; and he sent him into his fields to feed swine. And he would fain have filled his belly with the husks that the swine did eat: and no man gave unto him. And when he came to himself, he said, How many hired servants of my father's have bread enough and to spare, and I perish with hunger! I will arise and go to my father, and will say unto him, Father I have sinned against heaven, and before thee, And am no more worthy to be called thy son; make me as one of thy hired servants. And he arose, and came to his father. But when he was yet a great way off, his father saw him, and had compassion, and ran, and fell on his neck, and kissed him. And the son said unto him, Father I have sinned against heaven, and in thy sight, and am no more worthy to be called thy son. But the father said to his servants, Bring forth the best robe, and put it on him; and put a ring on his hand, and shoes on his feet: And bring hither the fatted calf, and kill it; and let us eat, and be merry: For this my son was dead, and is alive again; he was lost, and is found. And they began to be merry. Now his elder son was in the field: and he came and drew nigh to the house, he heard music and dancing. And he called one of the servants, and asked what these things meant. And he said unto him, Thy brother is come; and thy father hath killed the fatted calf, because he hath received him safe and sound. And he was angry, and would not go in: therefore came his father out, and entreated him. And he answering said to his father, Lo, these many years do I serve thee, neither transgressed I at any time thy commandment; and yet thou never gavest me a kid, that I might make merry with my friends: But as soon as this thy son was come, which hath devoured thy living with harlots, thou hast killed for him the fatted calf. And he said unto him, Son thou art

---

The King James Bible was first printed in 1611.

ever with me, and all that I have is thine. It was meet that we should make merry, and be glad: for this thy brother was dead, and is alive again; and was lost, and is found.

[1611]

QUESTIONS

THE KING JAMES BIBLE, *The Parable of the Prodigal Son*

1. Why has the son chosen to take his inheritance and leave his father's house? Why does he return? Why is his brother angry? What does the father say about his own behavior?

2. Some people want to spend what they have right away, and some want to save every penny. Is one way of life more noble than the other? What are the benefits and pitfalls of both ways?

3. The older brother does not answer his father in the story. Do you think that he changes his mind in response to the father's argument about what is lost and then found? Why or why not?

4. Write about a time when you spent money and then wished you had not. What caused you to spend? Why do you regret your action? What would you do differently next time?

John Updike
[1932–2009]

JOHN UPDIKE *was born and raised in Shillington, Pennsylvania, where his early academic success led to a scholarship to Harvard University. After graduating in 1954, Updike studied at the Ruskin School of Drawing and Fine Arts in Oxford, England, returning to the United States the following year to take a position on the staff of* The New Yorker, *where he worked under James Thurber for two years.*

The New Yorker *was also the venue for Updike's earliest publications, and he continued publishing fiction, poems, and essays in the magazine for decades after he left its staff. Updike is numbered among the most prolific contemporary writers, having published some fifty books. His second novel,* Rabbit, Run *(1960), inspired three sequels,* Rabbit Redux *(1972),* Rabbit is Rich *(1981), and* Rabbit at Rest, *(1990); each of the last two was awarded the Pulitzer Prize for fiction. Updike also received the Rosenthal Award from the National Institute of Arts and Letters (1959); the National Book Award in Fiction (1964); the O. Henry Prize (1967); the American Book Award (1982); the National Book Critics Circle Award for fiction (1982 and 1990); the National Arts Club Medal of Honor (1984); and both the National Medal of the Arts (1989) and the National Medal for the Humanities (2003).*

Among Updike's dozens of other notable publications include Bech: A Book *(1970), which introduced Henry Bech, a moderately successful Jewish-American novelist whom many read as Updike's fictional alter ego, and who returned in* Bech is Back *(1982) and* Bech at Bay *(1998). Updike's novel* The Witches of Eastwick *(1984) was adapted for a major motion picture starring Jack Nicholson. Many of his best short stories, such as "A&P," feature an eye for detail and an interest in sexuality and its repressions. These themes have characterized Updike's work throughout his career.*

For nearly five decades, Updike moved fluidly between multiple genres— novels, short stories, poetry, criticism, and other nonfiction—with equal grace. His realistic style, his masterful exploration of the conventions of prose narrative, and his attention to the nuances of life in postwar suburbia make Updike among the most beloved writers of the twentieth century.

A & P

JOHN UPDIKE

IN WALKS THESE THREE girls in nothing but bathing suits. I'm in the third check-out slot, with my back to the door, so I don't see them until they're over by the bread. The one that caught my eye first was the one in the plaid green two-piece. She was a chunky kid, with a good tan and a sweet broad soft-looking can with those two crescents of white just under it, where the sun never seems to hit, at the top of the backs of her legs. I stood there with my hand on a box of HiHo crackers trying to remember if I rang it up or not. I ring it up again and the customer starts giving me hell. She's one of these cash-register-watchers, a witch about fifty with rouge on her cheekbones and no eyebrows, and I know it made her day to trip me up. She'd been watching cash registers for fifty years and probably never seen a mistake before.

By the time I got her feathers smoothed and her goodies into a bag—she gives me a little snort in passing, if she'd been born at the right time they would have burned her over in Salem—by the time I get her on her way the girls had circled around the bread and were coming back, without a pushcart, back my way along the counters, in the aisle between the checkouts and the Special bins. They didn't even have shoes on. There was this chunky one, with the two-piece—it was bright green and the seams on the bra were still sharp and her belly was still pretty pale so I guessed she just got it (the suit)—there was this one, with one of those chubby berry-faces, the lips all bunched together under her nose, this one, and a tall one, with black hair that hadn't quite frizzed right, and one of these sunburns right across under the eyes, and a chin that was too long—you know, the kind of girl other girls think is very "striking" and "attractive" but never quite makes it, as they very well know, which is why they like her so much—and then the third one, that wasn't quite so tall. She was the queen. She kind of led them, the other two peeking around and making their shoulders round. She didn't look around, not this queen, she just walked straight on slowly, on these long white primadonna legs. She came down a little hard on her heels, as if she didn't walk in bare feet that much, putting down her heels and then letting the weight move along to her toes as if she was testing the floor with every step, putting a little deliberate extra action into it. You never know for sure how girls' minds work (do you really think it's a mind in there or just a little buzz like a bee in a glass jar?) but you got the idea she had talked the other two into coming in here with her, and now she was showing them how to do it, walk slow and hold yourself straight.

She had on a kind of dirty-pink—beige maybe, I don't know—bathing suit with a little nubble all over it and, what got me, the straps were down. They were off her shoulders looped loose around the cool tops of her arms, and I guess as a result the suit had slipped a little on her, so all around the top of the cloth there was this shining rim. If it hadn't been there you wouldn't have known there could have been anything whiter than those shoulders. With the straps pushed off, there was nothing between the top of the suit and the top of her head except just *her* this clean bare plane of the top of her chest down from the shoulder bones like a dented sheet of metal tilted in the light. I mean, it was more than pretty.

She had a sort of oaky hair that sun and salt had bleached, done up in a bun that was unravelling, and a kind of prim face. Walking into the A & P with your straps down, I suppose it's the only kind of face you *can* have. She held her head so high her neck, coming up out of those white shoulders, looked kind of stretched, but I didn't mind. The longer her neck was, the more of her there was.

She must have felt in the corner of her eye me and over my shoulder Stokesie in the second slot watching, but she didn't tip. Not this queen. She kept her eyes moving across the racks, and stopped, and turned so slow it made my stomach rub the inside of my apron, and buzzed to the other two, who kind of huddled against her for relief, and then they all three of them went up the cat-and-dog-food-breakfast-cereal-macaroni-rice-raisins-seasonings-spreads-spaghetti-soft-drinks-crackers-and-cookies aisle. From the third slot I look straight up this aisle to the meat counter, and I watched them all the way. The fat one with the tan sort of fumbled with the cookies, but on second thought she put the package back. The sheep pushing their carts down the aisle—the girls were walking against the usual traffic (not that we have one-way signs or anything)—were pretty hilarious. You could see them, when Queenie's white shoulders dawned on them, kind of jerk, or hop, or hiccup, but their eyes snapped back to their own baskets and on they pushed. I bet you could set off dynamite in an A & P and the people would by and large keep reaching and checking oatmeal off their lists and muttering "Let me see, there was a third thing, began with A, asparagus, no, ah, yes, applesauce!" or whatever it is they do mutter. But there was no doubt, this jiggled them. A few house-slaves in pin curlers even looked around after pushing their carts past to make sure what they had seen was correct.

You know, it's one thing to have a girl in a bathing suit down on the beach, where what with the glare nobody can look at each other much anyway, and another thing in the cool of the A & P, under the fluorescent lights, against all those stacked packages, with her feet paddling along naked over our checkerboard green-and-cream rubber-tile floor.

"Oh Daddy," Stokesie said beside me. "I feel so faint."

"Darling," I said. "Hold me tight." Stokesie's married, with two babies chalked up on his fuselage already, but as far as I can tell that's the only difference. He's twenty-two, and I was nineteen this April.

"Is it done?" he asks, the responsible married man finding his voice. I forgot to say he thinks he's going to be manager some sunny day, maybe in 1990 when it's called the Great Alexandrov and Petrooshki Tea Company or something.

What he meant was, our town is five miles from a beach, with a big summer colony out on the Point, but we're right in the middle of town, and the women generally put on a shirt or shorts or something before they get out of the car into the street. And anyway these are usually women with six children and varicose veins mapping their legs and nobody, including them, could care less. As I say, we're right in the middle of town, and if you stand at our front doors you can see two banks and the Congregational church and the newspaper store and three real-estate offices and about twenty-seven old freeloaders tearing up Central Street because the sewer broke again. It's not as if we're on the Cape; we're north of Boston and there's people in this town haven't seen the ocean for twenty years.

The girls had reached the meat counter and were asking McMahon something. He pointed, they pointed, and they shuffled out of sight behind a pyramid of Diet Delight peaches. All that was left for us to see was old McMahon patting his mouth and looking after them sizing up their joints. Poor kids, I began to feel sorry for them, they couldn't help it.

Now here comes the sad part of the story, at least my family says it's sad, but I don't think it's so sad myself. The store's pretty empty, it being Thursday afternoon, so there was nothing much to do except lean on the register and wait for the girls to show up again. The whole store was like a pinball machine and I didn't know which tunnel they'd come out of. After a while they come around out of the far aisle, around the light bulbs, records at discount of the Caribbean Six or Tony Martin Sings or some such gunk you wonder they waste wax on, six-packs of candy bars, and plastic toys done up in cellophane that fall apart when a kid looks at them anyway. Around they come, Queenie still leading the way, and holding a little gray jar in her hand. Slots Three through Seven are unmanned and I could see her wondering between Stokes and me, but Stokesie with his usual luck draws an old party in baggy gray pants who stumbles up with four giant cans of pineapple juice (what do these bums *do* with all that pineapple juice? I've often asked myself) so the girls come to me. Queenie puts down the jar and I take it into my fingers icy cold. Kingfish Fancy Herring Snacks in Pure Sour Cream: 49¢. Now her hands are empty, not a ring or a bracelet, bare as God made them, and I wonder where the money's coming from. Still with that prim look she lifts a folded dollar bill out of the hollow at the center of her nubbled pink top. The jar went heavy in my hand. Really, I thought that was so cute.

Then everybody's luck begins to run out. Lengel comes in from haggling with a truck full of cabbages on the lot and is about to scuttle into the door marked MANAGER behind which he hides all day when the girls touch his eye. Lengel's pretty dreary, teaches Sunday school and the rest, but he doesn't miss that much. He comes over and says, "Girls, this isn't the beach."

Queenie blushes, though maybe it's just a brush of sunburn I was noticing for the first time, now that she was so close. "My mother asked me to pick up a jar of herring snacks." Her voice kind of startled me, the way voices do when you see the people first, coming out so flat and dumb yet kind of tony, too, the way it ticked over "pick up" and "snacks." All of a sudden I slid right down her voice into her living room. Her father and the other men were standing around in ice-cream coats and bow ties and the women were in sandals picking up herring snacks on toothpicks off a big glass plate and they were all holding drinks the color of water with olives and sprigs of mint in them. When my parents have somebody over they get lemonade and if it's a real racy affair Schlitz in tall glasses with "They Do It Every Time" cartoons stencilled on.

"That's all right," Lengel said. "But this isn't the beach." His repeating this struck me as funny, as if it had just occurred to him, and he had been thinking all these years the A & P was a great big dune and he was the head lifeguard. He didn't like my smiling—as I say he doesn't miss much—but he concentrates on giving the girls that sad Sunday-school-superintendent stare.

Queenie's blush is no sunburn now, and the plump one in plaid, that I liked better from the back—a really sweet can—pipes up, "We weren't doing any shopping. We just came in for one thing."

"That makes no difference," Lengel tells her, and I could see from the way his eyes went that he hadn't noticed she was wearing a two-piece before. "We want you decently dressed when you come in here."

"We *are* decent," Queenie says suddenly, her lower lip pushing, getting sore now that she remembers her place, a place from which the crowd that runs the A & P must look pretty crummy. Fancy Herring Snacks flashed in her very blue eyes.

"Girls, I don't want to argue with you. After this come in here with your shoulders covered. It's our policy." He turns back. That's policy for you. Policy is what the kingpins want. What the others want is juvenile delinquency.

All this while, the customers had been showing up with their carts but, you know, sheep, seeing a scene, they had all bunched up on Stokesie, who shook open a paper bag as gently as peeling a peach, not wanting to miss a word. I could feel in the silence everybody getting nervous, most of all Lengel, who asks me, "Sammy, have you rung up their purchase?"

I thought and said "No" but it wasn't about that I was thinking. I go through the punches, 4, 9, GROC, TOT—it's more complicated than you think, and after you do it often enough, it begins to make a little song, that you hear words to, in my case "Hello (*bing*) there, you (*gung*) hap-py peepul (*splat*)"— the *splat* being the drawer flying out. I uncreased the bill, tenderly as you may imagine, it just having come from between the two smoothest scoops of vanilla I had ever known there were, and pass a half and a penny into her narrow pink palm, and nestle the herrings in a bag and twist its neck and hand it over, all the time thinking.

The girls, and who'd blame them, are in a hurry to get out, so I say "I quit" to Lengel quick enough for them to hear, hoping they'll stop and watch me, their unsuspected hero. They keep right on going, into the electric eye; the door flies open and they flicker across the lot to their car, Queenie and Plaid and Big Tall Goony-Goony (not that as raw material she was so bad), leaving me with Lengel and a kink in his eyebrow.

"Did you say something, Sammy?"

"I said I quit."

"I thought you did."

"You didn't have to embarrass them."

"It was they who were embarrassing us."

I started to say something that came out "Fiddle-de-doo." It's a saying of my grandmother's, and I know she would have been pleased.

"I don't think you know what you're saying." Lengel said.

"I know you don't," I said. "But I do." I pull the bow at the back of my apron and start shrugging it off my shoulders. A couple of customers that had been heading for my slot begin to knock against each other, like scared pigs in a chute.

Lengel sighs and begins to look very patient and old and gray. He's been a friend of my parents for years. "Sammy, you don't want to do this to your Mom and Dad," he tells me. It's true, I don't. But it seems to me that once you begin a gesture it's fatal not to go through with it. I fold the apron, "Sammy" stitched in red on the pocket, and put it on the counter, and drop the bow tie on top of it. The bow tie is theirs, if you've ever wondered. "You'll feel this for the rest of your life," Lengel says, and I know that's true, too, but remembering how he made that pretty girl blush makes me so scrunchy inside I punch the No Sale tab and the machine whirs "pee-pul" and the drawer splats out. One advantage to this scene taking place in summer, I can follow this up with a clean exit, there's no fumbling around getting your coat and galoshes, I just saunter into the electric eye in my white shirt that my mother ironed the night before, and the door heaves itself open, and outside the sunshine is skating around on the asphalt.

I look around for my girls, but they're gone, of course. There wasn't anybody but some young married screaming with her children about some candy they didn't get by the door of a powder-blue Falcon station wagon. Looking back in the big windows, over the bags of peat moss and aluminum lawn furniture stacked on the pavement, I could see Lengel in my place in the slot, checking the sheep through. His face was dark gray and his back stiff, as if he's just had an injection of iron, and my stomach kind of fell as I felt how hard the world was going to be to me hereafter.

[1961]

QUESTIONS

JOHN UPDIKE, *A & P*

1. How is the narrator's voice in the story constructed? In what ways is Sammy's character revealed through his narration? Do his actions parallel or contrast with that character?

2. What details does Updike use to set the scene of the supermarket? How do those details contribute to the richness of the story?

3. Does the narrator's attention to the girls give you a sense of their characters? What details of the narrator's descriptions of them seem objectively rendered, and what details seem more revealing of Sammy's own character?

4. Why does the narrator's family say that the incident at the A&P is sad? Why doesn't Sammy find it sad himself?

5. Sammy feels, at the story's end, "how hard the world was going to be to [him] thereafter." How do Sammy's earlier observations—of the supermarket, the customers, and the girls—lead you to understand what he means here, and why the world is going to be hard to him?

6. How does Updike's apparently objective, realistic portrait of suburbia function as a kind of cultural criticism? What is his critique, and how is it developed in the story?

Guy de Maupassant
[1850–1893]

GUY DE MAUPASSANT *came from Château de Miromesniel, Dieppe. His youth was varied, moving from the study of law in Paris around 1869 but giving that up to serve in the army during the Franco-Prussian War. Later, around 1872, he became a civil servant, working for the ministry of maritime affairs and then at the ministry of education. He left the public employ in 1880. His poetry first appeared that year with Des Vers (1880), and his fiction with "Boule De Suif" (or "Ball of Fat" in the anthology Soirées de Medan edited by Emile Zola. During the next ten years, de Maupassant wrote over three hundred short stories, as well as six novels.*

De Maupassant created a rich irony in his work, often characterized by a kind of humor that creates both amusement and discomfort at the same time. He was a "Naturalist," who showed life as it was for the middle class and poor who surrounded him in his life. The stories ring true because they reflect human foibles and frailties that do not change with time and place. De Maupassant helps the reader see humans as they are and hope that they are not. He also wrote about the sadness of a life of toil in A Woman's Life, *1883, and family struggles and conflicts in* Peter and John, *1888.*

De Maupassant became a victim of syphilis when he was in his twenties, a condition that eventually led to madness and death, but not before it first led to stories of horror and distress. The later stories resemble those of the American writer Poe, showing the dark side of human life and the nightmarish qualities that can haunt an author in distress. His quite unpleasant story "The Horror" (1887) displays his movement toward madness and death.

In 1892 de Maupassant attempted suicide. He spent the final year of his life in a mental institution in Paris and died there at the end of the following year.

The Necklace

GUY DE MAUPASSANT

SHE WAS ONE OF THOSE PRETTY and charming girls, born by a blunder of destiny in a family of employees. She had no dowry, no expectations, no means of being known, understood, loved, married by a man rich and distinguished; and she let them make a match for her with a little clerk in the Department of Education.

She was simple since she could not be adorned; but she was unhappy as though kept out of her own class; for women have no caste and no descent, their beauty, their grace, and their charm serving them instead of birth and fortune. Their native keenness, their instinctive elegance, their flexibility of mind, are their only hierarchy; and these make the daughters of the people the equals of the most lofty dames.

She suffered intensely, feeling herself born for every delicacy and every luxury. She suffered from the poverty of her dwelling, from the worn walls, the abraded chairs, the ugliness of the stuffs. All these things, which another woman of her caste would not even have noticed, tortured her and made her indignant. The sight of the little girl from Brittany who did her humble housework awoke in her desolated regrets and distracted dreams. She let her mind dwell on the quiet vestibules, hung with Oriental tapestries, lighted by tall lamps of bronze, and on the two tall footmen in knee breeches who dozed in the large armchairs, made drowsy by the heat of the furnace. She let her mind dwell on the large parlors, decked with old silk, with their delicate furniture, supporting precious bric-a-brac, and on the coquettish little rooms, perfumed, prepared for the five o'clock chat with the most intimate friends, men well known and sought after, whose attentions all women envied and desired.

When she sat down to dine, before a tablecloth three days old, in front of her husband, who lifted the cover of the tureen, declaring with an air of satisfaction, "Ah, the good *pot-au-feu*. I don't know anything better than that," she was thinking of delicate repasts, with glittering silver, with tapestries peopling the walls with ancient figures and with strange birds in a fairy-like forest; she was thinking of exquisite dishes, served in marvelous platters, of compliment whispered and heard with a sphinx-like smile, while she was eating the rosy flesh of a trout or the wings of a quail.

She had no dresses, no jewelry, nothing. And she loved nothing else; she felt herself made for that only. She would so much have liked to please, to be envied, to be seductive and sought after.

She had a rich friend, a comrade of her convent days, whom she did not want to go and see any more, so much did she suffer as she came away. And she wept all day long, from chagrin, from regret, from despair, and from distress.

But one evening her husband came in with a proud air, holding in his hand a large envelope.

"There," said he, "there's something for you."

She quickly tore the paper and took out of it a printed card which bore these words:—

"The Minister of Education and Mme. Georges Rampouneau beg M. and Mme. Loisel to do them the honor to pass the evening with them at the palace of the Ministry, on Monday, January 18."

Instead of being delighted, as her husband hoped, she threw the invitation on the table with annoyance, murmuring—

"What do you want me to do with that?"

"But, my dear, I thought you would be pleased. You never go out, and here's a chance, a fine one. I had the hardest work to get it. Everybody is after them; they are greatly sought for and not many are given to the clerks. You will see there all the official world."

She looked at him with an irritated eye and she declared with impatience:—

"What do you want me to put on my back to go there?"

He had not thought of that; he hesitated:—

"But the dress in which you go to the theater. That looks very well to me—"

He shut up, astonished and distracted at seeing that his wife was weeping. Two big tears were descending slowly from the corners of the eyes to the corners of the mouth. He stuttered:—

"What's the matter? What's the matter?"

But by a violent effort she had conquered her trouble, and she replied in a calm voice as she wiped her damp cheeks:—

"Nothing. Only I have no clothes, and in consequence I cannot go to this party. Give your card to some colleague whose wife has a better outfit than I."

He was disconsolate. He began again:—

"See here, Mathilde, how much would this cost, a proper dress, which would do on other occasions; something very simple?"

She reflected a few seconds, going over her calculations, and thinking also of the sum which she might ask without meeting an immediate refusal and a frightened exclamation from the frugal clerk.

"At last, she answered hesitatingly:—

"I don't know exactly, but it seems to me that with four hundred francs I might do it."

He grew a little pale, for he was reserving just that sum to buy a gun and treat himself to a little shooting, the next summer, on the plain of Nanterre, with some friends who used to shoot larks there on Sundays.

But he said:—

"All right. I will give you four hundred francs. But take care to have a pretty dress."

The day of the party drew near, and Mme. Loisel seemed sad, restless, anxious. Yet her dress was ready. One evening her husband said to her:—

"What's the matter? Come, now, you have been quite queer these last three days."

And she answered:—

"It annoys me not to have a jewel, not a single stone, to put on. I shall look like distress.

I would almost rather not go to this party."

He answered:—

"You will wear some natural flowers. They are very stylish this time of the year. For ten francs you will have two or three magnificent roses."

But she was not convinced.

"No; there's nothing more humiliating than to look poor among a lot of rich women."

But her husband cried:—

"What a goose you are! Go find your friend, Mme. Forester, and ask her to lend you some jewelry. You know her well enough to do that."

She gave a cry of joy:—

"That's true. I had not thought of it."

The next day she went to her friend's and told her about her distress.

Mme. Forester went to her mirrored wardrobe, took out a large casket, brought it, opened it, and said to Mme. Loisel:—

"Choose, my dear."

She saw at first bracelets, then a necklace of pearls, then a Venetian cross of gold set with precious stones of an admirable workmanship. She tried on the ornaments before the glass, hesitated, and could not decide to take them off and to give them up. She kept on asking:—

"You haven't anything else?"

"Yes, yes. Look. I do not know what will happen to please you."

All at once she discovered, in a box of black satin, a superb necklace of diamonds, and her heart began to beat with boundless desire. Her hands trembled in taking it up. She fastened it round her throat, on her high dress, and remained in ecstasy before herself.

Then, she asked, hesitating, full of anxiety:—

"Can you lend me this, only this?"

"Yes, yes, certainly."

She sprang to her friend's neck, kissed her with ardor, and then escaped with her treasure.

The day of the party arrived. Mme. Loisel was a success. She was the prettiest of them all, elegant, gracious, smiling, and mad with joy. All the men were looking at her, inquiring her name, asking to be introduced. All the attaches of the Cabinet wanted to dance with her. The Minister took notice of her. She danced with delight, with passion, intoxicated with pleasure, thinking of nothing, in the triumph of her beauty, in the glory of her success, in a sort of cloud of happiness made up of all these tributes, of all the admirations, of all these awakened desires, of this victory so complete and so sweet to a woman's heart.

She went away about four in the morning. Since midnight—her husband has been dozing in a little anteroom with three other men whose wives were having a good time.

He threw over her shoulders the wraps he had brought to go home in, modest garments of every-day life, the poverty of which was out of keeping with the elegance of the ball dress. She felt this, and wanted to fly so as not to be noticed by the other women, who were wrapping themselves up in rich furs. Loisel kept her back—

"Wait a minute; you will catch cold outside; I'll call a cab."

But she did not listen to him, and went downstairs rapidly. When they were in the street, they could not find a carriage, and they set out in search of one, hailing the drivers whom they saw passing in the distance.

They went down toward the Seine, disgusted, shivering. Finally, they found on the Quai one of those old night-hawk cabs which one sees in Paris only after night has fallen, as though they are ashamed of their misery in the daytime.

It brought them to their door, rue des Martyrs; and they went up their own stairs sadly. For her it was finished. And he was thinking that he would have to be at the Ministry at ten o'clock.

She took off the wraps with which she had covered her shoulders, before the mirror, so as to see herself once more in her glory. But suddenly she gave a cry. She no longer had the necklace around her throat!

Her husband, half undressed already, asked—

"What is the matter with you?"

She turned to him, terror-stricken:—

"I—I—I have not Mme. Forester's diamond necklace!"

He jumped up, frightened—

"What? How? It is not possible!"

And they searched in the folds of the dress, in the folds of the wrap, in the pockets, everywhere. They did not find it.

He asked:—

"Are you sure you still had it when you left the ball?"

"Yes, I touched it in the vestibule of the Ministry."

"But if you had lost it in the street, we should have heard it fall. It must be in the cab."

"Yes. That is probable. Did you take the number?"

"No. And you—you did not even look at it?"

"No."

They gazed at each other, crushed. At last Loisel dressed himself again.

"I'm going," he said, "back the whole distance we came on foot, to see if I cannot find it."

And he went out. She stayed there, in her ball dress, without strength to go to bed, overwhelmed, on a chair, without a fire, without a thought.

Her husband came back about seven o'clock. He had found nothing.

Then he went to police headquarters, to the newspapers to offer a reward, to the cab company; he did everything, in fact, that a trace of hope could urge him to.

She waited all day, in the same dazed state in face of this horrible disaster. Loisel came back in the evening, with his face worn and white; he had discovered nothing.

"You must write to your friend," he said, "that you have broken the clasp of her necklace and that you are having it repaired. That will give us time to turn around."

She wrote as he dictated.

At the end of a week they had lost all hope. And Loisel, aged by five years, declared:—

"We must see how we can replace those jewels."

The next day they took the case which had held them to the jeweler whose name was in the cover. He consulted his books.

"It was not I, madam, who sold this necklace. I only supplied the case."

Then they went from jeweler to jeweler, looking for a necklace like the other, consulting their memory,—sick both of them with grief and anxiety.

In a shop in the Palais Royal, they found a diamond necklace that seemed to them absolutely like the one they were seeking. It was priced forty thousand francs. They could have it for thirty-six.

They begged the jeweler not to sell it for three days. And they made a bargain that he should take it back for thirty-four thousand, if the first was found before the end of February.

Loisel possessed eighteen thousand francs which his father had left him. He had to borrow the remainder.

He borrowed, asking a thousand francs from one, five hundred from another, five here, three louis there. He gave promissory notes, made ruinous agreements, dealt with usurers, with all kinds of lenders. He compromised the end of his life, risked his signature without even knowing whether it could be honored; and, frightened by all the anguish of the future, by the black misery which was about to settle down on him, by the perspective of all sorts of physical deprivations and of all sorts of moral tortures, he went to buy the new diamond necklace, laying down on the jeweler's counter thirty-six thousand francs.

When Mme. Loisel took back the necklace to Mme. Forester, the latter said, with an irritated air:—

"You ought to have brought it back sooner, for I might have needed it."

She did not open the case, which her friend had been fearing. If she had noticed the substitution, what would she have thought? What would she have said? Might she not have been taken for a thief?

Mme. Loisel learned the horrible life of the needy. She made the best of it, moreover, frankly, heroically. The frightful debt must be paid. She would pay it. They dismissed the servant; they changed their rooms; they took an attic under the roof.

She learned the rough work of the household, the odious labors of the kitchen. She washed the dishes, wearing out her pink nails on the greasy pots and the bottoms of the pans. She washed the dirty linen, the shirts and the towels, which she dried on a rope; she carried down the garbage to the street every morning, and she carried up the water, pausing for breath on every floor. And, dressed like a woman of the people, she went to the fruiterer, the grocer, the butcher, a basket on her arm, bargaining, insulted, fighting for her wretched money, sou by sou.

Every month they had to pay notes, to renew others to gain time. The husband worked in the evening keeping up the books of a shopkeeper, and at night often he did copying at five sous the page.

And this life lasted ten years.

At the end of ten years they had paid everything back, everything, with the rates of usury and all the accumulation of heaped-up interest.

Mme. Loisel seemed aged now. She had become the robust woman, hard and rough, of a poor household. Badly combed, with her skirts awry and her hands red, her voice was loud, and she washed the floor with splashing water.

But sometimes, when her husband was at the office, she sat down by the window and she thought of that evening long ago, of that ball, where she had been so beautiful and so admired.

What would have happened if she had not lost that necklace? Who knows? Who knows? How singular life is, how changeable! What a little thing it takes to save you or to lose you.

Then, one Sunday, as she was taking a turn in the Champs Elysées, as a recreation after the labors of the week, she perceived suddenly a woman walking with a child. It was Mme. Forester, still young, still beautiful, still seductive.

Mme. Loisel felt moved. Should she speak to her? Yes, certainly. And now that she had paid up, she would tell her all. Why not?

She drew near.

"Good morning, Jeanne."

The other did not recognize her, astonished to be hailed thus familiarly by this woman of the people. She hesitated—

"But—madam—I don't know—are you not making a mistake?"

"No. I am Mathilde Loisel."

Her friend gave a cry—

"Oh!—My poor Mathilde, how you are changed."

"Yes, I have had hard days since I saw you, and many troubles,—and that because of you."

"Of me?—How so?"

"You remember that diamond necklace that you lent me to go to the ball at the Ministry?"

"Yes. And then?"

"Well, I lost it."

"How can that be?—since you brought it back to me?"

"I brought you back another just like it. And now for ten years we have been paying for it. You will understand that it was not easy for us, who had nothing. At last, it is done, and I am mighty glad."

Mme. Forester had guessed.

"You say that you bought a diamond necklace to replace mine?"

"Yes. You did not notice it, even, did you? They were exactly alike?"

And she smiled with proud and naïve joy.

Mme. Forester, much moved, took her by both hands:—

"Oh, my poor Mathilde. But mine were false. At most they were worth five hundred francs!"

[1907]

TRANSLATED BY BRANDER MATTHEWS (1852–1929)

QUESTIONS

GUY DE MAUPASSANT, *The Necklace*

1. Mme. Loisel is proud and will not go to a ball without a proper necklace, though her husband has struggled to get an invitation for them. Mme. Loisel borrows a necklace from her friend Mme. Foster to wear to the ball. What happens to the necklace?

2. In order to replace the necklace, what do the Loisels do? What happens to their lives? What happens to Mme. Loisel's pride and vanity?

3. What does Mme. Loisel find out about the necklace at the end of the story?

4. What are the consequences of trying to live above one's income? Why do we suffer when we overuse credit cards and other kinds of credit?

5. Social pressures can force us to do truly silly things. Why do we let ourselves be drawn in by fashion and style, even when we cannot afford new clothes?

6. How does irony of the kind we see in this story affect the reader? What is the feeling when the irony becomes clear? Does it caution the reader to be careful?

7. Why does the beginning of the story say that Mme. Loisel was born into a working class family by a "blunder of destiny"? What kind of family would Mme. Loisel have preferred?

8. How does the husband's indulgence lead to the problems in the story? Is he to blame for being so willing to please his wife at all costs? Is he likely still so indulgent after she has worked so hard at the end of the story?

9. In what ways does the final twist of the story reflect on what has gone before? Why does such an ending make such a story so memorable?

10. What kinds of people drive the entertainment industry? How do they dress, and what expectations do they set up in the young? Pick a particular entertainer, and write about how that person influences those who admire her or him.

11. Have you ever borrowed something from someone else or lent something to someone and have it go wrong? Write about the experience and its effect on your relationship.

12. Have you ever spent far too much for something that later did not mean much to you? How did you feel about your mistake? What did you learn from the experience?

Charlotte Perkins Gilman
[1860–1935]

Born in Hartford, Connecticut to a branch of the famous New England Beecher family, CHARLOTTE PERKINS GILMAN *grew up in near poverty after her father abandoned the family. Her sense of independence may well have been fostered by her encounters with great-aunt Harriet Beecher Stowe, author of the abolitionist novel* Uncle Tom's Cabin; *and feminist/suffragist great-aunts Catherine Beecher and Isabella Beecher Hooker. Despite a childhood pledge to retain her independence by remaining single, Gilman married at twenty-three, had a child a year later, and immediately plunged into depression. The treatment prescribed by the highly respected nerve specialist S. Weir Mitchell was for her to avoid writing and intellectual activity of any kind, and this only served to deepen her depression. She divorced her husband and took her mother and daughter to California. There Gilman resumed writing and lecturing on women's rights, and eventually married a cousin, George Gilman, in 1900.*

The year 1894 found Gilman in San Francisco, where she helped to organize the California Women's Congresses of 1894–1895; she and social reformer Jane Addams cofounded the Women's Peace Party in 1895. Her activism on behalf of women's rights took her to cities and towns throughout the United States and England. She argued that women were not biologically inferior to men, but rather had been conditioned to behave subserviently. "Women are human beings as much as men, by nature; and as women, are even more sympathetic with human processes," she argued. "To develop human life in its true powers we need fully equal citizenship for women." Toward that end, Gilman advocated communal living in which women could leave household duties and childcare to trained domestic workers, and then participate fully in the public sphere.

In 1935, a year after her husband's death and with a diagnosis of breast cancer, Gilman committed suicide, explaining her choice in the most rational terms: "When one is assured of unavoidable and imminent death, it is the simplest of human rights to choose a quick and easy death in place of a slow and horrible one."

Gilman was a prolific writer, and published a highly acclaimed exploration of women's status in Women and Economics *(1898) and a thoughtful, witty feminist-utopian novel in* Herland *(1915). She also published the magazine* The Forerunner, *for which she was the sole contributor, from 1910 to 1916; and wrote several novels, a poetry collection, and over two hundred short stories. "The Yellow Wallpaper," published in 1892 in* New England Magazine, *after a rejection from the* Atlantic Monthly, *draws from her experience with the common treatment of depression in women at the turn of the century. Carrie Chapman Catt, one of the most revered pioneers of the women's rights movement, called Charlotte Perkins Gilman, "the most original and challenging mind the movement produced." That sentiment was echoed by contemporary feminists in 1994, when Gilman was inducted into the National Women's Hall of Fame in Seneca Falls, New York.*

The Yellow Wall-Paper

CHARLOTTE PERKINS GILMAN

IT IS VERY SELDOM that mere ordinary people like John and myself secure halls for the summer.

A colonial mansion, a hereditary estate, I would say a haunted house, and reach the height of romantic felicity—but that would be asking too much of fate!

Still I will proudly declare that there is something queer about it.

Else, why should it be let so cheaply? And why have stood so long untenanted?

John laughs at me, of course, but one expects that in marriage.

John is practical in the extreme. He has no patience with faith, an intense horror of superstition, and he scoffs openly at any talk of things not to be felt and seen and put down in figures.

John is a physician, and *perhaps*—(I would not say it to a living soul, of course, but this is dead paper and a great relief to my mind—) *perhaps* that is one reason I do not get well faster.

You see he does not believe I am sick!

And what can one do?

If a physician of high standing, and one's own husband, assures friends and relatives that there is really nothing the matter with one but temporary nervous depression—a slight hysterical tendency—what is one to do?

My brother is also a physician, and also of high standing, and he says the same thing.

So I take phosphates or phosphites—whichever it is, and tonics, and journeys, and air, and exercise, and am absolutely forbidden to "work" until I am well again.

Personally, I disagree with their ideas.

Personally, I believe that congenial work, with excitement and change, would do me good.

But what is one to do?

I did write for a while in spite of them; but it *does* exhaust me a good deal—having to be so sly about it, or else meet with heavy opposition.

First published in *New England Magazine*, August 1892.

I sometimes fancy that in my condition if I had less opposition and more society and stimulus—but John says the very worst thing I can do is to think about my condition, and I confess it always makes me feel bad.

So I will let it alone and talk about the house.

The most beautiful place! It is quite alone, standing well back from the road, quite three miles from the village. It makes me think of English places that you read about, for there are hedges and walls and gates that lock, and lots of separate little houses for the gardeners and people.

There is a *delicious* garden! I never saw such a garden—large and shady, full of box-bordered paths, and lined with long grape-covered arbors with seats under them.

There were greenhouses, too, but they are all broken now.

There was some legal trouble, I believe, something about the heirs and coheirs; anyhow, the place has been empty for years.

That spoils my ghostliness, I am afraid, but I don't care—there is something strange about the house—I can feel it.

I even said so to John one moonlight evening, but he said what I felt was a *draught*, and shut the window.

I get unreasonably angry with John sometimes. I'm sure I never used to be so sensitive. I think it is due to this nervous condition.

But John says if I feel so, I shall neglect proper self-control; so I take pains to control myself—before him, at least, and that makes me very tired.

I don't like our room a bit. I wanted one downstairs that opened on the piazza and had roses all over the window, and such pretty old-fashioned chintz hangings! but John would not hear of it.

He said there was only one window and not room for two beds, and no near room for him if he took another.

He is very careful and loving, and hardly lets me stir without special direction.

I have a schedule prescription for each hour in the day; he takes all care from me, and so I feel basely ungrateful not to value it more.

He said we came here solely on my account, that I was to have perfect rest and all the air I could get. "Your exercise depends on your strength, my dear," said he, "and your food somewhat on your appetite; but air you can absorb all the time." So we took the nursery at the top of the house.

It is a big, airy room, the whole floor nearly, with windows that look all ways, and air and sunshine galore. It was nursery first and then playroom and gymnasium, I should judge; for the windows are barred for little children, and there are rings and things in the walls.

The paint and paper look as if a boys' school had used it. It is stripped off—the paper—in great patches all around the head of my bed, about as far as I can reach, and in a great place on the other side of the room low down. I never saw a worse paper in my life.

One of those sprawling flamboyant patterns committing every artistic sin.

It is dull enough to confuse the eye in following, pronounced enough to constantly irritate and provoke study, and when you follow the lame uncertain curves for a little distance they suddenly commit suicide—plunge off at outrageous angles, destroy themselves in unheard of contradictions.

The color is repellant, almost revolting; a smouldering unclean yellow, strangely faded by the slow-turning sunlight.

It is a dull yet lurid orange in some places, a sickly sulphur tint in others.

No wonder the children hated it! I should hate it myself if I had to live in this room long.

There comes John, and I must put this away,—he hates to have me write a word.

We have been here two weeks, and I haven't felt like writing before, since that first day.

I am sitting by the window now, up in this atrocious nursery, and there is nothing to hinder my writing as much as I please, save lack of strength.

John is away all day, and even some nights when his cases are serious.

I am glad my case is not serious!

But these nervous troubles are dreadfully depressing.

John does not know how much I really suffer. He knows there is no *reason* to suffer, and that satisfies him.

Of course it is only nervousness. It does weigh on me so not to do my duty in any way!

I meant to be such a help to John, such a real rest and comfort, and here I am a comparative burden already!

Nobody would believe what an effort it is to do what little I am able,—to dress and entertain, and order things.

It is fortunate Mary is so good with the baby. Such a dear baby!

And yet I *cannot* be with him, it makes me so nervous.

I suppose John never was nervous in his life. He laughs at me so about this wall-paper!

At first he meant to repaper the room, but afterwards he said that I was letting it get the better of me, and that nothing was worse for a nervous patient than to give way to such fancies.

He said that after the wall-paper was changed it would be the heavy bedstead, and then the barred windows, and then that gate at the head of the stairs, and so on.

"You know the place is doing you good," he said, "and really, dear, I don't care to renovate the house just for a three months' rental."

"Then do let us go downstairs," I said, "there are such pretty rooms there."

Then he took me in his arms and called me a blessed little goose, and said he would go down cellar, if I wished, and have it whitewashed into the bargain.

But he is right enough about the beds and windows and things.

It is an airy and comfortable room as any one need wish, and, of course, I would not be so silly as to make him uncomfortable just for a whim.

I'm really getting quite fond of the big room, all but that horrid paper.

Out of one window I can see the garden, those mysterious deep-shaded arbors, the riotous old-fashioned flowers, and bushes and gnarly trees.

Out of another I get a lovely view of the bay and a little private wharf belonging to the estate. There is a beautiful shaded lane that runs down there from the house. I always fancy I see people walking in these numerous paths and arbors, but John has cautioned me not to give way to fancy in the least. He says that with my imaginative power and habit of story-making, a nervous weakness like mine is sure to lead to all manner of excited fancies, and that I ought to use my will and good sense to check the tendency. So I try.

I think sometimes that if I were only well enough to write a little it would relieve the press of ideas and rest me.

But I find I get pretty tired when I try.

It is so discouraging not to have any advice and companionship about my work. When I get really well, John says we will ask cousin Henry and Julia down for a long visit; but he says he would as soon put fireworks in my pillow-case as to let me have those stimulating people about now.

I wish I could get well faster.

But I must not think about that. This paper looks to me as if it *knew* what a vicious influence it had!

There is a recurrent spot where the pattern lolls like a broken neck and two bulbous eyes stare at you upside down.

I get positively angry with the impertinence of it and the everlastingness. Up and down and sideways they crawl, and those absurd, unblinking eyes are everywhere. There is one place where two breadths didn't match, and the eyes go all up and down the line, one a little higher than the other.

I never saw so much expression in an inanimate thing before, and we all know how much expression they have! I used to lie awake as a child and get more entertainment and terror out of blank walls and plain furniture than most children could find in a toy-store.

I remember what a kindly wink the knobs of our big, old bureau used to have, and there was one chair that always seemed like a strong friend.

I used to feel that if any of the other things looked too fierce I could always hop into that chair and be safe.

The furniture in this room is no worse than inharmonious, however, for we had to bring it all from downstairs. I suppose when this was used as a play-room they had to take the nursery things out, and no wonder! I never saw such ravages as the children have made here.

The wall-paper, as I said before, is torn off in spots, and it sticketh closer than a brother—they must have had perseverance as well as hatred.

Then the floor is scratched and gouged and splintered, the plaster itself is dug out here and there, and this great heavy bed which is all we found in the room, looks as if it had been through the wars.

But I don't mind it a bit—only the paper.

There comes John's sister. Such a dear girl as she is, and so careful of me! I must not let her find me writing.

She is a perfect and enthusiastic housekeeper, and hopes for no better profession. I verily believe she thinks it is the writing which made me sick!

But I can write when she is out, and see her a long way off from these windows.

There is one that commands the road, a lovely shaded winding road, and one that just looks off over the country. A lovely country, too, full of great elms and velvet meadows.

This wall-paper has a kind of subpattern in a different shade, a particularly irritating one, for you can only see it in certain lights, and not clearly then.

But in the places where it isn't faded and where the sun is just so—I can see a strange, provoking, formless sort of figure, that seems to skulk about behind that silly and conspicuous front design.

There's sister on the stairs!

Well, the Fourth of July is over! The people are all gone and I am tired out. John thought it might do me good to see a little company, so we just had mother and Nellie and the children down for a week.

Of course I didn't do a thing. Jennie sees to everything now.

But it tired me all the same.

John says if I don't pick up faster he shall send me to Weir Mitchell[1] in the fall.

But I don't want to go there at all. I had a friend who was in his hands once, and she says he is just like John and my brother, only more so!

Besides, it is such an undertaking to go so far.

---

[1]Dr. S. Weir Mitchell (1829–1914), physician famous for his "rest cures" for "hysterical" women. Mitchell treated Gilman for a time.

I don't feel as if it was worth while to turn my hand over for anything, and I'm getting dreadfully fretful and querulous.

I cry at nothing, and cry most of the time.

Of course I don't when John is here, or anybody else, but when I am alone.

And I am alone a good deal just now. John is kept in town very often by serious cases, and Jennie is good and lets me alone when I want her to.

So I walk a little in the garden or down that lovely lane, sit on the porch under the roses, and lie down up here a good deal.

I'm getting really fond of the room in spite of the wall-paper. Perhaps *because* of the wall-paper.

It dwells in my mind so!

I lie here on this great immovable bed—it is nailed down, I believe—and follow that pattern about by the hour. It is as good as gymnastics, I assure you. I start, we'll say, at the bottom, down in the corner over there where it has not been touched, and I determine for the thousandth time that I *will* follow that pointless pattern to some sort of a conclusion.

I know a little of the principle of design, and I know this thing was not arranged on any laws of radiation, or alternation, or repetition, or symmetry, or anything else that I ever heard of.

It is repeated, of course, by the breadths, but not otherwise.

Looked at in one way each breadth stands alone, the bloated curves and flourishes—a kind of "debased Romanesque" with *delirium tremens*—go waddling up and down in isolated columns of fatuity.

But, on the other hand, they connect diagonally, and the sprawling outlines run off in great slanting waves of optic horror, like a lot of wallowing seaweeds in full chase.

The whole thing goes horizontally, too, at least it seems so, and I exhaust myself in trying to distinguish the order of its going in that direction.

They have used a horizontal breadth for a frieze, and that adds wonderfully to the confusion.

There is one end of the room where it is almost intact, and there, when the crosslights fade and the low sun shines directly upon it, I can almost fancy radiation after all,—the interminable grotesques seem to form around a common centre and rush off in headlong plunges of equal distraction.

It makes me tired to follow it. I will take a nap I guess.

I don't know why I should write this.

I don't want to.

I don't feel able.

And I know John would think it absurd. But I *must* say what I feel and think in some way—it is such a relief!

But the effort is getting to be greater than the relief.

Half the time now I am awfully lazy, and lie down ever so much.

John says I mustn't lose my strength, and has me take cod liver oil and lots of tonics and things, to say nothing of ale and wine and rare meat.

Dear John! He loves me very dearly, and hates to have me sick. I tried to have a real earnest reasonable talk with him the other day, and tell him how I wish he would let me go and make a visit to Cousin Henry and Julia.

But he said I wasn't able to go, nor able to stand it after I got there; and I did not make out a very good case for myself, for I was crying before I had finished.

It is getting to be a great effort for me to think straight. Just this nervous weakness I suppose.

And dear John gathered me up in his arms, and just carried me upstairs and laid me on the bed, and sat by me and read to me till it tired my head.

He said I was his darling and his comfort and all he had, and that I must take care of myself for his sake, and keep well.

He says no one but myself can help me out of it, that I must use my will and self-control and not let any silly fancies run away with me.

There's one comfort, the baby is well and happy, and does not have to occupy this nursery with the horrid wall-paper.

If we had not used it, that blessed child would have! What a fortunate escape! Why, I wouldn't have a child of mine, an impressionable little thing, live in such a room for worlds.

I never thought of it before, but it is lucky that John kept me here after all, I can stand it so much easier than a baby, you see.

Of course I never mention it to them any more—I am too wise,—but I keep watch of it all the same.

There are things in that paper that nobody knows but me, or ever will.

Behind that outside pattern the dim shapes get clearer every day.

It is always the same shape, only very numerous.

And it is like a woman stooping down and creeping about behind that pattern. I don't like it a bit. I wonder—I begin to think—I wish John would take me away from here!

It is so hard to talk with John about my case, because he is so wise, and because he loves me so.

But I tried it last night.

It was moonlight. The moon shines in all around just as the sun does.

I hate to see it sometimes, it creeps so slowly, and always comes in by one window or another.

John was asleep and I hated to waken him, so I kept still and watched the moonlight on that undulating wall-paper till I felt creepy.

The faint figure behind seemed to shake the pattern, just as if she wanted to get out.

I got up softly and went to feel and see if the paper *did* move, and when I came back John was awake.

"What is it, little girl?" he said. "Don't go walking about like that—you'll get cold."

I thought it was a good time to talk, so I told him that I really was not gaining here, and that I wished he would take me away.

"Why, darling!" said he, "our lease will be up in three weeks, and I can't see how to leave before.

"The repairs are not done at home, and I cannot possibly leave town just now. Of course if you were in any danger, I could and would, but you really are better, dear, whether you can see it or not. I am a doctor, dear, and I know. You are gaining flesh and color, your appetite is better, I feel really much easier about you."

"I don't weigh a bit more," said I, "nor as much; and my appetite may be better in the evening when you are here, but it is worse in the morning when you are away!"

"Bless her little heart!" said he with a big hug, "she shall be as sick as she pleases! But now let's improve the shining hours by going to sleep, and talk about it in the morning!"

"And you won't go away?" I asked gloomily.

"Why, how can I, dear? It is only three weeks more and then we will take a nice little trip of a few days while Jennie is getting the house ready. Really dear you are better!"

"Better in body perhaps—" I began, and stopped short, for he sat up straight and looked at me with such a stern, reproachful look that I could not say another word.

"My darling," said he, "I beg of you, for my sake and for our child's sake, as well as for your own, that you will never for one instant let that idea enter your mind! There is nothing so dangerous, so fascinating, to a temperament like yours. It is a false and foolish fancy. Can you not trust me as a physician when I tell you so?"

So of course I said no more on that score, and we went to sleep before long. He thought I was asleep first, but I wasn't, and lay there for hours trying to decide whether that front pattern and the back pattern really did move together or separately.

On a pattern like this, by daylight, there is a lack of sequence, a defiance of law, that is a constant irritant to a normal mind.

The color is hideous enough, and unreliable enough, and infuriating enough, but the pattern is torturing.

You think you have mastered it, but just as you get well underway in following, it turns a back-somersault and there you are. It slaps you in the face, knocks you down, and tramples upon you. It is like a bad dream.

The outside pattern is a florid arabesque, reminding one of a fungus. If you can imagine a toadstool in joints, an interminable string of toadstools, budding and sprouting in endless convolutions—why, that is something like it.

That is, sometimes!

There is one marked peculiarity about this paper, a thing nobody seems to notice but myself, and that is that it changes as the light changes.

When the sun shoots in through the east window—I always watch for that first long, straight ray—it changes so quickly that I never can quite believe it.

That is why I watch it always.

By moonlight—the moon shines in all night when there is a moon—I wouldn't know it was the same paper.

At night in any kind of light, in twilight, candlelight, lamplight, and worst of all by moonlight, it becomes bars! The outside pattern I mean, and the woman behind it is as plain as can be.

I didn't realize for a long time what the thing was that showed behind, that dim sub-pattern, but now I am quite sure it is a woman.

By daylight she is subdued, quiet. I fancy it is the pattern that keeps her so still. It is so puzzling. It keeps me quiet by the hour.

I lie down ever so much now. John says it is good for me, and to sleep all I can.

Indeed he started the habit by making me lie down for an hour after each meal.

It is a very bad habit I am convinced, for you see I don't sleep.

And that cultivates deceit, for I don't tell them I'm awake—O no!

The fact is I am getting a little afraid of John.

He seems very queer sometimes, and even Jennie has an inexplicable look.

It strikes me occasionally, just as a scientific hypothesis,—that perhaps it is the paper!

I have watched John when he did not know I was looking, and come into the room suddenly on the most innocent excuses, and I've caught him several times *looking at the paper!* And Jennie too. I caught Jennie with her hand on it once.

She didn't know I was in the room, and when I asked her in a quiet, a very quiet voice, with the most restrained manner possible, what she was doing with the paper—she turned around as if she had been caught stealing, and looked quite angry—asked me why I should frighten her so!

Then she said that the paper stained everything it touched, that she had found yellow smooches on all my clothes and John's, and she wished we would be more careful!

Did not that sound innocent? But I know she was studying that pattern, and I am determined that nobody shall find it out but myself!

Life is very much more exciting now than it used to be. You see I have something more to expect, to look forward to, to watch. I really do eat better, and am more quiet than I was.

John is so pleased to see me improve! He laughed a little the other day, and said I seemed to be flourishing in spite of my wall-paper.

I turned it off with a laugh. I had no intention of telling him it was *because* of the wall-paper—he would make fun of me. He might even want to take me away.

I don't want to leave now until I have found it out. There is a week more, and I think that will be enough.

I'm feeling ever so much better! I don't sleep much at night, for it is so interesting to watch developments; but I sleep a good deal in the daytime.

In the daytime it is tiresome and perplexing.

There are always new shoots on the fungus, and new shades of yellow all over it. I cannot keep count of them, though I have tried conscientiously.

It is the strangest yellow, that wall-paper! It makes me think of all the yellow things I ever saw—not beautiful ones like buttercups, but old foul, bad yellow things.

But there is something else about that paper—the smell! I noticed it the moment we came into the room, but with so much air and sun it was not bad. Now we have had a week of fog and rain, and whether the windows are open or not, the smell is here.

It creeps all over the house.

I find it hovering in the dining-room, skulking in the parlor, hiding in the hall, lying in wait for me on the stairs.

It gets into my hair.

Even when I go to ride, if I turn my head suddenly and surprise it—there is that smell!

Such a peculiar odor, too! I have spent hours in trying to analyze it, to find what it smelled like.

It is not bad—at first, and very gentle, but quite the subtlest, most enduring odor I ever met.

In this damp weather it is awful, I wake up in the night and find it hanging over me.

It used to disturb me at first. I thought seriously of burning the house—to reach the smell.

But now I am used to it. The only thing I can think of that it is like is the *color* of the paper! A yellow smell.

There is a very funny mark on this wall, low down, near the mopboard. A streak that runs round the room. It goes behind every piece of furniture, except the bed, a long, straight, even *smooch*, as if it had been rubbed over and over.

I wonder how it was done and who did it, and what they did it for. Round and round and round—round and round and round—it makes me dizzy!

I really have discovered something at last.

Through watching so much at night, when it changes so, I have finally found out.

The front pattern *does* move—and no wonder! The woman behind shakes it!

Sometimes I think there are a great many women behind, and sometimes only one, and she crawls around fast, and her crawling shakes it all over.

Then in the very bright spots she keeps still, and in the very shady spots she just takes hold of the bars and shakes them hard.

And she is all the time trying to climb through. But nobody could climb through that pattern—it strangles so; I think that is why it has so many heads.

They get through, and then the pattern strangles them off and turns them upside down, and makes their eyes white!

If those heads were covered or taken off it would not be half so bad.

I think that woman gets out in the daytime!

And I'll tell you why—privately—I've seen her!

I can see her out of every one of my windows!

It is the same woman, I know, for she is always creeping, and most women do not creep by daylight.

I see her in that long shaded lane, creeping up and down. I see her in those dark grape arbors, creeping all around the garden.

I see her on that long road under the trees, creeping along, and when a carriage comes she hides under the blackberry vines.

I don't blame her a bit. It must be very humiliating to be caught creeping by daylight!

I always lock the door when I creep by daylight. I can't do it at night, for I know John would suspect something at once.

And John is so queer now, that I don't want to irritate him. I wish he would take another room! Besides, I don't want anybody to get that woman out at night but myself.

I often wonder if I could see her out of all the windows at once.

But, turn as fast as I can, I can only see out of one at one time.

And though I always see her, she *may* be able to creep faster than I can turn!

I have watched her sometimes away off in the open country, creeping as fast as a cloud shadow in a high wind.

If only that top pattern could be gotten off from the under one! I mean to try it, little by little.

I have found out another funny thing, but I shan't tell it this time! It does not do to trust people too much.

There are only two more days to get this paper off, and I believe John is beginning to notice. I don't like the look in his eyes.

And I heard him ask Jennie a lot of professional questions about me. She had a very good report to give.

She said I slept a good deal in the daytime.

John knows I don't sleep very well at night, for all I'm so quiet!

He asked me all sorts of questions, too, and pretended to be very loving and kind.

As if I couldn't see through him!

Still, I don't wonder he acts so, sleeping under this paper for three months.

It only interests me, but I feel sure John and Jennie are secretly affected by it.

Hurrah! This is the last day, but it is enough. John is to stay in town over night, and won't be out until this evening.

Jennie wanted to sleep with me—the sly thing! but I told her I should undoubtedly rest better for a night all alone.

That was clever, for really I wasn't alone a bit! As soon as it was moonlight and that poor thing began to crawl and shake the pattern, I got up and ran to help her.

I pulled and she shook, I shook and she pulled, and before morning we had peeled off yards of that paper.

A strip about as high as my head and half around the room.

And then when the sun came and that awful pattern began to laugh at me, I declared I would finish it to-day!

We go away to-morrow, and they are moving all my furniture down again to leave things as they were before.

Jennie looked at the wall in amazement, but I told her merrily that I did it out of pure spite at the vicious thing.

She laughed and said she wouldn't mind doing it herself, but I must not get tired.

How she betrayed herself that time!

But I am here, and no person touches this paper but me,—not *alive*!

She tried to get me out of the room—it was too patent! But I said it was so quiet and empty and clean now that I believed I would lie down again and sleep all I could; and not to wake me even for dinner—I would call when I woke.

So now she is gone, and the servants are gone, and the things are gone, and there is nothing left but that great bedstead nailed down, with the canvas mattress we found on it.

We shall sleep downstairs to-night, and take the boat home to-morrow.

I quite enjoy the room, now it is bare again.

How those children did tear about here!

This bedstead is fairly gnawed!

But I must get to work.

I have locked the door and thrown the key down into the front path.

I don't want to go out, and I don't want to have anybody come in, till John comes.

I want to astonish him.

I've got a rope up here that even Jennie did not find. If that woman does get out, and tries to get away, I can tie her!

But I forgot I could not reach far without anything to stand on!

This bed will *not* move!

I tried to lift and push it until I was lame, and then I got so angry I bit off a little piece at one corner—but it hurt my teeth.

Then I peeled off all the paper I could reach standing on the floor. It sticks horribly and the pattern just enjoys it! All those strangled heads and bulbous eyes and waddling fungus growths just shriek with derision!

I am getting angry enough to do something desperate. To jump out of the window would be admirable exercise, but the bars are too strong even to try.

Besides I wouldn't do it. Of course not. I know well enough that a step like that is improper and might be misconstrued.

I don't like to *look* out of the windows even—there are so many of those creeping women, and they creep so fast.

I wonder if they all come out of that wall-paper as I did?

But I am securely fastened now by my well-hidden rope—you don't get *me* out in the road there!

I suppose I shall have to get back behind the pattern when it comes night, and that is hard!

It is so pleasant to be out in this great room and creep around as I please!

I don't want to go outside. I won't, even if Jennie asks me to.

For outside you have to creep on the ground, and everything is green instead of yellow.

But here I can creep smoothly on the floor, and my shoulder just fits in that long smooch around the wall, so I cannot lose my way.

Why there's John at the door!

It is no use, young man, you can't open it!

How he does call and pound!

Now he's crying for an axe.

It would be a shame to break down that beautiful door!

"John dear!" said I in the gentlest voice, "the key is down by the front steps, under a plantain leaf!"

That silenced him for a few moments.

Then he said—very quietly indeed, "Open the door, my darling!"

"I can't," said I. "The key is down by the front door under a plantain leaf!"

And then I said it again, several times, very gently and slowly, and said it so often that he had to go and see, and he got it of course, and came in. He stopped short by the door.

"What is the matter?" he cried. "For God's sake, what are you doing!"

I kept on creeping just the same, but I looked at him over my shoulder.

"I've got out at last," said I, "in spite of you and Jane. And I've pulled off most of the paper, so you can't put me back!"

Now why should that man have fainted? But he did, and right across my path by the wall, so that I had to creep over him every time!

[1892]

QUESTIONS

CHARLOTTE PERKINS GILMAN, *The Yellow Wall-Paper*

1. At what point do you begin to suspect that the narrator is losing touch with objective reality? Trace her decline, and cite passages that indicate a progressive separation from the world around her.

2. What leads the narrator to determine that there is a woman behind the wallpaper? Why does she eventually refer to the woman as herself?

3. Of all the adult characters mentioned in this story, only the narrator remains nameless. Her husband refers to her as "my dear," "my darling," "little girl," and "she." Of what significance is the narrator's namelessness? How is the story affected by the fact that even the narrator herself does not offer her name?

4. The narrator is clearly invested her writing; just as clearly, her husband considers this occupation dangerous to her. Precisely what does writing mean to the narrator? To her husband? How does the notion of writing and creativity contribute to the theme of the story?

5. Early in the story, the narrator suggests that the house might be haunted; as the story progresses she obviously senses the presence of the woman behind the wallpaper. The story can be read as a supernatural tale or as the chronicle of a woman's descent into madness. How does the meaning of the story change, depending on which interpretation you accept?

6. In what ways is the narrator's situation comparable to the imprisonment of a convict? How do the descriptions of the room, the behavior of John and Jennie, and the narrator's language contribute to this impression?

7. The narrator's descriptions of the wallpaper are both vivid and disturbing. How do the images she conjures up reflect her state of mind? How do they reflect the oppression she feels as a result of her confinement?

8. In order to understand the importance of perspective in this story, consider how the narrator's actions must appear to her sister-in-law and husband. Compose a letter from Jennie to John describing the narrator's behavior. Just as the narrator's language reveals her condition, consider the language Jennie would use as a reflection of her attitude and position.

9. Research the treatment of women's nervous disorders at the turn of the last century, particularly those therapies promoted by Dr. S. Weir Mitchell, who treated Charlotte Perkins Gilman and whose treatment is feared by the narrator in the story. Using this information, write an essay analyzing the story as a feminist commentary on the oppression of women.

Susan Glaspell
[1876–1948]

Heralded mainly for her playwriting, SUSAN GLASPELL *was an adept editor, as well as a prolific author of children's stories, short stories, novels, and a memoir. As the co-founder of the Provincetown Players, she is one of the most important figures in early twentieth-century theater. Born in 1876, Glaspell grew up in the small, Midwestern town of Davenport, Iowa. Following college and a brief stint in journalism, she began writing full-time and was immediately successful in this endeavor, publishing short stories in* Ladies' Home Journal *and other popular magazines. In 1909, she published her first novel, a bestselling romance titled* The Glory of the Conquered.

Glaspell and her husband, George Cram (Jig) Cook, were deeply involved in the cultural and artistic avant-garde centered in New York's Greenwich Village, a world that Glaspell critiqued in a series of short dramas. Around this time she also helped found the Provincetown Players, a small group of artists (including Edna St. Vincent Millay and Eugene O'Neill) committed to the communal production of experimental drama. This company worked to reject Broadway's popular commercial theater, but it nonetheless pleased audiences well enough to survive for eight years and to serve as the genesis of a national "little theater" movement. Glaspell not only wrote many plays for the company, but also directed and ably performed in a number of its productions.

Trifles, a one-act play depicting the investigation of a small-town murder, is Glaspell's most famous and most studied work. She wrote the play in only ten days, basing it on a murder investigation and trial she had reported on for the Des Moines Daily News *in 1901. The play opened at the Provincetown Players' Wharf Theater on August 8, 1916, with Glaspell taking the role of Mrs. Hale. A year after the American premiere of* Trifles, *she rewrote the play as a short story titled, "A Jury of Her Peers" (1917). Both works—by demonstrating how two women solve a murder case simply by looking at the domestic "trifles" men overlook—illustrate ways of viewing things with a critical eye. They also present the influences of patriarchy on how the world is perceived.*

Glaspell and Cook moved to Greece in 1922, where they lived until his death two years later. In 1931, Glaspell became the second woman ever to win a Pulitzer Prize for her three-act play Alison's House *(1930), which was inspired by the life of the poet Emily Dickinson. It was the last play she completed. However, she published seven novels between 1928 and 1945. Most of these novels were set in the American Midwest, where Glaspell was born, and explored the tension for individuals between traditional regional values and modern ways of living.*

Toward the end of her life, Glaspell synthesized two important aspects of her identity—her Midwestern roots and her passion for American theater—when she became director of the Midwest Play Bureau of the Federal Theater Project (1936–1938). She died of viral pneumonia in 1948.

A Jury of Her Peers

SUSAN GLASPELL

WHEN MARTHA HALE opened the storm-door and got the north wind, she ran back for her big woollen scarf. As she hurriedly wound that round her head her eye made a scandalized sweep of her kitchen. It was no ordinary thing that called her away—it was probably farther from ordinary than anything that had ever happened in Dickson County. But her kitchen was in no shape for leaving: bread ready for mixing, half the flour sifted and half unsifted.

She hated to see things half done; but she had been at that when they stopped to get Mr. Hale, and the sheriff came in to say his wife wished Mrs. Hale would come too—adding, with a grin, that he guessed she was getting scarey and wanted another woman along. So she had dropped everything right where it was.

"Martha!" now came her husband's impatient voice. "Don't keep folks waiting out here in the cold."

She joined the three men and the one woman waiting for her in the sheriff's car.

After she had the robes tucked in she took another look at the woman beside her. She had met Mrs. Peters the year before, at the county fair, and the thing she remembered about her was that she didn't seem like a sheriff's wife. She was small and thin and didn't have a strong voice. Mrs. Gorman, sheriff's wife before Gorman went out and Peters came in, had a voice that seemed to be backing up the law with every word. But if Mrs. Peters didn't look like a sheriff's wife, Peters made it up in looking like a sheriff—a heavy man with a big voice, who was particularly genial with the law-abiding, as if to make it plain that he knew the difference between criminals and non-criminals. And right there it came into Mrs. Hale's mind that this man who was so lively with all of them was going to the Wrights' now as a sheriff.

"The country's not very pleasant this time of year," Mrs. Peters at last ventured.

Mrs. Hale scarcely finished her reply, for they had gone up a little hill and could see the Wright place, and seeing it did not make her feel like talking. It looked very lonely this cold March morning. It had always been a lonesome-looking place. It was down in a hollow, and the poplar trees around it were lonely-looking trees. The men were looking at it and talking about what had happened. The county attorney was bending to one side, scrutinizing the place as they drew up to it.

"I'm glad you came with me," Mrs. Peters said nervously, as the two women were about to follow the men in through the kitchen door.

Even after she had her foot on the doorstep, Martha Hale had a moment of feeling she could not cross this threshold. And the reason it seemed she couldn't cross it now was because she hadn't crossed it before. Time and time again it had been in her mind, "I ought to go over and see Minnie Foster"— she still thought of her as Minnie Foster, though for twenty years she had been Mrs. Wright. And then there was always something to do and Minnie Foster would go from her mind. But now she could come.

The men went over to the stove. The women stood close together by the door. Young Henderson, the county attorney, turned around and said, "Come up to the fire, ladies."

Mrs. Peters took a step forward, then stopped. "I'm not—cold," she said.

And so the two women stood by the door, at first not even so much as looking around the kitchen.

The men talked about what a good thing it was the sheriff had sent his deputy out that morning to make a fire for them, and then Sheriff Peters stepped back from the stove, unbuttoned his outer coat, and leaned his hands on the kitchen table in a way that seemed to mark the beginning of official business. "Now, Mr. Hale," he said in a sort of semi-official voice, "before we move things about, you tell Mr. Henderson just what it was you saw when you came here yesterday morning."

The county attorney was looking around the kitchen.

"By the way," he asked, "has anything been moved?" He turned to the sheriff. "Are things just as you left them yesterday?"

Peters looked from cupboard to sink; to a small worn rocker a little to one side of the kitchen table.

"It's just the same."

"Well, Mr. Hale," said the county attorney, "tell just what happened when you came here yesterday morning."

Mrs. Hale, still leaning against the door, had that sinking feeling of the mother whose child is about to speak a piece. Lewis often wandered along and got things mixed up in a story. She hoped he would tell this straight and plain, and not say unnecessary things that would make it harder for Minnie Foster. He didn't begin at once, and she noticed that he looked queer, as if thinking of what he had seen here yesterday.

"Yes, Mr. Hale?" the county attorney reminded.

"Harry and I had started to town with a load of wood," Mrs. Hale's husband began.

Harry was Mrs. Hale's oldest boy. He wasn't with them now, for the wood never got to town yesterday and he was taking it this morning, so he hadn't been home when the sheriff stopped to say he wanted Mr. Hale to come over to the Wright place and tell the county attorney his story there, where he could point it all out. With all Mrs. Hale's other emotions came the fear Harry wasn't dressed warm enough—they hadn't any of them realized how that north wind did bite.

"We come along this road," Hale was going on, "and as we got in sight of the house I says to Harry, 'I'm goin' to see if I can't get John Wright to take a telephone.' You see," he explained to Henderson, "unless *I* can get somebody to go in with me they won't come out this branch road except for a price I can't pay. I'd spoke to Wright about it before; but he put me off, saying folks talked too much anyway, and all he asked was peace and quiet—guess you know about how much he talked himself. But I thought maybe if I went to the house and talked about it before his wife, and said all the women-folks liked the telephones, and that in this lonesome stretch of road it would be a good thing— well, I said to Harry that that was what I was going to say—though I said at the same time that I didn't know as what his wife wanted made much difference to John—"

Now, there he was!—saying things he didn't need to say. Mrs. Hale tried to catch her husband's eye, but fortunately the county attorney interrupted with:

"Let's talk about that a little later, Mr. Hale. I do want to talk about that, but I'm anxious now to know just what happened when you got here."

When he began this time, it was deliberately, as if he knew it were important.

"I didn't see or hear anything. I knocked at the door. And still it was all quiet inside. I knew they must be up—it was past eight o'clock. So I knocked again, louder, and I thought I heard somebody say, 'Come in.' I wasn't sure—I'm not sure yet. But I opened the door—this door," jerking a hand toward the door by which the two women stood, "and there, in that rocker"—pointing to it—"sat Mrs. Wright."

Everyone in the kitchen looked at the rocker. It came into Mrs. Hale's mind that this chair didn't look in the least like Minnie Foster—the Minnie Foster of twenty years before. It was a dingy red, with wooden rungs up the back, and the middle rung gone; the chair sagged to one side.

"How did she—look?" the county attorney was inquiring.

"Well," said Hale, "she looked—queer."

"How do you mean—queer?"

He took out note-book and pencil. Mrs. Hale did not like the sight of that pencil. She kept her eye on her husband, as if to keep him from saying unnecessary things that would go into the book and make trouble.

Hale spoke guardedly: "Well, as if she didn't know what she was going to do next. And kind of—done up."

"How did she seem to feel about your coming?"

"Why, I don't think she minded—one way or other. She didn't pay much attention. I said, 'Ho'do, Mrs. Wright. It's cold, ain't it?' And she said, 'Is it?'— And went on pleatin' of her apron.

"Well, I was surprised. She didn't ask me to come up to the stove, but just set there, not even lookin' at me. And so I said, 'I want to see John.'

"And then she—laughed. I guess you would call it a laugh.

"I thought of Harry and the team outside, so I said, a little sharp, 'Can I see John?' 'No,' says she kind of dull like. 'Ain't he home?' says I. Then she looked at me. 'Yes,' says she, 'he's home.' 'Then why can't I see him?' I asked her, out of patience with her now. ''Cause he's dead,' says she just as quiet and dull—and fell to pleatin' her apron. 'Dead?' says I, like you do when you can't take in what you've heard.

"She just nodded her head, not getting a bit excited, but rockin' back and forth.

"Why—where is he?" says I, not knowing *what* to say.

"She just pointed upstairs—like this"—pointing to the room above.

"I got up, with the idea of going up there myself. By this time I—didn't know what to do. I walked from there to here, then I says 'Why, what did he die of?'

"'He died of a rope round his neck,' says she; and just went on pleatin' at her apron."

Hale stopped speaking, staring at the rocker. Nobody spoke; it was as if all were seeing the woman who had sat there the morning before.

"And what did you do then?" the attorney asked.

"I went out and called Harry. I thought I might—need help. I got Harry in, and we went upstairs." His voice fell almost to a whisper. "There he was— lying over the—

"I think I'd rather have you go into that upstairs," the county attorney interrupted, "where you can point it all out. Just go on now with the rest of the story."

"Well, my first thought was to get that rope off. It looked—"

He stopped; he did not say how it looked.

"But Harry, he went up to him and he said, 'No, he's dead all right, and we'd better not touch anythin'.' So we went downstairs.

"She was still sitting that same way. 'Has anybody been notified?' I asked. 'No,' says she, unconcerned.

"'Who did this, Mrs. Wright?' said Harry. He said it business-like, and she stopped pleatin' at her apron. 'I don't know,' she says. 'You don't *know*?' says Harry. 'Weren't you sleepin' in the bed with him?' 'Yes,' says she, 'but I was on the inside.' 'Somebody slipped a rope round his neck and strangled him, and you didn't wake up?' says Harry. 'I didn't wake up,' she said after him.

"We may have looked as if we didn't see how that could be, for after a minute she said, 'I sleep sound.'

"Harry was going to ask her more questions, but I said maybe that weren't our business; maybe we ought to let her tell her story first to the coroner or the sheriff. So Harry went as fast as he could over to High Road—the Rivers' place, where there's a telephone."

"And what did she do when she knew you had gone for the coroner?"

"She moved from that chair to this one over here, and just sat there with her hands held together and looking down. I got a feeling that I ought to make some conversation, so I said I had come in to see if John wanted to put in a telephone; and at that she started to laugh, and then she stopped and looked at me—scared."

At sound of a moving pencil the man who was telling the story looked up.

"I dunno—maybe it wasn't scared; I wouldn't like to say it was. Soon Harry got back, and then Dr. Lloyd came, and you, Mr. Peters, and so I guess that's all I know that you don't."

He said this with relief, moved as if relaxing. The county attorney walked to the stair door.

"I guess we'll go upstairs first—then out to the barn and around there."

He paused and looked around the kitchen.

"You're convinced there was nothing important here?" he asked. "Nothing that would—point to any motive?"

The sheriff too looked all around. "Nothing here but kitchen things," he said, with a little laugh for the insignificance of kitchen things.

The county attorney was looking at the cupboard. He opened the upper part and looked in. After a moment he drew his hand away sticky.

"Here's a nice mess," he said resentfully.

The two women had drawn nearer, and now the sheriff's wife spoke.

"Oh—her fruit," she said, looking to Mrs. Hale for understanding. "She worried about that when it turned so cold last night. She said the fire would go out and her jars might burst."

Mrs. Peters' husband broke into a laugh.

"Well, can you beat the women! Held for murder, and worrying about her preserves!"

The young attorney set his lips.

"I guess before we're through with her she may have something more serious than preserves to worry about."

"Oh, well," said Mrs. Hale's husband, with good-natured superiority, "women are used to worrying over trifles."

The two women moved a little closer together. Neither of them spoke. The county attorney seemed to remember his manners—and think of his future.

"And yet," said he, with the gallantry of a young politician, "for all their worries, what would we do without the ladies?"

The women did not speak. He went to the sink to wash his hands, turned to wipe them on the roller towel, pulled it for a cleaner place.

"Dirty towels! Not much of a housekeeper, would you say, ladies?" He kicked his foot against some dirty pans under the sink.

"There's a great deal of work to be done on a farm," said Mrs. Hale stiffly.

"To be sure. And yet"—with a little bow to her—"I know there are some Dickson County farm-houses that do not have such roller towels."

"Those towels get dirty awful quick. Men's hands aren't always as clean as they might be."

"Ah, loyal to your sex, I see," he laughed. He gave her a keen look. "But you and Mrs. Wright were neighbors. I suppose you were friends too."

Martha Hale shook her head.

"I've seen little enough of her of late years. I've not been in this house—it's more than a year."

"And why was that? You didn't like her?"

"I liked her well enough," she replied with spirit. "Farmers' wives have their hands full, Mr. Henderson. And then—" She looked around the kitchen.

"Yes?" he encouraged.

"It never seemed a very cheerful place," said she, more to herself than to him.

"No," he agreed; "I don't think anyone would call it cheerful. I shouldn't say she had the home-making instinct."

"Well, I don't know as Wright had either," she muttered.

"You mean they didn't get on very well?"

"No; I don't mean anything," she answered, with decision. "But I don't think a place would be any the cheerfuler for John Wright's bein' in it."

"I'd like to talk to you about that a little later, Mrs. Hale." He moved towards the stair door, followed by the two men.

"I suppose anything Mrs. Peters does'll be all right?" the sheriff inquired. "She was to take in some clothes for her, you know—and a few little things. We left in such a hurry yesterday."

The county attorney looked at the two women they were leaving alone among the kitchen things.

"Yes—Mrs. Peters," he said, his glance resting on the woman who was not Mrs. Peters, the big farmer woman who stood behind the sheriff's wife. "Of course Mrs. Peters is one of us," he added in a manner of entrusting responsibility. "And keep your eye out, Mrs. Peters, for anything that might be of use. No telling; you women might come upon a clue to the motive—and that's the thing we need."

Mr. Hale rubbed his face in the fashion of a slow man getting ready for a pleasantry. "But would the women know a clue if they did come upon it?" he said. Having delivered himself of this, he followed the others through the stair door.

The women stood motionless, listening to the footsteps, first upon the stairs, then in the room above them.

Then, as if releasing herself from something too strange, Mrs. Hale began to arrange the dirty pans under the sink, which the county attorney's disdainful push of the foot had upset.

"I'd hate to have men coming into my kitchen, snoopin' round and criticizing."

"Of course it's no more than their duty," said the sheriff's wife, in her timid manner.

"Duty's all right, but I guess that deputy sheriff that come out to make the fire might have got a little of this on." She gave the roller towel a pull. "Wish I'd thought of that sooner! Seems mean to talk about her for not having things slicked up, when she had to come away in such a hurry."

She looked around the kitchen. Certainly it was not "slicked up." Her eye was held by a bucket of sugar on a low shelf. The cover was off the wooden bucket, and beside it was a paper bag—half full.

Mrs. Hale moved towards it.

"She was putting this in there," she said to herself—slowly.

She thought of the flour in her kitchen at home half sifted, half not sifted. She had been interrupted, and had left things half done. What had interrupted Minnie Foster? Why had that work been left half done? She made a move as if to finish it—unfinished things always bothered her, and then she saw that Mrs. Peters was watching her, and she didn't want Mrs. Peters to get that feeling she had of work begun and then—for some reason—not finished.

"It's a shame about her fruit," she said, going to the cupboard. "I wonder if it's all gone.

"Here's one that's all right," she said at last. She held it towards the light. "This is cherries, too." She looked again. "I declare I believe that's the only one.

"She'll feel awful bad, after all her hard work in the hot weather. I remember the afternoon I put up my cherries last summer."

She put the bottle on the table, and was about to sit down in the rocker. But something kept her from sitting in that chair. She stood looking at it, seeing the woman who had sat there "pleatin' at her apron."

The thin voice of the sheriff's wife broke in upon her: "I must be getting those things from the front room closet." She opened the door into the other room, started in, stepped back. "You coming with me, Mrs. Hale?" she asked nervously.

"You—you could help me get them."

They were soon back. "My!" said Mrs. Peters, dropping the things on the table and hurrying to the stove.

Mrs. Hale stood examining the clothes the woman who was being detained in town had said she wanted.

"Wright was close!" she exclaimed, holding up a shabby black skirt that bore the marks of much making over. "I think maybe that's why she kept so much to herself. I s'pose she felt she couldn't do her part; and then, you don't enjoy things when you feel shabby. She used to wear pretty clothes and be lively—when she was Minnie Foster, one of the town girls, singing in the choir. But that—oh, that was twenty years ago."

With a carefulness in which there was something tender, she folded the shabby clothes and piled them at one corner of the table. She looked up at Mrs. Peters, and there was something in the other woman's look that irritated her.

"She don't care," she said to herself. "Much difference it makes to her whether Minnie Foster had pretty clothes when she was a girl."

Then she looked again, and she wasn't so sure; in fact, she hadn't at any time been sure about Mrs. Peters. She had that shrinking manner, and yet her eyes looked as if they could see a long way into things.

"This all you was to take in?" asked Mrs. Hale.

"No," said the sheriff's wife; "she said she wanted an apron. Funny thing to want," she ventured in her nervous way, "for there's not much to get you dirty in jail, goodness knows. But I suppose just to make her feel more natural. She said they were in the bottom drawer of this cupboard. Yes—here they are. And then her little shawl that always hung on the stair door."

She took the small grey shawl from behind the door leading upstairs.

Suddenly Mrs. Hale took a quick step towards the other woman.

"Mrs. Peters!"

"Yes, Mrs. Hale?"

"Do you think she—did it?"

Mrs. Peters looked frightened. "Oh, I don't know," she said, in a voice that seemed to shrink from the subject.

"Well, I don't think she did," affirmed Mrs. Hale. "Asking for an apron, and her little shawl. Worryin' about her fruit."

"Mr. Peters says—" Footsteps were heard in the room above; she stopped, looked up, then went on in a lowered voice: "Mr. Peters says—it looks bad for her. Mr. Henderson is awful sarcastic in a speech, and he's going to make fun of her saying she didn't wake up."

For a moment Mrs. Hale had no answer. Then, "Well, I guess John Wright didn't wake up—when they was slippin' that rope under his neck," she muttered.

"No, it's *strange*," breathed Mrs. Peters. "They think it was such a—funny way to kill a man."

"That's just what Mr. Hale said," said Mrs. Hale, in a resolutely natural voice. "There was a gun in the house. He says that's what he can't understand."

"Mr. Henderson said, coming out, that what was needed for the case was a motive. Something to show anger—or sudden feeling."

"Well, I don't see any signs of anger around here," said Mrs. Hale. "I don't—" She stopped. Her eye was caught by a dishtowel in the middle of the kitchen table. Slowly she moved towards the table. One half of it was wiped clean, the other half untidy. Her eyes made a slow, almost unwilling turn to the bucket of sugar and the half-empty bag beside it. Things begun—and not finished.

She stepped back. "Wonder how they're finding things upstairs? I hope she had it in better shape up there. Seems kind of sneaking, locking her up in town and coming out here to get her own house to turn against her!"

"But, Mrs. Hale," said the sheriff's wife, "the law is the law."

"I s'pose it is," answered Mrs. Hale shortly.

She turned to the stove, saying something about that fire not being much to brag of.

"The law is the law—and a bad stove is a bad stove. How'd you like to cook on this?" with the poker pointing to the broken lining. She opened the oven door. The thought of Minnie Foster trying to bake in that oven—and the thought of her never going over to see Minnie Foster—

She was startled by hearing Mrs. Peters say, "A person gets discouraged—and loses heart."

The sheriff's wife had looked from the stove to the sink—the pail of water which had been carried in from outside. The two women stood there silent, above them the footsteps of the men who were looking for evidence against the woman who had worked in that kitchen. That look of seeing into things, of seeing through a thing to something else, was in the eyes of the sheriff's wife now. When Mrs. Hale next spoke to her, it was gently.

"Better loosen up your things, Mrs. Peters. We'll not feel them when we go out."

Mrs. Peters went to the back of the room to hang up the fur tippet she was wearing. "Why, she was piecing a quilt," she exclaimed, and held up a large sewing basket piled high with quilt pieces.

Mrs. Hale spread some of the blocks on the table.

"It's log-cabin pattern," she said, putting several of them together. "Pretty, isn't it?"

They were so engaged with the quilt that they did not hear the footsteps on the stairs. As the stair door opened Mrs. Hale was saying, "Do you suppose she was going to quilt it, or just knot it?"

The sheriff threw up his hands.

"They wonder whether she was going to quilt it, or just knot it!"

There was a laugh for the ways of women, a warming of hands over the stove, and then the county attorney said briskly, "Well, let's go right out to the barn and get that cleared up."

"I don't see as there's anything so strange," Mrs. Hale said resentfully, after the outside door had closed on the three men— "our taking up our time with little things while we're waiting for them to get the evidence. I don't see as it's anything to laugh about."

"Of course they've got awful important things on their minds," said the sheriff's wife apologetically.

They returned to an inspection of the blocks for the quilt. Mrs. Hale was looking at the fine, even sewing, preoccupied with thoughts of the woman who had done that sewing, when she heard the sheriff's wife say, in a startled tone, "Why, look at this one."

"The sewing," said Mrs. Peters, in a troubled way. "All the rest of them have been so nice and even—but—this one. Why, it looks as if she didn't know what she was about!"

Their eyes met—something flashed to life, passed between them; then, as if with an effort, they seemed to pull away from each other. A moment Mrs. Hale sat there, her fingers upon those stitches so unlike the rest of the sewing. Then she had pulled a knot and drawn the threads.

"Oh, what are you doing, Mrs. Hale?" asked the sheriff's wife.

"Just pulling out a stitch or two that's not sewed very good," said Mrs. Hale mildly.

"I don't think we ought to touch things," Mrs. Peters said.

"I'll just finish up this end," answered Mrs. Hale.

She threaded a needle and started to replace bad sewing with good. Then in that thin, timid voice, she heard: "Mrs. Hale!"

"Yes, Mrs. Peters?"

"What do you suppose she was so—nervous about?"

"Oh, *I* don't know," said Mrs. Hale, as if dismissing a thing not important enough to spend much time on. "I don't know as she was—nervous. I sew awful queer sometimes when I'm just tired."

"Well, I must get these clothes wrapped. They may be through sooner than we think. I wonder where I could find a piece of paper—and string."

"In that cupboard, maybe," suggested Mrs. Hale.

One piece of the crazy sewing remained unripped. Mrs. Peters' back turned, Martha Hale scrutinized that piece, compared it with the dainty, accurate stitches of the other blocks. The difference was startling. Holding this block it was hard to remain quiet, as if the distracted thoughts of the woman who had perhaps turned to it to try and quiet herself were communicating themselves to her.

"Here's a bird-cage," Mrs. Peters said. "Did she have a bird, Mrs. Hale?"

"Why, I don't know whether she did or not." She turned to took at the cage Mrs. Peters was holding up. "I've not been here in so long." She sighed. "There was a man round last year selling canaries cheap—but I don't know as she took one. Maybe she did. She used to sing real pretty herself."

"Seems kind of funny to think of a bird here. But she must have had one— or why would she have a cage? I wonder what happened to it."

"I suppose maybe the cat got it," suggested Mrs. Hale, resuming her sewing.

"No; she didn't have a cat. She's got that feeling some people have about cats—being afraid of them. When they brought her to our house yesterday, my cat got in the room, and she was real upset and asked me to take it out."

"My sister Bessie was like that," laughed Mrs. Hale.

The sheriff's wife did not reply. The silence made Mrs. Hale turn. Mrs. Peters was examining the bird-cage.

"Look at this door," she said slowly. "It's broke. One hinge has been pulled apart."

Mrs. Hale came nearer.

"Looks as if someone must have been—rough with it."

Again their eyes met—startled, questioning, apprehensive. For a moment neither spoke nor stirred. Then Mrs. Hale, turning away, said brusquely, "If they're going to find any evidence, I wish they'd be about it. I don't like this place."

"But I'm awful glad you came with me, Mrs. Hale." Mrs. Peters put the bird-cage on the table and sat down. "It would be lonesome for me—sitting here alone."

"Yes, it would, wouldn't it?" agreed Mrs. Hale. She had picked up the sewing, but now it dropped to her lap, and she murmured: "But I tell you what I do wish, Mrs. Peters. I wish I had come over sometimes when she was here. I wish— I had."

"But of course you were awful busy, Mrs. Hale. Your house—and your children."

"I could've come. I stayed away because it weren't cheerful—and that's why I ought to have come. I"—she looked around—"I've never liked this place. Maybe because it's down in a hollow and you don't see the road. I don't know what it is, but it's a lonesome place, and always was. I wish I had come over to see Minnie Foster sometimes. I can see now—"

"Well, you mustn't reproach yourself. Somehow we just don't see how it is with other folks till—something comes up."

"Not having children makes less work," mused Mrs. Hale, "but it makes a quiet house. And Wright out to work all day—and no company when he did come in. Did you know John Wright, Mrs. Peters?"

"Not to know him. I've seen him in town. They say he was a good man."

"Yes—good," conceded John Wright's neighbor grimly. "He didn't drink, and kept his word as well as most, I guess, and paid his debts. But he was a hard man, Mrs. Peters. Just to pass the time of day with him—" she shivered. "Like a raw wind that gets to the bone." Her eye fell upon the cage on the table before her, and she added, "I should think she would've wanted a bird!"

Suddenly she leaned forward, looking intently at the cage. "But what do you s'pose went wrong with it?"

"I don't know," returned Mrs. Peters; "unless it got sick and died."

But after she said this she reached over and swung the broken door. Both women watched it.

"You didn't know—her?" Mrs. Hale asked.

"Not till they brought her yesterday," said the sheriff's wife.

"She—come to think of it, she was kind of like a bird herself. Real sweet and pretty, but kind of timid and—flutterly. How—she—did—change."

Finally, as if struck with a happy thought and relieved to get back to everyday things: "Tell you what, Mrs. Peters, why don't you take the quilt in with you? It might take up her mind."

"Why, I think that's a real nice idea, Mrs. Hale. There couldn't possibly be any objection to that, could there? Now, just what will I take? I wonder if her patches are in here?" They turned to the sewing basket.

"Here's some red," said Mrs. Hale, bringing out a roll of cloth. Underneath this was a box. "Here, maybe her scissors are in here—and her things." She held it up. "What a pretty box! I'll warrant that was something she had a long time ago—when she was a girl."

She held it in her hand a moment; then, with a little sigh, opened it.

Instantly her hand went to her nose. "Why!"

Mrs. Peters drew nearer—then turned away.

"There's something wrapped up in this piece of silk," faltered Mrs. Hale.

"This isn't her scissors," said Mrs. Peters, in a shrinking voice.

Mrs. Hale raised the piece of silk. "Oh, Mrs. Peters!" she cried. "It's—"

Mrs. Peters bent closer.

"It's the bird," she whispered.

"But, Mrs. Peters!" cried Mrs. Hale. "Look at it! Its neck—look at its neck! It's all—other side *to*."

The sheriff's wife again bent closer.

"Somebody wrung its neck," said she, in a voice that was slow and deep.

The eyes of the two women met—this time clung together in a look of dawning comprehension, of growing horror. Mrs. Peters looked from the dead bird to the broken door of the cage. Again their eyes met. And just then there was a sound at the outside door.

Mrs. Hale slipped the box under the quilt pieces in the basket. The county attorney and sheriff came in.

"Well, ladies," said the attorney, as one turning from serious things to little pleasantries, "have you decided whether she was going to quilt it or knot it?"

"We think," said the sheriff's wife hastily, "that she was going to knot it."

"Well, that's very interesting, I'm sure." He caught sight of the cage. "Has the bird flown?"

"We think the cat got it," said Mrs. Hale in a prosaic voice.

He was walking up and down, as if thinking something out.

"Is there a cat?" he asked absently.

Mrs. Hale shot a look up at the sheriff's wife.

"Well, not *now*," said Mrs. Peters. "They're superstitious, you know; they leave."

The county attorney did not heed her. "No sign at all of anyone having come in from the outside," he said to Peters, continuing an interrupted conversation. "Their own rope. Now let's go upstairs again and go over it, piece by piece. It would have to have been someone who knew just the—"

The stair door closed behind them and their voices were lost.

The two women sat motionless, not looking at each other, but as if peering into something and at the same time holding back. When they spoke now it was as if they were afraid of what they were saying, but could not help saying it.

"She liked the bird," said Martha Hale. "She was going to bury it in that pretty box."

"When I was a girl," said Mrs. Peters, under her breath, "my kitten—there was a boy took a hatchet, and before my eyes—before I could get there—" She covered her face an instant. "If they hadn't held me back I would have"—she caught herself, and finished weakly—"hurt him."

Then they sat without speaking or moving.

"I wonder how it would seem," Mrs. Hale began, as if feeling her way over strange ground—"never to have had any children around." Her eyes made a sweep of the kitchen. "No, Wright wouldn't like the bird—a thing that sang. She used to sing. He killed that too."

Mrs. Peters moved. "Of course we don't know who killed the bird."

"I knew John Wright," was the answer.

"It was an awful thing was done in this house that night, Mrs. Hale," said the sheriff's wife. "Killing a man while he slept—slipping a thing round his neck that choked the life out of him."

Mrs. Hale's hand went to the bird-cage. "His neck. Choked the life out of him."

"We don't *know* who killed him," whispered Mrs. Peters wildly. "We don't *know.*"

Mrs. Hale had not moved. "If there had been years and years of nothing, then a bird to sing to you, it would be awful—still, after the bird was still."

"I know what stillness is," whispered Mrs. Peters. "When we homesteaded in Dakota, and my first baby died—after he was two years old—and me with no other then—"

Mrs. Hale stirred. "How soon do you suppose they'll be through looking for the evidence?"

"I know what stillness is," repeated Mrs. Peters. Then she too pulled back. "The law has got to punish crime, Mrs. Hale."

"I wish you'd seen Minnie Foster when she wore a white dress with blue ribbons, and stood up there in the choir and sang."

The picture of that girl, the thought that she had lived neighbor to her for twenty years, and had let her die for lack of life, was suddenly more than the woman could bear.

"Oh, I *wish* I'd come over here once in a while!" she cried. "That was a crime! That was a crime! Who's going to punish *that?*"

"We mustn't—take on," said Mrs. Peters, with a frightened look towards the stairs.

"I might 'a' *known* she needed help! I tell you, it's *queer*, Mrs. Peters. We live close together, and we live far apart. We all go through the same things— it's all just a different kind of the same thing! If it weren't—why do you and I *know*—what we know this minute?"

Seeing the jar of fruit on the table, she reached for it. "If I was you I wouldn't *tell* her her fruit was gone! Tell her it *ain't.* Tell her it's all right—all of it. Here—take this in to prove it to her! She—she may never know whether it was broke or not."

Mrs. Peters took the bottle of fruit as if glad to take it—as if touching a familiar thing, having something to do, could keep her from something else. She looked about for something to wrap the fruit in, took a petticoat from the pile of clothes she had brought from the front room, nervously started winding that round the bottle.

"My!" she began, in a high voice, "it's a good thing the men couldn't hear us! Getting all stirred up over a little thing like a—dead canary. As if that could have anything to do with—with—My, wouldn't they *laugh?*"

There were footsteps on the stairs.

"Maybe they would," muttered Mrs. Hale—"maybe they wouldn't."

"No, Peters," said the county attorney, "it's all perfectly clear, except the reason for doing it. But you know juries when it comes to women. If there was some definite thing—something to *show*. Something to make a story about. A thing that would connect up with this clumsy way of doing it."

Mrs. Hale looked at Mrs. Peters. Mrs. Peters was looking at her. Quickly they looked away from one another. The outer door opened and Mr. Hale came in.

"I've nailed back that board we ripped off," he said.

"Much obliged, Mr. Hale," said the sheriff. "We'll be getting along now."

"I'm going to stay here awhile by myself," the county attorney suddenly announced. "You can send Frank out for me, can't you?" he asked the sheriff. "I want to go over everything. I'm not satisfied we can't do better."

Again, for one brief moment, the women's eyes met.

The sheriff came up to the table.

"Did you want to see what Mrs. Peters was going to take in?"

The county attorney picked up the apron. He laughed.

"Oh, I guess they're not very dangerous things the ladies have picked out."

Mrs. Hale's hand was on the sewing basket in which the box was concealed. She felt that she ought to take her hand off the basket. She did not seem able to. She picked up one of the quilt blocks she had piled on to cover the box. She had a fear that if he took up the basket she would snatch it from him.

But he did not take it. With another laugh he turned away, saying, "No, Mrs. Peters doesn't need supervising. For that matter, a sheriff's wife is married to the law. Ever think of it that way, Mrs. Peters?"

Mrs. Peters had turned her face away. "Not—just that way," she said.

"Married to the law!" chuckled Mrs. Peters' husband. He moved towards the door into the front room, and said to the county attorney, "I just want you to come here a minute, George. We ought to take a look at these windows."

"Oh—windows!" scoffed the county attorney.

"We'll be leaving in a second, Mr. Hale," Mr. Peters told the farmer, as he followed the county attorney into the other room.

"Can't be leavin' too soon to suit me," muttered Hale, and went out.

Again, for one final moment, the two women were alone in that kitchen.

Martha Hale sprang up, her hands tight together, looking at that other woman, with whom it rested. At first she could not see her eyes, for the sheriff's wife had not turned back since she turned away at that suggestion of being married to the law. Slowly, unwillingly, Mrs. Peters turned her head until her eyes met the eyes of the other woman. There was a moment when they held each other in a steady, burning look in which there was no evasion nor flinching. Then Martha Hale's eyes pointed the way to the basket in which was hidden the thing that would convict the third woman—that woman who was not there, and yet who had been there with them through that hour.

For a moment Mrs. Peters did not move. And then she did it. Threw back the quilt pieces, got the box, tried to put it in her hand-bag. It was too big. Desperately she opened it, started to take the bird out. But there she broke— she could not touch the bird. She stood there helpless, foolish.

There was a sound at the door. Martha Hale snatched the box from the sheriff's wife and got it in the pocket of her big coat just as the sheriff and the county attorney came back into the kitchen.

"Well, Henry," said the county attorney, facetiously, "at least we found out that she was not going to quilt it. She was going to—what is it you call it, ladies?"

Mrs. Hale's hand was against the pocket of her coat.

"We call it—knot it," was her answer.

[1917]

QUESTIONS

1. What is the significance of the title of this story? How does your perception of the title change as you read the story?

2. Martha Hale is bothered about leaving her kitchen in disarray; she then bristles at the men's comments about Minnie Wright's kitchen. What does a clean, orderly kitchen mean to Mrs. Hale? Why does she attach more significance than the men do to the state of Mrs. Wright's kitchen?

3. Twice Mrs. Peters recalls incidents in her own life: her kitten's death and her baby's death. What is the significance of these recollections? What role do they play in her ultimate decision to protect Mrs. Wright?

4. Throughout this story Glaspell compares the reactions of men and women to ordinary household items. How do these reactions contribute to the theme of the story?

5. Neither John nor Minnie Wright appears in this story, and yet each character comes through quite clearly as the story progresses. How does Glaspell develop the characters of John and Minnie?

6. Much of the women's attention centers on the quilt that Mrs. Wright has been working on. How does the image of a quilt, particularly the materials and methods involved in its construction, contribute to the theme of the story?

7. Analyze the conversation between Mrs. Peters and Mrs. Hale after they discover the bird. Which specific lines indicate their sense of duty to the law? Which lines suggest their solidarity with Mrs. Wright? How do the references to their own lives contribute to their conclusions about Mrs. Wright?

8. In addition to guilt and innocence, this story also explores concepts of community and isolation, personal and public responsibility, loyalty and betrayal. Analyze the story as a commentary on the complexity of human relations with regard to these concepts, focusing on relationships between husbands and wives, men and women, friends, and citizens of a community.

9. Susan Glaspell also wrote the play *Trifles*, a leaner, dramatic version of this story. Read that play, noting what is omitted from the story form and what appears more immediate because of the dramatic form. Write an essay analyzing the differences between the play and the story. Which version do you consider more compelling? Why?

John Steinbeck
[1902–1968]

JOHN STEINBECK *was born in 1902 in Salinas, California. He attended Stanford University intermittently while working as a farm laborer and a ranch hand. His desire to be a writer led him to New York City and a job as a journalist for a newspaper, but he soon returned to California and began writing fiction.* Cup of Gold *appeared in 1929, followed by* The Pastures of Heaven *(1932) and* To a God Unknown *(1933). However, it was not until the publication of* Tortilla Flat *(1935) that Steinbeck's work received critical and popular notice. The next year the* San Francisco News *asked Steinbeck to write a series of reports on the migration to California by people escaping the effects of the dust bowl in the Midwest. The focus of his reports, titled "The Harvest Gypsies," was on the exploitation of migrant farm workers. Steinbeck drew upon his observations for* In Dubious Battle *(1936) and* Of Mice and Men *(1937). His classic work on this subject,* The Grapes of Wrath *(1939), solidified Steinbeck's reputation as a major American author and earned him the Pulitzer Prize in 1940. During World War II he worked again as a journalist in Italy and Russia and continued producing popular works, such as* Cannery Row *(1945) and* The Wayward Bus *(1947). With* East of Eden *(1952) Steinbeck produced another major work on life in the Salinas Valley. In 1962 Steinbeck was awarded the Nobel Prize for Literature, acknowledging the importance of his work in this way: "His sympathies always go out to the oppressed, to the misfits and the distressed; he likes to contrast the simple joy of life with the brutal and cynical craving for money. But in him we find the American temperament also in his great feeling for nature, for the tilled soil, the wasteland, the mountains, and the ocean coasts, all an inexhaustible source of inspiration to Steinbeck in the midst of, and beyond, the world of human beings." Steinbeck died in New York City in 1968.*

The Chrysanthemums

JOHN STEINBECK

THE HIGH GREY-FLANNEL fog of winter closed off the Salinas Valley from the sky and from all the rest of the world. On every side it sat like a lid on the mountains and made of the great valley a closed pot. On the broad, level land floor the gang plows bit deep and left the black earth shining like metal where the shares had cut. On the foothill ranches across the Salinas River, the yellow stubble fields seemed to be bathed in pale cold sunshine, but there was no sunshine in the valley now in December. The thick willow scrub along the river flamed with sharp and positive yellow leaves.

It was a time of quiet and of waiting. The air was cold and tender. A light wind blew up from the southwest so that the farmers were mildly hopeful of a good rain before long; but fog and rain do not go together.

Across the river, on Henry Allen's foothill ranch there was little work to be done, for the hay was cut and stored and the orchards were plowed up to receive the rain deeply when it should come. The cattle on the higher slopes were becoming shaggy and rough-coated.

Elisa Allen, working in her flower garden, looked down across the yard and saw Henry, her husband, talking to two men in business suits. The three of them stood by the tractor shed, each man with one foot on the side of the little Fordson. They smoked cigarettes and studied the machine as they talked.

Elisa watched them for a moment and then went back to her work. She was thirty-five. Her face was lean and strong and her eyes were as clear as water. Her figure looked blocked and heavy in her gardening costume, a man's black hat pulled low down over her eyes, clod-hopper shoes, a figured print dress almost completely covered by a big corduroy apron with four big pockets to hold the snips, the trowel and scratcher, the seeds and the knife she worked with. She wore heavy leather gloves to protect her hands while she worked.

She was cutting down the old year's chrysanthemum stalks with a pair of short and powerful scissors. She looked down toward the men by the tractor shed now and then. Her face was eager and mature and handsome; even her work with the scissors was over-eager, over-powerful. The chrysanthemum stems seemed too small and easy for her energy.

She brushed a cloud of hair out of her eyes with the back of her glove, and left a smudge of earth on her cheek in doing it. Behind her stood the neat white farm house with red geraniums close-banked around it as high as the windows. It was a hard-swept looking little house with hard-polished windows, and a clean mud-mat on the front steps.

Elisa cast another glance toward the tractor shed. The strangers were getting into their Ford coupe. She took off a glove and put her strong fingers down into the forest of new green chrysanthemum sprouts that were growing around the old roots. She spread the leaves and looked down among the close-growing stems. No aphids were there, no sowbugs or snails or cutworms. Her terrier fingers destroyed such pests before they could get started.

Elisa started at the sound of her husband's voice. He had come near quietly, and he leaned over the wire fence that protected her flower garden from cattle and dogs and chickens.

"At it again," he said. "You've got a strong new crop coming."

Elisa straightened her back and pulled on the gardening glove again. "Yes. They'll be strong this coming year." In her tone and on her face there was a little smugness.

"You've got a gift with things," Henry observed. "Some of those yellow chrysanthemums you had this year were ten inches across. I wish you'd work out in the orchard and raise some apples that big."

Her eyes sharpened. "Maybe I could do it, too. I've a gift with things, all right. My mother had it. She could stick anything in the ground and make it grow. She said it was having planters' hands that knew how to do it."

"Well, it sure works with flowers," he said.

"Henry, who were those men you were talking to?"

"Why, sure, that's what I came to tell you. They were from the Western Meat Company. I sold those thirty head of three-year-old steers. Got nearly my own price, too."

"Good," she said. "Good for you."

"And I thought," he continued, "I thought how it's Saturday afternoon, and we might go into Salinas for dinner at a restaurant, and then to a picture show— to celebrate, you see."

"Good," she repeated. "Oh, yes. That will be good."

Henry put on his joking tone. "There's fights tonight. How'd you like to go to the fights?"

"Oh, no," she said breathlessly. "No, I wouldn't like fights."

"Just fooling, Elisa. We'll go to a movie. Let's see. It's two now. I'm going to take Scotty and bring down those steers from the hill. It'll take us maybe two hours. We'll go in town about five and have dinner at the Cominos Hotel. Like that?"

"Of course I'll like it. It's good to eat away from home."

"All right, then. I'll go get up a couple of horses."

She said, "I'll have plenty of time to transplant some of these sets, I guess."

She heard her husband calling Scotty down by the barn. And a little later she saw the two men ride up the pale yellow hillside in search of the steers.

There was a little square sandy bed kept for rooting the chrysanthemums. With her trowel she turned the soil over and over, and smoothed it and patted it firm. Then she dug ten parallel trenches to receive the sets. Back at the chrysanthemum bed she pulled out the little crisp shoots, trimmed off the leaves of each one with her scissors and laid it on a small orderly pile.

A squeak of wheels and plod of hoofs came from the road. Elisa looked up. The country road ran along the dense bank of willows and cottonwoods that bordered the river, and up this road came a curious vehicle, curiously drawn. It was an old spring-wagon, with a round canvas top on it like the corner of a prairie schooner. It was drawn by an old bay horse and a little grey-and-white burro. A big stubble-bearded man sat between the cover flaps and drove the crawling team. Underneath the wagon, between the hind wheels, a lean and rangy mongrel dog walked sedately. Words were painted on the canvas, in clumsy, crooked letters. "Pots, pans, knives, sisors, lawn mores, Fixed." Two rows of articles, and the triumphantly definitive "Fixed" below. The black paint had run down in little sharp points beneath each letter.

Elisa, squatting on the ground, watched to see the crazy, loose-jointed wagon pass by. But it didn't pass. It turned into the farm road in front of her house, crooked old wheels skirling and squeaking. The rangy dog darted from between the wheels and ran ahead. Instantly the two ranch shepherds flew out at him. Then all three stopped, and with stiff and quivering tails, with taut straight legs, with ambassadorial dignity, they slowly circled, sniffing daintily. The caravan pulled up to Elisa's wire fence and stopped. Now the newcomer dog, feeling out-numbered, lowered his tail and retired under the wagon with raised hackles and bared teeth.

The man on the wagon seat called out, "That's a bad dog in a fight when he gets started."

Elisa laughed. "I see he is. How soon does he generally get started?"

The man caught up her laughter and echoed it heartily. "Sometimes not for weeks and weeks," he said. He climbed stiffly down, over the wheel. The horse and the donkey drooped like unwatered flowers.

Elisa saw that he was a very big man. Although his hair and beard were greying, he did not look old. His worn black suit was wrinkled and spotted with grease. The laughter had disappeared from his face and eyes the moment his laughing voice ceased. His eyes were dark, and they were full of the brooding that gets in the eyes of teamsters and of sailors. The calloused hands he rested on the wire fence were cracked, and every crack was a black line. He took off his battered hat.

"I'm off my general road, ma'am," he said. "Does this dirt road cut over across the river to the Los Angeles highway?"

Elisa stood up and shoved the thick scissors in her apron pocket. "Well, yes, it does, but it winds around and then fords the river. I don't think your team could pull through the sand."

He replied with some asperity, "It might surprise you what them beasts can pull through."

"When they get started?" she asked.

He smiled for a second. "Yes. When they get started."

"Well," said Elisa, "I think you'll save time if you go back to the Salinas road and pick up the highway there."

He drew a big finger down the chicken wire and made it sing. "I ain't in any hurry, ma'am. I go from Seattle to San Diego and back every year. Takes all my time. About six months each way. I aim to follow nice weather."

Elisa took off her gloves and stuffed them in the apron pocket with the scissors. She touched the under edge of her man's hat, searching for fugitive hairs. "That sounds like a nice kind of a way to live," she said.

He leaned confidentially over the fence. "Maybe you noticed the writing on my wagon. I mend pots and sharpen knives and scissors. You got any of them things to do?"

"Oh, no," she said, quickly. "Nothing like that." Her eyes hardened with resistance.

"Scissors is the worst thing," he explained. "Most people just ruin scissors trying to sharpen 'em, but I know how. I got a special tool. It's a little bobbit kind of thing, and patented. But it sure does the trick."

"No. My scissors are all sharp."

"All right, then. Take a pot," he continued earnestly, "a bent pot, or a pot with a hole. I can make it like new so you don't have to buy no new ones. That's a saving for you."

"No," she said shortly. "I tell you I have nothing like that for you to do."

His face fell to an exaggerated sadness. His voice took on a whining undertone. "I ain't had a thing to do today. Maybe I won't have no supper tonight. You see I'm off my regular road. I know folks on the highway clear from Seattle to San Diego. They save their things for me to sharpen up because they know I do it so good and save them money."

"I'm sorry," Elisa said irritably. "I haven't anything for you to do."

His eyes left her face and fell to searching the ground. They roamed about until so they came to the chrysanthemum bed where she had been working. "What's them plants, ma'am?"

The irritation and resistance melted from Elisa's face. "Oh, those are chrysanthemums, giant whites and yellows. I raise them every year, bigger than anybody around here."

"Kind of a long-stemmed flower? Looks like a quick puff of colored smoke?" he asked.

"That's it. What a nice way to describe them."

"They smell kind of nasty till you get used to them," he said.

"It's a good bitter smell," she retorted, "not nasty at all."

He changed his tone quickly. "I like the smell myself."

"I had ten-inch blooms this year," she said.

The man leaned farther over the fence, "Look. I know a lady down the road a piece, has got the nicest garden you ever seen. Got nearly every kind of flower but no chrysanthemums. Last time I was mending a copper-bottom washtub for her (that's a hard job but I do it good), she said to me, 'If you ever run acrost some nice chrysanthemums I wish you'd try to get me a few seeds.' That's what she told me."

Elisa's eyes grew alert and eager. "She couldn't have known much about chrysanthemums. You *can* raise them from seed, but it's much easier to root the little sprouts you see there."

"Oh," he said. "I s'pose I can't take none to her, then."

"Why yes you can," Elisa cried. "I can put some in damp sand, and you can carry them right along with you. They'll take root in the pot if you keep them damp. And then she can transplant them."

"She'd sure like to have some, ma'am. You say they're nice ones?"

"Beautiful," she said. "Oh, beautiful." Her eyes shone. She tore off the battered hat and shook out her dark pretty hair. "I'll put them in a flower pot, and you can take them right with you. Come into the yard."

While the man came through the picket gate Elisa ran excitedly along the geranium-bordered path to the back of the house. And she returned carrying a big red flower pot. The gloves were forgotten now. She kneeled on the ground by the starting bed and dug up the sandy soil with her fingers and scooped it into the bright new flower pot. Then she picked up the little pile of shoots she had prepared. With her strong fingers she pressed them into the sand and tamped around them with her knuckles. The man stood over her. "I'll tell you what to do," she said. "You remember so you can tell the lady."

"Yes, I'll try to remember."

"Well, look. These will take root in about a month. Then she must set them out, about a foot apart in good rich earth like this, see?" She lifted a handful of dark soil for him to look at. "They'll grow fast and tall. Now remember this: In July tell her to cut them down, about eight inches from the ground."

"Before they bloom?" he asked.

"Yes, before they bloom." Her face was tight with eagerness. "They'll grow right up again. About the last of September the buds will start."

She stopped and seemed perplexed. "It's the budding that takes the most care," she said hesitantly. "I don't know how to tell you." She looked deep into his eyes, searchingly. Her mouth opened a little, and she seemed to be listening. "I'll try to tell you," she said. "Did you ever hear of planting hands?"

"Can't say I have, ma'am."

"Well, I can only tell you what it feels like. It's when you're picking off the buds you don't want. Everything goes right down into your fingertips. You watch your fingers work. They do it themselves. You can feel how it is. They pick and pick the buds. They never make a mistake. They're with the plant. Do you see? Your fingers and the plant. You can feel that, right up your arm. They know. They never make a mistake. You can feel it. When you're like that you can't do anything wrong. Do you see that? Can you understand that?"

She was kneeling on the ground looking up at him. Her breast swelled passionately.

The man's eyes narrowed. He looked away self-consciously. "Maybe I know," he said. "Sometimes in the night in the wagon there—"

Elisa's voice grew husky. She broke in on him, "I've never lived as you do, but I know what you mean. When the night is dark—why, the stars are sharp-pointed, and there's quiet. Why, you rise up and up! Every pointed star gets driven into your body. It's like that. Hot and sharp and—lovely."

Kneeling there, her hand went out toward his leg in the greasy black trousers. Her hesitant fingers almost touched the cloth. Then her hand dropped to the ground. She crouched low like a fawning dog.

He said, "It's nice, just like you say. Only when you don't have no dinner, it ain't."

She stood up then, very straight, and her face was ashamed. She held the flower pot out to him and placed it gently in his arms. "Here. Put it in your wagon, on the seat, where you can watch it. Maybe I can find something for you to do."

At the back of the house she dug in the can pile and found two old and battered aluminum saucepans. She carried them back and gave them to him. "Here, maybe you can fix these."

His manner changed. He became professional. "Good as new I can fix them." At the back of his wagon he set a little anvil, and out of an oily tool box dug a small machine hammer. Elisa came through the gate to watch him while he pounded out the dents in the kettles. His mouth grew sure and knowing. At a difficult part of the work he sucked his upper-lip.

"You sleep right in the wagon?" Elisa asked.

"Right in the wagon, ma'am. Rain or shine I'm dry as a cow in there."

"It must be nice," she said. "It must be very nice, I wish women could do such things."

"It ain't the right kind of a life for a woman."

Her upper lip raised a little, showing her teeth. "How do you know? How can you tell?" she said.

"I don't know, ma'am," he protested. "Of course I don't know. Now here's your kettles, done. You don't have to buy no new ones."

"How much?"

"Oh, fifty cents'll do. I keep my prices down and my work good. That's why I have all them satisfied customers up and down the highway."

Elisa brought him a fifty-cent piece from the house and dropped it in his hand. "You might be surprised to have a rival some time. I can sharpen scissors, too. And I can beat the dents out of little pots. I could show you what a woman might do."

He put his hammer back in the oily box and shoved the little anvil out of sight. "It would be a lonely life for a woman, ma'am, and a scarey life, too, with animals creeping under the wagon all night." He climbed over the singletree, steadying himself with a hand on the burro's white rump. He settled himself in the seat, picked up the lines. "Thank you kindly, ma'am," he said. "I'll do like you told me; I'll go back and catch the Salinas road."

"Mind," she called, "if you're long in getting there, keep the sand damp."

"Sand, ma'am? . . . Sand? Oh, sure. You mean around the chrysanthemums. Sure I will." He clucked his tongue. The beasts leaned luxuriously into their collars. The mongrel dog took his place between the back wheels. The wagon turned and crawled out the entrance road and back the way it had come, along the river.

Elisa stood in front of her wire fence watching the slow progress of the caravan. Her shoulders were straight, her head thrown back, her eyes half-closed, so that the scene came vaguely into them. Her lips moved silently, forming the words "Good-bye—good-bye." Then she whispered, "That's a bright direction. There's a glowing there." The sound of her whisper startled her. She shook herself free and looked about to see whether anyone had been listening. Only the dogs had heard. They lifted their heads toward her from their sleeping in the dust, and then stretched out their chins and settled asleep again. Elisa turned and ran hurriedly into the house.

In the kitchen she reached behind the stove and felt the water tank. It was full of hot water from the noonday cooking. In the bathroom she tore off her soiled clothes and flung them into the corner, And then she scrubbed herself with a little block of pumice, legs and thighs, loins and chest and arms, until her skin was scratched and red. When she had dried herself she stood in front of a mirror in her bedroom and looked at her body. She tightened her stomach and threw out her chest. She turned and looked over her shoulder at her back.

After a while she began to dress, slowly. She put on her newest under-clothing and her nicest stockings and the dress which was the symbol of her prettiness. She worked carefully on her hair, penciled her eyebrows and rouged her lips.

Before she was finished she heard the little thunder of hoofs and the shouts of Henry and his helper as they drove the red steers into the corral. She heard the gate bang shut and set herself for Henry's arrival.

His step sounded on the porch. He entered the house calling, "Elisa, where are you?"

"In my room, dressing. I'm not ready. There's hot water for your bath. Hurry up. It's getting late."

When she heard him splashing in the tub, Elisa laid his dark suit on the bed, and shirt and socks and tie beside it. She stood his polished shoes on the floor beside the bed. Then she went to the porch and sat primly and stiffly down. She looked toward the river road where the willow-line was still yellow with frosted leaves so that under the high grey fog they seemed a thin band of sunshine. This was the only color in the grey afternoon. She sat unmoving for a long time. Her eyes blinked rarely.

Henry came banging out of the door, shoving his tie inside his vest as he came. Elisa stiffened and her face grew tight, Henry stopped short and looked at her.

"Why—why, Elisa. You look so nice!"

"Nice? You think I look nice? What do you mean by 'nice'?"

Henry blundered on. "I don't know. I mean you look different, strong and happy."

"I am strong? Yes, strong. What do you mean 'strong'?"

He looked bewildered. "You're playing some kind of a game," he said help-lessly. "It's a kind of play. You look strong enough to break a calf over your knee, happy enough to eat it like a watermelon."

For a second she lost her rigidity. "Henry! Don't talk like that. You didn't know what you said." She grew complete again. "I'm strong," she boasted. "I never knew before how strong."

Henry looked down toward the tractor shed, and when he brought his eyes back to her, they were his own again. "I'll get out the car. You can put on your coat while I'm starting."

Elisa went into the house. She heard him drive to the gate and idle down his motor, and then she took a long time to put on her hat. She pulled it here and pressed it there. When Henry turned the motor off she slipped into her coat and went out.

The little roadster bounced along on the dirt road by the river, raising the birds and driving the rabbits into the brush. Two cranes flapped heavily over the willow-line and dropped into the river-bed.

Far ahead on the road Elisa saw a dark speck. She knew.

She tried not to look as they passed it, but her eyes would not obey. She whispered to herself sadly, "He might have thrown them off the road. That wouldn't have been much trouble, not very much. But he kept the pot," she explained. "He had to keep the pot. That's why he couldn't get them off the road."

The roadster turned a bend and she saw the caravan ahead. She swung full around toward her husband so she could not see the little covered wagon and the mismatched team as the car passed them.

In a moment it was over. The thing was done. She did not look back.

She said loudly, to be heard above the motor, "It will be good, tonight, a good dinner."

"Now you're changed again," Henry complained. He took one hand from the wheel and patted her knee. "I ought to take you in to dinner oftener. It would be good for both of us. We get so heavy out on the ranch."

"Henry," she asked, "could we have wine at dinner?"

"Sure we could. Say! That will be fine."

She was silent for a while; then she said, "Henry, at those prize fights, do the men hurt each other very much?"

"Sometimes a little, not often. Why?"

"Well, I've read how they break noses, and blood runs down their chests. I've read how the fighting gloves get heavy and soggy with blood."

He looked around at her. "What's the matter, Elisa? I didn't know you read things like that." He brought the car to a stop, then turned to the right over the Salinas River bridge,

"Do any women ever go to the fights?" she asked.

"Oh, sure, some. What's the matter, Elisa? Do you want to go? I don't think you'd like it, but I'll take you if you really want to go."

She relaxed limply in the seat. "Oh, no. No. I don't want to go. I' m sure I don't." Her face was turned away from him. "It will be enough if we can have wine. It will be plenty," She turned up her coat collar so he could not see that she was crying weakly—like an old woman.

QUESTIONS

JOHN STEINBECK, *The Chrysanthemums*

1. How does the description in the opening two paragraphs set the tone for the rest of the story, particularly Steinbeck's description of the Salinas Valley? What other images serve to reflect Elisa's state of mind and situation?

2. Describe Elisa's physical appearance. What kind of person is she and how does Steinbeck's description of her establish her character? Why is her talent for growing chrysanthemums important to the story?

3. Why does Steinbeck include the scene in which Elisa is standing behind the wire fence looking at her husband and the two men? What does this scene convey about her feelings?

4. What is the symbolic significance of the chrysanthemums? What particular qualities does this flower have that mirror Elisa's perspective?

5. What is the significance of her meeting with the tinker? What kind of person is he? How does this part of the story bring her conflict to light? Why is he an unnamed character?

6. How has Elisa changed as a result of her meeting with the tinker? How is this reflected in the bathing scene? Why does she scrub herself "until her skin was scratched and red"? Why does she look at herself in the mirror?

7. The plot of Steinbeck's story is structured according to the basic principles of exposition, complication, crisis, and resolution. Write an essay outlining how the story conforms to these principles.

8. Write an essay describing how the setting of the story—the time and place in which it occurs—serves to reflect the changes in the main character and advance its major theme.

Eudora Welty

[1909–2001]

In her 1984 memoir One Writer's Beginnings, **EUDORA WELTY** *reminisces about her childhood introduction to books: "I learned from the age of two or three that any room in our house, at any time of day, was there to read in, or to be read to." Welty's father read to gather information; her mother, according to the writer, "sank as a hedonist into novels." This literary heritage is evident in everything Eudora Welty published during a career that spanned seven decades, a career that established her as one of the most revered writers of the Southern Literary Renaissance.*

Eudora Welty was born in Jackson, Mississippi, the eldest child and only daughter of Christian Welty and Mary Chestina Andrews Welty. She was educated at the Mississippi State College for Women (1925–1927), the University of Wisconsin (Bachelor of Arts, 1929), and the Columbia University Graduate School of Business (1930–1931). Welty left Columbia when her father died, and except for time spent traveling, she never moved away from Jackson again. During the Depression she worked for the Works Progress Administration (WPA), traveling throughout Mississippi taking photographs and writing about the sometimes desperate lives of its people. This job brought her into contact with a wide range of rural Southern personalities, who would later appear in her stories and novels. The literary magazine Southern Review *published several of her stories in the late 1930s, and her first collection,* A Curtain of Green, *appeared in 1941. By that time she had garnered the attention of a number of prominent writers, including Robert Penn Warren, Cleanth Brooks, and Katherine Anne Porter, who wrote the introduction to* A Curtain of Green. *This book was followed by a novella,* The Robber Bridegroom, *in 1942, and another story collection,* The Wide Net, *in 1943. During this period Welty won two O. Henry Short Story Prizes, one for "A Worn Path" (1942) and one for "The Wide Net" (1943). In 1944 she was awarded a grant in literature from the National Institute of Arts and Letters.*

Welty continued her exploration of Southern sensibility with novels including The Ponder Heart *(1954, winner of the William Dean Howells Medal);* Losing Battles *(1970, nominated for a National Book Award for fiction); and* The Optimist's Daughter *(1972, winner of the 1973 Pulitzer Prize for fiction); and short story collections including* The Bride of Inisfallen, and Other Stories *(1955) and* Moon Lake and Other Stories *(1980). Her essays and book reviews appeared in a number of periodicals, and she lectured across the country until shortly before her death. In 1980 Welty was awarded both the National Medal for Literature and the Presidential Medal of Freedom, and in 2000 she was inducted into the National Women's Hall of Fame.*

   Welty's best work offers readers a glimpse into the ordinary, everyday lives of hairdressers, postmistresses, musicians, and housewives; while some characters may veer into the grotesque, most live quiet, uneventful lives. But those lives are steeped in interior mystery; as critic Ruth Vande Kieft notes, "Inside is where all the mystery lies, and Eudora Welty's great pursuit has been to explore the mysteries of identity and meaning—of the essential self, which is inviolable." Few American writers have been as prolific as Eudora Welty, and few so beloved. A woman who claimed to have lived "a sheltered life," Welty has enriched the lives of generations of readers.

A Worn Path

EUDORA WELTY

IT WAS DECEMBER—a bright frozen day in the early morning. Far out in the country there was an old Negro woman with her head tied in a red rag, coming along a path through the pinewoods. Her name was Phoenix Jackson. She was very old and small and she walked, slowly in the dark pine shadows, moving a little from side to side in her steps, with the balanced heaviness and lightness of a pendulum in a grandfather clock. She carried a thin, small cane made from an umbrella, and with this she kept tapping the frozen earth in front of her. This made a grave and persistent noise in the still air, that seemed meditative, like the chirping of a solitary little bird.

She wore a dark striped dress reaching down to her shoetops, and an equally long apron of bleached sugar sacks, with a full pocket; all, neat and tidy, but every time she took a step she might have fallen over her shoelaces, which dragged from her unlaced shoes. She looked straight ahead. Her eyes were blue with age. Her skin had a pattern all its own of numberless branching wrinkles and as though a whole little tree stood in the middle of her forehead, but a golden color ran underneath, and the two knobs of her cheeks were illuminated by a yellow burning under the dark. Under the red rag her hair came down on her neck in the frailest of ringlets, still black, and with an odor like copper.

Now and then there was a quivering in the thicket. Old Phoenix said, "Out of my way, all you foxes, owls, beetles, jack rabbits, coons, and wild animals! . . . Keep out from under these feet, little bobwhites. . . . Keep the big wild hogs out of my path. Don't let none of those come running in my direction. I got a long way." Under her small black-freckled hand her cane, limber as a buggy whip, would switch at the brush as if to rouse up any hiding things.

On she went. The woods were deep and still. The sun made the pine needles almost too bright to look at, up where the wind rocked. The cones dropped as light as feathers. Down in the hollow was the mourning dove—it was not too late for him.

The path ran up a hill. "Seem like there is chains about my feet, time I get this far," she said, in the voice of argument old people keep to use with themselves. "Something always take a hold on this hill—pleads I should stay."

After she got to the top she turned and gave a full, severe look behind her where she had come. "Up through pines," she said at length. "Now down through oaks."

Her eyes opened their widest and she started down gently. But before she got to the bottom of the hill a bush caught her dress.

Her fingers were busy and intent, but her skirts were full and long, so that before she could pull them free in one place they were caught in another. It was not possible to allow the dress to tear. "I in the thorny bush," she said. "Thorns, you doing your appointed work. Never want to let folks past—no sir. Old eyes thought you was a pretty little *green* bush."

Finally, trembling all over, she stood free, and after a moment dared to stoop for her cane.

"Sun so high!" she cried, leaning back and looking, while the thick tears went over her eyes. "The time getting all gone here."

At the foot of this hill was a place where a log was laid across the creek.

"Now comes the trial," said Phoenix.

Putting her right foot out, she mounted the log and shut her eyes. Lifting her skirt, leveling her cane fiercely before her, like a festival figure in some parade, she began to march across. Then she opened her eyes and she was safe on the other side.

"I wasn't as old as I thought," she said.

But she sat down to rest. She spread her skirts on the bank around her and folded her hands over her knees. Up above her was a tree in a pearly cloud of mistletoe. She did not dare to close her eyes, and when a little boy brought her a little plate with a slice of marble-cake on it she spoke to him. "That would be acceptable," she said. But when she went to take it there was just her own hand in the air.

So she left that tree, and had to go through a barbed-wire fence. There she had to creep and crawl, spreading her knees and stretching her fingers like a baby trying to climb the steps. But she talked loudly to herself: she could not let her dress be torn now, so late in the day, and she could not pay for having her arm or leg sawed off if she got caught fast where she was.

At last she was safe through the fence and risen up out in the clearing. Big dead trees, like black men with one arm, were standing in the purple stalks of the withered cotton field. There sat a buzzard.

"Who you watching?"

In the furrow she made her way along

"Glad this not the season for bulls," she said, looking sideways, "and the good Lord made his snakes to curl up and sleep in the winter. A pleasure I don't see no two-headed snake coming around that tree, where it come once. It took a while to get by him, back in the summer."

She passed through the old cotton and went into a field of dead corn. It whispered and shook, and was taller than her head. "Through the maze now," she said, for there was no path.

Then there was something tall, black, and skinny there, moving before her.

At first she took it for a man. It could have been a man dancing in the field. But she stood still and listened, and it did not make a sound. It was as silent as a ghost.

"Ghost," she said sharply, "who be you the ghost of? For I have heard of nary death close by."

But there was no answer, only the ragged dancing in the wind.

She shut her eyes, reached out her hand, and touched a sleeve. She found a coat and inside that an emptiness, cold as ice.

"You scarecrow," she said. Her face lighted. "I ought to be shut up for good," she said with laughter. "My senses is gone. I too old. I the oldest people I ever know. Dance, old scarecrow," she said, "while I dancing with you."

She kicked her foot over the furrow, and with mouth drawn down shook her head once or twice in a little strutting way. Some husks blew down and whirled in streamers about her skirts.

Then she went on, parting her way from side to side with the cane, through the whispering field. At last she came to the end, to a wagon track, where the silver grass blew between the red ruts. The quail were walking around like pullets, seeming all dainty and unseen.

"Walk pretty," she said. "This the easy place. This the easy going."

She followed the track, swaying through the quiet bare fields, through the little strings of trees silver in their dead leaves, past cabins silver from weather, with the doors and windows boarded shut, all like old women under a spell sitting there. "I walking in their sleep," she said, nodding her head vigorously.

In a ravine she went where a spring was silently flowing through a hollow log. Old Phoenix bent and drank. "Sweetgum makes the water sweet," she said, and drank more. "Nobody knows who made this well, for it was here when I was born."

The track crossed a swampy part where the moss hung as white as lace from every limb. "Sleep on, alligators, and blow your bubbles." Then the track went into the road.

Deep, deep the road went down between the high green-colored banks. Overhead the live-oaks met, and it was as dark as a cave.

A black dog with a lolling tongue came up out of the weeds by the ditch. She was meditating, and not ready, and when he came at her she only hit him a little with her cane. Over she went in the ditch, like a little puff of milk-weed.

Down there, her senses drifted away. A dream visited her, and she reached her hand up, but nothing reached down and gave her a pull. So she lay there and presently went to talking. "Old woman," she said to herself, "that black dog come up out of the weeds to stall you off, and now there he sitting on his fine tail, smiling at you."

A white man finally came along and found her—a hunter, a young man, with his dog on a chain.

"Well, Granny!" he laughed. "What are you doing there?"

"Lying on my back like a June-bug waiting to be turned over, mister," she said, reaching up her hand.

He lifted her up, gave her a swing in the air, and set her down. "Anything broken, Granny?"

"No, sir, them old dead weeds is springy enough," said Phoenix, when she had got her breath. "I thank you for your trouble."

"Where do you live, Granny?" he asked, while the two dogs were growling at each other.

"Away back yonder, sir, behind that ridge. You can't even see it from here."

"On your way home?"

"No, sir, I going to town."

"Why that's too far! That's as far as I walk when I come out myself, and I get something for my trouble." He patted the stuffed bag he carried, and there hung down a little closed claw. It was one of the bobwhites, with its beak hooked bitterly to show it was dead. "Now you go on home, Granny!"

"I bound to go to town, mister," said Phoenix. "The time come around."

He gave another laugh, filling the whole landscape. "I know you colored people! Wouldn't miss going to town to see Santa Claus!"

But something held Old Phoenix very still. The deep lines in her face went into a fierce and different radiation. Without warning she had seen with her own eyes a flashing nickel fall out of the man's pocket on to the ground.

"How old are you, Granny?" he was saying.

"There is no telling, mister," she said, "no telling."

Then she gave a little cry and clapped her hands, and said, "Git on away from here, dog! Look! Look at that dog!" She laughed as if in admiration. "He ain't scared of nobody. He a big black dog." She whispered, "Sick him!"

"Watch me get rid of that cur," said the man. "Sick him, Pete! Sick him!"

Phoenix heard the dogs fighting and heard the man running and throwing sticks. She even heard a gunshot. But she was slowly bending forward by that time, further and further forward, the lids stretched down over her eyes, as if she were doing this in her sleep. Her chin was lowered almost to her knees. The yellow palm of her hand came out from the fold of her apron. Her fingers slid down and along the ground under the piece of money with the grace and care they would have in lifting an egg from under a sitting hen. Then she slowly straightened up, she stood erect, and the nickel was in her apron pocket. A bird flew by. Her lips moved. "God watching me the whole time. I come to stealing."

The man came back, and his own dog panted about them. "Well, I scared him off that time," he said, and then he laughed and lifted his gun and pointed it at Phoenix.

She stood straight and faced him.

"Doesn't the gun scare you?" he said, still pointing it.

"No, sir, I seen plenty go off closer by, in my day, and for less what I done," she said, holding utterly still.

He smiled, and shouldered the gun. "Well, Granny," he said, "you must be a hundred years old, and scared of nothing. I'd give you a dime if I had any money with me. But you take my advice and stay home, and nothing will happen to you."

"I bound to go on my way, mister," said Phoenix. She inclined her head in the red rag. Then they went in different directions, but she could hear the gun shooting again and again over the hill.

She walked on. The shadows hung from the oak trees to the road like curtains. Then she smelled wood-smoke, and smelled the river, and she saw a steeple and the cabins on their steep steps. Dozens of little black children whirled around her. There ahead was Natchez shining. Bells were ringing. She walked on.

In the paved city it was Christmas time. There were red and green electric lights strung and crisscrossed everywhere, and all turned on in the daytime. Old Phoenix would have been lost if she had not distrusted her eyesight and depended on her feet to know where to take her.

She paused quietly on the sidewalk, where people were passing by. A lady came along in the crowd, carrying an armful of red-, green-, and silver-wrapped presents; she gave off perfume like the red roses in hot summer, and Phoenix stopped her.

"Please, missy, will you lace up my shoe?" She held up her foot.

"What do you want, Grandma?"

"See my shoe," said Phoenix. "Do all right for out in the country, but wouldn't look right to go in a big building."

"Stand still then, Grandma," said the lady. She put her packages down carefully on the sidewalk beside her and laced and tied both shoes tightly.

"Can't lace 'em with a cane," said Phoenix. "Thank you, missy. I doesn't mind asking a nice lady to tie up my shoe when I gets out on the street."

Moving slowly and from side to side, she went into the stone building and into a tower of steps, where she walked up and around and around until her feet knew to stop.

She entered a door, and there she saw nailed up on the wall the document that had been stamped with the gold seal and framed in the gold frame which matched the dream that was hung up in her head.

"Here I be," she said. There was a fixed and ceremonial stiffness over her body.

"A charity case, I suppose," said an attendant who sat at the desk before her.

But Phoenix only looked above her head. There was sweat on her face; the wrinkles shone like a bright net.

"Speak up, Grandma" the woman said. "What's your name? We must have your history, you know. Have you been here before? What seems to be the trouble with you?"

Old Phoenix only gave a twitch to her face as if a fly were bothering her.

"Are you deaf?" cried the attendant.

But then the nurse came in.

"Oh, that's just old Aunt Phoenix," she said. "She doesn't come for herself—she has a little grandson. She makes these trips just as regular as clockwork. She lives away back off the Old Natchez Trace." She bent down. "Well, Aunt Phoenix, why don't you just take a seat? We won't keep you standing after your long trip." She pointed.

The old woman sat down, bolt upright in the chair.

"Now, how is the boy?" asked the nurse.

Old Phoenix did not speak.

"I said, how is the boy?"

But Phoenix only waited and stared straight ahead, her face very solemn and withdrawn into rigidity.

"Is his throat any better?" asked the nurse. "Aunt Phoenix, don't you hear me? Is your grandson's throat any better since the last time you came for the medicine?"

With her hand on her knees, the old woman waited, silent, erect, and motionless, just as if she were in armor.

"You mustn't take up our time this way, Aunt Phoenix," the nurse said. "Tell us quickly about your grandson, and get it over. He isn't dead, is he?"

At last there came a flicker and then a flame of comprehension across her face, and she spoke.

"My grandson. It was my memory had left me. There I sat and forgot why I made my long trip."

"Forgot?" The nurse frowned. "After you came so far?"

Then Phoenix was like an old woman begging a dignified forgiveness for waking up frightened in the night. "I never did go to school—I was too old at the Surrender," she said in a soft voice. "I'm an old woman without an education. It was my memory fail me. My little grandson, he is just the same, and I forgot it in the coming."

"Throat never heals, does it?" said the nurse, speaking in a loud, sure voice to Old Phoenix. By now she had a card with something written on it, a little list. "Yes. Swallowed lye. When was it—January—two—three years ago—"

Phoenix spoke unasked now. "No, missy, he not dead, he just the same. Every little while his throat begin to close up again, and he not able to swallow. He not get his breath. He not able to help himself. So the time come around, and I go on another trip for soothing medicine."

"All right. The doctor said as long as you came to get it you could have it," said the nurse. "But it's an obstinate case."

"My little grandson, he sit up there in the house all wrapped up, waiting by himself," Phoenix went on. "We is the only two left in the world. He suffer and it don't seem to put him back at all. He got a sweet look. He going to last. He wear a little patch quilt and peep out, holding his mouth open like a little bird. I remembers so plain now. I not going to forget him again, no, the whole enduring time. I could tell him from all the others in creation."

"All right." The nurse was trying to hush her now. She brought her a bottle of medicine. "Charity," she said, making a check mark in a book.

Old Phoenix held the bottle close to her eyes and then carefully put it into her pocket.

"I thank you," she said.

"It's Christmas time, Grandma," said the attendant. "Could I give you a few pennies out of my purse?"

"Five pennies is a nickel," said Phoenix stiffly.

"Here's a nickel," said the attendant.

Phoenix rose carefully and held out her hand. She received the nickel and then fished the other nickel out of her pocket and laid it beside the new one. She stared at her palm closely, with her head on one side.

Then she gave a tap with her cane on the floor.

"This is what come to me to do," she said. "I going to the store and buy my child a little windmill they sells, make out of paper. He going to find it hard to believe there such a thing in the world. I'll march myself back where he waiting, holding it straight up in this hand."

She lifted her free hand, gave a little nod, turned round, and walked out of the doctor's office. Then her slow step began on the stairs, going down.

[1941]

1. How does Phoenix Jackson's habit of talking to herself help to establish her character? In what ways is her monologue more dignified than humorous?

2. What does Phoenix's encounter with the hunter reveal about her cleverness and sense of purpose?

3. How do the hunter, the shopper, the attendant, and the nurse react to Phoenix? How does their behavior toward her convey their sense of superiority? How does the narrator undermine that superiority?

4. In what ways does Phoenix's journey resemble an epic quest? How does the narrator's description of the terrain and the obstacles contribute to that effect?

5. Why does Phoenix become less sure of herself once she enters the city? How does her uncertainty manifest itself?

6. Phoenix undertakes her journey at Christmastime. What is the significance of this timing? Of her decision to use the two nickels to buy her grandson a toy?

7. Welty has said that Phoenix's victory "is when she sees the diploma in the doctor's office," that her return journey "can now go without saying." How do you interpret this statement?

8. What is the significance of the title, "The Worn Path"? What does it suggest about Phoenix's determination?

9. When reminded of the reason for her journey—her grandson's condition—Phoenix says, "I not going to forget him again, no, the whole enduring time. I could tell him from all the others in creation." Write an essay analyzing this pronouncement as the central truth of the story. How does it reflect the powerful love that provides Phoenix with the strength to undertake her journey?

10. Research the legend of the Phoenix, and analyze the significance of Phoenix's name. How does an understanding of this legend lend further nobility to the old woman's quest?

James Joyce
[1882–1941]

JAMES JOYCE *was born at Rathgar outside of Dublin, Ireland. Joyce's father was musical and charming but given to losing money, or at least not keeping it. Joyce's young life was spent watching the family fortunes dwindle. The combination of a charming but unreliable father and a strong and demanding mother may have set the scenes for much of his later writing. Joyce attended boarding school where he suffered the abuses of Jesuit discipline as it was practiced in the late 1800s. In his first novel,* A Portrait of the Artist as a Young Man, *he describes beatings and verbal abuse. Joyce joined the Faculty of Arts in University College, Dublin, but soon found that he was meant for the life in early twentieth century Paris. In Ireland Joyce spent time with such notable writers as William Butler Yeats and developed a strong interest in the Irish independence movement though he never actually participated in the rebellion. Joyce's collection of short stories,* Dubliners, *is a kind of farewell to Ireland, since the portraits that he draws in these tales all suggest a kind of moral and political paralysis in the Irish mind. Joyce sympathized with his countrymen but was unable to find interest or energy in joining their battles with the British.*

After his mother's death in 1902, Joyce and his lover Nora Barnacle departed for Paris and Europe permanently. They became the parents of a son and daughter and did eventually marry in 1931, despite Joyce's objections to formal marriage. Joyce taught in Switzerland, but the Paris appeal was always strong. The American poet Ezra Pound encouraged Joyce in his writing and acted as coach and editor as well as literary supporter. Joyce spent most of the rest of his life working on his two major works, Ulysses *and* Finnegans Wake. *The American courts fought over the pornographic nature of* Ulysses, *the case having elicited the famous quotation by a judge that he "knew pornography when he saw it."* Ulysses *would hardly be considered shocking by twenty-first century MTV standards, but in its day the novel was controversial.*

In the meantime, Joyce's eyesight deteriorated, but he continued to write, supported by patrons, or people who were willing to give money to important artists to encourage their writing. Harriet Weaver, a wealthy woman who supported the Joyces for most of Joyce's writing life, was willing to continue to offer patronage even when his works were threatened by American disapproval. Both wars caused the Joyces to move to neutral Switzerland. Joyce lived in Switzerland during World War I and went there again as World War II threatened. It was there that he died during the war. He is now thought of as one of the greatest writers of the twentieth century. His contributions to the changes in the way that novels and stories tell about life began what was to become a postmodern way of writing despite the modernist centrality of Joyce's attitudes and artistic temperament.

Araby

JAMES JOYCE

NORTH RICHMOND STREET, being blind, was a quiet street except at the hour when the Christian Brothers' School set the boys free. An uninhabited house of two storeys stood at the blind end, detached from its neighbours in a square ground. The other houses of the street, conscious of decent lives within them, gazed at one another with brown imperturbable faces.

The former tenant of our house, a priest, had died in the back drawing room. Air, musty from having long been enclosed, hung in all the rooms, and the waste room behind the kitchen was littered with old useless papers. Among these I found a few paper-covered books, the pages of which were curled and damp: *The Abbott*, by Walter Scott, *The Devout Communicant* and *The Memoirs of Vidocq*. I liked the last best because its leaves were yellow. The wild garden behind the house contained a central apple-tree and a few straggling bushes under one of which I found the late tenant's rusty bicycle-pump. He had been a very charitable priest; in his will he had left all his money to institutions and the furniture of his house to his sister.

When the short days of winter came dusk fell before we had well eaten our dinners. When we met in the street the houses had grown sombre. The space of sky above us was the colour of ever-changing violet and towards it the lamps of the street lifted their feeble lanterns. The cold air stung us and we played till our bodies glowed. Our shouts echoed in the silent street. The career of our play brought us through the dark muddy lanes behind the houses where we ran the gauntlet of the rough tribes from the cottages, to the back doors of the dark dripping gardens where odours arose from the ashpits, to the dark odorous stables where a coachman smoothed and combed the horse or shook music from the buckled harness. When we returned to the street light from the kitchen windows had filled the areas. If my uncle was seen turning the corner we hid in the shadow until we had seen him safely housed. Or if Mangan's sister came out on the doorstep to call her brother in to his tea we watched her from our shadow peer up and down the street. We waited to see whether she would remain or go in and, if she remained, we left our shadow and walked up to Mangan's steps resignedly. She was waiting for us, her figure defined by the light from the half-opened door. Her brother always teased her before he obeyed and I stood by the railings looking at her. Her dress swung as she moved her body and the soft rope of her hair tossed from side to side.

Every morning I lay on the floor in the front parlor watching her door. The blind was pulled down within an inch of the sash so that I could not be seen. When she came out on the doorstep my heart leaped. I ran to the hall, seized my books and followed her. I kept her brown figure always in my eye and, when we came near the point at which our ways diverged, I quickened my pace and passed her. This happened morning after morning. I had never spoken to her, except for a few casual words, and yet her name was like a summons to all my foolish blood.

Her image accompanied me even in places the most hostile to romance. On Saturday evenings when my aunt went marketing I had to go to carry some of the parcels. We walked through the flaring street, jostled by drunken men and bargaining women, amid the curses of labourers, the shrill litanies of shop-boys who stood on guard by the barrels of pigs' cheeks, the nasal chanting of street singers, who sang a *come-all-you* about O'Donovan Rossa, or a ballad about the troubles in our native land. These noises converged in a single sensation of life for me: I imagined that I bore my chalice safely through the throng of foes. Her name sprang to my lips at moments in strange prayers and praises which I myself did not understand. My eyes were often full of tears (I could not tell why) and at times a flood from my heart seemed to pour itself out into my bosom. I thought little of the future. I did not know whether I would ever speak to her or not or, if I spoke to her, how I could tell her of my confused adoration. But my body was like a harp and her words and gestures were like fingers running upon the wires.

One evening I went into the back drawing-room in which the priest had died. It was a dark rainy evening and there was no sound in the house. Through one of the broken panes I heard the rain impinge upon the earth, the fine incessant needles of water playing in the sodden beds. Some distant lamp or lighted window gleamed below me. I was thankful that I could see so little. All my senses seemed to desire to veil themselves and, feeling that I was about to slip from them, I pressed the palms of my hands together until they trembled, murmuring: "*O love! O love!*" many times.

At last she spoke to me. When she addressed the first words to me I was so confused that I did not know what to answer. She asked me was I going to *Araby*. I forget whether I answered yes or no. It would be a splendid bazaar, she said; she would love to go.

—And why can't you? I asked.

While she spoke she turned a silver bracelet round and round her wrist. She could not go, she said, because there would be a retreat that week in her convent. Her brother and two other boys were fighting for their caps and I was alone at the railings. She held one of the spikes, bowing her head towards me. The light from the lamp opposite our door caught the white curve of her neck, lit up her hair that rested there and, falling, lit up the hand upon the railing. It fell over one side of her dress and caught the white border of a petticoat, just visible as she stood at ease.

—It's well for you, she said.

—If I go, I said, I will bring you something.

What innumerable follies laid waste my waking and sleeping thoughts after that evening! I wished to annihilate the tedious intervening days. I chafed against the work of school. At night in my bedroom and by day in the classroom her image came between me and the page I strove to read. The syllables of the word *Araby* were called to me through the silence in which my soul luxuriated and cast an Eastern enchantment over me. I asked for leave to go to the bazaar on Saturday night. My aunt was surprised and hoped it was not some Freemason affair. I answered few questions in class. I watched my master's face pass from amiability to sternness; he hoped I was not beginning to idle. I could not call my wandering thoughts together. I had hardly any patience with the serious work of life which, now that it stood between me and my desire, seemed to me child's play, ugly monotonous child's play.

On Saturday morning I reminded my uncle that I wished to go to the bazaar in the evening. He was fussing at the hallstand, looking for the hatbrush, and answered me curtly:

—Yes, boy, I know.

As he was in the hall I could not go into the front parlour and lie at the window. I left the house in bad humour and walked slowly towards the school. The air was pitilessly raw and already my heart misgave me.

When I came home to dinner my uncle had not yet been home. Still, it was early. I sat staring at the clock for some time and, when its ticking began to irritate me, I left the room. I mounted the staircase and gained the upper part of the house. The high cold empty gloomy rooms liberated me and I went from room to room singing. From the front window I saw my companions playing below in the street. Their cries reached me weakened and indistinct and, leaning my forehead against the cool glass, I looked over at the dark house where she lived. I may have stood there for an hour, seeing nothing but the brown-clad figure cast by my imagination, touched discreetly by the lamplight at the curved neck, at the hand upon the railing and at the border below the dress.

When I came downstairs again I found Mrs. Mercer sitting at the fire. She was an old garrulous woman, a pawnbroker's widow, who collected used stamps for some pious purpose. I had to endure the gossip of the tea-table. The meal was prolonged beyond an hour and still my uncle did not come. Mrs. Mercer stood up to go: she was sorry she couldn't wait any longer, but it was after eight o'clock and she did not like to be out late, as the night air was bad for her. When she had gone I began to walk up and down the room, clenching my fists. My aunt said:

—I'm afraid you may put off your bazaar for this night of Our Lord.

At nine o'clock I heard my uncle's latchkey in the halldoor. I heard him talking to himself and heard the hallstand rocking when it had received the weight of his overcoat. I could interpret these signs. When he was midway through his dinner I asked him to give me the money to go to the bazaar. He had forgotten.

—The people are in bed and after their first sleep now, he said.

I did not smile. My aunt said to him energetically:

—Can't you give him the money and let him go? You've kept him late enough as it is.

My uncle said he was very sorry he had forgotten. He said he believed in the old saying: "All work and no play makes Jack a dull boy." He asked me where I was going and, when I had told him a second time he asked me did I know *The Arab's Farewell to his Steed*. When I left the kitchen he was about to recite the opening lines of the piece to my aunt.

I held a florin tightly in my hand as I strode down Buckingham Street towards the station. The sight of the streets thronged with buyers and glaring with gas recalled to me the purpose of my journey. I took my seat in a third-class carriage of a deserted train. After an intolerable delay the train moved out of the station slowly. It crept onward among ruinous houses and over the twinkling river. At Westland Row Station a crowd of people pressed to the carriage doors; but the porters moved them back, saying that it was a special train for the bazaar. I remained alone in the bare carriage. In a few minutes the train drew up beside an improvised wooden platform. I passed out on to the road and saw by the lighted dial of a clock that it was ten minutes to ten. In front of me was a large building which displayed the magical name.

I could not find any sixpenny entrance and, fearing that the bazaar would be closed, I passed in quickly through a turnstile, handing a shilling to a weary-looking man. I found myself in a big hall girdled at half its height by a gallery. Nearly all the stalls were closed and the greater part of the hall was in darkness. I recognized a silence like that which pervades a church after a service. I walked into the centre of the bazaar timidly. A few people were gathered about the stalls which were still open. Before a curtain, over which the words *Café Chantant* were written in coloured lamps, two men were counting money on a salver. I listened to the fall of the coins.

Remembering with difficulty why I had come I went over to one of the stalls and examined porcelain vases and flowered tea-sets. At the door of the stall a young lady was talking and laughing with two young gentlemen. I remarked their English accents and listened vaguely to their conversation.

—O, I never said such a thing!

—O, but you did!

—O, but I didn't!

—Didn't she say that?

—Yes I heard her.

—O, there's a . . . fib!

Observing me the young lady came over and asked me did I wish to buy anything. The tone in her voice was not encouraging; she seemed to have spoken to me out of a sense of duty. I looked humbly at the great jars that stood like eastern guards at either side of the dark entrance to the stall and murmured:

—No, thank you.

The young lady changed the position of one of the vases and went back to the two young men. They began to talk of the same subject. Once or twice the young lady glanced at me over her shoulder.

I lingered before her stall, though I knew my stay was useless, to make my interest in her wares seem the more real. Then I turned away slowly and walked down the middle of the bazaar. I allowed the two pennies to fall against the sixpence in my pocket. I heard a voice call from one end of the gallery that the light was out. The upper part of the hall was now completely dark.

Gazing up into the darkness I saw myself as a creature driven and derided by vanity; and my eyes burned with anguish and anger.

[1914]

QUESTIONS

1. What kind of living conditions does the young narrator describe? What is his fascination with Mangan's sister?

2. The girl asks him to bring her something from the local bazaar (a cross between a fair and an outdoor sale) called Araby. Why can't the girl go to the bazaar herself?

3. Why does the narrator fail to buy something for the girl? How does he feel when his mission fails?

4. Joyce said that there are only three stories that are told over and over: first love, first encounter with death, and first encounter with mystery. This story suggests all three "firsts" as the boy moves through a cloud of powerful emotions. How do these themes thread through his experiences in the story?

5. Poverty features in many tales about Ireland, but this story only hints at the issues of poverty as it affects the lives of youngsters in its grasp. How do the themes of poverty and its toll on people appear in this story?

6. Religion had powerful effects on those who grew up in Catholic Ireland at the turn of the 20th century. In what ways does the tug of religious rules and feelings exert itself in this story?

7. The boy begins his tale by telling of the books he finds in the house where he lives, a house where a priest had died. He says he likes one of the priest's books, *The Memoirs of Vidocq* because its leaves were yellow. What do yellow leaves tell about a book? What kinds of associations does the color yellow have?

8. The word Araby suggests romance and adventure. How does the actual life of the boy compare to the romance that he imagines? How does his experience at the bazaar emphasize the lack of romance in his real life experience?

9. Choose a current book or movie that deals with "first love." Contrast the story with the story that Joyce's young narrator tells in "Araby." Analyze the reasons for the differences.

10. Look up the history of the Irish immigration to the United States. What caused so many Irish people to leave Ireland? What is the

relationship of their descendants to the "mother land" now? Write about this affection for a place.

11. The tale has to do with racing against time. The boy waits to go to the bazaar, then rushes to get there, then misses the chance to do as he had planned. Write about missed chances in your life or a race with time that you have experienced. How did the experience affect your future actions?

Katherine Mansfield
[1888–1923]

Born in Wellington, New Zealand, under the name Kathleen Mansfield Beaucamp, **KATHERINE MANSFIELD** *displayed her talents as a writer at a young age. In 1903, she was sent to Queen's College, London, to complete her education. She edited the college literary magazine and participated in musical activities. Her return to New Zealand was short, for she persuaded her father to provide her a living while she endeavored to succeed as a writer in London. There she married briefly, had financial difficulties, traveled with an opera company, and quickly damaged her fragile health. While in Germany recuperating, she wrote and published her first stories under the title of* In a German Pension *(1911). She also wrote articles for* The Westminster Gazette *to a supplement her income. In 1918 Mansfield then met and married the critic John Middleton Murry. They co-edited a journal called* Rhythm *where several of her stories first appeared. These were later collected in* Something Childish and Other Stories *(in the United States:* The Little Girl*) in 1924. Mansfield and Murry made their home in Buckinghamshire, but in early 1914 Mansfield again fell ill and traveled to the Continent to improve her health. Her brother, Leslie Beauchamp, was killed in action in World War I, further contributing to her distress but spurring on her creative impulses. She vowed to write much and well in his memory, determined that her own life, though likely to be short, would be vital and productive. She wrote* Prelude *(1918) in France and then contributed to D. H. Lawrence's journal* Signature *under the pen name of Matilda Berry.*

In 1918 Mansfield was diagnosed with tuberculosis and knew that her health was on the decline. She published Bliss and Other Stories *in 1920 and wrote reviews for her husband's journal,* Athenaeum, *most of which were published after her death in 1930 as* Novels and Novelists. *In 1920 she went to Switzerland where she wrote a group of stories,* The Garden Party and Other Stories *(1922). These received critical acclaim, but her career was to go no further, for her health was rapidly failing. She traveled to Paris and its environs to study with the Russian mystic Gurdjieff, one of the many spiritual thinkers working and writing in Europe at the time. She died in France. After her death, her husband, who wrote of her as the most delicate and spontaneous of creatures, published the rest of her works in* The Dove's Nest and Other Stories *(1923),* Journal *(1927),* Letters *(1928),* Selected Stories *(1929),* Poems *(1930), and* Scrapbook *(1939). Katherine Mansfield remains one of the brightest, funniest, and most sensitive of writers of the twentieth century.*

🗝 🗝 🗝

Miss Brill

KATHERINE MANSFIELD

ALTHOUGH IT WAS SO brilliantly fine—the blue sky powdered with gold and great spots of light like white wine splashed over the Jardins Publiques—Miss Brill was glad that she had decided on her fur. The air was motionless, but when you opened your mouth there was just a faint chill, like a chill from a glass of iced water before you sip, and now and again a leaf came drifting—from nowhere, from the sky. Miss Brill put up her hand and touched her fur. Dear little thing! It was nice to feel it again. She had taken it out of its box that afternoon, shaken out the moth-powder, given it a good brush, and rubbed the life back into the dim little eyes. "What has been happening to me"? said the sad little eyes. Oh, how sweet it was to see them snap at her again from the red eiderdown! . . . But the nose, which was of some black composition, wasn't at all firm. It must have had a knock, somehow. Never mind—a little dab of black sealing-wax when the time came—when it was absolutely necessary. . . . Little rogue! Yes, she really felt like that about it. Little rogue biting its tail just by her left ear. She could have taken it off and laid it on her lap and stroked it. She felt a tingling in her hands and arms, but that came from walking, she supposed. And when she breathed, something light and sad—no, not sad, exactly—something gentle seemed to move in her bosom.

There were a number of people out this afternoon, far more than last Sunday. And the band sounded louder and gayer. That was because the Season had begun. For although the band played all the year round on Sundays, out of season it was never the same. It was like some one playing with only the family to listen; it didn't care how it played if there weren't any strangers present. Wasn't the conductor wearing a new coat, too? She was sure it was new. He scraped with his foot and flapped his arms like a rooster about to crow, and the bandsmen sitting in the green rotunda blew out their cheeks and glared at the music. Now there came a little "flutey" bit—very pretty!—a little chain of bright drops. She was sure it would be repeated. It was; she lifted her head and smiled.

Only two people shared her "special" seat: a fine old man in a velvet coat, his hands clasped over a huge carved walking-stick, and a big old woman, sitting upright, with a roll of knitting on her embroidered apron. They did not speak. This was disappointing, for Miss Brill always looked forward to the

First published in 1922.

conversation. She had become really quite expert, she thought, at listening as though she didn't listen, at sitting in other people's lives just for a minute while they talked round her.

She glanced, sideways, at the old couple. Perhaps they would go soon. Last Sunday, too, hadn't been as interesting as usual. An English-man and his wife, he wearing a dreadful Panama hat and she button boots. And she'd gone on the whole time about how she ought to wear spectacles; she knew she needed them; but that it was no good getting any; they'd be sure to break and they'd never keep on. And he'd been so patient. He'd suggested everything—gold rims, the kind that curved round your ears, little pads inside the bridge. No, nothing would please her. "They'll always be sliding down my nose!" Miss Brill had wanted to shake her.

The old people sat on the bench, still as statues. Never mind, there was always the crowd to watch. To and fro, in front of the flower-beds and the band rotunda, the couples and groups paraded, stopped to talk, to greet, to buy a handful of flowers from the old beggar who had his tray fixed to the railings. Little children ran among them, swooping and laughing; little boys with big white silk bows under their chins, little girls, little French dolls, dressed up in velvet and lace. And sometimes a tiny staggerer came suddenly rocking into the open from under the trees, stopped, stared, as suddenly sat down "flop," until its small high-stepping mother, like a young hen, rushed scolding to its rescue. Other people sat on the benches and green chairs, but they were nearly always the same, Sunday after Sunday, and—Miss Brill had often noticed—there was something funny about nearly all of them. They were odd, silent, nearly all old, and from the way they stared they looked as though they'd just come from dark little rooms or even—even cupboards!

Behind the rotunda the slender trees with yellow leaves down drooping, and through them just a line of sea, and beyond the blue sky with gold-veined clouds.

Tum-tum-tum tiddle-um! tiddle-um! tum tiddley-um tum ta! blew the band.

Two young girls in red came by and two young soldiers in blue met them, and they laughed and paired and went off arm-in-arm. Two peasant women with funny straw hats passed, gravely, leading beautiful smoke-coloured donkeys. A cold, pale nun hurried by. A beautiful woman came along and dropped her bunch of violets, and a little boy ran after to hand them to her, and she took them and threw them away as if they'd been poisoned. Dear me! Miss Brill didn't know whether to admire that or not! And now an ermine toque and a gentleman in grey met just in front of her. He was tall, stiff, dignified, and she was wearing the ermine toque she'd bought when her hair was yellow. Now everything, her hair, her face, even her eyes, was the same colour as the shabby ermine, and her hand, in its cleaned glove, lifted to dab her lips, was a tiny yellowish paw. Oh, she was so pleased to see him—delighted! She rather thought they were going to meet that afternoon. She described where she'd been—everywhere, here, there, along by the sea. The day was so charming—didn't he agree? And wouldn't he, perhaps? . . . But he shook his head, lighted a cigarette, slowly breathed a great deep puff into her face, and, even while she was still talking and laughing, flicked the match away and walked on. The ermine toque was alone; she smiled more brightly than ever. But even the band seemed to know what she was feeling and played more softly, played tenderly, and the drum beat, "The Brute! The Brute!" over and over. What would she do? What was going to happen now? But as Miss Brill wondered, the ermine toque turned, raised her hand as though she'd seen some one else, much nicer, just over there and pattered away. And the band changed again and played more quickly, more gaily than ever, and the old couple on Miss Brill's seat got up and marched away, and such a funny old man with long whiskers hobbled along in time to the music and was nearly knocked over by four girls walking abreast.

Oh, how fascinating it was! How she enjoyed it! How she loved sitting here, watching it all! It was exactly like a play. Who could believe the sky at the back wasn't painted? But it wasn't till a little brown dog trotted on solemn and then slowly trotted off, like a little "theatre" dog, a little dog that had been drugged, that Miss Brill discovered what it was that made it so exciting. They were all on the stage. They weren't only the audience, not only looking on; they were acting. Even she had a part and came every Sunday. No doubt somebody would have noticed if she hadn't been there; she was part of the performance after all. How strange she's never thought of it like that before! And yet it explained why she made such a point of starting from home at just the same time each week—so as not to be late for the performance—and it also explained why she had quite a queer, shy feeling at telling her English pupils how she spent her Sunday afternoons. No wonder! Miss Brill nearly laughed out loud. She was on the stage. She thought of the old invalid gentleman to whom she read the newspaper four afternoons a week while he slept in the garden. She had got quite used to the frail head on the cotton pillow, the hollowed eyes, the open mouth and the high pinched nose. If he'd been dead she mightn't have noticed for weeks; she wouldn't have minded. But suddenly he knew he was having the paper read to him by an actress! "An actress!" The old head lifted; two points of light quivered in the old eyes. "An actress—are ye?" And Miss Brill smoothed the newspaper as though it were the manuscript of her part and said gently: "Yes, I have been an actress for a long time."

The band had been having a rest. Now they started again. And what they played was warm, sunny, yet there was just a faint chill—a something, what was it?—not sadness—no, not sadness—a something that made you want to sing. The tune lifted, lifted, the light shone; and it seemed to Miss Brill that in another moment all of them, all the whole company, would begin singing. The young ones, the laughing ones who were moving together, they would begin, and the men's voices, very resolute and brave, would join them. And then she too, she too, and the others on the benches—they would come in with a kind of accompaniment—something low, that scarcely rose or fell, something so beautiful—moving. . . . And Miss Brill's eyes filled with tears and she looked smiling at all the other members of the company. Yes, we understand, we understand, she thought—though what they understood she didn't know.

Just at that moment a boy and a girl came and sat down where the old couple had been. They were beautifully dressed; they were in love. The hero and heroine, of course, just arrived from his father's yacht. And still soundlessly singing, still with that trembling smile, Miss Brill prepared to listen.

"No, not now," said the girl. "Not here, I can't."

"But why? Because of that stupid old thing at the end there?" asked the boy. "Why does she come here at all—who wants her? Why doesn't she keep her silly old mug at home?"

"It's her fu-fur which is so funny," giggled the girl. "It's exactly like a fried whiting."

"Ah, be off with you!" said the boy in an angry whisper. Then: "Tell me, ma petite chère—"

"No, not here," said the girl. "Not *yet*."

On her way home she usually bought a slice of honey-cake at the baker's. It was her Sunday treat. Sometimes there was an almond in her slice, sometimes not. It made a great difference. If there was an almond it was like carrying home a tiny present—a surprise—something that might very well not have been there. She hurried on the almond Sundays and struck the match for the kettle in quite a dashing way.

But to-day she passed the baker's by, climbed the stairs, went into the little dark room—her room like a cupboard—and sat down on the red eiderdown. She sat there for a long time. The box that the fur came out of was on the bed. She unclasped the necklet quickly; quickly, without looking, laid it inside. But when she put the lid on she thought she heard something crying.

[1922]

QUESTIONS

1. What is Miss Brill doing with her afternoon? What kind of person is she? What are her financial circumstances?

2. The story is about living one's life through the imagination and through other people. How does Miss Brill live her life in this way?

3. What do the young people think of her? What do they say, and why is their commentary so hurtful? How do we know that she is devastated?

4. Writers often write about people who live their lives through fantasy because that is what they themselves do. How can this fantasy life create loneliness in the person with the fantasies?

5. The young are often indifferent to the feelings of elderly people. Why are the elderly discounted and ignored or even abused? What does such treatment say about the values of a culture?

6. The fur is the focus of the story in a variety of ways. Why does the crying in the box at the end of the story carry strong symbolism?

7. Throughout the story, Miss Brill tells stories to herself about the people she sees. What stories does she tell, and what do the stories say about her?

8. In the middle of the story, Miss Brill thinks that someone would have noticed had she not been at the band concert. Would anyone have noticed? Why does that supposition sit at the center of the story?

9. What percentage of the population in the United States is elderly? How many of those people live in poverty? Find out the answers to these questions, and write about the issue.

10. The symbolism in the story centers around the fur that Miss Brill wears, but it could as easily have centered on other circumstances of her life. What objects do you own that speak about your life? Pick one and write about it.

11. Take a walk around your campus or your town. Describe the people you see. Then write about the lives of people in your world. What kinds of people live in your "neighborhood"? What guesses can you make about them?

Edgar Allan Poe
[1809–1849]

The son of traveling actors, **EDGAR ALLAN POE** *was probably abandoned by his father shortly after his birth. In any case, his father died in 1810, and his mother continued to act, moving frequently with her children until 1811, when she too died, leaving Poe and his siblings destitute. Poe was adopted by the family of John and Frances Allan, and at his baptism assumed his benefactor's name. Despite this early gesture of connectedness, Poe's relationship with the Allans was fractious, especially after Poe began attending the University of Virginia in 1836. Here Poe was known both for his writing and also for his gambling and drinking. His repeated, abusive pleas for money caused John Allan to cut him off periodically. After one such incident Poe left the university and joined the army. During his service he published his first book of poetry,* Tamerlane and Other Poems *(1827). His second,* Al Aaraaf, *was published in 1829. In 1830, through Allan's influence, Poe was awarded an appointment to West Point, but he was soon expelled. Among cadets the legend still circulates that he forced this himself by showing up naked for morning formation, but it is more likely that drinking and gambling lay at the heart of the matter. In any event, this disgrace seems to have been fortuitous, because at this time Poe began to devote himself to writing, publishing several stories and winning a fiction contest in 1832.*

In 1833 he became editor of the Southern Literary Messenger, *one of several important literary posts he would fill in his life. In 1839 he became editor of* Burton's Gentleman's Magazine; *in 1840 editor of* Graham's; *and in 1845 editor of the* Broadway Journal. *He published a great deal of his own poetry and fiction in these journals, as well as numerous reviews (many of them quite strident), and in this way had a significant impact on literary trends and tastes. However, despite the fact that he continued to be awarded editorial positions, the same kind of behavior that resulted in his dismissal from West Point—drinking, gambling, and a disinclination to bow to authority—led him regularly into conflict with his employers. And although he published his work regularly, he was never far from poverty. He also had a tendency to pick literary fights, and was most famously dismissive of the New England transcendentalists. Some speculate that this kind of controversy may have been a ploy to sell magazines.*

Although his writing career was relatively brief and his habits were self-destructive, Poe managed to amass an impressive canon before his death in 1849. In addition to such works as "Ligeia" (1838); "The Fall of the House of Usher" (1839); Tales of the Grotesque and Arabesque *(1840); and the popular "The Raven" (1844); Poe is credited with the invention of the detective story. His character C. Auguste Dupin from "The Murders in the Rue Morgue"; "The Mystery* of Marie Roget"; and "The Purloined Letter" served as type for Sherlock Holmes and countless other detectives. In these and other stories Poe demonstrates an obsession with the dark side of human psychology. Many of his tales explore a concept he labeled "the spirit of perverseness . . . the unfathomable longing of the soul to vex itself." This phenomenon can be seen in stories such as "The Black Cat" and "The Tell-Tale Heart," in which seemingly rational characters are drawn to commit ghastly crimes for reasons they cannot explain. While his last years were clouded by the death of his wife from tuberculosis in 1846, he seemed on the road to recovery when, in 1849, he stopped in Baltimore on his way to Philadelphia and was found on the street four days later, unconscious and near death. The exact cause of his death on October 7 remains a mystery.

—David L. G. Arnold, *University of Wisconsin, Stevens Point*

The Masque of the Red Death

EDGAR ALLAN POE

THE "RED DEATH" HAD long devastated the country. No pestilence had ever been so fatal, or so hideous. Blood was its Avatar[1] and its seal—the redness and the horror of blood. There were sharp pains, and sudden dizziness, and then profuse bleeding at the pores, with dissolution. The scarlet stains upon the body and especially upon the face of the victim, were the pest ban which shut him out from the aid and from the sympathy of his fellow-men. And the whole seizure, progress and termination of the disease, were the incidents of half an hour.

But the Prince Prospero[2] was happy and dauntless and sagacious. When his dominions were half depopulated, he summoned to his presence a thousand hale and light-hearted friends from among the knights and dames of his court, and with these retired to the deep seclusion of one of his castellated abbeys. This was an extensive and magnificent structure, the creation of the prince's own eccentric yet august taste. A strong and lofty wall girdled it in. This wall had gates of iron. The courtiers, having entered, brought furnaces and massy hammers and welded the bolts. They resolved to leave means neither of ingress or egress to the sudden impulses of despair or of frenzy from within. The abbey was amply provisioned. With such precautions the courtiers might bid defiance to contagion. The external world could take care of itself. In the meantime it was folly to grieve, or to think. The prince had provided all the appliances of pleasure. There were buffoons, there were improvisatori,[3] there were ballet-dancers, there were musicians, there was Beauty, there was wine. All these and security were within. Without was the "Red Death."

It was toward the close of the fifth or sixth month of his seclusion, and while the pestilence raged most furiously abroad, that the Prince Prospero

---

[1] Hindu incarnation of a god.

[2] A character from Shakespeare's *The Tempest* (1611).

[3] An improvisatori composes music spontaneously, "on the spot."

First published in *Graham's Magazine* in May, 1842.

entertained his thousand friends at a masked ball of the most unusual magnificence.

It was a voluptuous scene, that masquerade. But first let me tell of the rooms in which it was held. There were seven—an imperial suite. In many palaces, however, such suites form a long and straight vista, while the folding doors slide back nearly to the walls on either hand, so that the view of the whole extent is scarcely impeded. Here the case was very different; as might have been expected from the duke's love of the *bizarre*. The apartments were so irregularly disposed that the vision embraced but little more than one at a time. There was a sharp turn at every twenty or thirty yards, and at each turn a novel effect. To the right and left, in the middle of each wall, a tall and narrow Gothic window looked out upon a closed corridor which pursued the windings of the suite. These windows were of stained glass whose color varied in accordance with the prevailing hue of the decorations of the chamber into which it opened. That at the eastern extremity was hung, for example, in blue—and vividly blue were its windows. The second chamber was purple in its ornaments and tapestries and here the panes were purple. The third was green throughout, and so were the casements. The fourth was furnished and lighted with orange—the fifth with white—the sixth with violet. The seventh apartment was closely shrouded in black velvet tapestries that hung all over the ceiling and down the walls, falling in heavy folds upon a carpet of the same material and hue. But in this chamber only, the color of the windows failed to correspond with the decorations. The panes here were scarlet—a deep blood color. Now in no one of the seven apartments was there any lamp or candelabrum, amid the profusion of golden ornaments that lay scattered to and fro or depended from the roof. There was no light of any kind emanating from lamp or candle within the suite of chambers. But in the corridors that followed the suite, there stood, opposite to each window, a heavy tripod, bearing a brazier of fire that projected its rays through the tinted glass and so glaringly illumined the room. And thus were produced a multitude of gaudy and fantastic appearances. But in the western or black chamber the effect of the firelight that streamed upon the dark hangings through the blood-tinted panes, was ghastly in the extreme, and produced so wild a look upon the countenances of those who entered, that there were few of the company bold enough to set foot within its precincts at all.

It was in this apartment, also, that there stood against the western wall, a gigantic clock of ebony. Its pendulum swung to and fro with a dull, heavy, monotonous clang; and when the minute-hand made the circuit of the face, and the hour was to be stricken, there came from the brazen lungs of the clock a sound which was clear and loud and deep and exceedingly musical, but of so peculiar a note and emphasis that, at each lapse of an hour, the musicians of the orchestra were constrained to pause, momentarily, in their performance, to hearken to the sound; and thus the waltzers perforce ceased their evolutions; and there was a brief disconcert of the whole gay company; and, while the chimes of the clock yet rang, it was observed that the giddiest grew pale, and the more aged and sedate passed their hands over their brows as if in confused reverie or meditation. But when the echoes had fully ceased, a light laughter at once pervaded the assembly; the musicians looked at each other and smiled as if at their own nervousness and folly, and made whispering vows, each to the other, that the next chiming of the clock should produce in them no similar emotion; and then, after the lapse of sixty minutes, (which embrace three thousand and six hundred seconds of the Time that flies,) there came yet another chiming of the clock, and then were the same disconcert and tremulousness and meditation as before.

But, in spite of these things, it was a gay and magnificent revel. The tastes of the duke were peculiar. He had a fine eye for colors and effects. He disregarded the *decora*[4] of mere fashion. His plans were bold and fiery, and his conceptions glowed with barbaric lustre. There are some who would have thought him mad. His followers felt that he was not. It was necessary to hear and see and touch him to be *sure* that he was not.

He had directed, in great part, the moveable embellishments of the seven chambers, upon occasion of this great *fête*, and it was his own guiding taste which had given character to the masqueraders. Be sure they were grotesque. There were much glare and glitter and piquancy and phantasm—much of what has been since seen in "Hernani." There were arabesque figures with unsuited limbs and appointments. There were delirious fancies such as the madman fashions. There was much of the beautiful, much of the wanton, much of the *bizarre*, something of the terrible, and not a little of that which might have excited disgust. To and fro in the seven chambers there stalked, in fact, a multitude of dreams. And these—the dreams—writhed in and about, taking hue from the rooms, and causing the wild music of the orchestra to seem as the echo of their steps. And, anon, there strikes the ebony clock which stands in the hall of the velvet. And then, for a moment, all is still, and all is silent save the voice of the clock. The dreams are stiff-frozen as they stand. But the echoes of the chime die away—they have endured but an instant—and a light, half-subdued laughter floats after them as they depart. And now again the music swells, and the dreams live, and writhe to and fro more merrily than

---

[4]Ornamentation

[5]Feast, festival

[6]1830 verse drama written by Victor Hugo (1802–1855).

ever, taking hue from the many-tinted windows through which stream the rays from the tripods. But to the chamber which lies most westwardly of the seven, there are now none of the maskers who venture; for the night is waning away; and there flows a ruddier light through the blood-colored panes; and the blackness of the sable drapery appals; and to him whose foot falls upon the sable carpet, there comes from the near clock of ebony a muffled peal more solemnly emphatic than any which reaches *their* ears who indulge in the more remote gaieties of the other apartments.

But these other apartments were densely crowded, and in them beat feverishly the heart of life. And the revel went whirlingly on, until at length there commenced the sounding of midnight upon the clock. And then the music ceased, as I have told; and the evolutions of the waltzers were quieted; and there was an uneasy cessation of all things as before. But now there were twelve strokes to be sounded by the bell of the clock; and thus it happened, perhaps, that more of thought crept, with more of time, into the meditations of the thoughtful among those who revelled. And thus, too, it happened, perhaps, that before the last echoes of the last chime had utterly sunk into silence, there were many individuals in the crowd who had found leisure to become aware of the presence of a masked figure which had arrested the attention of no single individual before. And the rumor of this new presence having spread itself whisperingly around, there arose at length from the whole company a buzz, or murmur, expressive of disapprobation and surprise—then, finally, of terror, of horror, and of disgust.

In an assembly of phantasms such as I have painted, it may well be supposed that no ordinary appearance could have excited such sensation. In truth the masquerade license of the night was nearly unlimited; but the figure in question had out-Heroded Herod,[7] and gone beyond the bounds of even the prince's indefinite decorum. There are chords in the hearts of the most reckless which cannot be touched without emotion. Even with the utterly lost, to whom life and death are equally jests, there are matters of which no jest can be made. The whole company, indeed, seemed now deeply to feel that in the costume and bearing of the stranger neither wit nor propriety existed. The figure was tall and gaunt, and shrouded from head to foot in the habiliments of the grave. The mask which concealed the visage was made so nearly to resemble the countenance of a stiffened corpse that the closest scrutiny must have had difficulty in detecting the cheat. And yet all this might have been endured, if not approved, by the mad revellers around. But the mummer[8] had gone so

---

[7]A reference to the notoriously violent Biblical King Herod; Shakespeare's Hamlet uses this phrase to describe over-acting.

[8]Masked actor

far as to assume the type of the Red Death. His vesture was dabbled in *blood*—and his broad brow, with all the features of the face, was besprinkled with the scarlet horror.

When the eyes of Prince Prospero fell upon this spectral image (which with a slow and solemn movement, as if more fully to sustain its *rôle*, stalked to and fro among the waltzers) he was seen to be convulsed, in the first moment with a strong shudder either of terror or distaste; but, in the next, his brow reddened with rage.

"Who dares?" he demanded hoarsely of the courtiers who stood near him—"who dares insult us with this blasphemous mockery? Seize him and unmask him—that we may know whom we have to hang at sunrise, from the battlements!"

It was in the eastern or blue chamber in which stood the Prince Prospero as he uttered these words. They rang throughout the seven rooms loudly and clearly—for the prince was a bold and robust man, and the music had become hushed at the waving of his hand.

It was in the blue room where stood the prince, with a group of pale courtiers by his side. At first, as he spoke, there was a slight rushing movement of this group in the direction of the intruder, who at the moment was also near at hand, and now, with deliberate and stately step, made closer approach to the speaker. But from a certain nameless awe with which the mad assumptions of the mummer had inspired the whole party, there were found none who put forth hand to seize him; so that, unimpeded, he passed within a yard of the prince's person; and, while the vast assembly, as if with one impulse, shrank from the centres of the rooms to the walls, he made his way uninterruptedly, but with the same solemn and measured step which had distinguished him from the first, through the blue chamber to the purple—through the purple to the green—through the green to the orange—through this again to the white—and even thence to the violet, ere a decided movement had been made to arrest him. It was then, however, that the Prince Prospero, maddening with rage and the shame of his own momentary cowardice, rushed hurriedly through the six chambers, while none followed him on account of a deadly terror that had seized upon all. He bore aloft a drawn dagger, and had approached, in rapid impetuosity, to within three or four feet of the retreating figure, when the latter, having attained the extremity of the velvet apartment, turned suddenly and confronted his pursuer. There was a sharp cry—and the dagger dropped gleaming upon the sable carpet, upon which, instantly afterwards, fell prostrate in death the Prince Prospero. Then, summoning the wild courage of despair, a throng of the revellers at once threw themselves into the black apartment, and, seizing the mummer, whose tall figure stood erect and motionless within the shadow of the ebony clock, gasped in unutterable horror at finding the grave-cerements[9] and corpse-like mask which they handled with so violent a rudeness, untenanted by any tangible form.

And now was acknowledged the presence of the Red Death. He had come like a thief in the night. And one by one dropped the revellers in the blood-bedewed halls of their revel, and died each in the despairing posture of his fall. And the life of the ebony clock went out with that of the last of the gay. And the flames of the tripods expired. And Darkness and Decay and the Red Death held illimitable dominion over all.

[1842]

---

[9]Shroud

QUESTIONS

EDGAR ALLAN POE, *The Masque of the Red Death*

1. Describe Prospero. What do you find noteworthy, significant, or even contradictory about this character?

2. Comment on the conspicuous image of the clock. What does this object symbolize within the larger context of the story?

3. The narrator of "The Masque of the Red Death" is preoccupied by Prospero's color-coded rooms. What is suggested or symbolized by these strange spaces?

4. To what extent is "The Masque of the Red Death" a story about politics and society? Discuss the story as a parable about power and government.

5. How does the demeanor of the Red Death set this guest apart from the other revellers?

6. Describe the ways in which Poe blends elements of literary realism and fantasy in "The Masque of the Red Death." What in your view is important or effective about this kind of combination?

7. Research and compose a biographical interpretation of "The Masque of the Red Death." How do the characters and events of the story reflect the author's life and experience? To what extent might Poe have understood the tale as a comment on his own society and/or culture?

8. Read William Shakespeare's play *The Tempest* (1610); pay careful attention to the central figure of Prospero. Write an essay in which you compare and contrast Shakespeare's Prospero with the Prospero of Poe's "The Masque of the Red Death."

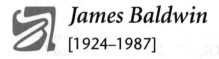 *James Baldwin*
[1924–1987]

JAMES BALDWIN *was renowned for his frank expression of personal, racial, and sexual identity, and for his blunt essays on the American civil rights struggle. Primarily a novelist, Baldwin also wrote three plays, many short stories, a children's book, essays, and literary criticism. Born in Harlem to a single mother, Baldwin grew up in extreme poverty. Despite his mother's marriage in 1927 to a factory worker and part-time preacher, their poverty went unabated as the family continued to grow. Being the eldest child, Baldwin was often left in charge of his seven siblings, and said once that "as they were born, I took them over with one hand and held a book with the other." Reading was his escape from the oppressive poverty as well as the contempt his stepfather directed toward him. Perhaps as a means to win his stepfather's favor, Baldwin became a preacher at fourteen at a Pentecostal church. His eventual rejection of Christianity played an important role in his later fiction and nonfiction.*

Baldwin was a precocious writer. By eight he was writing plays and at twelve he won a contest for his church newspaper for a short story. After graduating from high school, Baldwin moved to Greenwich Village in New York to pursue a career in writing. There he met fellow African-American writer Richard Wright, who sponsored the young Baldwin for the Eugene Saxton Fellowship. Baldwin won the fellowship as well as the Rosenwald Fellowship, which allowed him to develop his craft, although the products of both fellowships were, according to Baldwin, "unsalable."

During this period Baldwin's consciousness of race was being enflamed with his frustration over the condition of blacks in the United States. Finally, after he was refused service in a restaurant because of his race, Baldwin decided to leave the United States and live in France. Recounting the incident later in life, Baldwin stated that it was the only time in his life that he wanted to injure someone in the way that he had been injured. On arrival in France, Baldwin's first piece of writing was "Everybody's Protest Novel," a biting attack on American society and race relations.

While traveling through Europe, Baldwin wrote his novel Go Tell It on the Mountain. *The largely autobiographical novel tells the story of a poor black family from Harlem, and especially the story of the adolescent protagonist's troubles with an abusive father, faith, and sexual identity. The novel set the stage for Baldwin's later writing in which these themes figured prominently.*

Baldwin's reputation as a writer is complex. While some (particularly in the white community) call him revolutionary or radical, many in the black community feel he did not go far enough in his criticism of entrenched racism. Baldwin,

*however, seems to have seen his art as a means of not only expressing the prob-
lems of race relations, but also as a means of expiating the pain and suffering that
humans undergo in life. Ultimately, like the blues that he so deftly represents in
"Sonny's Blues," Baldwin's writing depicts the complexities of the pain and
beauty of African-American life.*

🦅 🦅 🦅

Sonny's Blues

JAMES BALDWIN

I READ ABOUT IT in the paper, in the subway, on my way to work. I read it, and I couldn't believe it, and I read it again. Then perhaps I just stared at it, at the newsprint spelling out his name, spelling out the story. I stared at it in the swinging lights of the subway car, and in the faces and bodies of the people, and in my own face, trapped in the darkness which roared outside.

It was not to be believed and I kept telling myself that, as I walked from the subway station to the high school. And at the same time I couldn't doubt it. I was scared, scared for Sonny. He became real to me again. A great block of ice got settled in my belly and kept melting there slowly all day long, while I taught my classes algebra. It was a special kind of ice. It kept melting, sending trickles of ice water all up and down my veins, but it never got less. Sometimes it hardened and seemed to expand until I felt my guts were going to come spilling out or that I was going to choke or scream. This would always be at a moment when I was remembering some specific thing Sonny had once said or done.

When he was about as old as the boys in my classes his face had been bright and open, there was a lot of copper in it; and he'd had wonderfully direct brown eyes, and great gentleness and privacy. I wondered what he looked like now. He had been picked up the evening before, in a raid on an apartment downtown, for peddling and using heroin.

I couldn't believe it: but what I mean by that is that I couldn't find any room for it anywhere inside me. I had kept it outside me for a long time. I hadn't wanted to know. I had had suspicions, but I didn't name them, I kept putting them away. I told myself that Sonny was wild, but he wasn't crazy. And he'd always been a good boy, he hadn't ever turned hard or evil or disrespectful, the way kids can, so quick, especially in Harlem. I didn't want to believe that I'd ever see my brother going down, coming to nothing, all that light in his face gone out, in the condition I'd already seen so many others. Yet it had happened and here I was, talking about algebra to a lot of boys who might, every one of them for all I knew, be popping off needles every time they went to the head.[1] Maybe it did more for them than algebra could.

---

[1]Bathroom

I was sure that the first time Sonny had ever had horse,[2] he couldn't have been much older than these boys were now. These boys, now, were living as we'd been living then, they were growing up with a rush and their heads bumped abruptly against the low ceiling of their actual possibilities. They were filled with rage. All they really knew were two darknesses, the darkness of their lives, which was now closing in on them, and the darkness of the movies, which had blinded them to that other darkness, and in which they now, vindictively, dreamed, at once more together than they were at any other time, and more alone.

When the last bell rang, the last class ended, I let out my breath. It seemed I'd been holding it for all that time. My clothes were wet—I may have looked as though I'd been sitting in a steam bath, all dressed up all afternoon. I sat alone in the classroom a long time. I listened to the boys outside, downstairs, shouting and cursing and laughing. Their laughter struck me for perhaps the first time. It was not the joyous laughter which—God knows why—one associates with children. It was mocking and insular, its intent was to denigrate. It was disenchanted, and in this, also, lay the authority of their curses. Perhaps I was listening to them because I was thinking about my brother and in them I heard my brother. And myself.

One boy was whistling a tune, at once very complicated and very simple, it seemed to be pouring out of him as though he were a bird, and it sounded very cool and moving through all that harsh, bright air, only just holding its own through all those other sounds.

I stood up and walked over to the window and looked down into the courtyard. It was the beginning of the spring and the sap was rising in the boys. A teacher passed through them every now and again, quickly, as though he or she couldn't wait to get out of that courtyard, to get those boys out of their sight and off their minds. I started collecting my stuff. I thought I'd better get home and talk to Isabel.

The courtyard was almost deserted by the time I got downstairs. I saw this boy standing in the shadow of a doorway, looking just like Sonny. I almost called his name. Then I saw that it wasn't Sonny, but somebody we used to know, a boy from around our block. He'd been Sonny's friend. He'd never been mine, having been too young for me, and, anyway, I'd never liked him. And now, even though he was a grown-up man, he still hung around that block, still spent hours on the street corners, was always high and raggy. I used to run into him from time to time and he'd often work around to asking me for a quarter or fifty cents. He always had some real good excuse too, and I always gave it to him, I don't know why.

---

[2]Heroin

But now, abruptly I hated him. I couldn't stand the way he looked at me, partly like a dog, partly like a cunning child. I wanted to ask him what the hell he was doing in the school courtyard.

He sort of shuffled over to me, and he said, "I see you got the papers. So you already know about it."

"You mean about Sonny? Yes, I already know about it. How come they didn't get you?"

He grinned. It made him repulsive and it also brought to mind what he'd looked like as a kid. "I wasn't there. I stay away from them people."

"Good for you." I offered him a cigarette and I watched him through the smoke. "You come all the way down here just to tell me about Sonny?"

"That's right." He was sort of shaking his head and his eyes looked strange, as though they were about to cross. The bright sun deadened his damp dark brown skin and it made his eyes look yellow and showed up the dirt in his kinked hair. He smelled funky. I moved a little way away from him and I said, "Well, thanks. But I already know about it and I got to get home."

"I'll walk you a little ways," he said. We started walking. There were a couple of kids still loitering in the courtyard and one of them said goodnight to me and looked strangely at the boy beside me.

"What're you going to do?" he asked me. "I mean, about Sonny?"

"Look. I haven't seen Sonny for over a year. I'm not sure I'm going to do anything. Anyway, what the hell *can* I do?"

"That's right," he said quickly, "ain't nothing you can do. Can't much help old Sonny no more, I guess."

It was what I was thinking and so it seemed to me he had no right to say it.

"I'm surprised at Sonny, though," he went on—he had a funny way of talking, he looked straight ahead as though he were talking to himself—"I thought Sonny was a smart boy, I thought he was too smart to get hung."

"I guess he thought so too," I said sharply, "and that's how he got hung. And how about you? You're pretty goddamn smart, I bet."

Then he looked directly at me, just for a minute. "I ain't smart," he said. "If I was smart, I'd have reached for a pistol a long time ago."

"Look. Don't tell *me* your sad story, if it was up to me, I'd give you one." Then I felt guilty—guilty, probably, for never having supposed that the poor bastard *had* a story of his own, much less a sad one, and I asked, quickly, "What's going to happen to him now?"

He didn't answer this. He was off by himself some place. "Funny thing," he said, and from his tone we might have been discussing the quickest way to get to Brooklyn, "when I saw the papers this morning, the first thing I asked myself was if I had anything to do with it. I felt sort of responsible."

I began to listen more carefully. The subway station was on the corner, just before us, and I stopped. He stopped, too. We were in front of a bar and he ducked slightly, peering in, but whoever he was looking for didn't seem to be there. The juke box was blasting away with something black and bouncy and I half watched the barmaid as she danced her way from the juke box to her place behind the bar. And I watched her face as she laughingly responded to something someone said to her, still keeping time to the music. When she smiled one saw the little girl, one sensed the doomed, still struggling woman beneath the battered face of the semi-whore.

"I never *give* Sonny nothing," the boy said finally, "but a long time ago I come to school high and Sonny asked me how it felt." He paused, I couldn't bear to watch him, I watched the barmaid, and I listened to the music which seemed to be causing the pavement to shake. "I told him it felt great." The music stopped, the barmaid paused and watched the juke box until the music began again. "It did."

All this was carrying me some place I didn't want to go. I certainly didn't want to know how it felt. It filled everything, the people, the houses, the music, the dark, quicksilver barmaid, with menace, and this menace was their reality.

"What's going to happen to him now?" I asked again.

"They'll send him away some place and they'll try to cure him." He shook his head. "Maybe he'll even think he's kicked the habit. Then they'll let him loose"—he gestured, throwing his cigarette into the gutter. "That's all."

"What do you mean that's *all*?"

But I knew what he meant.

"I *mean*, that's *all*." He turned his head and looked at me, pulling down the corners of his mouth. "Don't you know what I mean?" he asked, softly.

"How the hell *would* I know what you mean?" I almost whispered it, I don't know why.

"That's right," he said to the air, "how would *he* know what I mean?" He turned toward me again, patient and calm, and yet I somehow felt him shaking, shaking as though he were going to fall apart. I felt that ice in my guts again, the dread I'd felt all afternoon; and again I watched the barmaid, moving about the bar, washing glasses, and singing. "Listen. They'll let him out and then it'll just start all over again. That's what I mean."

"You mean—they'll let him out. And then he'll just start working his way back in again. You mean he'll never kick the habit. Is that what you mean?"

"That's right," he said cheerfully. "*You* see what I mean."

"Tell me," I said at last, "why does he want to die? He must want to die, he's killing himself, why does he want to die?"

He looked at me in surprise. He licked his lips. "He don't want to die. He wants to live. Don't nobody want to die, ever."

Then I wanted to ask him—too many things. He could not have answered, or if he had, I could not have borne the answers. I started walking. "Well, I guess it's none of my business."

"It's going to be rough on old Sonny," he said. We reached the subway station. "This is your station?" he asked. I nodded. I took one step down. "Damn!" he said suddenly. I looked up at him. He grinned again. "Damn it if I didn't leave all my money home. You ain't got a dollar on you, have you? Just for a couple of days, is all."

All at once something inside gave and threatened to come pouring out of me. I didn't hate him any more. I felt that in another moment I'd start crying like a child.

"Sure," I said. "Don't sweat." I looked in my wallet and didn't have a dollar, I only had five. "Here," I said. "That hold you?"

He didn't look at it—he didn't want to look at it. A terrible closed look came over his face, as though he were keeping the number on the bill a secret from him and me. "Thanks," he said, and now he was dying to see me go. "Don't worry about Sonny. Maybe I'll write him or something."

"Sure," I said. "You do that. So long."

"Be seeing you," he said. I went on down the steps.

And I didn't write Sonny or send him anything for a long time. When I finally did, it was just after my little girl died, he wrote me back a letter which made me feel like a bastard.

Here's what he said:

Dear brother,

You don't know how much I needed to hear from you. I wanted to write you many a time but I dug how much I must have hurt you and so I didn't write. But now I feel like a man who's been trying to climb up out of some deep, real deep and funky hole and just saw the sun up there, outside. I got to get outside.

I can't tell you much about how I got here. I mean I don't know how to tell you. I guess I was afraid of something or I was trying to escape from something and you know I have never been very strong in the head (smile). I'm glad Mama and Daddy are dead and can't see what's happened to their son and I swear if I'd known what I was doing I would never have hurt you so, you and a lot of other fine people who were nice to me and who believed in me.

I don't want you to think it had anything to do with me being a musician. It's more than that. Or maybe less than that. I can't get anything straight in my head down here and I try not to think about what's going to happen to me when I get outside again. Sometime I think I'm going to flip and *never* get outside and sometime I think I'll come straight back. I tell you one thing, though, I'd rather blow my brains out than go through this again. But that's what they all say, so they tell me. If I tell you when I'm coming to New York and if you could meet me, I sure would appreciate it. Give my love to Isabel and the kids and I was sure sorry to hear about little Gracie. I wish I could be like Mama and say the Lord's will be done, but I don't know it seems to me that trouble is the one thing that never does get stopped and I don't know what good it does to blame it on the Lord. But maybe it does some good if you believe it.

Your brother,
Sonny

Then I kept in constant touch with him and I sent him whatever I could and I went to meet him when he came back to New York. When I saw him many things I thought I had forgotten came flooding back to me. This was because I had begun, finally, to wonder about Sonny, about the life that Sonny lived inside. This life, whatever it was, had made him older and thinner and it had deepened the distant stillness in which he had always moved. He looked very unlike my baby brother. Yet, when he smiled, when we shook hands, the baby brother I'd never known looked out from the depths of his private life, like an animal waiting to be coaxed into the light.

"How you been keeping?" he asked me.

"All right. And you?"

"Just fine." He was smiling all over his face. "It's good to see you again."

"It's good to see you."

The seven years' difference in our ages lay between us like a chasm: I wondered if these years would ever operate between us as a bridge. I was remembering, and it made it hard to catch my breath, that I had been there when he was born; and I had heard the first words he had ever spoken. When he started to walk, he walked from our mother straight to me. I caught him just before he fell when he took the first steps he ever took in this world.

"How's Isabel?"

"Just fine. She's dying to see you."

"And the boys?"

"They're fine, too. They're anxious to see their uncle."

"Oh, come on. You know they don't remember me."

"Are you kidding? Of course they remember you."

He grinned again. We got into a taxi. We had a lot to say to each other, far too much to know how to begin.

As the taxi began to move, I asked, "You still want to go to India?"

He laughed. "You still remember that. Hell, no. This place is Indian enough for me."

"It used to belong to them," I said.

And he laughed again. "They damn sure knew what they were doing when they got rid of it."

Years ago, when he was around fourteen, he'd been all hipped on the idea of going to India. He read books about people sitting on rocks, naked, in all kinds of weather, but mostly bad, naturally, and walking barefoot through hot coals and arriving at wisdom. I used to say that it sounded to me as though they were getting away from wisdom as fast as they could. I think he sort of looked down on me for that.

"Do you mind," he asked, "if we have the driver drive alongside the park? On the west side—I haven't seen the city in so long."

"Of course not," I said. I was afraid that I might sound as though I were humoring him, but I hoped he wouldn't take it that way.

So we drove along, between the green of the park and the stony, lifeless elegance of hotels and apartment buildings, toward the vivid, killing streets of our childhood. These streets hadn't changed, though housing projects jutted up out of them now like rocks in the middle of a boiling sea. Most of the houses in which we had grown up had vanished, as had the stores from which we had stolen, the basements in which we had first tried sex, the rooftops from which we had hurled tin cans and bricks. But houses exactly like the houses of our past yet dominated the landscape, boys exactly like the boys we once had been found themselves smothering in these houses, came down into the streets for light and air and found themselves encircled by disaster. Some escaped the trap, most didn't. Those who got out always left something of themselves behind, as some animals amputate a leg and leave it in the trap. It might be said, perhaps, that I had escaped, after all, I was a school teacher; or that Sonny had, he hadn't lived in Harlem for years. Yet, as the cab moved uptown through streets which seemed, with a rush, to darken with dark people, and as I covertly studied Sonny's face, it came to me that what we both were seeking through our separate cab windows was that part of ourselves which had been left behind. It's always at the hour of trouble and confrontation that the missing member aches.

We hit 110th Street and started rolling up Lenox Avenue. And I'd known this avenue all my life, but it seemed to me again, as it had seemed on the day I'd first heard about Sonny's trouble, filled with a hidden menace which was its very breath of life.

"We almost there," said Sonny.

"Almost." We were both too nervous to say anything more.

We live in a housing project. It hasn't been up long. A few days after it was up it seemed uninhabitably new, now, of course, it's already rundown. It looks like a parody of the good, clean, faceless life—God knows the people who live in it do their best to make it a parody. The beat-looking grass lying around isn't enough to make their lives green, the hedges will never hold out the streets, and they know it. The big windows fool no one, they aren't big enough to make space out of no space. They don't bother with the windows, they watch the TV screen instead. The playground is most popular with the children who don't play at jacks, or skip rope, or roller skate, or swing, and they can be found in it after dark. We moved in partly because it's not too far from where I teach, and partly for the kids; but it's really just like the houses in which Sonny and I grew up. The same things happen, they'll have the same things to remember. The moment Sonny and I started into the house I had the feeling that I was simply bringing him back into the danger he had almost died trying to escape.

Sonny has never been talkative. So I don't know why I was sure he'd be dying to talk to me when supper was over the first night. Everything went fine, the oldest boy remembered him, and the youngest boy liked him, and Sonny had remembered to bring something for each of them; and Isabel, who is really much nicer than I am, more open and giving, had gone to a lot of trouble about dinner and was genuinely glad to see him. And she's always been able to tease Sonny in a way that I haven't. It was nice to see her face so vivid again and to hear her laugh and watch her make Sonny laugh. She wasn't, or, anyway, she didn't seem to be, at all uneasy or embarrassed. She chatted as though there were no subject which had to be avoided and she got Sonny past his first, faint stiffness. And thank God she was there, for I was filled with that icy dread again. Everything I did seemed awkward to me, and everything I said sounded freighted with hidden meaning. I was trying to remember everything I'd heard about dope addiction and I couldn't help watching Sonny for signs. I wasn't doing it out of malice. I was trying to find out something about my brother. I was dying to hear him tell me he was safe.

"Safe!" my father grunted, whenever Mama suggested trying to move to a neighborhood which might be safer for children. "Safe, hell! Ain't no place safe for kids, nor nobody."

He always went on like this, but he wasn't, ever, really as bad as he sounded, not even on weekends, when he got drunk. As a matter of fact, he was always on the lookout for "something a little better," but he died before he found it. He died suddenly, during a drunken weekend in the middle of the war, when Sonny was fifteen. He and Sonny hadn't ever got on too well. And this was partly because Sonny was the apple of his father's eye. It was because he loved Sonny so much and was frightened for him, that he was always fighting with him. It doesn't do any good to fight with Sonny. Sonny just moves back, inside himself, where he can't be reached. But the principal reason that they never hit it off is that they were so much alike. Daddy was big and rough and loud-talking, just the opposite of Sonny, but they both had—that same privacy.

Mama tried to tell me something about this, just after Daddy died. I was home on leave from the army.

This was the last time I ever saw my mother alive. Just the same, this picture gets all mixed up in my mind with pictures I had of her when she was younger. The way I always see her is the way she used to be on a Sunday afternoon, say, when the old folks were talking after the big Sunday dinner. I always see her wearing pale blue. She'd be sitting on the sofa. And my father would be sitting in the easy chair, not far from her. And the living room would be full of church folks and relatives. There they sit, in chairs all around the living room, and the night is creeping up outside, but nobody knows it yet. You can see the darkness growing against the windowpanes and you hear the street noises every now and again, or maybe the jangling beat of a tambourine from one of the churches close by, but it's real quiet in the room. For a moment nobody's talking, but every face looks darkening, like the sky outside. And my mother rocks a little from the waist, and my father's eyes are closed. Everyone is looking at something a child can't see. For a minute they've forgotten the children. Maybe a kid is lying on the rug, half asleep. Maybe somebody's got a kid in his lap and is absent-mindedly stroking the kid's head. Maybe there's a kid, quiet and big-eyed, curled up in a big chair in the corner. The silence, the darkness coming, and the darkness in the faces frightens the child obscurely. He hopes that the hand which strokes his forehead will never stop—will never die. He hopes that there will never come a time when the old folks won't be sitting around the living room, talking about where they've come from, and what they've seen, and what's happened to them and their kinfolk.

But something deep and watchful in the child knows that this is bound to end, is already ending. In a moment someone will get up and turn on the light. Then the old folks will remember the children and they won't talk any more that day. And when light fills the room, the child is filled with darkness. He knows that every time this happens he's moved just a little closer to that darkness outside. The darkness outside is what the old folks have been talking about. It's what they've come from. It's what they endure. The child knows that they won't talk any more because if he knows too much about what's happening to *them*, he'll know too much too soon, about what's going to happen to *him*.

The last time I talked to my mother, I remember I was restless. I wanted to get out and see Isabel. We weren't married then and we had a lot to straighten out between us.

There Mama sat, in black, by the window. She was humming an old church song, *Lord you brought me from a long ways off.* Sonny was out somewhere. Mama kept watching the streets.

"I don't know," she said, "if I'll ever see you again, after you go off from here. But I hope you'll remember the things I tried to teach you."

"Don't talk like that," I said, and smiled. "You'll be here a long time yet."

She smiled, too, but she said nothing. She was quiet for a long time. And I said, "Mama, don't you worry about nothing. I'll be writing all the time, and you be getting the checks. . . ."

"I want to talk to you about your brother," she said, suddenly. "If anything happens to me he ain't going to have nobody to look out for him."

"Mama," I said, "ain't nothing going to happen to you *or* Sonny. Sonny's all right. He's a good boy and he's got good sense."

"It ain't a question of his being a good boy," Mama said, "nor of his having good sense. It ain't only the bad ones, nor yet the dumb ones that gets sucked under." She stopped, looking at me. "Your Daddy once had a brother," she said, and she smiled in a way that made me feel she was in pain. "You didn't never know that, did you?"

"No," I said, "I never knew that," and I watched her face.

"Oh, yes," she said, "your Daddy had a brother." She looked out of the window again. "I know you never saw your Daddy cry. But *I* did—many a time, through all these years."

I asked her, "What happened to his brother? How come nobody's ever talked about him?"

This was the first time I ever saw my mother look old.

"His brother got killed," she said, "when he was just a little younger than you are now. I knew him. He was a fine boy. He was maybe a little full of the devil, but he didn't mean nobody no harm."

Then she stopped and the room was silent, exactly as it had sometimes been on those Sunday afternoons. Mama kept looking out into the streets.

"He used to have a job in the mill," she said, "and, like all young folks, he just liked to perform on Saturday nights. Saturday nights, him and your father would drift around to different places, go to dances and things like that, or just sit around with people they knew, and your father's brother would sing, he had a fine voice, and play along with himself on his guitar. Well, this particular Saturday night, him and your father was coming home from some place, and they were both a little drunk and there was a moon that night, it was bright like day. Your father's brother was feeling kind of good, and he was whistling to himself, and he had his guitar slung over his shoulder. They was coming down a hill and beneath them was a road that turned off from the highway. Well, your father's brother, being always kind of frisky, decided to run down this hill, and he did, with that guitar banging and clanging behind him, and he ran across the road, and he was making water behind a tree. And your father was sort of amused at him and he was still coming down the hill, kind of slow. Then he heard a car motor and that same minute his brother stepped from behind the tree, into the road, in the moonlight. And he started to cross the road. And your father started to run down the hill, he says he don't know why. This car was full of white men. They was all drunk, and when they seen your father's brother they let out a great whoop and holler and they aimed the car straight at him. They was having fun, they just wanted to scare him, the way they do sometimes, you know. But they was drunk. And I guess the boy, being drunk, too, and scared, kind of lost his head. By the time he jumped it was too late. Your father says he heard his brother scream when the car rolled over him, and he heard the wood of that guitar when it give, and he heard them strings go flying, and he heard them white men shouting, and the car kept on a-going and it ain't stopped till this day. And, time your father got down the hill, his brother weren't nothing but blood and pulp."

Tears were gleaming on my mother's face. There wasn't anything I could say.

"He never mentioned it," she said, "because I never let him mention it before you children. Your Daddy was like a crazy man that night and for many a night thereafter. He says he never in his life seen anything as dark as that road after the lights of that car had gone away. Weren't nothing, weren't nobody on that road, just your Daddy and his brother and that busted guitar. Oh, yes. Your Daddy never did really get right again. Till the day he died he weren't sure but that every white man he saw was the man that killed his brother."

She stopped and took out her handkerchief and dried her eyes and looked at me.

"I ain't telling you all this," she said, "to make you scared or bitter or to make you hate nobody. I'm telling you this because you got a brother. And the world ain't changed."

I guess I didn't want to believe this. I guess she saw this in my face. She turned away from me, toward the window again, searching those streets.

"But I praise my Redeemer," she said at last, "that He called your Daddy home before me. I ain't saying it to throw no flowers at myself, but, I declare, it keeps me from feeling too cast down to know I helped your father get safely through this world. Your father always acted like he was the roughest, strongest man on earth. And everybody took him to be like that. But if he hadn't had *me* there—to see his tears!"

She was crying again. Still I couldn't move. I said, "Lord, Lord, Mama, I didn't know it was like that."

"Oh, honey," she said, "there's a lot that you don't know. But you are going to find it out." She stood up from the window and came over to me. "You got to hold on to your brother," she said, "and don't let him fall, no matter what it looks like is happening to him and no matter how evil you gets with him. You going to be evil with him many a time. But don't you forget what I told you, you hear?"

"I won't forget," I said. "Don't you worry, I won't forget. I won't let nothing happen to Sonny."

My mother smiled as though she were amused at something she saw in my face. Then, "You may not be able to stop nothing from happening. But you got to let him know you's *there*."

Two days later I was married, and then I was gone. And I had a lot of things on my mind and I pretty well forgot my promise to Mama until I got shipped home on a special furlough for her funeral.

And, after the funeral, with just Sonny and me alone in the empty kitchen, I tried to find out something about him.

"What do you want to do?" I asked him.

"I'm going to be a musician," he said.

For he had graduated, in the time I had been away, from dancing to the juke box to finding out who was playing what, and what they were doing with it, and he had bought himself a set of drums.

"You mean, you want to be a drummer?" I somehow had the feeling that being a drummer might be all right for other people but not for my brother Sonny.

"I don't think," he said, looking at me very gravely, "that I'll ever be a good drummer. But I think I can play a piano."

I frowned. I'd never played the role of the older brother quite so seriously before, had scarcely ever, in fact, *asked* Sonny a damn thing. I sensed myself in the presence of something I didn't really know how to handle, didn't understand. So I made my frown a little deeper as I asked: "What kind of musician do you want to be?"

He grinned. "How many kinds do you think there are?"

"Be *serious*," I said.

He laughed, throwing his head back, and then looked at me. "I *am* serious."

"Well, then, for Christ's sake, stop kidding around and answer a serious question. I mean, do you want to be a concert pianist, or want to play classical music and all that, or—or what?" Long before I finished he was laughing again. "For Christ's *sake*, Sonny!"

He sobered, but with difficulty. "I'm sorry. But you sound so—*scared!*" and he was off again.

"Well, you may think it's funny now, baby, but it's not going to be so funny when you have to make your living at it, let me tell you *that*." I was furious because I knew he was laughing at me and I didn't know why.

"No," he said, very sober now, and afraid, perhaps, that he'd hurt me, "I don't want to be a classical pianist. That isn't what interests me. I mean"—he paused, looking hard at me, as though his eyes would help me to understand, and then gestured helplessly, as though perhaps his hand would help—"I mean, I'll have a lot of studying to do, and I'll have to study *everything*, but, I mean, I want to play *with*—jazz musicians." He stopped. "I want to play jazz," he said.

Well, the word had never before sounded as heavy, as real, as it sounded that afternoon in Sonny's mouth. I just looked at him and I was probably frowning a real frown by this time. I simply couldn't see why on earth he'd want to spend his time hanging around nightclubs, clowning around on bandstands, while people pushed each other around a dance floor. It seemed—beneath him, somehow. I had never thought about it before, had never been forced to, but I suppose I had always put jazz musicians in a class with what Daddy called "goodtime people."

"Are you *serious*?"

"Hell, *yes*, I'm serious."

He looked more helpless than ever, and annoyed, and deeply hurt.

I suggested helpfully: "You mean—like Louis Armstrong?"[3]

His face closed as though I'd struck him. "No. I'm not talking about none of that old-time, down home crap."

"Well, look Sonny, I'm sorry, don't get mad. I just don't altogether get it, that's all. Name somebody—you know, a jazz musician you admire."

"Bird."

"Who?"

"Bird! Charlie Parker![4] Don't they teach you nothing in the god-damn army?" I lit a cigarette. I was surprised and then a little amused to discover that I was trembling. "I've been out of touch," I said. "You'll have to be patient with me. Now. Who's this Parker character?"

"He's just one of the greatest jazz musicians alive," said Sonny, sullenly, his hands in his pockets, his back to me. "Maybe *the* greatest," he added, bitterly, "that's probably why *you* never heard of him."

---

[3]Important jazz musician and singer (1900–1971).

[4]Charles Christopher Parker (1920–1955). Known as "Bird" or "Yardbird," he was one of the most influential saxophonists and jazz musicians of the 1940s.

"All right," I said, "I'm ignorant. I'm sorry. I'll go out and buy all the cat's records right away, all right?"

"It don't," said Sonny, with dignity, "make any difference to me. I don't care what you listen to. Don't do me no favors."

I was beginning to realize that I'd never seen him so upset before. With another part of my mind I was thinking that this would probably turn out to be one of those things kids go through and that I shouldn't make it seem important by pushing it too hard. Still, I didn't think it would do any harm to ask: "Doesn't all this take a lot of time? Can you make a living at it?"

He turned back to me and half leaned, half sat, on the kitchen table. "Everything takes time," he said, "and—well, yes, sure, I can make a living at it. But what I don't seem to be able to make you understand is that it's the only thing I want to do."

"Well, Sonny," I said gently, "you know people can't always do exactly what they *want* to do—"

"*No*, I don't know that," said Sonny, surprising me. "I think people *ought* to do what they want to do, what else are they alive for?"

"You are getting to be a big boy," I said desperately, "it's time you started thinking about your future."

"I'm thinking about my future," said Sonny, grimly. "I think about it all the time."

I gave up. I decided, if he didn't change his mind, that we could always talk about it later. "In the meantime," I said, "you got to finish school." We had already decided that he'd have to move in with Isabel and her folks. I knew this wasn't the ideal arrangement because Isabel's folks are inclined to be dicty[5] and they hadn't especially wanted Isabel to marry me. But I didn't know what else to do. "And we have to get you fixed up at Isabel's."

There was a long silence. He moved from the kitchen table to the window. "That's a terrible idea. You know it yourself."

"Do you have a *better* idea?"

He just walked up and down the kitchen for a minute. He was as tall as I was. He had started to shave. I suddenly had the feeling that I didn't know him at all.

He stopped at the kitchen table and picked up my cigarettes. Looking at me with a kind of mocking, amused defiance, he put one between his lips. "You mind?"

"You smoking already?"

He lit the cigarette and nodded, watching me through the smoke. "I just wanted to see if I'd have the courage to smoke in front of you." He grinned and

---

[5]Snobbish

blew a great cloud of smoke to the ceiling. "It was easy." He looked at my face. "Come on, now. I bet you was smoking at my age, tell the truth."

I didn't say anything but the truth was on my face, and he laughed. But now there was something very strained in his laugh. "Sure. And I bet that ain't all you was doing."

He was frightening me a little. "Cut the crap," I said. "We already decided that you was going to go and live at Isabel's. Now what's got into you all of a sudden?"

"*You* decided it," he pointed out. "*I* didn't decide nothing." He stopped in front of me, leaning against the stove, arms loosely folded. "Look, brother. I don't want to stay in Harlem no more, I really don't." He was very earnest. He looked at me, then over toward the kitchen window. There was something in his eyes I'd never seen before, some thoughtfulness, some worry all his own. He rubbed the muscle of one arm. "It's time I was getting out of here."

"Where do you want to *go*, Sonny?"

"I want to join the army. Or the navy, I don't care. If I say I'm old enough, they'll believe me."

Then I got mad. It was because I was so scared. "You must be crazy. You goddamn fool, what the hell do you want to go and join the *army* for?"

"I just told you. To get out of Harlem."

"Sonny, you haven't even finished *school*. And if you really want to be a musician, how do you expect to study if you're in the *army*?"

He looked at me, trapped, and in anguish. "There's ways. I might be able to work out some kind of deal. Anyway, I'll have the G.I. Bill when I come out."

"*If* you come out." We stared at each other. "Sonny, please. Be reasonable. I know the setup is far from perfect. But we got to do the best we can."

"I ain't learning nothing in school," he said. "Even when I go." He turned away from me and opened the window and threw his cigarette out into the narrow alley. I watched his back. "At least, I ain't learning nothing you'd want me to learn." He slammed the window so hard I thought the glass would fly out, and turned back to me. "And I'm sick of the stink of these garbage cans!"

"Sonny," I said, "I know how you feel. But if you don't finish school now, you're going to be sorry later that you didn't." I grabbed him by the shoulders. "And you only got another year. It ain't so bad. And I'll come back and I swear I'll help you do *whatever* you want to do. Just try to put up with it till I come back. Will you please do that? For me?"

He didn't answer and he wouldn't look at me.

"Sonny. You hear me?"

He pulled away. "I hear you. But you never hear anything I say."

I didn't know what to say to that. He looked out of the window and then back at me. "OK," he said, and sighed. "I'll try."

Then I said, trying to cheer him up a little, "They got a piano at Isabel's. You can practice on it."

And as a matter of fact, it did cheer him up for a minute. "That's right," he said to himself. "I forgot that." His face relaxed a little. But the worry, the thoughtfulness, played on it still, the way shadows play on a face which is staring into the fire.

But I thought I'd never hear the end of that piano. At first, Isabel would write me, saying how nice it was that Sonny was so serious about his music and how, as soon as he came in from school, or wherever he had been when he was supposed to be at school, he went straight to that piano and stayed there until suppertime. And, after supper, he went back to that piano and stayed there until everybody went to bed. He was at the piano all day Saturday and all day Sunday. Then he bought a record player and started playing records. He'd play one record over and over again, all day long sometimes, and he'd improvise along with it on the piano. Or he'd play one section of the record, one chord, one change, one progression, then he'd do it on the piano. Then back to the record. Then back to the piano.

Well, I really don't know how they stood it. Isabel finally confessed that it wasn't like living with a person at all, it was like living with sound. And the sound didn't make any sense to her, didn't make any sense to any of them—naturally. They began, in a way, to be afflicted by this presence that was living in their home. It was as though Sonny were some sort of god, or monster. He moved in an atmosphere which wasn't like theirs at all. They fed him and he ate, he washed himself, he walked in and out of their door; he certainly wasn't nasty or unpleasant or rude, Sonny isn't any of those things; but it was as though he were all wrapped up in some cloud, some fire, some vision all his own; and there wasn't any way to reach him.

At the same time, he wasn't really a man yet, he was still a child, and they had to watch out for him in all kinds of ways. They certainly couldn't throw him out. Neither did they dare to make a great scene about that piano because even they dimly sensed, as I sensed, from so many thousands of miles away, that Sonny was at that piano playing for his life.

But he hadn't been going to school. One day a letter came from the school board and Isabel's mother got it—there had, apparently, been other letters but Sonny had torn them up. This day, when Sonny came in, Isabel's mother showed him the letter and asked where he'd been spending his time. And she finally got it out of him that he'd been down in Greenwich Village, with musicians and other characters, in a white girls' apartment. And this scared her and she started to scream at him and what came up, once she began—though she denies it to this day—was what sacrifices they were making to give Sonny a decent home and how little he appreciated it.

Sonny didn't play the piano that day. By evening, Isabel's mother had calmed down but then there was the old man to deal with, and Isabel herself. Isabel says she did her best to be calm but she broke down and started crying. She says she just watched Sonny's face. She could tell, by watching him, what was happening with him. And what was happening was that they penetrated his cloud, they had reached him. Even if their fingers had been a thousand times more gentle than human fingers ever are, he could hardly help feeling that they had stripped him naked and were spitting on that nakedness. For he also had to see that his presence, that music, which was life or death to him, had been torture for them and that they had endured it, not at all for his sake, but only for mine. And Sonny couldn't take that. He can take it a little better today than he could then but he's still not very good at it and, frankly, I don't know anybody who is.

The silence of the next few days must have been louder than the sound of all the music ever played since time began. One morning, before she went to work, Isabel was in his room for something and she suddenly realized that all of his records were gone. And she knew for certain that he was gone. And he was. He went as far as the navy would carry him. He finally sent me a postcard from some place in Greece and that was the first I knew that Sonny was still alive. I didn't see him any more until we were both back in New York and the war had long been over.

He was a man by then, of course, but I wasn't willing to see it. He came by the house from time to time, but we fought almost every time we met. I didn't like the way he carried himself, loose and dreamlike all the time, and I didn't like his friends, and his music seemed to be merely an excuse for the life he led. It sounded just that weird and disordered.

Then we had a fight, a pretty awful fight, and I didn't see him for months. By and by I looked him up, where he was living, in a furnished room in the Village, and I tried to make it up. But there were lots of other people in the room and Sonny just lay on his bed, and he wouldn't come downstairs with me, and he treated these other people as though they were his family and I weren't. So I got mad and then he got mad, and then I told him that he might just as well be dead as live the way he was living. Then he stood up and he told me not to worry about him any more in life, that he *was* dead as far as I was concerned. Then he pushed me to the door and the other people looked on as though nothing were happening, and he slammed the door behind me. I stood in the hallway, staring at the door. I heard somebody laugh in the room and then the tears came to my eyes. I started down the steps, whistling to keep from crying, I kept whistling to myself, *You going to need me, baby, one of these cold, rainy days.*

I read about Sonny's trouble in the spring. Little Grace died in the fall. She was a beautiful little girl. But she only lived a little over two years. She died of polio and she suffered. She had a slight fever for a couple of days, but it didn't seem like anything and we just kept her in bed. And we would certainly have called the doctor, but the fever dropped, she seemed to be all right. So we thought it had just been a cold. Then, one day, she was up, playing, Isabel was in the kitchen fixing lunch for the two boys when they'd come in from school, and she heard Grace fall down in the living room. When you have a lot of children you don't always start running when one of them falls, unless they start screaming or something. And, this time, Grace was quiet. Yet, Isabel says that when she heard that *thump* and then that silence, something happened in her to make her afraid. And she ran to the living room and there was little Grace on the floor, all twisted up, and the reason she hadn't screamed was that she couldn't get her breath. And when she did scream, it was the worst sound, Isabel says, that she'd ever heard in all her life, and she still hears it sometimes in her dreams. Isabel will sometimes wake me up with a low, moaning, strangled sound and I have to be quick to awaken her and hold her to me and where Isabel is weeping against me seems a mortal wound.

I think I may have written Sonny the very day that little Grace was buried. I was sitting in the living room in the dark, by myself, and I suddenly thought of Sonny. My trouble made his real.

One Saturday afternoon, when Sonny had been living with us, or, anyway, been in our house, for nearly two weeks, I found myself wandering aimlessly about the living room, drinking from a can of beer, and trying to work up the courage to search Sonny's room. He was out, he was usually out whenever I was home, and Isabel had taken the children to see their grandparents. Suddenly I was standing still in front of the living room window, watching Seventh Avenue. The idea of searching Sonny's room made me still. I scarcely dared to admit to myself what I'd be searching for. I didn't know what I'd do if I found it. Or if I didn't.

On the sidewalk across from me, near the entrance to a barbecue joint, some people were holding an old-fashioned revival meeting. The barbecue cook, wearing a dirty white apron, his *conked*[6] hair reddish and metallic in the pale sun, and a cigarette between his lips, stood in the doorway, watching them. Kids and older people paused in their errands and stood there, along with some older men and a couple of very tough-looking women who

---

[6]Chemically straightened

watched everything that happened on the avenue, as though they owned it, or were maybe owned by it. Well, they were watching this, too, The revival was being carried on by three sisters in black, and a brother. All they had were their voices and their Bibles and a tambourine. The brother was testifying and while he testified two of the sisters stood together, seeming to say, amen, and the third sister walked around with the tambourine outstretched and a couple of people dropped coins into it. Then the brother's testimony ended and the sister who had been taking up the collection dumped the coins into her palm and transferred them to the pocket of her long black robe. Then she raised both hands, striking the tambourine against the air, and then against one hand, and she started to sing. And the two other sisters and the brother joined in.

It was strange, suddenly, to watch, though I had been seeing these street meetings all my life. So, of course, had everybody else down there. Yet, they paused and watched and listened and I stood still at the window. *"Tis the old ship of Zion,"* they sang, and the sister with the tambourine kept a steady, jangling beat, *"it has rescued many a thousand!"* Not a soul under the sound of their voices was hearing this song for the first time, not one of them had been rescued. Nor had they seen much in the way of rescue work being done around them. Neither did they especially believe in the holiness of the three sisters and the brother, they knew too much about them, knew where they lived, and how. The woman with the tambourine, whose voice dominated the air, whose face was bright with joy, was divided by very little from the woman who stood watching her, a cigarette between her heavy, chapped lips, her hair a cuckoo's nest, her face scarred and swollen from many beatings, and her black eyes glittering like coal. Perhaps they both knew this, which was why, when, as rarely, they addressed each other, they addressed each other as Sister. As the singing filled the air the watching, listening faces underwent a change, the eyes focusing on something within; the music seemed to soothe a poison out of them; and time seemed, nearly, to fall away from the sullen, belligerent, battered faces, as though they were fleeing back to their first condition, while dreaming of their last. The barbecue cook half shook his head and smiled, and dropped his cigarette and disappeared into his joint. A man fumbled in his pockets for change and stood holding it in his hand impatiently, as though he had just remembered a pressing appointment further up the avenue. He looked furious. Then I saw Sonny, standing on the edge of the crowd. He was carrying a wide, flat notebook with a green cover, and it made him look, from where I was standing, almost like a schoolboy. The coppery sun brought out the copper in his skin, he was very faintly smiling, standing very still. Then the singing stopped, the tambourine turned into a collection plate again. The furious man dropped in his coins and vanished, so did a couple of the women, and Sonny dropped some change in the plate, looking directly at the woman with a little smile. He started across the avenue, toward the house. He has a slow, loping walk, something like the way Harlem hipsters walk, only he's imposed on this his own half-beat. I had never really noticed it before.

I stayed at the window, both relieved and apprehensive. As Sonny disappeared from my sight, they began singing again. And they were still singing when his key turned in the lock.

"Hey," he said.

"Hey, yourself. You want some beer?"

"No. Well, maybe." But he came up to the window and stood beside me, looking out. "What a warm voice," he said.

They were singing *If I could only hear my mother pray again!*

"Yes," I said, "and she can sure beat that tambourine."

"But what a terrible song," he said, and laughed. He dropped his notebook on the sofa and disappeared into the kitchen. "Where's Isabel and the kids?"

"I think they went to see their grandparents. You hungry?"

"No." He came back into the living room with his can of beer. "You want to come some place with me tonight?"

I sensed, I don't know how, that I couldn't possibly say no. "Sure. Where?"

He sat down on the sofa and picked up his notebook and started leafing through it. "I'm going to sit in with some fellows in a joint in the Village."

"You mean, you're going to play, tonight?"

"That's right." He took a swallow of his beer and moved back, to the window. He gave me a sidelong look. "If you can stand it."

"I'll try," I said.

He smiled to himself and we both watched as the meeting across the way broke up. The three sisters and the brother, heads bowed, were singing *God be with you till we meet again*. The faces around them were very quiet. Then the song ended. The small crowd dispersed. We watched the three women and the lone man walk slowly up the avenue.

"When she was singing before," said Sonny, abruptly, "her voice reminded me for a minute of what heroin feels like sometimes—when it's in your veins. It makes you feel sort of warm and cool at the same time. And distant. And—and sure." He sipped his beer, very deliberately not looking at me. I watched his face. "It makes you feel—in control. Sometimes you've got to have that feeling."

"Do you?" I sat down slowly in the easy chair.

"Sometimes." He went to the sofa and picked up his notebook again. "Some people do."

"In order," I asked, "to play?" And my voice was very ugly, full of contempt and anger.

"Well"—he looked at me with great, troubled eyes, as though, in fact, he hoped his eyes would tell me things he could never otherwise say—"they *think* so. And *if* they think so—!"

"And what do *you* think?" I asked.

He sat on the sofa and put his can of beer on the floor. "I don't know," he said, and I couldn't be sure if he were answering my question or pursuing his thoughts. His face didn't tell me. "It's not so much to *play*. It's to *stand* it, to be able to make it at all. On any level." He frowned and smiled: "In order to keep from shaking to pieces."

"But these friends of yours," I said, "they seem to shake themselves to pieces pretty goddamn fast."

"Maybe." He played with the notebook. And something told me that I should curb my tongue, that Sonny was doing his best to talk, that I should listen. "But of course you only know the ones that've gone to pieces. Some don't—or at least they haven't *yet* and that's just about all *any* of us can say." He paused. "And then there are some who just live, really, in hell, and they know it and they see what's happening, and they go right on. I don't know." He sighed, dropped the notebook, folded his arms. "Some guys, you can tell from the way they play, they on something *all* the time. And you can see that, well, it makes something real for them. But of course," he picked up his beer from the floor and sipped it and put the can down again, "they *want* to, too, you've got to see that. Even some of them that say they don't—*some*, not all."

"And what about you?" I asked—I couldn't help it. "What about you? Do *you* want to?"

He stood up and walked to the window and remained silent for a long time. Then he sighed. "Me," he said. Then: "While I was downstairs before, on my way here, listening to that woman sing, it struck me all of a sudden how much suffering she must have had to go through—to sing like that. It's *repulsive* to think you have to suffer that much."

I said: "But there's no way not to suffer—is there, Sonny?"

"I believe not," he said and smiled, "but that's never stopped anyone from trying." He looked at me. "Has it?" I realized, with this mocking look, that there stood between us, forever, beyond the power of time or forgiveness, the fact that I had held silence—so long!—when he had needed human speech to help him. He turned back to the window. "No, there's no way not to suffer. But you try all kinds of ways to keep from drowning in it, to keep on top of it, and to make it seem—well, like *you*. Like you did something, all right, and now you're suffering for it. You know?" I said nothing. "Well you know," he said, impatiently, "why *do* people suffer? Maybe it's better to do something to give it a reason, *any* reason."

"But we just agreed," I said, "that there's no way not to suffer. Isn't it better, then, just to—take it?"

"But nobody just takes it," Sonny cried, "that's what I'm telling you! *Everybody* tries not to. You're just hung up on the *way* some people try—it's not *your* way!"

The hair on my face began to itch, my face felt wet. "That's not true," I said, "that's not true. I don't give a damn what other people do, I don't even care how they suffer. I just care how *you* suffer." And he looked at me. "Please believe me," I said. "I don't want to see you—die—trying not to suffer."

"I won't," he said, flatly, "die trying not to suffer. At least, not any faster than anybody else."

"But there's no need," I said, trying to laugh, "is there? in killing yourself."

I wanted to say more, but I couldn't. I wanted to talk about will power and how life could be—well, beautiful. I wanted to say that it was all within; but was it? or, rather, wasn't that exactly the trouble? And I wanted to promise that I would never fail him again. But it would all have sounded—empty words and lies.

So I made the promise to myself and prayed that I would keep it.

"It's terrible sometimes, inside," he said, "that's what's the trouble. You walk these streets, black and funky and cold, and there's not really a living ass to talk to, and there's nothing shaking, and there's no way of getting it out—that storm inside. You can't talk it and you can't make love with it, and when you finally try to get with it and play it, you realize *nobody's* listening. So *you've* got to listen. You got to find a way to listen."

And then he walked away from the window and sat on the sofa again, as though all the wind had suddenly been knocked out of him. "Sometimes you'll do *anything* to play, even cut your mother's throat." He laughed and looked at me. "Or your brother's." Then he sobered. "Or your own." Then: "Don't worry. I'm all right now and I think I'll *be* all right. But I can't forget—where I've been. I don't mean just the physical place I've been, I mean where I've *been*. And *what* I've been."

"What have you been, Sonny?" I asked.

He smiled—but sat sideways on the sofa, his elbow resting on the back, his fingers playing with his mouth and chin, not looking at me. "I've been something I didn't recognize, didn't know I could be. Didn't know anybody could be." He stopped, looking inward, looking helplessly young, looking old. "I'm not talking about it now because I feel *guilty* or anything like that—maybe it would be better if I did, I don't know. Anyway, I can't really talk about it. Not to you, not to anybody," and now he turned and faced me. "Sometimes, you know and it was actually when I was most *out* of the world. I felt that I was in it, that I was *with* it, really, and I could play or I didn't really have to *play*, it just came out of me, it was there. And I don't know how I played, thinking about it now, but I know I did awful things, those times, sometimes, to people. Or it wasn't that I *did* anything to them—it was that they weren't real." He picked up the beer can; it was empty; he rolled it between his palms: "And other times—well, I needed a fix, I needed to find a place to lean, I needed to clear a space to *listen*—and I couldn't find it, and I—went crazy, I did terrible things to *me*, I was terrible *for* me." He began pressing the beer can between his hands, I watched the metal begin to give. It glittered, as he played with it, like a knife, and I was afraid he would cut himself, but I said nothing. "Oh well. I can never tell you. I was all by myself at the bottom of something, stinking and sweating and crying and shaking, and I smelled it, you know? *my* stink, and I thought I'd die if I couldn't get away from it and yet, all the same, I knew that everything I was doing was just locking me in with it. And I didn't know," he paused, still flattening the beer can, "I didn't know, I still *don't* know, something kept telling me that maybe it was good to smell your own stink, but I didn't think that *that* was what I'd been trying to do—and—who can stand it?" and he abruptly dropped the ruined beer can, looking at me with a small, still smile, and then rose, walking to the window as though it were the lodestone rock. I watched his face, he watched the avenue. "I couldn't tell you when Mama died—but the reason I wanted to leave Harlem so bad was to get away from drugs. And then, when I ran away, that's what I was running from—really. When I came back, nothing had changed, *I* hadn't changed, I was just—older." And he stopped drumming with his fingers on the windowpane. The sun had vanished, soon darkness would fall. I watched his face. "It can come again," he said, almost as though speaking to himself. Then he turned to me. "It can come again," he repeated. "I just want you to know that."

"All right," I said, at last. "So it can come again. All right."

He smiled, but the smile was sorrowful. "I had to try to tell you," he said.

"Yes," I said. "I understand that."

"You're my brother," he said, looking straight at me, and not smiling at all.

"Yes," I repeated, "yes. I understand that."

He turned back to the window, looking out. "All that hatred down there," he said, "all that hatred and misery and love. It's a wonder it doesn't blow the avenue apart."

We went to the only nightclub on a short, dark street, downtown. We squeezed through the narrow, chattering, jam-packed bar to the entrance of the big room, where the bandstand was. And we stood there for a moment, for the lights were very dim in this room and we couldn't see. Then, "Hello, boy," said a voice and an enormous black man, much older than Sonny or myself, erupted out of all that atmospheric lighting and put an arm around Sonny's shoulder. "I been sitting right here," he said, "waiting for you."

He had a big voice, too, and heads in the darkness turned toward us.

Sonny grinned and pulled a little away, and said, "Creole, this is my brother. I told you about him."

Creole shook my hand. "I'm glad to meet you, son," he said, and it was clear that he was glad to meet me *there*, for Sonny's sake. And he smiled, "You got a real musician in *your* family," and he took his arm from Sonny's shoulder and slapped him, lightly, affectionately, with the back of his hand.

"Well. Now I've heard it all," said a voice behind us. This was another musician, and a friend of Sonny's, a coal-black, cheerful-looking man, built close to the ground. He immediately began confiding to me, at the top of his lungs, the most terrible things about Sonny, his teeth gleaming like a lighthouse and his laugh coming up out of him like the beginning of an earthquake. And it turned out that everyone at the bar knew Sonny, or almost everyone; some were musicians, working there, or nearby, or not working, some were simply hangers-on, and some were there to hear Sonny play. I was introduced to all of them and they were all very polite to me. Yet, it was clear that, for them, I was only Sonny's brother. Here, I was in Sonny's world. Or, rather: his kingdom. Here, it was not even a question that his veins bore royal blood.

They were going to play soon and Creole installed me, by myself, at a table in a dark corner. Then I watched them, Creole, and the little black man, and Sonny, and the others, while they horsed around, standing just below the bandstand. The light from the bandstand spilled just a little short of them and, watching them laughing and gesturing and moving about, I had the feeling that they, nevertheless, were being most careful not to step into that circle of light too suddenly: that if they moved into the light too suddenly, without thinking, they would perish in flame. Then, while I watched, one of them, the small, black man, moved into the light and crossed the bandstand and started fooling around with his drums. Then—being funny and being, also, extremely ceremonious—Creole took Sonny by the arm and led him to the piano. A woman's voice called Sonny's name and a few hands started clapping. And Sonny, also being funny and being ceremonious, and so touched, I think, that he could have cried, but neither hiding it nor showing it, riding it like a man, grinned, and put both hands to his heart and bowed from the waist.

Creole then went to the bass fiddle and a lean, very bright-skinned brown man jumped up on the bandstand and picked up his horn. So there they were, and the atmosphere on the bandstand and in the room began to change and tighten. Someone stepped up to the microphone and announced them. Then there were all kinds of murmurs. Some people at the bar shushed others. The waitress ran around, frantically getting in the last orders, guys and chicks got closer to each other, and the lights on the bandstand, on the quartet, turned to a kind of indigo. Then they all looked different there. Creole looked about him for the last time, as though he were making certain that all his chickens were in the coop, and then he—jumped and struck the fiddle. And there they were.

All I know about music is that not many people ever really hear it. And even then, on the rare occasions when something opens within, and the music enters, what we mainly hear, or hear corroborated, are personal, private, vanishing evocations. But the man who creates the music is hearing something else, is dealing with the roar rising from the void and imposing order on it as it hits the air. What is evoked in him, then, is of another order, more terrible because it has no words, and triumphant, too, for that same reason. And his triumph, when he triumphs, is ours. I just watched Sonny's face. His face was troubled, he was working hard, but he wasn't with it. And I had the feeling that, in a way, everyone on the bandstand was waiting for him, both waiting for him and pushing him along. But as I began to watch Creole, I realized that it was Creole who held them all back. He had them on a short rein. Up there, keeping the beat with his whole body, wailing on the fiddle, with his eyes half closed, he was listening to everything, but he was listening to Sonny. He was having a dialogue with Sonny. He wanted Sonny to leave the shoreline and strike out for the deep water. He was Sonny's witness that deep water and drowning were not the same thing—he had been there, and he knew. And he wanted Sonny to know. He was waiting for Sonny to do the things on the keys which would let Creole know that Sonny was in the water.

And, while Creole listened, Sonny moved, deep within, exactly like someone in torment. I had never before thought of how awful the relationship must be between the musician and his instrument. He has to fill it, this instrument, with the breath of life, his own. He has to make it do what he wants it to do. And a piano is just a piano. It's made out of so much wood and wires and little hammers and big ones, and ivory. While there's only so much you can do with it, the only way to find this out is to try; to try and make it do everything.

And Sonny hadn't been near a piano for over a year. And he wasn't on much better terms with his life, not the life that stretched before him now. He and the piano stammered, started one way, got scared, stopped; started another way, panicked, marked time, started again; then seemed to have found a direction, panicked again, got stuck. And the face I saw on Sonny I'd never seen before. Everything had been burned out of it, and, at the same time, things usually hidden were being burned in, by the fire and fury of the battle which was occurring in him up there.

Yet, watching Creole's face as they neared the end of the first set, I had the feeling that something had happened, something I hadn't heard. Then they finished, there was scattered applause, and then, without an instant's warning, Creole started into something else, it was almost sardonic, it was *Am I Blue.* And, as though he commanded, Sonny began to play. Something began to happen. And Creole let out the reins. The dry, low, black man said something awful on the drums, Creole answered, and the drums talked back. Then the horn insisted, sweet and high, slightly detached perhaps, and Creole listened, commenting now and then, dry, and driving, beautiful and calm and old. Then they all came together again, and Sonny was part of the family again. I could tell this from his face. He seemed to have found, right there beneath his fingers, a damn brand-new piano. It seemed that he couldn't get over it. Then, for awhile, just being happy with Sonny, they seemed to be agreeing with him that brand-new pianos certainly were a gas.

Then Creole stepped forward to remind them that what they were play-ing was the blues. He hit something in all of them, he hit something in me, myself, and the music tightened and deepened, apprehension began to beat the air. Creole began to tell us what the blues were all about. They were not about anything very new. He and his boys up there were keeping it new, at the risk of ruin, destruction, madness, and death, in order to find new ways to make us listen. For, while the tale of how we suffer, and how we are delighted, and how we may triumph is never new, it always must be heard. There isn't any other tale to tell, it's the only light we've got in all this darkness.

And this tale, according to that face, that body, those strong hands on those strings, has another aspect in every country, and a new depth in every generation. Listen, Creole seemed to be saying, listen. Now these are Sonny's blues. He made the little black man on the drums know it, and the bright, brown man on the horn. Creole wasn't trying any longer to get Sonny in the water. He was wishing him Godspeed. Then he stepped back, very slowly, fill-ing the air with the immense suggestion that Sonny speak for himself.

Then they all gathered around Sonny and Sonny played. Every now and again one of them seemed to say, amen. Sonny's fingers filled the air with life, his life. But that life contained so many others. And Sonny went all the way back, he really began with the spare, flat statement of the opening phrase of the song. Then he began to make it his. It was very beautiful because it wasn't hurried and it was no longer a lament. I seemed to hear with what burning he had made it his, with what burning we had yet to make it ours, how we could cease lamenting. Freedom lurked around us and I understood, at last, that he could help us to be free if we would listen, that he would never be free until we did. Yet, there was no battle in his face now. I heard what he had gone through, and would continue to go through until he came to rest in earth. He had made it his: that long line, of which we knew only Mama and Daddy. And he was giving it back, as everything must be given back, so that, passing through death, it can live forever. I saw my mother's face again, and felt, for the first time, how the stones of the road she had walked on must have bruised her feet. I saw the moonlit road where my father's brother died. And it brought something else back to me, and carried me past it, I saw my little girl again and felt Isabel's tears again, and I felt my own tears begin to rise. And I was yet aware that this was only a moment, that the world waited outside, as hungry as a tiger, and that trouble stretched above us, longer than the sky.

Then it was over. Creole and Sonny let out their breath, both soaking wet, and grinning. There was a lot of applause and some of it was real. In the dark, the girl came by and I asked her to take drinks to the bandstand. There was a long pause, while they talked up there in the indigo light and after awhile I saw the girl put a Scotch and milk on top of the piano for Sonny. He didn't seem to notice it, but just before they started playing again he sipped from it and looked toward me, and nodded. Then he put it back on top of the piano. For me, then, as they began to play again, it glowed and shook above my brother's head like the very cup of trembling.[7]

[1957]

---

[7]See Isaiah 51:17, 22.

QUESTIONS

1. Describe the relationship of the two brothers. How does the narrator represent that relationship?

2. What event in the narrator's life causes him to make contact with his brother Sonny? What significance does his motivation have to the story?

3. What are possible reasons the narrator buys Sonny a drink at the end of the story?

4. Examine the passages in which the story makes use of music. What words or phrases stand out most to you?

5. Near the end of the story, Sonny tells the narrator that all people try to escape pain, including the narrator. What are the narrator's ways of escaping pain?

6. What is the role of race to the pain that Sonny describes?

7. What connection does "Sonny's Blues" make between art and suffering?

8. What role does the musical genre "the blues" play in the story? How do the blues shape the events in the story?

9. Write an essay in which you investigate the relationship of Sonny and the narrator. How do they reflect one another's worldview? What similarities and differences do they have?

10. Explain connections between the narrator's realization and the earlier stories he tells about Sonny. What does this realization show about the narrator and about Sonny?

Gabriel García Márquez
[1928–   ]

GABRIEL GARCÍA MÁRQUEZ *was born in 1928 in Aracataca, Colombia. Born into poverty, he was raised by his grandparents who greatly influenced García Márquez's life and work. His grandfather was a veteran of the civil war that occurred in Colombia in the late 1920s in response to the so-called "banana massacres." His grandmother was a natural storyteller, influencing García Márquez's writing style—magical realism—with ghost stories and other superstitions. In 1954 he began working as a journalist for* El Espectador *until the government shut down the paper. By this time, García Márquez had already settled in Paris after having traveled through Switzerland, Italy, Poland, and Hungary. In 1955 he published his first collection of stories, titled* Leaf Storm and Other Stories, *stories heavily influenced by the American writer William Faulkner. Soon after, he published* No One Writes to the Colonel *(1961) and* An Evil Hour *(1962). However, he was not yet satisfied with his writing and suffered great disappointment about his output until he finally experienced the inspiration that would lead to his masterwork,* One Hundred Years of Solitude *(1967), which was written in a creative burst that lasted eighteen months. In this novel, which brought him great fame, García Márquez felt he had achieved mythic expression and a way of storytelling akin to the stories told him by his grandmother. In 1975 he published* Autumn of the Patriarch, *followed by* Operacion Carlotta *(1977), a collection of essays about Cuba. In 1981 he was given the French Legion of Honor medal, and in 1982 he was awarded the Nobel Prize for Literature.* Love in a Time of Cholera *appeared in 1986 to rave reviews and served to enhance García Márquez's ability to take the world stage against political oppression and dictatorship.* News of a Kidnapping *(1996), a journalistic work, dealt with the subject of the Colombian drug trade. In 1999, García Márquez bought the Colombian news magazine,* Cambio, *which continues to advance progressive political themes.*

A Very Old Man with Enormous Wings

GABRIEL GARCÍA MÁRQUEZ

ON THE THIRD day of rain they had killed so many crabs inside the house that Pelayo had to cross his drenched courtyard and throw them into the sea, because the newborn child had a temperature all night and they thought it was due to the stench. The world had been sad since Tuesday. Sea and sky were a single ash-gray thing and the sands of the beach, which on March nights glimmered like powdered light, had become a stew of mud and rotten shellfish. The light was so weak at noon that when Pelayo was coming back to the house after throwing away the crabs, it was hard for him to see what it was that was moving and groaning in the rear of the courtyard. He had to go very close to see that it was an old man, a very old man, lying face down in the mud, who, in spite of his tremendous efforts, couldn't get up, impeded by his enormous wings.

Frightened by that nightmare, Pelayo ran to get Elisenda, his wife, who was putting compresses on the sick child, and he took her to the rear of the courtyard. They both looked at the fallen body with mute stupor. He was dressed like a ragpicker. There were only a few faded hairs left on his bald skull and very few teeth in his mouth, and his pitiful condition of a drenched, great-grandfather had taken away any sense of grandeur he might have had. His huge buzzard wings, dirty and half-plucked, were forever entangled in the mud. They looked at him so long and so closely that Pelayo and Elisenda very soon overcame their surprise and in the end found him familiar. Then they dared speak to him, and he answered in an incomprehensible dialect with a strong sailor's voice. That was how they skipped over the inconvenience of the wings and quite intelligently concluded that he was a lonely castaway from some foreign ship wrecked by the storm. And yet, they called in a neighbor woman who knew everything about life and death to see him, and all she needed was one look to show them their mistake.

"He's an angel," she told them. "He must have been coming for the child, but the poor fellow is so old that the rain knocked him down."

On the following day everyone knew that a flesh-and-blood angel was held captive in Pelayo's house. Against the judgment of the wise neighbor woman, for whom angels in those times were the fugitive survivors of a celestial conspiracy, they did not have the heart to club him to death. Pelayo watched over him all afternoon from the kitchen, armed with his bailiff's club, and before going to bed he dragged him out of the mud and locked him up with the hens in the wire chicken coop. In the middle of the night, when the rain stopped, Pelayo and Elisenda were still killing crabs. A short time afterward the child woke up without a fever and with a desire to eat. Then they felt magnanimous and decided to put the angel on a raft with fresh water and provisions for three days and leave him to his fate on the high seas. But when they went out into the courtyard with the first light of dawn, they found the whole neighborhood in front of the chicken coop having fun with the angel, without the slightest reverence, tossing him things to eat through the openings in the wire as if he weren't a supernatural creature but a circus animal.

Father Gonzaga arrived before seven o'clock, alarmed at the strange news. By that time onlookers less frivolous than those at dawn had already arrived and they were making all kinds of conjectures concerning the captive's future. The simplest among them thought that he should be named mayor of the world. Others of sterner mind felt that he should be promoted to the rank of five-star general in order to win all wars. Some visionaries hoped that he could be put to stud in order to implant on earth a race of winged wise men who could take charge of the universe. But Father Gonzaga, before becoming a priest, had been a robust woodcutter. Standing by the wire, he reviewed his catechism in an instant and asked them to open the door so that he could take a close look at that pitiful man who looked more like a huge decrepit hen among the fascinated chickens. He was lying in a corner drying his open wings in the sunlight among the fruit peels and breakfast leftovers that the early risers had thrown him. Alien to the impertinences of the world, he only lifted his antiquarian eyes and murmured something in his dialect when Father Gonzaga went into the chicken coop and said good morning to him in Latin. The parish priest had his first suspicion of an impostor when he saw that he did not understand the language of God or know how to greet His ministers. Then he noticed that seen close up he was much too human: he had an unbearable smell of the outdoors, the back side of his wings was strewn with parasites and his main feathers had been mistreated by terrestrial winds, and nothing about him measured up to the proud dignity of angels. Then he came out of the chicken coop and in a brief sermon warned the curious against the risks of being ingenuous. He reminded them that the devil had the bad habit of making use of carnival tricks in order to confuse the unwary. He argued that if wings were not the essential element in determining the difference between hawk and an airplane, they were even less so in the recognition of angels. Nevertheless, he promised to write a letter to his bishop so that the latter would write to his primate so that the latter would write to the Supreme Pontiff in order to get the final verdict from the highest courts.

His prudence fell on sterile hearts. The news of the captive angel spread with such rapidity that after a few hours the courtyard had the bustle of a marketplace and they had to call in troops with fixed bayonets to disperse the mob that was about to knock the house down. Elisenda, her spine all twisted from sweeping up so much marketplace trash, then got the idea of fencing in the yard and charging five cents admission to see the angel.

The curious came from far away. A traveling carnival arrived with a flying acrobat who buzzed over the crowd several times, but no one paid any attention to him because his wings were not those of an angel but, rather, those of a sidereal bat. The most unfortunate invalids on earth came in search of health: a poor woman who since childhood had been counting her heartbeats and had run out of numbers; a Portuguese man who couldn't sleep because the noise of the stars disturbed him; a sleepwalker who got up at night to undo the things he had done while awake; and many others with less serious ailments. In the midst of that shipwreck disorder that made the earth tremble, Pelayo and Elisenda were happy with fatigue, for in less than a week they had crammed their rooms with money and the line of pilgrims waiting their turn to enter still reached beyond the horizon.

The angel was the only one who took no part in his own act. He spent his time trying to get comfortable in his borrowed nest, befuddled by the hellish heat of the oil lamps and sacramental candles that had been placed along the wire. At first they tried to make him eat some mothballs, which, according to the wisdom of the wise neighbor woman, were the food prescribed for angels. But he turned them down, just as he turned down the papal lunches that the penitents brought him, and they never found out whether it was because he was an angel or because he was an old man that in the end he ate nothing but eggplant mush. His only supernatural virtue seemed to be patience. Especially during the first days, when the hens pecked at him, searching for the stellar parasites that proliferated in his wings, and the cripples pulled out feathers to touch their defective parts with, and even the most merciful threw stones at him, trying to get him to rise so they could see him standing. The only time they succeeded in arousing him was when they burned his side with an iron for branding steers, for he had been motionless for so many hours that they thought he was dead. He awoke with a start, ranting in his hermetic language and with tears in his eyes, and he flapped his wings a couple of times, which brought on a whirlwind of chicken dung and lunar dust and a gale of panic that did not seem to be of this world. Although many thought that his reaction had been one not of rage but of pain, from then on they were careful not to annoy him, because the majority understood that his passivity was not that of a hero taking his ease but that of a cataclysm in repose.

Father Gonzaga held back the crowd's frivolity with formulas of maidservant inspiration while awaiting the arrival of a final judgment on the nature of the captive. But the mail from Rome showed no sense of urgency. They spent their time finding out if the prisoner had a navel, if his dialect had any connection with Aramaic, how many times he could fit on the head of a pin, or whether he wasn't just a Norwegian with wings. Those meager letters might have come and gone until the end of time if a providential event had not put an end to the priest's tribulations.

It so happened that during those days, among so many other carnival attractions, there arrived in town the traveling show of the woman who had been changed into a spider for having disobeyed her parents. The admission to see her was not only less than the admission to see the angel, but people were permitted to ask her all manner of questions about her absurd state and to examine her up and down so that no one would ever doubt the truth of her horror. She was a frightful tarantula the size of a ram and with the head of a sad maiden. What was most heartrending, however, was not her outlandish shape but the sincere affliction with which she recounted the details of her misfortune. While still practically a child she had sneaked out of her parents' house to go to a dance, and while she was coming back through the woods after having danced all night without permission, a fearful thunderclap rent the sky in two and through the crack came the lightning bolt of brimstone that changed her into a spider. Her only nourishment came from the meatballs that charitable souls chose to toss into her mouth. A spectacle like that, full of so much human truth and with such a fearful lesson, was bound to defeat without even trying that of a haughty angel who scarcely deigned to look at mortals. Besides, the few miracles attributed to the angel showed a certain mental disorder, like the blind man who didn't recover his sight but grew three new teeth, or the paralytic who didn't get to walk but almost won the lottery, and the leper whose sores sprouted sunflowers. Those consolation miracles, which were more like mocking fun, had already ruined the angel's reputation when the woman who had been changed into a spider finally crushed him completely. That was how Father Gonzaga was cured forever of his insomnia and Pelayo's courtyard went back to being as empty as during the time it had rained for three days and crabs walked through the bedrooms.

The owners of the house had no reason to lament. With the money they saved they built a two-story mansion with balconies and gardens and high netting so that crabs wouldn't get in during the winter, and with iron bars on the windows so that angels wouldn't get in. Pelayo also set up a rabbit warren close to town and gave up his job as bailiff for good, and Elisenda bought some satin pumps with high heels and many dresses of iridescent silk, the kind worn on Sunday by the most desirable women in those times. The chicken coop was the only thing that didn't receive any attention. If they washed it down with creolin and burned tears of myrrh inside it every so often, it was not in homage to the angel but to drive away the dungheap stench that still hung everywhere like a ghost and was turning the new house into an old one. At first, when the child learned to walk, they were careful that he not get too close to the chicken coop. But then they began to lose their fears and got used to the smell, and before the child got his second teeth he'd gone inside the chicken coop to play, where the wires were falling apart. The angel was no less standoffish with him than with other mortals, but he tolerated the most ingenious infamies with the patience of a dog who had no illusions. They both came down with chicken pox at the same time. The doctor who took care of the child couldn't resist the temptation to listen to the angel's heart, and he found so much whistling in the heart and so many sounds in his kidneys that it seemed impossible for him to be alive. What surprised him most, however, was the logic of his wings. They seemed so natural on that completely human organism that he couldn't understand why other men didn't have them too.

When the child began school it had been some time since the sun and rain had caused the collapse of the chicken coop. The angel went dragging himself about here and there like a stray dying man. They would drive him out of the bedroom with a broom and a moment later find him in the kitchen. He seemed to be in so many places at the same time that they grew to think that he'd been duplicated, that he was reproducing himself all through the house, and the exasperated and unhinged Elisenda shouted that it was awful living in that hell full of angels. He could scarcely eat and his antiquarian eyes had also become so foggy that he went about bumping into posts. All he had left were the bare cannulae of his last feathers. Pelayo threw a blanket over him and extended him the charity of letting him sleep in the shed, and only then did they notice that he had a temperature at night, and was delirious with the tongue twisters of an old Norwegian. That was one of the few times they became alarmed, for they thought he was going to die and not even the wise neighbor woman had been able to tell them what to do with dead angels.

And yet he not only survived his worst winter, but seemed improved with the first sunny days. He remained motionless for several days in the farthest corner of the courtyard, where no one would see him, and at the beginning of December some large, stiff feathers began to grow on his wings, the feathers of a scarecrow, which looked more like another misfortune of decrepitude. But he must have known the reason for those changes, for he was quite careful that no one should notice them, that no one should hear the sea chanteys that he sometimes sang under the stars. One morning Elisenda was cutting some bunches of onions for lunch when a wind that seemed to come from the high seas blew into the kitchen. Then she went to the window and caught the angel in his first attempts at flight. They were so clumsy that his fingernails opened a furrow in the vegetable patch and he was on the point of knocking the shed down with the ungainly flapping that slipped on the light and couldn't get a grip on the air. But he did manage to gain altitude. Elisenda let out a sigh of relief, for herself and for him, when she saw him pass over the last houses, holding himself up in some way with the risky flapping of a senile vulture. She kept watching him even when she was through cutting the onions and she kept on watching until it was no longer possible for her to see him, because then he was no longer an annoyance in her life but an imaginary dot on the horizon of the sea.

[1968]

QUESTIONS

GABRIEL GARCÍA MÁRQUEZ, *A Very Old Man with Enormous Wings*

1. What is an allegory? How is the García Márquez story an example of an allegorical tale? What was your initial response to the story?

2. How does García Márquez combine realistic detail and plot line with the fantastical and surreal?

3. The point of view of the story is offered by a third-person omniscient narrator. How does the narrator's attitude towards the townspeople shift in the course of the plot?

4. What statement might García Márquez be making given the cruel treatment of the angel by the people in the village? Were you surprised by their response? Why or why not?

5. What is the role of the priest in the story? What happens when he seeks guidance as to the meaning of the angel?

6. Why does the plot shift—spin off really—to the account of the girl changed into a spider for disobeying her parents?

7. This story is an example of what is referred to as "magical realism." Research this literary movement and explain its significance in a brief report.

8. Some critics have asserted that the angel represents the artist and an impoverishment of the imagination. Are there any signs of such conditions in our culture today? Is there reason to be cynical about the state of the imagination? Explore possible justifications for this view in a short essay. Cite pertinent examples of social or moral disorder.

Katherine Anne Porter
[1890–1980]

Now considered among the most accomplished American writers of the twentieth century, **KATHERINE ANNE PORTER** *was forty years old before her first collection of stories* (Flowering Judas) *was published. Indeed, Porter never considered writing as a profession until she met journalist Kitty Barry Crawford while recovering from tuberculosis in 1916. Following Crawford to Denver, Porter embarked on a journalism career that took her from Denver to Greenwich Village to Mexico City, where she reported on post-Civil War unrest for* The Magazine of Mexico. *It was only after she returned to New York in 1921 that she began writing fiction in earnest; her first published story* ("María Concepción"), *based on her experiences in Mexico, appeared in* Century Magazine *in 1922.*

Much of Porter's fiction is based on her own life experiences—and much of her autobiography, critics have learned, is fiction. Portraying herself as an aristocratic Southern belle, Porter was actually born on a poor farm in Indian Creek, Texas. After her mother's death when Porter was two years old, her father brought his five children to live with his mother in Kyle, Texas. Glimpses of this severe, fiercely independent woman can be seen in Porter's stories "The Jilting of Granny Weatherall"; "The Old Order"; and "Old Mortality." Her death when Porter was eleven resulted in yet another move for the family, when her father brought the children to San Antonio. The unhappy teenager excelled in drama classes (although apparently not in other subjects), and began teaching drama before marrying at sixteen. The young woman's flair for the dramatic, as well as her romantic nature, can be seen in the character of Miranda from "The Old Order"; "Old Mortality"; and "Pale Horse, Pale Rider." Like Porter, Miranda learns life lessons at the feet of a strong grandmother and, like Porter, she leaves her husband, works as a journalist, and nearly dies in the influenza pandemic of 1918. Perhaps most important, however, Miranda suffers from a chronic disillusionment with herself and those around her. Porter's own disillusionment resulted in constant motion: In addition to Mexico, Denver, and New York, she also lived in New England, Germany, France, and a number of other places in the United States. In a sporadic but critically acclaimed career, she published stories in the Southern Review *and the* Virginia Quarterly, *as well as the collections* Pale Horse, Pale Rider *(1939) and* The Leaning Tower, and Other Stories *(1944), and one novel, the best-selling* Ship of Fools *(1962), which was made into a successful feature film in 1965.*

1965 also saw publication of Porter's Collected Stories, *for which she won both the Pulitzer Prize and the National Book Award. These capped a career peppered with awards: Guggenheim and Library of Congress fellowships; Ford*

Foundation and State Department grants; honorary degrees; and writer-in-residence appointments at the University of Michigan, Stanford University, Smith College, and the University of Maryland. On her death at age ninety, critics acknowledged her as one of the great literary talents of the twentieth century. Friend and poet Robert Penn Warren, writing for the Saturday Review, *recalled a body of work that bore "the stamp of a personality distinctive, delicately perceptive, keenly aware of the depth and darkness of human experience, delighted by the . . . triumphs of human kindness and warmth, and thoroughly committed to a quest for meaning in the midst of the ironic complexities of man's lot."*

The Jilting of Granny Weatherall

KATHERINE ANNE PORTER

SHE FLICKED HER WRIST neatly out of Doctor Harry's pudgy careful fingers and pulled the sheet up to her chin. The brat ought to be in knee breeches. Doctoring around the country with spectacles on his nose! "Get along now, take your schoolbooks and go. There's nothing wrong with me."

Doctor Harry spread a warm paw like a cushion on her forehead where the forked green vein danced and made her eyelids twitch. "Now, now, be a good girl, and we'll have you up in no time."

"That's no way to speak to a woman nearly eighty years old just because she's down. I'd have you respect your elders, young man."

"Well, Missy, excuse me." Doctor Harry patted her cheek. "But I've got to warn you, haven't I? You're a marvel, but you must be careful or you're going to be good and sorry."

"Don't tell me what I'm going to be. I'm on my feet now, morally speaking. It's Cornelia. I had to go to bed to get rid of her."

Her bones felt loose, and floated around in her skin, and Doctor Harry floated like a balloon around the foot of the bed. He floated and pulled down his waistcoat and swung his glasses on a cord. "Well, stay where you are, it certainly can't hurt you."

"Get along and doctor your sick," said Granny Weatherall. "Leave a well woman alone. I'll call for you when I want you. . . . Where were you forty years ago when I pulled through milk-leg and double pneumonia? You weren't even born. Don't let Cornelia lead you on," she shouted, because Doctor Harry appeared to float up to the ceiling and out. "I pay my own bills, and I don't throw my money away on nonsense!"

She meant to wave good-by, but it was too much trouble. Her eyes closed of themselves, it was like a dark curtain drawn around the bed. The pillow rose and floated under her, pleasant as a hammock in a light wind. She listened to the leaves rustling outside the window. No, somebody was swishing newspapers: no, Cornelia and Doctor Harry were whispering together. She leaped broad awake, thinking they whispered in her ear.

"She was never like this, *never* like this!" "Well, what can we expect?" "Yes, eighty years old. . . ."

Well, and what if she was? She still had ears. It was like Cornelia to whisper around doors. She always kept things secret in such a public way. She was always being tactful and kind. Cornelia was dutiful; that was the trouble with her. Dutiful and good: "So good and dutiful," said Granny, "that I'd like to spank her." She saw herself spanking Cornelia and making a fine job of it.

"What'd you say, Mother?"

Granny felt her face tying up in hard knots.

"Can't a body think, I'd like to know?"

"I thought you might want something."

"I do. I want a lot of things. First off, go away and don't whisper."

She lay and drowsed, hoping in her sleep that the children would keep out and let her rest a minute. It had been a long day. Not that she was tired. It was always pleasant to snatch a minute now and then. There was always so much to be done, let me see: tomorrow.

Tomorrow was far away and there was nothing to trouble about. Things were finished somehow when the time came; thank God there was always a little margin over for peace: then a person could spread out the plan of life and tuck in the edges orderly. It was good to have everything clean and folded away, with the hair brushes and tonic bottles sitting straight on the white embroidered linen: the day started without fuss and the pantry shelves laid out with rows of jelly glasses and brown jugs and white stone-china jars with blue whirligigs and words painted on them: coffee, tea, sugar, ginger, cinnamon, allspice: and the bronze clock with the lion on top nicely dusted off. The dust that lion could collect in twenty-four hours! The box in the attic with all those letters tied up, well, she'd have to go through that tomorrow. All those letters—George's letters and John's letters and her letters to them both—lying around for the children to find afterwards made her uneasy. Yes, that would be tomorrow's business. No use to let them know how silly she had been once.

While she was rummaging around she found death in her mind and it felt clammy and unfamiliar. She had spent so much time preparing for death there was no need for bringing it up again. Let it take care of itself now. When she was sixty she had felt very old, finished, and went around making farewell trips to see her children and grandchildren, with a secret in her mind: This is the very last of your mother, children! Then she made her will and came down with a long fever. That was all just a notion like a lot of other things, but it was lucky too, for she had once for all got over the idea of dying for a long time. Now she couldn't be worried. She hoped she had better sense now. Her father had lived to be one hundred and two years old and had drunk a noggin of strong hot toddy on his last birthday. He told the reporters it was his daily habit, and he owed his long life to that. He had made quite a scandal and was very pleased about it. She believed she'd just plague Cornelia a little.

"Cornelia! Cornelia!" No footsteps, but a sudden hand on her cheek. "Bless you, where have you been?"

"Here, Mother."

"Well, Cornelia, I want a noggin of hot toddy."

"Are you cold, darling?"

"I'm chilly, Cornelia. Lying in bed stops the circulation. I must have told you that a thousand times."

Well, she could just hear Cornelia telling her husband that Mother was getting a little childish and they'd have to humor her. The thing that most annoyed her was that Cornelia thought she was deaf, dumb, and blind. Little hasty glances and tiny gestures tossed around her and over her head saying, "Don't cross her, let her have her way, she's eighty years old," and she sitting there as if she lived in a thin glass cage. Sometimes Granny almost made up her mind to pack up and move back to her own house where nobody could remind her every minute that she was old. Wait, wait, Cornelia, till your own children whisper behind your back!

In her day she had kept a better house and had got more work done. She wasn't too old yet for Lydia to be driving eighty miles for advice when one of the children jumped the track, and Jimmy still dropped in and talked things over: "Now, Mammy, you've a good business head, I want to know what you think of this? . . ." Old. Cornelia couldn't change the furniture around without asking. Little things, little things! They had been so sweet when they were little. Granny wished the old days were back again with the children young and everything to be done over. It had been a hard pull, but not too much for her. When she thought of all the food she had cooked, and all the clothes she had cut and sewed, and all the gardens she had made—well, the children showed it. There they were, made out of her, and they couldn't get away from that. Sometimes she wanted to see John again and point to them and say, Well, I didn't do so badly, did I? But that would have to wait. That was for tomorrow. She used to think of him as a man, but now all the children were older than their father, and he would be a child beside her if she saw him now. It seemed strange and there was something wrong in the idea. Why, he couldn't possibly recognize her. She had fenced in a hundred acres once, digging the post holes herself and clamping the wires with just a negro boy to help. That changed a woman. John would be looking for a young woman with the peaked Spanish comb in her hair and the painted fan. Digging post holes changed a woman. Riding country roads in the winter when women had their babies was another thing: sitting up nights with sick horses and sick negroes and sick children and hardly ever losing one. John, I hardly ever lost one of them! John would see that in a minute, that would be something he could understand, she wouldn't have to explain anything!

It made her feel like rolling up her sleeves and putting the whole place to rights again. No matter if Cornelia was determined to be everywhere at once, there were a great many things left undone on this place. She would start tomorrow and do them. It was good to be strong enough for everything, even if all you made melted and changed and slipped under your hands, so that by the time you finished you almost forgot what you were working for. What was it I set out to do? she asked herself intently, but she could not remember. A fog rose over the valley, she saw it marching across the creek swallowing the trees and moving up the hill like an army of ghosts. Soon it would be at the near edge of the orchard, and then it was time to go in and light the lamps. Come in, children, don't stay out in the night air.

Lighting the lamps had been beautiful. The children huddled up to her and breathed like little calves waiting at the bars in the twilight. Their eyes followed the match and watched the flame rise and settle in a blue curve, then they moved away from her. The lamp was lit, they didn't have to be scared and hang on to mother any more. Never, never, never more. God, for all my life I thank Thee. Without Thee, my God, I could never have done it. Hail, Mary, full of grace.

I want you to pick all the fruit this year and see that nothing is wasted. There's always someone who can use it. Don't let good things rot for want of using. You waste life when you waste good food. Don't let things get lost. It's bitter to lose things. Now, don't let me get to thinking, not when I am tired and taking a little nap before supper. . . .

The pillow rose about her shoulders and pressed against her heart and the memory was being squeezed out of it: oh, push down the pillow, somebody: it would smother her if she tried to hold it. Such a fresh breeze blowing and such a green day with no threats in it. But he had not come, just the same. What does a woman do when she has put on the white veil and set out the white cake for a man and he doesn't come? She tried to remember. No, I swear he never harmed me but in that. He never harmed me but in that . . . and what if he did? There was the day, the day, but a whirl of dark smoke rose and covered it, crept up and over into the bright field where everything was planted so carefully in orderly rows. That was hell, she knew hell when she saw it. For sixty years she had prayed against remembering him and against losing her soul in the deep pit of hell, and now the two things were mingled in one and the thought of him was a smoky cloud from hell that moved and crept in her head when she had just got rid of Doctor Harry and was trying to rest a minute. Wounded vanity, Ellen, said a sharp voice in the top of her mind. Don't let your wounded vanity get the upper hand of you. Plenty of girls get jilted. You were jilted, weren't you? Then stand up to it. Her eyelids wavered and let in streamers of blue-gray light like tissue paper over her eyes. She must get up and pull the shades down or she'd never sleep. She was in bed again and the shades were not down. How could that happen? Better turn over, hide from the light, sleeping in the light gave you nightmares. "Mother, how do you feel now?" and a stinging wetness on her forehead. But I don't like having my face washed in cold water!

Hapsy? George? Lydia? Jimmy? No, Cornelia, and her features were swollen and full of little puddles. "They're coming, darling, they'll all be here soon." Go wash your face, child, you look funny.

Instead of obeying, Cornelia knelt down and put her head on the pillow. She seemed to be talking but there was no sound. "Well, are you tongue-tied? Whose birthday is it? Are you going to give a party?"

Cornelia's mouth moved urgently in strange shapes. "Don't do that, you bother me, daughter."

"Oh, no, Mother. Oh, no. . . ."

Nonsense. It was strange about children. They disputed your every word. "No what, Cornelia?"

"Here's Doctor Harry."

"I won't see that boy again. He just left five minutes ago."

"That was this morning, Mother. It's night now. Here's the nurse."

"This is Doctor Harry, Mrs. Weatherall. I never saw you look so young and happy!"

"Ah, I'll never be young again—but I'd be happy if they'd let me lie in peace and get rested."

She thought she spoke up loudly, but no one answered. A warm weight on her forehead, a warm bracelet on her wrist, and a breeze went on whispering, trying to tell her something. A shuffle of leaves in the everlasting hand of God, He blew on them and they danced and rattled. "Mother, don't mind, we're going to give you a little hypodermic." "Look here, daughter, how do ants get in this bed? I saw sugar ants yesterday." Did you send for Hapsy too?

It was Hapsy she really wanted. She had to go a long way back through a great many rooms to find Hapsy standing with a baby on her arm. She seemed to herself to be Hapsy also, and the baby on Hapsy's arm was Hapsy and himself and herself, all at once, and there was no surprise in the meeting. Then Hapsy melted from within and turned flimsy as gray gauze and the baby was a gauzy shadow, and Hapsy came up close and said, "I thought you'd never come," and looked at her very searchingly and said, "You haven't changed a bit!" They leaned forward to kiss, when Cornelia began whispering from a long way off, "Oh, is there anything you want to tell me? Is there anything I can do for you?"

Yes, she had changed her mind after sixty years and she would like to see George. I want you to find George. Find him and be sure to tell him I forgot him. I want him to know I had my husband just the same and my children and my house like any other woman. A good house too and a good husband that I loved and fine children out of him. Better than I hoped for even. Tell him I was given back everything he took away and more. Oh, no, oh, God, no, there was something else besides the house and the man and the children. Oh, surely they were not all? What was it? Something not given back. . . . Her breath crowded down under her ribs and grew into a monstrous frightening shape with cutting edges; it bored up into her head, and the agony was unbelievable: Yes, John, get the Doctor now, no more talk my time has come.

When this one was born it should be the last. The last. It should have been born first, for it was the one she had truly wanted. Everything came in good time. Nothing left out, left over. She was strong, in three days she would be as well as ever. Better. A woman needed milk in her to have her full health.

"Mother, do you hear me?"

"I've been telling you—"

"Mother, Father Connolly's here."

"I went to Holy Communion only last week. Tell him I'm not so sinful as all that."

"Father just wants to speak to you."

He could speak as much as he pleased. It was like him to drop in and inquire about her soul as if it were a teething baby, and then stay on for a cup of tea and a round of cards and gossip. He always had a funny story of some sort, usually about an Irishman who made his little mistakes and confessed them, and the point lay in some absurd thing he would blurt out in the confessional showing his struggles between native piety and original sin. Granny felt easy about her soul. Cornelia, where are your manners? Give Father Connolly a chair. She had her secret comfortable understanding with a few favorite saints who cleared a straight road to God for her. All as surely signed and sealed as the papers for the new Forty Acres. Forever . . . heirs and assigns forever. Since the day the wedding cake was not cut, but thrown out and wasted. The whole bottom dropped out of the world, and there she was blind and sweating with nothing under her feet and the walls falling away. His hand had caught her under the breast, she had not fallen, there was the freshly polished floor with the green rug on it, just as before. He had cursed like a sailor's parrot and said, "I'll kill him for you." Don't lay a hand on him, for my sake leave something to God. "Now, Ellen, you must believe what I tell you. . . ."

So there was nothing, nothing to worry about any more, except sometimes in the night one of the children screamed in a nightmare, and they both hustled out shaking and hunting for the matches and calling, "There, wait a minute, here we are!" John, get the doctor now, Hapsy's time has come. But there was Hapsy standing by the bed in a white cap. "Cornelia, tell Hapsy to take off her cap. I can't see her plain."

Her eyes opened very wide and the room stood out like a picture she had seen somewhere. Dark colors with the shadows rising towards the ceiling in long angles. The tall black dresser gleamed with nothing on it but John's picture, enlarged from a little one, with John's eyes very black when they should have been blue. You never saw him, so how do you know how he looked? But the man insisted the copy was perfect, it was very rich and handsome. For a picture, yes, but it's not my husband. The table by the bed had a linen cover and a candle and a crucifix. The light was blue from Cornelia's silk lampshades. No sort of light at all, just frippery. You had to live forty years with kerosene lamps to appreciate honest electricity. She felt very strong and she saw Doctor Harry with a rosy nimbus around him.

"You look like a saint, Doctor Harry, and I vow that's as near as you'll ever come to it."

"She's saying something."

"I heard you, Cornelia. What's all this carrying-on?"

"Father Connolly's saying—"

Cornelia's voice staggered and bumped like a cart in a bad road. It rounded corners and turned back again and arrived nowhere. Granny stepped up in the cart very lightly and reached for the reins, but a man sat beside her and she knew him by his hands, driving the cart. She did not look in his face, for she knew without seeing, but looked instead down the road where the trees leaned over and bowed to each other and a thousand birds were singing a Mass. She felt like singing too, but she put her hand in the bosom of her dress and pulled out a rosary, and Father Connolly murmured Latin in a very solemn voice and tickled her feet. My God, will you stop that nonsense? I'm a married woman. What if he did run away and leave me to face the priest by myself? I found another a whole world better. I wouldn't have exchanged my husband for anybody except St. Michael himself, and you may tell him that for me with a thank you in the bargain.

Light flashed on her closed eyelids, and a deep roaring shook her. Cornelia, is that lightning? I hear thunder. There's going to be a storm. Close all the windows. Call the children in. . . . "Mother, here we are, all of us." "Is that you, Hapsy?" "Oh, no, I'm Lydia. We drove as fast as we could." Their faces drifted above her, drifted away. The rosary fell out of her hands and Lydia put it back. Jimmy tried to help, their hands fumbled together, and Granny closed two fingers around Jimmy's thumb. Beads wouldn't do, it must be something alive. She was so amazed her thoughts ran round and round. So, my dear Lord, this is my death and I wasn't even thinking about it. My children have come to see me die. But I can't, it's not time. Oh, I always hated surprises. I wanted to give Cornelia the amethyst set—Cornelia, you're to have the amethyst set, but Hapsy's to wear it when she wants, and, Doctor Harry, do shut up. Nobody sent for you. Oh, my dear Lord, do wait a minute. I meant to do something about the Forty Acres, Jimmy doesn't need it and Lydia will later on, with that worthless husband of hers. I meant to finish the altar cloth and send six bottles of wine to Sister Borgia for her dyspepsia. I want to send six bottles of wine to Sister Borgia, Father Connolly, now don't let me forget.

Cornelia's voice made short turns and tilted over and crashed. "Oh, Mother, oh, Mother, oh, Mother. . . ."

"I'm not going, Cornelia. I'm taken by surprise. I can't go."

You'll see Hapsy again. What about her? "I thought you'd never come." Granny made a long journey outward, looking for Hapsy. What if I don't find her? What then? Her heart sank down and down, there was no bottom to death, she couldn't come to the end of it. The blue light from Cornelia's lampshade drew into a tiny point in the center of her brain, it flickered and winked like an eye, quietly it fluttered and dwindled. Granny lay curled down within herself, amazed and watchful, staring at the point of light that was herself; her body was now only a deeper mass of shadow in an endless darkness and this darkness would curl around the light and swallow it up. God, give a sign!

For a second time there was no sign. Again no bridegroom and the priest in the house. She could not remember any other sorrow because this grief wiped them all away. Oh, no, there's nothing more cruel than this—I'll never forgive it. She stretched herself with a deep breath and blew out the light.

[1929]

QUESTIONS

KATHERINE ANNE PORTER, *The Jilting of Granny Weatherall*

1. At what point does it become obvious that Granny Weatherall is drifting in and out of reality? How do the observations of the doctor and her daughter help to determine reality?

2. Why does Granny keep recalling Hapsy? What can be inferred about Hapsy from this reverie?

3. When Granny wants to tell George, "I was given back everything [you] took away and more," she suddenly thinks, "Oh, no, oh, God, no, there was something else. . . . Something not given back." What is that something? How does it explain Granny's inability to forget George?

4. Granny states twice, "Digging post holes changed a woman." What is the significance of this statement? How does it help to establish the complexity of Granny's character?

5. What is the significance of Granny's obsession with order? What is the cause of this obsession, and how has it served her throughout her life?

6. Identify the points in the story when Granny refers to religion or to the priest. How significant is religion to her? How is it tied in with her other reveries, for example, about having been jilted or about lighting the lamps at night?

7. When Granny recalls the portrait of John, she remembers that it did not resemble her husband. The artist insisted that it was a perfect copy, but Ellen objected, "but it's not my husband." What is the significance of this memory? How does it relate to Granny's recollections of George and of her children?

8. What sign is Granny waiting for at her death? Why does she say, "Again no bridegroom and the priest in the house"? What can she never forgive?

9. Write a character analysis of Ellen Weatherall. Focus on the traits that become apparent through her reverie, as well as on her relationships with her husband and her children.

10. This story uses the literary technique stream of consciousness. Explain this technique and analyze its impact on the story. How would the impact have been different if Ellen Weatherall's story had been told by an objective narrator, or even from her perspective but with more clarity?

How to Read a Poem

POETRY HAS APPARENTLY BEEN a part of human life, in the form of song, dating so far back we can't really tell if any civilization ever developed without it. Certainly we have all kinds of songs from the Greeks, from the Hebrews, from Africa, from China, and from India—poetry as song is a very ancient art. In the most ancient traditions, poetic song has been associated with ceremonial occasions, as well as with ordinary life, always bringing together the potent elements of rhythm and elevated, musical or ornate language, and the human voice.

Despite the enduring nature of this art, reading poetry for many people is an utterly alien activity. The resemblance between literary writing and the way people talk is, and has never been, exact; however, the norms of contemporary drama and fiction have changed over the last century so that the resemblance is much closer. Not so for poetry. Although there is certainly a "plain style" school among contemporary poets, the features of poetry seem in some ways to be permanently different from ordinary language. Why is poetry divided into lines, and beyond that, into stanzas? Why does some poetry rhyme (and why don't all poems rhyme)? Why does it circle around overhead without settling down to say what it means?

Moreover, daily life for many is not filled with opportunities to casually make the acquaintance of poetry, unless it's in the form of popular music lyrics or, occasionally, ad slogans. So, a person such as yourself sits down with a poem. You sigh. The poem, for its part, sits sphinx-like, or so it appears to the would-be reader, you. Where, oh where, is the magic decoder ring? How will you and the poem communicate with one another?

Here are some strategies for learning to hear what the poem has to say to you. To begin, let's take Jorie Graham's "Short History of the West," a challenging poem to be sure.

Short History of the West

Tap tap.
   A blue sky. A sun and a moon in it
Peel it back.
   The angles in ranks, the *about*.
Peel it back.
   Tap tap the underneath.
Blood where the sky has opened.
   And numbers in there—god how they sing—tap tap—

and the little hammer underneath
   and a hand holding the lid true.
What are you building little man?

   What's it like, what's it for?
We're going now, you stay in there.
   Deep in, nail at a time.
We're putting this back down, down over you, you stay in there,
   and then the storyline which starts where the gold doors

fold over the grassy curtain, click,
   and then the *and so*—hair falling
down all over—and the sky on now and red sun on and the
      sunbeam,
   and the thing at the end of its reach—the girl
in the room down there, at her kitchen table,
   the last pool of light on her plate,

and how you must think of her now—tired, or free,
   or full of *feeling*—and the light she should rise
to switch on now,
   and how she will not rise.

Read it Aloud

The first thing a reader of poetry can do is give the poem voice. Why is this important—and more practically, what benefit will derive from reading the poem aloud? Lyric poems are said to work through creating the effect of a voice speaking or singing, overheard. Lending the poem your voice can help you hear that effect more fully; it can also help your ear to register differences—in the *register* of the poem's language, in its diction, in its syntax. Try pausing slightly at the ends of lines. Some poets think that such pauses—especially at the ends of lines whose syntax does not naturally end at that point—are artificial; but you can see for yourself whether the poem seems to want you to pause, or whether it appears to want you to go on.

In Graham's poem, the reader can hear, for instance, in the first stanza, the sharply interrupted lines ("Tap tap. A blue sky. A sun and moon in it."), and also how, by the end of the second stanza, the lines start to run together or enjamb— that is, they're no longer separate sentences. You can also notice, then, that because of the enjambment, the poem seems to speed up quite a bit toward the end, to have a kind of breathlessness, especially as the lines get longer.

You can do the same thing with a more traditional poem. Take, for instance, Hart Crane's sonnet "To Emily Dickinson." Here are the first five lines.

You who desired so much—in vain to ask—
Yet fed your hunger like an endless task,
Dared dignify the labor, bless the quest—
Achieved that stillness ultimately best,

Being, of all, least sought for: Emily, hear!

These lines are very even, with none of the short line/long line rhythmic interruptions of Graham's poem. You can also notice how long the poem takes to finish its first sentence. Two of the lines end in dashes, and as you read these lines, you should be able to hear how those dashes effectively postpone the moment when the poem arrives at that imperative, "Emily, hear!"

Hearing these facts about the poem by way of reading it aloud can help to prepare you for a more analytic look at the poem. It helps you get closer to the poem, and although the poem may still seem reticent, you will have approached it directly, in effect creating your own invitation to hear the poem out.

Look at The Poem on The Page

What does the poem look like? Sometimes, the look of the poem on the page can give the reader some useful information. Does the poem look like it has regular forms or sections? Does the poem occupy the whole page, or does it align itself with one margin? Are the lines mostly the same length, or do they differ quite a bit?

This can seem like a very superficial aspect of the poem, but seeing how the poem resides on its page can help you begin to assess its form. Does it look like a form you've seen before, or does it seem new or different? Why does the poem have the divisions it does? Why are the poem's lines even or uneven?

In Graham's poem, notice that the first and second stanzas have eight lines apiece, but the third stanza has just six lines, and the fourth has only four lines. This might lead you to wonder why the stanzas get shorter toward the end; you can speculate something about the closure of the poem, that perhaps a shorter stanza means a sharper or more honed conclusion. You will probably also notice that every second line is slightly indented. You can also speculate that perhaps this embodies some small expectation about how the lines will be read; perhaps the poem works in pairs of lines.

Obviously, different poems present themselves differently on the page, and thus you'll notice or predict different things, depending on which poem you're scanning. With Wallace Stevens's poem "Thirteen Ways of Looking at a Blackbird," for instance, you'll notice that the poem is written in thirteen sections, which in turn predicts that the poem can be something like a theme and its variations, or even thirteen small poems organized around the same idea—

the blackbird. You might also notice that the first four sections are either two, three, or four lines long; this might remind you of other very short verse forms, such as haiku.

Regularize The Poem

Poems can feel very elliptical to the reader—that is, it can feel like there are things missing that the reader needs to understand the poem. This means, often, that if you create your own working hypothesis about the poem, you'll be able to understand what's there to begin with. There are a lot of things a reader can do to normalize the poem: Fill in or translate the syntax so that the poem seems more like regular sentences; look up unfamiliar words in the dictionary; and try to construct a situation or frame for the poem.

Much of the syntax in Graham's poem is not particularly hard to understand in and of itself. However, it can feel like the poem leaves a lot out—any frame of reference that would help us understand the "you" and the "we" of the poem. So let's start by constructing a working situation. The poem begins with sounds, written out as words—"Tap, tap." These taps might be a polite knock on a door—that is, an indication that whoever is tapping would like entrance—or they could be the sounds of building, of construction. As we go a little further on, we see these lines: "and the little hammer underneath / and a hand holding the lid true." This seems to indicate that something is being built, and from the inside of some sort of box. The "we," then, appears to be on the outside of the box; the "you," the "little man," seems to be on the inside.

Now, what's inside the box? A sky, a sun, a moon, angels, a "grassy curtain"—perhaps a small world. If there is a man inside a small world inside a box, then who might the "we" be? We could guess that these figures are godlike—they exist outside the human world. Does this work? The "we" figures "peel back" the top of the box-world—its heavens, with sun, moon, sky—to take a look at the humans within, then decide to leave them alone to their fate. Meanwhile, the humans are building their world.

The way you can tell if the situation you've constructed is adequate to the poem is to test it against that poem. Does it raise more questions than it answers? Do you have to work too hard to make the situation fit? If so, then you will want to reconsider your tentative situation. Here, in testing the situation we have devised against the poem, we might ask, what sort of god would leave human beings to themselves and their own devices? In asking this question, you might realize that you're asking a philosophical or a theological question; that might connect with the title, "Short History of the West."

Again, if we take another look at Hart Crane's poem, we can see that this strategy of regularizing the poem can be very helpful. When Crane says, "You who desired so much—in vain to ask— / Yet fed your hunger like an endless task, / Dared dignify the labor, bless the quest— / Achieved that stillness ulti-mately best," the reader can most helpfully construct the situation as one poet, Hart Crane, speaking in direct address to another, who is dead, Emily Dickinson. And the reader might also mentally insert the pronoun *you* to help the syntax work more clearly: "You who desired so much, though it was vain for you to ask, yet you fed hunger like an endless task. You dared to dignify the labor, you dared to bless the quest. You achieved that stillness that was ulti-mately best." Mentally regularizing the grammar helps the reader do two things: It helps you to understand the basic meaning of the poem, but it also helps you to see and appreciate the great compression and spareness of poetry.

Take Into Account The Poem's Anomalies
Anomalies are the things that seem odd, or that don't fit. Here, the poem has several words or phrases that are italicized: "the *about*," "and then the *and so*," and "full of *feelings*." What is Graham doing when she inserts these italics? You might not be able to answer this question, either immediately or perhaps ever; but raising the question can help you to see what the poem's project is, what it is concerned with. Here, you might surmise that the first two itali-cized words/phrases have something to do with storytelling—a story is *about* something; we use the phrase *and so* to suggest narrative movement and per-haps narrative causation (*and so* that led to this next thing). If this is so, then perhaps there is a connection with "the storyline which starts where the gold doors / fold over the grassy curtain, click."

Reading poems can be demanding work. A reader of Graham's poem can feel that the poet left blank places that the reader must fill in with conjecture. Other poets can give the reader the feeling of a great density of language, which is hard to decipher. And sometimes a whole poem can feel anomalous—that is, the whole arrangement of language, the situation, can feel quite different from what the reader has come to expect from written texts. When Wallace Stevens says, in "The Emperor of Ice-Cream," "Call the roller of big cigars, / The mus-cular one, and bid him whip / In kitchen cups concupiscent curds. / Let the wenches dawdle in such dress / As they are used to wear," the reader can feel, frankly, flummoxed. On the one hand, what situation calls for "the roller of big cigars"? On the other hand, who calls women "wenches," or says so grandly, "Let [them] dawdle in such dress / As they are used to wear"? When you're con-fronted with such anomalies, one strategy is to surmise that the speaker's odd-ness must be part of the point of the poem. The poem might be inventing deliberately unfamiliar language to draw attention to a common situation by making it feel uncommon. In any case, even identifying that the language is odd or anomalous can be helpful in assessing the poem and its project.

Now that you've done the work of trying to fill in some blanks, you can look at the more traditional elements of the poem: its **sounds**, its **figures**, and its **rhythms**. When we read poems for their sounds, we look for rhymes, of course, but also for other ways that the poem might contain densities and echoes of sound. We can see in Graham's poem, for instance, that although she doesn't use any end rhymes, she does use other repetitions, both exact repetitions, but also sound-echoes. Here's a passage:

> and the little hammer underneath
>   and a hand holding the lid true.
> What are you building little man?
>
>   What's it like, what's it for?
> We're going now, you stay in there.
>   Deep in, nail at a time.
> We're putting this back down, down over you, you stay in there,
>   and then the storyline which starts where the gold doors
>   . . .

In the first two lines, you can see the repetition of the *h* sound (*h*ammer, *h*and *h*olding) and also of the *l* sound in the first three lines—*l*ittle, *l*id, and *l*ike; you can also see, within the words, the repetition of the *d* sound (han*d* hol*d*ing the li*d*). Moreover, there are repetitions of words: *What* at the beginning of lines three and four, as well as within line four, and with that, also the repetition of the *wh/w* sound, including the "*We*'re" at the beginning of lines five and seven. And look at line seven: You have the repetition of "down, down" and "you, you." So, without any rhymes, you have a passage that is dense with the repetition of sound. You might want to think about what the effect of all these echoing and repetition is on you as the reader.

When we speak of figurative language, we mean its metaphors (and other related figures of speech). We've already started to account for some of them—the world figured as a box or other kind of lidded container, for instance; the human search for meaning figured as a kind of construction, perhaps. We might also look at figures such as those that occur at the end of the poem, after the lid has been put back on the box, and "the sky on now and the red sun on and the sunbeam, / and the thing at the end of its reach—the girl." The "red sun" probably signifies the sun at the end of the day. This is an image, certainly, but might also be metaphoric—we often think of the end of the day as a metaphor for the end of something else—a life, often, or perhaps of a way of life. Light itself has a long tradition as a metaphor for knowledge.

Putting these metaphors together might help us focus even further our sense of the poem's subject and what it might want to say to us.

Nearly every literature student learns something about how to ascertain the rhythmic pattern of a poem. Often, when you're working with a traditional poem, one whose meter is more or less regular, you can assign an appropriate name for that meter. In poems like this one, however, you won't be able to do that—the lines are too irregular. It can nonetheless be useful to try to understand where the stresses fall in the lines, and how the poem works with stresses to create an overall sense of the poem for the reader. Here's a passage:

> Tap tap.
>   A blue sky. A sun and a moon in it.
> Peel it back.
>   The angles in ranks, the *about*.
> Peel it back.
>   Tap tap the underneath.
> Blood where the sky has opened.
>   And numbers in there—god how they sing—tap tap—

If we try to hear where the stresses fall in these lines, it might go something like this (with stressed syllables in caps):

Tap TAP. / a BLUE SKY. a SUN and a MOON in it. / PEEL it BACK. / The ANgels in RANKS, the aBOUT. / PEEL it BACK. / Tap TAP the underNEATH. / BLOOD where the SKY has Opened. / And NUMbers there—GOD how they SING—tap TAP

The first line has one strong stress; the second has four; the third (and fifth) have two; the fourth has three; the sixth has two; the seventh has three; the eighth has four. This all looks pretty uneven, with no pattern. You might, however, notice that the shorter lines tend to end with a stressed syllable. This might mean that those short lines, which already seem to punctuate and sharpen the poem, are even more emphatic, as they end with those accented syllables. You could see if this is true throughout the poem. For instance, in the last stanza, note how three of the four lines end with an accented syllable. This might help to close the poem with a stronger feeling of finality.

Different poets and different poems work differently with sound, figure, and rhythm, which are the great resources of poetry. As a brief example to contrast with Graham's poem, you might look at Seamus Heaney's "Digging." Here's a stanza that occurs near the end of the poem:

> The cold smell of potato mould, the squelch and slap
> Of soggy peat, the curt cuts of an edge
> Through living roots awaken in my head.
> But I've no spade to follow men like them.

Here, you have words like "squelch" and "slap," which have an almost physical effect on the reader, with their wet sounds; the alliterations of "curt cuts," with the effect of doubling the echo effect because of the repetition of the *t* sound at the ends of both word; and the slant rhymes of "edge," "head," and "them." Notice the way the first line in this stanza has twelve syllables, whereas the remaining three have ten apiece, which fall into a fairly predictable iambic pattern. And, in the context of the rest of the poem, you see how this representation of the work of his father contrasts with his own kind of work, and understand that the pen—the implement of writing—becomes metaphorically analogous to a spade, implement of digging. In any poem, looking closely at the language for its sounds, rhythms, and metaphors helps you to get closest of all to the ways poems work.

This is how to read poetry. You try to hear it, understand its sounds and the patterns of sound; you try to understand its overall scene, what is implied by its minimal furnishings; you try to understand its figurative language, what turns of thought the poem ventures. At each turn you find yourself with new questions, rather than straightforward answers. Experienced readers of poetry say that the questions are part of the pleasure of reading poetry. As you read more poetry, you'll acquire a wider repertoire of reading strategies, and your enjoyment will also increase.

One last bit of advice: Find a poem you like and learn it, at least some of it, by heart. Recite it to yourself. Your comfort with poetic language will grow as you live with just one poem. You can add a new poem when you feel the old one needs company.

Robert Frost
[1874–1963]

The son of a journalist who died when **ROBERT FROST** *was only eleven, the now well-known poet lived with his mother in Lawrence, Massachusetts, where he worked at many jobs while finishing high school, where he was co-valedictorian of his class. While in school, he wrote for the* Lawrence High School Bulletin. *He married his co-valedictorian, Elinor White, and began his college career. Frost attended Dartmouth and Harvard, but dropped out of both shortly before the deaths of his three-year-old son and his mother. In search of financial stability, Frost bought a farm in Derry, New Hampshire, where he and Elinor had four more children while he wrote poetry and taught at the Pinkerton Academy. His first book,* A Boy's Will *appeared in 1913. Frost then sold the farm and moved his family to London where he met Ezra Pound who viewed Frost as a follower and composer of "Imagist" poems—poems of vivid pictoral language and minimal sentiment. However, Frost developed his own theory of the sound of poetry, that is, catching the word as it is heard and spoken. His* North of Boston *(1914) poems characterize his particular view of the purpose and practice of poetry. These poems use dramatic monologues to capture the realities of human life and words.*

Frost returned to the United States in 1915 and bought another farm in New Hampshire, but this time he was not dependent on farm income and minimal teaching. While in Europe, Frost had become friends with powerful editors and publishers, including Ellery Sedgwick editor of the Atlantic Monthly *and Henry Holt of the* New Republic. *He also became friends with the powerful poet and critic Louis Untermeyer. Frost taught at Amherst College and published his third book,* Mountain Interval *(1916). His fourth book,* New Hampshire, *won the Pulitzer Prize, followed by* West-Running Brook *in 1928, and* Collected Poems *in 1930, which won a second Pulitzer. Frost refused to join the political literary movements of the thirties but chose to write another personal and individual book,* A Further Range *(1936), which the critics attacked for lack of social relevance. In spite of its critics, the book also won a Pulitzer. In the late thirties, he suffered the deaths of two children and his wife, and he collapsed for a time. By 1942, however, he completed* A Witness Tree, *winner of yet another Pulitzer. This book was followed by* The Steeple Bush *in 1947 and* In the Clearing *in 1962. Frost spoke to the nation by reading "The Gift Outright" at President Kennedy's inauguration in 1961. He died two years later, a poet whose characters questioned their own comfortable assumptions about the world. With many well-wrought poems that demonstrate effective revisions of years of working and reworking, Frost was above all a craftsman.*

Stopping by Woods on a Snowy Evening

ROBERT FROST

Whose woods these are I think I know.
His house is in the village though;
He will not see me stopping here
To watch his woods fill up with snow.

My little horse must think it queer   5
To stop without a farmhouse near
Between the woods and frozen lake
The darkest evening of the year.

He gives his harness bells a shake
To ask if there is some mistake.   10
The only other sound's the sweep
Of easy wind and downy flake.

The woods are lovely, dark and deep,
But I have promises to keep,
And miles to go before I sleep,   15
And miles to go before I sleep.

[1923]

QUESTIONS

ROBERT FROST, *Stopping by Woods on a Snowy Evening*

1. This poem is famous in many ways, because it asks questions about life and death. What does snow seem to represent here?

2. The poet is lost in musing about death and life, but the horse is having none of it. What does the horse do for the narrator?

3. Everyone has "miles to go" every day, and sometimes the road is not easy. Why should we not end our lives? What lines in Frost's poem suggest his opinion on the subject?

4. The horse's body is life and warmth for the man, as well as company. A cowboy saying is that there is nothing so good for the inside of a man as the outside of a horse. How does Frost personify the horse in this poem? What is the effect of this poetic technique?

5. The quatrains in this poem link with an aaba, bbcb, ccdc pattern until the end when the pattern is dddd, not an easy rhyme to write. How does the repetition of the *eep* sound help to settle the poem's statement about life?

6. How do the words "lovely, dark, and deep" work together to suggest the temptations in the poem?

7. Psychologists sometimes describe moments of despair or sadness as "going into the woods" to discover something about ourselves. In this poem the poet discovers that he has obligations that will keep him alive and working for many years to come. Talk to older friends or family members about how they made it through rough times in their lives. Write about their trials and their solutions and triumphs.

Emily Dickinson
[1830–1886]

Born to an Amherst, Massachusetts, family in the early Victorian era, EMILY DICKINSON has been analyzed and reanalyzed for nearly two hundred years. She was one of three children of Edward and Emily Norcross Dickinson. Both her parents encouraged her education, sending her to Amherst Academy and Mount Holyoke Female Seminary, which she attended until her homesickness sent her home to stay. Her father served a term in Congress, giving Dickinson the opportunity to visit Washington, D.C. briefly, and an eye problem sent her to Boston to stay with cousins during treatment. Otherwise, she spent nearly all her life in Amherst. Her brother, Austin, was a justice of the peace and then succeeded his father as treasurer of Amherst College, while her sister Lavinia (Vinnie) led a lively social life in the town. Neither Emily or Vinnie married, both living in the family home, called the Evergreens, until their deaths.

Dickinson has often been described as a reclusive poet whose fame came only after her death, but she actually lived an exciting life of the mind, corresponding with many of the poets and intellectuals of her day and discussing world events and poetry with friends and family in the rich intellectual circle surrounding the family. Austin married Susan Gilbert and built a stately house, the Homestead, next door to the Evergreens. Emily and Susan became close friends and writing collaborators, Susan reading and responding to Dickinson's poems throughout their lives. Dickinson also exchanged correspondence with Samuel Bowles, editor of the Springfield Republican; Josiah Holland, editor at Scribner's publishing company; poet and novelist Helen Hunt Jackson; and Thomas Wentworth Higginson, poet and critic. She lived the life of a private intellectual whose letters recount a rich life of the mind.

Dickinson wrote throughout her life, but dating her poems can be done only through analysis of her handwriting and though analysis of booklets of her poems she called fascicles. Also, references to current events sometimes give clues to the timing of her writing. For example, her most productive time seems to have been from 1858 to 1865 when the Civil War provided her with both motivation and topic for many a poem. Some have noted that she wrote about death and sadness, but these Civil War poems clearly reflect the tragic times through which she lived. She continued to produce poetry until her death, completing over 1,800 poems. In 1890, after her death, a family friend, Mabel Loomis Todd, and Higginson published Poems, followed by a second volume in 1890, and a third in 1896. No other editors saw her manuscripts until Ralph W. Franklin was given access to them and produced a version, Poems in 1998, which followed her particular punctuation *and spelling patterns. These patterns give her poetry an extremely postmodern feel and flavor, for Dickinson was experimental in a variety of ways, using complex ideas in simple styles and creating new metaphors that challenge and intrigue readers as much in this century as in the last.*

Because I could not stop for Death–

EMILY DICKINSON

Because I could not stop for Death–
He kindly stopped for me–
The Carriage held but just Ourselves–
And Immortality.

We slowly drove–He knew no haste   5
And I had put away
My labor and my leisure too,
For His Civility–

We passed the School, where Children strove
At Recess–in the Ring–   10
We passed the Fields of Gazing Grain–
We passed the Setting Sun–

Or rather–He passed Us–
The Dews drew quivering and Chill–
For only Gossamer, my Gown–   15
My Tippet–only Tulle–[1]

We paused before a House that seemed
A Swelling of the Ground–
The Roof was scarcely visible–
The Cornice–in the Ground–   20

Since then–'tis Centuries–and yet
Feels shorter than the Day
I first surmised the Horses' Heads
Were toward Eternity–

[c. 1862]

---

[1]A tippet is a cape, and tulle is fine, filmy material.

QUESTIONS

EMILY DICKINSON, *Because I could not stop for Death–*

1. Death is compared to a carriage driver who picks up the speaker in a carriage. What route does the carriage take, and what is its destination?

2. What has time become for the speaker? What does it mean that the horse's heads were "turned toward Eternity"?

3. The speaker accepts death calmly. What view of the afterlife is presented in this poem? Is it a comforting view?

4. Some writers have speculated that people who live in small towns or in the country live closer to life and death, closer to nature. Are country people better able to deal with the reality of death? Why might this be?

5. Many of Dickinson's poems could be sung as hymns. Try singing this poem or at least reading it aloud. What is the effect of the lilting tone of the words? How does it blend with the meaning of the poem?

6. The poem begins with Death and ends with Eternity. These are both grand concepts. How does framing the poem this way link the death and the afterlife?

7. Visit an old cemetery. Read the tomb stones and then write about the lives of the people who are buried in the tombs.

8. Walk through a familiar place, and write down a description as you might see it if you were a ghost wandering through the town. What is precious? What would be best remembered? Write a description of what you see and think.

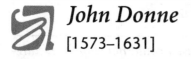

John Donne
[1573–1631]

The son of a wealthy London merchant and a noblewoman, a relative of Sir Thomas More, JOHN DONNE began life with great advantage. He attended both Cambridge and Oxford and studied law. His father's death when he was nearing twenty left him a wealthy and independent young man. Donne is a fascinating study for he displays many features of the early modern period that coincide with the writing of Shakespeare's plays. He was both a wild young man about town, and a serious religious writer who struggled with the conflicts between his early Catholicism and the Anglicanism that blew in on the winds of change, dominating England throughout the first decade of the 1600s. By the time he was twenty, he had finished the poems in his Divine Poems *as well as the first three poems in his* Satires. *By 1594 he wandered through Europe and by 1596 and 1597, he had served as a soldier in Cadiz and traveled to the Azores. In addition, his travels to Italy and Spain introduced him to the excitement of the literary and artistic Renaissance that swept through the south of Europe. Upon his return to London, he secretly married the daughter of Sir George Moore, lord lieutenant of the Tower of London, an act for which he was thrown in prison by his outraged father-in-law. Sir Francis Wooley rescued him and provided a home for the couple. The poetry he wrote to his wife is among the most treasured of personal writing from husband to wife. He finished his* Satires *and* The Progress of the Soul *during this time (1601). He also wrote a defense of suicide,* Biathanatos, *which was not published until after his death.*

Donne then embarked on a mental and spiritual struggle that brought him to take holy orders in the Anglican Church in 1611. He wrote prose against Catholicism, Pseudo-Martyr *(1610) and* Ignatius His Conclave *(1611), as well as his great mystical treatise,* The Anatomy of the World. *He was a favorite preacher of King James I and was appointed the Dean of St. Paul's Cathedral in 1621, a post he held until his death. His collected poems were printed in 1633, but his prose works, including his* Letters *and more than 150* Sermons *were published in assorted venues from 1633 to 1651.*

Donne displayed a range of intellectual and poetic talents as well as a multitude of personal faces. Thus he is remembered and admired as one of the great poets and thinkers of his own era and of the twentieth century as well. Donne has been appreciated for his conceits, his satire, his profound mysticism, and his political insight. Few poets have been so complete and so essentially paradoxical as John Donne.

Batter my heart, three-personed God, for You

JOHN DONNE

Batter my heart, three-personed God, for You
As yet but knock, breathe, shine, and seek to mend.
That I may rise and stand, o'erthrow me, and bend
Your force to break, blow, burn, and make me new.
I, like an usurped town to another due,   5
Labor to admit You, but Oh! to no end.
Reason, Your viceroy in me, me should defend,
But is captived, and proves weak or untrue.
Yet dearly I love You, and would be lovèd fain,
But am betrothed unto Your enemy;   10
Divorce me, untie or break that knot again;
Take me to You, imprison me, for I,
Except You enthrall me, never shall be free,
Nor ever chaste, except You ravish me.

[C. 1610]

Published 1635 in *Poems*.

QUESTIONS

JOHN DONNE, *Batter my heart, three-personed God, for You*

1. God's love is compared to a battering ram forcing itself into the poet's heart and then finally compared to a ravisher. What kinds of images are these for a religious poem? Read through the argument carefully to understand how the speaker uses such images to make a seemingly contradictory argument.

2. This Petrarchan sonnet follows a demanding rhyme scheme, abbaab-bacdcdccc, not an easy task in English (sonnets were easier to write in Italian in which many words end in vowels; English is far less accommodating). How do these rhyme schemes tie together the form of the argument?

3. Interview a person you think of as very religious (in a good way). Ask about the ways in which the person came to his or her feelings and convictions. Then write about what you learn, analyzing your own response to the experience of the interview.

A Valediction: Forbidding Mourning

JOHN DONNE

As virtuous men pass mildly away,
And whisper to their souls to go,
Whilst some of their sad friends do say
The breath goes now, and some say no:

So let us melt, and make no noise,   5
No tear-floods, nor sigh-tempests move;
'Twere profanation of our joys
To tell the laity[1] our love.

Moving of th' earth brings harms and fears;
Men reckon what it did and meant;   10
But trepidation of the spheres,
Though greater far, is innocent.

Dull sublunary lovers' love
(Whose soul is sense) cannot admit
Absence, because it doth remove   15
Those things which elemented[2] it.

But we, by a love so much refined
That ourselves know not what it is,
Inter-assurèd of the mind,
Care less, eyes, lips, and hands to miss.   20

Our two souls, therefore, which are one,
Though I must go, endure not yet

----

[1]Those not ordained.

[2]From which it was made.

Published 1635 in *Poems*.

A breach, but an expansiòn,
Like gold to airy thinness beat.

If they be two, they are two so   25
As stiff twin compasses are two:
Thy soul, the fixed foot, makes no show
To move, but doth, if th' other do.

And though it in the center sit,
Yet when the other far doth roam,   30
It leans and harkens after it,
And grows erect as that comes home.

Such wilt thou be to me, who must,
Like th' other foot, obliquely run;
Thy firmness makes my circle just,   35
And makes me end where I begun.

[1611]

QUESTIONS

JOHN DONNE, *A Valediction: Forbidding Mourning*

1. This poem has two conceits, or complex comparisons, that express the feelings of the speaker. He is leaving on a trip but bids his wife not to worry for their love is not just of the body but of the spirit. How does he explain this idea?

2. He compares his departure to that of a draftsman's compass with a center and a moving arm. How is his leaving like the moving arm?

3. Parting is always sweet sorrow, but there are many ways of saying good-bye. Why is the method chosen in this poem effective?

4. Great love between long married partners always draws admiration. In what ways does this poem draw that admiration from the reader?

5. In simple measured quatrains, the poet forms rhymes that drive the poem from argument to argument. How does this form facilitate the reading of the sometimes difficult ideas?

6. The poem turns at line twenty when the speaker dismisses the importance of the physical and turns to the power of the spiritual. The argument has powerful logic. Do you think that his wife was persuaded?

7. Construct an argument that rests on the "if this, then that" basis of the argument in this poem. Try to use comparisons to illustrate your points as well.

8. The divorce rate is quite high in the United States. Look at the statistics on who divorces. If you can find data on church attendance, note the effect of "spiritual" connections on relationships. Do those who share religions tend to have stronger commitments? Write about this data and its implications for courtship.

The Sun Rising

JOHN DONNE

Busy old fool, unruly sun,
Why dost thou thus,
Through windows, and through curtains, call on us?
Must to thy motions lovers' seasons run?
Saucy pedantic wretch, go chide   5
Late schoolboys, and sour prentices,
Go tell court-huntsmen that the king will ride,
Call country ants[1] to harvest offices;
Love, all alike, no season knows, nor clime,
Nor hours, days, months, which are the rags of time.   10

Thy beams, so reverend and strong
Why shouldst thou think?
I could eclipse and cloud them with a wink,
But that I would not lose her sight so long:
If her eyes have not blinded thine,   15
Look, and tomorrow late, tell me
Whether both the Indias[2] of spice and mine
Be where thou left'st them, or lie here with me.
Ask for those kings whom thou saw'st yesterday,
And thou shalt hear, all here in one bed lay.   20

She is all states, and all princes I,
Nothing else is.
Princes do but play us; compared to this,
All honor's mimic, all wealth alchemy.
Thou, sun, art half as happy as we,   25

---

[1]Farm workers

[2]East and West Indies.

Published 1635 in *Poems*.

In that the world's contracted thus;
Thine age asks ease, and since thy duties be
To warm the world, that's done in warming us.
Shine here to us, and thou art every where;
This bed thy center[3] is, these walls thy sphere.   *30*

[c. 1633]

---

[3]Of orbit

QUESTIONS

JOHN DONNE, *The Sun Rising*

1. The speaker is having a wonderful time chiding the sun for shedding its morning light on him and his lady love. He argues that when the sun shines on them, it shines on all the world, because they are the only world to one another. Is the sun likely to pay attention to the speaker? Why does this fact make the poem amusing?

2. Lovers ignore the world in order to be with one another. How does this poem illustrate the feelings of lovers when the world dares to intrude?

3. Each stanza of this poem has its own mini-argument. Why does the speaker say that the sun is not so powerful because he can make the sun go away with a wink? Why does he not want to wink? Why finally would everyone like to be these lovers, according to the speaker?

4. Write about a great love story such as that of Romeo and Juliet or Anthony and Cleopatra. What attitude did these lovers have toward the rest of the world? What was the result?

Gerard Manley Hopkins
[1844–1889]

GERARD MANLEY HOPKINS *was educated by his family to become a prelate in the Church of England. He was sent to the best schools and cut a figure as the "Star of Balliol" at Oxford. He seemed to be in line to become a famous leader of the English Church; then in 1866 he came under the influence of the great Roman Catholic thinker, Cardinal John Henry Newman. Hopkins converted to the Roman church and was accepted into the Society of Jesus in 1868, much to the surprise and amazement of his friends and colleagues. He burned the writing that he had done up to that time and gave up writing for seven years. He became a missionary to the slums of Liverpool where he was saddened and shocked by the conditions in which the poor of the city lived. Eventually, he moved on to a church in Dublin and then in 1884 he was appointed professor of classics at the Catholic University College, Dublin. This was the time of great unrest in Ireland. Charles Stewart Parnell was leading the national movement toward self-government and the country was still recovering from the Famine (1844–1847) and the loss of population due to deaths and emigration. Thus Hopkins found Dublin depressing and joyless. His time in Ireland was short for he contracted typhoid fever and died in 1889. He is buried in the Jesuit plot, Glasnevin cemetery, Dublin.*

Hopkins produced many complex and challenging poems that used what he called "Sprung Rhythm," a form that used one to four syllables with the stress always on the first syllable. The purpose of this form was to make the poetry flow easily from one line to another and to increase the music of the lines. None of this poetry, however, appeared for the public during Hopkins's lifetime nor for a very long time thereafter. Father Hopkins left his poetic legacy in the hands of his good friend Robert Bridges who felt that the Victorian public was not ready for the poetic tricks and verbal eccentricities of Hopkins's poetry. Bridges therefore kept the poems from publication for thirty or more years until 1918 when the poetic winds had shifted. At that time the poems were published to great praise by the postwar poets whose work resembled that of the long-since departed Hopkins. Suddenly, the work that would have been too obscure and too convoluted for readers was current and lively. Hopkins became a celebrated and appreciated poet in a world that he himself would not have known nor understood.

God's Grandeur

GERARD MANLEY HOPKINS

THE world is charged with the grandeur of God.
    It will flame out, like shining from shook foil;
    It gathers to a greatness, like the ooze of oil
Crushed. Why do men then now not reck his rod?
Generations have trod, have trod, have trod;   5
    And all is seared with trade; bleared, smeared with toil;
    And wears man's smudge and shares man's smell: the soil
Is bare now, nor can foot feel, being shod.

And for all this, nature is never spent;
    There lives the dearest freshness deep down things;   10
And though the last lights off the black West went
    Oh, morning, at the brown brink eastward, springs—
Because the Holy Ghost over the bent
    World broods with warm breast and with ah! bright wings.

[1877]

Composed in 1877, and collected in *The Later Poetic Manuscripts of Gerard Manley Hopkins in Facsimile* in 1918.

QUESTIONS

GERARD MANLEY HOPKINS, *God's Grandeur*

1. This poem expresses the power of God through nature. What does the speaker suggest of how God can been seen in nature?

2. This poem expresses the kinds of vivid images that sometimes appear in the visions in the Bible, visions where prophets see bright vivid images and lights. How do these images affect the contemporary reader?

3. This sonnet demonstrates the interesting rhythms that Hopkins uses in his poetry. Notice the ways that the words sound in the poem. How do the rhymes emphasize the interesting variations in the poem?

4. Describe a scene that strikes you as particularly vivid and meaningful. Explain to your reader why the scene is important to you. Be as specific as possible as you create both the scene and your reasons.

Matthew Arnold
[1822–1888]

MATTHEW ARNOLD *was born in a small town outside of London, Laleham on Themes. His family moved to Rugby School where his father, Thomas Arnold, was headmaster and where Arnold received his early education. He matriculated at Balliol College, Oxford, in 1841 where his poem "Cromwell, A Prize Poem" won a poetry award. He was a lively youth in college, sometimes thought by his friends to be less than serious, an unlikely beginning for a poet and critic who was to become known for his weighty thought. He even managed to graduate with less than top honors. He moved to Paris where he met female author George Sand, and his close friend the poet Arthur Clough, and tasted the sophisticated life of the Paris literary elite. In 1847 he became Lord Lansdowne's secretarial assistant, a post that gave him financial advantages, and in 1951 he received an appointment as school inspector, a post that allowed him enough funds to marry Frances Wightman, a prominent judge's daughter. In 1847 he published* The Tragic Reveler and Other Poems *and in 1852* Empedocles on Etna and Other Poems. *Both books lacked literary acclaim and soon disappeared from the scene, but the preface to the latter—with affinities to Greek thought, Goethe's romanticism, and the ideas of Wordsworth—began his career as a critic. Two volumes of poetry,* Poems: A New Edition *(1853–1854) and* New Poems *(1867) established him as a poet. In 1857 he was appointed at Oxford as professor of poetry where he wrote and published* Essays on Criticism *(1865, 1888) and* Culture and Anarchy *(1869). These essays reflect his ideas about romanticism and about those he called Philistines (those who do not appreciate fine art and fine literature, a concept he adopted from Scottish philosopher and critic Thomas Carlisle). At this point he turned to theology in* Literature and Dogma *(1872) and with* Last Essay on Church and Religion *(1877). His theology argued for the existence of a God who seemed to give his creatures more questions than answers. These ideas met with some resistance by his peers.*

In 1883 he received a pension and was able to leave teaching and the university life to become a man of leisure and to travel and lecture widely throughout Europe and America, where he lectured as far west as St. Louis. He wrote Discourses in America, *the book for which he said he would most like to be remembered. His daughter married an American, so he traveled back to America with some frequency. He died, during one of her visits to England, as he ran for a tram car. He is remembered for embodying the Romantic tradition that characterized the last part of the Victorian era and for his dark vision of the century to come.*

Dover Beach

MATTHEW ARNOLD

The sea is calm to-night.
The tide is full, the moon lies fair
Upon the straits;—on the French coast the light
Gleams and is gone; the cliffs of England stand,
Glimmering and vast, out in the tranquil bay.   *5*
Come to the window, sweet is the night-air!

Only, from the long line of spray
Where the sea meets the moon-blanch'd land,
Listen! you hear the grating roar
Of pebbles which the waves draw back, and fling,   *10*
At their return, up the high strand,
Begin, and cease, and then again begin,
With tremulous cadence slow, and bring
The eternal note of sadness in.

Sophocles long ago   *15*
Heard it on the Aegean, and it brought
Into his mind the turbid ebb and flow
Of human misery; we
Find also in the sound a thought,
Hearing it by this distant northern sea.   *20*

The Sea of Faith
Was once, too, at the full, and round earth's shore
Lay like the folds of a bright girdle furl'd.
But now I only hear
Its melancholy, long, withdrawing roar,   *25*
Retreating, to the breath
Of the night-wind, down the vast edges drear
And naked shingles of the world.

First published in *New Poems* in 1867.

Ah, love, let us be true
To one another! for the world, which seems   30
To lie before us like a land of dreams,
So various, so beautiful, so new,
Hath really neither joy, nor love, nor light,
Nor certitude, nor peace, nor help for pain;
And we are here as on a darkling plain   35
Swept with confused alarms of struggle and flight,
Where ignorant armies clash by night.

[1867]

QUESTIONS

MATTHEW ARNOLD, *Dover Beach*

1. What is the setting for the poem? Why does the sea evoke such sadness in the speaker of the poem? The speaker talks to a lover. What are the requests at the beginning and end of the poem?

2. What is the Sea of Faith? What does the speaker say about the nature of faith in the modern world? Why has it ebbed?

3. Who are the armies? Do we know? Are there always armies clashing somewhere?

4. Lovers usually feel that they are alone against the world, especially young lovers. How does the poem express this feeling of isolation?

5. The end of the nineteenth century hinted at the devastation to come in the twentieth century. How does this poem express that anticipation of conflict?

6. Scientists say that all humans came from the sea and long to return. How does the poem play with that idea?

7. This poem follows no particular metric form or rhyme pattern, yet it leans heavily on the use of rhymes and sounds. Look at the vowel sounds at the ends of lines in each stanza. Note that they are the same in the stanzas. What does each collection of sounds do to carry the meaning of the poem, especially the last rhyme of *fight* and *night*?

8. Note that the poem itself ebbs and flows like the waves and that the sound moves as waves move. How does this motion affect the reading of the poem?

9. Why is "Sea of Faith" in the middle of the poem capitalized? Can you propose some reasons why this might be?

10. Describe a moment you spent alone with someone who is significant to you. Let the reader understand the ideas that were communicated in that moment.

11. Research the end of the nineteenth century. Then write about the kinds of attitudes and energies that were expressed at that time, especially the rise of nationalism and threats of war.

12. Compare a place that you enjoy, as Arnold does the cliffs at Dover, with some social or political event in the world.

William Shakespeare
[1564–1616]

WILLIAM SHAKESPEARE *was born in Stratford-upon-Avon, the son of a glove-maker and wool dealer. Though his father, John, held some status in the city, at some point the family lost its position and thus, though his eldest son William attended Stratford Grammar School and may have had hopes of attending university, he did not. When Shakespeare was eighteen years old, he married Anne Hathaway and had three children before his twenty-first birthday. By the early 1590s he was established in London as an actor and a playwright, as well as the part-owner and manager of a theater company. He was a prolific writer, having written (or, in a couple of cases, co-written) at the time of his death thirty-eight plays and several volumes of poetry—*The Sonnets *(1609),* Venus and Adonis *(1593), and* The Rape of Lucrece *(1593).*

Perhaps the most pored-over of all authors, Shakespeare fascinates in part because of the lack of detail known about his life. However, a good deal is discernable about the social milieu surrounding his life and work. By the time Shakespeare emerged as an actor and a playwright in the theater scene in London of the early 1590s, he must have spent some time as an apprentice actor, and tried his hand at playwriting. Theater-going at that time spanned all social classes. His earliest plays draw heavily on classical sources and models, suggesting something about his early education. Playwriting at that time was probably considered more a professional skill than an art. When theaters were shut down because of the plague (1592–1593), he wrote his narrative poems, probably dedicated to the Earl of Southampton, a patron. When Shakespeare retired to Stratford-upon-Avon, he had seen to the publication of the poems, though not his plays. Plays at that time were written for a fee, with the rights retained by production companies. Shakespeare owned a share of the theater company, which had Lord Chamberlain as its patron and was under the royal sponsorship of King James. The company built the Globe Theater, where many of the plays were produced. He was buried in the same parish church where he was baptized. Not until seven years after his death were most of the plays collected and published by two of his partners.

The sonnets have a special place in the Shakespeare oeuvre. They are still considered models of the form, and are part of a vibrant sonnet-writing tradition in the Renaissance. The kind of sonnet Shakespeare—and other Renaissance writers such as Sir Thomas Wyatt, Henry Howard, Earl of Surrey, Edmund Spenser, and Sir Philip Sidney—wrote is often called the Elizabethan or Shakespearean sonnet. Differing from the Italian or Petrarchan sonnet, the

Elizabethan sonnet was organized in quatrains, with a concluding couplet. (The Petrarchan sonnet had an octave and a sestet.) Typically, the quatrains created an argument of examples, with each set of four lines offering an instance or amplification of the poem's central idea.

My Mistress' Eyes are Nothing Like the Sun

WILLIAM SHAKESPEARE

My mistress' eyes are nothing like the sun;
Coral is far more red than her lips' red;
If snow be white, why then her breasts are dun;
If hairs be wires, black wires grow on her head.
I have seen roses damasked red and white,   5
But no such roses see I in her cheeks;
And in some perfumes is there more delight
Than in the breath that from my mistress reeks.
I love to hear her speak, yet well I know
That music hath a far more pleasing sound;   10
I grant I never saw a goddess go:
My mistress, when she walks, treads on the ground.
   And yet, by heaven, I think my love as rare
   As any she belied with false compare.

[1609]

First published in the 1609 *Shake-speares sonnets*.

QUESTIONS

WILLIAM SHAKESPEARE, *My Mistress' Eyes are Nothing Like the Sun*

1. What strategies does the poet use to create comparisons? For instance, he negates extravagant comparisons—" . . . no such roses see I in her cheeks."

2. What words in this poem seem to have negative connotations to a reader today? What did those words mean when Shakespeare wrote them?

3. Divide the poem into its three quatrains. What ideas does each quatrain elaborate? What cumulative effect do they have by the time the poem reaches its concluding couplet?

4. This sonnet playfully satirizes the commonplaces of the courtly love tradition, wherein the beloved is praised in idealized terms. What role does the satiric impulse play in a love poem? Is it a love poem?

5. The concluding couplet contains an oath—"by heaven." Why does the poet swear by heaven? What effect does this gesture have? What is the tone of this oath?

6. Note the paradoxes in the poem—for instance, that by calling his mistress ordinary, the poet deems his love "rare." When a poem tries to advance its argument by means of contradictory impulses as this poem does, what is the effect on the reader?

7. In an exploratory essay compare this poem with another love poem, either another sonnet by Shakespeare or one by another writer. What strategies does each poem employ to describe the beloved? To what extent do love poems appear to praise themselves—their artistry, their own wit—in addition to praising the beloved?

8. In a brief essay, discuss the descriptive and argumentative resources of the sonnet form, using this poem as an exemplar. For what sorts of descriptions and arguments does the sonnet appear to be uniquely suited?

Shall I Compare Thee to a Summer's Day?

WILLIAM SHAKESPEARE

Shall I compare thee to a summer's day?
Thou art more lovely and more temperate.
Rough winds do shake the darling buds of May,
And summer's lease hath all too short a date.
Sometime too hot the eye of heaven shines,   5
And often is his gold complexion dimmed;
And every fair from fair sometimes declines,
By chance, or nature's changing course, untrimmed.
But thy eternal summer shall not fade,
Nor lose possession of that fair thou ow'st;   10
Nor shall death brag thou wand'rest in his shade,
When in eternal lines to time thou grow'st.
　　So long as men can breathe or eyes can see,
　　So long lives this, and this gives life to thee.

[1609]

First published in the 1609 *Shake-speares sonnets*.

QUESTIONS

WILLIAM SHAKESPEARE, *Shall I Compare Thee to a Summer's Day?*

1. Using a historical dictionary, such as the *Oxford English Dictionary*, look up the words "day," "lease," and "untrimm'd." How are the sixteenth century meanings connected to, and different from, the meanings these words have for us today?

2. Notice that the poem begins with a rhetorical question. As the poet answers his own question, what path does his logic take? How would you outline the argument of the poem?

3. Outline the poem's rhyme scheme. How do the rhymes serve to unify sections of the poem? How would you say the poem's sections become connected with one another—that is, what are the transitions of the poem?

4. The poem focuses on the act of comparing a beloved to something else. What does the poem seem to say about the value of comparison?

5. The poem offers itself as a substitute for physical beauty, which will fade. What does the poem seem to claim about the value of the work of art, in comparison to the experience it claims to immortalize?

6. The poem moves from asserting the greater loveliness of the beloved, to asserting that 'her loveliness, like all loveliness will fade—though not her "eternal summer." What is the nature of this eternal summer?

7. Write an essay in which you explore the poem as a sonnet. What ideas; requests to the reader; and relationship between the speaker and the beloved does the sonnet form enable?

8. Write an exploratory essay in which you consider the triangle the poem proposes between the lover/speaker, the beloved, and the idea of immortality.

Edwin Arlington Robinson
[1869–1935]

EDWIN ARLINGTON ROBINSON *was born in Head Tide, Maine into a family whose wealth came from the timber industry, though the national depression of the 1890s left his family virtually penniless. Though Robinson attended Harvard, he left after only two years of study due to his family's declining fortune and the deaths of his father in 1892 and his mother in 1896. He began writing by the age of eleven and was, as a high school student, the youngest member of the poetry society in the town of Gardiner, where his family had moved shortly after his birth. Robinson's first two books were published during these years—*The Torrent and the Night Before *(1896) and *The Children of the Night *(1897). Though the first book received some good reviews, the second did not. After its publication, Robinson moved to New York to live in Greenwich Village where he worked at temporary jobs until the publication of *Captain Craig *in 1902, which drew the attention of Theodore Roosevelt, then the president. Roosevelt arranged for Robinson to work in a secure government job. Robinson dedicated his next volume, *The Town down the River *(1909) to Roosevelt, and this began his most productive phase. Robinson wrote an Arthurian series, *Merlin *(1917), *Lancelot *(1920), and *Tristram *(1927), and won the Pulitzer Prize three times: the first time in 1921 for his *Collected Poems, *the second for *The Man Who Died Twice *(1924), and the third for *Tristram. *The Man against the Sky *(1916) was described by Amy Lowell as powerful and dynamic. Robinson continuously wrote and published throughout his life. By the time he died, Robinson had published twenty volumes of poetry. His later volumes of narrative verse included *Dionysus in Doubt *(1925), *Matthias at the Door *(1931), and *King Jasper *(1953). He is best known for formal verse in traditional forms, with an intense psychological focus. Opposed to the Puritanism of his day, which he saw as repressive, Robinson was critical of the kind of materialism that conspired against average citizens.*

Richard Cory

EDWIN ARLINGTON ROBINSON

Whenever Richard Cory went down town,
We people on the pavement looked at him:
He was a gentleman from sole to crown,
Clean favored, and imperially slim.

And he was always quietly arrayed,   5
And he was always human when he talked;
But still he fluttered pulses when he said,
"Good-morning," and he glittered when he walked.

And he was rich—yes, richer than a king—
And admirably schooled in every grace: 10
In fine, we thought that he was everything
To make us wish that we were in his place.

So on we worked, and waited for the light,
And went without the meat, and cursed the bread;
And Richard Cory, one calm summer night,   15
Went home and put a bullet through his head.

[1897]

First published in *The Children of the Night: A Book of Poems* by Edward Arlington Robinson, in 1897.

EDWIN ARLINGTON ROBINSON, *Richard Cory*

1. The poetic form of "Richard Cory" is the ballad—four-line stanzas, here in iambic pentameter (for the most part), with a rhyme scheme of *abab, cdcd, abab*. This is one of the oldest forms of poetry in English. What effect does the very song-like character of the form have on your reading of it?

2. What sense do you have of the word *imperially* in line four? What does this imply about Cory? About the *we* who are the speakers of the poem? About the relation between the two?

3. Does the poem have a turn—a place where the tone appears to shift? Where would you locate it?

4. What features of the language account for the intensity of the last stanza? For instance, what about the syntax of the first two lines of the stanza? The shift in perspective? Devices of sound, such as consonance (*worked, waited, went without*)?

5. The crux of the poem seems to be a question: Why, given all he had, would Richard Cory kill himself? Does the poem offer any hints to answer the question? Why do you think the poem declines to speculate explicitly?

6. One might also say that the poem derives from a wish: "In fine we thought that he was everything / To make us wish that we were in his place." Does the poem's ending abolish this wish? What evidence is there for the idea that, in the poem, the wish to assume the position of another's privilege outlasts that person's tragic, or mysterious, end?

7. Write an exploratory essay in which you consider the idea of social class as exemplified in the poem. In what ways does this poem appear to be an American poem?

8. Write a brief essay discussing the ballad form, using "Richard Cory" as an example. You might contrast the poem with another ballad; consider looking at a ballad from the earliest British tradition, such as "Edward" or "Twa Corbies." What ideas do the formal features of the ballad seem to invite in these poems?

Percy Bysshe Shelley
[1792–1822]

PERCY BYSSHE SHELLEY'S *name is often equated with passion of every kind. Born in Horsham, Sussex, to a country squire of means, he quickly displayed his chief traits: great intelligence, high feelings, intense love of beauty, and total rejection of all authority. He was sent to Eton where he was bullied by the more manly boys. He rebelled against their bullying in every possible way and became known as "Mad Shelley." Up at Oxford, he and his friend, Thomas Jefferson Hogg, wrote a tract in 1811,* The Necessity of Atheism, *for which they were promptly expelled. At home he broke his own rules against marriage and ran off to Edinburgh with his sister's friend, Harriet Westbrook. As the couple wandered around England, Shelley finished his first great work,* Queen Mab, *at the same time that the couple's first child was born (1813). At about that time, he began to correspond with William Godwin, whose work on the eighteenth century philosopher Jean-Jacques Rousseau greatly influenced many of the Romantic poets. Upon his meeting with Godwin, Shelley fell in love with Godwin's daughter, Mary, and ran off to the Continent with her in 1814. In 1816 Harriet committed suicide, leaving the way open for Mary Godwin and Shelley to marry, but the courts took Shelley's two children from him and put them in the hands of their maternal grandfather. In March 1818, the Shelleys left England for Italy, never to return. At that time, Shelley began a flurry of writing that produced most of his great works. His famous* Prometheus Unbound *appeared in 1819. This tale follows the adventures of Prometheus in Aeschylus's* Prometheus Bound *(Prometheus was chained to a rock by Zeus but freed by Asia and Demogorgon). For Shelley, Zeus represented all tyranny, and Asia and Demogorgon represented nature and necessity. That year he also wrote the play that is referred to as the last great Elizabethan drama,* The Cenci, *about Renaissance Italy's bloody incestuous history. His famous* Adonais *appeared in 1821, his elegy to his friend John Keats, who he thought had been hounded to death by bad critics (it was actually tuberculosis). Shelley's* Hellas *is an allegory about the Greek struggle for independence that also captivated the Romantic poets and cost writer Lord George Gordon Byron his life in 1824. Shelley himself was drowned while sailing off the west coast of Italy with a friend. A storm blew up and overwhelmed the boat, forcing poor swimmer Shelley into the sea. His body was washed ashore, cremated, and buried in the Protestant burial grounds in Rome. Shelley is probably best known for his great lyric poems, especially* The Ode to the West Wind *and* To a Skylark, *because these captured the imagination and fancy of the Romantics more subtly and sweetly than any of the Romantic poets.*

Ozymandias

PERCY BYSSHE SHELLEY

I met a traveler from an antique land
Who said: Two vast and trunkless legs of stone
Stand in the desert. Near them, on the sand,
Half sunk, a shattered visage lies, whose frown,
And wrinkled lip, and sneer of cold command,   5
Tell that its sculptor well those passions read
Which yet survive, stamped on these lifeless things,
The hand that mocked them and the heart that fed;
And on the pedestal these words appear:
"My name is Ozymandias, king of kings: 10
Look on my works, ye Mighty, and despair!"
Nothing beside remains. Round the decay
Of that colossal wreck, boundless and bare
The lone and level sands stretch far away.

[1818]

Composed in 1817. First published in *The Examiner,* January 11, 1818.

QUESTIONS

PERCY BYSSHE SHELLEY, *Ozymandias*

1. The speaker in this poem relates what is effectively hearsay. Why does Shelley choose to relate the story this way? What is the effect of reading the poem by a narrator once-removed from the action?

2. What did the traveler see in the desert? What does the inscription on the statue say? What is the irony in this statement?

3. This sonnet, like all of Shelley's work, uses the form to express the idea and is not bound by the rules. Note the rhyme scheme in this poem and the way in which the quotation is used. How does Shelley highjack this constrained form to make his point?

4. Study some present or past dictator (Hitler, Stalin, Nero, etc.). What happened to the dictator's power in the end? What happened to his life? How does history remember him?

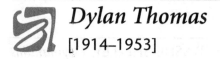

Dylan Thomas
[1914–1953]

A popular image of the poet is, perhaps, as a hard-drinking, womanizing, rabble-rousing, egotistic, irresponsible, and ultimately tragic figure. No poet more conformed to this image than **DYLAN THOMAS.** *Born in the town of Swansea, Wales, Thomas attended Swansea Grammar School, dropped out of school at sixteen, and became a reporter for* The South Wales Daily Post. *By the age of twenty, he published his first book of poems, drawing high praise. Between 1936 and 1946 he published several more books of poems and prose, made radio broadcasts for the BBC, and by 1950 embarked on the first of his legendary reading tours of the United States. These readings captivated American audiences who were entranced by the force of Thomas's personality, his theatrical performances, and the emotional, lyrical intensity of his poetry.*

Thomas was, as another poet described him, "the maddest of the word-mad poets." Consistent with the Romantic, self-destructive image he cast, Thomas died at thirty-nine after a heavy bout of drinking at the renowned White Horse Tavern in New York City. Always productive, Thomas published In Country Sleep, And Other Poems *and his* Collected Poems *in 1952. In 1954 he published the memoir of his Welsh childhood,* A Child's Christmas in Wales *and a radio play,* Under Milk Wood, *which also recalls memories of the coastal town where he was raised.*

Do Not Go Gentle into That Good Night

DYLAN THOMAS

Do not go gentle into that good night,
Old age should burn and rave at close of day;
Rage, rage against the dying of the light.

Though wise men at their end know dark is right,
Because their words had forked no lightning they   5
Do not go gentle into that good night.

Good men, the last wave by, crying how bright
Their frail deeds might have danced in a green bay,
Rage, rage against the dying of the light.

Wild men who caught and sang the sun in flight,   10
And learn, too late, they grieved it on its way,
Do not go gentle into that good night.

Grave men, near death, who see with blinding sight
Blind eyes could blaze like meteors and be gay,
Rage, rage against the dying of the light.   15

And you, my father, there on the sad height,
Curse, bless, me now with your fierce tears, I pray.
Do not go gentle into that good night.
Rage, rage against the dying of the light.

[1952]

DYLAN THOMAS, *Do Not Go Gentle into That Good Night*

1. This poem is one of the most famous examples of a *villanelle*. Examine the form carefully for its structure and rhythm; summarize how it is designed. Does your examination influence your appreciation of the poem? How does the form lend it emotional intensity?

2. Thomas wrote this poem during his father's final illness. What is the poet's mood or frame of mind as reflected in the poem?

3. Name the different kinds of men described in the poem. How does each of them confront death? What is the poet attempting to convey to his father?

4. The lines "Do not go gentle into that good night" and "Rage, rage against the dying of the light" are each repeated twice. Why? How is the meaning enhanced the second time?

5. What does Thomas suggest about regret and how people confront it? What is the connection between regret and the reasons why death is resented?

6. How does the poem treat social concepts of illness, death, and grief?

7. What is the poet's perspective on the role of spirituality in the lives of humans? Does the poem make an argument for a particular point of view?

8. Write an essay explaining how each man in the poem stands in contrast to forces larger than himself. What does the poem have to say about human agency and fate?

9. Write an essay in which you explore cultural views of grief and death. What is our attitude about them? How is that attitude reflected in the various rituals or practices, and expressions that surround them?

Gwendolyn Brooks
[1917–2000]

GWENDOLYN ELIZABETH BROOKS *was born and grew up in Topeka, Kansas, where her mother, Keziah Corine Wims Brooks, taught school and her father, David Anderson Brooks, provided her with a desk and allowed writing time early in her life. She published her first poem in a local newspaper,* Hyde Parker, *at age eleven and published poems again at age thirteen in* American Childhood. *At sixteen, she was publishing poems regularly in the* Chicago Defender. *At twenty-one she married Henry Lovington Blakeley II, with whom she had two children, Henry III and Nora. They moved to Chicago where she expanded her acquaintances and met famous writers of the Harlem Renaissance, including Langston Hughes who came to give a poetry reading in Chicago, and agreed to read her early poetry. Hughes later became a family friend as well as a mentor. By 1953, when she wrote an autobiographical novel,* Maud Martha, *she was a well-established poet. Her* A Street in Bronzeville *(1945) expressed the development of her powerful voice as she described the traumatized soldiers returning from World War II and the oppressed poor blacks who lived in rundown neighborhoods. In this collection she used the sonnet form to sing the woes of blacks in urban America during the thirties and forties. She described what she saw in Chicago and New York with a power that brought a wider community to feel and comprehend the plight of poor people.*

In The Bean Eaters *(1960) Brooks turned her attention to the civil rights movement, recounting the horrors of that time, for example, the murder of fourteen-year-old Emmet Till, in "A Bronzeville Mother Loiters in Mississippi. Meanwhile a Mississippi Mother Burns Bacon." She was accused by some as having become a political poet, but she wrote with a voice that was needed in the sixties. In* the Mecca *(1968) is a collection of her poems about false spirituality and deception, partially written about the time she worked for a spiritual leader who deceived his followers. During the first twenty-five years of her career, she also wrote many reviews for the* Chicago Daily News, *the* Sun Times, Black World, *the* New York Times, *and the* Tribune. *She taught poetry in colleges in Chicago (Columbia, Elmhurst, Northeastern Illinois) and at Wisconsin-Madison. In 1968, she became Poet Laureate of Illinois. In 1971, she wrote her first autobiography,* Report from Part One. *After this, she began to publish only with black presses and to write even more intensely about the lives of black people in the cities. Two volumes,* To Disembark *(1981) and* Children Coming Home *(1991), collect the poems that speak to black people about their lives. In 1996 she pro-*

duced a second autobiography, Report from Part Two, *which introduces and discusses some of her most well-known poems. Throughout the last years of her life, Brooks was generous with her time, traveling to give readings and to receive the scores of awards she received from admiring readers and listeners. Her work is loved and admired by both academics and non-academics, both in her adopted state and beyond.*

We Real Cool

GWENDOLYN BROOKS

The Pool Players.
Seven at the Golden Shovel.

We real cool. We
Left school. We

Lurk late. We   5
Strike straight. We

Sing sin. We
Thin gin. We

Jazz June. We
Die soon.   10

[1960]

QUESTIONS

GWENDOLYN BROOKS, *We Real Cool*

1. Who are the speakers in the poem, other than pool players? What evidence do you have as to their identity?

2. The poem was written in the later fifties. What would young men like this be doing now? Would they still be playing pool?

3. Does Brooks feel sympathy for these young men? How can you tell?

4. Young men have always "hung out" in groups—from ancient Greece to any modern city. Why are these young men particularly dangerous to themselves?

5. Every line but the last ends with "We" as both the end of the line and the beginning of a new sentence, except the last. What is the effect of this form?

6. This poem is perhaps the best known of Brooks's poems. Some of the words, though, have several meanings and have been debated for forty years. For example, what do you think "strike-straight" means? "Thin gin"? "Jazz June"? All of these have been debated.

7. Choose a group of young people with whom you are acquainted. Write about the activities of the group and about their potential for success or failure in life. What causes you to make your judgments?

8. Look up the word "cool" in the *Oxford English Dictionary* or another good dictionary. What are the possible meanings? Write about the way the word has changed, and its meaning for you and your generation.

Robert Browning
[1812–1889]

ROBERT BROWNING *was born to a wealthy banker whose library became the playground for the eager young scholar. Browning's schooling consisted of a few years at Peckham and some lectures at London University in 1830. Otherwise he was educated by private tutors and by himself, reading his father's vast collection of books. His father had his son's first small volume of verses privately printed as* Incondita, *while Browning was still a child. Browning's first real publication was* Pauline *in 1833. Shortly after the publication of this poem, he left on the first of his many travels to Europe. While in Italy, he wrote* Paracelsus, *a poem about a sorcerer's experiences and motivations. This poem was published in 1835. His next two works did not enhance his reputation, a play called* Strafford *that closed after five nights and a dense poem* Sordello *(1840) that was so learned and complex that it gave Browning the reputation of being unintelligible to the reading public. In 1846 he met, fell in love with, and married the much more successful poet Elizabeth Barrett. They moved to Florence and had one son. They lived in Florence until her death in 1861. There he wrote* Christmas Eve and Easter Day *(1850) and* Men and Women *(1855). Browning had begun the writing that would build the reputation which he now holds. He was not much appreciated by the Victorians, who admired sentiment and feeling, while his poetry took a tactile view of the human psyche, often letting his speakers reveal damaging information about themselves while apparently boasting or reporting events. He is considered one of the great psychological poets.*

After Barrett Browning's death, he moved to London where he withdrew for a short time but then began to travel and give presentations widely. He published Dramatis Personae *(1864) and* The Ring and the Book *four years later. The latter is one of the longest and most complex poems in English. It deals with a trial for a murder of a young woman, but the real content of the poem includes dramatic monologues of everyone involved in the crime. Each speaker has seen and experienced something different, making the poem a testimony to modern psychological research into the unreliability of eyewitnesses. The poem never resolves the truth of the murder, for there is not truth, only the many perspectives of those involved, truly a postmodern perspective on reality. After completing this poem Browning began to write mysterious and grotesque poems and also began to translate Greek tragedies, but none of these was successful. At the end of his life he moved to Venice to live, dying at his son's palazzo. He is buried in poet's corner in Westminster Abbey. He remains one of the brilliant thinkers and philosophers of his era, as well as a great poet.*

My Last Duchess

ROBERT BROWNING

Ferrara[1]

That's my last Duchess painted on the wall,
Looking as if she were alive. I call
That piece a wonder, now; Frà Pandolf's hands
Worked busily a day, and there she stands.
Will't please you sit and look at her? I said   5
"Frà Pandolf" by design, for never read
Strangers like you that pictured countenance,
The depth and passion of its earnest glance,
But to myself they turned (since none puts by
The curtain I have drawn for you, but I)   10
And seemed as they would ask me, if they durst,
How such a glance came there; so, not the first
Are you to turn and ask thus. Sir, 'twas not
Her husband's presence only, called that spot
Of joy into the Duchess' cheek; perhaps   15
Frà Pandolf chanced to say, "Her mantle laps
Over my lady's wrist too much," or "Paint
Must never hope to reproduce the faint
Half-flush that dies along her throat." Such stuff
Was courtesy, she thought, and cause enough   20
For calling up that spot of joy. She had
A heart—how shall I say?—too soon made glad,
Too easily impressed; she liked whate'er
She looked on, and her looks went everywhere.
Sir, 'twas all one! My favor at her breast,   25
The dropping of the daylight in the West,

---

[1]Ferrara, a city in northern Italy, is the scene.

First published in *Dramatic Lyrics* 1842 and retitled as printed in the 1849 *Dramatic Romances and Lyrics*.

The bough of cherries some officious fool
Broke in the orchard for her, the white mule
She rode with round the terrace—all and each
Would draw from her alike the approving speech,   *30*
Or blush, at least. She thanked men,—good! but thanked
Somehow—I know not how—as if she ranked
My gift of a nine-hundred-years-old name
With anybody's gift. Who'd stoop to blame
This sort of trifling? Even had you skill   *35*
In speech—which I have not—to make your will
Quite clear to such an one, and say "Just this
Or that in you disgusts me; here you miss,
Or there exceed the mark"—and if she let
Herself be lessoned so, nor plainly set   *40*
Her wits to yours, forsooth, and made excuse—
E'en then would be some stooping; and I choose
Never to stoop. Oh, sir, she smiled, no doubt,
Whene'er I passed her; but who passed without
Much the same smile? This grew; I gave commands;   *45*
Then all smiles stopped together. There she stands
As if alive. Will't please you rise? We'll meet
The company below, then. I repeat,
The Count your master's known munificence
Is ample warrant that no just pretense   *50*
Of mine for dowry will be disallowed;
Though his fair daughter's self, as I avowed
At starting, is my object. Nay, we'll go
Together down, sir. Notice Neptune, though,
Taming a sea-horse, thought a rarity,   *55*
Which Claus of Innsbruck cast in bronze for me!

[1842]

QUESTIONS

ROBERT BROWNING, *My Last Duchess*

1. This poem is a dramatic monologue. That means that the speaker is a character who, like a character in a play, presents a long speech. Who is the speaker in this poem? What is his status? Who is the listener?

2. What has the Duke done to his deceased wife? How does the reader know? What are the Duke and the ambassador doing while the Duke talks? Why is this significant?

3. Men of great power often see their families as extensions of their power. What kind of abuse follows from this attitude?

4. What is the motivation for collecting great private art collections? Should great art be in the hands of one person or in the hands of the public? Why?

5. Why is Fra Pandolf so important in the poem? What relationship has he had with the Duke's wife? Does the Duke suspect an affair? How do you know?

6. Line 25 shows why the Duke was offended by his wife. What does he say that she did wrong? Why is this a warning to the ambassador who is negotiating the Duke's next marriage?

7. Read about Henry VIII of England. Write about his reasons for beheading three of his wives and divorcing two others. What gave him the authority to take such actions?

8. What causes domestic violence today? Are there men and women who think that they own their partners? What is the result? Write about this issue.

John Keats
[1795–1821]

JOHN KEATS'S *father kept a London livery stable—not a very auspicious beginning for the Romantic poet of the sublimely beautiful. His father died when he
was nine, and when he was fifteen, he lost his mother to tuberculosis. His brother
died of the same disease a few years later, and it took Keats, too, at age twenty-
six. Tuberculosis was common in the early 1800s, and was especially prevelant
among those who lived in London's smoggy interior. Despite these challenges, and
his early death, Keats produced a large volume of memorable poetry.*

*He attended school at Enfield, but in 1810 was apprenticed to a surgeon. The
medical profession did not have the status that it has today, and this change was
not a social improvement for the young Keats. Despite his removal from school,
he read and fell in love with Edmund Spenser's* Faerie Queen, *and even as he finished his apprenticeship and began work in a London hospital, his heart and
imagination were with Spenser's world of elves and knights. He met all the
Romantic writers, including Percy Byssche Shelley and Samuel Taylor Coleridge,
and became friends with Leigh Hunt, editor of* The Examiner, *which published
some of his early sonnets. Keats dedicated his first volume of poems to Hunt in
1817. His first long poem,* Endymion, *appeared in 1818, but his friendship with
Hunt, who was on the outs with the London critics, drew criticism of the poem.
Keats was hurt, but continued to write, despite Shelley's later argument in*
Adonais *that the critics had killed Keats with their reviews. At the same time he
fell hopelessly in love with Fanny Brawne, whose social position would not allow
her to marry a stable-boy-turned-physician, whatever poetic talents he possessed.
These losses seemed to fuel his poetic passion. In 1819, he published* The Eve of
St. Agnes, *arguably the signature poem of the sensuous and fanciful wing of the
Romantic movement. This poem tells the story of a young knight who brings
beautiful food to his lady's chamber, and appears to her as if in a dream to persuade her to run away with him, which she does. His next two poems,* La Belle
Dame sans Merci (The Beautiful Woman Without Mercy), *a poem about a
witch, and* Lamia, *a poem about a woman who can become a snake, followed in
1820.* Isabella, or The Pot of Basil, *followed, a tale taken from Boccaccio's*
Decameron *about a woman who plants her unfaithful lover's head in a pot of
herbs. His last poem, the unfinished* Hyperion, *recounts a classical myth, and
throughout the last years of his life, he wrote the sonnets that have become the
jewels of the Romantic movement.*

Bright Star! Would I were steadfast as thou art

JOHN KEATS

Bright star! would I were steadfast as thou art—
  Not in lone splendor hung aloft the night,
And watching, with eternal lids apart,
  Like nature's patient, sleepless Eremite
The moving waters at their priest-like task   5
  Of pure ablution round earth's human shores,
Or gazing on the new soft-fallen mask
  Of snow upon the mountains and the moors—
No—yet still steadfast, still unchangeable,
  Pillowed upon my fair love's ripening breast,   10
To feel for ever its soft fall and swell,
  Awake for ever in a sweet unrest,
Still, still to hear her tender-taken breath,
And so live ever—or else swoon to death.

[1819]

For over century, this sonnet was thought to be Keats' last written poem, but it was probably written no later than 1819. First published in a Plymouth newspaper in 1838, it was
later collected by Richard Monckton Milnes in *Life, Letters and Literary Remains of John
Keats* in 1848.

QUESTIONS

1. What advantage does the star have over the speaker in the poem? What can the star see and do that the poet cannot?

2. Humans wink in and out of life, whereas the stars stay the same for billions of years. Why do poets look at the stars and wish for immortality? What do stars lack that poets possess?

3. This sonnet presents the problem in its first four quatrains. What is the problem and what does the resolution in the final couplets make clear?

4. Would it really be a good idea to live forever, especially in the arms of a beloved? What is wrong with trying to hold on to a single moment? Write about a time when you had trouble letting go of something.

Ode to a Nightingale

JOHN KEATS

I

My heart aches, and a drowsy numbness pains
   My sense, as though of hemlock[1] I had drunk,
Or emptied some dull opiate to the drains
   One minute past, and Lethe-wards[2] had sunk:
'Tis not through envy of thy happy lot,   5
   But being too happy in thine happiness—
      That thou, light-wingèd Dryad[3] of the trees,
         In some melodious plot
Of beechen green, and shadows numberless,
      Singest of summer in full-throated ease.   10

II

O, for a draught of vintage! that hath been
   Cooled a long age in the deep-delved earth,
Tasting of Flora[4] and the country green,
   Dance, and Provençal song, and sunburnt mirth!
O for a beaker full of the warm South,   15
   Full of the true, the blushful Hippocrene,[5]
      With beaded bubbles winking at the brim,
         And purple-stainèd mouth;
That I might drink, and leave the world unseen,
      And with thee fade away into the forest dim.   20

---

[1]Poison

[2]Lethe, river of forgetfulness in Greek mythic Hades.

[3]Wood nymph

[4]Flower goddess

[5]Fountain of the muses.

First published in *Annals of the Fine Arts* in July, 1819. Republished in *John Keats, Lamia, Isabella, The Eve of St. Agnes, and Other Poems* in 1820.

III

Fade far away, dissolve, and quite forget
   What thou, among the leaves hast never known,
The weariness, the fever, and the fret
   Here, where men sit and hear each other groan;
Where palsy shakes a few, sad, last gray hairs,   *25*
     Where youth grows pale, and specter-thin, and dies,
       Where but to think is to be full of sorrow
         And leaden-eyed despairs,
     Where Beauty cannot keep her lustrous eyes;
       Or new Love pine at them beyond tomorrow.   *30*

IV

Away! away! for I will fly to thee,
   Not charioted by Bacchus and his pards,[6]
But on the viewless wings of Poesy,
   Though the dull brain perplexes and retards:
Already with thee! tender is the night,   *35*
     And haply the Queen-Moon is on her throne,
       Clustered around by all her starry Fays;
         But here there is no light,
     Save what from heaven is with the breezes blown
       Through verdurous glooms and winding mossy ways.   *40*

V

I cannot see what flowers are at my feet,
   Nor what soft incense hangs upon the boughs,
But, in embalmed[7] darkness, guess each sweet
   Wherewith the seasonable month endows
The grass, the thicket, and the fruit-tree wild;   *45*
     What hawthorn, and the pastoral eglantine;
       Fast fading violets covered up in leaves;
         And mid-May's eldest child,
     The coming musk-rose, full of dewy wine,
       The murmurous haunt of flies on summer eves.   *50*

---

[6]God of wine, whose chariot was drawn by leopards.

[7]Wrapped in sweet scent.

VI

Darkling I listen; and for many a time
  I have been half in love with easeful Death,
Called him soft names in many a musèd rhyme,
  To take into the air my quiet breath;
Now more than ever seems it rich to die,   55
    To cease upon the midnight with no pain,
      While thou art pouring forth thy soul abroad
        In such an ecstasy!
  Still wouldst thou sing, and I have ears in vain—
    To thy high requiem become a sod.   60

VII

Thou wast not born for death, immortal Bird!
  No hungry generations tread thee down;
The voice I hear this passing night was heard
  In ancient days by emperor and clown:
Perhaps the selfsame song that found a path   65
    Through the sad heart of Ruth[8] when, sick for home,
      She stood in tears amid the alien corn:
        The same that oft-times hath
  Charmed magic casements, opening on the foam
    Of perilous seas, in faery lands forlorn.   70

VIII

Forlorn! the very word is like a bell
  To toll me back from thee to my sole self!
Adieu! the fancy cannot cheat so well
  As she is famed to do, deceiving elf.
Adieu! adieu! thy plaintive anthem fades   75
    Past the near meadows, over the still stream,
      Up the hill side; and now 'tis buried deep
        In the next valley-glades:
  Was it a vision, or a waking dream?
    Fled is that music:—Do I wake or sleep?   80

[1819]

---

[8]The Book of Ruth in the Bible tells of a young woman far from home.

QUESTIONS

1. What is the speaker in the poem doing? Where is he? What does he see and hear?

2. The sound of the nightingale carries the speaker further and further into fantasy as night comes on. What happens to the speaker's mood as darkness falls?

3. Why is it that "the fancy cannot cheat so well"? Why can't our imaginations give us what we yearn for, no matter how much art and music we produce? Why is it impossible to forget the troubles of the world, even with the strongest drugs and obsessions?

4. Close your eyes and have someone read this poem to you. Then look carefully at the complex rhyming pattern in this poem. Note the shapes of each stanza on the page. What are the effects of the sounds and patterns? How do they work together to evoke the bird being described?

5. As the poem progresses, it becomes increasingly dark, and the sounds and scents become more intense. How does this increasing darkness lead to a feeling of disappointment at the end of the poem? What effect does the word "Forlorn" have?

6. In this poem, Keats refers to many mythological places and characters. Read about at least one of them, and write about the myth you have chosen. What importance does it have for you?

7. Write about a memory that you have of a place that was magical for you. How did you experience this place with all of your senses? Describe your experience and analyze your responses in retrospect.

To Autumn

JOHN KEATS

I

Season of mists and mellow fruitfulness,
   Close bosom-friend of the maturing sun;
Conspiring with him how to load and bless
   With fruit the vines that round the thatch-eaves run;
To bend with apples the mossed cottage-trees,   *5*
   And fill all fruit with ripeness to the core;
     To swell the gourd, and plump the hazel shells
With a sweet kernel; to set budding more,
And still more, later flowers for the bees,
Until they think warm days will never cease,   *10*
   For Summer has o'er-brimmed their clammy cells.

II

Who hath not seen thee oft amid thy store?
   Sometimes whoever seeks abroad may find
Thee sitting careless on a granary floor,
   Thy hair soft-lifted by the winnowing wind;   *15*
Or on a half-reaped furrow sound asleep,
   Drowsed with the fume of poppies, while thy hook[1]
     Spares the next swath and all its twinèd flowers:
And sometimes like a gleaner thou dost keep
   Steady thy laden head across a brook;   *20*
   Or by a cider-press, with patient look,
     Thou watchest the last oozings hours by hours.

---

[1]Sickle

Composed in 1819 and first published in *Lamia, Isabella, The Eve of St. Agnes, and Other Poems* in 1820.

III

Where are the songs of Spring? Ay, where are they?
    Think not of them, thou hast thy music too,—
While barrèd clouds bloom the soft-dying day,   25
    And touch the stubble-plains with rosy hue;
Then in a wailful choir the small gnats mourn
    Among the river sallows[2], borne aloft
        Or sinking as the light wind lives or dies;
And full-grown lambs loud bleat from hilly bourn;   30
Hedge-crickets sing; and now with treble soft
The red-breast whistles from a garden-croft[3]
    And gathering swallows twitter in the skies.

[1820]

---

[2]River willows

[3]Garden plot

QUESTIONS

1. How does Keats describe the various stages of autumn? How does he contrast autumn with spring?

2. What mood does Keats convey about autumn? What lines in the poem offer the strongest evidence of the narrator's response to this season?

3. Each of the stanzas is eleven lines long. Look carefully at the rhyme scheme, and note how the rhymes change as the poem progresses from late summer to nearly winter. Note rhymes such as "hazel shells" and "clammy cells," "flowers" and "by hours," and "or dies" and "the skies." What happens to the mood?

4. British school children were often given the assignment to write about a season, or compare two different seasons. Choose an ordinary kind of writing activity such as comparing and contrasting high school and college or discussing the causes of the Gulf War. Then write the assignment in such a way that you challenge the ease of the assignment, and make it your own, as Keats did the simple autumn assignment.

On First Looking into Chapman's Homer[1]

JOHN KEATS

Much have I traveled in the realms of gold,
   And many goodly states and kingdoms seen;
   Round many western islands have I been
Which bards in fealty[2] to Apollo[3] hold.
Oft of one wide expanse had I been told   5
   That deep-browed Homer ruled as his demesne,[4]
   Yet did I never breathe its pure serene
Till I heard Chapman speak out loud and bold.
Then felt I like some watcher of the skies
   When a new planet swims into his ken;   10
Or like stout Cortez[5] when with eagle eyes
   He stared at the Pacific—and all his men
Looked at each other with a wild surmise—
   Silent, upon a peak in Darien.[6]

[1816]

---

[1]Keats recounts the excitement he felt reading George Chapman's Elizabethan translations of *The Iliad* and *The Odyssey*.

[2]Loyalty

[3]The god of the sun and of poetry.

[4]Domain

[5]Not, unfortunately, the first Spaniard to see the Pacific; Keats goofed.

[6]Isthmus of Panama.

First published in London's *The Examiner,* Dec. 1, 1816.

QUESTIONS

JOHN KEATS, *On First Looking Into Chapman's Homer*

1. Keats had certainly read the Greek epics, but George Chapman's translations of *The Illiad* and *The Odyssey* enthralled him. How does he compare his earlier readings of these classics to Chapman's versions?

2. A translator always brings something of him or herself to the text, and thus makes old stories new. How does Keats express the excitement of finding the new in the old?

3. The first eight lines of this sonnet explain how Keats felt about the classics before Chapmans translation. How does the sextet explain the new experience?

4. Write about a movie that has been made into a book or vice versa, and analyze the two different versions. Which did you experience first? How did that effect your thoughts about which was more powerful?

George Herbert
[1593-1633]

GEORGE HERBERT, *one of the metaphysical poets, (so named because of their inward-looking poetry), was born in northern England in Montgomery. He was from an important border family, and though his father died three years after his birth, he was given a good education and was encouraged in his academic interests. He was a poet of the Puritan era in British literature but was far more complex than that affiliation might suggest. He attended Westminster School and Trinity College, Cambridge. He was a brilliant student and great speaker who became university orator at only eighteen when he was fairly new at Cambridge. He was a man of great religious fervor who spoke his faith both in public debate and in the privacy of his poetry. In 1626 he was made deacon of Lincoln Cathedral, giving him responsibility for one of the great cathedrals of England when he was only thirty-three years old. Four years later, ordained as an Anglican priest, he was assigned to the rectory of Fulston St. Peter's, Bemerton, Wiltshire. He died three years later and was buried under the altar of this church, which he had served with great devotion and reverence.*

As a priest he had not published his poems during his lifetime, but after his death, his poems were published in a work entitled The Temple. *This work contains 129 poems, which, taken together, trace the spiritual history of a great religious man in search of his own way of expressing and understanding his faith. His poetry was an introduction into what would later become a long tradition of religious poetry that would be taken up by John Donne the poet and great dean of St. Paul's, and later such writers as T.S. Eliot. Herbert broke new ground in creating an understanding of the poem as a way to express the mysteries of religious feeling through the complex ambiguity and nuance of the poem. One of his most famous poems,* The Collar, *expresses this complexity by showing a man at odds with God. In the poem the speaker raves at the idea of religious obligation, comparing it to the yoke that an ox might wear as it trods the grain. The speaker becomes more and more agitated as the poem proceeds and then hears the quiet voice of the Divine calling him "child" and he quiets and submits to the gentle yoke of one who has always had his best interests at heart. The poem exemplifies the writing of the metaphysical poets, a sensitivity to realities outside the world of sensory experience and logic.*

The Collar[1]

GEORGE HERBERT

I struck the board and cried, "No more;
     I will abroad!
What? shall I ever sigh and pine?
My lines and life are free, free as the road,
     Loose as the wind, as large as store.[2]   5
        Shall I be still in suit?[3]
     Have I no harvest but a thorn
     To let me blood, and not restore
What I have lost with cordial fruit?
        Sure there was wine   10
     Before my sighs did dry it; there was corn
        Before my tears did drown it.
     Is the year only lost to me?
        Have I no bays[4] to crown it,
No flowers, no garlands gay? All blasted?   15
        All wasted?
     Not so, my heart; but there is fruit,
        And thou hast hands.
     Recover all thy sigh-blown age
On double pleasures: leave thy cold dispute   20
Of what is fit, and not. Forsake thy cage,
        Thy rope of sands,
Which petty thoughts have made, and made to thee
     Good cable, to enforce and draw,
        And be thy law,

---

[1]The collar itself is the yoke that Christ tells his followers is light when worn for him.

[2]Storehouse

[3]Service to another.

[4]Circles of bay leaves worn by heroes or poets.

First published in *The Temple* in 1633.

While thou didst wink and wouldst not see.   *25*
          Away! Take heed;
          I will abroad.
Call in thy death's-head[5] there; tie up thy fears.
          He that forbears
      To suit and serve his need,   *30*
          Deserves his load."
But as I raved and grew more fierce and wild
          At every word,
Methought I heard one calling, *Child!*
         And I replied, *My Lord.*   *35*

[1633]

---

[5]A skull; reminder of mortality.

QUESTIONS

1. The speaker in the poem struggles with the idea that he must obey God's will and that he wants to remain an individual. He then hears the "still small voice" and turns quietly. What personal experiences does this reflect?

2. Authority can be most difficult to accept when humans have taken vows to obey. Why do we chafe against the very commitments that keep our lives whole? Where in the poem is this conflict apparent?

3. In the last four lines of the poem, the speaker describes his words as raving and as fierce and wild. What does he say that is so fierce? What does he want to do? Why?

4. Write about authority that you must deal with: school, military, work, church. How do you cope with authority? Analyze your own responses to authority.

Easter Wings

GEORGE HERBERT

Lord, who createdst man in wealth and store,
Though foolishly he lost the same,
Decaying more and more
Till he became
Most poor;
With thee
Oh, let me rise
As larks, harmoniously,
And sing this day thy victories;
Then shall the fall further the flight in me.

My tender age in sorrow did begin;
And still with sicknesses and shame
Thou didst so punish sin,
That I became
Most thin.
With thee
Let me combine,
And feel this day thy victory;
For if I imp¹ my wing on thine,
Affliction shall advance the flight in me.

[1633]

---

¹To repair a wing by adding a feather.

First published in *The Temple* in 1633.

QUESTIONS

1. "Easter Wings" recounts the speaker's feelings of sin and inadequacy, feelings that can be spirited away on the wings of the Easter dove. How does the shape of the poem contribute to this meaning?

2. The joy of rebirth is celebrated throughout all cultures, as spring or new rains or the end of war always bring new hope to humans. Birds, and in particular doves, are often used to indicate this hope. What is the significance of Herbert's use of bird imagery here?

3. The poem begins on the right so that it must be turned counterclockwise to be read. How does this choice of shape affect the picture of the poem as it appears? What does the image itself contribute to the reading?

4. Form has been debated among writers and writing teachers probably since writing began. Choose a form that you find useful, and write a piece within that form. Try to create an organic whole so that the form and the meaning enhance each other.

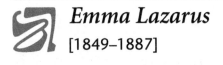

Emma Lazarus
[1849–1887]

EMMA LAZARUS *was one of seven children born to a sugar merchant in New York City. She spent her youth in New York and Newport, Rhode Island, and was tutored privately in music, languages, and literature; her family was wealthy enough to afford not only this education, but also the publication of her first book,* Poems and Translations *(1866), which contained poems she wrote as a teenager. This book received praise by none other than the writer and philosopher Ralph Waldo Emerson, who then acted as her mentor. In 1871 she published* Admetus and Other Poems; *she also produced a novel,* Alide: An Episode of Goethe's Life *(1874). Usually considered to be the first noteworthy Jewish-American writer, Lazarus wrote and translated tirelessly throughout her short life, and was known as an activist and a reformer as well as a poet. She explored her Jewish roots in* Songs of a Semite: The Dance to Death and Other Poems *(1882), and became an advocate of a Jewish homeland and created the Society for the Improvement and Colonization of Eastern European Jews. As a spokeswoman for improving the working conditions of immigrants, she was invited to contribute a poem as part of a fundraising activity for the Statue of Liberty. The poem "The New Colossus" was chosen to be inscribed on the base of the statue in 1903.*

The New Colossus

EMMA LAZARUS

Not like the brazen giant of Greek fame,
With conquering limbs astride from land to land;
Here at our sea-washed, sunset gates shall stand
A mighty woman with a torch, whose flame
Is the imprisoned lightning, and her name   5
Mother of Exiles. From her beacon-hand
Glows world-wide welcome; her mild eyes command
The air-bridged harbor that twin cities frame.
"Keep, ancient lands, your storied pomp!" cries she
With silent lips. "Give me your tired, your poor,   10
Your huddled masses yearning to breathe free,
The wretched refuse of your teeming shore.
Send these, the homeless, tempest-tost to me,
I lift my lamp beside the golden door!"

[1883]

Written for the "In Aid of the Bartholdi Pedastal Fund" art auction in 1883.

QUESTIONS

EMMA LAZARUS, *The New Colossus*

1. Though Americans typically know this poem only for the lines, "Give me your tired, your poor, Your huddled masses yearning to breathe free," the whole poem is typical of nineteenth-century romantic poetry, including its use of ancient cultural and mythological references. In an encyclopedia, look up the Colossus of Rhodes; what use does Lazarus make of this figure from the ancient world?

2. The poem begins with a negation: "Not like. . . ." What *is* the New Colossus like? How is this figure different from the old one? On what points do they differ?

3. This poem contains an example of the figure *prosopopoeia*, in which a writer gives human features and capabilities to an inanimate figure. Lazarus's use of this figure occurs when she has the statue speak, "with silent lips." What is the effect of this figure of speech?

4. Lazarus's comparison of the old Colossus to the Statue of Liberty reflects the contrast she sees between the old world—Europe—and the new. What are the implicit points of comparison between the two places?

5. In what sense were the immigrants who came to the United States, "homeless"?

6. Track Lazarus's use of light and fire imagery in the poem. How does she use this imagery to make her argument?

7. In an exploratory essay, consider the ways that Lazarus's poem embodies the larger narrative the United States as a place of refuge and opportunity. What role do you suppose poems, stories, songs, and other cultural productions play in the narratives a country creates of itself?

8. In a brief essay, describe the ways Lazarus's poem fits into the historical circumstances of its composition. To do this, you will need to do some research into the conditions for immigrants in Europe as well as in the cities of the United States. Is Lazarus's metaphorical account of the United States realistic or idealistic?

William Blake

[1757–1827]

WILLIAM BLAKE *was born in London to a middle class family, but his bent toward seeing the world in terms of visions quickly appeared. Blake saw more than the dirty world of a big city; rather he saw angels and other spiritual beings as he walked through life. He considered the world he lived in to be corrupted by its lack of imagination, and he set about creating his own Golden Age of art and poetry. Showing great artistic talent early in life, by age ten he began drawing in school and later became an engraver and design artist. He did not earn great sums as an artist, because his work was strange in an era that loved landscapes and careful representations of classic events such as Bible stories and historic battles. Blake's art illustrated more that could not be seen than that which could be seen.*

He married his wife, Catherine, in 1782. She was devoted to him though the story goes that she nearly fainted when she first saw him due to his fiery eyes and passionate presence. From that early era came his first collection of poetry, Poetical Sketches *(1783). When his younger brother Robert died, Blake's sense of connection to the spiritual world was strengthened. He wrote the* Songs of Experience *(1789) during this time of elation and spiritual growth, and these poems express his sense of the heavenly and spiritual. This bliss, however, was short-lived as Blake first followed and then rejected the Swedish theologian, Emanuel Swendenborg. Blake rejected Swendenborg's ideas about predestination, and wrote* The Marriage of Heaven and Hell *(1790–1793) as an attack on any such doctrine.*

Blake then became connected with the champions of the French Revolution, including William Godwin, Tom Paine, and the Romantic poets, William Wordsworth, Samuel Coleridge, Robert Southey, and William Hazlitt. His protest against those who interfere with the rights of their fellow humans expressed itself in the most famous of his collections, Songs of Experience *(1798–1794), and in* The French Revolution, America, *and the* Visions of the Daughters of Albion. *The last poem attacks marriage, which Blake disapproved of while he continued to be a faithful and devoted husband. The* Book of Thel *(1783) followed, a tale of a soul that refuses to be born into this wicked world. His mythology was elaborated and illustrated in* The Book of Urizen, The Song of Los, The Book of Ahania, *and* The Book of Los.

From 1800 to 1803, the Blakes lived in a small town called Felpham, supported by a patron and poet friend named William Hayley, but Blake and Hayley differed in the nature of the poetry the two wrote, Hayley's being simple and sentimental, Blake's being mystical and complex. While at Felpham, Blake finished

The Four Zoas *and* Milton; *upon returning to London, he wrote the third of his* "prophetic" *works,* Jerusalem. *After that he spent many years in poverty, even painting dishes for Wedgwood, but was finally rediscovered in 1818 by a younger generation of painters, John Linnell, Samuel Palmer, John Varley, and George Richmond. He began to illustrate Dante and the book of Job, but these remained unfinished at the time of his death in 1827.*

The Lamb

WILLIAM BLAKE

Little Lamb, who made thee?
  Dost thou know who made thee?
Gave thee life, and bid thee feed
By the stream and o'er the mead;
Gave thee clothing of delight,   5
Softest clothing, wooly, bright;
Gave thee such a tender voice,
Making all the vales rejoice?
  Little Lamb, who made thee?
  Dost thou know who made thee?   10

Little Lamb, I'll tell thee,
  Little Lamb, I'll tell thee:
He is callèd by thy name,
For he calls himself a Lamb.
He is meek, and he is mild;   15
He became a little child.
I a child, and thou a lamb,
We are callèd by his name.
  Little Lamb, God bless thee!
  Little Lamb, God bless thee!   20

[1789]

First published in *Songs of Innocence* in 1789.

QUESTIONS

1. Who is the speaker in this poem? Read it aloud to more easily gauge the age of the voice.

2. Why was Christ called the Lamb of God? What happens to a sacrificial lamb? How does that fact contribute to the reading of this poem?

3. The poem is similar to a nursery rhyme. Each couplet leads on to the next in a simple and sometimes repetitive form. The child voice answers its own question. Who did make both the lamb and the child, according to the poem?

4. What do Easter and Passover celebrate? What was the command to the families in the first Passover? What danger do those who are too innocent face? How can we protect them?

The Tyger

WILLIAM BLAKE

Tyger, Tyger, burning bright
In the forests of the night,
What immortal hand or eye
Could frame thy fearful symmetry?

In what distant deeps or skies   5
Burnt the fire of thine eyes?
On what wings dare he aspire?
What the hand dare seize the fire?

And what shoulder and what art
Could twist the sinews of thy heart?   10
And, when thy heart began to beat,
What dread hand and what dread feet?

What the hammer? What the chain?
In what furnace was thy brain?
What the anvil? What dread grasp   15
Dare its deadly terror clasp?

When the stars threw down their spears,
And watered heaven with their tears,
Did he smile his work to see?
Did he who made the Lamb make thee?   20

Tyger, Tyger, burning bright
In the forests of the night,
What immortal hand or eye
Dare frame thy fearful symmetry?

[1794]

First published in *Songs of Experience* in 1794.

QUESTIONS

1. What words describe the power of the tiger? What are his eyes like? His brain?

2. Notice the changes that occur throughout the poem. These are intentional, for Blake wrote many versions of this poem before deciding on this exact order. What changes occur, and where?

3. Humans have long wondered why life works the way that it does with predators and prey. Why do you think nature is so cruel?

4. Each lines ends with a question. Follow the sequence of the questions. Where do they lead?

5. Note the change from *could* in line four to *dare* in line twenty-four. What does this change indicate? What questions do the changed questions ask?

6. Consider the arguments of hunters in justification of their hunting. What do hunters give to nature? What do they take away? Write about this argument.

7. Is it possible to see the universe as finally benevolent toward life? Write about this philosophical question, tackling the same dilemma that Blake tackles in this poem.

London

WILLIAM BLAKE

I wander through each chartered street,[1]
Near where the chartered Thames does flow,
And mark in every face I meet
Marks of weakness, marks of woe.

In every cry of every man,   5
In every infant's cry of fear,
In every voice, in every ban,
The mind-forged manacles I hear.

How the chimney-sweeper's cry[2]
Every black'ning church appalls   10
And the hapless soldier's sigh
Runs in blood down palace walls.

But most through midnight streets I hear
How the youthful harlot's curse
Blasts the new born infant's tear   15
And blights with plagues the marriage hearse.

[1794]

---

[1]*Chartered* can mean mapped, but it can also mean constricted, under control. The use of the word in line 2 refers to the *chartered Thames,* meaning that the river is hemmed by ugly buildings and streets.

[2]Small boys had to go through the city crying out "Chimneys swept," but also cried because they were forced to do dirty and dangerous work because they were small enough to go up (or down) chimneys.

First published in *Songs of Experience* in 1794.

QUESTIONS

1. This poem describes the grim London that Blake knew, the London of the poor. The town is dirty indeed, but what does "mind-forged manacles" mean? Who does Blake blame for putting people in bad conditions?

2. The poem ends on a dark note. What has the young harlot done to her child?

3. Cities inevitably attract those who look for the darker side of life, but they also cause the innocent to fall victim to the evils already present. How does this poem characterize both groups?

4. Does weakness always lead to woe? The church is blackened and the soldier's blood runs down palace walls. What happens to religious, political, and military organizations when those who lead them are weak or corrupt?

5. The poem is written in quatrains with a\b\a\b rhymes. How does the rhyme pattern contribute to the effects of the poem? Consider the power of the words used: appalls, walls, curse, hearse. What do these words suggest?

6. What effect does the final image cast over the entire poem? What can be hoped for in a world where a mother curses her infant, and whose father is likely unknown at its birth?

7. London is one of the oldest cities in England. It was called Londinium by the Romans when they ruled it. Read about London today. Does it still have its dark side? How has it improved?

8. Write about a social problem in your town. What are the possible causes? What can ordinary people do to contribute to a solution?

Wilfred Owen
[1893–1917]

WILFRED OWEN *was born at Plas Wilmot, Oswestry. The family moved to Birkenhead in 1897 and to Shrewsbury in 1906. He became a lay assistant at Dunsden but returned home in 1913, ill and unable to continue his duties. In September of the same year he went to Bordeaux to teach in the Berlitz School. He then moved on, in 1914, to the Pyrenees where he tutored at Bagneres de Bigorre. There Owen met the French poet Laurent Tailhade and began to write in earnest. In 1915 he went home briefly but quickly returned to France. In the fall with the war in full force, he returned to England to enlist in the 2nd Artists Rifles Officers Training Corp, and in June 1916, he was commissioned into the 5th (Reserve) Manchester Regiment at Milford Camp, Near Witley. Once Owen left teaching and writing to become a soldier, he found himself classified as a 1st Class Shot and embedded in a military career. In this position, he saw some of the Battle of the Somme, the most horrible battle of World War I and one of the most horrible battles of all wars. Hundreds of thousands of young men were thrown into an unceasing and unending conflict; no one won but many died. By this time in 1916 the Battle of the Somme was officially ended, but Owen was still with his regiment, which was down to 156 officers and men. He took command first of a firing range party and then of a Musketry Party on the range at Crossens, near Southport. At Christmas he had embarkation leave but by January he arrived back in France, being sent to the dangerous Infantry Base Depot at Etaples and then to the 2nd Manchesters as an Officer reinforcement. On January 12 he was sent into the frontline at Serre in charge of "A" Company. His platoon occupied a former German bunker in No Man's Land and posted a sentry who during a bombardment was blinded, an incident that became the subject of his poem, "The Sentry."*

Out of the battle line for a time, he suffered a concussion following a fall but rejoined his battalion near Manchester Hill, Selency, where he was in and out of battle for several weeks. In May he was evacuated with shell shock and taken to hospital in Hampshire and then on to Edinburgh where he met fellow poets Siegfried Sassoon and Robert Graves and wrote, "Anthem for Doomed Youth" and "Dulce et Decorum Est." In January 1918 Owen attended Robert Graves's wedding and by June was deemed fit for service and joined the 5th Manchesters. Prior to his return to the french battle fields, Owen visited Siegfried Sassoon in hospital in August of that year. He was in the Brigade attack on the Beaurevoir-Fonsomme Line at Joncourt for which Owen was recommended for a Military Cross. In October his group, the 2nd Manchesters, took over the line west of the

Sambre-Oise canal, near Ors. He wrote his last letter to his mother from the cellar of the Maison Forestier (Forester's House) at Pommereuil and on November 4 was killed in action on the banks of the Sambre-Oise canal. In 1919 seven of his poems were published in Wheels *and in 1920 the* Poems of Wilfred Owen, *with an introduction by Siegfried Sassoon appeared. In 1931, his complete poems were edited by Edmund Blunden.*

Dulce et Decorum Est

WILFRED OWEN

Bent double, like old beggars under sacks,
Knock-kneed, coughing like hags, we cursed through sludge,
Till on the haunting flares we turned our backs
And towards our distant rest began to trudge.
Men marched asleep. Many had lost their boots   5
But limped on, blood-shod. All went lame; all blind;
Drunk with fatigue; deaf even to the hoots
Of tired, outstripped Five-Nines that dropped behind.

Gas! Gas! Quick, boys!—An ecstasy of fumbling,
Fitting the clumsy helmets just in time;   10
But someone still was yelling out and stumbling
And flound'ring like a man in fire or lime . . .
Dim, through the misty panes and thick green light,
As under a green sea, I saw him drowning.

In all my dreams, before my helpless sight,   15
He plunges at me, guttering, choking, drowning.
If in some smothering dreams you too could pace
Behind the wagon that we flung him in,
And watch the white eyes writhing in his face,
His hanging face, like a devil's sick of sin;   20
If you could hear, at every jolt, the blood
Come gargling from the froth-corrupted lungs,
Obscene as cancer, bitter as the cud
Of vile, incurable sores on innocent tongues,—
My friend, you would not tell with such high zest   25
To children ardent for some desperate glory,
The old Lie: Dulce et decorum est
Pro patria mori.[1]

[1920]

---

[1]From Horace: It is sweet and fitting....(to die for one's country).

Written in October of 1917.

QUESTIONS

WILFRED OWEN, *Dulce et Decorum Est*

1. In the poem the soldiers move backward from enemy bombardment. Then the poison gas comes, and one soldier does not get his gas mask on in time. What happens to him?

2. Old men talk of duty and of glory when serving one's country. According to Owen, what do the young men say, who must suffocate in poison gas?

3. The couplet in the middle of this poem and the chilling last line control the form of these stanzas. Why is the image of the dream so horrible at the end of the poem? Why is the last line so ironic? Is it worse to see death or to dream about it night after night?

4. Is it worthwhile to suffer if one is doing the right thing? Pick a specific instance of suffering that has come from doing the right thing. Write about whether the sacrifice was worth it.

William Wordsworth
[1770–1850]

Born in Cockermouth, Cumberland, a country village, WILLIAM WORDSWORTH
*was the child of an attorney who was well educated and wealthy. He sent his son to
Cambridge in 1787 at the age of seventeen. Wordsworth excelled at school but took
time off to travel to Switzerland and northern Italy and then on to France. In
France he became excited about the French Revolution and met the philosopher
Jean-Jacques Rousseau, whose ideas about nature and humanity greatly influenced
the young poet. He lived in France during the turbulent year of 1792, fathering a
child, Caroline, with Annette Vallon. He wrote romantically about the affair in
later years but seems to have decided after a second visit in 1802 to end the relationship. He married his sister Dorothy's friend Mary Hutchinson shortly thereafter
and settled in Grasmere in the Lake Country. In the meantime, around 1795, he
met and became extremely close to Samuel Taylor Coleridge. From 1795 to 1798,
in quiet Somersetshire, the two men created what was to become the touchstone
work for the Romantic movement, the* Lyrical Ballads, *followed by its famous*
Preface *in 1800. This work contains the most famous of Wordsworth's and
Coleridge's poems as well as Wordsworth's clear statement of their literary values
and beliefs. At first light this work was not well received because it was both revolutionary (not a good thing to be so closely after the American Revolution) in that
it supported the rights of the common person and was religiously challenging.
Wordsworth propounded a love of nature so strong that it could be said to look
almost pagan. Needless to say, opinion changed over the centuries, and the work is
now considered one of literary history's most important milestones. Some literary
historians set the date of 1798 as the great change in the direction of British literature.*

*After a trip to Germany with Coleridge and Coleridge's wife, Wordsworth
settled at Rydal Mount near Lake Windermere, where he spent the rest of his life
in peace and serenity. As the years passed, he became more and more conservative, rejecting the French Revolution with the advent of Napoleon and returning
to the church of England. In 1813 he became distributor of stamps, a conservative governmental office, having completely joined the conservatives and turned
away from Romantic ideals. During his last years, in 1843 he became Poet
Laureate and held the post until his death. His most famous works include the*
Lucy poems, Tintern Abbey, *and the* Ode on Intimations of Immortality, *all
written in his youth. He is also known for his two autobiographical poems,* The
Prelude *and* The Excursion, *both of which were included in a longer unfinished
work,* The Recluse.

London, 1802

WILLIAM WORDSWORTH

Milton![1] thou shouldst be living at this hour:
England hath need of thee: she is a fen
Of stagnant waters: altar, sword, and pen,
Fireside, the heroic wealth of hall and bower,
Have forfeited their ancient English dower   *5*
Of inward happiness. We are selfish men:
Oh! raise us up, return to us again;
And give us manners, virtue, freedom, power.
Thy soul was like a Star, and dwelt apart:
Thou hadst a voice whose sound was like the sea,   *10*
Pure as the naked heavens, majestic, free;
So didst thou travel on life's common way
In cheerful godliness; and yet thy heart
The lowliest duties on herself did lay.

[1802; 1807]

---

[1]John Milton (1608–1674) wrote great religious poetry (*Paradise Lost*) but also powerful political tracts on literary and political freedom.

Composed in 1802. First published in *Poems in Two Volumes* in 1807.

QUESTIONS

WILLIAM WORDSWORTH, *London, 1802*

1. In the early 1800s English life turned from an agrarian, countryside-based society to one of industrial-focused city life. How does Wordsworth express his disgust with the move from nobility to money making? What has been lost? Why does the speaker suggest that religious and political power are needed?

2. John Milton lived in an era of great political turmoil and change, as did Wordsworth. What was happening in France and the United States in the late 1700s and early 1800s? What was going on in England at this time?

3. The sonnet presents the problem of the lack of character in Wordsworth's contemporaries in the first eight lines (as a sonnet often does) and then presents the solution in the last six: bring back Milton. What qualities of Milton are needed?

4. If you could bring back a character in history whom you admire, who would it be? Write about why you admire this person and what you think this person could contribute to the world as we know it.

Lines

COMPOSED A FEW MILES ABOVE TINTERN ABBEY

WILLIAM WORDSWORTH

Five years have past; five summers, with the length
Of five long winters! and again I hear
These waters, rolling from their mountain-springs
With a soft inland murmur.—Once again
Do I behold these steep and lofty cliffs,   5
That on a wild secluded scene impress
Thoughts of more deep seclusion; and connect
The landscape with the quiet of the sky.
The day is come when I again repose
Here, under this dark sycamore, and view   10
These plots of cottage-ground, these orchard-tufts,
Which at this season, with their unripe fruits,
Are clad in one green hue, and lose themselves
'Mid groves and copses. Once again I see
These hedge-rows, hardly hedge-rows, little lines   15
Of sportive wood run wild: these pastoral farms,
Green to the very door; and wreaths of smoke
Sent up, in silence, from among the trees!
With some uncertain notice, as might seem
Of vagrant dwellers in the houseless woods,   20
Or of some Hermit's cave, where by his fire
The Hermit sits alone.
                    These beauteous forms,
Through a long absence, have not been to me
As is a landscape to a blind man's eye: 25
But oft, in lonely rooms, and 'mid the din
Of towns and cities, I have owed to them
In hours of weariness, sensations sweet,
Felt in the blood, and felt along the heart;

And passing even into my purer mind,   *30*
With tranquil restoration:—feelings too
Of unremembered pleasure: such, perhaps,
As have no slight or trivial influence
On that best portion of a good man's life,
His little, nameless, unremembered, acts   *35*
Of kindness and of love. Nor less, I trust,
To them I may have owed another gift,
Of aspect more sublime; that blessed mood,
In which the burthen of the mystery,
In which the heavy and the weary weight   *40*
Of all this unintelligible world,
Is lightened:—that serene and blessed mood,
In which the affections gently lead us on,—
Until, the breath of this corporeal frame
And even the motion of our human blood   *45*
Almost suspended, we are laid asleep
In body, and become a living soul:
While with an eye made quiet by the power
Of harmony, and the deep power of joy,
We see into the life of things.   *50*
                  If this
Be but a vain belief, yet, oh! how oft—
In darkness and amid the many shapes
Of joyless daylight; when the fretful stir
Unprofitable, and the fever of the world,   *55*
Have hung upon the beatings of my heart—
How oft, in spirit, have I turned to thee,
O sylvan Wye! thou wanderer thro' the woods,
How often has my spirit turned to thee!
   And now, with gleams of half-extinguished thought   *60*
With many recognitions dim and faint,
And somewhat of a sad perplexity,
The picture of the mind revives again:
While here I stand, not only with the sense
Of present pleasure, but with pleasing thoughts   *65*
That in this moment there is life and food
For future years. And so I dare to hope,
Though changed, no doubt, from what I was when first
I came among these hills; when like a roe
I bounded o'er the mountains, by the sides   *70*

Of the deep rivers, and the lonely streams,
Wherever nature led: more like a man
Flying from something that he dreads, than one
Who sought the thing he loved. For nature then
(The coarser pleasures of my boyish days, 75
And their glad animal movements all gone by)
To me was all in all.—I cannot paint
What then I was. The sounding cataract
Haunted me like a passion: the tall rock,
The mountain, and the deep and gloomy wood, 80
Their colours and their forms, were then to me
An appetite; a feeling and a love,
That had no need of a remoter charm,
By thought supplied, nor any interest
Unborrowed from the eye.—That time is past, 85
And all its aching joys are now no more,
And all its dizzy raptures. Not for this
Faint I, nor mourn nor murmur; other gifts
Have followed; for such loss, I would believe,
Abundant recompense. For I have learned 90
To look on nature, not as in the hour
Of thoughtless youth; but hearing oftentimes
The still, sad music of humanity,
Nor harsh nor grating, though of ample power
To chasten and subdue. And I have *felt* 95
A presence that disturbs me with the joy
Of elevated thoughts; a sense sublime
Of something far more deeply interfused,
Whose dwelling is the light of setting suns,
And the round ocean and the living air, 100
And the blue sky, and in the mind of man:
A motion and a spirit, that impels
All thinking things, all objects of all thought,
And rolls through all things. Therefore am I still
A lover of the meadows and the woods, 105
And mountains; and of all that we behold
From this green earth; of all the mighty world
Of eye, and ear,—both what they half create,
And what perceive; well pleased to recognise
In nature and the language of the sense 110
The anchor of my purest thoughts, the nurse,

The guide, the guardian of my heart, and soul
Of all my moral being.
                              Nor perchance,
If I were not thus taught, should I the more   115
suffer my genial spirits to decay:
For thou art with me here upon the banks
Of this fair river; thou my dearest Friend,
My dear, dear Friend: and in thy voice I catch
The language of my former heart, and read   120
My former pleasures in the shooting lights
Of thy wild eyes. Oh! yet a little while
May I behold in thee what I was once,
My dear, dear Sister! and this prayer I make,
Knowing that Nature never did betray   125
The heart that loved her; 'tis her privilege,
Through all the years of this our life, to lead
From joy to joy: for she can so inform
The mind that is within us, so impress
With quietness and beauty, and so feed   130
With lofty thoughts, that neither evil tongues,
Rash judgments, nor the sneers of selfish men,
Nor greetings where no kindness is, nor all
The dreary intercourse of daily life,
Shall e'er prevail against us, or disturb   135
Our cheerful faith, that all which we behold
Is full of blessings. Therefore let the moon
Shine on thee in thy solitary walk;
And let the misty mountain-winds be free
To blow against thee: and, in after years,   140
When these wild ecstasies shall be matured
Into a sober pleasure; when thy mind
Shall be a mansion for all lovely forms,
Thy memory be as a dwelling-place
For all sweet sounds and harmonies; oh! then,   145
If solitude, or fear, or pain, or grief,
Should be thy portion, with what healing thoughts
Of tender joy wilt thou remember me,
And these my exhortations! Nor, perchance—
If I should be where I no more can hear   150
Thy voice, nor catch from thy wild eyes these gleams
Of past existence—wilt thou then forget

That on the banks of this delightful stream
We stood together; and that I, so long
A worshipper of Nature, hither came   155
Unwearied in that service: rather say
With warmer love—oh! with far deeper zeal
Of holier love. Nor wilt thou then forget
That after many wanderings, many years
Of absence, these steep woods and lofty cliffs,   160
And this green pastoral landscape, were to me
More dear, both for themselves and for thy sake!

[1798]

QUESTIONS

1. Wordsworth and his sister return to a favorite spot in southwestern England, the hills around the ruins of Tintern Abbey. In the poem Wordsworth recalls earlier visits to the hills and the lovely Wye River. How does he describe the countryside? What feelings does he have for it?

2. What does he hope for future years and future visits to this countryside? How does nature help to cheer human beings even when life seems dreary?

3. How does being with his sister improve the experience for him, and what does he hope for the two of them?

4. It is no accident that Wordsworth is considered the leader of the Romantic movement, at least the part of it that sees nature as the spirit and salvation of human beings. How does nature lighten the "heavy and weary weight" of life?

5. The poem talks of nature as transcending the ordinary world's daily activities. From this reference and others like it, the great American transcendental movement began to take form. How does nature produce spiritual experiences?

6. Wordsworth remembers his own early years when he saw his sister's pleasure in nature. How do children and young adults convey a sense of being a part of nature as older adults are not?

7. Wordsworth himself said that this poem is almost an ode, that is, a poem in praise and contemplation of something beautiful. Is Wordsworth talking about nature itself or about his feelings in the face of nature?

8. This poem contains many famous lines, but perhaps the most famous and often quoted is "The still, sad music of humanity" (l. 91). What contrast is Wordsworth highlighting in the use of these words?

9. He ends the poem with the hope that he and his sister will come again to the country around Tintern Abbey and that they will live long in touch with nature, but he ends with a tribute to her, that nature is more dear because he enjoys it in her company. Why is it that we want to take our good friends with us to see places in which we most delight?

10. Describe a place where you love to camp or hike. Talk about your experiences there and the people who have gone there with you.

11. What happens to people who become cut off from nature? Why do we spend so much of our lives in high-rise buildings, airplanes, and automobiles? What would happen to us if we were to walk more and ride less? Write about the effects of nature on humans in the twenty-first century.

12. Write to a family member or friend telling him or her how much you like traveling or spending time in nature with that person. Perhaps you hunt or fish with a buddy, or perhaps you ski regularly with a group. Write to them about the meaning of the experience to you.

Dudley Randall
[1914–2000]

Born in Washington, D.C. DUDLEY RANDALL, *son of a minister and a teacher, moved to Detroit at the age of six. He had a varied career as a worker in a foundry, poet, translator, publisher, editor, and founder of Broadside Press in 1965, which he ran out of his home. He served in the military during WWII. While attending college he worked in a post office and later worked as a librarian at Morgan State University and Lincoln University. He earned a B.A. from Wayne State University in 1949, an M.A. from the University of Michigan in 1951, and later studied briefly at the University of Ghana. In 1956 he took a position in the Wayne County Federated Library System. He briefly held a teaching position in 1969, but in that year he became librarian and poet in residence at the University of Detroit, from which he retired in 1974. Randall published his first poem in the* Detroit Free Press *when he was thirteen and at that early age was already being influenced by the work of the writers such as Countee Cullen and Jean Toomer. His interest in Russia led him to translate the work of Alexander Pushkin and to visit the Soviet Union in 1966.*

All of Randall's sizeable efforts as a publisher and editor were designed to promote and support black writers. Broadside Press was inspired by key events from the civil rights movement, such as the bombing of a church in Birmingham, Alabama in 1963. The tragedy of that event—in which four young girls were killed—was captured in what is perhaps Randall's most famous poem, "Ballad of Birmingham." The other major event that fueled his commitment to civil rights was the assassination of President John F. Kennedy. This event prompted Randall to write the poem "Dressed in Pink," which recalls the image of Jacqueline Kennedy's outfit stained with the blood of her husband. These poems and other were published as "broadsides." The tradition of broadsides goes back to the sixteenth century. Typically, as ballads, they were intended to be put to music. They appeared on one side of a single sheet of paper, and dealt with a specific event. Randall's broadsides carried on this tradition and were used to call attention to culturally important events, such as the funeral of the four little girls and Kennedy's assassination. Randall's first book of poetry, titled Poem Counterpoem, *appeared in 1966. In 1967 he co-edited* For Malcolm: Poems on the Life and Death of Malcolm X, *a collection of poems written by various black authors in honor of the slain black leader, who was assassinated in 1965. Another edited collection, titled* Black Poetry, *appeared in 1969, and in 1971, he published another collection,* The Black Poets. *In 1975 Randall published* Broadside Memories: Poets I Have Known. *This appeared at the time he sold Broadside Press, a fact that caused him great sadness. Among his other books of his own poetry were* More to

Remember: Poems of Four Decades *(1971)*, After the Killing (1973), *and* A Litany of Friends: New and Selected Poems *(1981). He won several awards in his lifetime, including a National Endowment for the Arts fellowship in 1981. His influence on the Black arts movement in the nineteen-sixties and -seventies cannot be denied.*

Ballad of Birmingham

DUDLEY RANDALL

(On the Bombing of a Church in Birmingham,
Alabama, 1963)

"Mother dear, may I go downtown
Instead of out to play,
And march the streets of Birmingham
In a Freedom March today?"

"No, baby, no, you may not go,   5
For the dogs are fierce and wild,
And clubs and hoses, guns and jails
Aren't good for a little child."

"But, mother, I won't be alone.
Other children will go with me,   10
And march the streets of Birmingham
To make our country free."

"No, baby, no, you may not go,
For I fear those guns will fire.
But you may go to church instead   15
And sing in the children's choir."

She has combed and brushed her night-dark hair,
And bathed rose petal sweet,
And drawn white gloves on her small brown hands,
And white shoes on her feet.   20

Reprinted from *Roses and Revolutions: The Selected Writings of Dudley Randall*, edited by
Melba Joyce Boyd (2009), by permission of the Dudley Randall Literary Estate.

The mother smiled to know her child
Was in the sacred place,
But that smile was the last smile
To come upon her face.

For when she heard the explosion,   25
Her eyes grew wet and wild.
She raced through the streets of Birmingham
Calling for her child.

She clawed through bits of glass and brick,
Then lifted out a shoe.   30
"O here's the shoe my baby wore,
But, baby, where are you?"

[1966]

QUESTIONS

DUDLEY RANDALL, *Ballad of Birmingham*

1. This poem recounts a critical historical event of the civil rights era: the bombing of a church in Alabama in which four little girls perished. What do you know about this event, and what was its significance?

2. The poem focuses on one of the girls as its subject rather than the four. Why might the poet have made this decision?

3. The poem is written in the form of a ballad. Traditionally, ballads have their origins in song and are intended to be transmitted orally. The literary ballad, of which this is an example, is intended to imitate the oral form of the traditional ballad. Explain how the poem accomplishes this.

4. Summarize the story told by the narrator in the poem. Why does the narrator appear dispassionate? How does it build emotionally energy in the telling?

5. What is the essential irony of the poem? How does that irony lend the poem its special poignancy and tragedy?

6. What is the effect created by the mother's discovery of the child's shoe in the last stanza? What sort of power does such an image possess?

7. Expand upon Question 1 by writing an essay in which you discuss the poem within its historical context. What events led up to the bombing of the church and what were its consequences?

8. This poem originally appeared as a broadside. Broadsides have a long-standing tradition going back to the sixteenth century. Write an essay exploring the history of the broadside ballad. What social purposes did it serve?

Alfred, Lord Tennyson
[1809–1892]

ALFRED TENNYSON'S *life spans most of the years of Queen Victoria's reign. He was born in a Lincolnshire rectory into a talented and literate family, the fourth child and one of eight sons and four daughters. All the children were brought up as intellectuals. Tennyson's publication of poetry included the works of his two brothers, Frederick and Charles* (Poems by Two Brothers, *1827). Tennyson looked the part of a poet, tall and slender with an elegant head, and he was quickly adopted by the artistic circle at school. At Trinity College, Cambridge, he became a member of the poets' club, The Apostles, where he met Arthur Henry Hallam, whose early death was to shape both Tennyson's temperament and his poetry. Before that event, however, Tennyson won the Chancellor's prize for a poem titled* Timbuctoo *and saw his first volume of poetry published in 1830,* Poems, Chiefly Lyrical. *His second volume appeared in 1832. In 1833, Hallam, by then engaged to Tennyson's sister, Emily, died in Vienna. Tennyson began his poem on faith and doubt,* In Memoriam, *that was eventually to make him famous. He worked on the poem for seventeen years. At the same time, he worked on* Idylls of the King, *a long work retelling the tales of King Arthur from Malory but molded into the Victorian mindset. In 1842, he published* Poems, *which included* Ulysses *and* Morte D'Arthur. *In 1847, his popular satire on women's place in the world,* Princess, *appeared. These were difficult times for Tennyson, despite the success of the latest poems. Then in 1850 he married Emily Sellwood and finally published* In Memoriam. *That year he was chosen to succeed Wordsworth as Poet Laureate. A long formal poem,* Ode on the Death of the Duke of Wellington *(1852) preceded* Maud *(1855), a romantic tale of love and death, followed by* Enoch Arden *and* Northern Farmer *(1964). He dedicated a new edition of* Idylls *to the memory of Queen Victoria's beloved husband Prince Albert, who had died in 1861, and became a great favorite of the queen. In 1884, he became Lord Tennyson and published* Becket, *a successful drama. In his last years, he wrote apace, publishing* Tiresias and Other Poems *in 1885,* Locksley Hall Sixty Years After *in 1886,* Demeter and Other Poems *in 1889, and* The Death of Oenone *in 1892, published just after his death. Assessments of Tennyson's work was, in turn, criticized and then praised in the past century. During most of the twentieth century, he was thought to be too ornate for most readers, but in time his poetic talent and his ability to bring sound and light to life were honored. Those who love a talented wordsmith and those who love a mythic vision of ancient England love Tennyson.*

The Eagle

ALFRED, LORD TENNYSON

He clasps the crag with crooked hands;
Close to the sun in lonely lands,
Ringed with the azure world, he stands.

The wrinkled sea beneath him crawls;
He watches from his mountain walls,   5
And like a thunderbolt he falls.

[1851]

First published in *Poems of Alfred Tennyson* in 1851.

QUESTIONS

ALFRED, LORD TENNYSON, *The Eagle*

1. What image of this noble bird do you get from reading this poem? How is he personified?

2. What do eagles symbolize? How do the loneliness and the power combine to make the image of the bird come to life? Why might Tennyson have chosen an eagle as the subject of his poem rather than another type of bird?

3. The two stanzas are tightly rhymed. What effect do the three rhymed words have on the movement and power of the poem? Read the last line again. How does the sound imitate the meaning?

4. Pick an animal that is somehow symbolic for you. Write a description that helps the reader to understand the symbolism that you attach to the animal.

Theodore Roethke
[1908–1963]

As a poet, **THEODORE ROETHKE** *is credited as being a strong influence on the tradition of confessional poetry that includes poets such as Sylvia Plath, Anne Sexton, Robert Lowell, and John Berryman. Roethke had a life complicated by bouts of depression and mania that both engaged and drove away friends, and caused turmoil in his career as a teacher and writer. Roethke was born in Saginaw, Michigan to German immigrant parents. His father, Otto Roethke owned a commercial greenhouse. The greenhouse in which Roethke spent much time as a child became a pervasive influence in Roethke's writing, as did his strained relationship with his over-bearing, stern father. Roethke's interior journeys into his own psyche generally include references to both. Of the poet's first collection of poems,* Open House *(1941), critic Walter Kalaidjian suggests it is Roethke's heart that is an "open house" and that the title poem represents the confessional aesthetic that Roethke followed for the rest of his life, and that influenced other poets who had little connection with the impersonal, idea-driven poetry in the tradition of T. S. Eliot, Ezra Pound, and their ilk.*

Throughout his life Roethke suffered from manic depression and was hospitalized several times. Never one to hide his emotional state from his readers, Roethke presented his illness with candor but tied it into an organic whole. Depression, it seemed, became a dark, organic place—although dank and full of decay, it also kept his ideas and poetry alive to sprout in more fertile times. In both 1945 and 1950 he received fellowships from the Guggenheim Foundation. In 1945 he suffered a major bout of depression for which he received shock treatments. By 1947 he was teaching at the University of Washington and the next year published The Lost Son and Other Poems. *In the 1950s he spent time in England and Europe on a Fulbright grant. In 1957 Roethke published* Words for the Wind. *That year he won the Bollingen Prize and the National Book Award. While in Europe he published* The Waking: Poems 1933–1953 *(1953), which received the Pulitzer Prize. By 1959 he suffered yet another mental breakdown and was admitted to a Seattle sanitarium. His last work was* The Far Field *(1962). His work remains popular today for its imagery, its rhythms, and its elegiac quality. Overall, it is Roethke's metaphoric sense of the relation between the psyche and the physical landscape that makes him engaging as a poet.*

My Papa's Waltz

THEODORE ROETHKE

The whiskey on your breath
Could make a small boy dizzy;
But I hung on like death:
Such waltzing was not easy.

We romped until the pans
Slid from the kitchen shelf;
My mother's countenance
Could not unfrown itself.

The hand that held my wrist
Was battered on one knuckle;   10
At every step you missed
My right ear scraped a buckle.

You beat time on my head
With a palm caked hard by dirt,
then waltzed me off to bed   15
Still clinging to your shirt.

[1948]

QUESTIONS

1. What effect does the rhyme and meter of the poem have on you? What do these qualities have on the poem's meaning?

2. What seems joyful in the poem? What seems dangerous? How does the poet establish the line between the two?

3. Who are the characters in the poem? What is their relationship? What prompts the poet to recall this moment?

4. Is this poem happy or sad? Or both? How so? How does it speak to the complexities of parent/child relationships?

5. What images in the poem seem particularly unsettling? Why are they?

6. Why can't the mother's "countenance unfrown itself?" What does this gesture suggest about the marriage?

7. What is the significance of being put to bed in the poem, culturally and symbolically? What does the poem suggest about the power of adults over children?

8. Roethke described his father elsewhere as being a violent alcoholic. Write an essay in which you explore how your response to this poem changed when you discovered that fact.

9. Parents have influence on our lives that reaches deep into our essential being. Write an essay considering your own experiences with your parents' influence, using your understanding of "My Papa's Waltz."

Jonathan Swift
[1667–1745]

Jonathan Swift's epitaph, which he wrote himself, reads
> Swift sailed into his rest;
> Savage indignation there
> Cannot lacerate his breast.
> Imitate him if you dare,
> World-besotted traveler; he
> Served human liberty.

In this epitaph, a translation from the Latin by W. B. Yeats, perhaps the expression "savage indignation" most captures the significance of Swift's life and writings. He was a true satirist in that he used humor and wit to critique humanity and its institutions for the purpose of holding people accountable for society's imperfections and in order to improve social conditions. At various times Swift used pseudonyms or published works anonymously to enhance his ends, such as with Gulliver's Travels *(1726) and* A Modest Proposal *(1729). By not using his actual name, readers of these great works were convinced of their authenticity. That is, for the satire to have its intended effect, readers had to accept the reality of Lemuel Gulliver's experiences. Further, they had to believe that the "modest" proposal of breeding infants as food for the wealthy was made in all sincerity— that the author of the pamphlet was an actual person. This famous essay was motivated by Swift's despair over England's mute response to the latest famine in Ireland. It was an unflinching indictment of England's policies toward Ireland.*

Swift was born in Dublin, received a degree from Trinity College in 1686 and furthered his studies at Oxford University, from which he earned a master of arts degree in 1692. In 1694 he returned to Ireland and in the following year was ordained in the Church of Ireland (Anglican), and eventually became Dean of St. Patrick's Cathedral. In 1704 Swift anonymously published A Tale of a Tub, *a satire on religious debates. Soon after, Swift published* The Battle of the Books *and* The Mechanical Operation of the Spirit. *The series of satirical pamphlets on church issues,* An Argument Against Abolishing Christianity, *appeared in 1708. Swift became the editor of the newspaper* The Examiner *siding with the Tories, (outlaw Irish), against the Whig party that supported English parliamentary rights. However, the Whigs gained power after the death of Queen Anne, which fueled Swift's sense of injustice experienced by the Irish people. By the time of* The Drapier's Letters *(1724), Swift was extremely popular in Ireland, having also donated much of his earnings to the establishment of St. Patrick's Hospital. Swift continued to resist English authority in* A Short View of the State of Ireland *(1728). By 1735 Swift's Ménière's disease became more pronounced, causing him bouts of dizziness and nausea. His memory was already beginning to fail, possibly due to Alzheimer's disease. Senility had set in by 1735 and eventually, after a stroke, he could no longer be deemed responsible to conduct his own affairs. When he died, Ireland mourned his passing.*

A Description of the Morning

JONATHAN SWIFT

Now hardly here and there an hackney-coach,
Appearing, showed the ruddy morn's approach.
Now Betty from her master's bed had flown
And softly stole to discompose her own.
The slipshod 'prentice from his master's door   5
Had pared the dirt, and sprinkled round the floor.
Now Moll had whirled her mop with dextrous airs,
Prepared to scrub the entry and the stairs.
The youth with broomy stumps began to trace
The kennel-edge, where wheels had worn the place.   10
The small-coal man was heard with cadence deep
Till drowned in shriller notes of chimneysweep,
Duns at his lordship's gate began to meet,
And Brickdust Moll had screamed through half the street.
The turnkey now his flock returning sees,   15
Duly let out a-nights to steal for fees;
The watchful bailiffs take their silent stands;
And schoolboys lag with satchels in their hands.

[1709]

First published in 1709.

JONATHAN SWIFT, *A Description of the Morning*

1. Boys' lesson books at that time often asked for assignments such as, "describe the morning or the evening." This poem addresses the typical assignment but with a rather nasty twist, since Swift was likely to see the worst in humanity. What images do you notice that criticize humanity and show its darker side?

2. Morning is usually thought to be a time of hope and promise, yet the morning in this poem tends to offer only dirt and work. Is the world in the eye of the beholder, and if so, what would you say about Swift's eye?

3. This poem consists of nine couplets, each rhymed in precise patterns and each indicating the mini-picture being presented. Trace the poem through its patterns, noting each place and person being described. What class of people is being shown? How can you tell?

4. Write a description of the morning in the world where you live. Use Swift's pattern of showing several people who make up the social world that you are describing, though you will have the luxury of describing each in more detail. Then comment on the world that you have described, noting the social and physical characteristics that strike you as important to an understanding of that world.

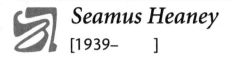

Seamus Heaney

[1939–   ]

SEAMUS HEANEY *was born in County Derry in Northern Ireland. He was the oldest of nine children, with a father who was a farmer and a cattle dealer. His mother's family had connections with the more industrial economy of Ulster's textile mills. Heaney's youngest years were spent in the country; he was a student in the local primary school, though at age twelve he won a scholarship to a Catholic boarding school, St. Columb's. Heaney has described this original move as from, "the earth of farm labour to the heaven of education," and many other moves followed: to Belfast, where he studied at Queen's University; to the Irish Republic, where he taught at Carysfort College, a teacher training institution; and to intermittent stints teaching in America. He was appointed as the Boylston Professor of Rhetoric and Oratory at Harvard University, where he teaches one semester each year, returning to his home in Dublin for the rest of the year. In 1995, he was awarded the Nobel Prize in Literature.*

Heaney shares with other Northern Irish poets (such as Michael Longley, Derek Mahon, Paul Muldoon, Medbh McGuckian and Ciaran Carson) the consciousness that comes from living and working in a society deeply divided along religious and political lines; a society that has suffered decades of violence. Heaney's work engages the question of poetry's obligations and agencies in the social world. In an essay, "Frontiers of Writing," Heaney quotes the poet Nadezha Mandelstam who discussed the "social character" of the work of poetry; Heaney echoes Mandelstam's phrases in his own statement: "To be a source of truth and at the same time a vehicle of harmony: this expresses what we would like poetry to be."

Heaney wants to attend to the particularities of poetic knowledge—how poetry, through its instruments of "metre and syntax, of tone and musical trueness," comprises its own answer to the world, but that practical knowledge of the world also compels its own ethical response; he says that "within ourselves we can reconcile two orders of knowledge which we might call the practical and poetic . . . [and] that each form of knowledge redresses the other and that the frontier between them is there for the crossing." Heaney's work, through its musical sound and the scope of its subjects, exemplifies as well as any living poet's that crossing a frontier can be most profitable.

Mid-Term Break

SEAMUS HEANEY

I sat all morning in the college sick bay
Counting bells knelling classes to a close.
At two o'clock our neighbors drove me home.

In the porch I met my father crying—
He had always taken funerals in his stride—   5
And Big Jim Evans saying it was a hard blow.

The baby cooed and laughed and rocked the pram
When I came in, and I was embarrassed
By old men standing up to shake my hand

And tell me they were "sorry for my trouble,"   10
Whispers informed strangers I was the eldest,
Away at school, as my mother held my hand
In hers and coughed out angry tearless sighs.
At ten o'clock the ambulance arrived
With the corpse, stanched and bandaged by the nurses.   15

Next morning I went up into the room. Snowdrops
And candles soothed the bedside; I saw him
For the first time in six weeks. Paler now,

Wearing a poppy bruise on his left temple,
He lay in the four foot box as in his cot.   20
No gaudy scars, the bumper knocked him clear.

A four foot box, a foot for every year.

[1980]

QUESTIONS

SEAMUS HEANEY, *Mid-Term Break*

1. The poem's title takes a matter-of-fact aspect of an academic year—the break a student might take in the middle of a term—and makes of it a metaphor for something else. What "terms" are broken off midway in the poem?

2. What can we say about the speaker of the poem? Where in time is he, in relation to the events related in the poem?

3. What details does Heaney assemble to characterize the grieving household?

4. Mark Strand and Eavan Boland describe an elegy, in *The Making of a Poem*, as "a lament . . . it sets out the circumstances and character of a loss. It mourns for a dead person, lists his or her virtues, and seeks consolation beyond the momentary event." We might call this poem an intimate elegy. Does this poem seem to exhibit these features?

5. Elegies for the deaths of children constitute a small subgenre of the elegy. Other examples include John Crowe Ransom's "Bells for John Whiteside's Daughter," or Dylan Thomas's "Refusal to Mourn the Death of a Child by Fire." What are the risks of elegizing the death of a child? How does the poem handle, for instance, the risk of over-sentimentality?

6. Why do you suppose the poet has the younger version of himself express so little emotion? Where would you locate the emotional core of the poem?

7. In a brief essay, compare this poem with another elegy. Why do you suppose the elegy has become a genre of poetry? What appears to be its typical gestures? What work does elegy do that other kinds of poems do not do?

8. In an exploratory essay, analyze the strategies that Heaney uses to create the persona of an adolescent boy. Why do you suppose the poet chooses this strategy?

Walt Whitman
[1819–1892]

WALT WHITMAN *was born in New York to Walter Whitman, a housebuilder, and Louisa Van Velsor. Both his parents descended from early settlers of Long Island. In Whitman's early childhood, his parents moved to Brooklyn, where he attended public school. As an adolescent, he worked as an office boy and learned the printing trade at the* Patriot *and* Star *newspapers in Brooklyn. He worked as a printer until 1836 until a fire destroyed much of the printing district, and he then took up school teaching on Long Island. In 1838 he founded a weekly newspaper,* Long-Islander, *which he published and edited. During this period, he wrote poetry and literary prose.*

During the 1840s, Whitman worked for various newspapers as an editor, writer, and compositor, while he continued to write in various genres, including a novel, stories, sketches, and poetry. He briefly edited a New Orleans newspaper in 1848, the Daily Crescent, *though the job was short-lived (he resigned just months after he arrived). He traveled back to Brooklyn via the Mississippi, the Great Lakes, and the Hudson River. Around this time, he wrote and published several poems that later appeared in the first edition of* Leaves of Grass. *Much of that work, however, existed only as fragments until it was collected and published in 1855. The first edition was 795 copies, and consisted of twelve untitled poems and a preface. A subsequent edition the next year contained thirty-three poems. Whitman added to and altered* Leaves of Grass *many times—in 1860, 1867, 1870, 1876, 1881, and 1891.*

The book achieved recognition almost immediately. Ralph Waldo Emerson sent Whitman a letter shortly after the book's publication, saying, "I greet you at the beginning of a great career." Many literary and other public figures hailed the work, and his writing was published in various well-known periodicals such as Harper's Magazine, Galaxy, *and* The Radical. *William Michael Rossetti published a selection of Whitman's work in London under the title* Poems of Walt Whitman *in 1868, which brought him to the attention of the literary lights of England, including Tennyson and Swinburne.*

During the Civil War, Whitman worked as a freelance journalist and as a visitor—a "wound-dresser"—in different hospitals. After the war, he worked in various government offices, and was fired from at least one of those positions, in part because some of the poems in Leaves of Grass *were considered obscene. In later years, his health was not good, though he continued writing, lecturing on diverse topics including Thomas Paine and Abraham Lincoln, and editing his own work. In 1884, he purchased a small house—a "little old shanty of my own"—on Mickle Street in Camden, New Jersey. Friends and admirers helped him financially and* otherwise. Active as a writer and lecturer till nearly the end of his life, Whitman died in 1892 and was buried in the Harleigh Cemetery.

Whitman is one of the great original poets, certainly of America but almost as certainly of all writers in English. His work is marked by the long exclamatory line, the oratorical, hortatory power of his voice, and the democratic inclusiveness of his subjects. In the preface to the first edition of Leaves of Grass, Whitman wrote, "The messages of great poets to each man and woman are, Come to us on equal terms, Only then can you understand us, We are no better than you, What we enclose you enclose, What we enjoy you may enjoy. Did you suppose there could be only one Supreme?" In his every gesture as a poet, Whitman's ardor, and the genuineness of this invitation, reach out afresh to the reader.

Facing West from California's Shores

WALT WHITMAN

Facing west, from California's shores,
Inquiring, tireless, seeking what is yet unfound,
I, a child, very old, over waves, towards the house of maternity,
    the land of migrations, look afar,
Look off the shores of my Western sea, the circle almost
    circled:
For starting westward from Hindustan, from the vales of
    Kashmere,   5
From Asia, from the north, from the God, the sage, and
    the hero,
From the south, from the flowery peninsulas and the spice
    islands,
Long having wandered since, round the earth having
    wandered,
Now I face home again, very pleased and joyous;
(But where is what I started for, so long ago?   10
And why is it yet unfound?)

[1860]

From *Leaves of Grass*, 1867.

QUESTIONS

WALT WHITMAN, *Facing West from California's Shores*

1. What is the situation of the speaker in this poem? Where is he located physically? At what point is he in his life?

2. Whitman was an Easterner—a New Yorker—yet this speaker appears to be casting his gaze out across the Pacific Ocean. Based on your reading, what significance do you find in this location?

3. Where does the speaker say he has journeyed? What makes him "pleas'd and joyous" at the end of the poem?

4. The poem makes reference to exotic locales—Hindustan, Kashmere, Asia, the "flowery peninsulas and the spice islands." What do these locales signify in the poem? Are they a contrast with his present location? With his homecoming?

5. The structure of the poem is relatively simple, built around two clauses of a compound-complex sentence: "I . . . look afar . . . ; . . . Now I face home again. . . ." Thus, the poem's subject has to do with something like archetypal journey of one's life. With what knowledge does the poem's speaker seem to have returned?

6. The poem ends with a parenthetical pair of questions:

   (But where is what I started for so long ago?

   And why is it yet unfound?)

   In a poem that maintains that the return to one's home is joyous and pleasing, what effect do these two questions have on the reader? Do they constitute a reversal, a complication?

8. The consciousness of the speaker is in a sense the whole of this poem: What we understand about his journey comes solely through his voice and his construction of that journey. In a brief essay, analyze what we know about this speaker from the way he explains himself, from what he says about his various destinations, and from his manner of speech.

9. In an exploratory essay, consider the role of paradox in the logic of this poem. For instance, the speaker says he is "a child, very old"; the poem's conclusion might also be said to be paradoxical. How does the poet use paradox to investigate the idea of a wisdom-quest?

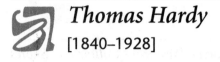

Thomas Hardy
[1840–1928]

THOMAS HARDY *was born on June 2, 1840, the first child of Thomas and Jemima Hardy. He would be followed by two sisters and a brother. The family lived at Higher Bockhampton, Dorset, England—a hamlet consisting of some ten houses situated in a wooded area on the edge of Puddletown Heath (which Hardy was later to christen Edgon Heath). As a young boy, Hardy memorized large swatches of the* Book of Common Prayer, *and on wet Sundays, he would wrap himself in a tablecloth and lead the family in the Service for Morning Prayer.*

Hardy's mother, not necessarily taken with the religious life, enrolled her son in a nonconformist school, and within a year or two had secured him additional tuition in Latin. He left school at sixteen, with a good grounding in Latin, drawing, ancient history, and various branches of mathematics. The same year he was apprenticed to the local architect in Dorchester, John Hicks. Five years later, in 1861, he set off for London to practice architecture on a larger scale.

In London, he worked at his architectural career while reading English literature and taking advantage of the city's museums, opera-houses, and concert halls. He began to write poems ("Hap" and "The Ruined Maid" date from this period). Desperate to find his way into print, he wrote a first novel, The Poor Man and the Lady, *which was rejected. But the publisher's reader, George Meredith, encouraged Hardy to write another, which resulted in his first published book,* Desperate Remedies (1871). *During this time, he read Darwin's* The Origin of Species *and became an agnostic, adopting a scientific world view touched with a sense of beauty and nostalgia.*

By 1870, he returned to Dorset where he continued to write fiction. His first major hit was Far From the Madding Crowd (1874). *On the strength of this success, he was able to marry Emma Lavinia Gifford, a woman he had met and fallen in love with in 1870. For the next 22 years he wrote and published fiction and became one of England's leading novelists, famous as the sexually frank and socially challenging author of* Return of the Native (1878), The Mayor of Casterbridge (1885), The Woodlanders (1887), Tess of the d'Urbervilles (1891), *and* Jude the Obscure (1895).

In 1898, after the stormy success of Jude the Obscure, *Hardy surprised his readers by presenting them with not another novel but instead,* Wessex Poems, *his first collection of verse—a collection that included a good number of those early poems rejected by editors in the 1860s. This book was followed by seven more,* Poems of the Past and the Present (1901—*which included "The Darkling Thrush"*), Time's Laughingstocks (1909), Satires of Circumstance (1914—

which included "The Convergence of the Twain"), Moments of Vision *(1917),* Late Lyrics and Earlier *(1922),* Human Shows *(1925), and* Winter Words *(posthumous, 1928). He died at age 87 on January 11, 1928, equally famous as novelist and poet.*

—Bill Morgan, *Illinois State University*

The Convergence of the Twain

THOMAS HARDY

Lines on the Loss of the "Titanic"

I

In a solitude of the sea
Deep from human vanity,
And the Pride of Life that planned her, stilly couches she.

II

Steel chambers, late the pyres
Of her salamandrine fires,   5
Cold currents thrid[1], and turn to rhythmic tidal lyres.

III

Over the mirrors meant
To glass the opulent
The sea-worm crawls—grotesque, slimed, dumb, indifferent.

IV

Jewels in joy designed   10
To ravish the sensuous mind
Lie lightless, all their sparkles bleared and black and blind.

V

Dim moon-eyed fishes near
Gaze at the gilded gear
And query: "What does this vaingloriousness down here?" . . .   15

---

[1]Thread

First published in 1912.

VI

Well: while was fashioning
This creature of cleaving wing,
The Immanent Will that stirs and urges everything

VII

Prepared a sinister mate
For her—so gaily great—   20
A Shape of Ice, for the time far and dissociate.

VIII

And as the smart ship grew
In stature, grace, and hue,
In shadowy silent distance grew the Iceberg too.

IX

Alien they seemed to be: 25
No mortal eye could see
The intimate welding of their later history,

X

Or sign that they were bent
By paths coincident
On being anon twin halves of one august event,   30

XI

Till the Spinner of the Years
Said "Now!" And each one hears,
And consummation comes, and jars two hemispheres.

[1912]

QUESTIONS

1. A member of the Titanic's staff is said to have answered a passenger's query about safety with, "Lady, even God couldn't sink this ship." Is Hardy perhaps reacting to that kind of human confidence?

2. The poem describes the iceberg as a suitor of the lady ship. Why is this image particularly frightening?

3. Is the Immanent Will in "The Convergence of the Twain" another name for God, or is there something more sinister in this line?

4. Why was the loss of the Titanic so big a news event in its day, and even in our own? Why is this story so powerful as a meditation on human expectations?

5. What is the difference between the language used to describe the iceberg and the ship in "The Convergence of the Twain"?

6. The last line describes the meeting of the iceberg and the ship as a consummation. What meanings does this word have? Why does it follow the image of a seducer and a lady?

7. In "The Convergence of the Twain," Hardy's Titanic, like most ships, is called *she*. Write about the ways gender and sexuality figure in the language of the poem.

8. Compare the imagery in this poem with disasters in our own day, the Challenger or the twin towers, for example. Write about how you would use imagery to describe a present day disaster. Why did you choose the imagery that you chose?

Ezra Pound
[1885–1972]

EZRA POUND *was a poet, translator, critic, essayist, editor, and mentor to many of the great writers of the twentieth century. He also created literary movements, and his most famous statement about art, "make it new", captured what Pound believed about how literature should reflect the conditions of modern society. Accordingly, many give him credit for having originated modern poetry, freeing it from the attitudes of the previous era.*

Pound was born in Idaho but soon moved with his parents to Philadelphia. When he was sixteen he entered the University of Pennsylvania. Two years later he transferred to Hamilton College where he studied several languages, particularly Italian and Spanish. His interest in languages would have considerable bearing on the texture of his poetry and his ideas about translating literary works into English. For a brief time he taught college in the United States, but in 1907 left for Europe, first settling in England and later in Italy.

His first book of poems, A Lume Spento, *was published in Italy in 1908. In 1912, Pound started a movement in poetry, called Imagism. His imagist manifesto stated that poetry should be free of sentimentality, be direct, concise, and musically varied. That movement resulted in the publication of an anthology of imagist poetry titled* Des Imagists *(1914). By 1915, his interests turned to translating Chinese poetry. He published his first translations that year in the volume,* Cathay. *In 1917 he began work on his epic poem, the* Cantos, *which he continued to expand throughout his life. It was published, along with a collection of his translations, in 1953. This work, with its nonnarrative structure, symbolism, and allusions to politics, history, and culture, is considered by many to be a major example of the principles of twentieth century Modernism.*

Pound's influence on literature cannot be understated. In his own work, and with his support of poets such as T. S. Eliot and William Carlos Williams, and novelists such as James Joyce and Ernest Hemingway, he changed the face of literature. His early interest in world literature put him ahead of his time, as witnessed today by the increasing focus on writers from non-English-speaking cultures.

In a Station of the Metro

EZRA POUND

The apparition of these faces in the crowd;
Petals on a wet, black bough.

[1913]

First published in *Poetry: A Magazine of Verse* in April, 1913.

QUESTIONS

EZRA POUND, *In a Station of the Metro*

1. The word "apparition" usually signifies something ghostly. What does it mean in the context of this poem? Why do the faces look ghostly to the poet?

2. What is the central metaphor of the poem? What correlation does the metaphor have with the natural world?

3. Why is the poem compressed into a single sentence broken up into two lines? What effect does it achieve as a result? Why is the beginning of each line capitalized?

4. Notice the rhyme between the words "crowd" and "bough." What quality does this lend to the poem?

5. By focusing on an image with such singular intensity, the poem establishes a relationship between the human and nature. Explain how the poem achieves this sense of unity.

6. Imagism as a poetry movement emphasizes the "thingness" of objects in reality. What statement is the poet making about the relationship between the mind and its function in the expression of reality?

7. As an example of Modernism, this poem makes its own statement about how literature as art treats its subject matter. Art, this suggests, perceives the world differently. What beliefs about poetry as art form are expressed in this poem?

8. Write a brief essay on the ancient poetry form of *haiku*. In your essay, discuss how "In a Station of the Metro" was influenced by this form. Also, discuss how the poem advances the form and adapts it to modern conditions.

9. Revisit your responses to the questions in number one in this list. In an exploratory essay, reconsider that response and discuss how your interpretation of the word "apparition" changes in view of those questions.

A. E. Housman
[1859–1936]

ALFRED EDWARD HOUSMAN *was born at Valley House, Fockbury, near Bromsgrove in Worcestershire. The child of a solicitor, Housman grew up in relative privilege. He attended King Edward's School, Bromsgrove, and St. John's College, Oxford. From 1882 to 1892 he worked at the Patent Office in London but continued to study classical literature and began writing poetry. He also produced brilliant articles on the Classics that were published in scholarly journals. In 1892 he was appointed Professor of Latin at University College, London. At about the same time, he published his first collection of poems,* A Shropshire Lad *(1896), a romantic study of youthful exuberance. This cycle of poems tells of the central character, Terence Hearsay, who leaves the countryside for life in London. The world these poems describe portrays Housman's idealized rural scenery and country life, filled with nostalgia and rustic sweetness. Ironically, a number of the poems were written before Housman had actually seen Shropshire. Later, Housman was surprised to find that people made literary pilgrimages to the places he described. These pilgrims were surprised at the license that Housman had taken with the actual landscape. For example he put a vane on one steeple that was actually on another church. In 1911 Housman became Kennedy Professor of Latin at Cambridge. He continued his notable scholarship and wrote more Shropshire poems, which were published in his* Last Poems *(1922). He died at Cambridge, and his ashes were buried in Shropshire near the north door of St. Laurence's Church in Ludlow.*

Housman is well known for creating a vision of country life that everyone wishes were true though it may in fact have never existed. Critics speculate that he presented a kind of divided consciousness, a man who came from a distinguished family (one of his younger brothers was the novelist and dramatist Laurence Housman) and whose livelihood and reputation in his own day rested on his serious Latin scholarship. Yet he is remembered for something quite other than social recognition and academic power. He is remembered for his ability to carry his readers back to a time that never was but that we all wish might have been. That time is the joyous time of a youth spent wandering through the trees and meadows of a mythical English countryside peopled with good-willed country folk, friendly wooly creatures, and children whose lives have never known a care.

Loveliest of trees, the cherry now

A. E. HOUSMAN

Loveliest of trees, the cherry now
Is hung with bloom along the bough,
And stands about the woodland ride[1]
Wearing white for Eastertide.

Now, of my threescore years and ten,   5
Twenty will not come again,
And take from seventy springs a score,
It only leaves me fifty more.

And since to look at things in bloom
Fifty springs are little room,   10
About the woodlands I will go
To see the cherry hung with snow.

[1896]

---

[1]Path

First published in *A Shropshire Lad* in 1896.

A. E. HOUSMAN, *Loveliest of trees, the cherry now*

1. How does Housman use the image of the cherry to demonstrate his views on aging?

2. The poem is written in deceptively simple couplets. What do the rhymed words do to illustrate the joyfulness of the imagery and optimism of the poem?

3. Consider the age that you are now. What do you intend to do with the next twenty years? What choices will you make? What ambitions do you have? What will you seize now, and what will you wait for until later?

Wallace Stevens
[1879–1955]

WALLACE STEVENS *was born in Reading, Pennsylvania. He attended Harvard University from 1897 to 1900, though he did not graduate. Instead, he graduated from New York Law School in 1903 and worked for various law firms until 1914, when he was hired as a vice president of the New York Office of the Equitable Surety Co. of St. Louis. As a result of mergers, his job was abolished in 1916, and he joined the Hartford Accident and Indemnity company. By 1934, he was named vice president of this company, for which he worked the rest of his life, residing in Hartford.*

By all accounts, Stevens was a successful businessman, but during the years when he was establishing his career, he was also establishing a career as a poet. His first work was published when he was thirty-six years old; he published poems in Poetry, *and his first book,* Harmonium, *was published in 1923 by Knopf. Stevens was discouraged by the reviews for* Harmonium *and did not write or publish much through the remainder of the twenties. However, he began to write again in the thirties, publishing* Ideas of Order *(1935);* Owl's Clover *(1937); and* The Man with the Blue Guitar *(1937).* Parts of a World, Notes Toward a Supreme Fiction, *and* Esthetique du Mal *followed in 1942. Many people see Stevens' last volumes as his greatest—all of which he wrote after he was sixty years old. This was poetry interested in the conditions of its own making, philosophical in some senses, inventive, playful, speculative.*

Stevens lived a cosmopolitan life, and took regular trips to New York from his Hartford home. He also frequently traveled to Havana and Florida. He loved fine food and other fleshly pleasures—pleasures that circulate just beneath the surface of his poems. In "Notes Toward a Supreme Fiction"—a poem which can be read as an artistic manifesto—one of the sections is titled, "It Must Be Abstract," but another is titled, "It Must Give Pleasure." And in a late poem, "A Quiet Normal Life," there is a quintessential Stevensian moment that perhaps expresses what he saw in poetry: The poem reveals a man sitting and thinking, listening to the sounds of the night:

> . . . above the crickets' chords,
> Babbling, each one, the uniqueness of its sound.
> There was no fury in transcendent forms.
> But his actual candle blazed with artifice.

That "actual candle"—the poet's instrument—ignites with the skill, and the will, to make poems. Stevens is known for that incandescence.

Disillusionment of Ten O'clock

WALLACE STEVENS

The houses are haunted
By white night-gowns.
None are green,
Or purple with green rings,
Or green with yellow rings,   5
Or yellow with blue rings.
None of them are strange,
With socks of lace
And beaded ceintures.
People are not going   10
To dream of baboons and periwinkles.
Only, here and there, an old sailor
Drunk and asleep in his boots,
Catches tigers
In red weather.   15

[1923]

QUESTIONS

WALLACE STEVENS, *Disillusionment of Ten O'clock*

1. This poem's diction has several registers: a plain, repetitive one ("Or purple with green rings, / Or green with yellow rings, / Or blue with yellow rings."); a slightly exotic one ("socks of lace / And beaded ceintures"); and a hint of a nautical one ("an old sailor . . . / Catches tigers / In red weather"). What do these shifts in register do for the reader? What effects does Stevens appear to be aiming for?

2. It's not hard to catch the note of longing that undergirds the poem. How does the poem achieve this effect? For instance, the speaker notes that "none [of the nightgowns] are green." How does this negation yield a sense of what the speaker longs for?

3. Who appears to be the speaker of the poem? How can you tell? What kind of speaker, for instance, speaks of "beaded ceintures"?

4. With what does the speaker of the poem appear to be disillusioned?

5. The opening line of the poem uses the word "haunted." What is the form of this haunting? What forms do the ghostly figures take?

6. The poet notes, with a tone of disappointment, that "None of them [the nightgowns] are strange." What are some possible meanings of "strange"? Why does the speaker of the poem wish for strange nightgowns—or other strange entities?

7. Robert Frost once said to Stevens that his poems were "too full of bric a brac." (Stevens, for his part, said to Frost that his poems were "full of subjects.") Richard Howard once said, at a literary panel that also included the poet William Stafford, "Here the great Plains meet the great Fancies." Stevens can be seen as an emblematic figure in that same dichotomy. In an essay, discuss the ways Stevens uses the contrast between the plain and the fancy—between what he sees as the mundane and the exotic.

8. One of the subjects of the poem appears to be the imagination. In an exploratory essay, consider the various forms the imagination takes in the poem. For instance, the main impulse of the poem—to wish for a more fanciful, colorful life—is embroidered with a rather fanciful construction of the unimaginative life.

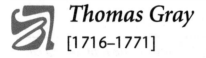

Thomas Gray
[1716–1771]

These familiar lines—"Full many a flower is born to blush unseen" and "Far from the madding Crowd's ignoble Strife"—are taken from THOMAS GRAY'S "Elegy Written in a Country Churchyard," one of the most frequently quoted poems in the English language. The poet and scholar Gray wrote little over the course of his life, but his use of varied poetic forms and straightforward speech, as well his love of nature and his fascination with history, had a profound influence on verse. Written in the middle of the eighteenth century, his poetry provided a useful segue from the restraint and polish of Neoclassicism into the sensitivity and love of nature that characterized British Romanticism.

Gray was the only surviving child of a middle-class London family. He had a privileged educational background, attending Eton College, then Cambridge University. Arriving at Cambridge, he found himself dissatisfied with the lectures and the other restrictions of university life. While he never took a degree, he formed close friendships that profoundly affected his life. Of these, his friendship with Horace Walpole, author of the early gothic romance The Castle of Otranto *(1765), was particularly influential. Throughout his life, Gray wrote his friends richly entertaining and personally illuminating letters; his correspondence offered not only humorous anecdotes, but also learned insights into various topics, especially classical and continental literature. After a grand tour of Europe with Walpole, Gray returned to Cambridge where he pursued further his intellectual interests. These ranged among classical languages, music, politics, architecture, metaphysics, painting, criticism, and history, to name a few. Though he studied in seclusion, for his erudition he was eventually appointed in 1768 the Regius Professor of Modern History.*

Though Gray longed for privacy and published only a few poems, his "Elegy Written in a Country Churchyard" (1751) became the representative poem of his age, and attracted to him unwanted fame. This melancholic poem, much studied and often anthologized, is a restrained meditative poem inspired by his contemplation of a country graveyard. Gray tended to speak in universals so, fittingly, this poem does not mourn the passing of a particular person but rather speaks more generally to the message that rich and poor alike inevitably die. This accessible poem muses on the villagers who have commemorated their dead in this graveyard, and suggests that their simplicity might have spared them greater toil—a message reflecting a familiar political justification of rural poverty articulated during this period.

In the midst of the unwanted fame attained from his "Elegy," Gray retreated into his studies and, in particular, into the study of Norse literature. He also crafted Pindaric odes, "The Bard" and "The Progress of Poesy," both published by Walpole in 1757. He died in 1771, and is buried in the churchyard in the village of Stokes Poges, which he described in his most famous poem.

Elegy Written in a Country Churchyard

THOMAS GRAY

The curfew tolls the knell of parting day,
    The lowing herd wind slowly o'er the lea,
The plowman homeward plods his weary way,
    And leaves the world to darkness and to me.

Now fades the glimmering landscape on the sight,   5
    And all the air a solemn stillness holds,
Save where the beetle wheels his droning flight,
    And drowsy tinklings lull the distant folds;

Save that from yonder ivy-mantled tower
    The moping owl does to the moon complain   10
Of such, as wandering near her secret bower,
    Molest her ancient solitary reign.

Beneath those rugged elms, that yew tree's shade,
    Where heaves the turf in many a moldering heap,
Each in his narrow cell forever laid,   15
    The rude[1] forefathers of the hamlet sleep.

The breezy call of incense-breathing Morn,
    The swallow twittering from the straw-built shed.
The cock's shrill clarion, or the echoing horn,[2]
    No more shall rouse them from their lowly bed.   20

For them no more the blazing hearth shall burn,
    Or busy housewife ply her evening care;

---

[1]Unsophisticated

[2]Hunter's horn

First published, anonymously, in 1751.

No children run to lisp their sire's return,
    Or climb his knees the envied kiss to share.

Oft did the harvest to their sickle yield,   25
    Their furrow oft the stubborn glebe[3] has broke;
How jocund did they drive their team afield!
    How bowed the woods beneath their sturdy stroke!

Let not Ambition mock their useful toil,
    Their homely joys, and destiny obscure;   30
Nor Grandeur hear with a disdainful smile
    The short and simple annals of the poor.

The boast of heraldry, the pomp of power,
    And all that beauty, all that wealth e'er gave,
Awaits alike the inevitable hour.   35
    The paths of glory lead but to the grave.

Nor you, ye proud, impute to these the fault,
    If Memory o'er their tomb no trophies raise,
Where through the long-drawn aisle and fretted[4] vault
    The pealing anthem swells the note of praise.   40

Can storied urn or animated[5] bust
    Back to its mansion call the fleeting breath?
Can Honor's voice provoke the silent dust,
    Or Flattery soothe the dull cold ear of Death?

Perhaps in this neglected spot is laid   45
    Some heart once pregnant with celestial fire;
Hands that the rod of empire might have swayed,
    Or waked to ecstasy the living lyre.

But Knowledge to their eyes her ample page
    Rich with the spoils of time did ne'er unroll;   50

---

[3]Ground

[4]Ornamentation of an interlacing pattern.

[5]The poet refers here to a Grecian urn decorated with a narrative in pictures. By "animated bust," he means a sculpture imbued with a lifelike quality.

Chill Penury repressed their noble rage,
   And froze the genial current of the soul.

Full many a gem of purest ray serene,
   The dark unfathomed caves of ocean bear:
Full many a flower is born to blush unseen,   *55*
   And waste its sweetness on the desert air.

Some village Hampden,[6] that with dauntless breast
   The little tyrant of his fields withstood;
Some mute inglorious Milton[7] here may rest,
   Some Cromwell[8] guiltless of his country's blood.   *60*

The applause of listening senates to command,
   The threats of pain and ruin to despise,
To scatter plenty o'er a smiling land,
   And read their history in a nation's eyes.

Their lot forbade: nor circumscribed alone   *65*
   Their growing virtues, but their crimes confined;
Forbade to wade through slaughter to a throne,
   And shut the gates of mercy on mankind,

The struggling pangs of conscious truth to hide,
   To quench the blushes of ingenuous shame,   *70*
Or heap the shrine of Luxury and Pride
   With incense kindled at the Muse's flame.

Far from the madding crowd's ignoble strife,
   Their sober wishes never learned to stray;
Along the cool sequestered vale of life   *75*
   They kept the noiseless tenor of their way.

Yet even these bones from insult to protect
   Some frail memorial still erected nigh,

---

[6]English politician John Hampden (c. 1595–1643) imprisoned in 1627 for his refusal to pay a tax levied by King Charles I.

[7]English poet John Milton (1608–1674) wrote the epic poem *Paradise Lost* (1667).

[8]Puritan Oliver Cromwell (1599–1658) led a rebellion against King Charles I to become Lord Protector of England from 1649–1658.

With uncouth[9] rhymes and shapeless sculpture decked,
    Implores the passing tribute of a sigh.   *80*

Their name, their years, spelt by the unlettered[10] Muse,
    The place of fame and elegy supply:
And many a holy text around she strews,
    That teach the rustic moralist to die.

For who to dumb Forgetfulness a prey,   *85*
    This pleasing anxious being e'er resigned,
Left the warm precincts of the cheerful day,
    Nor cast one longing lingering look behind?

On some fond breast the parting soul relies,
    Some pious drops[11] the closing eye requires;   *90*
Even from the tomb the voice of Nature cries,
    Even in our ashes live their wonted[12] fires.

For thee, who mindful of the unhonored dead
    Dost in these lines their artless tale relate;
If chance,[13] by lonely contemplation led,   *95*
    Some kindred spirit shall inquire thy fate,

Haply some hoary-headed swain may say,
    "Oft have we seen him at the peep of dawn
Brushing with hasty steps the dews away
    To meet the sun upon the upland lawn.   *100*

"There at the foot of yonder nodding beech
    That wreathes its old fantastic roots so high,
His listless length at noontide would he stretch,
    And pore upon the brook that babbles by.

"Hard by yon wood, now smiling as in scorn,   *105*
    Muttering his wayward fancies he would rove,

---

[9]Awkward, uncultivated.

[10]Lacking formal education.

[11]Tears

[12]Accustomed

[13]In other words, "If it should happen that."

Now drooping, woeful wan, like one forlorn,
    Or crazed with care, or crossed in hopeless love.

"One morn I missed him on the customed hill,
    Along the heath and near his favorite tree;   110
Another came; nor yet beside the rill,
    Nor up the lawn, nor at the wood was he;

"The next with dirges due in sad array
    Slow through the churchway path we saw him borne.
Approach and read (for thou canst read) the lay,   115
    Graved on the stone beneath yon aged thorn."

    The Epitaph

Here rests his head upon the lap of Earth
    A youth to Fortune and to Fame unknown,
Fair Science[14] *frowned not on his humble birth,*
    And Melancholy marked him for her own.   120

Large was his bounty, and his soul sincere,
    Heaven did a recompense as largely send:
He gave to Misery all he had, a tear,
    He gained from Heaven ('twas all he wished) a friend.

No farther seek his merits to disclose.   125
    Or draw his frailties from their dread abode
(There they alike in trembling hope repose),
    The bosom of his Father and his God.

                                     [1751]

---

[14]Pursuit of knowledge, in general.

QUESTIONS

THOMAS GRAY, *Elegy Written in a Country Churchyard*

1. Comment on the ways in which the first three stanzas establish the mood of the poem as a whole.

2. Summarize stanzas 4–7. What is the subject of these quatrains?

3. Define the literary tactic of allegory and describe its relevance to Gray's "Elegy Written in a Country Churchyard."

4. In what ways does Gray use the device of historical allusion as a means of celebrating those buried in the churchyard?

5. At what point does the speaker begin to reflect on his own death? How do these meditations relate to the preceding stanzas?

6. Consider the significance of "The Epitaph" in relation to the poem as a whole.

7. After conducting research, compose an essay about the relevance of Gray's "Elegy" to literary romanticism. You might find it particularly useful to examine the poet's representations of nature, rural life, and human emotion.

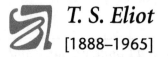

T. S. Eliot
[1888–1965]

T. S. ELIOT *was the seventh child of successful St. Louis merchant, Henry Ware Eliot, and school teacher, Charlotte Sterns Eliot. He showed such great intellectual abilities that he entered Harvard at age eighteen. There he studied English, Latin, Greek, German, and French literature. He also studied history, art, and philosophy, and wrote for the Harvard* Advocate. *After college he traveled in Europe and spent a year at the Sorbonne and wrote his first great poem, "The Love Song of J. Alfred Prufrock" at age twenty-three. He went home to America and studied for a doctorate at Harvard, returned to Germany to do doctoral research, but moved to London and Oxford at the beginning of World War I. In London he met Ezra Pound who championed Eliot's abilities as a poet and helped him publish "Prufrock" in* Poetry *in June 1915. Eliot also published "Preludes" and "Rhapsody on a Windy Night" in* Blast, *and "Portrait of a Lady" in* Others. *The following year he finished his doctorate but did not return to the United States to become a professor as his parents had expected. Instead he married Vivienne Haigh-Wood and took a job as a clerk in Lloyds Bank. During this era he wrote literary journalism for important newspapers and journals such as the* New Statesman, *the* Monist, *and the* Times Literary Supplement. *He became an assistant editor for the* Egoist *and wrote a short book on Pound,* Ezra Pound: His Metric and Poetry *(1918). His first book of poetry,* Prufrock and Other Observations *had appeared a year earlier. In 1920 he published* Poems *and a volume of essays,* The Sacred Wood.

In 1921, Eliot collapsed from over-work and spent a few months resting in Germany and traveling in France where he wrote The Waste Land *in consultation with Ezra Pound, (Pound mostly crossed out passages of a much longer draft; passages that were to become the starting points for later poems), that appeared in 1922. By 1925 Eliot was a literary celebrity, able to leave the bank and join the publishing house of Faber and Gwyer (later Faber and Faber). In 1927 he became a devout Anglican after years of meditation and study. In 1932, following years of Haigh-Wood's acute depressions, he and his first wife divorced. She died in a mental hospital in 1947. He published* The Hollow Men *and* Ash Wednesday *in 1930 and "Journey of the Magi" in 1931. His selected essays,* The Use of Poetry *and* The Use of Criticism, *were published in 1933. At that time also Eliot began to write drama, becoming a noted dramatist with* Murder in the Cathedral *in 1935 and* The Family Reunion *in 1939. His last great poems were "The Four Quartets: Burnt Norton" (1936), "East Coker" (1940), "The Dry Salvages" (1941), and "Little Gidding" (1942). He married Esme Valerie Fletcher in 1957 and lived as a celebrated writer until his death in 1965. He received the Nobel Prize for Literature and England's Order of Merit among many other honors.*

The Love Song of J. Alfred Prufrock

T. S. ELIOT

S'io credessi che mia risposta fosse
a persona che mai tornasse al mondo,
questa fiamma staria senza più scosse.
Ma per ciò che giammai di questo fondo
non tornò vivo alcun, s'i'odo il vero,
senza tema d'infamia ti rispondo.[1]

Let us go then, you and I,
When the evening is spread out against the sky
Like a patient etherised upon a table;
Let us go, through certain half-deserted streets,
The muttering retreats   5
Of restless nights in one-night cheap hotels
And sawdust restaurants with oyster-shells:
Streets that follow like a tedious argument
Of insidious intent
To lead you to an overwhelming question . . .   10
Oh, do not ask, 'What is it?'
Let us go and make our visit.

---

[1] "If I thought my answer were to one who would ever return to the world, this flame should stay without another movement; but since none ever returned alive from this depth, if what I hear is true, I answer thee without fear of infamy." Eliot's epigraph comes from Canto 27 of Dante's *Inferno*, in which Dante visits the eighth circle of hell, reserved for evil counselors. The words are uttered by Count Guido de Montefeltrano, also known in Dante's time as The Fox. Montefeltrano is condemned to burn in a prison of fire because of his destructive advice to Pope Boniface. A brilliant political and military tactician, Guido in his youth led troops against the Papacy and was excommunicated. He then repented his sins and retired to a monastery. The corrupt Pope Boniface, however, lured Guido out of retirement by offering him reinstatement in the church in exchange for his cunning services in suppressing the Pope's enemies. Seduced by the Pope's promises of a ticket to heaven, Guido aided the Pope's corrupt designs, only to find upon his death that he had been double-crossed and sent to hell for his efforts. Dante imagines Guido as a man "taken in by his own craftiness."

Published in *Prufrock and Other Observations* in 1917.

In the room the women come and go
Talking of Michelangelo,[2]

The yellow fog that rubs its back upon the window-panes,   *15*
The yellow smoke that rubs its muzzle on the window-panes,
Licked its tongue into the corners of the evening,
lingered upon the pools that stand in drains,
Let fall upon its back the soot that falls from chimneys,
Slipped by the terrace, made a sudden leap,   *20*
And seeing that it was a soft October night,
Curled once about the house, and fell asleep.

For indeed there will be time
For the yellow smoke that slides along the street
Rubbing its back upon the window-panes;   *25*
There will be time, there will be time
To prepare a face to meet the faces that you meet;
There will be time to murder and create,
And time for all the works and days of hands
That lift and drop a question on your plate;   *30*
Time for you and time for me,
And time yet for a hundred indecisions,
And for a hundred visions and revisions,
Before the taking of a toast and tea.

In the room the women come and go   *35*
Talking of Michelangelo.

And indeed there will be time
To wonder, 'Do I dare?' and, 'Do I dare?'
Time to turn back and descend the stair,
With a bald spot in the middle of my hair—   *40*
(They will say: 'How his hair is growing thin!')
My morning coat, my collar mounting firmly to the chin,
My necktie rich and modest, but asserted by a simple pin—
(They will say: 'But how his arms and legs are thin!')
Do I dare   *45*
Disturb the universe?

---

[2]Michelangelo (1475–1564), the revered Italian sculptor, painter, architect, and poet.

In a minute there is time
For decisions and revisions which a minute will reverse.
For I have known them all already, known them all—
Have known the evenings, mornings, afternoons,　　　　　　　*50*
I have measured out my life with coffee spoons;
I know the voices dying with a dying fall
Beneath the music from a farther room.
　　So how should I presume?

And I have known the eyes already, known them all—　　　　*55*
The eyes that fix you in a formulated phrase,
And when I am formulated, sprawling on a pin,
When I am pinned and wriggling on the wall,
Then how should I begin
to spit out all the butt-ends of my days and ways?　　　　*60*
　　And how should I presume?

And I have known the arms already, known them all—
Arms that are braceleted and white and bare
(But in the lamplight, downed with light brown hair!)
Is it perfume from a dress　　　　　　　　　　　　　　*65*
That makes me so digress?
Arms that lie along a table, or wrap about a shawl.
　　And should I then presume?
　　And how should I begin?

. . . . .

Shall I say, I have gone at dusk through narrow streets　　*70*
And watched the smoke that rises from the pipes
Of lonely men in shirt-sleeves, leaning out of windows? . . .

I should have been a pair of ragged claws
Scuttling across the floors of silent seas.

. . . . .

And the afternoon, the evening, sleeps so peacefully!　　　*75*
Smoothed by long fingers,
Asleep . . . tired . . . or it malingers,
Stretched on the floor, here beside you and me.
Should I, after tea and cakes and ices,
Have the strength to force the moment to its crisis?　　　*80*

But though I have wept and fasted, wept and prayed,
Though I have seen my head (grown slightly bald) brought in
    upon a platter,[3]
I am no prophet—and here's no great matter;
I have seen the moment of my greatness flicker,
And I have seen the eternal Footman hold my coat, and snicker,   *85*
And in short, I was afraid.

And would it have been worth it, after all,
After the cups, the marmalade, the tea,
Among the porcelain, among some talk of you and me,
Would it have been worth while,   *90*
To have bitten off the matter with a smile,
To have squeezed the universe into a ball
To roll it towards some overwhelming question,
To say: 'I am Lazarus,[4] come from the dead,
Come back to tell you all, I shall tell you all'—   *95*
If one, settling a pillow by her head,
    Should say: 'That is not what I meant at all.
    That is not it, at all.'

And would it have been worth it, after all,
Would it have been worth while,   *100*
After the sunsets and the dooryards and the sprinkled streets,
After the novels, after the teacups, after the skirts that trail along
    the floor—
And this, and so much more?—
It is impossible to say just what I mean!
But as if a magic lantern[5] threw the nerves in patterns on a   *105*
    screen:
Would it have been worth while

---

[3]In the Biblical story of Salome and John the Baptist (see Mark VI:17–28) Salome, the daughter of
Queen Herodias hated John the Baptist. Herod, to please Herodias, imprisoned John. Salome
danced before Herod and he promised to give anything she wished. Salome asked for the head of
John the Baptist on a platter.

[4]Lazarus: Prufrock uses Jesus' parable of Lazarus and Dives told in Luke XVI:19–31. In the parable,
Dives, a rich man, ignores the suffering of a poor man, Lazarus, who begs for crumbs from Dives's
table. Lazarus dies and he goes to heaven. Dives goes to hell. Dives implores God to allow Lazarus to
return from the dead to warn Dives's relatives to repent.

[5]An early form of optical projector.

If one, settling a pillow or throwing off a shawl,
And turning toward the window, should say:
   'That is not it at all,
   That is not what I meant, at all.'   *110*

  . . . . .

No! I am not Prince Hamlet,[6] nor was meant to be;
Am an attendant lord, one that will do
To swell a progress, start a scene or two,
Advise the prince; no doubt, an easy tool,
Deferential, glad to be of use,   *115*
Politic, cautious, and meticulous;
Full of high sentence, but a bit obtuse;
At times, indeed, almost ridiculous—
Almost, at times, the Fool[7]

I grow old . . . I grow old . . .   *120*
I shall wear the bottoms of my trousers rolled.

Shall I part my hair behind? Do I dare to eat a peach?
I shall wear white flannel trousers, and walk upon the beach.
I have heard the mermaids singing, each to each.

I do not think that they will sing to me.   *125*

I have seen them riding seaward on the waves
Combing the white hair of the waves blown back
When the wind blows the water white and black.

We have lingered in the chambers of the sea
By sea-girls wreathed with seaweed red and brown   *130*
Till human voices wake us, and we drown.

                    [1915]

---

[6]Prince Hamlet: the protagonist of William Shakespeare's tragedy, *Hamlet*.

[7]The Fool, or jester, was a stock character of Elizabethan drama.

QUESTIONS

T. S. ELIOT, *The Love Song of J. Alfred Prufrock*

1. This poem was Eliot's first major achievement. He wrote it when he was a young man of twenty-three, yet the speaker in the poem appears to be a middle-aged man. How does this man, who appears to be in midlife crisis, explain the central problem of his life?

2. The introduction of the poem is in Italian, taken from Canto 27 of Dante's *Inferno* and reads roughly something like, "I'll tell you the truth only because you cannot take it back to the living." The speaker of these lines is Count Guido de Montefeltrano, who was a soldier and politician, repented, and then returned to serve a corrupt pope, only to find himself in hell. How does the beginning of "Prufrock" suggest hell? What kind of hell is the speaker experiencing? Why?

3. T. S. Eliot loved cats. Lines 15–25 suggest a comparison with a cat. What image does an ally cat or feral cat suggest? How does that fit with the mood of the poem?

4. The speaker in the poem is a modest and mild man who is afraid of the kinds of women he would like to meet. How does this problem suggest the eternal "battle of the sexes"?

5. The poem uses Biblical references: line 82 ("my head brought in upon a platter) refers to John the Baptist who was beheaded at the wish of princess Salome. Line 94 & 95 ("I am Lazarus, come from the dead/Come back to tell you all, I shall tell you all") refer to the follower of Jesus whom Jesus raised from the dead. These lines suggest the questions about the nature of life and death, heaven and hell, that the poem addresses. What do we learn about the life beyond death from Lazarus, or from John the Baptist for that matter? What can we know in this life? Why is that a problem for the speaker in the poem?

6. The final part of the poem (1.111) mentions Prince Hamlet, the Shakespearian character who questions the honesty of his father's ghost who comes to seek revenge. Hamlet's question is, "Can a ghost be trusted to tell the truth; could it be a demon instead?" This is the poet's question in the poem, but it is not the narrator's question. What is it that the narrator wants?

7. Lines 92–94 refer to a famous "seduction" poem by poet Andrew Marvell, "To His Coy Mistress," a poem in which the speaker urges a young woman to take advantage of her youth while she can and roll all

their sweetness "into one ball." This suggestive image indicates the worry of Prufrock: Would a woman want him at his age and in his state? What do you think?

8. "Do I dare to eat a peach?" (1. 122) is perhaps one of the most over-interpreted lines in poetry. Eve dares to eat the apple that will eventually bring her to death (beyond this world), but the speaker in the poem cannot quite get himself to consider even a peach, let alone an apple. The poet seems to ask, "What have we come to?" What indeed have we come to in the two thousands? Does the question of good and evil still catch our attention as it did in 1915? How and why?

9. Nearly every line of "Prufrock" refers to some literary text or other reference, partly because Eliot had just finished working on a degree in classical literature. It was filling his head. If a young poet were to write such a poem, what literature would fill his or her head? Write about the literary influences that form the young scholar of the twenty-first century.

10. Do we still worry about what happens after death? Many people argue that America especially has become a secular country in which owning things and making money is more important than anything else. Write about the conflicts between the drive to become rich and successful and to lead a good life in spiritual or religious terms.

11. What are the courting rituals in your cultural group? How do young people meet? What happens to the shy guy or girl? Does anyone end up alone and lonely like Prufrock? Write about how the effort to find a good mate affects people in your generation.

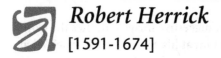

Robert Herrick
[1591-1674]

ROBERT HERRICK *of all poets best displays the transition from the grand atti-*
tudes of the Renaissance—as displayed by William Shakespeare and Herrick's
mentor, the great dramatist Ben Jonson—to the repression of the Puritan inter-
lude and back to the rollicking good humor of the Restoration. Born in London,
he was the son of a goldsmith who died soon after his birth. Herrick's mother took
him off to the village of Hampton to enjoy a childhood in the country. He was
then briefly apprenticed to a jeweler but quickly rejected the work and was sent
on to St. John's College, Cambridge, from which he graduated in 1617. He wrote
poetry with the "tribe of Ben" and enjoyed the life of the city but failed to gain a
court appointment. He then took orders in the Anglican church and served as a
military chaplain to the Duke of Buckingham. Shortly after, in 1629, King
Charles II appointed him Prior in Devonshire where he settled in comfortably
and began to write pastoral songs in addition to his lighthearted courtly lyrics.
These were collected in his first publication, Hesperides, *in 1648. The previous*
year he had refused to sign the Solemn League and Covenant, (a binding agree-
ment between Scotland swearing loyalty to the English Parliament), and was thus
relieved of his role as prior. When the Restoration brought back the crown,
Herrick regained his appointment in Devonshire parish and served there until his
death.

Herrick has been described as thoroughly pagan, a lover of life and good liv-
ing. His poems sing of wine, women, and song, not necessarily in that order. He
commanded all about him to live joyfully and seize the day whenever possible.
His conscience may have bothered him at times, for he was also the author of
Noble Numbers, *poems of praise to the Divine and repentance for transgressions.*
Most of all, though, he was the poet of the joys of the simple life, praising the
English countryside where he grew up and where he spent his happiest years as a
village priest. Herrick was the opposite of the metaphysical poets who dwelt on the
life of the spirit and soul. Herrick dwelt instead on the life of the senses, praising
all of life's richness and all the blessings that come from time spent at the dining
table and wandering through fields of daisies and sunflowers. He also was most
able at praising the beauties of a young woman whether clad or unclad, perhaps
not the ideal image for a priest but certainly the ultimate expression of one who
followed the great tradition of the Renaissance.

Upon Julia's Clothes

ROBERT HERRICK

Whenas in silks my Julia goes,
Then, then, methinks, how sweetly flows
That liquefaction of her clothes.

Next, when I cast mine eyes and see
That brave vibration each way free,   5
O how that glittering taketh me!

[1648]

First published in *Hesperides* in 1648.

QUESTIONS

ROBERT HERRICK, *Upon Julia's Clothes*

1. In this poem the speaker describes his response when his lady wears silk. What does he see and feel on these occasions?

2. Why do people like to wear silk? What qualities does it have that no other fabric has? What symbolic value does silk have? Why is it sexy?

3. These triplets are about rhyme, six lines, two rhymes. How do the rhymes reflect the quality of the fabric and the woman being described?

4. What power does the fashion industry have over young people? Write about the fashion ads that appear in your favorite magazine. What do they say about the people who wear them? What is the rhetoric of the fashion?

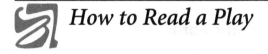 *How to Read a Play*

As A LITERARY GENRE, drama is particularly challenging to readers because it is both a literary text—a written work to be studied much like a poem or short story—and the script for a performative event that is a work of art intended to be staged before a live audience. It is a text meant to be embodied, to be seen and heard. Therefore, drama involves more than simply the give-and-take between an author and a reader. As an art form, the performance of drama demands a collaborative relationship among at least three parties: 1) the playwright who authors the script, 2) the individuals who help stage the production, including the director, stage manager, lighting and set designers, actors, and musicians, among others, and 3) those who watch the production, the audience.

In some ways, drama is the most difficult genre to read and study because it demands a particular investment of imagination and attention. The playwright encourages you to envision the rich visual images of a theatrical production, but all you have at hand are the words on the page of the dramatic script. As a reader of drama, you will find in the text the rich figurative language of poetry, but without the abundant narrative description found in prose. To imagine the world of the play, you must read closely all of the elements of drama, particularly the dialogue and the stage directions. You need to engage with the text not only as a reader, but also as the director, the actor, the set designer—and still maintain your role as an audience member. You also have to keep in mind the particular context in which the play was written and how that shapes the form and content of the play. It's a tricky task, but immensely rewarding.

By reading drama critically, you will be called on to develop your own interpretation of how the play might be staged. Based on your close reading and analysis, try to imagine which performers should be cast in the roles, where the action of the play should be set, what the costumes might look like. You can mentally stage your own production of the play you've read. Plus, you will have the opportunity to see many of these plays produced on stage, as well as in television and film adaptations. One of the great pleasures drama affords is the opportunity to look critically at different interpretations of a given play in performance. For instance, how does Shakespeare's troubled young hero *Hamlet* seem different when performed by Sir Laurence Olivier—and by Ethan Hawke? How does Molière's *Tartuffe*, with its satire of religious hypocrisy, speak to us differently when staged in its original setting of the seventeenth-century French court—and when set in contemporary America?

Dramatic Form

Because plays are intended to be performed, they are written in **dialogue**, which depicts the conversation between two or more characters. A **monologue** provides the spoken thoughts of a single character. A **soliloquy** is a speech delivered by a single character on stage while alone or isolated from the other characters. In a soliloquy, a character is basically speaking to himself and sharing his innermost thoughts and feelings with the audience. In a short **aside**, a character similarly speaks aloud without the other characters hearing him, and this bit of dialogue is directed toward himself or to the audience.

Though generally intended to be spoken aloud by actors before a live audience, drama also encompasses **closet drama**, a dramatic form primarily (if not exclusively) intended only to be read, as well as **pantomime** and **mime**, which are forms of drama based strictly on movement with no words at all.

Because most plays are intended to be performed before a live audience, they usually run no more than two hours in performance. Therefore, the dramatic script is relatively short and compact; as with a short story or poem, readers must attend to each word and symbol, every entrance and exit. The length of a play also provides another way to categorize it. Plays are generally divided into **acts**, which are divisions in plays much like chapters in novels. These acts are sometimes further divided into **scenes**, which are smaller units akin to subchapters.

Plays are generally categorized by their **genre**, a term that signals its type. In a **tragedy**, the central character is usually an eminent person who struggles with a morally significant problem or encounters a series of disastrous events; these unhappy events eventually lead to a tragic ending, in which the hero either suffers miserably or dies. In Shakespeare's tragedy *Othello*, for instance, the main character struggles with jealousy and betrayal, and ultimately kills both his wife and himself. In a **comedy**, the characters similarly struggle with important issues, but the problems are resolved and the play ends happily. In Shakespeare's comedy *A Midsummer Night's Dream*, the young lovers—like *Othello*'s young lovers—struggle with jealously and betrayal. Yet the problems in this comedy are happily resolved, and the play concludes with a set of joyful weddings. There are many different types of comic drama, ranging from the social and political critique offered by **satire** to the practical jokes that characterize **slapstick**. You may find as you read that these categories are not completely distinct: there are comic moments in tragedy, tragic moments in comedy. A **tragicomedy** is a play that combines elements of comedy and tragedy: It is a serious play that generally ends without catastrophe.

Reading Drama Critically

Before you encounter the first bit of dramatic dialogue, you can already begin reading a play critically. What, for instance, does the title lead you to expect? Who is the play's author? When was it written? What does the date of the play's publication or production lead you to expect? How, for instance, might a play written in 1600 differ from one written in 2005? Who might be the intended audience for this play? Is the play a translation? Will it invite you into a familiar or unfamiliar world?

By immediately locating the historical and cultural context of a particular drama, you will also become alert to differences in form and content among the plays you read. You will be prepared, for instance, to think about why the chorus interrupts the action of an ancient Greek play by Euripides, why Shakespeare sometimes offers a "play within a play"; why the plot of Dion Boucicault's melodrama appears ridiculous; or why Bertold Brecht's epic drama employs such unusual stage devices. You don't need to jump into in-depth research about the play's context. Just be aware that the unfamiliar stage devices might reflect the expectations of a different type of audience, and that the thematic concerns introduced by the play engaged with issues important to that historical audience. Even if the play appears odd or perplexing at first glance, it likely also engages you with contemporary concerns meaningful to you.

When you read past the title, author, and publication (or performance) date of a play, notice that the author usually provides a list of **characters**. This list may offer you detailed explanations of the characters, details like those found in a novel or short story, or it may offer you little beyond a name. Generally, you will also be provided the details of the play's scene or **setting—** its time, place, and occasion.

Information such as this reminds us that a dramatic text is also a **script**, a plan intended to instruct theater companies on how to produce, cast, and stage the written text. Yet this information can also help readers by providing additional descriptions of the characters and the setting. In drama, it can sometimes be hard to remember who is saying what the first time you read a play. For help, you can look to the descriptions offered in the list of characters or in the stage directions. Sometimes, as in the case of work by the playwright Tennessee Williams, the descriptions of the characters will be long and detailed. But in Susan Glaspell's drama *Trifles*, she tells us only that "George Henderson" is the "county attorney." Yet, as we read his dialogue, we discover that this brash young man assumes too much due to his position as an authority, one unfamiliar with the community he visits. As a result, he overlooks some of the clues that are crucial to his attempt to solve the murder of John

Wright. The dialogue and the stage directions work together to create the world of the play.

When you first approach the text of a play, you can read it much like you read fiction. Of course, a play looks different from a short story or poem because it is written in dialogue. As readers of drama, we move between the words spoken by a particular character and the **stage directions**. As you read, especially at the opening of scenes or acts, attend to these stage directions. These are the author's instructions, to be interpreted by the director and cast—and they often vanish in performance. The stage directions might be minimal, consisting only of a few words. Or they might be elaborate, running for pages and pages. When reading the stage directions, pay close attention to the world the author tries to create. Note the descriptions of scenery and costumes, the **stage properties** (the props, or moveable objects on stage); the stage positions recommended for the actors, the **stage business** (the action on stage without dialogue and usually involving props), and the lighting and sound effects. In a dramatic text, the stage directions are usually bracketed and in italics; they interrupt the flow of the dialogue, the words spoken by the actors on stage. Nonetheless, play close attention to them: They offer crucial insights into the dialogue, the words delivered on stage.

In additional to the dialogue and the stage directions, playwrights offer other bits of information that can help you to understand the text or to see the play in your mind's eye. Some authors offer a **preface** and/or an **afterword** to explain their intentions for the play. In the case of George Bernard Shaw's *Pygmalion*, the play on which the stage musical *My Fair Lady* was based, the playwright offers an extended account of the study of phonetics in the preface. In the play's afterword, Shaw informs us of the fates of the two main characters, Henry Higgins and Eliza Doolittle. On the stage, *Pygmalion* looks like a romantic comedy; it concludes with the apparent suggestion that Higgins and Eliza have fallen in love and will marry. But considered in the context of its afterword, the play reads like a dark—if humorous—critique of middle-class mores in early twentieth-century England.

When you begin to read the play's dialogue, think closely about the language. Is the drama written in prose or poetry? Do a few characters speak for long periods, or are there brief exchanges among many characters? Does the language seem familiar—or is it alien? If the language seems alien to you, is it because of difficult words, unfamiliar references, strange rhythms? Be sure to look up any unfamiliar words and references in the dictionary or an encyclopedia.

As you work through the dramatic text, read it as you would read poetry or fiction: Attend to devices such as style, plot, tone, and characterization. As you read the dialogue, also attend to the use of figurative language. For instance, the prologue of *Oedipus Rex* provides us with an extended metaphor in which a priest describes the blighted city of Thebes as being like a ship. Just as you might do in a poem or short story or novel, you can explore the importance of this extended metaphor. How does it contribute to your understanding of this ancient Greek city, the setting for the play?

You should also attend to the form of the drama. Is the play organized in longer acts or shorter scenes? The division marked between acts frequently suggests a change in locale or time. A scene is a smaller component of the play: a change of scene does not necessarily signal a change in locale or time, but it does frequently mark the departure or entrance of a new character. Is this a longer play, consisting of three or more acts or many scenes? Or is a shorter play: a sketch or a one-act play?

As you read the dialogue and stage directions, you will inevitably become familiar with the **characters** who people the drama. The characters are the literary figures represented on stage by **actors**. As you read, you might want to jot down some obvious particulars to help you keep the various characters straight in your head: Who are they? Where are they from? What's the relationship among these characters? What do they want? What gets in the way of their desires? On some level, these questions seem silly. But remember, you don't have the rich narrative detail of fiction to help you place the characters in their setting and situation.

As you work your way through the play, determine who the **protagonist** is. The protagonist is the central character of the drama, the character whose desires or interests drive the plot. In the classical tradition, the protagonist was a noble hero—but that is not always the case in later forms of drama. The **antagonist** is the character or force that prevents the protagonist from attaining his or her desires. You may find more than one protagonist or antagonist, and sometimes the protagonist or antagonist is not a person, but something more abstract. For instance, in Lorraine Hansberry's *A Raisin in the Sun*, you might consider Karl Lindner the antagonist because he tries to prevent the play's black characters from moving into his white neighborhood. But in fact, racism is the antagonist in Hansberry's drama. In some ways, Lindner is just a **stock character**, a flat character whose behavior is stereotypical and whose presence merely advances the plot; he is the "bigoted white guy."

The dramatic action of a play usually stems from the conflict between the protagonist and the antagonist. In most cases, the conflict creates the suspense that propels you to the end of the play; it makes you wonder what will happen, and encourages you to care about the events on the page and on the stage. The **plot** is simply the events that unfold in the narrative on stage. The elements of the plot include the **exposition** (when we first meet characters, learn what happened previously and what's happening now), the **rising action** (the events that lead to the climax), the **climax** (the turning point or crisis of the plot, the highest point of emotion or intensity in the play), the **falling action** (the events that follow the climax), and the **conclusion** (the resolution of the play, also known as the denouement).

As you follow the plot to its conclusion, you may notice some interesting techniques that playwrights employ. Some drama begins *in medias res,* which means the play begins in the middle of ongoing action. The author can introduce **foreshadowing,** a hint of what's to come in future events; or **dramatic irony,** in which we in the audience knows more about events to come than the characters on stage. Some plays offer a **double plot,** in which two plots function simultaneously; or a **subplot** (or underplot), which is a second, minor plot that involves characters other than the protagonist. In tragedy, dramatists sometimes provide a humorous subplot as relief from the dark tragic plot that drives the play.

One of the unique aspects of drama can be found through its use of **symbols.** As you likely know, fiction and poetry frequently employ symbols to convey meaning. A symbol is an object that conveys an excess of meaning; it carries a symbolic importance beyond its obvious literal function. For instance, in poetry, a rose is frequently not just a rose—despite Gertrude Stein's insistence to the contrary. A rose can serve as a symbol of love or beauty or a host of other things. In drama, a symbol serves this same function. In J. M. Synge's play *Riders to the Sea,* the rope is more than just a rope; it also represents Bartley's attachment to his mother. When Bartley takes the rope to use as a halter, he leaves behind his connection to his home and the women who sustain it. But in drama, the rope is also a prop and part of the play's **mise-en-scène.** The mise-en-scène refers to everything that occupies the stage, including the scenery, props, and stage movement.

As you read drama closely and critically, you need to attend to the elements listed here, to the play's form, characterization, setting, plot, and figurative language. But don't forget to look at the big picture. What is the **theme** of the play, the central idea it advances? Why did the playwright choose this particular subject matter, these particular formal devices? What makes the play's story compelling? Why have audiences responded so powerfully to this play, sometimes for centuries? What specifically about this play has inspired actors to perform it, readers and critics to study it, theatergoers to applaud it? When you read a text, attend to your instincts. Frequently, the strongest and most creative critical insights start with an initial gut reaction to a moment in the play. Just remember, you can only transform that gut reaction into a compelling argument by supporting it with concrete evidence from the text, the words on the page, and strong analysis.

Tennessee Williams
[1911–1983]

The American playwright **TENNESSEE WILLIAMS** *was born Thomas Lanier Williams, in Columbus, Mississippi. After a particularly gloomy childhood in St. Louis, he attended and subsequently dropped out of both the University of Missouri and Washington University. He eventually graduated, at age twenty-four, from the State University of Iowa, with a degree in playwriting. After he graduated, the prestigious Theatre Guild produced his play* Battle of Angels *(1940), in Boston. Though the play failed to connect with audiences, this production nonetheless launched the career of one of the most significant post-World War II playwrights.*

In 1944, Williams achieved his first major theatrical success with his memory play, The Glass Menagerie. *It was first produced in Chicago, and moved to New York a year later, where it won Williams the New York Drama Critics' Circle Award for the first of four times. The Glass Menagerie is considered to be somewhat autobiographical, based on his childhood experiences in the tenements of St. Louis. His parents were miserable; he toiled unhappily at a shoe factory, writing in his free time; and both he and his older sister (upon whom the character Laura was based) suffered breakdowns. In the play, Tom, son of the controlling Amanda and brother to the fragile Laura, recounts his home life from memory. As Tom himself cautions in his opening speech, the play cannot be read strictly as realistic. Consequently, the stage directions incorporate avant-garde stage techniques to depict this highly personal tale: Brechtian devices such as a performer's direct address to the audience and visual images flashed on stage during the performance interrupt the flow of the narrative.*

Williams's second Broadway play attracted even more acclaim. A Streetcar Named Desire *(1947) ran for 855 performances, and introduced the brooding actor Marlon Brando to audiences as Stanley, the brash and seductive husband in this drama set in New Orleans. Throughout his career, Williams continued to write plays that garnered commercial success and critical acclaim, including* The Rose Tattoo *(1951),* Cat on a Hot Tin Roof *(1955), and* The Night of the Iguana *(1961). Many of these works reached larger audiences when translated into successful films, starring luminaries such as Vivien Leigh, Burt Lancaster, and Katherine Hepburn.*

Immensely productive until his accidental death in 1983, Williams left behind not only a raft of brilliant plays, but a rich collection of work in other genres, including autobiography, poetry, the short story and novel. His haunting invocation of the American South in his work—as well as his fearless thematic exploration of sexuality, addiction, and madness—powerfully influenced subsequent writers and continues to appeal to audiences.

The Glass Menagerie

TENNESSEE WILLIAMS

NOBODY, NOT EVEN THE RAIN, HAS SUCH
SMALL HANDS[1]

—e.e. cummings

SCENE: AN ALLEY IN ST. LOUIS

Part I. Preparation for a Gentleman Caller.
Part II. The Gentleman calls.

Time: Now and the Past.

THE CHARACTERS

Amanda Wingfield (the mother): A little woman of great but confused vitality clinging frantically to another time and place. Her characterization must be carefully created, not copied from type. She is not paranoiac, but her life is paranoia. There is much to admire in Amanda, and as much to love and pity as there is to laugh at. Certainly she has endurance and a kind of heroism, and though her foolishness makes her unwittingly cruel at times, there is tenderness in her slight person.

Laura Wingfield (her daughter): Amanda, having failed to establish contact with reality, continues to live vitally in her illusions, but Laura's situation is even graver. A childhood illness has left her crippled, one leg slightly shorter than the other, and held in a brace. This defect need not be more than suggested on the stage. Stemming from this, Laura's separation increases till she is like a piece of her own glass collection, too exquisitely fragile to move from the shelf.

Tom Wingfield (her son): And the narrator of the play. A poet with a job in a warehouse. His nature is not remorseless, but to escape from a trap he has to act without pity.

Jim O'Connor (the gentleman caller): A nice, ordinary, young man.

---

[1]Final line of the American poet e. e. cummings's poem, "somewhere i have never traveled, gladly beyond" (1923).

SCENE ONE

The Wingfield apartment is in the rear of the building, one of those vast hive-like conglomerations of cellular living-units that flower as warty growths in overcrowded urban centers of lower middle-class population and are symptomatic of the impulse of this largest and fundamentally enslaved section of American society to avoid fluidity and differentiation and to exist and function as one interfused automatism.

The apartment faces an alley and is entered by a fire escape, a structure whose name is a touch of accidental poetic truth, for all of these huge buildings are always burning with the slow and implacable fires of human desperation. The fire escape is part of what we see—that is, the landing of it and steps descending from it.

The scene is memory and is therefore nonrealistic. Memory takes a lot of poetic license. It omits some details; others are exaggerated, according to the emotional value of the articles it touches, for memory is seated predominantly in the heart. The interior is therefore rather dim and poetic.

At the rise of the curtain, the audience is faced with the dark, grim rear wall of the Wingfield tenement. This building is flanked on both sides by dark, narrow alleys which run into murky canyons of tangled clotheslines, garbage cans, and the sinister latticework of neighboring fire escapes. It is up and down these side alleys that exterior entrances and exits are made during the play. At the end of Tom's opening commentary, the dark tenement wall slowly becomes transparent and reveals the interior of the ground-floor Wingfield apartment.

Nearest the audience is the living room, which also serves as a sleeping room for Laura, the sofa unfolding to make her bed. Just beyond, separated from the living room by a wide arch or second proscenium with transparent faded portieres (or second curtain), is the dining room. In an old-fashioned whatnot in the living room are seen scores of transparent glass animals. A blown-up photograph of the father hangs on the wall of the living room, to the left of the archway. It is the face of a very handsome young man in a doughboy's First World War cap. He is gallantly smiling, ineluctably smiling, as if to say "I will be smiling forever."

Also hanging on the wall, near the photograph, are a typewriter keyboard chart and a Gregg shorthand diagram. An upright typewriter on a small table stands beneath the charts.

The audience hears and sees the opening scene in the dining room through both the transparent fourth wall of the building and the transparent gauze portieres of the dining-room arch. It is during this revealing scene that the fourth wall slowly ascends, out of sight. This transparent exterior wall is not brought down again until the very end of the play, during Tom's final speech.

The narrator is an undisguised convention of the play. He takes whatever license with dramatic convention is convenient to his purposes.

Tom enters, dressed as a merchant sailor, and strolls across to the fire escape. There he stops and lights a cigarette. He addresses the audience.

TOM. Yes, I have tricks in my pocket, I have things up my sleeve. But I am the opposite of a stage magician. He gives you illusion that has the appearance of truth. I give you truth in the pleasant disguise of illusion.

   To begin with, I turn back time. I reverse it to that quaint period, the thirties, when the huge middle class of America was matriculating in a school for the blind. Their eyes had failed them, or they had failed their eyes, and so they were having their fingers pressed forcibly down on the fiery Braille alphabet of a dissolving economy.

   In Spain there was a revolution. Here there was only shouting and confusion. In Spain there was Guernica.[2] Here there were disturbances of labor, sometimes pretty violent, in otherwise peaceful cities such as Chicago, Cleveland, Saint Louis . . .

   This is the social background of the play.

(Music begins to play.)

   The play is memory. Being a memory play, it is dimly lighted, it is sentimental, it is not realistic. In memory everything seems to happen to music. That explains the fiddle in the wings.

   I am the narrator of the play, and also a character in it. The other characters are my mother, Amanda, my sister, Laura, and a gentleman caller who appears in the final scenes. He is the most realistic character in the play, being an emissary from a world of reality that we were somehow set apart from. But since I have a poet's weakness for symbols, I am using this character also as a symbol; he is the long-delayed but always expected something that we live for. There is a fifth character in the play who doesn't appear except in this larger-than-life-size photograph over the mantel. This is our father who left us a long time ago. He was a telephone man who fell in love with long distances; he gave up his job with the telephone company and skipped the light fantastic out of town . . .

   The last we heard of him was a picture postcard from Mazatlan, on the Pacific coast of Mexico, containing a message of two words: "Hello—Goodbye!" and no address.

   I think the rest of the play will explain itself. . . .

---

[2]Town in northern Spain destroyed during the Spanish Civil War (1936–1939).

(Amanda's voice becomes audible through the portieres.)

(Legend on screen: "Ou sont les neiges d'antan?")[3]

(Tom divides the portieres and enters the dining room. Amanda and Laura are seated at a drop-leaf table. Eating is indicated by gestures without food or utensils. Amanda faces the audience. Tom and Laura are seated in Profile. The interior is lit up softly and through the scrim we see Amanda and Laura seated at the table.)

AMANDA *(calling)*. Tom?
TOM. Yes, Mother.
AMANDA. We can't say grace until you come to the table!
TOM. Coming, Mother. *(He bows slightly and withdraws, reappearing a few moments later in his place at the table.)*
AMANDA *(to her son)*. Honey, don't *push* with your *fingers*. If you have to push with something, the thing to push with is a crust of bread. And chew—chew! Animals have secretions in their stomachs which enable them to digest food without mastication, but human beings are supposed to chew their food before they swallow it down. Eat food leisurely, son, and really enjoy it. A well-cooked meal has lots of delicate flavors that have to be held in the mouth for appreciation. So chew your food and give your salivary glands a chance to function!

(Tom deliberately lays his imaginary fork down and pushes his chair back from the table.)

TOM. I haven't enjoyed one bite of this dinner because of your constant directions on how to eat it. It's you that make me rush through meals with your hawklike attention to every bite I take. Sickening—spoils my appetite—all this discussion of—animals' secretion—salivary glands—mastication!
AMANDA *(lightly)*. Temperament like a Metropolitan star!

(Tom rises and walks toward the living room.)

You're not excused from the table.
TOM. I'm getting a cigarette.
AMANDA. You smoke too much.

(Laura rises.)

LAURA. I'll bring in the blanc mange.

---

[3]"Where are the snows of yesteryear?" in French. Drawn from poem by French medieval writer François Villon.

(Tom remains standing with his cigarette by the portieres.)

AMANDA *(rising)*. No, sister, no, sister—you be the lady this time and I'll be the darky.

LAURA. I'm already up.

AMANDA. Resume your seat, little sister—I want you to stay fresh and pretty—for gentlemen callers!

LAURA *(sitting down)*. I'm not expecting any gentlemen callers.

AMANDA *(crossing out to the kitchenette, airily)*. Sometimes they come when they are least expected! Why, I remember one Sunday afternoon in Blue Mountain—

(She enters the kitchenette.)

TOM. I know what's coming!

LAURA. Yes. But let her tell it.

TOM. Again?

LAURA. She loves to tell it.

(Amanda returns with a bowl of dessert.)

AMANDA. One Sunday afternoon in Blue Mountain—your mother received—*seventeen!*—gentlemen callers! Why, sometimes there weren't chairs enough to accommodate them all. We had to send the nigger over to bring in folding chairs from the parish house.

TOM *(remaining at the portieres)*. How did you entertain those gentlemen callers?

AMANDA. I understood the art of conversation!

TOM. I bet you could talk.

AMANDA. Girls in those days *knew* how to talk, I can tell you.

TOM. Yes?

(Image on screen: Amanda as a girl on a porch, greeting callers.)

AMANDA. They knew how to entertain their gentlemen callers. It wasn't enough for a girl to be possessed of a pretty face and a graceful figure—although I wasn't slighted in either respect. She also needed to have nimble wit and a tongue to meet all occasions.

TOM. What did you talk about?

AMANDA. Things of importance going on in the world! Never anything coarse or common or vulgar.

(She addresses Tom as though he were seated in the vacant chair at the table though he remains by the portieres. He plays this scene as though reading from a script.)

My callers were gentlemen—all! Among my callers were some of the most prominent young planters of the Mississippi Delta—planters and sons of planters!

(Tom motions for music and a spot of light on Amanda. Her eyes lift, her face glows, her voice becomes rich and elegiac.)

(Screen legend: "Ou sont les neiges d'antan?"*)*

There was young Champ Laughlin who later became vice-president of the Delta Planters Bank. Hadley Stevenson who was drowned in Moon Lake and left his widow one hundred and fifty thousand in Government bonds. There were the Cutrere brothers, Wesley and Bates. Bates was one of my bright particular beaux! He got in a quarrel with that wild Wainwright boy. They shot it out on the floor of Moon Lake Casino. Bates was shot through the stomach. Died in the ambulance on his way to Memphis. His widow was also well provided-for, came into eight or ten thousand acres, that's all. She married him on the rebound—never loved her—carried my picture on him the night he died! And there was that boy that every girl in the Delta had set her cap for! That beautiful, brilliant young Fitzhugh boy from Greene County!

TOM. What did he leave his widow?

AMANDA. He never married! Gracious, you talk as though all of my old admirers had turned up their toes to the daisies!

TOM. Isn't this the first you've mentioned that still survives?

AMANDA. That Fitzhugh boy went North and made a fortune—came to be known as the Wolf of Wall Street! He had the Midas touch, whatever he touched turned to gold! And I could have been Mrs. Duncan J. Fitzhugh, mind you! But—I picked your *father!*

LAURA *(rising)*. Mother, let me clear the table.

AMANDA. No, dear, you go in front and study your typewriter chart. Or practice your shorthand a little. Stay fresh and pretty!—It's almost time for our gentlemen callers to start arriving. *(She flounces girlishly toward the kitchenette)* How many do you suppose we're going to entertain this afternoon?

(Tom throws down the paper and jumps up with a groan.)

LAURA *(alone in the dining room)*. I don't believe we're going to receive any, Mother.

AMANDA *(reappearing, airily)*. What? No one—not one? You must be joking!

(Laura nervously echoes her laugh. She slips in a fugitive manner through the half-open portieres and draws them gently behind her A shaft of very clear light

is thrown on her face against the faded tapestry of the curtains. Faintly the music of "The Glass Menagerie" is heard as she continues, lightly:)

> Not one gentleman caller? It can't be true! There must be a flood, there must have been a tornado!

LAURA. It isn't a flood, it's not a tornado, Mother. I'm just not popular like you were in Blue Mountain. . . .

(Tom utters another groan. Laura glances at him with a faint, apologetic smile. Her voice catches a little:)

> Mother's afraid I'm going to be an old maid.

(The scene dims out with the "Glass Menagerie" music.)

SCENE TWO

On the dark stage the screen is lighted with the image of blue roses. Gradually Laura's figure becomes apparent and the screen goes out. The music subsides.

Laura is seated in the delicate ivory chair at the small claw-foot table. She wears a dress of soft violet material for a kimono—her hair is tied back from her forehead with a ribbon. She is washing and polishing her collection of glass. Amanda appears on the fire escape steps. At the sound of her ascent, Laura catches her breath, thrusts the bowl of ornaments away, and sets herself stiffly before the diagram of the typewriter keyboard as though it held her spellbound. Something has happened to Amanda. It is written in her face as she climbs to the landing: a look that is grim and hopeless and a little absurd. She has on one of those cheap or imitation velvety-looking cloth coats with imitation fur collar. Her hat is five or six years old, one of those dreadful cloche hats that were worn in the late Twenties, and she is clutching an enormous black patent-leather pocketbook with nickel clasps and initials. This is her full-dress outfit, the one she usually wears to the D.A.R.[4] Before entering she looks through the door. She purses her lips, opens her eyes very wide, rolls them upward and shakes her head. Then she slowly lets herself in the door. Seeing her mother's expression Laura touches her lips with a nervous gesture.

LAURA. Hello, Mother, I was—*(She makes a nervous gesture toward the chart on the wall. Amanda leans against the shut door and stares at Laura with a martyred look.)*

AMANDA. Deception? Deception? *(She slowly removes her hat and gloves, continuing the sweet suffering stare. She lets the hat and gloves fall on the floor—a bit of acting.)*

---

[4]Daughters of the American Revolution, an elite women's patriotic and social organization.

LAURA *(shakily)*. How was the D.A.R. meeting?

(Amanda slowly opens her purse and removes a dainty white handkerchief which she shakes out delicately and delicately touches to her lips and nostrils.)

Didn't you go to the D.A.R. meeting, Mother?

AMANDA *(faintly, almost inaudibly)*. —No.—No. *(then more forcibly:)* I did not have the strength—to go to the D.A.R. In fact, I did not have the courage! I wanted to find a hole in the ground and hide myself in it forever! *(She crosses slowly to the wall and removes the diagram of the typewriter keyboard. She holds it in front of her for a second, staring at it sweetly and sorrowfully—then bites her lips and tears it in two pieces.)*

LAURA *(faintly)*. Why did you do that, Mother?

(Amanda repeats the same procedure with the chart of the Gregg Alphabet.)[5]

Why are you—

AMANDA. Why? Why? How old are you, Laura?

LAURA. Mother, you know my age.

AMANDA. I thought that you were an adult; it seems that I was mistaken.

(She crosses slowly to the sofa and sinks down and stares at Laura.)

LAURA. Please don't stare at me, Mother.

(Amanda closes her eyes and lowers her head. There is a ten-second pause.)

AMANDA. What are we going to do, what is going to become of us, what is the future?

(There is another pause.)

LAURA. Has something happened, Mother?

(Amanda draws a long breath, takes out the handkerchief again, goes through the dabbing process.)

Mother, has—something happened?

AMANDA. I'll be all right in a minute, I'm just bewildered—*(She hesitates.)*— by life. . . .

LAURA. Mother, I wish that you would tell me what's happened!

AMANDA. As you know, I was supposed to be inducted into my office at the D.A.R. this afternoon.

(Screen image: A swarm of typewriters.)

---

[5]Symbols for the shorthand writing system invented by John Robert Gregg.

But I stopped off at Rubicam's Business College to speak to your teachers about your having a cold and ask them what progress they thought you were making down there.

LAURA. Oh. . . .

AMANDA. I went to the typing instructor and introduced myself as your mother. She didn't know who you were. "Wingfield," she said, "We don't have any such student enrolled at the school!"

I assured her she did, that you had been going to classes since early in January. "I wonder," she said, "if you could be talking about that terribly shy little girl who dropped out of school after only a few days' attendance?"

"No," I said, "Laura, my daughter, has been going to school every day for the past six weeks!"

"Excuse me," she said. She took the attendance book out and there was your name, unmistakably printed, and all the dates you were absent until they decided you had dropped out of school.

I still said, "No, there must have been some mistake! There must have been some mix-up in the records!"

And she said, "No—I remember her perfectly now. Her hands shook so that she couldn't hit the right keys! The first time we gave a speed test, she broke down completely—was sick at the stomach and almost had to be carried into the wash room! After that morning she never showed up any more. We phoned the house but never got any answer"—While I was working at Famous-Barr,[6] I suppose, demonstrating those—

(She indicates a brassiere with her hands.)

Oh! I felt so weak I could barely keep on my feet! I had to sit down while they got me a glass of water! Fifty dollars' tuition, all of our plans—my hopes and ambitions for you—just gone up the spout, just gone up the spout like that.

(Laura draws a long breath and gets awkwardly to her feet. She crosses to the Victrola and winds it up.)

What are you doing?

LAURA. Oh! *(She releases the handle and returns to her seat.)*

AMANDA. Laura, where have you been going when you've gone out pretending that you were going to business college?

LAURA. I've just been going out walking.

AMANDA. That's not true.

---

[6]Department store chain.

LAURA. It is. I just went walking.

AMANDA. Walking? Walking? In winter? Deliberately courting pneumonia in that light coat? Where did you walk to, Laura?

LAURA. All sorts of places—mostly in the park.

AMANDA. Even after you'd started catching that cold?

LAURA. It was the lesser of two evils, Mother.

(Screen image: Winter scene in a park.*)*

I couldn't go back there. I—threw up—on the floor!

AMANDA. From half past seven till after five every day you mean to tell me you walked around in the park, because you wanted to make me think that you were still going to Rubicam's Business College?

LAURA. It wasn't as bad as it sounds. I went inside places to get warmed up.

AMANDA. Inside where?

LAURA. I went in the art museum and the bird houses at the Zoo. I visited the penguins every day! Sometimes I did without lunch and went to the movies. Lately I've been spending most of my afternoons in the Jewel Box, that big glass house where they raise tropical flowers.

AMANDA. You did all this to deceive me, just for deception?

(Laura looks down.)

Why?

LAURA. Mother, when you're disappointed, you get that awful suffering look on your face, like the picture of Jesus' mother in the museum!

AMANDA. Hush!

LAURA. I couldn't face it.

(There is a pause. A whisper of strings is heard. Legend on screen: "The Crust of Humility."*)*

AMANDA *(hopelessly fingering the huge pocketbook).* So what are we going to do the rest of our lives? Stay home and watch the parades go by? Amuse ourselves with the glass menagerie, darling? Eternally play those wornout phonograph records your father left as a painful reminder of him? We won't have a business career—we've given that up because it gave us nervous indigestion! *(She laughs wearily.)* What is there left but dependency all our lives? I know so well what becomes of unmarried women who aren't prepared to occupy a position. I've seen such pitiful cases in the South—barely tolerated spinsters living upon the grudging patronage of sister's husband or brother's wife!—stuck away in some little mousetrap of a room—encouraged by one in-law to visit another—little birdlike women without any nest—eating the crust of humility all their life! Is that the future that we've mapped out for ourselves? I swear it's the only alternative I can think of! *(She pauses.)* It isn't a very pleasant alternative, is it? *(She pauses again.)* Of course—some girls *do marry.*

(Laura twists her hands nervously.)

Haven't you ever liked some boy?

LAURA. Yes. I liked one once. *(She rises.)* I came across his picture a while ago.

AMANDA *(with some interest).* He gave you his picture?

LAURA. No, it's in the yearbook.

AMANDA *(disappointed).* Oh—a high school boy.

(Screen image: Jim as the high school hero bearing a silver cup.)

LAURA. Yes. His name was Jim. *(She lifts the heavy annual from the clawfoot table.)* Here he is in *The Pirates of Penzance.*

AMANDA *(absently).* The what?

LAURA. The operetta the senior class put on. He had a wonderful voice and we sat across the aisle from each other Mondays, Wednesdays and Fridays in the Aud.[7] Here he is with the silver cup for debating! See his grin?

AMANDA *(absently).* He must have had a jolly disposition.

LAURA. He used to call me—Blue Roses.

(Screen image: Blue roses.)

AMANDA. Why did he call you such a name as that?

LAURA. When I had that attack of pleurosis—he asked me what was the matter when I came back. I said pleurosis—he thought I said Blue Roses! So that's what he always called me after that. Whenever he saw me, he'd holler, "Hello, Blue Roses!" I didn't care for the girl that he went out with. Emily Meisenbach. Emily was the best-dressed girl at Soldan. She never struck me, though, as being sincere . . . It says in the Personal Section—they're engaged. That's—six years ago! They must be married by now.

AMANDA. Girls that aren't cut out for business careers usually wind up married to some nice man. *(She gets up with a spark of revival.)* Sister, that's what you'll do!

(Laura utters a startled, doubtful laugh. She reaches quickly for a piece of glass.)

LAURA. But, Mother—

AMANDA. Yes? *(She goes over to the phonograph.)*

LAURA *(in a tone of frightened apology).* I'm—crippled!

AMANDA. Nonsense! Laura, I've told you never, never to use that word. Why,

---

[7]Auditorium

you're not crippled, you just have a little defect—hardly noticeable, even! When people have some slight disadvantage like that, they cultivate other things to make up for it—develop charm—and vivacity—and—*charm!* That's all you have to do! *(She turns again to the phonograph.)* One thing your father had *plenty of*—was *charm!*

(The scene fades out with music.)

SCENE THREE

Legend on screen: "After the fiasco—"

(Tom speaks from the fire escape landing.)

TOM. After the fiasco at Rubicam's Business College, the idea of getting a gentleman caller for Laura began to play a more and more important part in Mother's calculations. It became an obsession. Like some archetype of the universal unconscious, the image of the gentleman caller haunted our small apartment. . . .

(Screen image: A young man at the door of a house with flowers.)

An evening at home rarely passed without some allusion to this image, this specter, this hope. . . . Even when he wasn't mentioned, his presence hung in Mother's preoccupied look and in my sister's frightened, apologetic manner—hung like a sentence passed upon the Wingfields!

Mother was a woman of action as well as words. She began to take logical steps in the planned direction. Late that winter and in the early spring—realizing that extra money would be needed to properly feather the nest and plume the bird—she conducted a vigorous campaign on the telephone, roping in subscribers to one of those magazines for matrons called *The Homemaker's Companion*, the type of journal that features the serialized sublimations of ladies of letters who think in terms of delicate cuplike breasts, slim, tapering waists, rich, creamy thighs, eyes like wood smoke in autumn, fingers that soothe and caress like strains of music, bodies as powerful as Etruscan sculpture.

(Screen image: The cover of a glamour magazine.)

(Amanda enters with the telephone on a long extension cord. She is spotlighted in the dim stage.)

AMANDA. Ida Scott? This is Amanda Wingfield! We *missed* you at the D.A.R. last Monday! I said to myself: She's probably suffering with that sinus condition! How is that sinus condition?

Horrors! Heaven have mercy!—You're a Christian martyr, yes, that's what you are, a Christian martyr!

Well, I just now happened to notice that your subscription to the *Companion's* about to expire! Yes, it expires with the next issue, honey!—just when that wonderful new serial by Bessie Mae Hopper is getting off to such an exciting start. Oh, honey, it's something that you can't miss! You remember how *Gone with the Wind* took everybody by storm? You simply couldn't go out if you hadn't read it. All everybody *talked* was Scarlett O'Hara. Well, this is a book that critics already compare to *Gone with the Wind*. It's the *Gone with the Wind* of the post–World-War generation!—What?—Burning?—Oh, honey, don't let them burn, go take a look in the oven and I'll hold the wire! Heavens—I think she's hung up!

(The scene dims out.)

(Legend on screen: "You think I'm in love with Continental Shoemakers?")

(Before the lights come up again, the violent voices of Tom and Amanda are heard. They are quarrelling behind the portieres. In front of them stands Laura with clenched hands and panicky expression. A clear pool of light is on her figure throughout this scene.)

TOM. What in Christ's name am I—
AMANDA *(shrilly)*. Don't you use that—
TOM. —supposed to do!
AMANDA. —expression! Not in my—
TOM. Ohhh!
AMANDA. —presence! Have you gone out of your senses?
TOM. I have, that's true, *driven* out!
AMANDA. What is the matter with you, you—big—big—IDIOT!
TOM. Look!—I've got *no thing*, no single thing—
AMANDA. Lower your voice!
TOM. —in my life here that I can call my OWN! Everything is—
AMANDA. Stop that shouting!
TOM. Yesterday you confiscated my books! You had the nerve to—
AMANDA. I took that horrible novel back to the library—yes! That hideous book by that insane Mr. Lawrence.[8]

(Tom laughs wildly.)

I cannot control the output of diseased minds or people who cater to them—

---

[8]D. H. Lawrence (1885–1930), a sometimes censored English poet and novelist who wrote about sexual themes.

(Tom laughs still more wildly.)

BUT I WON'T ALLOW SUCH FILTH BROUGHT INTO MY HOUSE! No, no, no, no, no!

TOM. House, house! Who pays rent on it, who makes a slave of himself to—

AMANDA *(fairly screeching)*. Don't you DARE to—

TOM. No, no, I mustn't say things! *I've* got to just—

AMANDA. Let me tell you—

TOM. I don't want to hear any more!

(He tears the portieres open. The dining-room area is lit with a turgid smoky red glow. Now we see Amanda; her hair is in metal curlers and she is wearing a very old bathrobe, much too large for her slight figure, a relic of the faithless Mr. Wingfield. The upright typewriter now stands on the drop-leaf table, along with a wild disarray of manuscripts. The quarrel was probably precipitated by Amanda's interruption of Tom's creative labor. A chair lies overthrown on the floor. Their gesticulating shadows are cast on the ceiling by the fiery glow.)

AMANDA. You *will* hear more, you—

TOM. No, I won't hear more, I'm going out!

AMANDA. You come right back in—

TOM. Out, out, out! Because I'm—

AMANDA. Come back here, Tom Wingfield! I'm not through talking to you!

TOM. Oh, go—

LAURA *(desperately)*.—Tom!

AMANDA. You're going to listen, and no more insolence from you! I'm at the end of my patience!

(He comes back toward her)

TOM. What do you think I'm at? Aren't I supposed to have any patience to reach the end of, Mother? I know, I know. It seems unimportant to you, what I'm *doing*—what I *want* to do—having a little *difference* between them! You don't think that—

AMANDA. I think you've been doing things that you're ashamed of. That's why you act like this. I don't believe that you go every night to the movies. Nobody goes to the movies night after night. Nobody in their right minds goes to the movies as often as you pretend to. People don't go to the movies at nearly midnight, and movies don't let out at two A.M.: Come in stumbling. Muttering to yourself like a maniac! You get three hours' sleep and then go to work. Oh, I can picture the way you're doing down there. Moping, doping, because you're in no condition.

TOM *(wildly)*. No, I'm in no condition!

AMANDA. What right have you got to jeopardize your job? Jeopardize the security of us all? How do you think we'd manage if you were—

TOM. Listen! You think I'm crazy about the *warehouse*? *(He bends fiercely toward her slight figure.)* You think I'm in love with the Continental Shoemakers? You think I want to spend fifty-five *years* down there in that—*celotex interior*! with—*fluorescent*—*tubes*! I'd rather somebody picked up a crowbar and battered out my brains—than go back mornings! I *go*! Every time you come in yelling that Goddamn *"Rise and Shine!"* *"Rise and Shine!"* I say to myself. "How *lucky dead* people are!" But I get up. I *go*! For sixty-five dollars a month I give up all that I dream of doing and being *ever*! And you say self—*self's* all I ever think of. Why, listen, if self is what I thought of, Mother, I'd be where he is—GONE! *(He points to his father's picture.)* As far as the system of transportation reaches! *(He starts past her. She grabs his arm.)* Don't grab at me, Mother!

AMANDA. Where are you going?

TOM. I'm going to the *movies*!

AMANDA. I don't believe that lie!

(Tom crouches toward her, overtowering her tiny figure. She backs away, gasping.)

TOM. I'm going to opium dens! Yes, opium dens, dens of vice and criminals' hangouts, Mother. I've joined the Hogan Gang,[9] I'm a hired assassin, I carry a tommy gun in a violin case! I run a string of cat houses[10] in the Valley! They call me Killer, Killer Wingfield, I'm leading a double-life, a simple, honest warehouse worker by day, by night a dynamic *czar* of the *underworld, Mother.* I go to gambling casinos, I spin away fortunes on the roulette table! I wear a patch over one eye and a false mustache, sometimes I put on green whiskers. On those occasions they call me— *El Diablo*![11] Oh, I could tell you many things to make you sleepless! My enemies plan to dynamite this place. They're going to blow us all sky-high some night! I'll be glad, very happy, and so will you! You'll go up, up on a broomstick, over Blue Mountain with seventeen gentlemen callers! You ugly—babbling old—*witch*. . . .

(He goes through a series of violent, clumsy movements, seizing his overcoat,

---

[9]St. Louis crime family.

[10]Brothels

[11]The devil, in Spanish.

lunging to the door, pulling it fiercely open. The women watch him, aghast. His arm catches in the sleeve of the coat as he struggles to pull it on. For a moment he is pinioned by the bulky garment. With an outraged groan he tears the coat off again, splitting the shoulder of it, and hurls it across the room. It strikes against the shelf of Laura's glass collection, and there is a tinkle of shattering glass. Laura cries out as if wounded.)

(Music.)

(Screen legend: "The Glass Menagerie.")

Laura *(shrilly).* My glass!—menagerie.... *(She covers her face and turns away.)*

(But Amanda is still stunned and stupefied by the "ugly witch" so that she barely notices this occurrence. Now she recovers her speech.)

AMANDA *(in an awful voice).* I won't speak to you—until you apologize!

(She crosses through the portieres and draws them together behind her. Tom is left with Laura. Laura clings weakly to the mantel with her face averted. Tom stares at her stupidly for a moment. Then he crosses to the shelf. He drops awkwardly on his knees to collect the fallen glass, glancing at Laura as if he would speak but couldn't.)

("The Glass Menagerie" music steals in as the scene dims out.)

SCENE FOUR

The interior of the apartment is dark. There is a faint light in the alley. A deep-voiced bell in a church is tolling the hour of five.

Tom appears at the top of the alley. After each solemn boom of the bell in the tower, he shakes a little noisemaker or rattle as if to express the tiny spasm of man in contrast to the sustained power and dignity of the Almighty. This and the unsteadiness of his advance make it evident that he has been drinking. As he climbs the few steps to the fire escape landing light steals up inside. Laura appears in the front room in a night-dress. She notices that Tom's bed is empty. Tom fishes in his pockets for his door key, removing a motley assortment of articles in his search, including a shower of movie ticket stubs and an empty bottle. At last he finds the key, but just as he is about to insert it, it slips from his fingers. He strikes a match and crouches below the door.

TOM *(bitterly).* One crack—and it falls through!

(Laura opens the door.)

LAURA. Tom! Tom, what are you doing?

TOM. Looking for a door key.

LAURA. Where have you been all this time?

TOM. I have been to the movies.

LAURA. All this time at the movies?

TOM. There was a very long program. There was a Garbo picture and a Mickey Mouse and a travelogue and a newsreel and a preview of coming attractions. And there was an organ solo and a collection for the Milk Fund[12]—simultaneously—which ended up in a terrible fight between a fat lady and an usher!

LAURA *(innocently)*. Did you have to stay through everything?

TOM. Of course! And, oh, I forgot! There was a big stage show! The headliner on this stage show was Malvolio the Magician. He performed wonderful tricks, many of them, such as pouring water back and forth between pitchers. First it turned to wine and then it turned to beer and then it turned to whisky. I know it was whisky it finally turned into because he needed somebody to come up out of the audience to help him, and I came up—both shows! It was Kentucky Straight Bourbon. A very generous fellow, he gave souvenirs. *(He pulls from his back pocket a shimmering rainbow-colored scarf.)* He gave me this. This is his magic scarf. You can have it, Laura. You wave it over a canary cage and you get a bowl of goldfish. You wave it over the goldfish bowl and they fly away canaries. . . . But the wonderfullest trick of all was the coffin trick. We nailed him into a coffin and he got out of the coffin without removing one nail. *(He has come inside.)* There is a trick that would come in handy for me—get me out of this two-by-four situation! *(He flops on the bed and starts removing his shoes.)*

LAURA. Tom—shhh!

TOM. What're you shushing me for?

LAURA. You'll wake up Mother.

TOM. Goody, goody! Pay 'er back for all those "Rise an' Shines." *(He lies down, groaning.)* You know it don't take much intelligence to get yourself into a nailed-up coffin, Laura. But who the hell ever got himself out of one without removing one nail?

(As if in answer, the father's grinning photograph lights up. The scene dims out.)
(Immediately following, the church bell is heard striking six. At the sixth stroke the alarm clock goes off in Amanda's room, and after a few moments we hear her

---

[12]Charity organization

calling: "Rise and Shine! Rise and Shine! Laura, go tell your brother to rise and shine!")

TOM *(sitting up slowly)*. I'll rise—but I won't shine.

(The light increases.)

AMANDA. Laura, tell your brother his coffee is ready.

(Laura slips into the front room.)

LAURA. Tom!—It's nearly seven. Don't make Mother nervous.

(He stares at her stupidly.)

   (beseechingly:) Tom, speak to Mother this morning. Make up with her, apologize, speak to her!
TOM. She won't to me. It's her that started not speaking.
LAURA. If you just say you're sorry she'll start speaking.
TOM. Her not speaking—is that such a tragedy?
LAURA. Please—please!
AMANDA *(calling from the kitchenette)*. Laura, are you going to do what I asked you to do, or do I have to get dressed and go out myself?
LAURA. Going, going—soon as I get on my coat!

(She pulls on a shapeless felt hat with a nervous, jerky movement, pleadingly glancing at Tom. She rushes awkwardly for her coat. The coat is one of Amanda's inaccurately made-over, the sleeves too short for Laura.)

   Butter and what else?
AMANDA *(entering from the kitchenette)*. Just butter. Tell them to charge it.
LAURA. Mother, they make such faces when I do that.
AMANDA. Sticks and stones can break our bones, but the expression on Mr. Garfinkel's face won't harm us! Tell your brother his coffee is getting cold.
LAURA *(at the door)*. Do what I asked you, will you, will you, Tom?

(He looks sullenly away.)

AMANDA. Laura, go now or just don't go at all!
LAURA *(rushing out)*. Going—going!

(A second later she cries out. Tom springs up and crosses to the door. Tom opens the door.)

TOM. Laura?
LAURA. I'm all right. I slipped, but I'm all right.
AMANDA *(peering anxiously after her)*. If anyone breaks a leg on those fire-

escape steps, the landlord ought to be sued for every cent he possesses! *(She shuts the door. Now she remembers she isn't speaking to Tom and returns to the other room.)*

(As Tom comes listlessly for his coffee, she turns her back to him and stands rigidly facing the window on the gloomy gray vault of the areaway. Its light on her face with its aged but childish features is cruelly sharp, satirical as a Daumier[13] print.)

(The music of "Ave Maria" is heard softly.)

(Tom glances sheepishly but sullenly at her averted figure and slumps at the table. The coffee is scalding hot; he sips it and gasps and spits it back in the cup. At his gasp, Amanda catches her breath and half turns. Then she catches herself and turns back to the window. Tom blows on his coffee, glancing sidewise at his mother, She clears her throat. Tom clears his. He starts to rise, sinks back down again, scratches his head, clears his throat again. Amanda coughs. Tom raises his cup in both hands to blow on it, his eyes staring over the rim of it at his mother for several moments. Then he slowly sets the cup down and awkwardly and hesitantly rises from the chair.)

TOM *(hoarsely)*. Mother. I—I apologize, Mother.

(Amanda draws a quick, shuddering breath. Her face works grotesquely. She breaks into childlike tears.)

I'm sorry for what I said, for everything that I said, I didn't mean it.

AMANDA *(sobbingly)*. My devotion has made me a witch and so I make myself hateful to my children!

TOM. No, you *don't*.

AMANDA. I worry so much, don't sleep, it makes me nervous!

TOM *(gently)*. I understand that.

AMANDA. I've had to put up a solitary battle all these years. But you're my right-hand bower![14] Don't fall down, don't fail!

TOM *(gently)*. I try, Mother.

AMANDA *(with great enthusiasm)*. Try and you will *succeed*! *(The notion makes her breathless.)* Why, you—you're just *full* of natural endowments! Both of my children—they're *unusual* children! Don't you think I know it? I'm so—*proud*! Happy and—feel I've—so much to be thankful for but—promise me one thing, son!

TOM. What, Mother?

AMANDA. Promise, son, you'll—never be a drunkard!

---

[13]Honoré Daumier (1808–1879), French cartoonist who in his work satirized the middle classes.

[14]Highest card in a game.

TOM (*turns to her grinning*). I will never be a drunkard, Mother.

AMANDA. That's what frightened me so, that you'd be drinking! Eat a bowl of Purina!

TOM. Just coffee, Mother.

AMANDA. Shredded wheat biscuit?

TOM. No. No, Mother, just coffee.

AMANDA. You can't put in a day's work on an empty stomach. You've got ten minutes—don't gulp! Drinking too-hot liquids makes cancer of the stomach. . . . Put cream in.

TOM. No, thank you.

AMANDA. To cool it.

TOM. No! No, thank you, I want it black.

AMANDA. I know, but it's not good for you. We have to do all that we can to build ourselves up. In these trying times we live in, all that we have to cling to is—each other. . . . That's why it's important to—Tom, I—I sent out your sister so I could discuss something with you. If you hadn't spoken I would have spoken to you. (*She sits down.*)

TOM (*gently*). What is it, Mother, that you want to discuss?

AMANDA. *Laura!*

(*Tom puts his cup down slowly.*)

(*Legend on screen: "Laura." Music: "The Glass Menagerie."*)

TOM. —Oh.—Laura . . .

AMANDA (*touching his sleeve*). You know how Laura is. So quiet but—still water runs deep! She notices things and I think she—broods about them.

(*Tom looks up.*)

A few days ago I came in and she was crying.

TOM. What about?

AMANDA. You.

TOM. Me?

AMANDA. She has an idea that you're not happy here.

TOM. What gave her that idea?

AMANDA. What gives her any idea? However, you do act strangely. I—I'm not criticizing, understand *that*! I know your ambitions do not lie in the warehouse, that like everybody in the whole wide world—you've had to—make sacrifices, but—Tom—Tom—life's not easy, it calls for—Spartan endurance! There's so many things in my heart that I cannot describe to you! I've never told you but I—*loved* your father. . . .

TOM *(gently)*. I know that, Mother.

AMANDA. And you—when I see you taking after his ways! Staying out late—and—well, you *had* been drinking the night you were in that—terrifying condition! Laura says that you hate the apartment and that you go out nights to get away from it! Is that true, Tom?

TOM. No. You say there's so much in your heart that you can't describe to me. That's true of me, too. There's so much in my heart that I can't describe to *you*! So let's respect each other's—

AMANDA. But, why—*why*, Tom—are you always so *restless*? Where do you go to, nights?

TOM. I—go to the movies.

AMANDA. Why do you go to the movies so much, Tom?

TOM. I go to the movies because—I like adventure. Adventure is something I don't have much of at work, so I go to the movies.

AMANDA. But, Tom, you go to the movies *entirely* too *much*!

TOM. I like a lot of adventure.

(Amanda looks baffled, then hurt. As the familiar inquisition resumes, Tom becomes hard and impatient again. Amanda slips back into her querulous attitude toward him.)

(Image on screen: A sailing vessel with Jolly Roger.)

AMANDA. Most young men find adventure in their careers.

TOM. Then most young men are not employed in a warehouse.

AMANDA. The world is full of young men employed in warehouses and offices and factories.

TOM. Do all of them find adventure in their careers?

AMANDA. They do or they do without it! Not everybody has a craze for adventure.

TOM. Man is by instinct a lover, a hunter, a fighter, and none of those instincts are given much play at the warehouse!

AMANDA. Man is by instinct! Don't quote instinct to me! Instinct is something that people have got away from! It belongs to animals! Christian adults don't want it!

TOM. What do Christian adults want, then, Mother?

AMANDA. Superior things! Things of the mind and the spirit! Only animals have to satisfy instincts! Surely your aims are somewhat higher than theirs! Than monkeys—pigs—

TOM. I reckon they're not.

AMANDA. You're joking. However, that isn't what I wanted to discuss.

TOM *(rising)*. I haven't much time.

AMANDA (*pushing his shoulders*). Sit down.

TOM. You want me to punch in red[15] at the warehouse, Mother?

AMANDA. You have five minutes. I want to talk about Laura.

(*Screen legend: "Plans and Provisions."*)

TOM. All right! What about Laura?

AMANDA. We have to be making some plans and provisions for her. She's older than you, two years, and nothing has happened. She just drifts along doing nothing. It frightens me terribly how she just drifts along.

TOM. I guess she's the type that people call home girls.

AMANDA. There's no such type, and if there is, it's a pity! That is unless the home is hers, with a husband!

TOM. What?

AMANDA. Oh, I can see the handwriting on the wall as plain as I see the nose in front of my face! It's terrifying! More and more you remind me of your father! He was out all hours without explanation!—Then *left! Goodbye!* And me with the bag to hold. I saw that letter you got from the Merchant Marine. I know what you're dreaming of. I'm not standing here blindfolded. (*She pauses.*) Very well, then. Then *do* it! But not till there's somebody to take your place.

TOM. What do you mean?

AMANDA. I mean that as soon as Laura has got somebody to take care of her, married, a home of her own, independent—why, then you'll be free to go wherever you please, on land, on sea, whichever way the wind blows you! But until that time you've got to look out for your sister. I don't say me because I'm old and don't matter! I say for your sister because she's young and dependent.

I put her in business college—a dismal failure! Frightened her so it made her sick at the stomach. I took her over to the Young People's League at the church. Another fiasco. She spoke to nobody, nobody spoke to her. Now all she does is fool with those pieces of glass and play those worn-out records. What kind of a life is that for a girl to lead?

TOM. What can I do about it?

AMANDA. Overcome selfishness! Self, self, self is all that you ever think of!

(*Tom springs up and crosses to get his coat. It is ugly and bulky. He pulls on a cap with earmuffs.*)

Where is your muffler? Put your wool muffler on!

---

[15]Late for work.

(He snatches it angrily from the closet, tosses it around his neck and pulls both ends tight.)

Tom! I haven't said what I had in mind to ask you.

TOM. I'm too late to—

AMANDA *(catching his arm—very importunately; then shyly)*. Down at the warehouse, aren't there some—nice young men?

TOM. No!

AMANDA. There *must* be—*some* . . .

TOM. Mother—*(He gestures.)*

AMANDA. Find out one that's clean-living—doesn't drink and ask him out for sister!

TOM. What?

AMANDA. For *sister*! To *meet*! Get *acquainted*!

TOM *(stamping to the door)*. Oh, my *go-osh*!

AMANDA. Will you?

(He opens the door. She says, imploringly:)

Will you?

(He starts down the fire escape.)

Will you? *Will* you, dear?

TOM *(calling back)*. Yes!

(Amanda closes the door hesitantly and with a troubled but faintly hopeful expression.)

(Screen image: The cover of a glamour magazine.)

(The spotlight picks up Amanda at the phone.)

AMANDA. Ella Cartwright? This is Amanda Wingfield!
How are you, honey?
How is that kidney condition?

(There is a five-second pause.)

Horrors!

(There is another pause.)

You're a Christian martyr, yes, honey, that's what you are, a Christian martyr! Well, I just now happened to notice in my little red book that your subscription to the *Companion* has just run out! I knew that you wouldn't want to miss out on the wonderful serial starting in this new issue. It's by

Bessie Mae Hopper, the first thing she's written since *Honeymoon for Three*. Wasn't that a strange and interesting story? Well, this one is even lovelier, I believe. It has a sophisticated, society background. It's all about the horsey set on Long Island!

(The light fades out.)

SCENE FIVE

Legend on the screen: "Annunciation."
Music is heard as the light slowly comes on.

It is early dusk of a spring evening. Supper has just been finished in the Wingfield apartment. Amanda and Laura, in light-colored dresses, are removing dishes from the table in the dining room, which is shadowy, their movements formalized almost as a dance or ritual, their moving forms as pale and silent as moths. Tom, in white shirt and trousers, rises from the table and crosses toward the fire escape.

AMANDA *(as he passes her).* Son, will you do me a favor?
TOM. What?
AMANDA. Comb your hair! You look so pretty when your hair is combed!

(Tom slouches on the sofa with the evening paper. Its enormous headline reads: "Franco Triumphs.")[16]

There is only one respect in which I would like you to emulate your father.
TOM. What respect is that?
AMANDA. The care he always took of his appearance. He never allowed himself to look untidy.

(He throws down the paper and crosses to the fire escape.)

Where are you going?
TOM. I'm going out to smoke.
AMANDA. You smoke too much. A pack a day at fifteen cents a pack. How much would that amount to in a month? Thirty times fifteen is how much Tom? Figure it out and you will be astounded at what you could save. Enough to give you a night-school course in accounting at Washington U.! Just think what a wonderful thing that would be for you, son!

(Tom is unmoved by the thought.)

---

[16]Francisco Franco's forces defeated the Loyalists, thus ending the Spanish Civil War in 1939.

TOM. I'd rather smoke. *(He steps out on the landing, letting the screen door slam.)*

AMANDA *(sharply)*. I know! That's the tragedy of it. . . . *(Alone, she turns to look at her husband's picture.)*

(Dance music: "The World Is Waiting for the Sunrise!")

TOM *(to the audience)*. Across the alley from us was the Paradise Dance Hall. On evenings in spring the windows and doors were open and the music came outdoors. Sometimes the lights were turned out except for a large glass sphere that hung from the ceiling. It would turn slowly about and filter the dusk with delicate rainbow colors. Then the orchestra played a waltz or a tango, something that had a slow and sensuous rhythm. Couples would come outside, to the relative privacy of the alley. You could see them kissing behind ash pits and telephone poles. This was the compensation for lives that passed like mine, without any change or adventure. Adventure and change were imminent in this year. They were waiting around the corner for all these kids. Suspended in the midst over Berchtesgaden,[17] caught in the folds of Chamberlain's umbrella.[18] In Spain there was Guernica! But here there was only hot swing music and liquor, dance halls, bars, and movies, and sex that hung in the gloom like a chandelier and flooded the world with brief, deceptive rainbows. . . . All the world was waiting for bombardments!

(Amanda turns from the picture and comes outside.)

AMANDA *(sighing)*. A fire escape landing's a poor excuse for a porch. *(She spreads a newspaper on a step and sits down, gracefully and demurely as if she were settling into a swing on a Mississippi veranda.)* What are you looking at?

TOM. The moon.

AMANDA. Is there a moon this evening?

TOM. It's rising over Garfinkel's Delicatessen.

AMANDA. So it is! A little silver slipper of a moon. Have you made a wish on it yet?

TOM. Um-hum.

AMANDA. What did you wish for?

TOM. That's a secret.

---

[17]Resort in the German Alps favored by Adolf Hitler.

[18]Neville Chamberlain (1869–1940), British Prime Minister who sought to negotiate with Hitler through appeasement. His ubiquitous umbrella became a popular symbol of his credulity.

AMANDA. A secret, huh? Well, I won't tell mine either. I will be just as mysterious as you.

TOM. I bet I can guess what yours is.

AMANDA. Is my head so transparent?

TOM. You're not a sphinx.

AMANDA. No, I don't have secrets. I'll tell you what I wished for on the moon. Success and happiness for my precious children! I wish for that whenever there's a moon, and when there isn't a moon, I wish for it, too.

TOM. I thought perhaps you wished for a gentleman caller.

AMANDA. Why do you say that?

TOM. Don't you remember asking me to fetch one?

AMANDA. I remember suggesting that it would be nice for your sister if you brought home some nice young man from the warehouse. I think that I've made that suggestion more than once.

TOM. Yes, you have made it repeatedly.

AMANDA. Well?

TOM. We are going to have one.

AMANDA. *What?*

TOM. A gentleman caller!

(The annunciation is celebrated with music.)

(Amanda rises.)

(Image on screen: A caller with a bouquet.)

AMANDA. You mean you have asked some nice young man to come over?

TOM. Yep. I've asked him to dinner.

AMANDA. You really did?

TOM. I did!

AMANDA. You did, and did he—*accept?*

TOM. He did!

AMANDA. Well, well—well, well! That's—lovely!

TOM. I thought that you would be pleased.

AMANDA. It's definite then?

TOM. Very definite.

AMANDA. Soon?

TOM. Very soon.

AMANDA. For heaven's sake, stop putting on and tell me some things, will you?

TOM. What things do you want me to tell you?

AMANDA. *Naturally* I would like to know when he's *coming!*

TOM. He's coming tomorrow.

AMANDA. *Tomorrow?*

TOM. Yep. Tomorrow.

AMANDA. But, Tom!

TOM. Yes, Mother?

AMANDA. Tomorrow gives me no time!

TOM. Time for what?

AMANDA. Preparations! Why didn't you phone me at once, as soon as you asked him, the minute that he accepted? Then, don't you see, I could have been getting ready!

TOM. You don't have to make any fuss.

AMANDA. Oh, Tom, Tom, Tom, of course I have to make a fuss! I want things nice, not sloppy! Not thrown together. I'll certainly have to do some fast thinking, won't I?

TOM. I don't see why you have to think at all.

AMANDA. You just don't know. We can't have a gentleman caller in a pigsty! All my wedding silver has to be polished, the monogrammed table linen ought to be laundered! The windows have to be washed and fresh curtains put up. And how about clothes? We have to *wear* something, don't we?

TOM. Mother, this boy is no one to make a fuss over!

AMANDA. Do you realize he's the first young man we've introduced to your sister? It's terrible, dreadful, disgraceful that poor little sister has never received a single gentleman caller! Tom, come inside!

(She opens the screen door.)

TOM. What for?

AMANDA. I want to ask you some things.

TOM. If you're going to make such a fuss, I'll call it off, I'll tell him not to come!

AMANDA. You certainly won't do anything of the kind. Nothing offends people worse than broken engagements. It simply means I'll have to work like a Turk! We won't be brilliant, but we will pass inspection. Come on inside.

(Tom follows her inside, groaning.)

Sit down.

TOM. Any particular place you would like me to sit?

AMANDA. Thank heavens I've got that new sofa! I'm also making payments on a floor lamp I'll have sent out! And put the chintz covers on, they'll brighten things up! Of course I'd hoped to have these walls repapered. . . . What is the young man's name?

TOM. His name is O'Connor.

AMANDA. That, of course, means fish—tomorrow is Friday! I'll have that salmon loaf—with Durkee's dressing! What does he do? He works at the warehouse?

TOM. Of course! How else would I—

AMANDA. Tom, he—doesn't drink?

TOM. Why do you ask me that?

AMANDA. Your father *did*!

TOM. Don't get started on that!

AMANDA. He *does* drink, then?

TOM. Not that I know of!

AMANDA. Make sure, be certain! The last thing I want for my daughter's a boy who drinks!

TOM. Aren't you being a little bit premature? Mr. O'Connor has not yet appeared on the scene!

AMANDA. But will tomorrow. To meet your sister, and what do I know about his character? Nothing! Old maids are better off than wives of drunkards!

TOM. Oh, my God!

AMANDA. Be still!

TOM *(leaning forward to whisper)*. Lots of fellows meet girls whom they don't marry!

AMANDA. Oh, talk sensibly, Tom—and don't be sarcastic! *(She has gotten a hairbrush.)*

TOM. What are you doing?

AMANDA. I'm brushing that cowlick down! *(She attacks his hair with the brush.)* What is this young man's position at the warehouse?

TOM *(submitting grimly to the brush and the interrogation)*. This young man's position is that of a shipping clerk, Mother.

AMANDA. Sounds to me like a fairly responsible job, the sort of a job you would be in if you just had more *get-up*. What is his salary? Have you any idea?

TOM. I would judge it to be approximately eighty-five dollars a month.

AMANDA. Well—not princely, but—

TOM. Twenty more than I make.

AMANDA. Yes, how well I know! But for a family man, eighty-five dollars a month is not much more than you can just get by on. . . .

TOM. Yes, but Mr. O'Connor is not a family man.

AMANDA. He might be, mightn't he? Some time in the future?

TOM. I see. Plans and provisions.

AMANDA. You are the only young man that I know of who ignores the fact that the future becomes the present, the present the past, and the past turns into everlasting regret if you don't plan for it!

TOM. I will think that over and see what I can make of it.

AMANDA. Don't be supercilious with your mother! Tell me some more about this—what do you call him?

TOM. James D. O'Connor. The D. is for Delaney.

AMANDA. Irish on *both* sides! *Gracious!* And doesn't drink?

TOM. Shall I call him up and ask him right this minute?

AMANDA. The only way to find out about those things is to make discreet inquiries at the proper moment. When I was a girl in Blue Mountain and it was suspected that a young man drank, the girl whose attentions he had been receiving, if any girl *was*, would sometimes speak to the minister of his church, or rather her father would if her father was living, and sort of feel him out on the young man's character. That is the way such things are discreetly handled to keep a young woman from making a tragic mistake!

TOM. Then how did you happen to make a tragic mistake?

AMANDA. That innocent look of your father's had everyone fooled! He *smiled*—the world was *enchanted*! No girl can do worse than put herself at the mercy of a handsome appearance! I hope that Mr. O'Connor is not too good-looking.

TOM. No, he's not too good-looking. He's covered with freckles and hasn't too much of a nose.

AMANDA. He's not right-down homely, though?

TOM. Not right-down homely. Just medium homely, I'd say.

AMANDA. Character's what to look for in a man.

TOM. That's what I've always said, Mother.

AMANDA. You've never said anything of the kind and I suspect you would never give it a thought.

TOM. Don't be so suspicious of me.

AMANDA. At least I hope he's the type that's up and coming.

TOM. I think he really goes in for self-improvement.

AMANDA. What reason have you to think so?

TOM. He goes to night school.

AMANDA *(beaming)*. Splendid! What does he do, I mean study?

TOM. Radio engineering and public speaking!

AMANDA. Then he has visions of being advanced in the world! Any young man who studies public speaking is aiming to have an executive job some day! And radio engineering! A thing for the future! Both of these facts are very illuminating. Those are the sort of things that a mother should know concerning any young man who comes to call on her daughter. Seriously or—not.

TOM. One little warning. He doesn't know about Laura. I didn't let on that we had dark ulterior motives. I just said, why don't you come and have dinner with us? He said okay and that was the whole conversation.

AMANDA. I bet it was! You're eloquent as an oyster. However, he'll know about Laura when he gets here. When he sees how lovely and sweet and pretty she is, he'll thank his lucky stars he was asked to dinner.

TOM. Mother, you mustn't expect too much of Laura.

AMANDA. What do you mean?

TOM. Laura seems all those things to you and me because she's ours and we love her. We don't even notice she's crippled any more.

AMANDA. Don't say crippled! You know that I never allow that word to be used!

TOM. But face facts, Mother. She is and—that's not all—

AMANDA. What do you mean "not all"?

TOM. Laura is very different from other girls.

AMANDA. I think the difference is to her advantage.

TOM. Not quite all—in the eyes of others—strangers—she's terribly shy and lives in a world of her own and those things make her seem a little peculiar to people outside the house.

AMANDA. Don't say peculiar.

TOM. Face the facts. She is.

(The dance hall music changes to a tango that has a minor and somewhat ominous tone.)

AMANDA. In what way is she peculiar—may I ask?

TOM *(gently)*. She lives in a world of her own—a world of little glass ornaments, Mother. . . .

(He gets up. Amanda remains holding the brush, looking at him, troubled.)

She plays old phonograph records and—that's about all—*(He glances at himself in the mirror and crosses to the door.)*

AMANDA *(sharply)*. Where are you going?

TOM. I'm going to the movies. *(He goes out the screen door.)*

AMANDA. Not to the movies, every night to the movies! *(She follows quickly to the screen door.)* I don't believe you always go to the movies!

(He is gone. Amanda looks worriedly after him for a moment. Then vitality and optimism return and she turns from the door, crossing the portieres.)

Laura! Laura!

(Laura answers from the kitchenette.)

LAURA. Yes, Mother.

AMANDA. Let those dishes go and come in front!

(Laura appears with a dish towel. Amanda speaks to her gaily.)

Laura, come here and make a wish on the moon!

(Screen image: The Moon.)

LAURA *(entering).* Moon—moon?
AMANDA. A little silver slipper of a moon. Look over your left shoulder, Laura, and make a wish!

(Laura looks faintly puzzled as if called out of sleep. Amanda seizes her shoulders and turns her at an angle by the door.)

Now! Now, darling, *wish!*
LAURA. What shall I wish for, Mother?
AMANDA *(her voice trembling and her eyes suddenly filling with tears).* Happiness! Good fortune!

(The sound of the violin rises and the stage dims out.)

SCENE SIX

The light comes up on the fire escape landing. Tom is leaning against the grill, smoking.

(Screen image: The high school hero.)

TOM. And so the following evening I brought Jim home to dinner. I had known Jim slightly in high school. In high school Jim was a hero. He had tremendous Irish good nature and vitality with the scrubbed and polished look of white chinaware. He seemed to move in a continual spotlight. He was a star in basketball, captain of the debating club, president of the senior class and the glee club and he sang the lead in the annual light operas. He was always running or bounding, never just walking. He seemed always at the point of defeating the law of gravity. He was shooting with such velocity through his adolescence that you would logically expect him to arrive at nothing short of the White House by the time he was thirty. But Jim apparently ran into more interference after his graduation from Soldan. His speed had definitely slowed. Six years after he left high school he was holding a job that wasn't much better than mine.

(Screen image: The Clerk.)

He was the only one at the warehouse with whom I was on friendly terms. I was valuable to him as someone who could remember his former glory, who had seen him win basketball games and the silver cup in debating. He knew of my secret practice of retiring to a cabinet of the washroom to work on poems when business was slack in the warehouse. He called me Shakespeare. And while the other boys in the warehouse regarded me with suspicious hostility, Jim took a humorous attitude toward me. Gradually his attitude affected the others, their hostility wore off and they also began to smile at me as people smile at an oddly fashioned dog who trots across their path at some distance.

I knew that Jim and Laura had known each other at Soldan, and I had heard Laura speak admiringly of his voice. I didn't know if Jim remembered her or not. In high school Laura had been as unobtrusive as Jim had been astonishing. If he did remember Laura, it was not as my sister, for when I asked him to dinner, he grinned and said, "You know, Shakespeare, I never thought of you as having folks!"

He was about to discover that I did. . . .

(*Legend on screen:* "The accent of a coming foot.")

(*The light dims out on Tom and comes up in the Wingfield living room—a delicate lemony light. It is about five on a Friday evening of late spring which comes "scattering poems in the sky."*)

(*Amanda has worked like a Turk in preparation for the gentleman caller. The results are astonishing, The new floor lamp with its rose silk shade is in place, a colored paper lantern conceals the broken light fixture in the ceiling, new billowing white curtains are at the windows, chintz covers are on the chairs and sofa, a pair of new sofa pillows make their initial appearance. Open boxes and tissue paper are scattered on the floor.*)

(*Laura stands in the middle of the room with lifted arms while Amanda crouches before her, adjusting the hem of a new dress, devout and ritualistic. The dress is colored and designed by memory. The arrangement of Laura's hair is changed; it is softer and more becoming. A fragile, unearthly prettiness has come out in Laura: she is like a piece of translucent glass touched by light, given a momentary radiance, not actual, not lasting.*)

AMANDA (*impatiently*). Why are you trembling?

LAURA. Mother, you've made me so nervous!

AMANDA. How have I made you nervous?

LAURA. By all this fuss! You make it seem so important!

AMANDA. I don't understand you, Laura. You couldn't be satisfied with just sitting home, and yet whenever I try to arrange something for you, you seem to resist it. (*She gets up.*) Now take a look at yourself. No, wait! Wait just a moment—I have an idea!

LAURA. What is it now?

(Amanda produces two powder puffs which she wraps in handkerchiefs and stuffs in Laura's bosom.)

LAURA. Mother, what are you doing?

AMANDA. They call them "Gay Deceivers"!

LAURA. I won't wear them!

AMANDA. You will!

LAURA. Why should I?

AMANDA. Because, to be painfully honest, your chest is flat.

LAURA. You make it seem like we were setting a trap.

AMANDA. All pretty girls are a trap, a pretty trap, and men expect them to be.

(Legend on screen: "A pretty trap.")

> Now look at yourself, young lady. This is the prettiest you will ever be! *(She stands back to admire Laura.)* I've got to fly now! You're going to be surprised by your mother's appearance!

(Amanda crosses through the portieres, humming gaily. Laura moves slowly to the long mirror and stares solemnly at herself. A wind blows the white curtains inward in a slow, graceful motion and with a faint, sorrowful sighing.)

AMANDA *(from somewhere behind the portieres)*. It isn't dark enough yet.

(Laura turns slowly before the mirror with a troubled look.)

(Legend on screen: "This is my sister: Celebrate her with strings!" Music plays.)

AMANDA *(laughing, still not visible)*. I'm going to show you something. I'm going to make a spectacular appearance!

LAURA. What is it, Mother?

AMANDA. Possess your soul in patience—you will see! Something I've resurrected from that old trunk! Styles haven't changed so terribly much after all. . . . *(She parts the portieres.)* Now just look at your mother! *(She wears a girlish frock of yellowed voile with a blue silk sash. She carries a bunch of jonquils—the legend of her youth is nearly revived. Now she speaks feverishly.)* This is the dress in which I led the cotillion. Won the cakewalk twice at Sunset Hill, wore one Spring to the Governor's Ball in Jackson! See how I sashayed around the ballroom, Laura? *(She raises her skirt and does a mincing step around the room.)* I wore it on Sundays for my gentlemen callers! I had it on the day I met your father. . . . I had malaria fever all that Spring. The change of climate from East Tennessee to the Delta—weakened resistance. I had a little temperature all the time—not enough to be serious—just enough to make me restless and giddy! Invitations poured in—parties all over the Delta! "Stay in bed," said Mother, "you have a fever!"—but I just wouldn't. I took quinine but kept on going, going! Evenings, dances! Afternoons, long, long rides! Picnics—lovely! So lovely, that country in May—all lacy with dogwood, literally flooded with jonquils! That was the spring I had the craze for jonquils. Jonquils became an absolute obsession. Mother said, "Honey, there's no more room for jonquils." And still I kept on bringing in more jonquils. Whenever, wherever I saw them, I'd say, "Stop! Stop! I see jonquils!" I made the young men help me gather the jonquils! It was a joke, Amanda and her jonquils. Finally there were no more vases to hold them, every available space was filled with jonquils. No vases to hold them? All right, I'll hold them myself! And then I—*(She stops in front of the picture. Music plays.)* met your father! Malaria fever and jonquils and then—this—boy.... *(She switches on the rose-colored lamp.)* I hope they get here before it starts to rain. *(She crosses the room and places the jonquils in a bowl on the table.)* I gave your brother a little extra change so he and Mr. O'Connor could take the service car home.

LAURA *(with an altered look)*. What did you say his name was?
AMANDA. O'Connor.
LAURA. What is his first name?
AMANDA. I don't remember. Oh, yes, I do. It was—Jim!

(Laura sways slightly and catches hold of a chair.)

(Legend on screen: "Not, Jim!")

LAURA *(faintly)*. Not—Jim!
AMANDA. Yes, that was it, it was Jim! I've never known a Jim that wasn't nice!
(The music becomes ominous.)
LAURA. Are you sure his name is Jim O'Connor?
AMANDA. Yes. Why?
LAURA. Is he the one that Tom used to know in high school?
AMANDA. He didn't say so. I think he just got to know him at the warehouse.
LAURA. There was a Jim O'Connor we both knew in high school—*(then, with effort)* If that is the one that Tom is bringing to dinner—you'll have to excuse me, I won't come to the table.
AMANDA. What sort of nonsense is this?
LAURA. You asked me once if I'd ever liked a boy. Don't you remember I showed you this boy's picture?
AMANDA. You mean the boy you showed me in the year-book?
LAURA. Yes, that boy.
AMANDA. Laura, Laura, were you in love with that boy?
LAURA. I don't know, Mother. All I know is I couldn't sit at the table if it was him!

AMANDA. It won't be him! It isn't the least bit likely. But whether it is or not, you will come to the table. You will not be excused.

LAURA. I'll have to be, Mother.

AMANDA. I don't intend to humor your silliness, Laura. I've had too much from you and your brother, both! So just sit down and compose yourself till they come. Tom has forgotten his key so you'll have to let them in, when they arrive.

LAURA *(panicky)*. Oh, Mother—*you* answer the door!

AMANDA *(lightly)*. I'll be in the kitchen—busy!

LAURA. Oh, Mother, please answer the door, don't make me do it!

AMANDA *(crossing into the kitchenette)*. I've got to fix the dressing for the salmon. Fuss, fuss—silliness!—over a gentleman caller!

(The door swings shut. Laura is left alone.)

(Legend on screen: "Terror!")

(She utters a low moan and turns off the lamp—sits stiffly on the edge of the sofa, knotting her fingers together.)

(Legend on screen: "The Opening of a Door!")

(Tom and Jim appear on the fire escape steps and climb to the landing. Hearing their approach, Laura rises with a panicky gesture. She retreats to the portieres. The doorbell rings. Laura catches her breath and touches her throat. Low drums sound.)

AMANDA *(calling)*. Laura, sweetheart! The door!

(Laura stares at it without moving.)

JIM. I think we just beat the rain.

TOM. Uh-huh. *(He rings again, nervously. Jim whistles and fishes for a cigarette.)*

AMANDA *(very, very gaily)*. Laura, that is your brother and Mr. O'Connor! Will you let them in, darling!

(Laura crosses toward the kitchenette door.)

LAURA *(breathlessly)*. Mother—you go to the door!

(Amanda steps out of the kitchenette and stares furiously at Laura. She points imperiously at the door)

LAURA. Please, please!

AMANDA *(in fierce whisper)*. What is the matter with you, you silly thing?

LAURA *(desperately)*. Please, you answer it, *please*!

AMANDA. I told you I wasn't going to humor you, Laura. Why have you chosen this moment to lose your mind?

LAURA. Please, please, please, you go!

AMANDA. You'll have to go to the door because I can't!

LAURA *(despairingly)*. I can't either!

AMANDA. *Why?*

LAURA. I'm *sick*!

AMANDA. I'm sick, too—of your nonsense! Why can't you and your brother be normal people? Fantastic whims and behavior!

(Tom gives a long ring.)

Preposterous goings on! Can you give me one reason—*(She calls out lyrically.) Coming! Just one second!*—why should you be afraid to open a door? Now you answer it, Laura!

LAURA. Oh, oh, oh . . . *(She returns through the portieres, darts to the Victrola, winds it frantically and turns it on.)*

AMANDA. Laura Wingfield, you march right to that door!

LAURA. Yes—yes, Mother!

(A faraway, scratchy rendition of "Dardanella" softens the air and gives her strength to move through it. She slips to the door and draws it cautiously open. Tom enters with the caller, Jim O'Connor.)

TOM. Laura, this is Jim. Jim, this is my sister, Laura.

JIM *(stepping inside)*. I didn't know that Shakespeare had a sister!

LAURA *(retreating, stiff and trembling, from the door)*. How—how do you do?

JIM *(heartily, extending his hand)*. Okay!

(Laura touches it hesitantly with hers.)

JIM. Your hand's *cold*, Laura!

LAURA. Yes, well—I've been playing the Victrola. . . .

JIM. Must have been playing classical music on it! You ought to play a little hot swing music to warm you up!

LAURA. Excuse me—I haven't finished playing the Victrola. . . . *(She awkwardly hurries into the front room. She pauses a second by the Victrola. Then she catches her breath and darts through the portieres like a frightened deer.)*

JIM *(grinning)*. What was the matter?

TOM. Oh—with Laura? Laura is—terribly shy.

JIM. Shy, huh? It's unusual to meet a shy girl nowadays. I don't believe you ever mentioned you had a sister.

TOM. Well, now you know. I have one. Here is the *Post Dispatch*. You want a piece of it?

JIM. Uh-huh.

TOM. What piece? The comics?

JIM. Sports! *(He glances at it.)* Ole Dizzy Dean is on his bad behavior.

TOM *(uninterested).* Yeah? *(He lights a cigarette and goes over to the fire-escape door.)*

JIM. Where are *you* going?

TOM. I'm going out on the terrace.

JIM *(going after him).* You know, Shakespeare—I'm going to sell you a bill of goods!

TOM. What goods?

JIM. A course I'm taking.

TOM. Huh?

JIM. In public speaking! You and me, we're not the warehouse type.

TOM. Thanks—that's good news. But what has public speaking got to do with it?

JIM. It fits you for—executive positions!

TOM. Awww.

JIM. I tell you it's done a helluva lot for me.

(Image on screen: Executive at his desk.*)*

TOM. In what respect?

JIM. In every! Ask yourself what is the difference between you an' me and men in the office down front? Brains?—No!—Ability?—No! Then what? Just one little thing—

TOM. What is that one little thing?

JIM. Primarily it amounts to—social poise! Being able to square up to people and hold your own on any social level!

AMANDA *(from the kitchenette).* Tom?

TOM. Yes, Mother?

AMANDA. Is that you and Mr. O'Connor?

TOM. Yes, Mother.

AMANDA. Well, you just make yourselves comfortable in there.

TOM. Yes, Mother.

AMANDA. Ask Mr. O'Connor if he would like to wash his hands.

JIM. Aw, no—no—thank you—I took care of that at the warehouse. Tom—

TOM. Yes?

JIM. Mr. Mendoza was speaking to me about you.

TOM. Favorably?

JIM. What do you think?

TOM. Well—

JIM. You're going to be out of a job if you don't wake up.

TOM. I am waking up—

JIM. You show no signs.

TOM. The signs are interior.

(Image on screen: The sailing vessel with the Jolly Roger again.)

TOM. I'm planning to change. *(He leans over the fire-escape rail, speaking with quiet exhilaration. The incandescent marquees and signs of the first-run movie houses light his face from across the alley. He looks like a voyager.)* I'm right at the point of committing myself to a future that doesn't include the warehouse and Mr. Mendoza or even a night-school course in public speaking.

JIM. What are you gassing about?

TOM. I'm tired of the movies.

JIM. Movies!

TOM. Yes, movies! Look at them—*(a wave toward the marvels of Grand Avenue)* All of those glamorous people—having adventures—hogging it all, gobbling the whole thing up! You know what happens? People go to the *movies* instead of *moving*! Hollywood characters are supposed to have all the adventures for everybody in America, while everybody in America sits in a dark room and watches them have them! Yes, until there's a war. That's when adventure becomes available to the masses! *Everyone's* dish, not only Gable's! Then the people in the dark room come out of the dark room to have some adventures themselves—goody, goody! It's our turn now, to go to the South Sea Island—to make a safari—to be exotic, far-off! But I'm not patient. I don't want to wait till then. I'm tired of the *movies* and I am *about* to *move*!

JIM *(incredulously)*. Move?

TOM. Yes.

JIM. When?

TOM. Soon!

JIM. Where? When?

(The music seems to answer the question, while Tom thinks it over. He searches in his pockets.)

TOM. I'm starting to boil inside. I know I seem dreamy, but inside—well, I'm boiling! Whenever I pick up a shoe, I shudder a little thinking how short life is and what I am doing! Whatever that means, I know it doesn't mean shoes—except as something to wear on a traveler's feet! *(He finds what he has been searching for in his pockets and holds out a paper to Jim.)* Look—

JIM. What?

TOM. I'm a member.

JIM *(reading)*. The Union of Merchant Seamen.

TOM. I paid my dues this month, instead of the light bill.

JIM. You will regret it when they turn the lights off.

TOM. I won't be here.

JIM. How about your mother?

TOM. I'm like my father. The bastard son of a bastard! Did you notice how he's grinning in his picture in there? And he's been absent going on sixteen years!

JIM. You're just talking, you drip. How does your mother feel about it?

TOM. Shhh! Here comes Mother! Mother is not acquainted with my plans!

AMANDA *(coming through the poitieres)*. Where are you all?

TOM. On the terrace, Mother,

(They start inside. She advances to them. Tom is distinctly shocked at her appearance. Even Jim blinks a little. He is making his first contact with girlish Southern vivacity and in spite of the night-school course in public speaking is somewhat thrown off the beam by the unexpected outlay of social charm. Certain responses are attempted by Jim but are swept aside by Amanda's gay laughter and chatter. Tom is embarrassed but after the first shock Jim reacts very warmly. He grins and chuckles, is altogether won over.)

(Image on screen: Amanda as a girl.)

AMANDA *(coyly smiling, shaking her girlish ringlets)*. Well, well, well, so this is Mr. O'Connor. Introductions entirely unnecessary. I've heard so much about you from my boy. I finally said to him, Tom—good gracious!—why don't you bring this paragon to supper? I'd like to meet this nice young man at the warehouse!—instead of just hearing him sing your praises so much! I don't know why my son is so stand-offish—that's not Southern behavior!

Let's sit down and—I think we could stand a little more air in here! Tom, leave the door open. I felt a nice fresh breeze a moment ago. Where has it gone to? Mmm, so warm already! And not quite summer, even. We're going to burn up when summer really gets started. However, we're having—we're having a very light supper. I think light things are better fo' this time of year. The same as light clothes are. Light clothes an' light food are what warm weather calls fo'. You know our blood gets so thick during th' winter—it takes a while fo' us to *adjust* ou'selves—when the season changes . . . It's come so quick this year. I wasn't prepared. All of a sudden—heavens! Already summer! I ran to the trunk an' pulled out this light dress—terribly old! Historical almost! But feels so good—so good an' co-ol, y' know. . . .

TOM. Mother—

AMANDA. Yes, honey?

TOM. How about—supper?

AMANDA. Honey, you go ask Sister if supper is ready! You know that Sister is in full charge of supper! Tell her you hungry boys are waiting for it. *(to Jim)* Have you met Laura?

JIM. She—

AMANDA. Let you in? Oh, good, you've met already! It's rare for a girl as sweet an' pretty as Laura to be domestic! But Laura is, thank heavens, not only pretty but also very domestic. I'm not at all. I never was a bit. I never could make a thing but angel-food cake. Well, in the South we had so many servants. Gone, gone, gone. All vestiges of gracious living! Gone completely! I wasn't prepared for what the future brought me. All of my gentlemen callers were sons of planters and so of course I assumed that I would be married to one and raise my family on a large piece of land with plenty of servants. But man proposes—and woman accepts the proposal! To vary that old, old saying a little bit—I married no planter! I married a man who worked for the telephone company! That gallantly smiling gentleman over there! *(She points to the picture.)* A telephone man who—fell in love with long-distance! Now he travels and I don't even know where! But what am I going on for about my—tribulations? Tell me yours—I hope you don't have any! Tom?

TOM *(returning)*. Yes, Mother?

AMANDA. Is supper nearly ready?

TOM. It looks to me like supper is on the table.

AMANDA. Let me look—*(She rises prettily and looks through the portieres.)* Oh, lovely! But where is Sister?

TOM. Laura is not feeling well and says that she thinks she'd better not come to the table.

AMANDA. What? Nonsense! Laura? Oh, Laura!

LAURA *(from the kitchenette, faintly)*. Yes, Mother.

AMANDA. You really must come to the table. We won't be seated until you come to the table! Come in, Mr. O'Connor. You sit over there, and I'll. . . . Laura? Laura Wingfield! You're keeping us waiting, honey! We can't say grace until you come to the table!

(The kitchenette door is pushed weakly open and Laura comes in. She is obviously quite faint, her lips trembling, her eyes wide and staring. She moves unsteadily toward the table.)

(Screen legend: "Terror!")

(Outside a summer storm is coming on abruptly. The white curtains billow inward at the windows and there is a sorrowful murmur from the deep blue dusk.)

(Laura suddenly stumbles; she catches at a chair with a faint moan.)

TOM. Laura!
AMANDA. Laura!

(There is a clap of thunder)

(Screen legend: "Ah!")

(despairingly) Why, Laura, you *are* ill, darling! Tom, help your sister into the living room, dear! Sit in the living room, Laura—rest on the sofa. Well! *(to Jim as Tom helps his sister to the sofa in the living room)* Standing over the hot stove made her ill! I told her that it was just too warm this evening, but—

(Tom comes back to the table.)

Is Laura all right now?
TOM. Yes.
AMANDA. What *is* that? Rain? A nice cool rain has come up! *(She gives Jim a frightened look.)* I think we may—have grace—now . . .
(Tom looks at her stupidly.) Tom, honey—you say grace!
TOM. Oh . . . "For these and all thy mercies—"

(They bow their heads, Amanda stealing a nervous glance at Jim. In the living room Laura, stretched on the sofa, clenches her hand to her lips, to hold back a shuddering sob.)

God's Holy Name be praised—

(The scene dims out.)

SCENE SEVEN

It is half an hour later. Dinner is just being finished in the dining room. Laura is still huddled upon the sofa, her feet drawn under her, her head resting on a pale blue pillow, her eyes wide and mysteriously watchful. The new floor lamp with its shade of rose-colored silk gives a soft, becoming light to her face, bringing out the fragile, unearthly prettiness which usually escapes attention. From outside there is a steady murmur of rain, but it is slackening and soon stops; the air outside becomes pale and luminous as the moon breaks through the clouds. A moment after the curtain rises, the lights in both rooms flicker and go out.

JIM. Hey, there, Mr. Light Bulb!

(Amanda laughs nervously.)

(Legend on screen: "Suspension of public service.")

AMANDA. Where was Moses when the lights went out? Ha-ha. Do you know the answer to that one, Mr. O'Connor?

JIM. No, Ma'am, what's the answer?

AMANDA. In the dark!

(Jim laughs appreciatively.)

Everybody sit still. I'll light the candles. Isn't it lucky we have them on the table? Where's a match? Which of you gentlemen can provide a match?

JIM. Here.

AMANDA. Thank you, Sir.

JIM. Not at all, Ma'am!

AMANDA *(as she lights the candles)*. I guess the fuse has burnt out. Mr. O'Connor, can you tell a burnt-out fuse? I know I can't and Tom is a total loss when it comes to mechanics.

(They rise from the table and go into the kitchenette, from where their voices are heard.)

Oh, be careful you don't bump into something. We don't want our gentleman caller to break his neck. Now wouldn't that be a fine howdy-do?

JIM. Ha-ha! Where is the fuse-box?

AMANDA. Right here next to the stove. Can you see anything?

JIM. Just a minute.

AMANDA. Isn't electricity a mysterious thing? Wasn't it Benjamin Franklin who tied a key to a kite? We live in such a mysterious universe, don't we? Some people say that science clears up all the mysteries for us. In my opinion it only creates more! Have you found it yet?

JIM. No, Ma'am. All these fuses look okay to me.

AMANDA. Tom!

TOM. Yes, Mother?

AMANDA. That light bill I gave you several days ago. The one I told you we got the notices about?

(Legend on screen: "Ha!")

TOM. Oh—yeah.

AMANDA. You didn't neglect to pay it by any chance?

TOM. Why, I—

AMANDA. Didn't! I might have known it!

JIM. Shakespeare probably wrote a poem on that light bill, Mrs. Wingfield.

AMANDA. I might have known better than to trust him with it! There's such a high price for negligence in this world!

JIM. Maybe the poem will win a ten-dollar prize!

AMANDA. We'll just have to spend the remainder of the evening in the nineteenth century, before Mr. Edison made the Mazda lamp!

JIM. Candlelight is my favorite kind of light.

AMANDA. That shows you're romantic! But that's no excuse for Tom. Well, we got through dinner. Very considerate of them to let us get through dinner before they plunged us into everlasting darkness, wasn't it, Mr. O'Connor?

JIM. Ha-ha!

AMANDA. Tom, as a penalty for your carelessness you can help me with the dishes.

JIM. Let me give you a hand.

AMANDA. Indeed you will not!

JIM. I ought to be good for something.

AMANDA. Good for something? (*Her tone is rhapsodic.*) Why, Mr. O'Connor, nobody, *nobody's* given me this much entertainment in years—as you have!

JIM. Aw, now, Mrs. Wingfield!

AMANDA. I'm not exaggerating, not one bit! But Sister is all by her lonesome. You go keep her company in the parlor! I'll give you this lovely old candelabrum that used to be on the altar at the Church of the Heavenly Rest. It was melted a little out of shape when the church burnt down. Lightning struck it one spring. Gypsy Jones was holding a revival at the time and he intimated that the church was destroyed because the Episcopalians gave card parties.

JIM. Ha-ha.

AMANDA. And how about you coaxing Sister to drink a little wine? I think it would be good for her! Can you carry both at once?

JIM. Sure. I'm Superman!

AMANDA. Now, Thomas, get into this apron!

(*Jim comes into the dining room, carrying the candelabrum, its candles lighted, in one hand and a glass of wine in the other. The door of the kitchenette swings closed on Amanda's gay laughter; the flickering light approaches the portieres. Laura sits up nervously as Jim enters. She can hardly speak from the almost intolerable strain of being alone with a stranger*)

(*Screen legend: "I don't suppose you remember me at all!"*)

(*At first, before Jim's warmth overcomes her paralyzing shyness, Laura's voice is thin and breathless, as though she had just run up a steep flight of stairs. Jim's attitude is gently humorous. While the incident is apparently unimportant, it is to Laura the climax of her secret life.)*

JIM. Hello there, Laura.
LAURA *(faintly)*. Hello.

(She clears her throat.)

JIM. How are you feeling now? Better?
LAURA. Yes. Yes, thank you.
JIM. This is for you. A little dandelion wine. *(He extends the glass toward her with extravagant gallantry.)*
LAURA. Thank you.
JIM. Drink it—but don't get drunk!

(He laughs heartily. Laura takes the glass uncertainly; she laughs shyly.)

Where shall I set the candles?
LAURA. Oh—oh, anywhere . . .
JIM. How about here on the floor? Any objections?
LAURA. No.
JIM. I'll spread a newspaper under to catch the drippings. I like to sit on the floor. Mind if I do?
LAURA. Oh, no.
JIM. Give me a pillow?
LAURA. What?
JIM. A pillow!
LAURA. Oh . . . *(She hands him one quickly.)*
JIM. How about you? Don't you like to sit on the floor?
LAURA. Oh—yes.
JIM. Why don't you, then?
LAURA. I—will.
JIM. Take a pillow!

(Laura does. She sits on the floor on the other side of the candelabrum. Jim crosses his legs and smiles engagingly at her.)

I can't hardly see you sitting way over there.
LAURA. I can—see you.
JIM. I know, but that's not fair, I'm in the limelight.

(Laura moves her pillow closer.)

Good! Now I can see you! Comfortable?
LAURA. Yes.

JIM. So am I. Comfortable as a cow! Will you have some gum?

LAURA. No thank you.

JIM. I think that I will indulge, with your permission. *(He musingly unwraps a stick of gum and holds it up.)* Think of the fortune made by the guy that invented the first piece of chewing gum. Amazing, huh? The Wrigley Building is one of the sights of Chicago—I saw it when I went up to the Century of Progress. Did you take in the Century of Progress[19]?

LAURA. No, I didn't.

JIM. Well, it was quite a wonderful exposition. What impressed me most was the Hall of Science. Gives you an idea of what the future will be in America, even more wonderful than the present time is! *(There is a pause. Jim smiles at her.)* Your brother tells me you're shy. Is that right, Laura?

LAURA. I—don't know.

JIM. I judge you to be an old-fashioned type of girl. Well, I think that's a pretty good type to be. Hope you don't think I'm being too personal—do you?

LAURA *(hastily, out of embarrassment).* I believe I *will* take a piece of gum, if you—don't mind. *(clearing her throat)* Mr. O'Connor, have you—kept up with your singing?

JIM. Singing? Me?

LAURA. Yes. I remember what a beautiful voice you had.

JIM. When did you hear me sing?

(Laura does not answer, and in the long pause which follows a man's voice is heard singing offstage.)

VOICE.

> O blow, ye winds, heigh-ho,
> A-roving I will go!
>   I'm off to my love
>   With a boxing glove—
> Ten thousand miles away!

JIM. You say you've heard me sing?

LAURA. Oh, yes! Yes, very often . . . I—don't suppose—you remember me—at all?

JIM *(smiling doubtfully).* You know I have an idea I've seen you before. I had that idea as soon as you opened the door. It seemed almost like I was about to remember your name. But the name that I started to call you—

---

[19]1933–1934 World's Fair, held in Chicago.

wasn't a name! And so I stopped myself before I said it.

LAURA. Wasn't it—Blue Roses?

JIM (*springing up, grinning*). Blue Roses! My gosh, yes—Blue Roses! That's what I had on my tongue when you opened the door! Isn't it funny what tricks your memory plays? I didn't connect you with high school some-how or other. But that's where it was; it was high school. I didn't even know you were Shakespeare's sister! Gosh, I'm sorry.

LAURA. I didn't expect you to. You—barely knew me!

JIM. But we did have a speaking acquaintance, huh?

LAURA. Yes, we—spoke to each other.

JIM. When did you recognize me?

LAURA. Oh, right away!

JIM. Soon as I came in the door?

LAURA. When I heard your name I thought it was probably you. I knew that Tom used to know you a little in high school. So when you came in the door—well, then I was—sure.

JIM. Why didn't you *say* something, then?

LAURA (*breathlessly*). I didn't know what to say, I was—too surprised!

JIM. For goodness sakes! You know, this sure is funny!

LAURA. Yes! Yes, isn't it, though . . .

JIM. Didn't we have a class in something together?

LAURA. Yes, we did.

JIM. What class was that?

LAURA. It was—singing—chorus!

JIM. Aw!

LAURA. I sat across the aisle from you in the Aud.

JIM. Aw.

LAURA. Mondays, Wednesdays, and Fridays.

JIM. Now I remember—you always came in late.

LAURA. Yes, it was so hard for me, getting upstairs. I had that brace on my leg—it clumped so loud!

JIM. I never heard any clumping.

LAURA (*wincing at the recollection*). To me it sounded like—thunder!

JIM. Well, well, well, I never even noticed.

LAURA. And everybody was seated before I came in. I had to walk in front of all those people. My seat was in the back row. I had to go clumping all the way up the aisle with everyone watching!

JIM. You shouldn't have been self-conscious.

LAURA. I know, but I was. It was always such a relief when the singing started.

JIM. Aw, yes, I've placed you now! I used to call you Blue Roses. How was it that I got started calling you that?

LAURA. I was out of school a little with pleurosis. When I came back you asked me what was the matter. I said I had pleurosis—you thought I said *Blue Roses.* That's what you always called me after that!

JIM. I hope you didn't mind.

LAURA. Oh, no—I liked it. You see, I wasn't acquainted with many—people. . . .

JIM. As I remember you sort of stuck by yourself.

LAURA. I—I—never have had much luck at—making friends.

JIM. I don't see why you wouldn't.

LAURA. Well, I—started out badly.

JIM. You mean being—

LAURA. Yes, it sort of—stood between me—

JIM. You shouldn't have let it!

LAURA. I know, but it did, and—

JIM. You were shy with people!

LAURA. I tried not to be but never could—

JIM. Overcome it?

LAURA. No, I—I never could!

JIM. I guess being shy is something you have to work out of kind of gradually.

LAURA *(sorrowfully).* Yes—I guess it—

JIM. Takes time!

LAURA. Yes—

JIM. People are not so dreadful when you know them. That's what you have to remember! And everybody has problems, not just you, but practically everybody has got some problems. You think of yourself as having the only problems, as being the only one who is disappointed. But just look around you and you will see lots of people as disappointed as you are. For instance, I hoped when I was going to high school that I would be further along at this time, six years later, than I am now. You remember that wonderful write-up I had in *The Torch*?

LAURA. Yes! *(She rises and crosses to the table.)*

JIM. It said I was bound to succeed in anything I went into!

(Laura returns with the high school yearbook.)

Holy Jeez! *The Torch!*

(He accepts it reverently. They smile across the book with mutual wonder. Laura crouches beside him and they begin to turn the pages. Laura's shyness is dissolving in his warmth.)

LAURA. Here you are in *The Pirates of Penzance!*

JIM *(wistfully).* I sang the baritone lead in that operetta.

LAURA *(raptly)*. So—*beautifully!*
JIM *(protesting)*. Aw—
LAURA. Yes, yes—beautifully—beautifully!
JIM. You heard me?
LAURA. All three times!
JIM. No!
LAURA. Yes!
JIM. All three performances?
LAURA *(looking down)*. Yes.
JIM. Why?
LAURA. I—wanted to ask you to—autograph my program.

(She takes the program from the back of the yearbook and shows it to him.)

JIM. Why didn't you ask me to?
LAURA. You were always surrounded by your own friends so much that I never had a chance to.
JIM. You should have just—
LAURA. Well, I—thought you might think I was—
JIM. Thought I might think you was—what?
LAURA. Oh—
JIM *(with reflective relish)*. I was beleaguered by females in those days.
LAURA. You were terribly popular!
JIM. Yeah—
LAURA. You had such a—friendly way—
JIM. I was spoiled in high school.
LAURA. Everybody—liked you!
JIM. Including you?
LAURA. I—yes, I—did, too—*(She gently closes the book in her lap.)*
JIM. Well, well, well! Give me that program, Laura.

(She hands it to him. He signs it with a flourish.)

There you are—better late than never!
LAURA. Oh, I—what a—surprise!
JIM. My signature isn't worth very much right now. But some day—maybe—it will increase in value! Being disappointed is one thing and being discouraged is something else. I am disappointed but I am not discouraged. I'm twenty-three years old. How old are you?
LAURA. I'll be twenty-four in June.
JIM. That's not old age!
LAURA. No, but—
JIM. You finished high school?

LAURA *(with difficulty)*. I didn't go back.

JIM. You mean you dropped out?

LAURA. I made bad grades in my final examinations. *(She rises and replaces the book and the program on the table. Her voice is strained.)* How is—Emily Meisenbach getting along?

JIM. Oh, that kraut-head!

LAURA. Why do you call her that?

JIM. That's what she was.

LAURA. You're not still—going with her?

JIM. I never see her.

LAURA. It said in the "Personal" section that you were—engaged!

JIM. I know, but I wasn't impressed by that—propaganda!

LAURA. It wasn't—the truth?

JIM. Only in Emily's optimistic opinion!

LAURA. Oh—

Legend: "What have you done since high school?")

(Jim lights a cigarette and leans indolently back on his elbows smiling at Laura with a warmth and charm which lights her inwardly with altar candles. She remains by the table, picks up a piece from the glass menagerie collection, and turns it in her hands to cover her tumult.)

JIM *(after several reflective puffs on his cigarette)*. What have you done since high school?

(She seems not to hear him.)

Huh?

(Laura looks up.)

I said what have you done since high school, Laura?

LAURA. Nothing much.

JIM. You must have been doing something these six long years.

LAURA. Yes.

JIM. Well, then, such as what?

LAURA. I took a business course at business college—

JIM. How did that work out?

LAURA. Well, not very—well—I had to drop out, it gave me—indigestion—

(Jim laughs gently.)

JIM. What are you doing now?

LAURA. I don't do anything—much. Oh, please don't think I sit around doing nothing! My glass collection takes up a good deal of time. Glass is something you have to take good care of.

JIM. What did you say—about glass?

LAURA. Collection I said—I have one—*(She clears her throat and turns away again, acutely shy.)*

JIM *(abruptly).* You know what I judge to be the trouble with you? Inferiority complex! Know what that is? That's what they call it when someone low-rates himself! I understand it because I had it, too. Although my case was not so aggravated as yours seems to be. I had it until I took up public speaking, developed my voice, and learned that I had an aptitude for science. Before that time I never thought of myself as being outstanding in any way whatsoever! Now I've never made a regular study of it, but I have a friend who says I can analyze people better than doctors that make a profession of it. I don't claim that to be necessarily true, but I can sure guess a person's psychology, Laura! *(He takes out his gum.)* Excuse me, Laura. I always take it out when the flavor is gone. I'll use this scrap of paper to wrap it in. I know how it is to get it stuck on a shoe. *(He wraps the gum in paper and puts it in his pocket.)* Yep—that's what I judge to be your principal trouble. A lack of confidence in yourself as a person. You don't have the proper amount of faith in yourself. I'm basing that fact on a number of your remarks and also on certain observations I've made. For instance that clumping you thought was so awful in high school. You say that you even dreaded to walk into class. You see what you did? You dropped out of school, you gave up an education because of a clump, which as far as I know was practically nonexistent! A little physical defect is what you have. Hardly noticeable even! Magnified thousands of times by imagination! You know what my strong advice to you is? Think of yourself as *superior* in some way!

LAURA. In what way would I think?

JIM. Why, man alive, Laura! just look about you a little. What do you see? A world full of common people! All of 'em born and all of 'em going to die! Which of them has one-tenth of your good points! Or mine! Or anyone else's, as far as that goes—gosh! Everybody excels in some one thing. Some in many! *(He unconsciously glances at himself in the mirror.)* All you've got to do is to discover in what! Take me, for instance. *(He adjusts his tie at the mirror.)* My interest happens to lie in electro-dynamics. I'm taking a course in radio engineering at night school, Laura, on top of a fairly responsible job at the warehouse. I'm taking that course and studying public speaking.

LAURA. Ohhhh.

JIM. Because I believe in the future of television! *(turning his back to her.)* I wish to be ready to go up right along with it. Therefore I'm planning to get in on the ground floor. In fact I've already made the right connections and all that remains is for the industry itself to get under way! Full steam—(*His eyes are starry.*) Knowledge—Zzzzzp! Money—Zzzzzzp!—Power! That's the cycle democracy is built on!

(*His attitude is convincingly dynamic. Laura stares at him, even her shyness eclipsed in her absolute wonder. He suddenly grins.*)

I guess you think I think a lot of myself?
LAURA. No—o-o-o, I—
JIM. Now how about you? Isn't there something you take more interest in than anything else?
LAURA. Well, I do—as I said—have my—glass collection—

(*A peal of girlish laughter rings from the kitchenette.*)

JIM. I'm not right sure I know what you're talking about. What kind of glass is it?
LAURA. Little articles of it, they're ornaments mostly! Most of them are little animals made out of glass, the tiniest little animals in the world. Mother calls them the glass menagerie! Here's an example of one, if you'd like to see it! This one is one of the oldest. It's nearly thirteen.

(*Music: "The Glass Menagerie."*)

Oh, be careful—if you breathe, it breaks!
JIM. I'd better not take it. I'm pretty clumsy with things.
LAURA. Go on, I trust you with him! (*She places the piece in his palm.*)
There now—you're holding him gently! Hold him over the light, he loves the light! You see how the light shines through him?
JIM. It sure does shine!
LAURA. I shouldn't be partial, but he is my favorite one.
JIM. What kind of a thing is this one supposed to be?
LAURA. Haven't you noticed the single horn on his forehead?
JIM. A unicorn, huh?
LAURA. Mmmm—hmmm!
JIM. Unicorns—aren't they extinct in the modern world?
LAURA. I know!
JIM. Poor little fellow, he must feel sort of lonesome.
LAURA (*smiling*). Well, if he does, he doesn't complain about it. He stays on a shelf with some horses that don't have horns and all of them seem to get along nicely together.
JIM. How do you know?
LAURA (*lightly*). I haven't heard any arguments among them!

JIM *(grinning)*. No arguments, huh? Well, that's a pretty good sign! Where shall I set him!

LAURA. Put him on the table. They all like a change of scenery once in a while!

JIM. Well, well, well, well—*(He places the glass piece on the table, then raises his arm and stretches.)* Look how big my shadow is when I stretch!

LAURA. Oh, oh, yes—it stretches across the ceiling!

JIM *(crossing to the door)*. I think it's stopped raining. *(He opens the fire-escape door and the background music changes to a dance tune.)* Where does the music come from?

LAURA. From the Paradise Dance Hall across the alley.

JIM. How about cutting the rug a little, Miss Wingfield?

LAURA. Oh, I—

JIM. Or is your program filled up? Let me have a look at it. *(He grasps an imaginary card.)* Why, every dance is taken! I'll just have to scratch some out.

(Waltz music: "La Golondrina.")

Ahhh, a waltz! *(He executes some sweeping turns by himself, then holds his arms toward Laura.*

LAURA *(breathlessly)*. I—can't dance!

JIM. There you go, that inferiority stuff!

LAURA. I've never danced in my life!

JIM. Come on, try!

LAURA. Oh, but I'd step on you!

JIM. I'm not made out of glass.

LAURA. How—how—how do we start?

JIM. Just leave it to me. You hold your arms out a little.

LAURA. Like this?

JIM *(taking her in his arms)*. A little bit higher. Right. Now don't tighten up, that's the main thing about it—relax.

LAURA *(laughing breathlessly)*. It's hard not to.

JIM. Okay.

LAURA. I'm afraid you can't budge me.

JIM. What do you bet I can't? *(He swings her into motion.)*

LAURA. Goodness, yes, you can!

JIM. Let yourself go, now, Laura, just let yourself go.

LAURA. I'm—

JIM. Come on!

LAURA. —trying!

JIM. Not so stiff—easy does it!

LAURA. I know but I'm—

JIM. Loosen th' backbone! There now, that's a lot better.

LAURA. Am I?

JIM. Lots, lots better! *(He moves her about the room in a clumsy waltz.)*

LAURA. Oh, my!

JIM. Ha-ha!

LAURA. Oh, my goodness!

JIM. Ha-ha-ha!

(They suddenly bump into the table, and the glass piece on it falls to the floor. Jim stops the dance.)

What did we hit on?

LAURA. Table.

JIM. Did something fall off it? I think—

LAURA. Yes.

JIM. I hope that it wasn't the little glass horse with the horn!

LAURA. Yes. *(She stoops to pick it up.)*

JIM. Aw, aw, aw. It is broken?

LAURA. Now it is just like all the other horses.

JIM. It's lost its—

LAURA. Horn! It doesn't matter. Maybe it's a blessing in disguise.

JIM. You'll never forgive me. I bet that that was your favorite piece of glass.

LAURA. I don't have favorites much. It's no tragedy, Freckles. Glass breaks so easily. No matter how careful you are. The traffic jars the shelves and things fall off them.

JIM. Still I'm awfully sorry that I was the cause.

LAURA *(smiling)*. I'll just imagine he had an operation. The horn was removed to make him feel less—freakish!

(They both laugh.)

Now he will feel more at home with the other horses, the ones that don't have horns.

JIM. Ha-ha, that's very funny! *(Suddenly he is serious.)* I'm glad to see that you have a sense of humor. You know—you're—well—very different! Surprisingly different from anyone else I know! *(His voice becomes soft and hesitant with a genuine feeling.)* Do you mind me telling you that?

(Laura is abashed beyond speech.)

I mean it in a nice way—

(Laura nods shyly, looking away.)

You make me feel sort of—I don't know how to put it! I'm usually pretty good at expressing things, but—this is something that I don't know how to say!

(Laura touches her throat and clears it—turns the broken unicorn in her hands. His voice becomes softer.)

Has anyone ever told you that you were pretty?

(There is a pause, and the music rises slightly. Laura looks up slowly, with wonder and shakes her head.)

Well, you are! In a very different way from anyone else. And all the nicer because of the difference, too.

(His voice becomes low and husky, Laura turns away, nearly faint with the novelty of her emotions.)

I wish that you were my sister. I'd teach you to have some confidence in yourself. The different people are not like other people, but being different is nothing to be ashamed of. Because other people are not such wonderful people. They're one hundred times one thousand. You're one times one! They walk all over the earth. You just stay here. They're common as—weeds, but—you—well, you're—*Blue Roses!*

(Image on screen: Blue Roses.*)*

(The music changes.)

LAURA. But blue is wrong for—roses. . . .
JIM. It's right for you! You're—pretty!
LAURA. In what respect am I pretty?
JIM. In all respects—believe me! Your eyes—your hair—are pretty! Your hands are pretty! *(He catches hold of her hand.)* You think I'm making this up because I'm invited to dinner and have to be nice. Oh, I could do that! I could put on an act for you, Laura, and say lots of things without being very sincere. But this time I am. I'm talking to you sincerely. I happened to notice you had this inferiority complex that keeps you from feeling comfortable with people. Somebody needs to build your confidence up and make you proud instead of shy and turning away and—blushing. Somebody—ought to—*kiss* you, Laura!

(His hand slips slowly up her arm to her shoulder as the music swells tumultuously. He suddenly turns her about and kisses her on the lips. When he releases her, Laura sinks on the sofa with a bright, dazed look. Jim backs away and fishes in his pocket for a cigarette.)

(Legend on screen: "A souvenir.")

Stumblejohn!

(He lights the cigarette, avoiding her look. There is a peal of girlish laughter from Amanda in the kitchenette. Laura slowly raises and opens her hand. It still contains the little broken glass animal. She looks at it with a tender, bewildered expression.)

Stumblejohn! I shouldn't have done that—that was way off the beam. You don't smoke, do you?

(She looks up, smiling, not hearing the question. He sits beside her rather gingerly. She looks at him speechlessly—waiting. He coughs decorously and moves a little farther aside as he considers the situation and senses her feelings, dimly, with perturbation. He speaks gently.)

Would you—care for a—mint?

(She doesn't seem to hear him but her look grows brighter even.)

Peppermint? Life Saver? My pocket's a regular drugstore—wherever I go. . . . *(He pops a mint in his mouth. Then he gulps and decides to make a clean breast of it. He speaks slowly and gingerly.)* Laura, you know, if I had a sister like you, I'd do the same thing as Tom. I'd bring out fellows and—introduce her to them. The right type of boys—of a type to—appreciate her. Only—well—he made a mistake about me. Maybe I've got no call to be saying this. That may not have been the idea in having me over. But what if it was? There's nothing wrong about that. The only trouble is that in my case—I'm not in a situation to—do the right thing. I can't take down your number and say I'll phone. I can't call up next week and—ask for a date. I thought I had better explain the situation in case you—mis-understood it and—I hurt your feelings. . . .

(There is a pause. Slowly, very slowly, Laura's look changes, her eyes returning slowly from his to the glass figure in her palm. Amanda utters another gay laugh in the kitchenette.)

LAURA *(faintly)*. You—won't—call again?

JIM. No, Laura, I can't. *(He rises from the sofa.)* As I was just explaining, I've—got strings on me. Laura, I've—been going steady! I go out all the time with a girl named Betty. She's a home-girl like you, and Catholic, and Irish, and in a great many ways we—get along fine. I met her last summer on a moonlight boat trip up the river to Alton, on the Majestic. Well—right away from the start it was—love!

(Legend: Love!)

(Laura sways slightly forward and grips the arm of the sofa. He fails to notice, now enrapt in his own comfortable being.)

Being in love has made a new man of me!

(Leaning stiffly forward, clutching the arm of the sofa, Laura struggles visibly with her storm. But Jim is oblivious; she is a long way off.)

The power of love is really pretty tremendous! Love is something that changes the whole world, Laura!

(The storm abates a little and Laura leans back. He notices her again.)

It happened that Betty's aunt took sick, she got a wire and had to go to Centralia. So Tom—when he asked me to dinner—I naturally just accepted the invitation, not knowing that you—that he—that I—*(He stops awkwardly.)* Huh—I'm a stumblejohn!

(He flops back on the sofa. The holy candles on the altar of Laura's face have been snuffed out. There is a look of almost infinite desolation. Jim glances at her uneasily.)

I wish that you would—say something.

(She bites her lip which was trembling and then bravely smiles. She opens her hand again on the broken glass figure. Then she gently takes his hand and raises it level with her own. She carefully places the unicorn in the palm of his hand, then pushes his fingers closed upon it.)

What are you—doing that for? You want me to have him? Laura?

(She nods.)

What for?
LAURA. A—souvenir. . . .

(She rises unsteadily and crouches beside the Victrola to wind it up.)

(Legend on screen: "Things have a way of turning out so badly!" Or image: "Gentleman caller waving goodbye—gaily.")

(At this moment Amanda rushes brightly back into the living room. She bears a pitcher of fruit punch in an old-fashioned cut-glass pitcher, and a plate of macaroons. The plate has a gold border and poppies painted on it.)

AMANDA. Well, well, well! Isn't the air delightful after the shower! I've made you children a little liquid refreshment. *(She turns gaily to Jim.)* Jim, do you know that song about lemonade?

"Lemonade, lemonade
Made in the shade and stirred with a spade—
Good enough for any old maid!"

JIM *(uneasily)*. Ha-ha! No—I never heard it.

AMANDA. Why, Laura! You look so serious!

JIM. We were having a serious conversation.

AMANDA. Good! Now you're better acquainted!

JIM *(uncertainly)*. Ha-ha! Yes.

AMANDA. You modern young people are much more serious-minded than my generation. I was so gay as a girl!

JIM. You haven't changed, Mrs. Wingfield.

AMANDA. Tonight I'm rejuvenated! The gaiety of the occasion, Mr. O'Connor! *(She tosses her head with a peal of laughter, spilling some lemonade.)* Oooo! I'm baptizing myself!

JIM. Here—let me—

AMANDA *(setting the pitcher down)*. There now. I discovered we had some maraschino cherries. I dumped them in, juice and all!

JIM. You shouldn't have gone to that trouble, Mrs. Wingfield.

AMANDA. Trouble, trouble? Why, it was loads of fun! Didn't you hear me cutting up in the kitchen? I bet your ears were burning! I told Tom how outdone with him I was for keeping you to himself so long a time! He should have brought you over much, much sooner! Well, now that you've found your way, I want you to be a very frequent caller! Not just occasional but all the time. Oh, we're going to have a lot of gay times together! I see them coming! Mmm, just breathe that air! So fresh, and the moon's so pretty! I'll skip back out—I know where my place is when young folks are having a—serious conversation!

JIM. Oh, don't go out, Mrs. Wingfield. The fact of the matter is I've got to be going.

AMANDA. Going, now? You're joking! Why, it's only the shank of the evening, Mr. O'Connor.

JIM. Well, you know how it is.

AMANDA. You mean you're a young workingman and have to keep workingmen's hours. We'll let you off early tonight. But only on the condition that next time you stay later. What's the best night for you? Isn't Saturday night the best night for you workingmen?

JIM. I have a couple of time-clocks to punch, Mrs. Wingfield. One at morning, another one at night!

AMANDA. My, but you *are* ambitious! You work at night, too?

JIM. No, Ma'am, not work but—Betty!

(He crosses deliberately to pick up his hat. The band at the Paradise Dance Hall goes into a tender waltz.)

AMANDA. Betty? Betty? Who's—Betty!

(There is an ominous cracking sound in the sky.)

JIM. Oh, just a girl. The girl I go steady with!

(He smiles charmingly. The sky falls.)

(Legend: "The Sky Falls.")

AMANDA *(a long-drawn exhalation)*. Ohhhh . . . Is it a serious romance, Mr. O'Connor?

JIM. We're going to be married the second Sunday in June.

AMANDA. Ohhhh—how nice! Tom didn't mention that you were engaged to be married.

JIM. The cat's not out of the bag at the warehouse yet. You know how they are. They call you Romeo and stuff like that. *(He stops at the oval mirror to put on his hat. He carefully shapes the brim and the crown to give a discreetly dashing effect.)* It's been a wonderful evening, Mrs. Wingfield. I guess this is what they mean by Southern hospitality.

AMANDA. It really wasn't anything at all.

JIM. I hope it don't seem like I'm rushing off. But I promised Betty I'd pick her up at the Wabash depot, an' by the time I get my jalopy down there her train'll be in. Some women are pretty upset if you keep 'em waiting.

AMANDA. Yes, I know—the tyranny of women! *(She extends her hand.)* Goodbye, Mr. O'Connor. I wish you luck—and happiness—and success! All three of them, and so does Laura! Don't you, Laura?

LAURA. Yes!

JIM *(taking Laura's hand)*. Goodbye, Laura. I'm certainly going to treasure that souvenir. And don't you forget the good advice I gave you. *(He raises his voice to a cheery shout.)* So long, Shakespeare! Thanks again, ladies. Good night!

(He grins and ducks jauntily out. Still barely grimacing, Amanda closes the door on the gentleman caller. Then she turns back to the room with a puzzled expression. She and Laura don't dare to face each other. Laura crouches beside the Victrola to wind it.)

AMANDA *(faintly)*. Things have a way of turning out so badly. I don't believe that I would play the Victrola. Well, well—well! Our gentleman caller was engaged to be married! *(She raises her voice.)* Tom!

TOM *(from the kitchenette)*. Yes, Mother?

AMANDA. Come in here a minute. I want to tell you something awfully funny.

TOM *(entering with a macaroon and a glass of the lemonade).* Has the gentleman caller gotten away already?

AMANDA. The gentleman caller has made an early departure. What a wonderful joke you played on us!

TOM. How do you mean?

AMANDA. You didn't mention that he was engaged to be married.

TOM. Jim? Engaged?

AMANDA. That's what he just informed us.

TOM. I'll be jiggered! I didn't know about that.

AMANDA. That seems very peculiar.

TOM. What's peculiar about it?

AMANDA. Didn't you call him your best friend down at the warehouse?

TOM. He is, but how did I know?

AMANDA. It seems extremely peculiar that you wouldn't know your best friend was going to be married!

TOM. The warehouse is where I work, not where I know things about people!

AMANDA. You don't know things anywhere! You live in a dream; you manufacture illusions!

(He crosses to the door.)

Where are you going?

TOM. I'm going to the movies.

AMANDA. That's right, now that you've had us make such fools of ourselves. The effort, the preparations, all the expense! The new floor lamp, the rug, the clothes for Laura! All for what? To entertain some other girl's fiancé! Go to the movies, go! Don't think about us, a mother deserted, an unmarried sister who's crippled and has no job! Don't let anything interfere with your selfish pleasure! Just go, go, go—to the movies!

TOM. All right, I will! The more you shout about my selfishness to me the quicker I'll go, and I won't go to the movies!

AMANDA. Go, then! Go to the moon—you selfish dreamer!

(Tom smashes his glass on the floor. He plunges out on the fire escape, slamming the door. Laura screams in fright. The dance-hall music becomes louder. Tom stands on the fire escape, gripping the rail. The moon breaks through the storm clouds, illuminating his face.)

(Legend on screen: "And so goodbye . . .")

(Tom's closing speech is timed with what is happening inside the house. We see,

as though through soundproof glass, that Amanda appears to be making a comforting speech to Laura, who is huddled upon the sofa. Now that we cannot hear the mother's speech, her silliness is gone and she has dignity and tragic beauty. Laura's hair hides her face until, at the end of the speech, she lifts her head to smile at her mother. Amanda's gestures are slow and graceful, almost dancelike, as she comforts her daughter. At the end of her speech she glances a moment at the father's picture—then withdraws through the portieres. At the close of Tom's speech, Laura blows out the candles, ending the play.)

TOM. I didn't go to the moon, I went much further—for time is the longest distance between two places. Not long after that I was fired for writing a poem on the lid of a shoe-box. I left Saint Louis. I descended the steps of this fire escape for a last time and followed, from then on, in my father's footsteps, attempting to find in motion what was lost in space. I traveled around a great deal. The cities swept about me like dead leaves, leaves that were brightly colored but torn away from the branches. I would have stopped, but I was pursued by something. It always came upon me unawares, taking me altogether by surprise. Perhaps it was a familiar bit of music. Perhaps it was only a piece of transparent glass. Perhaps I am walking along a street at night, in some strange city, before I have found companions. I pass the lighted window of a shop where perfume is sold. The window is filled with pieces of colored glass, tiny transparent bottles in delicate colors, like bits of a shattered rainbow. Then all at once my sister touches my shoulder. I turn around and look into her eyes. Oh, Laura, Laura, I tried to leave you behind me, but I am more faithful than I intended to be! I reach for a cigarette, I cross the street, I run into the movies or a bar, I buy a drink, I speak to the nearest stranger—anything that can blow your candles out!

(Laura bends over the candles.)

For nowadays the world is lit by lightning! Blow out your candles, Laura—and so goodbye. . . .

(She blows the candles out.)

[1945]

QUESTIONS

1. *The Glass Menagerie* is a "memory play," told from Tom's perspective. Find the non-naturalistic elements of this play. What effect do they have on the narrative? How do they help to establish the play's tone?

2. How does Amanda's coming of age in the American South influence her perception of the contemporary world?

3. What is the symbolic significance of Laura's glass menagerie in this play? In particular, what does the broken unicorn symbolize? How do these symbols help advance the larger them of *The Glass Menagerie*?

4. Why does Tom choose to escape to the movies? What does this fact tell us about his character?

5. Explain Jim's philosophy of life. What are its strengths? Its weaknesses? In what ways are Tom and Amanda alike? Amanda and Laura? Tom and Laura?

6. Who is the protagonist of *The Glass Menagerie*? Explain your choice.

7. The play opens with a direct address to the audience from Tom, the son whose memory spawns the events we see on stage. This direct address to the audience is sometimes called "breaking the fourth wall," because the character breaks the invisible wall separating the fictional events on stage from the real-life audience in the stalls. What is the point of this stage effect? Why does Williams have his narrator directly address the audience?

8. How does this play seem to regard the American Dream, the fantasy that individuals can achieve affluence and happiness through hard work and self-reliance?

9. *The Glass Menagerie* employs some of the stage techniques developed by the German playwright and director Bertolt Brecht. For instance, the stage directions call for images to be flashed on-screen during the performance. These techniques sought to achieve what Brecht called "the alienation effect"; they sought to distance the spectator from the events on stage, so that he or she would react intellectually, rather than emotionally, to the performance. However, many contemporary directors of *The Glass Menagerie* opt not to use the screen images. As a result, the play takes on a more realistic—and pointedly, a less symbolic—mood. Given your close reading of the play, make a case to either use or discard these projected images in a production.

10. Imagine the fate of Tom, Laura, and Amanda following Tom's departure from their tenement home. Use evidence from the play's text, particularly material from Williams's rich characterizations, to support your predictions.

Henrik Ibsen
[1828–1906]

The playwright **HENRIK IBSEN** *was born into a provincial Norwegian family. As a young man, he studied medicine but soon began working as a stage manager at a local theater. While serving as the artistic director for the National Theater in Oslo, he wrote his first plays. Unfortunately, he met with little early success in his homeland. Consequently, he moved to Italy and to Germany, where he lived for twenty-seven years.*

During his early career, Ibsen wrote verse plays based on Norwegian myth and history, including Brand *(1866) and* Peer Gynt *(1867). He soon turned his attention to contemporary social problems and to dramatic realism. Dramatic realism endeavors to portray onstage an accurate representation of everyday life. These plays depict the details of contemporary existence through their dialogue, setting, and costumes; in doing so, they seek to produce the illusion of objectivity for their audiences. Created in opposition to the well-made play and to the popular melodrama, realism resisted the simple cause-and-effect plot structure and the sentimentality of those popular dramatic forms.*

Ibsen's three-act realist drama A Doll's House *(1879) addresses the "woman problem." As women became increasingly public and political during the nineteenth century, society grappled with the radical transformation of feminine roles—and with its consequent effects on the private sphere of the home. A Doll's House engages with these concerns by staging the marriage of Torvald and Nora Helmer in which the patronizing Torvald treats his wife Nora like a mindless child. This fictional marriage asked audiences to think critically about the oppressive roles to which women are confined. When Nora discovers her husband is a hypocrite, she leaves him, slamming the door in the final act of the play. Nineteenth century audiences, shocked by this conclusion, were challenged to speculate on Nora's fate. Audiences and readers are still intrigued by what happens to Nora once she leaves her home. (In a satirical sketch, the English comedy troupe Monty Python hypothesized that Nora walked out of the door . . . only to be met on the other side by a marching band, which promptly ran over her.)*

Like A Doll's House, *much of Ibsen's later work tackled social problems and the individuals affected by them. The plays—many of which continue to be produced regularly—include* An Enemy of the People *(1882);* The Wild Duck *(1884);* Hedda Gabler *(1890); and* The Master Builder *(1892). During the late nineteenth and early twentieth centuries, Ibsen's drama actively contributed to social debate. His critiques of society moved beyond the realm of the strictly artistic; they powerfully influenced society and politics. In fact, the term "Ibsenism" became a catchphrase for the critique of society, even as the playwright himself avoided politics. Notably, the content of these plays was frequently shocking and often bravely tackled subjects once taboo on the stage. For instance,* Ghosts *(1881) critiqued religious values and addressed frankly the issue of venereal disease.*

Ibsen has had a profound and enduring effect on modern drama. His contemporaries rapidly embraced his dramatic innovations, and his work was quickly translated and produced throughout Europe and the United States. He died in Norway in 1906.

A Doll's House

HENRIK IBSEN

DRAMATIS PERSONÆ

TORVALD HELMER.
NORA, his wife.
DR. RANK.
MRS. LINDE.
NILS KROGSTAD.
THE HELMER'S THREE YOUNG CHILDREN.
ANNE, their nurse.
A HOUSEMAID.
A PORTER.

SCENE

The action takes place in HELMER'S *house.*

ACT I

SCENE—*A room furnished comfortably and tastefully but not extravagantly. At the back a door to the right leads to the entrance hall; another to the left leads to* HELMER'S *study. Between the doors stands a piano. In the middle of the left-hand wall is a door and beyond a window. Near the window are a round table, armchairs and a small sofa. In the right-hand wall, at the farther end, another door; and on the same side, nearer the footlights, a stove, two easy chairs and a rocking chair; between the stove and the door a small table. Engravings on the walls; a cabinet with china and other small objects; a small bookcase with well-bound books. The floors are carpeted, and a fire burns in the stove. It is winter.*

A bell rings in the hall; shortly afterward the door is heard to open. Enter NORA, *humming a tune and in high spirits. She is in outdoor dress and carries a number of parcels; these she lays on the table to the right. She leaves the outer door open after her, and through it is seen a* PORTER *who is carrying a Christmas tree and a basket, which he gives to the* MAID *who has opened the door.*

NORA. Hide the Christmas tree carefully, Helen. Be sure the children do not see it till this evening, when it is dressed. (*To the* PORTER, *taking out her purse.*) How much?

POR. Sixpence.

NORA. There is a shilling. No, keep the change. (*The* PORTER *thanks her and goes out.* NORA *shuts the door. She is laughing to herself as she takes off her hat and coat. She takes a packet of macaroons from her pocket and eats one or two, then goes cautiously to her husband's door and listens.*) Yes, he is in. (*Still humming, she goes to the table on the right.*)

HEL. (*calls out from his room*). Is that my little lark twittering out there?

NORA (*busy opening some of the parcels*). Yes, it is!

HEL. Is it my little squirrel bustling about?

NORA. Yes!

HEL. When did my squirrel come home?

NORA. Just now. (*Puts the bag of macaroons into her pocket and wipes her mouth.*) Come in here, Torvald, and see what I have bought.

HEL. Don't disturb me. (*A little later he opens the door and looks into the room, pen in hand.*) Bought, did you say? All these things? Has my little spend-thrift been wasting money again?

NORA. Yes, but, Torvald, this year we really can let ourselves go a little. This is the first Christmas that we have not needed to economize.

HEL. Still, you know, we can't spend money recklessly.

NORA. Yes, Torvald, we may be a wee bit more reckless now, mayn't we? Just a tiny wee bit! You are going to have a big salary and earn lots and lots of money.

HEL. Yes, after the new year; but then it will be a whole quarter before the salary is due.

NORA. Pooh! We can borrow till then.

HEL. Nora! (*Goes up to her and takes her playfully by the ear.*) The same little featherhead! Suppose, now, that I borrowed fifty pounds today and you spent it all in the Christmas week and then on New Year's Eve a slate fell on my head and killed me and——

NORA (*putting her hands over his mouth*). Oh! don't say such horrid things.

HEL. Still, suppose that happened,—what then?

NORA. If that were to happen, I don't suppose I should care whether I owed money or not.

HEL. Yes, but what about the people who had lent it?

NORA. They? Who would bother about them? I should not know who they were.

HEL. That is like a woman! But seriously, Nora, you know what I think about that. No debt, no borrowing. There can be no freedom or beauty about a home life that depends on borrowing and debt. We two have kept bravely on the straight road so far, and we will go on the same way for the short time longer that there need be any struggle.

NORA (*moving toward the stove*). As you please, Torvald.

HEL. (*following her*). Come, come, my little skylark must not droop her wings. What is this! Is my little squirrel out of temper? (*Taking out his purse.*) Nora, what do you think I have got here?

NORA (*turning round quickly*). Money!

HEL. There you are. (*Gives her some money.*) Do you think I don't know what a lot is wanted for housekeeping at Christmas time?

NORA (*counting*). Ten shillings—a pound—two pounds! Thank you, thank you, Torvald; that will keep me going for a long time.

HEL. Indeed it must.

NORA. Yes, yes, it will. But come here and let me show you what I have bought. And all so cheap! Look, here is a new suit for Ivar and a sword, and a horse and a trumpet for Bob, and a doll and dolly's bedstead for Emmy—they are very plain, but anyway she will soon break them in pieces. And here are dress lengths and handkerchiefs for the maids; old Anne ought really to have something better.

HEL. And what is in this parcel?

NORA (*crying out*). No, no! You mustn't see that till this evening.

HEL. Very well. But now tell me, you extravagant little person, what would you like for yourself?

NORA. For myself? Oh, I am sure I don't want anything.

HEL. Yes, but you must. Tell me something reasonable that you would particularly like to have.

NORA. No, I really can't think of anything—unless, Torvald——

HEL. Well?

NORA (*playing with his coat buttons and without raising her eyes to his*). If you really want to give me something, you might—you might——

HEL. Well, out with it!

NORA (*speaking quickly*). You might give me money, Torvald. Only just as much as you can afford; and then one of these days I will buy something with it.

HEL. But, Nora——

NORA. Oh, do! dear Torvald; please, please do! Then I will wrap it up in beautiful gilt paper and hang it on the Christmas tree. Wouldn't that be fun?

HEL. What are little people called that are always wasting money?

NORA. Spendthrifts—I know. Let us do as I suggest, Torvald, and then I shall have time to think what I am most in want of. That is a very sensible plan, isn't it?

HEL. (*smiling*). Indeed it is—that is to say, if you were really to save out of the money I give you and then really buy something for yourself. But if you spend it all on the housekeeping and any number of unnecessary things, then I merely have to pay up again.

NORA. Oh, but, Torvald——

HEL. You can't deny it, my dear little Nora. (*Puts his arm around her waist.*) It's a sweet little spendthrift, but she uses up a deal of money. One would hardly believe how expensive such little persons are!

NORA. It's a shame to say that. I do really save all I can.

HEL. (*laughing*). That's very true—all you can. But you can't save anything!

NORA (*smiling quietly and happily*). You haven't any idea how many expenses we skylarks and squirrels have, Torvald.

HEL. You are an odd little soul. Very like your father. You always find some new way of wheedling money out of me, and as soon as you have got it it seems to melt in your hands. You never know where it has gone. Still, one must take you as you are. It is in the blood; for indeed it is true that you can inherit these things, Nora.

NORA. Ah, I wish I had inherited many of Papa's qualities.

HEL. And I would not wish you to be anything but just what you are, my sweet little skylark. But, do you know, it strikes me that you are looking rather— what shall I say?—rather uneasy today.

NORA. Do I?

HEL. You do, really. Look straight at me.

NORA (*looks at him*). Well?

HEL. (*wagging his finger at her*). Hasn't Miss Sweet Tooth been breaking rules in town today?

NORA. No; what makes you think that?

HEL. Hasn't she paid a visit to the confectioner's?

NORA. No, I assure you, Torvald——

HEL. Not been nibbling sweets?

NORA. No, certainly not.

HEL. Not even taken a bite at a macaroon or two?

NORA. No, Torvald, I assure you, really——

HEL. There, there, of course I was only joking.

NORA (*going to the table on the right*). I should not think of going against your wishes.

HEL. No, I am sure of that; besides, you gave me your word. (*Going up to her.*) Keep your little Christmas secrets to yourself, my darling. They will all be revealed tonight when the Christmas tree is lit, no doubt.

NORA. Did you remember to invite Doctor Rank?

HEL. No. But there is no need; as a matter of course he will come to dinner with us. However, I will ask him when he comes in this morning. I have ordered some good wine. Nora, you can't think how I am looking forward to this evening.

NORA. So am I! And how the children will enjoy themselves, Torvald!

HEL. It is splendid to feel that one has a perfectly safe appointment and a big enough income. It's delightful to think of, isn't it?

NORA. It's wonderful!

HEL. Do you remember last Christmas? For a full three weeks before hand you shut yourself up every evening till long after midnight, making ornaments for the Christmas tree and all the other fine things that were to be a surprise to us. It was the dullest three weeks I ever spent!

NORA. I didn't find it dull.

HEL. (*smiling*). But there was precious little result, Nora.

NORA. Oh, you shouldn't tease me about that again. How could I help the cat's going in and tearing everything to pieces?

HEL. Of course you couldn't, poor little girl. You had the best of intentions to please us all, and that's the main thing. But it is a good thing that our hard times are over.

NORA. Yes, it is really wonderful.

HEL. This time I needn't sit here and be dull all alone and you needn't ruin your dear eyes and your pretty little hands——

NORA (*clapping her hands*). No, Torvald, I needn't any longer, need I! It's wonderfully lovely to hear you say so! (*Taking his arm.*) Now I will tell you how I have been thinking we ought to arrange things, Torvald. As soon as Christmas is over——(*A bell rings in the hall.*) There's the bell. (*She tidies the room a little.*) There's someone at the door. What a nuisance!

HEL. If it is a caller, remember I am not at home.

MAID (*in the doorway*). A lady to see you, ma'am—a stranger.

NORA. Ask her to come in.

MAID (*to* HELMER). The doctor came at the same time, sir.

HEL. Did he go straight into my room?

MAID. Yes sir.

(HELMER *goes into his room. The* MAID *ushers in* MRS. LINDE, *who is in traveling dress, and shuts the door.*)

MRS. L. (*in a dejected and timid voice*). How do you do, Nora?

NORA (*doubtfully*). How do you do——

MRS. L. You don't recognize me, I suppose.

NORA. No, I don't know—yes, to be sure, I seem to——(*Suddenly.*) Yes! Christine! Is it really you?

MRS. L. Yes, it is I.

NORA. Christine! To think of my not recognizing you! And yet how could I? (*In a gentle voice.*) How you have altered, Christine!

MRS. L. Yes, I have indeed. In nine, ten long years——

NORA. Is it so long since we met? I suppose it is. The last eight years have been a happy time for me, I can tell you. And so now you have come into the town and have taken this long journey in winter—that was plucky of you.

MRS. L. I arrived by steamer this morning.

NORA. To have some fun at Christmas time, of course. How delightful! We will have such fun together! But take off your things. You are not cold, I hope. (*Helps her.*) Now we will sit down by the stove and be cozy. No, take this armchair; I will sit here in the rocking chair. (*Takes her hands.*) Now you look like your old self again; it was only the first moment——You are a little paler, Christine, and perhaps a little thinner.

MRS. L. And much, much older, Nora.

NORA. Perhaps a little older; very, very little; certainly not much. (*Stops suddenly and speaks seriously*). What a thoughtless creature I am, chattering away like this. My poor, dear Christine, do forgive me.

MRS. L. What do you mean, Nora?

NORA (*gently*). Poor Christine, you are a widow.

MRS. L. Yes; it is three years ago now.

NORA. Yes, I knew; I saw it in the papers. I assure you, Christine, I meant ever so often to write to you at the time, but I always put it off and something always prevented me.

MRS. L. I quite understand, dear.

NORA. It was very bad of me, Christine. Poor thing, how you must have suffered. And he left you nothing?

MRS. L. No.

NORA. And no children?

MRS. L. No.

NORA. Nothing at all, then?

MRS. L. Not even any sorrow or grief to live upon.

NORA (*looking incredulously at her*). But, Christine, is that possible?

MRS. L. (*smiles sadly and strokes her hair*). It sometimes happens, Nora.

NORA. So you are quite alone. How dreadfully sad that must be. I have three lovely children. You can't see them just now, for they are out with their nurse. But now you must tell me all about it.

MRS. L. No, no; I want to hear about you.

NORA. No, you must begin. I mustn't be selfish today; today I must only think of your affairs. But there is one thing I must tell you. Do you know we have just had a great piece of good luck?

MRS. L. No, what is it?

NORA. Just fancy, my husband has been made manager of the bank!

MRS. L. Your husband? What good luck!

NORA. Yes, tremendous! A barrister's profession is such an uncertain thing, especially if he won't undertake unsavory cases; and naturally Torvald has never been willing to do that, and I quite agree with him. You may imagine how pleased we are! He is to take up his work in the bank at the new year, and then he will have a big salary and lots of commissions. For the future we can live quite differently—we can do just as we like. I feel so relieved and so happy, Christine! It will be splendid to have heaps of money and not need to have any anxiety, won't it?

MRS. L. Yes, anyhow I think it would be delightful to have what one needs.

NORA. No, not only what one needs but heaps and heaps of money.

MRS. L. (*smiling*). Nora, Nora, haven't you learned sense yet? In our schooldays you were a great spendthrift.

NORA (*laughing*). Yes, that is what Torvald says now. (*Wags her finger at her.*) But "Nora, Nora" is not so silly as you think. We have not been in a position for me to waste money. We have both had to work.

MRS. L. You too?

NORA. Yes; odds and ends, needlework, crochet work, embroidery and that kind of thing. (*Dropping her voice.*) And other things as well. You know Torvald left his office when we were married? There was no prospect of promotion there, and he had to try and earn more than before. But during the first year he overworked himself dreadfully. You see, he had to make money every way he could; and he worked early and late; but he couldn't stand it and fell dreadfully ill, and the doctors said it was necessary for him to go south.

MRS. L. You spent a whole year in Italy, didn't you?

NORA. Yes. It was no easy matter to get away, I can tell you. It was just after Ivar was born; but naturally we had to go. It was a wonderfully beautiful journey, and it saved Torvald's life. But it cost a tremendous lot of money, Christine.

MRS. L. So I should think.

NORA. It cost about two hundred and fifty pounds. That's a lot, isn't it?

MRS. L. Yes, and in emergencies like that it is lucky to have the money.

NORA. I ought to tell you that we had it from Papa.

MRS. L. Oh, I see. It was just about that time that he died, wasn't it?

NORA. Yes; and, just think of it, I couldn't go and nurse him. I was expecting little Ivar's birth every day and I had my poor sick Torvald to look after. My dear, kind father—I never saw him again, Christine. That was the saddest time I have known since our marriage.

MRS. L. I know how fond you were of him. And then you went off to Italy?

NORA. Yes; you see, we had money then, and the doctors insisted on our going, so we started a month later.

MRS. L. And your husband came back quite well?

NORA. As sound as a bell!

MRS. L. But—the doctor?

NORA. What doctor?

MRS. L. I thought your maid said the gentleman who arrived here just as I did was the doctor.

NORA. Yes, that was Doctor Rank, but he doesn't come here professionally. He is our greatest friend and comes in at least once every day. No, Torvald has not had an hour's illness since then, and our children are strong and healthy and so am I. (*Jumps up and claps her hands.*) Christine! Christine! It's good to be alive and happy! But how horrid of me; I am talking of nothing but my own affairs. (*Sits on a stool near her and rests her arms on her knees.*) You mustn't be angry with me. Tell me, is it really true that you did not love your husband? Why did you marry him?

MRS. L. My mother was alive then and was bedridden and helpless, and I had to provide for my two younger brothers; so I did not think I was justified in refusing his offer.

NORA. No, perhaps you were quite right. He was rich at that time, then?

MRS. L. I believe he was quite well off. But his business was a precarious one, and when he died it all went to pieces and there was nothing left.

NORA. And then?

MRS. L. Well, I had to turn my hand to anything I could find—first a small shop, then a small school and so on. The last three years have seemed like one long working day, with no rest. Now it is at an end, Nora. My poor mother needs me no more, for she is gone; and the boys do not need me either; they have got situations and can shift for themselves.

NORA. What a relief you must feel it.

MRS. L. No indeed; I only feel my life unspeakably empty. No one to live for any more. (*Gets up restlessly.*) That was why I could not stand the life in my little backwater any longer. I hope it may be easier here to find something which will busy me and occupy my thoughts. If only I could have the good luck to get some regular work—office work of some kind——

NORA. But, Christine, that is so frightfully tiring, and you look tired out now. You had far better go away to some watering place.

MRS. L. (*walking to the window*). I have no father to give me money for a journey, Nora.

NORA (*rising*). Oh, don't be angry with me.

MRS. L. (*going up to her*). It is you that must not be angry with me, dear. The worst of a position like mine is that it makes one so bitter. No one to work for and yet obliged to be always on the lookout for chances. One must live, and so one becomes selfish. When you told me of the happy turn your fortunes have taken—you will hardly believe it—I was delighted not so much on your account as on my own.

NORA. How do you mean? Oh, I understand. You mean that perhaps Torvald could get you something to do.

MRS. L. Yes, that was what I was thinking of.

NORA. He must, Christine. Just leave it to me; I will broach the subject very cleverly—I will think of something that will please him very much. It will make me so happy to be of some use to you.

MRS. L. How kind you are, Nora, to be so anxious to help me! It is doubly kind in you, for you know so little of the burdens and troubles of life.

NORA. I? I know so little of them?

MRS. L. (*smiling*). My dear! Small household cares and that sort of thing! You are a child, Nora.

NORA (*tosses her head and crosses the stage*). You ought not to be so superior.

MRS. L. No?

NORA. You are just like the others. They all think that I am incapable of anything really serious——

MRS. L. Come, come.

NORA. —that I have gone through nothing in this world of cares.

MRS. L. But, my dear Nora, you have just told me all your troubles.

NORA. Pooh!—those were trifles. (*Lowering her voice.*) I have not told you the important thing.

MRS. L. The important thing? What do you mean?

NORA. You look down upon me altogether, Christine—but you ought not to. You are proud, aren't you, of having worked so hard and so long for your mother?

MRS. L. Indeed, I don't look down on anyone. But it is true that I am both proud and glad to think that I was privileged to make the end of my mother's life almost free from care.

NORA. And you are proud to think of what you have done for your brothers.

MRS. L. I think I have the right to be.

NORA. I think so too. But now listen to this; I too have something to be proud and glad of.

MRS. L. I have no doubt you have. But what do you refer to?

NORA. Speak low. Suppose Torvald were to hear! He mustn't on any account—no one in the world must know, Christine, except you.

MRS. L. But what is it?

NORA. Come here. (*Pulls her down on the sofa beside her.*) Now I will show you that I too have something to be proud and glad of. It was I who saved Torvald's life.

MRS. L. "Saved"? How?

NORA. I told you about our trip to Italy. Torvald would never have recovered if he had not gone there.

MRS. L. Yes, but your father gave you the necessary funds.

NORA (*smiling*). Yes, that is what Torvald and the others think, but——

MRS. L. But——

NORA. Papa didn't give us a shilling. It was I who procured the money.

MRS. L. You? All that large sum?

NORA. Two hundred and fifty pounds. What do you think of that?

MRS. L. But, Nora, how could you possibly do it? Did you win a prize in the lottery?

NORA (*contemptuously*). In the lottery? There would have been no credit in that.

MRS. L. But where did you get it from, then?

NORA (*humming and smiling with an air of mystery*). Hm, hm! Aha!

MRS. L. Because you couldn't have borrowed it.

NORA. Couldn't I? Why not?

MRS. L. No, a wife cannot borrow without her husband's consent.

NORA (*tossing her head*). Oh, if it is a wife who has any head for business—a wife who has the wit to be a little bit clever——

MRS. L. I don't understand it at all, Nora.

NORA. There is no need you should. I never said I had borrowed the money. I may have got it some other way. (*Lies back on the sofa.*) Perhaps I got it from some other admirers. When anyone is as attractive as I am——

MRS. L. You are a mad creature.

NORA. Now you know you're full of curiosity, Christine.

MRS. L. Listen to me, Nora dear. Haven't you been a little bit imprudent?

NORA (*sits up straight*). Is it imprudent to save your husband's life?

MRS. L. It seems to me imprudent, without his knowledge, to——

NORA. But it was absolutely necessary that he should not know! My goodness, can't you understand that? It was necessary he should have no idea what a dangerous condition he was in. It was to me that the doctors came and said that his life was in danger and that the only thing to save him was to live in the south. Do you suppose I didn't try, first of all, to get what I wanted as if it were for myself? I told him how much I should love to travel abroad like other young wives; I tried tears and entreaties with him; I told him that he ought to remember the condition I was in and that he ought to be kind and indulgent to me; I even hinted that he might raise a loan. That nearly made him angry, Christine. He said I was thoughtless and that it was his duty as my husband not to indulge me in my whims and caprices—as I believe he called them. Very well, I thought, you must be saved—and that was how I came to devise a way out of the difficulty.

MRS. L. And did your husband never get to know from your father that the money had not come from him?

NORA. No, never. Papa died just at that time. I had meant to let him into the secret and beg him never to reveal it. But he was so ill then—alas, there never was any need to tell him.

MRS. L. And since then have you never told your secret to your husband?

NORA. Good heavens, no! How could you think so? A man who has such strong opinions about these things! And besides, how painful and humiliating it would be for Torvald, with his manly independence, to know that he owed me anything! It would upset our mutual relations altogether; our beautiful happy home would no longer be what it is now.

MRS. L. Do you mean never to tell him about it?

NORA (*meditatively and with a half-smile*). Yes—someday, perhaps, after many years, when I am no longer as nice looking as I am now. Don't laugh at me! I mean, of course, when Torvald is no longer as devoted to me as he is now; when my dancing and dressing-up and reciting have palled on him; then it may be a good thing to have something in reserve——(*Breaking off.*) What nonsense! That time will never come. Now what do you think of my great secret, Christine? Do you still think I am of no use? I can tell you, too, that this affair has caused me a lot of worry. It has been by no means easy for me to meet my engagements punctually. I may tell you that there is something that is called, in business, quarterly interest and another thing called payment in installments, and it is always so dreadfully difficult to manage them. I have had to save a little here and there, where I could, you understand. I have not been able to put aside much from my housekeeping money, for Torvald must have a good table. I couldn't let my children be shabbily dressed; I have felt obliged to use up all he gave me for them, the sweet little darlings!

MRS. L. So it has all had to come out of your own necessaries of life, poor Nora?

NORA. Of course. Besides, I was the one responsible for it. Whenever Torvald has given me money for new dresses and such things I have never spent more than half of it; I have always bought the simplest and cheapest things. Thank heaven any clothes look well on me, and so Torvald has never noticed it. But it was often very hard on me, Christine—because it is delightful to be really well dressed, isn't it?

MRS. L. Quite so.

NORA. Well, then I have found other ways of earning money. Last winter I was lucky enough to get a lot of copying to do, so I locked myself up and sat writing every evening until quite late at night. Many a time I was desperately tired, but all the same it was a tremendous pleasure to sit there working and earning money. It was like being a man.

MRS. L. How much have you been able to pay off in that way?

NORA. I can't tell you exactly. You see, it is very difficult to keep an account of a business matter of that kind. I only know that I have paid every penny that I could scrape together. Many a time I was at my wits' end. (*Smiles.*) Then I used to sit here and imagine that a rich old gentleman had fallen in love with me——

MRS. L. What! Who was it?

NORA. Be quiet!—that he had died and that when his will was opened it contained, written in big letters, the instruction: "The lovely Mrs. Nora Helmer is to have all I possess paid over to her at once in cash."

MRS. L. But, my dear Nora—who could the man be?

NORA. Good gracious, can't you understand? There was no old gentleman at all; it was only something that I used to sit here and imagine, when I couldn't think of any way of procuring money. But it's all the same now; the tiresome old person can stay where he is as far as I am concerned; I don't care about him or his will either, for I am free from care now. (*Jumps up.*) My goodness, it's delightful to think of, Christine! Free from care! To be able to be free from care, quite free from care; to be able to play and romp with the children; to be able to keep the house beautifully and have everything just as Torvald likes it! And, think of it, soon the spring will come and the big blue sky! Perhaps we shall be able to take a little trip—perhaps I shall see the sea again! Oh, it's a wonderful thing to be alive and be happy. (*A bell is heard in the hall.*)

MRS. L. (*rising*). There is the bell; perhaps I had better go.

NORA. No, don't go; no one will come in here; it is sure to be for Torvald.

SERVANT (*at the hall door*). Excuse me, ma'am—there is a gentleman to see the master, and as the doctor is with him——

NORA. Who is it?

KROG. (*at the door*). It is I, Mrs. Helmer. (MRS. LINDE *starts, trembles and turns to the window.*)

NORA (*takes a step toward him and speaks in a strained, low voice*). You? What is it? What do you want to see my husband about?

KROG. Bank business—in a way. I have a small post in the bank, and I hear your husband is to be our chief now.

NORA. Then it is——

KROG. Nothing but dry business matters, Mrs. Helmer; absolutely nothing else.

NORA. Be so good as to go into the study then. (*She bows indifferently to him and shuts the door into the hall, then comes back and makes up the fire in the stove.*)

MRS. L. Nora—who was that man?

NORA. A lawyer of the name of Krogstad.

MRS. L. Then it really was he.

NORA. Do you know the man?

MRS. L. I used to—many years ago. At one time he was a solicitor's clerk in our town.

NORA. Yes, he was.

MRS. L. He is greatly altered.

NORA. He made a very unhappy marriage.

MRS. L. He is a widower now, isn't he?

NORA. With several children. There now, it is burning up. (*Shuts the door of the stove and moves the rocking chair aside.*)

MRS. L. They say he carries on various kinds of business.

NORA. Really! Perhaps he does; I don't know anything about it. But don't let us think of business; it is so tiresome.

DR. RANK (*comes out of* HELMER'S *study. Before he shuts the door he calls to him*). No, my dear fellow, I won't disturb you; I would rather go in to your wife for a little while. (*Shuts the door and sees* MRS. LINDE.) I beg your pardon; I am afraid I am disturbing you too.

NORA. No, not at all. (*Introducing him.*) Doctor Rank, Mrs. Linde.

RANK. I have often heard Mrs. Linde's name mentioned here. I think I passed you on the stairs when I arrived, Mrs. Linde?

MRS. L. Yes, I go up very slowly; I can't manage stairs well.

RANK. Ah! Some slight internal weakness?

MRS. L. No, the fact is I have been overworking myself.

RANK. Nothing more than that? Then I suppose you have come to town to amuse yourself with our entertainments?

MRS. L. I have come to look for work.

RANK. Is that a good cure for overwork?

MRS. L. One must live, Doctor Rank.

RANK. Yes, the general opinion seems to be that it is necessary.

NORA. Look here, Doctor Rank—you know you want to live.

RANK. Certainly. However wretched I may feel, I want to prolong the agony as long as possible. All my patients are like that. And so are those who are morally diseased; one of them, and a bad case too, is at this very moment with Helmer——

MRS. L. (*sadly*). Ah!

NORA. Whom do you mean?

RANK. A lawyer of the name of Krogstad, a fellow you don't know at all. He suffers from a diseased moral character, Mrs. Helmer, but even he began talking of its being highly important that he should live.

NORA. Did he? What did he want to speak to Torvald about?

RANK. I have no idea; I only heard that it was something about the bank.

NORA. I didn't know this—what's his name?—Krogstad had anything to do with the bank.

RANK. Yes, he has some sort of appointment there. (*To* MRS. LINDE.) I don't know whether you find also in your part of the world that there are certain people who go zealously snuffing about to smell out moral corruption and, as soon as they have found some, put the person concerned into some lucrative position where they can keep their eye on him. Healthy natures are left out in the cold.

MRS. L. Still I think the sick are those who most need taking care of.

RANK (*shrugging his shoulders*). Yes, there you are. That is the sentiment that is turning society into a sick house.

(NORA, *who has been absorbed in her thoughts, breaks out into smothered laughter and claps her hands.*)

RANK. Why do you laugh at that? Have you any notion what society really is?

NORA. What do I care about tiresome society? I am laughing at something quite different, something extremely amusing. Tell me, Doctor Rank, are all the people who are employed in the bank dependent on Torvald now?

RANK. Is that what you find so extremely amusing?

NORA (*smiling and humming*). That's my affair! (*Walking about the room.*) It's perfectly glorious to think that we have—that Torvald has so much power over so many people. (*Takes the packet from her pocket.*) Doctor Rank, what do you say to a macaroon?

RANK. What, macaroons? I thought they were forbidden here.

NORA. Yes, but these are some Christine gave me.

MRS. L. What! I?

NORA. Oh well, don't be alarmed! You couldn't know that Torvald had forbidden them. I must tell you that he is afraid they will spoil my teeth. But, bah!—once in a way——That's so, isn't it, Doctor Rank? By your leave! (*Puts a macaroon into his mouth.*) You must have one too, Christine. And I shall have one, just a little one—or at most two. (*Walking about.*) I am tremendously happy. There is just one thing in the world now that I should dearly love to do.

RANK. Well, what is that?

NORA. It's something I should dearly love to say if Torvald could hear me.

RANK. Well, why can't you say it?

NORA. No, I daren't; it's so shocking.

MRS. L. Shocking?

RANK. Well, I should not advise you to say it. Still, with us you might. What is it you would so much like to say if Torvald could hear you?

NORA. I should just love to say—Well, I'm damned!

RANK. Are you mad?

MRS. L. Nora dear!

RANK. Say it, here he is!

NORA (*hiding the packet*). Hush! Hush! Hush!

(HELMER *comes out of his room with his coat over his arm and his hat in his hand.*)

NORA. Well, Torvald dear, have you got rid of him?

HEL. Yes, he has just gone.

NORA. Let me introduce you—this is Christine, who has come to town.

HEL. Christine? Excuse me, but I don't know——

NORA. Mrs. Linde, dear; Christine Linde.

HEL. Of course. A school friend of my wife's, I presume?

MRS. L. Yes, we have known each other since then.

NORA. And just think, she has taken a long journey in order to see you.

HEL. What do you mean?

MRS. L. No, really, I——

NORA. Christine is tremendously clever at bookkeeping, and she is frightfully anxious to work under some clever man, so as to perfect herself——

HEL. Very sensible, Mrs. Linde.

NORA. And when she heard you had been appointed manager of the bank—the news was telegraphed, you know—she traveled here as quick as she could. Torvald, I am sure you will be able to do something for Christine, for my sake, won't you?

HEL. Well, it is not altogether impossible. I presume you are a widow, Mrs. Linde?

MRS. L. Yes.

HEL. And have had some experience of bookkeeping?

MRS. L. Yes, a fair amount.

HEL. Ah well, it's very likely I may be able to find something for you.

NORA (*clapping her hands*). What did I tell you?

HEL. You have just come at a fortunate moment, Mrs. Linde.

MRS. L. How am I to thank you?

HEL. There is no need. (*Puts on his coat.*) But today you must excuse me——

RANK. Wait a minute; I will come with you. (*Brings his fur coat from the hall and warms it at the fire.*)

NORA. Don't be long away, Torvald dear.

HEL. About an hour, not more.

NORA. Are you going too, Christine?

MRS. L. (*putting on her cloak*). Yes, I must go and look for a room.

HEL. Oh well, then, we can walk down the street together.

NORA (*helping her*). What a pity it is we are so short of space here; I am afraid it is impossible for us——

MRS. L. Please don't think of it! Good-by, Nora dear, and many thanks.

NORA. Good-by for the present. Of course you will come back this evening. And you too, Doctor Rank. What do you say? If you are well enough? Oh, you must be! Wrap yourself up well. (*They go to the door all talking together. Children's voices are heard on the staircase.*)

NORA. There they are. There they are! (*She runs to open the door. The* NURSE *comes in with the children.*) Come in! Come in! (*Stoops and kisses them.*) Oh, you sweet blessings! Look at them, Christine! Aren't they darlings?

RANK. Don't let us stand here in the draught.

HEL. Come along, Mrs. Linde; the place will only be bearable for a mother now!

(RANK, HELMER *and* MRS. LINDE *go downstairs. The* NURSE *comes forward with the children;* NORA *shuts the hall door.*)

NORA. How fresh and well you look! Such red cheeks!—like apples and roses. (*The children all talk at once while she speaks to them.*) Have you had great fun? That's splendid! What, you pulled both Emmy and Bob along on the sledge? Both at once? That *was* good. You are a clever boy, Ivar. Let me take her for a little, Anne. My sweet little baby doll! (*Takes the baby from the* MAID *and dances it up and down.*) Yes, yes, Mother will dance with Bob too. What! Have you been snowballing? I wish I had been there too! No, no, I will take their things off, Anne; please let me do it, it is such fun. Go in now, you look half frozen. There is some hot coffee for you on the stove.

(*The* NURSE *goes into the room on the left.* NORA *takes off the children's things and throws them about while they all talk to her at once.*)

NORA. Really! Did a big dog run after you? But it didn't bite you? No, dogs don't bite nice little dolly children. You mustn't look at the parcels, Ivar. What are they? Ah, I daresay you would like to know. No, no—it's something nasty! Come, let us have a game! What shall we play at? Hide and seek? Yes, we'll play hide and seek. Bob shall hide first. Must I hide? Very well, I'll hide first. (*She and the children laugh and shout and romp in and out of the room; at last* NORA *hides under the table; the children rush in and look for her but do not see her; they hear her smothered laughter, run to the table, lift up the cloth and find her. Shouts of laughter. She crawls forward and pretends to frighten them. Fresh laughter. Meanwhile there has been a knock at the hall door but none of them has noticed it. The door is half opened and* KROGSTAD *appears. He waits a little; the game goes on.*)

KROG. Excuse me, Mrs. Helmer.

NORA (*with a stifled cry turns round and gets up onto her knees*). Ah! What do you want?

KROG. Excuse me, the outer door was ajar; I suppose someone forgot to shut it.

NORA (*rising*). My husband is out, Mr. Krogstad.

KROG. I know that.

NORA. What do you want here then?

KROG. A word with you.

NORA. With me? (*To the children, gently.*) Go in to Nurse. What? No, the strange man won't do Mother any harm. When he has gone we will have another game. (*She takes the children into the room on the left and shuts the door after them.*) You want to speak to me?

KROG. Yes, I do.

NORA. Today? It is not the first of the month yet.

KROG. No, it is Christmas Eve, and it will depend on yourself what sort of a Christmas you will spend.

NORA. What do you want? Today it is absolutely impossible for me——

KROG. We won't talk about that till later on. This is something different. I presume you can give me a moment?

NORA. Yes—yes, I can—although——

KROG. Good. I was in Olsen's Restaurant and saw your husband going down the street——

NORA. Yes?

KROG. With a lady.

NORA. What then?

KROG. May I make so bold as to ask if it was a Mrs. Linde?

NORA. It was.

KROG. Just arrived in town?

NORA. Yes, today.

KROG. She is a great friend of yours, isn't she?

NORA. She is. But I don't see——

KROG. I knew her too, once upon a time.

NORA. I am aware of that.

KROG. Are you? So you know all about it; I thought as much. Then I can ask you, without beating about the bush—is Mrs. Linde to have an appointment in the bank?

NORA. What right have you to question me, Mr. Krogstad? You, one of my husband's subordinates! But since you ask, you shall know. Yes, Mrs. Linde *is* to have an appointment. And it was I who pleaded her cause, Mr. Krogstad, let me tell you that.

KROG. I was right in what I thought then.

NORA (*walking up and down the stage*). Sometimes one has a tiny little bit of influence, I should hope. Because one is a woman it does not necessarily follow that——When anyone is in a subordinate position, Mr. Krogstad, they should really be careful to avoid offending anyone who—who——

KROG. Who has influence?

NORA. Exactly.

KROG. (*changing his tone*). Mrs. Helmer, you will be so good as to use your influence on my behalf.

NORA. What? What do you mean?

KROG. You will be so kind as to see that I am allowed to keep my subordinate position in the bank.

NORA. What do you mean by that? Who proposes to take your post away from you?

KROG. Oh, there is no necessity to keep up the pretense of ignorance. I can quite understand that your friend is not very anxious to expose herself to the chance of rubbing shoulders with me, and I quite understand, too, whom I have to thank for being turned off.

NORA. But I assure you——

KROG. Very likely; but, to come to the point, the time has come when I should advise you to use your influence to prevent that.

NORA. But, Mr. Krogstad, I *have* no influence.

KROG. Haven't you? I thought you said yourself just now——

NORA. Naturally I did not mean you to put that construction on it. I! What should make you think I have any influence of that kind with my husband?

KROG. Oh, I have known your husband from our student days. I don't suppose he is any more unassailable than other husbands.

NORA. If you speak slightingly of my husband, I shall turn you out of the house.

KROG. You are bold, Mrs. Helmer.

NORA. I am not afraid of you any longer. As soon as the New Year comes I shall in a very short time be free of the whole thing.

KROG. (*controlling himself*). Listen to me, Mrs. Helmer. If necessary, I am prepared to fight for my small post in the bank as if I were fighting for my life.

NORA. So it seems.

KROG. It is not only for the sake of the money; indeed, that weighs least with me in the matter. There is another reason—well, I may as well tell you. My position is this. I daresay you know, like everybody else, that once, many years ago, I was guilty of an indiscretion.

NORA. I think I have heard something of the kind.

KROG. The matter never came into court, but every way seemed to be closed to me after that. So I took to the business that you know of. I had to do something; and, honestly, I don't think I've been one of the worst. But now I must cut myself free from all that. My sons are growing up; for their sake I must try and win back as much respect as I can in the town. This post in the bank was like the first step up for me—and now your husband is going to kick me downstairs again into the mud.

NORA. But you must believe me, Mr. Krogstad; it is not in my power to help you at all.

KROG. Then it is because you haven't the will, but I have means to compel you.

NORA. You don't mean that you will tell my husband that I owe you money?

KROG. Hm! Suppose I were to tell him?

NORA. It would be perfectly infamous of you. (*Sobbing.*) To think of his learning my secret, which has been my joy and pride, in such an ugly, clumsy way—that he should learn it from you! And it would put me in a horribly disagreeable position.

KROG. Only disagreeable?

NORA (*impetuously*). Well, do it then!—and it will be the worse for you. My husband will see for himself what a blackguard you are, and you certainly won't keep your post then.

KROG. I asked you if it was only a disagreeable scene at home that you were afraid of?

NORA. If my husband does get to know of it, of course he will at once pay you what is still owing, and we shall have nothing more to do with you.

KROG. (*coming a step nearer*). Listen to me, Mrs. Helmer. Either you have a very bad memory or you know very little of business. I shall be obliged to remind you of a few details.

NORA. What do you mean?

KROG. When your husband was ill you came to me to borrow two hundred and fifty pounds.

NORA. I didn't know anyone else to go to.

KROG. I promised to get you that amount——

NORA. Yes, and you did so.

KROG. I promised to get you that amount on certain conditions. Your mind was so taken up with your husband's illness and you were so anxious to get the money for your journey that you seem to have paid no attention to the conditions of our bargain. Therefore it will not be amiss if I remind you of them. Now I promised to get the money on the security of a bond which I drew up.

NORA. Yes, and which I signed.

KROG. Good. But below your signature there were a few lines constituting your father a surety for the money; those lines your father should have signed.

NORA. Should? He did sign them.

KROG. I had left the date blank; that is to say your father should himself have inserted the date on which he signed the paper. Do you remember that?

NORA. Yes, I think I remember.

KROG. Then I gave you the bond to send by post to your father. Is that not so?

NORA. Yes.

KROG. And you naturally did so at once, because five or six days afterward you brought me the bond with your father's signature. And then I gave you the money.

NORA. Well, haven't I been paying it off regularly?

KROG. Fairly so, yes. But—to come back to the matter in hand—that must have been a very trying time for you, Mrs. Helmer?

NORA. It was, indeed.

KROG. Your father was very ill, wasn't he?

NORA. He was very near his end.

KROG. And died soon afterward?

NORA. Yes.

KROG. Tell me, Mrs. Helmer, can you by any chance remember what day your father died?—on what day of the month, I mean.

NORA. Papa died on the twenty-ninth of September.

KROG. That is correct; I have ascertained it for myself. And, as that is so, there is a discrepancy (*taking a paper from his pocket*) which I cannot account for.

NORA. What discrepancy? I don't know—— ⌐

KROG. The discrepancy consists, Mrs. Helmer, in the fact that your father signed this bond three days after his death.

NORA. What do you mean? I don't understand.

KROG. Your father died on the twenty-ninth of September. But look here; your father has dated his signature the second of October. It is a discrepancy, isn't it? (NORA *is silent.*) Can you explain it to me? (NORA *is still silent.*) It is a remarkable thing, too, that the words "second of October," as well as the year, are not written in your father's handwriting but in one that I think I know. Well, of course it can be explained; your father may have forgotten to date his signature and someone else may have dated it haphazard before they knew of his death. There is no harm in that. It all depends on the signature of the name, and *that* is genuine, I suppose, Mrs. Helmer? It was your father himself who signed his name here?

NORA (*after a short pause, throws her head up and looks defiantly at him*). No, it was not. It was I that wrote Papa's name.

KROG. Are you aware that is a dangerous confession?

NORA. In what way? You shall have your money soon.

KROG. Let me ask you a question: why did you not send the paper to your father?

NORA. It was impossible; Papa was so ill. If I had asked him for his signature, I should have had to tell him what the money was to be used for; and when he was so ill himself I couldn't tell him that my husband's life was in danger—it was impossible.

KROG. It would have been better for you if you had given up your trip abroad.

NORA. No, that was impossible. That trip was to save my husband's life; I couldn't give that up.

KROG. But did it never occur to you that you were committing a fraud on me?

NORA. I couldn't take that into account; I didn't trouble myself about you at all. I couldn't bear you because you put so many heartless difficulties in my way although you knew what a dangerous condition my husband was in.

KROG. Mrs. Helmer, you evidently do not realize clearly what it is that you have been guilty of. But I can assure you that my one false step, which lost me all my reputation, was nothing more or nothing worse than what you have done.

NORA. You? Do you ask me to believe that you were brave enough to run a risk to save your wife's life?

KROG. The law cares nothing about motives.

NORA. Then it must be a very foolish law.

KROG. Foolish or not, it is the law by which you will be judged if I produce this paper in court.

NORA. I don't believe it. Is a daughter not to be allowed to spare her dying father anxiety and care? Is a wife not to be allowed to save her husband's life? I don't know much about law, but I am certain that there must be laws permitting such things as that. Have you no knowledge of such laws—you who are a lawyer? You must be a very poor lawyer, Mr. Krogstad.

KROG. Maybe. But matters of business—such business as you and I have had together—do you think I don't understand that? Very well. Do as you please. But let me tell you this—if I lose my position a second time, you shall lose yours with me. (*He bows and goes out through the hall.*)

NORA (*appears buried in thought for a short time, then tosses her head*). Nonsense! Trying to frighten me like that! I am not so silly as he thinks. (*Begins to busy herself putting the children's things in order.*) And yet—— No, it's impossible! I did it for love's sake.

THE CHILDREN (*in the doorway on the left*). Mother, the stranger man has gone out through the gate.

NORA. Yes, dears, I know. But don't tell anyone about the stranger man. Do you hear? Not even Papa.

CHILDREN. No, Mother; but will you come and play again?

NORA. No, no—not now.

CHILDREN. But, Mother, you promised us.

NORA. Yes, but I can't now. Run away in; I have such a lot to do. Run away in, my sweet little darlings. (*She gets them into the room by degrees and shuts the door on them, then sits down on the sofa, takes up a piece of needlework and sews a few stitches but soon stops.*) No! (*Throws down the work, gets up, goes to the hall door and calls out.*) Helen! bring the tree in. (*Goes to the table on the left, opens a drawer and stops again.*) No, no! It is quite impossible!

MAID (*coming in with the tree*). Where shall I put it, ma'am?

NORA. Here, in the middle of the floor.

MAID. Shall I get you anything else?

NORA. No, thank you. I have all I want.

(*Exit* MAID.)

NORA (*begins dressing the tree*). A candle here—and flowers here—— The horrible man! It's all nonsense—there's nothing wrong. The tree shall be splendid! I will do everything I can think of to please you, Torvald! I will sing for you, dance for you—— (HELMER *comes in with some papers under his arm.*) Oh, are you back already?

HEL. Yes. Has anyone been here?

NORA. Here? No.

HEL. That is strange. I saw Krogstad going out of the gate.

NORA. Did you? Oh yes, I forgot, Krogstad was here for a moment.

HEL. Nora, I can see from your manner that he has been here begging you to say a good word for him.

NORA. Yes.

HEL. And you were to appear to do it of your own accord; you were to conceal from me the fact of his having been here; didn't he beg that of you too?

NORA. Yes, Torvald, but——

HEL. Nora, Nora, and you would be a party to that sort of thing? To have any talk with a man like that and give him any sort of promise? And to tell me a lie into the bargain?

NORA. A lie?

HEL. Didn't you tell me no one had been here? (*Shakes his finger at her.*) My little songbird must never do that again. A songbird must have a clean beak to chirp with—no false notes! (*Puts his arm around her waist.*) That is so, isn't it? Yes, I am sure it is. (*Lets her go.*) We will say no more about it. (*Sits down by the stove.*) How warm and snug it is here! (*Turns over his papers.*)

NORA (*after a short pause during which she busies herself with the Christmas tree*). Torvald!

HEL. Yes.

NORA. I am looking forward tremendously to the fancy-dress ball at the Stenborgs' the day after tomorrow.

HEL. And I am tremendously curious to see what you are going to surprise me with.

NORA. It was very silly of me to want to do that.

HEL. What do you mean?

NORA. I can't hit upon anything that will do; everything I think of seems so silly and insignificant.

HEL. Does my little Nora acknowledge that at last?

NORA (*standing behind his chair with her arms on the back of it*). Are you very busy, Torvald?

HEL. Well——

NORA. What are all those papers?

HEL. Bank business.

NORA. Already?

HEL. I have got authority from the retiring manager to undertake the necessary changes in the staff and in the rearrangement of the work, and I must make use of the Christmas week for that, so as to have everything in order for the new year.

NORA. Then that was why this poor Krogstad——

HEL. Hm!

NORA (*leans against the back of his chair and strokes his hair*). If you hadn't been so busy, I should have asked you a tremendously big favor, Torvald.

HEL. What is that? Tell me.

NORA. There is no one has such good taste as you. And I do so want to look nice at the fancy-dress ball. Torvald, couldn't you take me in hand and decide what I shall go as and what sort of a dress I shall wear?

HEL. Aha! So my obstinate little woman is obliged to get someone to come to her rescue?

NORA. Yes, Torvald, I can't get along a bit without your help.

HEL. Very well, I will think it over; we shall manage to hit upon something.

NORA. That is nice of you. (*Goes to the Christmas tree. A short pause.*) How pretty the red flowers look! But tell me, was it really something very bad that this Krogstad was guilty of?

HEL. He forged someone's name. Have you any idea what that means?

NORA. Isn't it possible that he was driven to do it by necessity?

HEL. Yes; or, as in so many cases, by imprudence. I am not so heartless as to condemn a man altogether because of a single false step of that kind.

NORA. No, you wouldn't, would you, Torvald?

HEL. Many a man has been able to retrieve his character if he has openly confessed his fault and taken his punishment.

NORA. Punishment?

HEL. But Krogstad did nothing of that sort; he got himself out of it by a cunning trick, and that is why he has gone under altogether.

NORA. But do you think it would——

HEL. Just think how a guilty man like that has to lie and play the hypocrite with everyone, how he has to wear a mask in the presence of those near and dear to him, even before his own wife and children. And about the children—that is the most terrible part of it all, Nora.

NORA. How?

HEL. Because such an atmosphere of lies infects and poisons the whole life of a home. Each breath the children take in such a house is full of the germs of evil.

NORA (*coming nearer him*). Are you sure of that?

HEL. My dear, I have often seen it in the course of my life as a lawyer. Almost everyone who has gone to the bad early in life has had a deceitful mother.

NORA. Why do you only say—mother?

HEL. It seems most commonly to be the mother's influence, though naturally a bad father's would have the same result. Every lawyer is familiar with the fact. This Krogstad, now, has been persistently poisoning his own children with lies and dissimulation; that is why I say he has lost all moral character. (*Holds out his hands to her.*) That is why my sweet little Nora must promise me not to plead his cause. Give me your hand on it. Come, come, what is this? Give me your hand. There now, that's settled. I assure you it would be quite impossible for me to work with him; I literally feel physically ill when I am in the company of such people.

NORA (*takes her hand out of his and goes to the opposite side of the Christmas tree*). How hot it is in here, and I have such a lot to do.

HEL. (*getting up and putting his papers in order*). Yes, and I must try and read through some of these before dinner, and I must think about your costume too. And it is just possible I may have something ready in gold paper to hang up on the tree. (*Puts his hand on her head.*) My precious little singing bird! (*He goes into his room and shuts the door after him.*)

NORA (*after a pause, whispers*). No, no—it isn't true. It's impossible; it must be impossible.

(*The* NURSE *opens the door on the left.*)

NURSE. The little ones are begging so hard to be allowed to come in to Mamma.

NORA. No, no, no! Don't let them come in to me! You stay with them, Anne.

NURSE. Very well, ma'am. (*Shuts the door.*)

NORA (*pale with terror*). Deprave my little children? Poison my home? (*A short pause. Then she tosses her head.*) It's not true. It can't possibly be true.

ACT II

THE SAME SCENE—*The Christmas tree is in the corner by the piano, stripped of its ornaments and with burned-down candle ends on its disheveled branches.* NORA'S *cloak and hat are lying on the sofa. She is alone in the room, walking about uneasily. She stops by the sofa and takes up her cloak.*

NORA (*drops the cloak*). Someone is coming now. (*Goes to the door and listens.*) No—it is no one. Of course no one will come today, Christmas Day—nor tomorrow either. But perhaps—— (*Opens the door and looks out.*) No, nothing in the letter box; it is quite empty. (*Comes forward.*) What rubbish! Of course he can't be in earnest about it. Such a thing couldn't happen; it is impossible—I have three little children.

(*Enter the* NURSE *from the room on the left, carrying a big cardboard box.*)

NURSE. At last I have found the box with the fancy dress.

NORA. Thanks; put it on the table.

NURSE (*in doing so*). But it is very much in want of mending.

NORA. I should like to tear it into a hundred thousand pieces.

NURSE. What an idea! It can easily be put in order—just a little patience.

NORA. Yes, I will go and get Mrs. Linde to come and help me with it.

NURSE. What, out again? In this horrible weather? You will catch cold, ma'am, and make yourself ill.

NORA. Well, worse than that might happen. How are the children?

NURSE. The poor little souls are playing with their Christmas presents, but——

NORA. Do they ask much for me?

NURSE. You see, they are so accustomed to having their mamma with them.

NORA. Yes—but, Nurse, I shall not be able to be so much with them now as I was before.

NURSE. Oh well, young children easily get accustomed to anything.

NORA. Do you think so? Do you think they would forget their mother if she went away altogether?

NURSE. Good heavens!—went away altogether?

NORA. Nurse, I want you to tell me something I have often wondered about— how could you have the heart to put your own child out among strangers?

NURSE. I was obliged to if I wanted to be little Nora's nurse.

NORA. Yes, but how could you be willing to do it?

NURSE. What, when I was going to get such a good place by it? A poor girl who has got into trouble should be glad to. Besides, that wicked man did- n't do a single thing for me.

NORA. But I suppose your daughter has quite forgotten you.

NURSE. No, indeed she hasn't. She wrote to me when she was confirmed and when she was married.

NORA (*putting her arms round her neck*). Dear old Anne, you were a good mother to me when I was little.

NURSE. Little Nora, poor dear, had no other mother but me.

NORA. And if my little ones had no other mother, I am sure you would—— What nonsense I am talking! (*Opens the box.*) Go in to them. Now I must—— You will see tomorrow how charming I shall look.

NURSE. I am sure there will be no one at the ball so charming as you, ma'am. (*Goes into the room on the left.*)

NORA (*begins to unpack the box but soon pushes it away from her*). If only I dared go out. If only no one would come. If only I could be sure nothing would happen here in the meantime. Stuff and nonsense! No one will come. Only I mustn't think about it. I will brush my muff. What lovely, lovely gloves! Out of my thoughts, out of my thoughts! One, two, three, four, five, six—— (*Screams.*) Ah! there is someone coming. (*Makes a movement toward the door but stands irresolute.*)

(*Enter* MRS. LINDE *from the hall, where she has taken off her cloak and hat.*)

NORA. Oh, it's you, Christine. There is no one else out there, is there? How good of you to come!

MRS. L. I heard you were up asking for me.

NORA. Yes, I was passing by. As a matter of fact, it is something you could help me with. Let us sit down here on the sofa. Look here. Tomorrow evening there is to be a fancy-dress ball at the Stenborgs', who live above us, and Torvald wants me to go as a Neapolitan fishergirl and dance the tarantella that I learnt at Capri.

MRS. L. I see; you are going to keep up the character.

NORA. Yes, Torvald wants me to. Look, here is the dress; Torvald had it made for me there, but now it is all so torn, and I haven't any idea——

MRS. L. We will easily put that right. It is only some of the trimming come unsewn here and there. Needle and thread? Now then, that's all we want.

NORA. It *is* nice of you.

MRS. L. (*sewing*). So you are going to be dressed up tomorrow, Nora. I will tell you what—I shall come in for a moment and see you in your fine feathers. But I have completely forgotten to thank you for a delightful evening yesterday.

NORA (*gets up and crosses the stage*). Well, I don't think yesterday was as pleasant as usual. You ought to have come down to town a little earlier, Christine. Certainly Torvald does understand how to make a house dainty and attractive.

MRS. L. And so do you, it seems to me; you are not your father's daughter for nothing. But tell me, is Doctor Rank always as depressed as he was yesterday?

NORA. No; yesterday it was very noticeable. I must tell you that he suffers from a very dangerous disease. He has consumption of the spine, poor creature. His father was a horrible man who committed all sorts of excesses, and that is why his son was sickly from childhood, do you understand?

MRS. L. (*dropping her sewing*). But, my dearest Nora, how do you know anything about such things?

NORA (*walking about*). Pooh! When you have three children you get visits now and then from—from married women who know something of medical matters, and they talk about one thing and another.

MRS. L. (*goes on sewing. A short silence*). Does Doctor Rank come here every day?

NORA. Every day regularly. He is Torvald's most intimate friend and a friend of mine too. He is just like one of the family.

MRS. L. But tell me this—is he perfectly sincere? I mean, isn't he the kind of man that is very anxious to make himself agreeable?

NORA. Not in the least. What makes you think that?

MRS. L. When you introduced him to me yesterday he declared he had often heard my name mentioned in this house, but afterward I noticed that your husband hadn't the slightest idea who I was. So how could Doctor Rank——

NORA. That is quite right, Christine. Torvald is so absurdly fond of me that he wants me absolutely to himself, as he says. At first he used to seem almost jealous if I mentioned any of the dear folks at home, so naturally I gave up doing so. But I often talk about such things with Doctor Rank because he likes hearing about them.

MRS. L. Listen to me, Nora. You are still very like a child in many things, and I am older than you in many ways and have a little more experience. Let me tell you this—you ought to make an end of it with Doctor Rank.

NORA. What ought I to make an end of?

MRS. L. Of two things, I think. Yesterday you talked some nonsense about a rich admirer who was to leave you money——

NORA. An admirer who doesn't exist, unfortunately! But what then?

MRS. L. Is Doctor Rank a man of means?

NORA. Yes, he is.

MRS. L. And has no one to provide for?

NORA. No, no one; but——

MRS. L. And comes here every day?

NORA. Yes, I told you so.

MRS. L. But how can this well-bred man be so tactless?

NORA. I don't understand you at all.

MRS. L. Don't prevaricate, Nora. Do you suppose I don't guess who lent you the two hundred and fifty pounds?

NORA. Are you out of your senses? How can you think of such a thing! A friend of ours, who comes here every day! Do you realize what a horribly painful position that would be?

MRS. L. Then it really isn't he?

NORA. No, certainly not. It would never have entered into my head for a moment. Besides, he had no money to lend then; he came into his money afterward.

MRS. L. Well, I think that was lucky for you, my dear Nora.

NORA. No, it would never have come into my head to ask Doctor Rank. Although I am quite sure that if I had asked him——

MRS. L. But of course you won't.

NORA. Of course not. I have no reason to think it could possibly be necessary. But I am quite sure that if I told Doctor Rank——

MRS. L. Behind your husband's back?

NORA. I must make an end of it with the other one, and that will be behind his back too. I *must* make an end of it with him.

MRS. L. Yes, that is what I told you yesterday, but——

NORA (*walking up and down*). A man can put a thing like that straight much easier than a woman.

MRS. L. One's husband, yes.

NORA. Nonsense! (*Standing still.*) When you pay off a debt you get your bond back, don't you?

MRS. L. Yes, as a matter of course.

NORA. And can tear it into a hundred thousand pieces and burn it up—the nasty dirty paper!

MRS. L. (*looks hard at her, lays down her sewing and gets up slowly*). Nora, you are concealing something from me.

NORA. Do I look as if I were?

MRS. L. Something has happened to you since yesterday morning. Nora, what is it?

NORA (*going nearer to her*). Christine! (*Listens.*) Hush! There's Torvald come home. Do you mind going in to the children for the present? Torvald can't bear to see dressmaking going on. Let Anne help you.

MRS. L. (*gathering some of the things together*). Certainly—but I am not going away from here till we have had it out with one another. (*She goes into the room on the left as* HELMER *comes in from the hall.*)

NORA (*going up to* HELMER). I have wanted you so much, Torvald dear.

HEL. Was that the dressmaker?

NORA. No, it was Christine; she is helping me to put my dress in order. You will see I shall look quite smart.

HEL. Wasn't that a happy thought of mine, now?

NORA. Splendid! But don't you think it is nice of me, too, to do as you wish?

HEL. Nice?—because you do as your husband wishes? Well, well, you little rogue, I am sure you did not mean it in that way. But I am not going to disturb you; you will want to be trying on your dress, I expect.

NORA. I suppose you are going to work.

HEL. Yes. (*Shows her a bundle of papers.*) Look at that. I have just been in to the bank. (*Turns to go into his room.*)

NORA. Torvald.

HEL. Yes.

NORA. If your little squirrel were to ask you for something very, very prettily——

HEL. What then?

NORA. Would you do it?

HEL. I should like to hear what it is first.

NORA. Your squirrel would run about and do all her tricks if you would be nice and do what she wants.

HEL. Speak plainly.

NORA. Your skylark would chirp, chirp about in every room, with her song rising and falling——

HEL. Well, my skylark does that anyhow.

NORA. I would play the fairy and dance for you in the moonlight, Torvald.

HEL. Nora—you surely don't mean that request you made of me this morning?

NORA (*going near him*). Yes, Torvald, I beg you so earnestly——

HEL. Have you really the courage to open up that question again?

NORA. Yes, dear, you *must* do as I ask; you *must* let Krogstad keep his post in the bank.

HEL. My dear Nora, it is his post that I have arranged Mrs. Linde shall have.

NORA. Yes, you have been awfully kind about that, but you could just as well dismiss some other clerk instead of Krogstad.

HEL. This is simply incredible obstinacy! Because you chose to give him a thoughtless promise that you would speak for him I am expected to——

NORA. That isn't the reason, Torvald. It is for your own sake. This fellow writes in the most scurrilous newspapers; you have told me so yourself. He can do you an unspeakable amount of harm. I am frightened to death of him.

HEL. Ah, I understand; it is recollections of the past that scare you.

NORA. What do you mean?

HEL. Naturally you are thinking of your father.

NORA. Yes—yes, of course. Just recall to your mind what these malicious creatures wrote in the papers about Papa and how horribly they slandered him. I believe they would have procured his dismissal if the Department had not sent you over to inquire into it and if you had not been so kindly disposed and helpful to him.

HEL. My little Nora, there is an important difference between your father and me. Your father's reputation as a public official was not above suspicion. Mine is, and I hope it will continue to be so as long as I hold my office.

NORA. You never can tell what mischief these men may contrive. We ought to be so well off, so snug and happy here in our peaceful home, and have no cares—you and I and the children, Torvald! That is why I beg you so earnestly——

HEL. And it is just by interceding for him that you make it impossible for me to keep him. It is already known at the bank that I mean to dismiss Krogstad. Is it to get about now that the new manager has changed his mind at his wife's bidding?

NORA. And what if it did?

HEL. Of course!—if only this obstinate little person can get her way! Do you suppose I am going to make myself ridiculous before my whole staff, to let people think I am a man to be swayed by all sorts of outside influence? I should very soon feel the consequences of it, I can tell you! And besides, there is one thing that makes it quite impossible for me to have Krogstad in the bank as long as I am manager.

NORA. Whatever is that?

HEL. His moral failings I might perhaps have overlooked if necessary——

NORA. Yes, you could—couldn't you?

HEL. And I hear he is a good worker too. But I knew him when we were boys. It was one of those rash friendships that so often prove an incubus in afterlife. I may as well tell you plainly, we were once on very intimate terms with one another. But this tactless fellow lays no restraint on himself when other people are present. On the contrary, he thinks it gives him the right to adopt a familiar tone with me, and every minute it is "I say, Helmer, old fellow!" and that sort of thing. I assure you it is extremely painful for me. He would make my position in the bank intolerable.

NORA. Torvald, I don't believe you mean that.

HEL. Don't you? Why not?

NORA. Because it is such a narrow-minded way of looking at things.

HEL. What are you saying? Narrow-minded? Do you think I am narrow-minded?

NORA. No, just the opposite, dear—and it is exactly for that reason——

HEL. It's the same thing. You say my point of view is narrow-minded, so I must be so too. Narrow-minded! Very well—I must put an end to this. (*Goes to the hall door and calls.*) Helen!

NORA. What are you going to do?

HEL. (*looking among his papers*). Settle it. (*Enter* MAID.) Look here; take this letter and go downstairs with it at once. Find a messenger and tell him to deliver it and be quick. The address is on it, and here is the money.

MAID. Very well, sir. (*Exit with the letter.*)

HEL. (*putting his papers together*). Now then, little Miss Obstinate.

NORA (*breathlessly*). Torvald—what was that letter?

HEL. Krogstad's dismissal.

NORA. Call her back, Torvald! There is still time. Oh, Torvald, call her back!

Do it for my sake—for your own sake—for the children's sake! Do you hear me, Torvald? Call her back! You don't know what that letter can bring upon us.

HEL. It's too late.

NORA. Yes, it's too late.

HEL. My dear Nora, I can forgive the anxiety you are in, although really it is an insult to me. It is, indeed. Isn't it an insult to think that I should be afraid of a starving quill driver's vengeance? But I forgive you nevertheless, because it is such eloquent witness to your great love for me. (*Takes her in his arms.*) And that is as it should be, my own darling Nora. Come what will, you may be sure I shall have both courage and strength if they be needed. You will see I am man enough to take everything upon myself.

NORA (*in a horror-stricken voice*). What do you mean by that?

HEL. Everything, I say.

NORA (*recovering herself*). You will never have to do that.

HEL. That's right. Well, we will share it, Nora, as man and wife should. That is how it shall be. (*Caressing her.*) Are you content now? There! there!— not these frightened dove's eyes! The whole thing is only the wildest fancy! Now you must go and play through the tarantella and practice with your tambourine. I shall go into the inner office and shut the door, and I shall hear nothing; you can make as much noise as you please. (*Turns back at the door.*) And when Rank comes tell him where he will find me. (*Nods to her, takes his papers and goes into his room and shuts the door after him.*)

NORA (*bewildered with anxiety, stands as if rooted to the spot and whispers*). He was capable of doing it. He will do it. He will do it in spite of everything. No, not that! Never, never! Anything rather than that! Oh, for some help, some way out of it! (*The doorbell rings.*) Doctor Rank! Anything rather than that—anything, whatever it is! (*She puts her hands over her face, pulls herself together, goes to the door and opens it. RANK is standing without, hanging up his coat. During the following dialogue it begins to grow dark.*)

NORA. Good day, Doctor Rank. I knew your ring. But you mustn't go in to Torvald now; I think he is busy with something.

RANK. And you?

NORA (*brings him in and shuts the door after him*). Oh, you know very well I always have time for you.

RANK. Thank you. I shall make use of as much of it as I can.

NORA. What do you mean by that? As much of it as you can?

RANK. Well, does that alarm you?

NORA. It was such a strange way of putting it. Is anything likely to happen?

RANK. Nothing but what I have long been prepared for. But I certainly didn't expect it to happen so soon.

NORA (*gripping him by the arm*). What have you found out? Doctor Rank, you must tell me.

RANK (*sitting down by the stove*). It is all up with me. And it can't be helped.

NORA (*with a sigh of relief*). Is it about yourself?

RANK. Who else? It is no use lying to one's self. I am the most wretched of all my patients, Mrs. Helmer. Lately I have been taking stock of my internal economy. Bankrupt! Probably within a month I shall lie rotting in the churchyard.

NORA. What an ugly thing to say!

RANK. The thing itself is cursedly ugly, and the worst of it is that I shall have to face so much more that is ugly before that. I shall only make one more examination of myself; when I have done that I shall know pretty certainly when it will be that the horrors of dissolution will begin. There is something I want to tell you. Helmer's refined nature gives him an unconquerable disgust at everything that is ugly; I won't have him in my sickroom.

NORA. Oh, but, Doctor Rank——

RANK. I won't have him there. Not on any account. I bar my door to him. As soon as I am quite certain that the worst has come I shall send you my card with a black cross on it, and then you will know that the loathsome end has begun.

NORA. You are quite absurd today. And I wanted you so much to be in a really good humor.

RANK. With death stalking beside me? To have to pay this penalty for another man's sin! Is there any justice in that? And in every single family, in one way or another, some such inexorable retribution is being exacted.

NORA (*putting her hands over her ears*). Rubbish! Do talk of something cheerful.

RANK. Oh, it's a mere laughing matter; the whole thing. My poor innocent spine has to suffer for my father's youthful amusements.

NORA (*sitting at the table on the left*). I suppose you mean that he was too partial to asparagus and pâté de foie gras, don't you?

RANK. Yes, and to truffles.

NORA. Truffles, yes. And oysters too, I suppose?

RANK. Oysters, of course; that goes without saying.

NORA. And heaps of port and champagne. It is sad that all these nice things should take their revenge on our bones.

RANK. Especially that they should revenge themselves on the unlucky bones of those who have not had the satisfaction of enjoying them.

NORA. Yes, that's the saddest part of it all.

RANK (*with a searching look at her*). Hm!

NORA (*after a short pause*). Why did you smile?

RANK. No, it was you that laughed.

NORA. No, it was you that smiled, Doctor Rank!

RANK (*rising*). You are a greater rascal than I thought.

NORA. I am in a silly mood today.

RANK. So it seems.

NORA (*putting her hands on his shoulders*). Dear, dear Doctor Rank, death mustn't take you away from Torvald and me.

RANK. It is a loss you would easily recover from. Those who are gone are soon forgotten.

NORA (*looking at him anxiously*). Do you believe that?

RANK. People form new ties, and then——

NORA. Who will form new ties?

RANK. Both you and Helmer, when I am gone. You yourself are already on the highroad to it, I think. What did that Mrs. Linde want here last night?

NORA. Oho! You don't mean to say that you are jealous of poor Christine?

RANK. Yes, I am. She will be my successor in this house. When I am done for, this woman will——

NORA. Hush! Don't speak so loud. She is in that room.

RANK. Today again. There, you see.

NORA. She has only come to sew my dress for me. Bless my soul, how unreasonable you are! (*Sits down on the sofa.*) Be nice now, Doctor Rank, and tomorrow you will see how beautifully I shall dance, and you can imagine I am doing it all for you—and for Torvald too, of course. (*Takes various things out of the box.*) Doctor Rank, come and sit down here, and I will show you something.

RANK (*sitting down*). What is it?

NORA. Just look at those!

RANK. Silk stockings.

NORA. Flesh colored. Aren't they lovely? It is so dark here now, but tomorrow—— No, no, no! You must only look at the feet. Oh well, you may have leave to look at the legs too.

RANK. Hm!

NORA. Why are you looking so critical? Don't you think they will fit me?

RANK. I have no means of forming an opinion about that.

NORA (*looks at him for a moment*). For shame! (*Hits him lightly on the ear with the stockings.*) That's to punish you. (*Folds them up again.*)

RANK. And what other nice things am I to be allowed to see?

NORA. Not a single thing more, for being so naughty. (*She looks among the things, humming to herself.*)

RANK (*after a short silence*). When I am sitting here talking to you as intimately as this I cannot imagine for a moment what would have become of me if I had never come into this house.

NORA (*smiling*). I believe you do feel thoroughly at home with us.

RANK (*in a lower voice, looking straight in front of him*). And to be obliged to leave it all——

NORA. Nonsense, you are not going to leave it.

RANK (*as before*). And not be able to leave behind one the slightest token of one's gratitude, scarcely even a fleeting regret—nothing but an empty place which the firstcomer can fill as well as any other.

NORA. And if I asked you now for a—— No!

RANK. For what?

NORA. For a big proof of your friendship——

RANK. Yes, yes!

NORA. I mean a tremendously big favor——

RANK. Would you really make me so happy for once?

NORA. Ah, but you don't know what it is yet.

RANK. No—— but tell me.

NORA. I really can't, Doctor Rank. It is something out of all reason; it means advice and help and a favor——

RANK. The bigger a thing it is, the better. I can't conceive what it is you mean. Do tell me. Haven't I your confidence?

NORA. More than anyone else. I know you are my truest and best friend, and so I will tell you what it is. Well, Doctor Rank, it is something you must help me to prevent. You know how devotedly, how inexpressibly deeply Torvald loves me; he would never for a moment hesitate to give his life for me.

RANK (*leaning toward her*). Nora—do you think he is the only one——

NORA (*with a slight start*). The only one——?

RANK. The only one who would gladly give his life for your sake.

NORA (*sadly*). Is that it?

RANK. I was determined you should know it before I went away, and there will never be a better opportunity than this. Now you know it, Nora. And now you know, too, that you can trust me as you would trust no one else.

NORA (*rises deliberately and quietly*). Let me pass.

RANK (*makes room for her to pass him but sits still*). Nora!

NORA (*at the hall door*). Helen, bring in the lamp. (*Goes over to the stove.*) Dear Doctor Rank, that was really horrid of you.

RANK. To have loved you as much as anyone else does? Was that horrid?

NORA. No, but to go and tell me so. There was really no need——

RANK. What do you mean? Did you know? (MAID *enters with lamp, puts it down on the table and goes out.*) Nora—Mrs. Helmer—tell me, had you any idea of this?

NORA. Oh, how do I know whether I had or whether I hadn't? I really can't tell you. To think you could be so clumsy, Doctor Rank! We were getting on so nicely.

RANK. Well, at all events you know that you can command me body and soul. So won't you speak out?

NORA (*looking at him*). After what happened?

RANK. I beg you to let me know what it is.

NORA. I can't tell you anything now.

RANK. Yes, yes. You mustn't punish me in that way. Let me have permission to do for you whatever a man may do.

NORA. You can do nothing for me now. Besides, I really don't need any help at all. You will find that the whole thing is merely fancy on my part. It really is so—of course it is! (*Sits down in the rocking chair and looks at him with a smile.*) You are a nice sort of man, Doctor Rank! Don't you feel ashamed of yourself now the lamp has come?

RANK. Not a bit. But perhaps I had better go—forever?

NORA. No indeed, you shall not. Of course you must come here just as before. You know very well Torvald can't do without you.

RANK. Yes, but you?

NORA. Oh, I am always tremendously pleased when you come.

RANK. It is just that that put me on the wrong track. You are a riddle to me. I have often thought that you would almost as soon be in my company as in Helmer's.

NORA. Yes—you see, there are some people one loves best and others whom one would almost always rather have as companions.

RANK. Yes, there is something in that.

NORA. When I was at home of course I loved Papa best. But I always thought it tremendous fun if I could steal down into the maids' room, because they never moralized at all and talked to each other about such entertaining things.

RANK. I see—it is *their* place I have taken.

NORA (*jumping up and going to him*). Oh, dear, nice Doctor Rank, I never meant that at all. But surely you can understand that being with Torvald is a little like being with Papa——

(*Enter* MAID *from the hall.*)

MAID. If you please, ma'am. (*Whispers and hands her a card.*)

NORA (*glancing at the card*). Oh! (*Puts it in her pocket.*)

RANK. Is there anything wrong?

NORA. No, no, not in the least. It is only something—it is my new dress——

RANK. What? Your dress is lying there.

NORA. Oh yes, that one; but this is another. I ordered it. Torvald mustn't know about it.

RANK. Oho! Then that was the great secret.

NORA. Of course. Just go in to him; he is sitting in the inner room. Keep him as long as——

RANK. Make your mind easy; I won't let him escape. (*Goes into* HELMER'S *room.*)

NORA (*to the* MAID). And he is standing waiting in the kitchen?

MAID. Yes; he came up the back stairs.

NORA. But didn't you tell him no one was in?

MAID. Yes, but it was no good.

NORA. He won't go away?

MAID. No; he says he won't until he has seen you, ma'am.

NORA. Well, let him come in—but quietly. Helen, you mustn't say anything about it to anyone. It is a surprise for my husband.

MAID. Yes, ma'am, I quite understand. (*Exit.*)

NORA. This dreadful thing is going to happen! It will happen in spite of me! No, no, no, it can't happen—it shan't happen! (*She bolts the door of* HELMER'S *room. The* MAID *opens the hall door for* KROGSTAD *and shuts it after him. He is wearing a fur coat, high boots and a fur cap.*)

NORA (*advancing toward him*). Speak low—my husband is at home.

KROG. No matter about that.

NORA. What do you want of me?

KROG. An explanation of something.

NORA. Make haste then. What is it?

KROG. You know, I suppose, that I have got my dismissal.

NORA. I couldn't prevent it, Mr. Krogstad. I fought as hard as I could on your side, but it was no good.

KROG. Does your husband love you so little then? He knows what I can expose you to, and yet he ventures——

NORA. How can you suppose that he has any knowledge of the sort?

KROG. I didn't suppose so at all. It would not be the least like our dear Torvald Helmer to show so much courage——

NORA. Mr. Krogstad, a little respect for my husband, please.

KROG. Certainly—all the respect he deserves. But since you have kept the matter so carefully to yourself, I make bold to suppose that you have a little clearer idea than you had yesterday of what it actually is that you have done?

NORA. More than you could ever teach me.

KROG. Yes, such a bad lawyer as I am.

NORA. What is it you want of me?

KROG. Only to see how you were, Mrs. Helmer. I have been thinking about you all day long. A mere cashier, a quill driver, a—well, a man like me—even he has a little of what is called feeling, you know.

NORA. Show it then; think of my little children.

KROG. Have you and your husband thought of mine? But never mind about that. I only wanted to tell you that you need not take this matter too seriously. In the first place there will be no accusation made on my part.

NORA. No, of course not; I was sure of that.

KROG. The whole thing can be arranged amicably; there is no reason why anyone should know anything about it. It will remain a secret between us three.

NORA. My husband must never get to know anything about it.

KROG. How will you be able to prevent it? Am I to understand that you can pay the balance that is owing?

NORA. No, not just at present.

KROG. Or perhaps that you have some expedient for raising the money soon?

NORA. No expedient that I mean to make use of.

KROG. Well, in any case it would have been of no use to you now. If you stood there with ever so much money in your hand, I would never part with your bond.

NORA. Tell me what purpose you mean to put it to.

KROG. I shall only preserve it—keep it in my possession. No one who is not concerned in the matter shall have the slightest hint of it. So that if the thought of it has driven you to any desperate resolution——

NORA. It has.

KROG. If you had it in your mind to run away from your home——

NORA. I had.

KROG. Or even something worse——

NORA. How could you know that?

KROG. Give up the idea.

NORA. How did you know I had thought of *that*?

KROG. Most of us think of that at first. I did too—but I hadn't the courage.

NORA (*faintly*). No more than I.

KROG. (*in a tone of relief*). No, that's it, isn't it—you hadn't the courage either?

NORA. No, I haven't—I haven't.

KROG. Besides, it would have been a great piece of folly. Once the first storm at home is over—— I have a letter for your husband in my pocket.

NORA. Telling him everything?

KROG. In as lenient a manner as I possibly could.

NORA (*quickly*). He mustn't get the letter. Tear it up. I will find some means of getting money.

KROG. Excuse me, Mrs. Helmer, but I think I told you just now——

NORA. I am not speaking of what I owe you. Tell me what sum you are asking my husband for, and I will get the money.

KROG. I am not asking your husband for a penny.

NORA. What do you want then?

KROG. I will tell you. I want to rehabilitate myself, Mrs. Helmer; I want to get on, and in that your husband must help me. For the last year and a half I have not had a hand in anything dishonorable, and all that time I have been struggling in most restricted circumstances. I was content to work my way up step by step. Now I am turned out, and I am not going to be satisfied with merely being taken into favor again. I want to get on, I tell you. I want to get into the bank again, in a higher position. Your husband must make a place for me——

NORA. That he will never do!

KROG. He will; I know him; he dare not protest. And as soon as I am in there again with him then you will see! Within a year I shall be the manager's right hand. It will be Nils Krogstad and not Torvald Helmer who manages the bank.

NORA. That's a thing you will never see!

KROG. Do you mean that you will——

NORA. I have courage enough for it now.

KROG. Oh, you can't frighten me. A fine, spoilt lady like you——

NORA. You will see, you will see.

KROG. Under the ice, perhaps? Down into the cold, coal-black water? And then, in the spring, to float up to the surface, all horrible and unrecognizable, with your hair fallen out——

NORA. You can't frighten me.

KROG. Nor you me. People don't do such things, Mrs. Helmer. Besides, what use would it be? I should have him completely in my power all the same.

NORA. Afterward? When I am no longer——

KROG. Have you forgotten that it is I who have the keeping of your reputation? (NORA *stands speechlessly looking at him.*) Well, now, I have warned you. Do not do anything foolish. When Helmer has had my letter I shall expect a message from him. And be sure you remember that it is your husband himself who has forced me into such ways as this again. I will never forgive him for that. Good-by, Mrs. Helmer. (*Exit through the hall.*)

NORA (*goes to the hall door, opens it slightly and listens*). He is going. He is not putting the letter in the box. Oh no, no! that's impossible! (*Opens the door by degrees.*) What is that? He is standing outside. He is not going downstairs. Is he hesitating? Can he—— (*A letter drops in the box; then* KROGSTAD'S *footsteps are heard, till they die away as he goes downstairs.* NORA *utters a stifled cry and runs across the room to the table by the sofa. A short pause.*)

NORA. In the letter box. (*Steals across to the hall door.*) There it lies—Torvald, Torvald, there is no hope for us now!

(MRS. LINDE *comes in from the room on the left, carrying the dress.*)

MRS. L. There, I can't see anything more to mend now. Would you like to try it on?

NORA (*in a hoarse whisper*). Christine, come here.

MRS. L. (*throwing the dress down on the sofa*). What is the matter with you? You look so agitated!

NORA. Come here. Do you see that letter? There, look—you can see it through the glass in the letter box.

MRS. L. Yes, I see it.

NORA. That letter is from Krogstad.

MRS. L. Nora—it was Krogstad who lent you the money!

NORA. Yes, and now Torvald will know all about it.

MRS. L. Believe me, Nora, that's the best thing for both of you.

NORA. You don't know all. I forged a name.

MRS. L. Good heavens!

NORA. I only want to say this to you, Christine—you must be my witness.

MRS. L. Your witness? What do you mean? What am I to——

NORA. If I should go out of my mind—and it might easily happen——

MRS. L. Nora!

NORA. Or if anything else should happen to me—anything, for instance, that might prevent my being here——

MRS. L. Nora! Nora! you are quite out of your mind.

NORA. And if it should happen that there were someone who wanted to take all the responsibility, all the blame, you understand——

MRS. L. Yes, yes—but how can you suppose——

NORA. Then you must be my witness, that it is not true, Christine. I am not out of my mind at all; I am in my right senses now, and I tell you no one else has known anything about it; I, and I alone, did the whole thing. Remember that.

MRS. L. I will, indeed. But I don't understand all this.

NORA. How should you understand it? A wonderful thing is going to happen.

MRS. L. A wonderful thing?

NORA. Yes, a wonderful thing! But it is so terrible. Christine, it *mustn't* happen, not for all the world.

MRS. L. I will go at once and see Krogstad.

NORA. Don't go to him; he will do you some harm.

MRS. L. There was a time when he would gladly do anything for my sake.

NORA. He?

MRS. L. Where does he live?

NORA. How should I know? Yes—(*feeling in her pocket*)—here is his card. But the letter, the letter!

HEL. (*calls from his room, knocking at the door*). Nora!

NORA (*cries out anxiously*). Oh, what's that? What do you want?

HEL. Don't be so frightened. We are not coming in; you have locked the door. Are you trying on your dress?

NORA. Yes, that's it. I look so nice, Torvald.

MRS. L. (*who has read the card*). I see he lives at the corner here.

NORA. Yes, but it's no use. It is hopeless. The letter is lying there in the box.

MRS. L. And your husband keeps the key?

NORA. Yes, always.

MRS. L. Krogstad must ask for his letter back unread, he must find some pretense——

NORA. But it is just at this time that Torvald generally——

MRS. L. You must delay him. Go in to him in the meantime. I will come back as soon as I can. (*She goes out hurriedly through the hall door.*)

NORA (*goes to* HELMER'S *door, opens it and peeps in*). Torvald!

HEL. (*from the inner room*). Well? May I venture at last to come into my own room again? Come along, Rank, now you will see—— (*Halting in the doorway.*) But what is this?

NORA. What is what, dear?

HEL. Rank led me to expect a splendid transformation.

RANK (*in the doorway*). I understood so, but evidently I was mistaken.

NORA. Yes, nobody is to have the chance of admiring me in my dress until tomorrow.

HEL. But, my dear Nora, you look so worn out. Have you been practicing too much?

NORA. No, I have not practiced at all.

HEL. But you will need to——

NORA. Yes, indeed I shall, Torvald. But I can't get on a bit without you to help me; I have absolutely forgotten the whole thing.

HEL. Oh, we will soon work it up again.

NORA. Yes, help me, Torvald. Promise that you will! I am so nervous about it—all the people—— You must give yourself up to me entirely this evening. Not the tiniest bit of business—you mustn't even take a pen in your hand. Will you promise, Torvald dear?

HEL. I promise. This evening I will be wholly and absolutely at your service, you helpless little mortal. Ah, by the way, first of all I will just—— (*Goes toward the hall door.*)

NORA. What are you going to do there?

HEL. Only see if any letters have come.

NORA. No, no! Don't do that, Torvald!

HEL. Why not?

NORA. Torvald, please don't. There is nothing there.

HEL. Well, let me look. (*Turns to go to the letter box.* NORA, *at the piano, plays the first bars of the tarantella.* HELMER *stops in the doorway.*) Aha!

NORA. I can't dance tomorrow if I don't practice with you.

HEL. (*going up to her*). Are you really so afraid of it, dear?

NORA. Yes, so dreadfully afraid of it. Let me practice at once; there is time now, before we go to dinner. Sit down and play for me, Torvald dear; criticize me and correct me as you play.

HEL. With great pleasure, if you wish me to. (*Sits down at the piano.*)

NORA (*takes out of the box a tambourine and a long variegated shawl. She hastily drapes the shawl round her. Then she springs to the front of the stage and calls out*). Now play for me! I am going to dance!

(HELMER *plays and* NORA *dances.* RANK *stands by the piano behind* HELMER *and looks on.*)

HEL. (*as he plays*). Slower, slower!

NORA. I can't do it any other way.

HEL. Not so violently, Nora!

NORA. This is the way.

HEL. (*stops playing*). No, no—that is not a bit right.

NORA. (*laughing and swinging the tambourine*). Didn't I tell you so?

RANK. Let me play for her.

HEL. (*getting up*). Yes, do. I can correct her better then.

(RANK *sits down at the piano and plays.* NORA *dances more and more wildly.* HELMER *has taken up a position by the stove and during her dance gives her frequent instructions. She does not seem to hear him; her hair comes down and falls over her shoulders; she pays no attention to it but goes on dancing. Enter* MRS. LINDE.)

MRS. L. (*standing as if spellbound in the doorway*). Oh!

NORA (*as she dances*). Such fun, Christine!

HEL. My dear darling Nora, you are dancing as if your life depended on it.

NORA. So it does.

HEL. Stop, Rank this is sheer madness. Stop, I tell you! (RANK *stops playing, and* NORA *suddenly stands still.* HELMER *goes up to her.*) I could never have believed it. You have forgotten everything I taught you.

NORA. (*throwing away the tambourine*). There, you see.

HEL. You will want a lot of coaching.

NORA. Yes, you see how much I need it. You must coach me up to the last minute. Promise me that, Torvald!

HEL. You can depend on me.

NORA. You must not think of anything but me, either today or tomorrow; you mustn't open a single letter—not even open the letter box——

HEL. Ah, you are still afraid of that fellow——

NORA. Yes, indeed I am.

HEL. Nora, I can tell from your looks that there is a letter from him lying there.

NORA. I don't know; I think there is; but you must not read anything of that kind now. Nothing horrid must come between us till this is all over.

RANK (*whispers to* HELMER). You mustn't contradict her.

HEL. (*taking her in his arms*). The child shall have her way. But tomorrow night, after you have danced——

NORA. Then you will be free. (*The* MAID *appears in the doorway to the right.*)

MAID. Dinner is served, ma'am.

NORA. We will have champagne, Helen.

MAID. Very good, ma'am. (*Exit.*)

HEL. Hullo!—are we going to have a banquet?

NORA. Yes, a champagne banquet till the small hours. (*Calls out.*) And a few macaroons. Helen—lots, just for once!

HEL. Come, come, don't be so wild and nervous. Be my own little skylark, as you used.

NORA. Yes, dear, I will. But go in now, and you too, Doctor Rank, Christine, you must help me to do up my hair.

RANK. (*whispers to* HELMER *as they go out*). I suppose there is nothing—she is not expecting anything?

HEL. Far from it, my dear fellow; it is simply nothing more than this childish nervousness I was telling you of. (*They go into the right-hand room.*)

NORA. Well!

MRS. L. Gone out of town.

NORA. I could tell from your face.

MRS. L. He is coming home tomorrow evening. I wrote a note for him.

NORA. You should have let it alone; you must prevent nothing. After all, it is splendid to be waiting for a wonderful thing to happen.

MRS. L. What is it that you are waiting for?

NORA. Oh, you wouldn't understand. Go in to them, I will come in a moment. (MRS. LINDE *goes into the dining room.* NORA *stands still for a little while, as if to compose herself. Then she looks at her watch.*) Five o'clock. Seven hours till midnight; and then four-and-twenty hours till the next midnight. Then the tarantella will be over. Twenty-four and seven? Thirty-one hours to live.

HEL. (*from the doorway on the right*). Where's my little skylark?

NORA (*going to him with her arms outstretched*). Here she is!

ACT III

THE SAME SCENE—*The table has been placed in the middle of the stage with chairs round it. A lamp is burning on the table. The door into the hall stands open. Dance music is heard in the room above.* MRS. LINDE *is sitting at the table idly turning over the leaves of a book; she tries to read but does not seem able to collect her thoughts. Every now and then she listens intently for a sound at the outer door.*

MRS. L. (*looking at her watch*). Not yet—and the time is nearly up. If only he does not—— (*Listens again.*) Ah, there he is. (*Goes into the hall and opens the outer door carefully. Light footsteps are heard on the stairs. She whispers.*) Come in. There is no one here.

KROG. (*in the doorway*). I found a note from you at home. What does this mean?

MRS. L. It is absolutely necessary that I should have a talk with you.

KROG. Really? And it is absolutely necessary that it should be here?

MRS. L. It is impossible where I live; there is no private entrance to my rooms. Come in; we are quite alone. The maid is asleep, and the Helmers are at the dance upstairs.

KROG. (*coming into the room*). Are the Helmers really at a dance tonight?

MRS. L. Yes, why not?

KROG. Certainly—why not?

MRS. L. Now, Nils, let us have a talk.

KROG. Can we two have anything to talk about?

MRS. L. We have a great deal to talk about.

KROG. I shouldn't have thought so.

MRS. L. No, you have never properly understood me.

KROG. Was there anything else to understand except what was obvious to all the world—a heartless woman jilts a man when a more lucrative chance turns up?

MRS. L. Do you believe I am as absolutely heartless as all that? And do you believe it with a light heart?

KROG. Didn't you?

MRS. L. Nils, did you really think that?

KROG. If it were as you say, why did you write to me as you did at the time?

MRS. L. I could do nothing else. As I had to break with you, it was my duty also to put an end to all that you felt for me.

KROG. (*wringing his hands*). So that was it. And all this—only for the sake of money!

MRS. L. You mustn't forget that I had a helpless mother and two little brothers. We couldn't wait for you, Nils; your prospects seemed hopeless then.

KROG. That may be so, but you had no right to throw me over for anyone else's sake.

MRS. L. Indeed, I don't know. Many a time did I ask myself if I had the right to do it.

KROG. (*more gently*). When I lost you it was as if all the solid ground went from under my feet. Look at me now—I am a shipwrecked man clinging to a bit of wreckage.

MRS. L. But help may be near.

KROG. It *was* near, but then you came and stood in my way.

MRS. L. Unintentionally, Nils. It was only today that I learned it was your place I was going to take in the bank.

KROG. I believe you, if you say so. But now that you know it, are you not going to give it up to me?

MRS. L. No, because that would not benefit you in the least.

KROG. Oh, benefit, benefit—I would have done it whether or no.

MRS. L. I have learned to act prudently. Life and hard, bitter necessity have taught me that.

KROG. And life has taught me not to believe in fine speeches.

MRS. L. Then life has taught you something very reasonable. But deeds you must believe in.

KROG. What do you mean by that?

MRS. L. You said you were like a shipwrecked man clinging to some wreckage.

KROG. I had good reason to say so.

MRS. L. Well, I am like a shipwrecked woman clinging to some wreckage—no one to mourn for, no one to care for.

KROG. It was your own choice.

MRS. L. There was no other choice—then.

KROG. Well, what now?

MRS. L. Nils, how would it be if we two shipwrecked people could join forces?

KROG. What are you saying?

MRS. L. Two on the same piece of wreckage would stand a better chance than each on their own.

KROG. Christine!

MRS. L. What do you suppose brought me to town?

KROG. Do you mean that you gave me a thought?

MRS. L. I could not endure life without work. All my life, as long as I can remember, I have worked, and it has been my greatest and only pleasure. But now I am quite alone in the world—my life is so dreadfully empty and I feel so forsaken. There is not the least pleasure in working for one's self. Nils, give me someone and something to work for.

KROG. I don't trust that. It is nothing but a woman's overstrained sense of generosity that prompts you to make such an offer of yourself.

MRS. L. Have you ever noticed anything of the sort in me?

KROG. Could you really do it? Tell me—do you know all about my past life?

MRS. L. Yes.

KROG. And do you know what they think of me here?

MRS. L. You seemed to me to imply that with me you might have been quite another man.

KROG. I am certain of it.

MRS. L. Is it too late now?

KROG. Christine, are you saying this deliberately? Yes, I am sure you are. I see it in your face. Have you really the courage, then——

MRS. L. I want to be a mother to someone, and your children need a mother. We two need each other. Nils, I have faith in your real character—I can dare anything with you.

KROG. (*grasps her hands*). Thanks, thanks, Christine! Now I shall find a way to clear myself in the eyes of the world. Ah, but I forgot——

MRS. L. (*listening*). Hush! The tarantella! Go, go!

KROG. Why? What is it?

MRS. L. Do you hear them up there? When that is over we may expect them back.

KROG. Yes, yes—I will go. But it is all no use. Of course you are not aware what steps I have taken in the matter of the Helmers.

MRS. L. Yes, I know all about that.

KROG. And in spite of that have you the courage to——

MRS. L. I understand very well to what lengths a man like you might be driven by despair.

KROG. If I could only undo what I have done!

MRS. L. You cannot. Your letter is lying in the letter box now.

KROG. Are you sure of that?

MRS. L. Quite sure, but——

KROG. (*with a searching look at her*). Is that what it all means?—that you want to save your friend at any cost? Tell me frankly. Is that it?

MRS. L. Nils, a woman who has once sold herself for another's sake doesn't do it a second time.

KROG. I will ask for my letter back.

MRS. L. No, no.

KROG. Yes, of course I will. I will wait here till Helmer comes; I will tell him he must give me my letter back—that it only concerns my dismissal—that he is not to read it——

MRS. L. No, Nils, you must not recall your letter.

KROG. But, tell me, wasn't it for that very purpose that you asked me to meet you here?

MRS. L. In my first moment of fright it was. But twenty-four hours have elapsed since then, and in that time I have witnessed incredible things in this house. Helmer must know all about it. This unhappy secret must be disclosed; they must have a complete understanding between them, which is impossible with all this concealment and falsehood going on.

KROG. Very well, if you will take the responsibility. But there is one thing I can do in any case, and I shall do it at once.

MRS. L. (*listening*). You must be quick and go! The dance is over; we are not safe a moment longer.

KROG. I will wait for you below.

MRS. L. Yes, do. You must see me back to my door.

KROG. I have never had such an amazing piece of good fortune in my life! (*Goes out through the outer door. The door between the room and the hall remains open.*)

MRS. L. (*tidying up the room and laying her hat and cloak ready*). What a difference! What a difference! Someone to work for and live for—a home to bring comfort into. That I will do, indeed. I wish they would be quick and come. (*Listens.*) Ah, there they are now. I must put on my things. (*Takes up her hat and cloak.* HELMER'S *and* NORA'S *voices are heard outside; a key is turned, and* HELMER *brings* NORA *almost by force into the hall. She is in an Italian costume with a large black shawl round her; he is in evening dress and a black domino which is flying open.*)

NORA (*hanging back in the doorway and struggling with him*). No, no, no!— don't take me in. I want to go upstairs again; I don't want to leave so early.

HEL. But, my dearest Nora——

NORA. Please, Torvald dear—please, *please*—only an hour more.

HEL. Not a single minute, my sweet Nora. You know that was our agreement. Come along into the room; you are catching cold standing there. (*He brings her gently into the room in spite of her resistance.*)

MRS. L. Good evening.

NORA. Christine!

HEL. You here so late, Mrs. Linde?

MRS. L. Yes, you must excuse me; I was so anxious to see Nora in her dress.

NORA. Have you been sitting here waiting for me?

MRS. L. Yes; unfortunately I came too late—you had already gone upstairs— and I thought I couldn't go away again without having seen you.

HEL. (*taking off* NORA'S *shawl*). Yes, take a good look at her. I think she is worth looking at. Isn't she charming, Mrs. Linde?

MRS. L. Yes, indeed she is.

HEL. Doesn't she look remarkably pretty? Everyone thought so at the dance. But she is terribly self-willed, this sweet little person. What are we to do with her? You will hardly believe that I had almost to bring her away by force.

NORA. Torvald, you will repent not having let me stay, even if it were only for half an hour.

HEL. Listen to her, Mrs. Linde! She had danced her tarantella, and it had been a tremendous success, as it deserved—although possibly the performance was a trifle too realistic—a little more so, I mean, than was strictly compatible with the limitations of art. But never mind about that! The chief thing is, she had made a success—she had made a tremendous success. Do you think I was going to let her remain there after that and spoil the effect? No indeed! I took my charming little Capri maiden—my capricious little Capri maiden, I should say—on my arm, took one quick turn round the room, a curtsey on either side, and, as they say in novels, the beautiful apparition disappeared. An exit ought always to be effective, Mrs. Linde; but that is what I cannot make Nora understand. Pooh! this room is hot. (*Throws his domino on a chair and opens the door of his room.*) Hullo! it's all dark in here. Oh, of course—excuse me. (*He goes in and lights some candles.*)

NORA (*in a hurried and breathless whisper*). Well?

MRS. L. (*in a low voice*). I have had a talk with him.

NORA. Yes, and——

MRS. L. Nora, you must tell your husband all about it.

NORA (*in an expressionless voice*). I knew it.

MRS. L. You have nothing to be afraid of as far as Krogstad is concerned, but you must tell him.

NORA. I won't tell him.

MRS. L. Then the letter will.

NORA. Thank you, Christine. Now I know what I must do. Hush!

HEL. (*coming in again*). Well, Mrs. Linde, have you admired her?

MRS. L. Yes, and now I will say good night.

HEL. What, already? Is this yours, this knitting?

MRS. L. (*taking it*). Yes, thank you. I had very nearly forgotten it.

HEL. So you knit?

MRS. L. Of course.

HEL. Do you know, you ought to embroider.

MRS. L. Really? Why?

HEL. Yes, it's far more becoming. Let me show you. You hold the embroidery thus in your left hand and use the needle with the right—like this—with a long easy sweep. Do you see?

MRS. L. Yes, perhaps——

HEL. Yes, but in the case of knitting—that can never be anything but ungraceful; look here—the arms close together, the knitting needles going up and down—it has a sort of Chinese effect. . . . That was really excellent champagne they gave us.

MRS. L. Well—good night, Nora, and don't be self-willed any more.

HEL. That's right, Mrs. Linde.

MRS. L. Good night, Mr. Helmer.

HEL. (*accompanying her to the door*). Good night, good night. I hope you will get home all right. I should be very happy to—— But you haven't any great distance to go. Good night, good night. (*She goes out; he shuts the door after her and comes in again.*) Ah!—at last we have got rid of her. She is a frightful bore, that woman.

NORA. Aren't you very tired, Torvald?

HEL. No, not in the least.

NORA. Nor sleepy?

HEL. Not a bit. On the contrary I feel extraordinarily lively. And you?—you really look both tired and sleepy.

NORA. Yes, I am very tired. I want to go to sleep at once.

HEL. There, you see it was quite right of me not to let you stay there any longer.

NORA. Everything you do is quite right, Torvald.

HEL. (*kissing her on the forehead*). Now my little skylark is speaking reasonably. Did you notice what good spirits Rank was in this evening?

NORA. Really? Was he? I didn't speak to him at all.

HEL. And I very little, but I have not for a long time seen him in such good form. (*Looks for a while at her and then goes nearer to her.*) It is delightful to be at home by ourselves again, to be all alone with you—you fascinating, charming little darling!

NORA. Don't look at me like that, Torvald.

HEL. Why shouldn't I look at my dearest treasure?—at all the beauty that is mine, all my very own?

NORA (*going to the other side of the table*). You mustn't say things like that to me tonight.

HEL. (*following her*). You have still got the tarantella in your blood, I see. And it makes you more captivating than ever. Listen—the guests are beginning to go now. (*In a lower voice.*) Nora—soon the whole house will be quiet.

NORA. Yes, I hope so.

HEL. Yes, my own darling Nora. Do you know, when I am out at a party with you like this, why I speak so little to you, keep away from you and only send a stolen glance in your direction now and then?—do you know why I do that? It is because I make believe to myself that we are secretly in love and you are my secretly promised bride and that no one suspects there is anything between us.

NORA. Yes, yes—I know very well your thoughts are with me all the time.

HEL. And when we are leaving and I am putting the shawl over your beautiful young shoulders—on your lovely neck—then I imagine that you are my young bride and that we have just come from our wedding and I am bringing you, for the first time, into our home—to be alone with you for the first time—quite alone with my shy little darling! All this evening I have longed for nothing but you. When I watched the seductive figures of the tarantella my blood was on fire; I could endure it no longer, and that was why I brought you down so early——

NORA. Go away, Torvald! You must let me go. I won't——

HEL. What's that? You're joking, my little Nora! You won't—you won't? Am I not your husband? (*A knock is heard at the outer door.*)

NORA (*starting*). Did you hear——

HEL. (*going into the hall*). Who is it?

RANK (*outside*). It is I. May I come in for a moment?

HEL. (*in a fretful whisper*). Oh, what does he want now? (*Aloud.*) Wait a minute. (*Unlocks the door.*) Come, that's kind of you not to pass by our door.

RANK. I thought I heard your voice, and I felt as if I should like to look in. (*With a swift glance round.*) Ah yes!—these dear familiar rooms. You are very happy and cosy in here, you two.

HEL. It seems to me that you looked after yourself pretty well upstairs too.

RANK. Excellently. Why shouldn't I? Why shouldn't one enjoy everything in this world?—at any rate as much as one can and as long as one can. The wine was capital——

HEL. Especially the champagne.

RANK. So you noticed that too? It is almost incredible how much I managed to put away!

NORA. Torvald drank a great deal of champagne tonight too.

RANK. Did he?

NORA. Yes, and he is always in such good spirits afterward.

RANK. Well, why should one not enjoy a merry evening after a well-spent day?

HEL. Well-spent? I am afraid I can't take credit for that.

RANK (*clapping him on the back*). But I can, you know!

HEL. Exactly.

NORA. Doctor Rank, you must have been occupied with some scientific investigation today.

HEL. Just listen!—little Nora talking about scientific investigations!

NORA. And may I congratulate you on the result?

RANK. Indeed you may.

NORA. Was it favorable, then?

RANK. The best possible, for both doctor and patient—certainty.

NORA (*quickly and searchingly*). Certainty?

RANK. Absolute certainty. So wasn't I entitled to make a merry evening of it after that?

NORA. Yes, you certainly were, Doctor Rank.

HEL. I think so too, so long as you don't have to pay for it in the morning.

RANK. Oh well, one can't have anything in this life without paying for it.

NORA. Doctor Rank—are you fond of fancy-dress balls?

RANK. Yes, if there is a fine lot of pretty costumes.

NORA. Tell me—what shall we two wear at the next?

HEL. Little featherbrain!—are you thinking of the next already?

RANK. We two? Yes, I can tell you. You shall go as a good fairy——

HEL. Yes, but what do you suggest as an appropriate costume for that?

RANK. Let your wife go dressed just as she is in everyday life.

HEL. That was really very prettily turned. But can't you tell us what you will be?

RANK. Yes, my dear friend, I have quite made up my mind about that.

HEL. Well?

RANK. At the next fancy-dress ball I shall be invisible.

HEL. That's a good joke!

RANK. There is a big black hat—have you ever heard of hats that make you invisible? If you put one on, no one can see you.

HEL. (*suppressing a smile*). Yes, you are quite right.

RANK. But I am clean forgetting what I came for. Helmer, give me a cigar— one of the dark Havanas.

HEL. With the greatest pleasure. (*Offers him his case.*)

RANK (*takes a cigar and cuts off the end*). Thanks.

NORA (*striking a match*). Let me give you a light.

RANK. Thank you. (*She holds the match for him to light his cigar.*) And now good-by!

HEL. Good-by, good-by, dear old man!

NORA. Sleep well, Doctor Rank.

RANK. Thank you for that wish.

NORA. Wish me the same.

RANK. You? Well, if you want me to sleep well! And thanks for the light. (*He nods to them both and goes out.*)

HEL. (*in a subdued voice*). He has drunk more than he ought.

NORA (*absently*). Maybe. (HELMER *takes a bunch of keys out of his pocket and goes into the hall.*) Torvald! What are you going to do there?

HEL. Empty the letter box; it is quite full; there will be no room to put the newspaper in tomorrow morning.

NORA. Are you going to work tonight?

HEL. You know quite well I'm not. What is this? Someone has been at the lock.

NORA. At the lock?

HEL. Yes, someone has. What can it mean? I should never have thought the maid—— Here is a broken hairpin. Nora, it is one of yours.

NORA (*quickly*). Then it must have been the children.

HEL. Then you must get them out of those ways. There, at last I have got it open. (*Takes out the contents of the letter box and calls to the kitchen.*) Helen! Helen, put out the light over the front door. (*Goes back into the room and shuts the door into the hall. He holds out his hand full of letters.*) Look at that—look what a heap of them there are. (*Turning them over.*) What on earth is that?

NORA (*at the window*). The letter—— No! Torvald, no!

HEL. Two cards—of Rank's.

NORA. Of Doctor Rank's?

HEL. (*looking at them*). Doctor Rank. They were on the top. He must have put them in when he went out.

NORA. Is there anything written on them?

HEL. There is a black cross over the name. Look there—what an uncomfortable idea! It looks as if he were announcing his own death.

NORA. It is just what he is doing.

HEL. What? Do you know anything about it? Has he said anything to you?

NORA. Yes. He told me that when the cards came it would be his leave-taking from us. He means to shut himself up and die.

HEL. My poor old friend. Certainly I knew we should not have him very long with us. But so soon! And so he hides himself away like a wounded animal.

NORA. If it has to happen, it is best it should be without a word—don't you think so, Torvald?

HEL. (*walking up and down*). He had so grown into our lives. I can't think of him as having gone out of them. He, with his sufferings and his loneliness, was like a cloudy background to our sunlit happiness. Well, perhaps it is best so. For him, anyway. (*Standing still.*) And perhaps for us too, Nora. We two are thrown quite upon each other now. (*Puts his arms round her.*) My darling wife, I don't feel as if I could hold you tight enough. Do you know, Nora, I have often wished that you might be threatened by some great danger, so that I might risk my life's blood and everything for your sake.

NORA (*disengages herself and says firmly and decidedly*). Now you must read your letters, Torvald.

HEL. No, no; not tonight. I want to be with you, my darling wife.

NORA. With the thought of your friend's death——

HEL. You are right; it has affected us both. Something ugly has come between us—the thought of the horrors of death. We must try and rid our minds of that. Until then—we will each go to our own room.

NORA (*hanging on his neck*). Good night, Torvald—good night!

HEL. (*kissing her on the forehead*). Good night, my little singing bird. Sleep sound, Nora. Now I will read my letters through. (*He takes his letters and goes into his room, shutting the door after him.*)

NORA (*gropes distractedly about, seizes* HELMER'S *domino, throws it about her while she says in quick, hoarse, spasmodic whispers*). Never to see him again. Never! Never! (*Puts her shawl over her head.*) Never to see my children again either—never again. Never! Never! Ah! the icy black water— the unfathomable depths—if only it were over! He has got it now—now he is reading it. Good-by, Torvald and my children! (*She is about to rush out through the hall when* HELMER *opens his door hurriedly and stands with an open letter in his hand.*)

HEL. Nora!

NORA. Ah!

HEL. What is this? Do you know what is in this letter?

NORA. Yes, I know. Let me go! Let me get out!

HEL. (*holding her back*). Where are you going?

NORA (*trying to get free*). You shan't save me, Torvald!

HEL. (*reeling*). True? Is this true, that I read here? Horrible! No, no—it is impossible that it is true.

NORA. It is true. I have loved you above everything else in the world.

HEL. Oh, don't let us have any silly excuses.

NORA (*taking a step toward him*). Torvald!

HEL. Miserable creature—what have you done?

NORA. Let me go. You shall not suffer for my sake. You shall not take it upon yourself.

HEL. No tragedy airs, please. (*Locks the hall door.*) Here you shall stay and give me an explanation. Do you understand what you have done? Answer me! Do you understand what you have done?

NORA (*looks steadily at him and says with a growing look of coldness in her face*). Yes, now I am beginning to understand thoroughly.

HEL. (*walking about the room*). What a horrible awakening! All these eight years—she who was my joy and pride—a hypocrite, a liar—worse, worse—a criminal! The unutterable ugliness of it all! For shame! For shame! (NORA *is silent and looks steadily at him. He stops in front of her.*) I ought to have suspected that something of the sort would happen. I ought to have foreseen it. All your father's want of principle—be silent!—all your father's want of principle has come out in you. No religion, no morality, no sense of duty—— How I am punished for having winked at what he did! I did it for your sake, and this is how you repay me.

NORA. Yes, that's just it.

HEL. Now you have destroyed all my happiness. You have ruined all my future. It is horrible to think of! I am in the power of an unscrupulous man; he can do what he likes with me, ask anything he likes of me, give me any orders he pleases—I dare not refuse. And I must sink to such miserable depths because of a thoughtless woman!

NORA. When I am out of the way you will be free.

HEL. No fine speeches, please. Your father always had plenty of those ready too. What good would it be to me if you were out of the way, as you say? Not the slightest. He can make the affair known everywhere; and if he does, I may be falsely suspected of having been a party to your criminal action. Very likely people will think I was behind it all—that it was I who prompted you! And I have to thank you for all this—you whom I have cherished during the whole of our married life. Do you understand now what it is you have done for me?

NORA (*coldly and quietly*). Yes.

HEL. It is so incredible that I can't take it in. But we must come to some understanding. Take off that shawl. Take it off, I tell you. I must try and appease
him in some way or another. The matter must be hushed up at any cost.
And as for you and me, it must appear as if everything between us were
just as before—but naturally only in the eyes of the world. You will still
remain in my house, that is a matter of course. But I shall not allow you
to bring up the children; I dare not trust them to you. To think that I
should be obliged to say so to one whom I have loved so dearly and whom
I still—— No, that is all over. From this moment happiness is not the
question; all that concerns us is to save the remains, the fragments, the
appearance——

(*A ring is heard at the front-door bell.*)

HEL. (*with a start*). What is that? So late! Can the worst—can he—— Hide
yourself, Nora. Say you are ill.

(NORA *stands motionless.* HELMER *goes and unlocks the hall door.*)

MAID (*half dressed, comes to the door*). A letter for the mistress.

HEL. Give it to me. (*Takes the letter and shuts the door.*) Yes, it is from him. You
shall not have it; I will read it myself.

NORA. Yes, read it.

HEL. (*standing by the lamp*). I scarcely have the courage to do it. It may mean
ruin for the both of us. No, I must know. (*Tears open the letter, runs his eye
over a few lines, looks at a paper enclosed and gives a shout of joy.*) Nora!
(*She looks at him questioningly.*) Nora! No, I must read it once again. Yes,
it is true! I am saved! Nora, I am saved!

NORA. And I?

HEL. You too, of course; we are both saved, both you and I. Look, he sends you
your bond back. He says he regrets and repents—that a happy change in
his life—— Never mind what he says! We are saved, Nora! No one can do
anything to you. Oh, Nora, Nora—— No, first I must destroy these hateful things. Let me see. (*Takes a look at the bond.*) No, no, I won't look at it.
The whole thing shall be nothing but a bad dream to me. (*Tears up the
bond and both letters, throws them all into the stove and watches them
burn.*) There—now it doesn't exist any longer. He says that since
Christmas Eve you—— These must have been three dreadful days for
you, Nora.

NORA. I have fought a hard fight these three days.

HEL. And suffered agonies and seen no way out, but—— No, we won't call
any of the horrors to mind. We will only shout with joy and keep saying,
"It's all over! It's all over!" Listen to me, Nora. You don't seem to realize

that it is all over. What is this?—such a cold, set face! My poor little Nora, I quite understand; you don't feel as if you could believe that I have forgiven you. But it is true, Nora, I swear it; I have forgiven you everything. I know that what you did you did out of love for me.

NORA. That is true.

HEL. You have loved me as a wife ought to love her husband. Only you had not sufficient knowledge to judge of the means you used. But do you suppose you are any the less dear to me because you don't understand how to act on your own responsibility? No, no; only lean on me; I will advise and direct you. I should not be a man if this womanly helplessness did not just give you a double attractiveness in my eyes. You must not think any more about the hard things I said in my first moment of consternation, when I thought everything was going to overwhelm me. I have forgiven you, Nora; I swear to you I have forgiven you.

NORA. Thank you for your forgiveness. (*She goes out through the door to the right.*)

HEL. No, don't go. (*Looks in.*) What are you doing in there?

NORA (*from within*). Taking off my fancy dress.

HEL. (*standing at the open door*). Yes, do. Try and calm yourself and make your mind easy again, my frightened little singing bird. Be at rest and feel secure; I have broad wings to shelter you under. (*Walks up and down by the door.*) How warm and cosy our home is, Nora. Here is shelter for you; here I will protect you like a hunted dove that I have saved from a hawk's claws; I will bring peace to your poor beating heart. It will come, little by little, Nora, believe me. Tomorrow morning you will look upon it all quite differently; soon everything will be just as it was before. Very soon you won't need me to assure you that I have forgiven you; you will yourself feel the certainty that I have done so. Can you suppose I should ever think of such a thing as repudiating you or even reproaching you? You have no idea what a true man's heart is like, Nora. There is something so indescribably sweet and satisfying, to a man, in the knowledge that he has forgiven his wife—forgiven her freely and with all his heart. It seems as if that had made her, as it were, doubly his own; he has given her a new life, so to speak, and she has in a way become both wife and child to him. So you shall be for me after this, my little scared, helpless darling. Have no anxiety about anything, Nora; only be frank and open with me, and I will serve as will and conscience both to you—— What is this? Not gone to bed? Have you changed your things?

NORA (*in everyday dress*). Yes, Torvald, I have changed my things now.

HEL. But what for?—so late as this.

NORA. I shall not sleep tonight.

HEL. But, my dear Nora——

NORA (*looking at her watch*). It is not so very late. Sit down here, Torvald. You and I have much to say to one another. (*She sits down at one side of the table.*)

HEL. Nora—what is this?—this cold, set face?

NORA. Sit down. It will take some time; I have a lot to talk over with you.

HEL. (*sits down at the opposite side of the table*). You alarm me, Nora!—and I don't understand you.

NORA. No, that is just it. You don't understand me, and I have never understood you either—before tonight. No, you mustn't interrupt me. You must simply listen to what I say. Torvald, this is a settling of accounts.

HEL. What do you mean by that?

NORA (*after a short silence*). Isn't there one thing that strikes you as strange in our sitting here like this?

HEL. What is that?

NORA. We have been married now eight years. Does it not occur to you that this is the first time we two, you and I, husband and wife, have had a serious conversation?

HEL. What do you mean, serious?

NORA. In all these eight years—longer than that—from the very beginning of our acquaintance we have never exchanged a word on any serious subject.

HEL. Was it likely that I would be continually and forever telling you about worries that you could not help me to bear?

NORA. I am not speaking about business matters. I say that we have never sat down in earnest together to try and get at the bottom of anything.

HEL. But, dearest Nora, would it have been any good to you?

NORA. That is just it; you have never understood me. I have been greatly wronged, Torvald—first by Papa and then by you.

HEL. What! By us two—by us two who have loved you better than anyone else in the world?

NORA (*shaking her head*). You have never loved me. You have only thought it pleasant to be in love with me.

HEL. Nora, what do I hear you saying?

NORA. It is perfectly true, Torvald. When I was at home with Papa he told me his opinion about everything, and so I had the same opinions; and if I differed from him I concealed the fact, because he would not have liked it. He called me his doll child, and he played with me just as I used to play with my dolls. And when I came to live with you——

HEL. What sort of an expression is that to use about our marriage?

NORA (*undisturbed*). I mean that I was simply transferred from Papa's hands to yours. You arranged everything according to your own taste, and so I got the same tastes as you—or else I pretended to. I am really not quite sure which—I think sometimes the one and sometimes the other. When I look back on it it seems to me as if I have been living here like a poor woman—just from hand to mouth. I have existed merely to perform tricks for you, Torvald. But you would have it so. You and Papa have committed a great sin against me. It is your fault that I have made nothing of my life.

HEL. How unreasonable and how ungrateful you are, Nora! Have you not been happy here?

NORA. No, I have never been happy. I thought I was, but it has never really been so.

HEL. Not—not happy!

NORA. No, only merry. And you have always been so kind to me. But our home has been nothing but a playroom. I have been your doll wife, just as at home I was Papa's doll child; and here the children have been my dolls. I thought it great fun when you played with me, just as they thought it great fun when I played with them. That is what our marriage has been, Torvald.

HEL. There is some truth in what you say—exaggerated and strained as your view of it is. But for the future it shall be different. Playtime shall be over and lesson time shall begin.

NORA. Whose lessons? Mine or the children's?

HEL. Both yours and the children's, my darling Nora.

NORA. Alas, Torvald, you are not the man to educate me into being a proper wife for you.

HEL. And you can say that!

NORA. And I—how am I fitted to bring up the children?

HEL. Nora!

NORA. Didn't you say so yourself a little while ago—that you dare not trust me to bring them up?

HEL. In a moment of anger! Why do you pay any heed to that?

NORA. Indeed, you were perfectly right. I am not fit for the task. There is another task I must undertake first. I must try and educate myself—you are not the man to help me in that. I must do that for myself. And that is why I am going to leave you now.

HEL. (*springing up*). What do you say?

NORA. I must stand quite alone if I am to understand myself and everything about me. It is for that reason that I cannot remain with you any longer.

HEL. Nora, Nora!

NORA. I am going away from here now, at once. I am sure Christine will take me in for the night.

HEL. You are out of your mind! I won't allow it! I forbid you!

NORA. It is no use forbidding me anything any longer. I will take with me what belongs to myself. I will take nothing from you, either now or later.

HEL. What sort of madness is this?

NORA. Tomorrow I shall go home—I mean to my old home. It will be easiest for me to find something to do there.

HEL. You blind, foolish woman!

NORA. I must try and get some sense, Torvald.

HEL. To desert your home your husband and your children! And you don't consider what people will say!

NORA. I cannot consider that at all. I only know that it is necessary for me.

HEL. It's shocking. This is how you would neglect your most sacred duties.

NORA. What do you consider my most sacred duties?

HEL. Do I need to tell you that? Are they not your duties to your husband and your children?

NORA. I have other duties just as sacred.

HEL. That you have not. What duties could those be?

NORA. Duties to myself.

HEL. Before all else you are a wife and a mother.

NORA. I don't believe that any longer. I believe that before all else I am a reasonable human being just as you are—or, at all events, that I must try and become one. I know quite well, Torvald, that most people would think you right and that views of that kind are to be found in books; but I can no longer content myself with what most people say or with what is found in books. I must think over things for myself and get to understand them.

HEL. Can you understand your place in your own home? Have you not a reliable guide in such matters as that?—have you no religion?

NORA. I am afraid, Torvald, I do not exactly know what religion is.

HEL. What are you saying?

NORA. I know nothing but what the clergyman said when I went to be confirmed. He told us that religion was this and that and the other. When I am away from all this and am alone I will look into that matter too. I will see if what the clergyman said is true, or at all events if it is true for me.

HEL. This is unheard of in a girl of your age! But if religion cannot lead you aright, let me try and awaken your conscience. I suppose you have some moral sense? Or—answer me—am I to think you have none?

NORA. I assure you, Torvald, that is not an easy question to answer. I really don't know. The thing perplexes me altogether. I only know that you and I look at it in quite a different light. I am learning, too, that the law is quite another thing from what I supposed; but I find it impossible to convince myself that the law is right. According to it a woman has no right to spare her old dying father or to save her husband's life. I can't believe that.

HEL. You talk like a child. You don't understand the conditions of the world in which you live.

NORA. No, I don't. But now I am going to try. I am going to see if I can make out who is right, the world or I.

HEL. You are ill, Nora; you are delirious; I almost think you are out of your mind.

NORA. I have never felt my mind so clear and certain as tonight.

HEL. And is it with a clear and certain mind that you forsake your husband and your children?

NORA. Yes, it is.

HEL. Then there is only one possible explanation.

NORA. What is that?

HEL. You do not love me any more.

NORA. No, that is just it.

HEL. Nora!—and you can say that?

NORA. It gives me great pain, Torvald, for you have always been so kind to me, but I cannot help it. I do not love you any more.

HEL. (*regaining his composure*). Is that a clear and certain conviction too?

NORA. Yes, absolutely clear and certain. That is the reason why I will not stay here any longer.

HEL. And can you tell me what I have done to forfeit your love?

NORA. Yes, indeed I can. It was to-night, when the wonderful thing did not happen; then I saw you were not the man I had thought you.

HEL. Explain yourself better—I don't understand you.

NORA. I have waited so patiently for eight years; for, goodness knows, I knew very well that wonderful things don't happen every day. Then this horrible misfortune came upon me, and then I felt quite certain that the wonderful thing was going to happen at last. When Krogstad's letter was lying out there never for a moment did I imagine that you would consent to accept this man's conditions. I was so absolutely certain that you would say to him: Publish the thing to the whole world. And when that was done——

HEL. Yes, what then?—when I had exposed my wife to shame and disgrace?

NORA. When that was done I was so absolutely certain you would come forward and take everything upon yourself and say: I am the guilty one.

HEL. Nora!

NORA. You mean that I would never have accepted such a sacrifice on your part? No, of course not. But what would my assurances have been worth against yours? That was the wonderful thing which I hoped for and feared, and it was to prevent that that I wanted to kill myself.

HEL. I would gladly work night and day for you, Nora—bear sorrow and want for your sake. But no man would sacrifice his honor for the one he loves.

NORA. It is a thing hundreds of thousands of women have done.

HEL. Oh, you think and talk like a heedless child.

NORA. Maybe. But you neither think nor talk like the man I could bind myself to. As soon as your fear was over—and it was not fear for what threatened me but for what might happen to you—when the whole thing was past, as far as you were concerned it was exactly as if nothing at all had happened. Exactly as before, I was your little skylark, your doll, which you would in the future treat with doubly gentle care because it was so brittle and fragile. (*Getting up.*) Torvald—it was then it dawned upon me that for eight years I had been living here with a strange man and had borne him three children. Oh, I can't bear to think of it! I could tear myself into little bits!

HEL. (*sadly*). I see, I see. An abyss has opened between us—there is no denying it. But, Nora, would it not be possible to fill it up?

NORA. As I am now, I am no wife for you.

HEL. I have it in me to become a different man.

NORA. Perhaps—if your doll is taken away from you.

HEL. But to part!—to part from you! No, no, Nora; I can't understand that idea.

NORA (*going out to the right*). That makes it all the more certain that it must be done. (*She comes back with her cloak and hat and a small bag which she puts on a chair by the table.*)

HEL. Nora. Nora, not now! Wait till tomorrow.

NORA (*putting on her cloak*). I cannot spend the night in a strange man's room.

HEL. But can't we live here like brother and sister?

NORA (*putting on her hat*). You know very well that would not last long. (*Puts the shawl round her.*) Good-by, Torvald. I won't see the little ones. I know they are in better hands than mine. As I am now, I can be of no use to them.

HEL. But someday, Nora—someday?

NORA. How can I tell? I have no idea what is going to become of me.

HEL. But you are my wife, whatever becomes of you.

NORA. Listen, Torvald. I have heard that when a wife deserts her husband's house, as I am doing now, he is legally freed from all obligations toward her. In any case I set you free from all your obligations. You are not to feel yourself bound in the slightest way, any more than I shall. There must be perfect freedom on both sides. See, here is your ring back. Give me mine.

HEL. That too?

NORA. That too.

HEL. Here it is.

NORA. That's right. Now it is all over. I have put the keys here. The maids know all about everything in the house—better than I do. Tomorrow, after I have left her, Christine will come here and pack up my own things that I brought with me from home. I will have them sent after me.

HEL. All over! All over! Nora, shall you never think of me again?

NORA. I know I shall often think of you and the children and this house.

HEL. May I write to you, Nora?

NORA. No—never. You must not do that.

HEL. But at least let me send you——

NORA. Nothing—nothing.

HEL. Let me help you if you are in want.

NORA. No. I can receive nothing from a stranger.

HEL. Nora—can I never be anything more than a stranger to you?

NORA (*taking her bag*). Ah, Torvald, the most wonderful thing of all would have to happen.

HEL. Tell me what that would be!

NORA. Both you and I would have to be so changed that—— Oh, Torvald, I don't believe any longer in wonderful things happening.

HEL. But I will believe in it. Tell me. So changed that——

NORA. That our life together would be a real wedlock. Good-by. (*She goes out through the hall.*)

HEL. (*sinks down on a chair at the door and buries his face in his hands*). Nora! Nora! (*Looks round and rises.*) Empty! She is gone. (*A hope flashes across his mind.*) The most wonderful thing of all—— ?

(*The sound of a door shutting is heard from below.*)

[1879]

QUESTIONS

1. What is the significance of the play's title? Some translations title the play *A Doll House*, while others (including this one) label it *A Doll's House*. What difference in meaning does the possessive convey?

2. Realism is characterized frequently by its focus on the protagonist's struggle against social restrictions. Who is the protagonist of this play? Against what forces does the protagonist struggle? How does the protagonist develop over the course of the play?

3. Describe the setting of *A Doll's House*. What symbolic import does the drawing room convey, as opposed to a kitchen or bedroom? What does this setting tell us about the Helmers and their values?

4. *A Doll's House* regularly invokes symbols to convey meaning. Explain the function of one or more of the following: the Christmas tree, Nora's pet names, macaroons, the tarentella, the silk stockings.

5. What is the crisis of this play? Explain why you believe this moment to be the turning point of the plot.

6. Many of the characters in *A Doll's House* are paired and contrasted: Nora and Mrs. Linde; Nora and Krogstad; Nora and Rank; Torvald and Rank; Torvald and Krogstad; Krogstad and Mrs. Linde. Pick one of these pairs and describe how they are similar and how they differ.

7. At the end of the play, are you sympathetic to Nora? To Torvald? Using evidence from the text, explain how Ibsen encourages or undermines your affective connection to these characters.

8. What makes this play realistic? Think here of aspects of stagecraft, as well as of characterization, plot, and dialogue.

9. Find all of the instances in which money becomes a subject of discussion for the middle class characters of *A Doll's House*. What do we learn about the characters as the result of their perceptions of money—and its power? What statement, if any, is Ibsen making about middle class values? Does the function of money or the values associated with it differ for men and for women? How? Discuss the thematic function of money in *A Doll's House*.

10. In many ways, *A Doll's House* can be read as a feminist manifesto, one articulating a theme of advancing women's rights. Does the focus on

women's issues render this play obsolete? How does this play speak to contemporary audiences, or does it? Make a case for (or against) the contemporary relevance of *A Doll's House.*

August Wilson
[1945–   ]

In his review of AUGUST WILSON'S Gem of the Ocean *(2004), Ben Brantley wrote, "For Black Americans to forget their past, Mr. Wilson has suggested . . . , it is to be without a compass in the present and a clear road to the future." Wilson's career has been dedicated to providing that compass and road through a ten-play cycle chronicling the experience of African Americans in the twentieth century. Born Frederick August Kittel to an African-American mother and a German father, August Wilson grew up in the Hill District of Pittsburgh. Abandoned by her husband, his mother worked various jobs to support her six children, and encouraged them to pursue education as a means of escaping the poverty to which they were born. Wilson learned to read at the age of four, and became such a proficient writer that a white teacher accused him of plagiarizing a high school paper on Napoleon Bonaparte. This incident, following years of racist abuse, led Wilson to drop out of school and continue his education on his own, in the city library.*

Profoundly influenced by such writers as Amiri Baraka, Langston Hughes, and Ralph Ellison, Wilson also found inspiration in the words of Nation of Islam leaders Malcolm X and Elijah Muhammad, as well as in the blues, particularly the songs of Bessie Smith. His own early writing took the form of poetry, but in 1968 he co-founded Black Horizon on the Hill Theater, where his first plays were produced. After ten years with the theater, he moved to Minneapolis, where his play, Jitney! *(set in the 1970s), appeared to critical acclaim in 1982. Two years later a second,* Ma Rainey's Black Bottom *(set in the 1920s), was accepted by the National Playwrights Conference of the Eugene O'Neill Theater Center in Connecticut. Collaborating with Lloyd Richards, dean of the Yale Drama School and director of the O'Neill center, Wilson has gone on to write seven more plays, each dealing with a different decade:* Fences *(1985), set in the 1950s;* Joe Turner's Come and Gone *(1986), set in the 1910s;* The Piano Lesson *(1987), set in the 1930s;* Two Trains Running *(1990), set in the 1960s;* Seven Guitars *(1995), set in the 1940s;* King Hedley II *(2000), set in the 1980s; and* Gem of the Ocean *(2004), set in the 1900s.*

All of August Wilson's plays have been presented on Broadway, and his work has garnered him numerous fellowships, awards, and prizes, including two Pulitzer Prizes and five New York Drama Critics Circle Awards. His incorporation of the blues, storytelling, mysticism, images of migration, and earthy humor have made his work resonate with audiences and critics alike. Scholars are equally laudatory: Jonathan Little, in the Dictionary of Literary Biography, *refers to Wilson's plays as "complex and mysterious," revealing "the poisonous effects of a bitter legacy on black individuals and their communities" and including "thrilling if infrequent moments of personal liberation"; and Henry Louis Gates, Jr. has called him "the most accomplished black playwright in this nation's history." Given the response to Wilson's work in the past quarter century, the playwright might well be considered, in Gates's words, "the dean of American dramatists."*

Fences

AUGUST WILSON

CHARACTERS IN THE PLAY

TROY MAXSON,
JIM BONO, *Troy's friend*
ROSE, *Troy's wife*
LYONS, *Troy's oldest son by previous marriage*
GABRIEL, *Troy's brother*
CORY, *Troy and Rose's son*
RAYNELL, *Troy's daughter*

SETTING

The setting is the yard which fronts the only entrance to the MAXSON *household, an ancient two-story brick house set back off a small alley in a big-city neighborhood. The entrance to the house is gained by two or three steps leading to a wooden porch badly in need of paint.*

A relatively recent addition to the house and running its full width, the porch lacks congruence. It is a sturdy porch with a flat roof. One or two chairs of dubious value sit at one end where the kitchen window opens onto the porch. An old-fashioned icebox stands silent guard at the opposite end.

The yard is a small dirt yard, partially fenced, except for the last scene, with a wooden sawhorse, a pile of lumber, and other fence-building equipment set off to the side. Opposite is a tree from which hangs a ball made of rags. A baseball bat leans against the tree. Two oil drums serve as garbage receptacles and sit near the house at right to complete the setting.

THE PLAY

Near the turn of the century, the destitute of Europe sprang on the city with tenacious claws and an honest and solid dream. The city devoured them. They swelled its belly until it burst into a thousand furnaces and sewing machines, a thousand butcher shops and bakers' ovens, a thousand churches and hospitals

---

and funeral parlors and money-lenders. The city grew. It nourished itself and offered each man a partnership limited only by his talent, his guile, and his will-ingness and capacity for hard work. For the immigrants of Europe, a dream dared and won true.

The descendants of African slaves were offered no such welcome or par-ticipation. They came from places called the Carolinas and the Virginias, Georgia, Alabama, Mississippi, and Tennessee. They came strong, eager, search-ing. The city rejected them and they fled and settled along the riverbanks and under bridges in shallow, ramshackle houses made of sticks and tar-paper. They collected rags and wood. They sold the use of their muscles and their bodies. They cleaned houses and washed clothes, they shined shoes, and in quiet des-peration and vengeful pride, they stole, and lived in pursuit of their own dream. That they could breathe free, finally, and stand to meet life with the force of dignity and whatever eloquence the heart could call upon.

By 1957, the hard-won victories of the European immigrants had solidi-fied the industrial might of America. War had been confronted and won with new energies that used loyalty and patriotism as its fuel. Life was rich, full, and flourishing. The Milwaukee Braves won the World Series, and the hot winds of change that would make the sixties a turbulent, racing, dangerous, and provocative decade had not yet begun to blow full.

ACT I

SCENE ONE

It is 1957. TROY *and* BONO *enter the yard, engaged in conversation.* TROY *is fifty-three years old, a large man with thick, heavy hands; it is this largeness that he strives to fill out and make an accommodation with. Together with his blackness, his largeness informs his sensibilities and the choices he has made in his life.*

Of the two men, BONO *is obviously the follower. His commitment to their friendship of thirty-odd years is rooted in his admiration of* TROY's *honesty, capacity for hard work, and his strength, which* BONO *seeks to emulate.*

It is Friday night, payday, and the one night of the week the two men engage in a ritual of talk and drink. TROY *is usually the most talkative and at times he can be crude and almost vulgar, though he is capable of rising to profound heights of expression. The men carry lunch buckets and wear or carry burlap aprons and are dressed in clothes suitable to their jobs as garbage collectors.*

BONO. Troy, you ought to stop that lying!

TROY. I ain't lying! The nigger had a watermelon this big. (*He indicates with his hands.*)

Talking about . . . "What watermelon, Mr. Rand?" I liked to fell out! "What watermelon, Mr. Rand?" . . . And it sitting there big as life.

BONO. What did Mr. Rand say?

TROY. Ain't said nothing. Figure if the nigger too dumb to know he carrying a watermelon, he wasn't gonna get much sense out of him. Trying to hide that great big old watermelon under his coat. Afraid to let the white man see him carry it home.

BONO. I'm like you . . . I ain't got no time for them kind of people.

TROY. Now what he look like getting mad cause he see the man from the union talking to Mr. Rand?

BONO. He come to me talking about . . . "Maxson gonna get us fired." I told him to get away from me with that. He walked away from me calling you a troublemaker. What Mr. Rand say?

TROY. Ain't said nothing. He told me to go down the Commissioner's office next Friday. They called me down there to see them.

BONO. Well, as long as you got your complaint filed, they can't fire you. That's what one of them white fellows tell me.

TROY. I ain't worried about them firing me. They gonna fire me cause I asked a question? That's all I did. I went to Mr. Rand and asked him, "Why? Why you got the white mens driving and the colored lifting?" Told him, "what's the matter, don't I count? You think only white fellows got sense enough to drive a truck. That ain't no paper job! Hell, anybody can drive a truck. How come you got all whites driving and the colored lifting?" He told me "take it to the union." Well, hell, that's what I done! Now they wanna come up with this pack of lies.

BONO. I told Brownie if the man come and ask him any questions . . . just tell the truth! It ain't nothing but something they done trumped up on you cause you filed a complaint on them.

TROY. Brownie don't understand nothing. All I want them to do is change the job description. Give everybody a chance to drive the truck. Brownie can't see that. He ain't got that much sense.

BONO. How you figure he be making out with that gal be up at Taylors' all the time . . . that Alberta gal?

TROY. Same as you and me. Getting just as much as we is. Which is to say nothing.

BONO. It is, huh? I figure you doing a little better than me . . . and I ain't saying what I'm doing.

TROY. Aw, nigger, look here . . . I know you. If you had got anywhere near that gal, twenty minutes later you be looking to tell somebody. And the first one you gonna tell . . . that you gonna want to brag to . . . is gonna be me.

BONO. I ain't saying that. I see where you be eyeing her.

TROY. I eye all the women. I don't miss nothing. Don't never let nobody tell you Troy Maxson don't eye the women.

BONO. You been doing more than eyeing her. You done bought her a drink or two.

TROY. Hell yeah, I bought her a drink! What that mean? I bought you one, too. What that mean cause I buy her a drink? I'm just being polite.

BONO. It's alright to buy her one drink. That's what you call being polite. But when you wanna be buying two or three . . . that's what you call eyeing her.

TROY. Look here, as long as you known me . . . you ever known me to chase after women?

BONO. Hell yeah! Long as I done known you. You forgetting I knew you when.

TROY. Naw, I'm talking about since I been married to Rose?

BONO. Oh, not since you been married to Rose. Now, that's the truth, there. I can say that.

TROY. Alright then! Case closed.

BONO. I see you be walking up around Alberta's house. You supposed to be at Taylors' and you be walking up around there.

TROY. What you watching where I'm walking for? I ain't watching after you.

BONO. I seen you walking around there more than once.

TROY. Hell, you liable to see me walking anywhere! That don't mean nothing cause you see me walking around there.

BONO. Where she come from anyway? She just kinda showed up one day.

TROY. Tallahassee. You can look at her and tell she one of them Florida gals. They got some big healthy women down there. Grow them right up out the ground. Got a little bit of Indian in her. Most of them niggers down in Florida got some Indian in them.

BONO. I don't know about that Indian part. But she damn sure big and healthy. Woman wear some big stockings. Got them great big old legs and hips as wide as the Mississippi River.

TROY. Legs don't mean nothing. You don't do nothing but push them out of the way. But them hips cushion the ride!

BONO. Troy, you ain't got no sense.

TROY. It's the truth! Like you riding on Goodyears!

(ROSE *enters from the house. She is ten years younger than* TROY, *her devotion to him stems from her recognition of the possibilities of her life without him: a succession of abusive men and their babies, a life of partying and running the streets, the Church, or aloneness with its attendant pain and frustration. She recognizes* TROY's *spirit as a fine and illuminating one and she either ignores or forgives his faults, only some of which she recognizes. Though she doesn't drink, her presence is an integral part of the Friday night rituals. She alternates between the porch and the kitchen, where supper preparations are under way.*)

ROSE. What you all out here getting into?

TROY. What you worried about what we getting into for? This is men talk, woman.

ROSE. What I care what you all talking about? Bono, you gonna stay for supper?

BONO. No, I thank you, Rose. But Lucille say she cooking up a pot of pigfeet.

TROY. Pigfeet! Hell, I'm going home with you! Might even stay the night if you got some pigfeet. You got something in there to top them pigfeet, Rose?

ROSE. I'm cooking up some chicken. I got some chicken and collard greens.

TROY. Well, go on back in the house and let me and Bono finish what we was talking about. This is men talk. I got some talk for you later. You know what kind of talk I mean. You go on and powder it up.

ROSE. Troy Maxson, don't you start that now!

TROY (*Puts his arm around her*). Aw, woman . . . come here. Look here, Bono . . . when I met this woman . . . I got out that place, say, "Hitch up my pony, saddle up my mare . . . there's a woman out there for me somewhere." I looked here. Looked there. Saw Rose and latched on to her. I latched on to her and told her—I'm gonna tell you the truth—I told her, "Baby, I don't wanna marry, I just wanna be your man." Rose told me . . . tell him what you told me, Rose.

ROSE. I told him if he wasn't the marrying kind, then move out the way so the marrying kind could find me.

TROY. That's what she told me. "Nigger, you in my way. You blocking the view! Move out the way so I can find me a husband." I thought it over two or three days. Come back—

ROSE. Ain't no two or three days nothing. You was back the same night.

TROY. Come back, told her . . . "Okay, baby . . . but I'm gonna buy me a banty rooster and put him out there in the backyard . . . and when he see a stranger come, he'll flap his wings and crow . . ." Look here, Bono, I could watch the front door by myself . . . it was that back door I was worried about.

ROSE. Troy, you ought not talk like that. Troy ain't doing nothing but telling a lie.

TROY. Only thing is . . . when we first got married . . . forget the rooster . . . we ain't had no yard!

BONO. I hear you tell it. Me and Lucille was staying down there on Logan Street. Had two rooms with the outhouse in the back. I ain't mind the outhouse none. But when that goddamn wind blow through there in the winter . . . that's what I'm talking about! To this day I wonder why in the hell I ever stayed down there for six long years. But see, I didn't know I could do no better. I thought only white folks had inside toilets and things.

ROSE. There's a lot of people don't know they can do no better than they doing now. That's just something you got to learn. A lot of folks still shop at Bella's.

TROY. Ain't nothing wrong with shopping at Bella's. She got fresh food.

ROSE. I ain't said nothing about if she got fresh food. I'm talking about what she charge. She charge ten cents more than the A&P.

TROY. The A&P ain't never done nothing for me. I spends my money where I'm treated right. I go down to Bella, say, "I need a loaf of bread, I'll pay you Friday." She give it to me. What sense that make when I got money to go and spend it somewhere else and ignore the person who done right by me? That ain't in the Bible.

ROSE. We ain't talking about what's in the Bible. What sense it make to shop there when she overcharge?

TROY. You shop where you want to. I'll do my shopping where the people been good to me.

ROSE. Well, I don't think it's right for her to overcharge. That's all I was saying.

BONO. Look here . . . I got to get on. Lucille going be raising all kind of hell.

TROY. Where you going, nigger? We ain't finished this pint. Come here, finish this pint.

BONO. Well, hell, I am . . . if you ever turn the bottle loose.

TROY (*Hands him the bottle*). The only thing I say about the A&P is I'm glad Cory got that job down there. Help him take care of his school clothes and things. Gabe done moved out and things getting tight around here. He got that job. . . . He can start to look out for himself.

ROSE. Cory done went and got recruited by a college football team.

TROY. I told that boy about that football stuff. The white man ain't gonna let him get nowhere with that football. I told him when he first come to me with it. Now you come telling me he done went and got more tied up in it. He ought to go and get recruited in how to fix cars or something where he can make a living.

ROSE. He ain't talking about making no living playing football. It's just something the boys in school do. They gonna send a recruiter by to talk to you. He'll tell you he ain't talking about making no living playing football. It's a honor to be recruited.

TROY. It ain't gonna get him nowhere. Bono'll tell you that.

BONO. If he be like you in the sports . . . he's gonna be alright. Ain't but two men ever played baseball as good as you. That's Babe Ruth and Josh Gibson. Them's the only two men ever hit more home runs than you.

TROY. What it ever get me? Ain't got a pot to piss in or a window to throw it out of.

ROSE. Times have changed since you was playing baseball, Troy. That was before the war. Times have changed a lot since then.

TROY. How in hell they done changed?

ROSE. They got lots of colored boys playing ball now. Baseball and football.

BONO. You right about that, Rose. Times have changed, Troy. You just come along too early.

TROY. There ought not never have been no time called too early! Now you take that fellow . . . what's that fellow they had playing right field for the Yankees back then? You know who I'm talking about, Bono. Used to play right field for the Yankees.

ROSE. Selkirk?

TROY. Selkirk! That's it! Man batting .269, understand? .269. What kind of sense that make? I was hitting .432 with thirty-seven home runs! Man batting .269 and playing right field for the Yankees! I saw Josh Gibson's daughter yesterday. She walking around with raggedy shoes on her feet. Now I bet you Selkirk's daughter ain't walking around with raggedy shoes on her feet! I bet you that!

ROSE. They got a lot of colored baseball players now. Jackie Robinson was the first. Folks had to wait for Jackie Robinson.

TROY. I done seen a hundred niggers play baseball better than Jackie Robinson. Hell, I know some teams Jackie Robinson couldn't even make! What you talking about Jackie Robinson. Jackie Robinson wasn't nobody. I'm talking about if you could play ball then they ought to have let you play. Don't care what color you were. Come telling me I come along too early. If you could play . . . then they ought to have let you play.

(TROY *takes a long drink from the bottle.*)

ROSE. You gonna drink yourself to death. You don't need to be drinking like that.

TROY. Death ain't nothing. I done seen him. Done wrassled with him. You can't tell me nothing about death. Death ain't nothing but a fastball on the outside corner. And you know what I'll do to that! Lookee here, Bono . . . am I lying? You get one of them fastballs, about waist high, over the outside corner of the plate where you can get the meat of the bat on it . . . and good god! You can kiss it goodbye. Now, am I lying?

BONO. Naw, you telling the truth there. I seen you do it.

TROY. If I'm lying . . . that 450 feet worth of lying! (*Pause.*)

That's all death is to me. A fastball on the outside corner.

ROSE. I don't know why you want to get on talking about death.

TROY. Ain't nothing wrong with talking about death. That's part of life. Everybody gonna die. You gonna die, I'm gonna die. Bono's gonna die. Hell, we all gonna die.

ROSE. But you ain't got to talk about it. I don't like to talk about it.

TROY. You the one brought it up. Me and Bono was talking about baseball . . . you tell me I'm gonna drink myself to death. Ain't that right, Bono? You know I don't drink this but one night out of the week. That's Friday night. I'm gonna drink just enough to where I can handle it. Then I cuts it loose. I leave it alone. So don't you worry about me drinking myself to death. 'Cause I ain't worried about Death. I done seen him. I done wrestled with him.

Look here, Bono . . . I looked up one day and Death was marching straight at me. Like Soldiers on Parade! The Army of Death was marching straight at me. The middle of July, 1941. It got real cold just like it be winter. It seem like Death himself reached out and touched me on the shoulder. He touch me just like I touch you. I got cold as ice and Death standing there grinning at me.

ROSE. Troy, why don't you hush that talk.

TROY. I say . . . What you want, Mr. Death? You be wanting me? You done brought your army to be getting me? I looked him dead in the eye. I wasn't fearing nothing. I was ready to tangle. Just like I'm ready to tangle now. The Bible say be ever vigilant. That's why I don't get but so drunk. I got to keep watch.

ROSE. Troy was right down there in Mercy Hospital. You remember he had pneumonia? Laying there with a fever talking plumb out of his head.

TROY. Death standing there staring at me . . . carrying that sickle in his hand. Finally he say, "You want bound over for another year?" See, just like that . . . "You want bound over for another year?" I told him, "Bound over hell ! Let's settle this now!"

It seem like he kinda fell back when I said that, and all the cold went out of me. I reached down and grabbed that sickle and threw it just as far as I could throw it . . . and me and him commenced to wrestling.

We wrestled for three days and three nights. I can't say where I found the strength from. Every time it seemed like he was gonna get the best of me, I'd reach way down deep inside myself and find the strength to do him one better.

ROSE. Every time Troy tell that story he find different ways to tell it. Different things to make up about it.

TROY. I ain't making up nothing. I'm telling you the facts of what happened. I wrestled with Death for three days and three nights and I'm standing here to tell you about it.

(*Pause.*)

Alright. At the end of the third night we done weakened each other to where we can't hardly move. Death stood up, throwed on his robe . . . had him a white robe with a hood on it. He threwed on that robe and went off to look for his sickle. Say, "I'll be back." Just like that. "I'll be back." I told him, say, "Yeah, but . . . you gonna have to find me!" I wasn't no fool. I wasn't going looking for him. Death ain't nothing to play with. And I know he's gonna get me. I know I got to join his army . . . his camp followers. But as long as I keep my strength and see him coming . . . as long as I keep up my vigilance . . . he's gonna have to fight to get me. I ain't going easy.

BONO. Well, look here, since you got to keep up your vigilance . . . let me have the bottle.

TROY. Aw hell, I shouldn't have told you that part. I should have left out that part.

ROSE. Troy be talking that stuff and half the time don't even know what he be talking about.

TROY. Bono know me better than that.

BONO. That's right. I know you. I know you got some Uncle Remus in your blood. You got more stories than the devil got sinners.

TROY. Aw hell, I done seen him too! Done talked with the devil.

ROSE. Troy, don't nobody wanna be hearing all that stuff.

(LYONS *enters the yard from the street. Thirty-four years old,* TROY's *son by a previous marriage, he sports a neatly trimmed goatee, sport coat, white shirt, tieless and buttoned at the collar. Though he fancies himself a musician, he is more caught up in the rituals and "idea" of being a musician than in the actual practice of the music. He has come to borrow money from* TROY, *and while he knows he will be successful, he is uncertain as to what extent his lifestyle will be held up to scrutiny and ridicule.*)

LYONS. Hey, Pop.

TROY. What you come "Hey, Popping" me for?

LYONS. How you doing, Rose? (*He kisses her.*) Mr. Bono. How you doing?

BONO. Hey, Lyons . . . how you been?

TROY. He must have been doing alright. I ain't seen him around here last week.

ROSE. Troy, leave your boy alone. He come by to see you and you wanna start all that nonsense.

TROY. I ain't bothering Lyons.

(*Offers him the bottle.*)

Here . . . get you a drink. We got an understanding. I know why he come by to see me and he know I know.

LYONS. Come on, Pop . . . I just stopped by to say hi . . . see how you was doing.

TROY. You ain't stopped by yesterday.

ROSE. You gonna stay for supper, Lyons? I got some chicken cooking in the oven.

LYONS. No, Rose . . . thanks. I was just in the neighborhood and thought I'd stop by for a minute.

TROY. You was in the neighborhood alright, nigger. You telling the truth there. You was in the neighborhood cause it's my payday.

LYONS. Well, hell, since you mentioned it . . . let me have ten dollars.

TROY. I'll be damned! I'll die and go to hell and play blackjack with the devil before I give you ten dollars.

BONO. That's what I wanna know about . . . that devil you done seen.

LYONS. What . . . Pop done seen the devil? You too much, Pops.

TROY. Yeah, I done seen him. Talked to him too!

ROSE. You ain't seen no devil. I done told you that man ain't had nothing to do with the devil. Anything you can't understand, you want to call it the devil.

TROY. Look here, Bono . . . I went down to see Hertzberger about some furniture. Got three rooms for two-ninety-eight. That what it say on the radio. "Three rooms . . . two-ninety-eight." Even made up a little song about it. Go down there . . . man tell me I can't get no credit. I'm working every day and can't get no credit. What to do? I got an empty house with some raggedy furniture in it. Cory ain't got no bed. He's sleeping on a pile of rags on the floor. Working every day and can't get no credit. Come back here— Rose'll tell you—madder than hell. Sit down . . . try to figure what I'm gonna do. Come a knock on the door. Ain't been living here but three days. Who know I'm here? Open the door . . . devil standing there bigger than life. White fellow . . . got on good clothes and everything. Standing there with a clipboard in his hand. I ain't had to say nothing. First words come out of his mouth was . . . "I understand you need some furniture and can't get no credit." I liked to fell over. He say "I'll give you all the credit you want, but you got to pay the interest on it." I told him, "Give me three rooms worth and charge whatever you want." Next day a truck pulled up here and two men unloaded them three rooms. Man what drove the truck give me a book. Say send ten dollars, first of every month to the address in the book and everything will be alright. Say if I miss a payment the devil was coming back and it'll be hell to pay. That was fifteen years ago. To this day . . . the first of the month I send my ten dollars, Rose'll tell you.

ROSE. Troy lying.

TROY. I ain't never seen that man since. Now you tell me who else that could have been but the devil? I ain't sold my soul or nothing like that, you understand. Naw, I wouldn't have truck with the devil about nothing like that. I got my furniture and pays my ten dollars the first of the month just like clockwork.

BONO. How long you say you been paying this ten dollars a month?

TROY. Fifteen years!

BONO. Hell, ain't you finished paying for it yet? How much the man done charged you.

TROY. Aw hell, I done paid for it. I done paid for it ten times over! The fact is I'm scared to stop paying it.

ROSE. Troy lying. We got that furniture from Mr. Glickman. He ain't paying no ten dollars a month to nobody.

TROY. Aw hell, woman. Bono know I ain't that big a fool.

LYONS. I was just getting ready to say . . . I know where there's a bridge for sale.

TROY. Look here, I'll tell you this . . . it don't matter to me if he was the devil. It don't matter if the devil give credit. Somebody has got to give it.

ROSE. It ought to matter. You going around talking about having truck with the devil . . . God's the one you gonna have to answer to. He's the one gonna be at the Judgment.

LYONS. Yeah, well, look here, Pop . . . let me have that ten dollars. I'll give it back to you. Bonnie got a job working at the hospital.

TROY. What I tell you, Bono? The only time I see this nigger is when he wants something. That's the only time I see him.

LYONS. Come on, Pop, Mr. Bono don't want to hear all that. Let me have the ten dollars. I told you Bonnie working.

TROY. What that mean to me? "Bonnie working." I don't care if she working. Go ask her for the ten dollars if she working. Talking about "Bonnie working." Why ain't you working?

LYONS. Aw, Pop, you know I can't find no decent job. Where am I gonna get a job at? You know I can't get no job.

TROY. I told you I know some people down there. I can get you on the rubbish if you want to work. I told you that the last time you came by here asking me for something.

LYONS. Naw, Pop . . . thanks. That ain't for me. I don't wanna be carrying nobody's rubbish. I don't wanna be punching nobody's time clock.

TROY. What's the matter, you too good to carry people's rubbish? Where you think that ten dollars you talking about come from? I'm just supposed to haul people's rubbish and give my money to you cause you too lazy to work. You too lazy to work and wanna know why you ain't got what I got.

ROSE. What hospital Bonnie working at? Mercy?

LYONS. She's down at Passavant working in the laundry.

TROY. I ain't got nothing as it is. I give you that ten dollars and I got to eat beans the rest of the week. Naw . . . you ain't getting no ten dollars here.

LYONS. You ain't got to be eating no beans. I don't know why you wanna say that.

TROY. I ain't got no extra money. Gabe done moved over to Miss Pearl's paying her the rent and things done got tight around here. I can't afford to be giving you every payday.

LYONS. I ain't asked you to give me nothing. I asked you to loan me ten dollars. I know you got ten dollars.

TROY. Yeah, I got it. You know why I got it? Cause I don't throw my money away out there in the streets. You living the fast life . . . wanna be a musician . . . running around in them clubs and things . . . then, you learn to take care of yourself. You ain't gonna find me going and asking nobody for nothing. I done spent too many years without.

LYONS. You and me is two different people, Pop.

TROY. I done learned my mistake and learned to do what's right by it. You still trying to get something for nothing. Life don't owe you nothing. You owe it to yourself. Ask Bono. He'll tell you I'm right.

LYONS. You got your way of dealing with the world . . . I got mine. The only thing that matters to me is the music.

TROY. Yeah, I can see that! It don't matter how you gonna eat . . . where your next dollar is coming from. You telling the truth there.

LYONS. I know I got to eat. But I got to live too. I need something that gonna help me to get out of the bed in the morning. Make me feel like I belong in the world. I don't bother nobody. I just stay with my music cause that's the only way I can find to live in the world. Otherwise there ain't no telling what I might do. Now I don't come criticizing you and how you live. I just come by to ask you for ten dollars. I don't wanna hear all that about how I live.

TROY. Boy, your mama did a hell of a job raising you.

LYONS. You can't change me, Pop. I'm thirty-four years old. If you wanted to change me, you should have been there when I was growing up. I come by to see you . . . ask for ten dollars and you want to talk about how I was raised. You don't know nothing about how I was raised.

ROSE. Let the boy have ten dollars, Troy.

TROY (*To* LYONS). What the hell you looking at me for? I ain't got no ten dollars. You know what I do with my money.

(*To* ROSE.)

Give him ten dollars if you want him to have it.

ROSE. I will. Just as soon as you turn it loose.

TROY (*Handing* ROSE *the money*). There it is. Seventy-six dollars and forty-two cents. You see this, Bono? Now, I ain't gonna get but six of that back.

ROSE. You ought to stop telling that lie. Here, Lyons. (*She hands him the money.*)

LYONS. Thanks, Rose. Look . . . I got to run . . . I'll see you later.

TROY. Wait a minute. You gonna say, "thanks, Rose" and ain't gonna look to see where she got that ten dollars from? See how they do me, Bono?

LYONS. I know she got it from you, Pop. Thanks. I'll give it back to you.

TROY. There he go telling another lie. Time I see that ten dollars . . . he'll be owing me thirty more.

LYONS. See you, Mr. Bono.

BONO. Take care, Lyons!

LYONS. Thanks, Pop. I'll see you again.

(LYONS *exits the yard.*)

TROY. I don't know why he don't go and get him a decent job and take care of that woman he got.

BONO. He'll be alright, Troy. The boy is still young.

TROY. The *boy* is thirty-four years old.

ROSE. Let's not get off into all that.

BONO. Look here . . . I got to be going. I got to be getting on. Lucille gonna be waiting.

TROY (*Puts his arm around* ROSE). See this woman, Bono? I love this woman. I love this woman so much it hurts. I love her so much . . . I done run out of ways of loving her. So I got to go back to basics. Don't you come by my house Monday morning talking about time to go to work . . . 'cause I'm still gonna be stroking!

ROSE. Troy! Stop it now!

BONO. I ain't paying him no mind, Rose. That ain't nothing but gin-talk. Go on, Troy. I'll see you Monday.

TROY. Don't you come by my house, nigger! I done told you what I'm gonna be doing.

(*The lights go down to black.*)

SCENE TWO

The lights come up on ROSE *hanging up clothes. She hums and sings softly to herself. It is the following morning.*

ROSE (*Sings*). Jesus, be a fence all around me every day Jesus, I want you to
            protect me as I travel on my way.
            Jesus, be a fence all around me every day.

(TROY *enters from the house.*)

ROSE (*continued*). Jesus, I want you to protect me
            As I travel on my way.

(*To* TROY)

'Morning. You ready for breakfast? I can fix it soon as I finish hanging up these clothes.

TROY. I got the coffee on. That'll be alright. I'll just drink some of that this morning.

ROSE. That 651 hit yesterday. That's the second time this month. Miss Pearl hit for a dollar . . . seem like those that need the least always get lucky. Poor folks can't get nothing.

TROY. Them numbers don't know nobody. I don't know why you fool with them. You and Lyons both.

ROSE. It's something to do.

TROY. You ain't doing nothing but throwing your money away.

ROSE. Troy, you know I don't play foolishly. I just play a nickel here and a nickel there.

TROY. That's two nickels you done thrown away.

ROSE. Now I hit sometimes . . . that makes up for it. It always comes in handy when I do hit. I don't hear you complaining then.

TROY. I ain't complaining now. I just say it's foolish. Trying to guess out of six hundred ways which way the number gonna come. If I had all the money niggers, these Negroes, throw away on numbers for one week—just one week—I'd be a rich man.

ROSE. Well, you wishing and calling it foolish ain't gonna stop folks from playing numbers. That's one thing for sure. Besides . . . some good things come from playing numbers. Look where Pope done bought him that restaurant off of numbers.

TROY. I can't stand niggers like that. Man ain't had two dimes to rub together. He walking around with his shoes all run over bumming money for cigarettes. Alright. Got lucky there and hit the numbers . . .

ROSE. Troy, I know all about it.

TROY. Had good sense, I'll say that for him. He ain't throwed his money away. I seen niggers hit the numbers and go through two thousand dollars in four days. Man brought him that restaurant down there . . . fixed it up real nice . . . and then didn't want nobody to come in it! A Negro go in there and can't get no kind of service. I seen a white fellow come in there and order a bowl of stew. Pope picked all the meat out the pot for him. Man ain't had nothing but a bowl of meat! Negro come behind him and ain't got nothing but the potatoes and carrots. Talking about what numbers do for people, you picked a wrong example. Ain't done nothing but make a worser fool out of him than he was before.

ROSE. Troy, you ought to stop worrying about what happened at work yesterday.

TROY. I ain't worried. Just told me to be down there at the Commissioner's office on Friday. Everybody think they gonna fire me. I ain't worried about them firing me. You ain't got to worry about that.

(*Pause.*)

Where's Cory? Cory in the house? (*Calls.*) Cory?

ROSE. He gone out.

TROY. Out, huh? He gone out 'cause he know I want him to help me with this fence. I know how he is. That boy scared of work.

(GABRIEL *enters. He comes halfway down the alley and, hearing* TROY's *voice, stops.*)

TROY (*Continues*). He ain't done a lick of work in his life.

ROSE. He had to go to football practice. Coach wanted them to get in a little extra practice before the season start.

TROY. I got his practice . . . running out of here before he get his chores done.

ROSE. Troy, what is wrong with you this morning? Don't nothing set right with you. Go on back in there and go to bed . . . get up on the other side.

TROY. Why something got to be wrong with me? I ain't said nothing wrong with me.

ROSE. You got something to say about everything. First it's the numbers . . . then it's the way the man runs his restaurant . . . then you done got on Cory. What's it gonna be next? Take a look up there and see if the weather suits you . . . or is it gonna be how you gonna put up the fence with the clothes hanging in the yard.

TROY. You hit the nail on the head then.

ROSE. I know you like I know the back of my hand. Go on in there and get you some coffee . . . see if that straighten you up. 'Cause you ain't right this morning.

(TROY *starts into the house and sees* GABRIEL. GABRIEL *starts singing.* TROY's *brother, he is seven years younger than* TROY. *Injured in World War II, he has a metal plate in his head. He carries an old trumpet tied around his waist and believes with every fiber of his being that he is the Archangel Gabriel. He carries a chipped basket with an assortment of discarded fruits and vegetables he has picked up in the strip district and which he attempts to sell.*)

GABRIEL (*Singing*).
   Yes, ma'am, I got plums
   You ask me how I sell them
   Oh ten cents apiece
   Three for a quarter
   Come and buy now
   'Cause I'm here today
   And tomorrow I'll be gone

(GABRIEL *enters.*)

   Hey, Rose!

ROSE. How you doing, Gabe?

GABRIEL. There's Troy . . . Hey, Troy!

TROY. Hey, Gabe.

(*Exit into kitchen.*)

ROSE (*To* GABRIEL). What you got there?

GABRIEL. You know what I got, Rose. I got fruits and vegetables.

ROSE (*Looking in basket*). Where's all these plums you talking about?

GABRIEL. I ain't got no plums today, Rose. I was just singing that. Have some tomorrow. Put me in a big order for plums. Have enough plums tomorrow for St. Peter and everybody.

(TROY *re-enters from kitchen, crosses to steps.*)

(*To* ROSE.)

    Troy's mad at me.

TROY. I ain't mad at you. What I got to be mad at you about? You ain't done nothing to me.

GABRIEL. I just moved over to Miss Pearl's to keep out from in your way. I ain't mean no harm by it.

TROY. Who said anything about that? I ain't said anything about that.

GABRIEL. You ain't mad at me, is you?

TROY. Naw . . . I ain't mad at you, Gabe. If I was mad at you I'd tell you about it.

GABRIEL. Got me two rooms. In the basement. Got my own door too. Wanna see my key?

(*He holds up a key.*)

    That's my own key! Ain't nobody else got a key like that.

    That's my key! My two rooms!

TROY. Well, that's good, Gabe. You got your own key . . . that's good.

ROSE. You hungry, Gabe? I was just fixing to cook Troy his breakfast.

GABRIEL. I'll take some biscuits. You got some biscuits? Did you know when I was in heaven . . . every morning me and St. Peter would sit down by the gate and eat some big fat biscuits? Oh, yeah! We had us a good time. We'd sit there and eat us them biscuits and then St. Peter would go off to sleep and tell me to wake him up when it's time to open the gates for the judgment.

ROSE. Well, come on . . . I'll make up a batch of biscuits.

(ROSE *exits into the house.*)

GABRIEL. Troy . . . St. Peter got your name in the book. I seen it. It say . . . Troy Maxson. I say . . . I know him! He got the same name like what I got. That's my brother!

TROY. How many times you gonna tell me that, Gabe?

GABRIEL. Ain't got my name in the book. Don't have to have my name. I done died and went to heaven. He got your name though. One morning St. Peter was looking at his book . . . marking it up for the judgment . . . and he let me see your name. Got it in there under M. Got Rose's name . . . I ain't seen it like I seen yours . . . but I know it's in there. He got a great big book. Got everybody's name what was ever been born. That's what he told me. But I seen your name. Seen it with my own eyes.

TROY. Go on in the house there. Rose going to fix you something to eat.

GABRIEL. Oh, I ain't hungry. I done had breakfast with Aunt Jemimah. She come by and cooked me up a whole mess of flapjacks. Remember how we used to eat them flapjacks?

TROY. Go on in the house and get you something to eat now.

GABRIEL. I got to go sell my plums. I done sold some tomatoes. Got me two
  quarters. Wanna see?

(*He shows* TROY *his quarters.*)

I'm gonna save them and buy me a new horn so St. Peter can hear me when
it's time to open the gates.

(GABRIEL *stops suddenly. Listens.*)

Hear that? That's the hellhounds. I got to chase them out of here. Go on get
out of here! Get out!

(GABRIEL *exits singing.*)

Better get ready for the judgment
Better get ready for the judgment
My Lord is coming down

(ROSE *enters from the house.*)

TROY. He gone off somewhere.
GABRIEL (*Offstage*):
Better get ready for the judgment
Better get ready for the judgment morning
Better get ready for the judgment
My God is coming down
ROSE. He ain't eating right. Miss Pearl say she can't get him to eat nothing.
TROY. What you want me to do about it, Rose? I done did everything I can for
  the man. I can't make him get well. Man got half his head blown away . . .
  what you expect?
ROSE. Seem like something ought to be done to help him.
TROY. Man don't bother nobody. He just mixed up from that metal plate he
  got in his head. Ain't no sense for him to go back into the hospital.
ROSE. Least he be eating right. They can help him take care of himself.
TROY. Don't nobody wanna be locked up, Rose. What you wanna lock him
  up for? Man go over there and fight the war . . . messin' around with them
  Japs, get half his head blown off . . . and they give him a lousy three thou-
  sand dollars. And I had to swoop down on that.
ROSE. Is you fixing to go into that again?
TROY. That's the only way I got a roof over my head . . . cause of that metal plate.
ROSE. Ain't no sense you blaming yourself for nothing. Gabe wasn't in no condition to manage that money. You done what was right by him. Can't
  nobody say you ain't done what was right by him. Look how long you took
  care of him . . . till he wanted to have his own place and moved over there
  with Miss Pearl.

TROY. That ain't what I'm saying, woman! I'm just stating the facts. If my
  brother didn't have that metal plate in his head . . . I wouldn't have a pot
  to piss in or a window to throw it out of. And I'm fifty-three years old. Now
  see if you can understand that!

(TROY *gets up from the porch and starts to exit the yard.*)

ROSE. Where you going off to? You been running out of here every Saturday
  for weeks. I thought you was gonna work on this fence?
TROY. I'm gonna walk down to Taylors'. Listen to the ball game. I'll be back in
  a bit. I'll work on it when I get back.

(*He exits the yard. The lights go to black.*)

SCENE THREE

The lights come up on the yard. It is four hours later. ROSE *is taking down the
clothes from the line.* CORY *enters carrying his football equipment.*

ROSE. Your daddy like to had a fit with you running out of here this morning
  without doing your chores.
CORY. I told you I had to go to practice.
ROSE. He say you were supposed to help him with this fence.
CORY. He been saying that the last four or five Saturdays, and then he don't
  never do nothing, but go down to Taylors'. Did you tell him about the
  recruiter?
ROSE. Yeah, I told him.
CORY. What he say?
ROSE. He ain't said nothing too much. You get in there and get started on your
  chores before he gets back. Go on and scrub down them steps before he
  gets back here hollering and carrying on.
CORY. I'm hungry. What you got to eat, Mama?
ROSE. Go on and get started on your chores. I got some meat loaf in there.
  Go on and make you a sandwich . . . and don't leave no mess in there.

(CORY *exits into the house.* ROSE *continues to take down the clothes.* TROY *enters
the yard and sneaks up and grabs her from behind.*)

  Troy! Go on, now. You liked to scared me to death. What was the score of
  the game? Lucille had me on the phone and I couldn't keep up with it.
TROY. What I care about the game? Come here, woman. (*He tries to kiss her.*)
ROSE. I thought you went down Taylors' to listen to the game. Go on, Troy!
  You supposed to be putting up this fence.
TROY (*Attempting to kiss her again*). I'll put it up when I finish with what is at
  hand.

ROSE. Go on, Troy. I ain't studying you.

TROY (*Chasing after her*). I'm studying you . . . fixing to do my homework!

ROSE. Troy, you better leave me alone.

TROY. Where's Cory? That boy brought his butt home yet?

ROSE. He's in the house doing his chores.

TROY (*Calling*). Cory! Get your butt out here, boy!

(ROSE *exits into the house with the laundry.* TROY *goes over to the pile of wood, picks up a board, and starts sawing.* CORY *enters from the house.*)

TROY. You just now coming in here from leaving this morning?

CORY. Yeah, I had to go to football practice.

TROY. Yeah, what?

CORY. Yessir.

TROY. I ain't but two seconds off you noway. The garbage sitting in there over-flowing . . . you ain't done none of your chores . . . and you come in here talking about "Yeah."

CORY. I was just getting ready to do my chores now, Pop . . .

TROY. Your first chore is to help me with this fence on Saturday. Everything else come after that. Now get that saw and cut them boards.

(CORY *takes the saw and begins cutting the boards.* TROY *continues working. There is a long pause.*)

CORY. Hey, Pop . . . why don't you buy a TV?

TROY. What I want with a TV? What I want one of them for?

CORY. Everybody got one. Earl, Ba Bra . . . Jesse!

TROY. I ain't asked you who had one. I say what I want with one?

CORY. So you can watch it. They got lots of things on TV. Baseball games and everything. We could watch the World Series.

TROY. Yeah . . . and how much this TV cost?

CORY. I don't know. They got them on sale for around two hundred dollars.

TROY. Two hundred dollars, huh?

CORY. That ain't that much, Pop.

TROY. Naw, it's just two hundred dollars. See that roof you got over your head at night? Let me tell you something about that roof. It's been over ten years since that roof was last tarred. See now . . . the snow come this winter and sit up there on that roof like it is . . . and it's gonna seep inside. It's just gonna be a little bit . . . ain't gonna hardly notice it. Then the next thing you know, it's gonna be leaking all over the house. Then the wood rot from all that water and you gonna need a whole new roof. Now, how much you think it cost to get that roof tarred?

CORY. I don't know.

TROY. Two hundred and sixty-four dollars . . . cash money. While you thinking about a TV, I got to be thinking about the roof . . . and whatever else go wrong around here. Now if you had two hundred dollars, what would you do . . . fix the roof or buy a TV?

CORY. I'd buy a TV. Then when the roof started to leak . . . when it needed fixing . . . I'd fix it.

TROY. Where you gonna get the money from? You done spent it for a TV. You gonna sit up and watch the water run all over your brand new TV.

CORY. Aw, Pop. You got money. I know you do.

TROY. Where I got it at, huh?

CORY. You got it in the bank.

TROY. You wanna see my bankbook? You wanna see that seventy-three dollars and twenty-two cents I got sitting up in there.

CORY. You ain't got to pay for it all at one time. You can put a down payment on it and carry it on home with you.

TROY. Not me. I ain't gonna owe nobody nothing if I can help it. Miss a payment and they come and snatch it right out your house. Then what you got? Now, soon as I get two hundred dollars clear, then I'll buy a TV. Right now, as soon as I get two hundred and sixty-four dollars, I'm gonna have this roof tarred.

CORY. Aw . . . Pop!

TROY. You go on and get you two hundred dollars and buy one if ya want it. I got better things to do with my money.

CORY. I can't get no two hundred dollars. I ain't never seen two hundred dollars.

TROY. I'll tell you what . . . you get you a hundred dollars and I'll put the other hundred with it.

CORY. Alright, I'm gonna show you.

TROY. You gonna show me how you can cut them boards right now.

(CORY *begins to cut the boards. There is a long pause.*)

CORY. The Pirates won today. That makes five in a row.

TROY. I ain't thinking about the Pirates. Got an all-white team. Got that boy . . . that Puerto Rican boy . . . Clemente. Don't even half-play him. That boy could be something if they give him a chance. Play him one day and sit him on the bench the next.

CORY. He gets a lot of chances to play.

TROY. I'm talking about playing regular. Playing every day so you can get your timing. That's what I'm talking about.

CORY. They got some white guys on the team that don't play every day. You can't play everybody at the same time.

TROY. If they got a white fellow sitting on the bench . . . you can bet your last dollar he can't play! The colored guy got to be twice as good before he get on the team. Tha's why I don't want you to get all tied up in them sports. Man on the team and what it get him? They got colored on the team and don't use them. Same as not having them. All them teams the same.

CORY. The Braves got Hank Aaron and Wes Covington. Hank Aaron hit two home runs today. That makes forty-three.

TROY. Hank Aaron ain't nobody. That's what you supposed to do. That's how you supposed to play the game. Ain't nothing to it. It's just a matter of timing . . . getting the right follow-through. Hell, I can hit forty-three home runs right now!

CORY. Not off no major-league pitching, you couldn't.

TROY. We had better pitching in the Negro leagues. I hit seven home runs off of Satchel Paige. You can't get no better than that!

CORY. Sandy Koufax. He's leading the league in strike-outs.

TROY. I ain't thinking of no Sandy Koufax.

CORY. You got Warren Spahn and Lew Burdette. I bet you couldn't hit no home runs off of Warren Spahn.

TROY. I'm through with it now. You go on and cut them boards.

(*Pause.*)

Your mama tell me you done got recruited by a college football team? Is that right?

CORY. Yeah. Coach Zellman say the recruiter gonna be coming by to talk to you. Get you to sign the permission papers.

TROY. I thought you supposed to be working down there at the A&P. Ain't you suppose to be working down there after school?

CORY. Mr. Stawicki say he gonna hold my job for me until after the football season. Say starting next week I can work weekends.

TROY. I thought we had an understanding about this football stuff? You suppose to keep up with your chores and hold that job down at the A&P. Ain't been around here all day on a Saturday. Ain't none of your chores done . . . and now you telling me you done quit your job.

CORY. I'm gonna be working weekends.

TROY. You damn right you are! And ain't no need for nobody coming around here to talk to me about signing nothing.

CORY. Hey, Pop . . . you can't do that. He's coming all the way from North Carolina.

TROY. I don't care where he coming from. The white man ain't gonna let you get nowhere with that football noway. You go on and get your book-learning so you can work yourself up in that A&P or learn how to fix cars or build houses or something, get you a trade. That way you have something can't nobody take away from you. You go on and learn how to put your hands to some good use. Besides hauling people's garbage.

CORY. I get good grades, Pop. That's why the recruiter wants to talk with you. You got to keep up your grades to get recruited. This way I'll be going to college. I'll get a chance . . .

TROY. First you gonna get your butt down there to the A&P and get your job back.

CORY. Mr. Stawicki done already hired somebody else 'cause I told him I was playing football.

TROY. You a bigger fool than I thought . . . to let somebody take away your job so you can play some football. Where you gonna get your money to take out your girlfriend and whatnot? What kind of foolishness is that to let somebody take away your job?

CORY. I'm still gonna be working weekends.

TROY. Naw . . . naw. You getting your butt out of here and finding you another job.

CORY. Come on, Pop! I got to practice. I can't work after school and play football too. The team needs me. That's what Coach Zellman say . . .

TROY. I don't care what nobody else say. I'm the boss . . . you understand? I'm the boss around here. I do the only saying what counts.

CORY. Come on, Pop!

TROY. I asked you . . . did you understand?

CORY. Yeah . . .

TROY. What?!

CORY. Yessir.

TROY. You go on down there to that A&P and see if you can get your job back. If you can't do both . . . then you quit the football team. You've got to take the crookeds with the straights.

CORY. Yessir.

(Pause.)

Can I ask you a question?

TROY. What the hell you wanna ask me? Mr. Stawicki the one you got the questions for.

CORY. How come you ain't never liked me?

TROY. Liked you? Who the hell say I got to like you? What law is there say I got to like you? Wanna stand up in my face and ask a damn fool-ass question like that. Talking about liking somebody. Come here, boy, when I talk to you.

(CORY *comes over to where* TROY *is working. He stands slouched over and* TROY *shoves him on his shoulder.*)

Straighten up, goddammit! I asked you a question . . . what law is there say I got to like you?

CORY. None.

TROY. Well, alright then! Don't you eat every day?

(*Pause.*)

Answer me when I talk to you! Don't you eat every day?

CORY. Yeah.

TROY. Nigger, as long as you in my house, you put that sir on the end of it when you talk to me!

CORY. Yes . . . sir.

TROY. You eat every day.

CORY. Yessir!

TROY. Got a roof over your head.

CORY. Yessir!

TROY. Got clothes on your back.

CORY. Yessir.

TROY. Why you think that is?

CORY. Cause of you.

TROY. Aw, hell I know it's 'cause of me . . . but why do you think that is?

CORY (*Hesitant*). Cause you like me.

TROY. Like you? I go out of here every morning . . . bust my butt . . . putting up with them crackers every day . . . cause I like you? You about the biggest fool I ever saw.

(*Pause.*)

It's my job. It's my responsibility! You understand that? A man got to take care of his family. You live in my house . . . sleep you behind on my bedclothes . . . fill you belly up with my food . . . cause you my son. You my flesh and blood. Not 'cause I like you! Cause it's my duty to take care of you. I owe a responsibility to you!

Let's get this straight right here . . . before it go along any further . . . I ain't got to like you. Mr. Rand don't give me my money come payday cause he likes me. He gives me cause he owe me. I done give you everything I had to give you. I gave you your life! Me and your mama worked that out between us. And liking your black ass wasn't part of the bargain. Don't you try and go through life worrying about if somebody like you or not. You best be making sure they doing right by you. You understand what I'm saying, boy?

CORY. Yessir.

TROY. Then get the hell out of my face, and get on down to that A&P.

(ROSE *has been standing behind the screen door for much of the scene. She enters as* CORY *exits.*)

ROSE. Why don't you let the boy go ahead and play football, Troy? Ain't no harm in that. He's just trying to be like you with the sports.

TROY. I don't want him to be like me! I want him to move as far away from my life as he can get. You the only decent thing that ever happened to me. I wish him that. But I don't wish him a thing else from my life. I decided seventeen years ago that boy wasn't getting involved in no sports. Not after what they did to me in the sports.

ROSE. Troy, why don't you admit you was too old to play in the major leagues? For once . . . why don't you admit that?

TROY. What do you mean too old? Don't come telling me I was too old. I just wasn't the right color. Hell, I'm fifty-three years old and can do better than Selkirk's .269 right now!

ROSE. How's was you gonna play ball when you were over forty? Sometimes I can't get no sense out of you.

TROY. I got good sense, woman. I got sense enough not to let my boy get hurt over playing no sports. You been mothering that boy too much. Worried about if people like him.

ROSE. Everything that boy do . . . he do for you. He wants you to say "Good job, son." That's all.

TROY. Rose, I ain't got time for that. He's alive. He's healthy. He's got to make his own way. I made mine. Ain't nobody gonna hold his hand when he get out there in that world.

ROSE. Times have changed from when you was young, Troy. People change. The world's changing around you and you can't even see it.

TROY (*Slow, methodical*). Woman . . . I do the best I can do. I come in here every Friday. I carry a sack of potatoes and a bucket of lard. You all line up at the door with your hands out. I give you the lint from my pockets. I give you my sweat and my blood. I ain't got no tears. I done spent them. We go upstairs in that room at night . . . and I fall down on you and try to blast a hole into forever. I get up Monday morning . . . find my lunch on the table. I go out. Make my way. Find my strength to carry me through to the next Friday.

(*Pause.*)

That's all I got, Rose. That's all I got to give. I can't give nothing else.

(TROY *exits into the house. The lights go down to black.*)

SCENE FOUR

It is Friday. Two weeks later. CORY *starts out of the house with his football equipment. The phone rings.*

CORY (*Calling*). I got it!

(*He answers the phone and stands in the screen door talking.*)

Hello? Hey, Jesse. Naw . . . I was just getting ready to leave now.
ROSE (*Calling*). Cory!
CORY. I told you, man, them spikes is all tore up. You can use them if you want, but they ain't no good. Earl got some spikes.
ROSE (*Calling*). Cory!
CORY (*Calling to* ROSE). Mam? I'm talking to Jesse.

(*Into phone.*)

When she say that? (*Pause.*) Aw, you lying, man. I'm gonna tell her you said that.
ROSE (*Calling*). Cory, don't you go nowhere!
CORY. I got to go to the game, Ma!

(*Into the phone.*)

Yeah, hey, look, I'll talk to you later. Yeah, I'll meet you over Earl's house. Later. Bye, Ma.

(CORY *exits the house and starts out the yard.*)

ROSE. Cory, where you going off to? You got that stuff all pulled out and thrown all over your room.
CORY (*In the yard*). I was looking for my spikes. Jesse wanted to borrow my spikes.
ROSE. Get up there and get that cleaned up before your daddy get back in here.
CORY. I got to go to the game! I'll clean it up *when I get back.*

(CORY *exits.*)

ROSE. That's all he need to do is see that room all messed up.

(ROSE *exits into the house.* TROY *and* BONO *enter the yard.* TROY *is dressed in clothes other than his work clothes.*)

BONO. He told him the same thing he told you. Take it to the union.
TROY. Brownie ain't got that much sense. Man wasn't thinking about nothing. He wait until I confront them on it . . . then he wanna come crying seniority.
(*Calls.*)
Hey, Rose!
BONO. I wish I could have seen Mr. Rand's face when he told you.

TROY. He couldn't get it out of his mouth! Liked to bit his tongue! When they called me down there to the Commissioner's office . . . he thought they was gonna fire me. Like everybody else.

BONO. I didn't think they was gonna fire you. I thought they was gonna put you on the warning paper.

TROY. Hey, Rose!

(*To* BONO.)

Yeah, Mr. Rand like to bit his tongue.

(TROY *breaks the seal on the bottle, takes a drink, and hands it to* BONO.)

BONO. I see you run right down to Taylors' and told that Alberta gal.

TROY (*Calling*). Hey Rose! (*To* BONO.) I told everybody. Hey, Rose! I went down there to cash my check.

ROSE (*Entering from the house*). Hush all that hollering, man! I know you out here. What they say down there at the Commissioner's office?

TROY. You supposed to come when I call you, woman. Bono'll tell you that.

(*To* BONO.)

Don't Lucille come when you call her?

ROSE. Man, hush your mouth. I ain't no dog . . . talk about "come when you call me."

TROY (*Puts his arm around* ROSE). You hear this, Bono? I had me an old dog used to get uppity like that. You say, "C'mere, Blue!" . . . and he just lay there and look at you. End up getting a stick and chasing him away trying to make him come.

ROSE. I ain't studying you and your dog. I remember you used to sing that old song.

TROY (*He sings*). Hear it ring! Hear it ring! I had a dog his name was Blue.

ROSE. Don't nobody wanna hear you sing that old song.

TROY (*Sings*). You know Blue was mighty true.

ROSE. Used to have Cory running around here singing that song.

BONO. Hell, I remember that song myself.

TROY (*Sings*). You know Blue was a good old dog. Blue treed a possum in a hollow log.

That was my daddy's song. My daddy made up that song.

ROSE. I don't care who made it up. Don't nobody wanna hear you sing it.

TROY (*Makes a song like calling a dog*). Come here, woman.

ROSE. You come in here carrying on, I reckon they ain't fired you. What they say down there at the Commissioner's office?

TROY. Look here, Rose . . . Mr. Rand called me into his office today when I got back from talking to them people down there . . . it come from up top . . . he called me in and told me they was making me a driver.

ROSE. Troy, you kidding!

TROY. No I ain't. Ask Bono.

ROSE. Well, that's great, Troy. Now you don't have to hassle them people no more.

(LYONS *enters from the street.*)

TROY. Aw hell, I wasn't looking to see you today. I thought you was in jail. Got it all over the front page of the *Courier* about them raiding Sefus' place . . . where you be hanging out with all them thugs.

LYONS. Hey, Pop . . . that ain't got nothing to do with me. I don't go down there gambling. I go down there to sit in with the band. I ain't got nothing to do with the gambling part. They got some good music down there.

TROY. They got some rogues . . . is what they got.

LYONS. How you been, Mr. Bono? Hi, Rose.

BONO. I see where you playing down at the Crawford Grill tonight.

ROSE. How come you ain't brought Bonnie like I told you. You should have brought Bonnie with you, she ain't been over in a month of Sundays.

LYONS. I was just in the neighborhood . . . thought I'd stop by.

TROY. Here he come . . .

BONO. Your daddy got a promotion on the rubbish. He's gonna be the first colored driver. Ain't got to do nothing but sit up there and read the paper like them white fellows.

LYONS. Hey, Pop . . . if you knew how to read you'd be alright.

BONO. Naw . . . naw . . . you mean if the nigger knew how to *drive* he'd be all right. Been fighting with them people about driving and ain't even got a license. Mr. Rand know you ain't got no driver's license?

TROY. Driving ain't nothing. All you do is point the truck where you want it to go. Driving ain't nothing.

BONO. Do Mr. Rand know you ain't got no driver's license? That's what I'm talking about. I ain't asked if driving was easy. I asked if Mr. Rand know you ain't got no driver's license.

TROY. He ain't got to know. The man ain't got to know my business. Time he find out, I have two or three driver's licenses.

LYONS (*Going into his pocket*). Say, look here, Pop . . .

TROY. I knew it was coming. Didn't I tell you, Bono? I know what kind of "Look here, Pop" that was. The nigger fixing to ask me for some money. It's Friday night. It's my payday. All them rogues down there on the avenue . . . the ones that ain't in jail . . . and Lyons is hopping in his shoes to get down there with them.

LYONS. See, Pop . . . if you give somebody else a chance to talk sometime, you'd see that I was fixing to pay you back your ten dollars like I told you. Here . . . I told you I'd pay you when Bonnie got paid.

TROY. Naw . . . you go ahead and keep that ten dollars. Put it in the bank. The next time you feel like you wanna come by here and ask me for something . . . you go on down there and get that.

LYONS. Here's your ten dollars, Pop. I told you I don't want you to give me nothing. I just wanted to borrow ten dollars.

TROY. Naw . . . you go on and keep that for the next time you want to ask me.

LYONS. Come on, Pop . . . here go your ten dollars.

ROSE. Why don't you go on and let the boy pay you back, Troy?

LYONS. Here you go, Rose. If you don't take it I'm gonna have to hear about it for the next six months.

(*He hands her the money.*)

ROSE. You can hand yours over here too, Troy.

TROY. You see this, Bono. You see how they do me.

BONO. Yeah, Lucille do me the same way.

(GABRIEL *is heard singing offstage. He enters.*)

GABRIEL. Better get ready for the Judgment! Better get ready for . . . Hey! . . . Hey! . . . There's Troy's boy!

LYONS. How you doing, Uncle Gabe?

GABRIEL. Lyons . . . The King of the Jungle! Rose . . . hey, Rose. Got a flower for you.

(*He takes a rose from his pocket.*)

Picked it myself. That's the same rose like you is!

ROSE. That's right nice of you, Gabe.

LYONS. What you been doing, Uncle Gabe?

GABRIEL. Oh, I been chasing hellhounds and waiting on the time to tell St. Peter to open the gates.

LYONS. You been chasing hellhounds, huh? Well . . . you doing the right thing, Uncle Gabe. Somebody got to chase them.

GABRIEL. Oh, yeah . . . I know it. The devil's strong. The devil ain't no pushover. Hellhounds snipping at everybody's heels. But I got my trumpet waiting on the judgment time.

LYONS. Waiting on the Battle of Armageddon, huh?

GABRIEL. Ain't gonna be too much of a battle when God get to waving that Judgment sword. But the people's gonna have a hell of a time trying to get into heaven if them gates ain't open.

LYONS (*Putting his arm around* GABRIEL). You hear this, Pop. Uncle Gabe, you alright!

GABRIEL (*Laughing with* LYONS). Lyons! King of the Jungle.

ROSE. You gonna stay for supper, Gabe. Want me to fix you a plate?

GABRIEL. I'll take a sandwich, Rose. Don't want no plate. Just wanna eat with my hands. I'll take a sandwich.

ROSE. How about you, Lyons? You staying? Got some short ribs cooking.

LYONS. Naw, I won't eat nothing till after we finished playing.

(Pause.)

You ought to come down and listen to me play, Pop.

TROY. I don't like that Chinese music. All that noise.

ROSE. Go on in the house and wash up, Gabe . . . I'll fix you a sandwich.

GABRIEL *(To* LYONS, *as he exits).* Troy's mad at me.

LYONS. What you mad at Uncle Gabe for, Pop.

ROSE. He thinks Troy's mad at him cause he moved over to Miss Pearl's.

TROY. I ain't mad at the man. He can live where he want to live at.

LYONS. What he move over there for? Miss Pearl don't like nobody.

ROSE. She don't mind him none. She treats him real nice. She just don't allow all that singing.

TROY. She don't mind that rent he be paying . . . that's what she don't mind.

ROSE. Troy, I ain't going through that with you no more. He's over there cause he want to have his own place. He can come and go as he please.

TROY. Hell, he could come and go as he please here. I wasn't stopping him. I ain't put no rules on him.

ROSE. It ain't the same thing, Troy. And you know it.

*(*GABRIEL *comes to the door.)*

Now, that's the last I wanna hear about that. I don't wanna hear nothing else about Gabe and Miss Pearl. And next week . . .

GABRIEL. I'm ready for my sandwich, Rose.

ROSE. And next week . . . when that recruiter come from that school . . . I want you to sign that paper and go on and let Cory play football. Then that'll be the last I have to hear about that.

TROY *(To* ROSE *as she exits into the house).* I ain't thinking about Cory nothing.

LYONS. What . . . Cory got recruited? What school he going to?

TROY. That boy walking around here smelling his piss . . . thinking he's grown. Thinking he's gonna do what he want, irrespective of what I say. Look here, Bono . . . I left the Commissioner's office and went down to the A&P . . . that boy ain't working down there. He lying to me. Telling me he got his job back . . . telling me he working weekends . . . telling me he working after school . . . Mr. Stawicki tell me he ain't working down there at all!

LYONS. Cory just growing up. He's just busting at the seams trying to fill out your shoes.

TROY. I don't care what he's doing. When he get to the point where he wanna disobey me . . . then it's time for him to move on. Bono'll tell you that. I bet he ain't never disobeyed his daddy without paying the consequences.

BONO. I ain't never had a chance. My daddy came on through . . . but I ain't never knew him to see him . . . or what he had on his mind or where he went. Just moving on through. Searching out the New Land. That's what the old folks used to call it. See a fellow moving around from place to place . . . woman to woman . . . called it searching out the New Land. I can't say if he ever found it. I come along, didn't want no kids. Didn't know if I was gonna be in one place long enough to fix on them right as their daddy. I figured I was going searching too. As it turned out I been hooked up with Lucille near about as long as your daddy been with Rose. Going on sixteen years.

TROY. Sometimes I wish I hadn't known my daddy. He ain't cared nothing about no kids. A kid to him wasn't nothing. All he wanted was for you to learn how to walk so he could start you to working. When it come time for eating . . . he ate first. If there was anything left over, that's what you got. Man would sit down and eat two chickens and give you the wing.

LYONS. You ought to stop that, Pop. Everybody feed their kids. No matter how hard times is . . . everybody care about their kids. Make sure they have something to eat.

TROY. The only thing my daddy cared about was getting them bales of cotton in to Mr. Lubin. That's the only thing that mattered to him. Sometimes I used to wonder why he was living. Wonder why the devil hadn't come and got him. "Get them bales of cotton in to Mr. Lubin" and find out he owe him money . . .

LYONS. He should have just went on and left when he saw he couldn't get nowhere. That's what I would have done.

TROY. How he gonna leave with eleven kids? And where he gonna go? He ain't knew how to do nothing but farm. No, he was trapped and I think he knew it. But I'll say this for him . . . he felt a responsibility toward us. Maybe he ain't treated us the way I felt he should have . . . but without that responsibility he could have walked off and left us . . . made his own way.

BONO. A lot of them did. Back in those days what you talking about . . . they walk out their front door and just take on down one road or another and keep on walking.

LYONS. There you go! That's what I'm talking about.

BONO. Just keep on walking till you come to something else. Ain't you never heard of nobody having the walking blues? Well, that's what you call it when you just take off like that.

TROY. My daddy ain't had them walking blues! What you talking about? He stayed right there with his family. But he was just as evil as he could be. My mama couldn't stand him. Couldn't stand that evilness. She run off when I was about eight. She sneaked off one night after he had gone to sleep.

Told me she was coming back for me. I ain't never seen her no more. All his women run off and left him. He wasn't good for nobody.

When my turn come to head out, I was fourteen and got to sniffing around Joe Canewell's daughter. Had us an old mule we called Greyboy. My daddy sent me out to do some plowing and I tied up Greyboy and went to fooling around with Joe Canewell's daughter. We done found us a nice little spot, got real cozy with each other. She about thirteen and we done figured we was grown anyway . . . so we down there enjoying ourselves . . . ain't thinking about nothing. We didn't know Greyboy had got loose and wandered back to the house and my daddy was looking for me. We down there by the creek enjoying ourselves when my daddy come up on us. Surprised us. He had them leather straps off the mule and commenced to whupping me like there was no tomorrow. I jumped up, mad and embarrassed. I was scared of my daddy. When he commenced to whupping on me . . . quite naturally I run to get out of the way.

(Pause.)

Now I thought he was mad cause I ain't done my work. But I see where he was chasing me off so he could have the gal for himself. When I see what the matter of it was, I lost all fear of my daddy. Right there is where I become a man . . . at fourteen years of age.

(Pause.)

Now it was my turn to run him off. I picked up them same reins that he had used on me. I picked up them reins and commenced to whupping on him. The gal jumped up and run off . . . and when my daddy turned to face me, I could see why the devil had never come to get him . . . cause he was the devil himself. I don't know what happened. When I woke up, I was laying right there by the creek, and Blue . . . this old dog we had . . . was licking my face. I thought I was blind. I couldn't see nothing. Both my eyes were swollen shut. I layed there and cried. I didn't know what I was gonna do. The only thing I knew was the time had come for me to leave my daddy's house. And right there the world suddenly got big. And it was a long time before I could cut it down to where I could handle it.

Part of that cutting down was when I got to the place where I could feel him kicking in my blood and knew that the only thing that separated us was the matter of a few years.

(GABRIEL *enters from the house with a sandwich.*)

LYONS. What you got there, Uncle Gabe?

GABRIEL. Got me a ham sandwich. Rose gave me a ham sandwich.

TROY. I don't know what happened to him. I done lost touch with everybody except Gabriel. But I hope he's dead. I hope he found some peace.

LYONS. That's a heavy story, Pop. I didn't know you left home when you was fourteen.

TROY. And didn't know nothing. The only part of the world I knew was the forty-two acres of Mr. Lubin's land. That's all I knew about life.

LYONS. Fourteen's kinda young to be out on your own. (*Phone rings.*) I don't even think I was ready to be out on my own at fourteen. I don't know what I would have done.

TROY. I got up from the creek and walked on down to Mobile. I was through with farming. Figured I could do better in the city. So I walked the two hundred miles to Mobile.

LYONS. Wait a minute . . . you ain't walked no two hundred miles, Pop. Ain't nobody gonna walk no two hundred miles. You talking about some walking there.

BONO. That's the only way you got anywhere back in them days.

LYONS. Shhh. Damn if I wouldn't have hitched a ride with somebody!

TROY. Who you gonna hitch it with? They ain't had no cars and things like they got now. We talking about 1918.

ROSE (*Entering*). What you all out here getting into?

TROY (*To* ROSE). I'm telling Lyons how good he got it. He don't know nothing about this I'm talking.

ROSE. Lyons, that was Bonnie on the phone. She say you supposed to pick her up.

LYONS. Yeah, okay, Rose.

TROY. I walked on down to Mobile and hitched up with some of them fellows that was heading this way. Got up here and found out . . . not only couldn't you get a job . . . you couldn't find no place to live. I thought I was in freedom. Shhh. Colored folks living down there on the riverbanks in whatever kind of shelter they could find for themselves. Right down there under the Brady Street Bridge. Living in shacks made of sticks and tarpaper. Messed around there and went from bad to worse. Started stealing. First it was food. Then I figured, hell, if I steal money I can buy me some food. Buy me some shoes too! One thing led to another. Met your mama. I was young and anxious to be a man. Met your mama and had you. What I do that for? Now I got to worry about feeding you and her. Got to steal three times as much. Went out one day looking for somebody to rob . . . that's what I was, a robber. I'll tell you the truth. I'm ashamed of it today. But it's the truth. Went to rob this fellow . . . pulled out my knife . . . and he pulled out a gun. Shot me in the chest. It felt just like somebody had taken a hot branding iron and laid it on me. When he shot me I jumped at him with my knife. They told me I killed him and they put me in the penitentiary and locked me up for fifteen years. That's where I met Bono. That's where I learned how to play baseball. Got out that place and your mama had taken you and went on to make life without me. Fifteen years was a long time for her to wait. But that fifteen years cured me of that robbing stuff. Rose'll tell you. She asked me when I met her if I had gotten all that foolishness out of my system. And I told her, "Baby, it's you and baseball all what count with me." You hear me, Bono? I meant it too. She say, "Which one comes first?" I told her, "Baby, ain't no doubt it's baseball . . . but you stick and get old with me and we'll both outlive this baseball." Am I right, Rose? And it's true.

ROSE. Man, hush your mouth. You ain't said no such thing. Talking about, "Baby, you know you'll always be number one with me." That's what you was talking.

TROY. You hear that, Bono. That's why I love her.

BONO. Rose'll keep you straight. You get off the track, she'll straighten you up.

ROSE. Lyons, you better get on up and get Bonnie. She waiting on you.

LYONS (*Gets up to go*). Hey, Pop, why don't you come on down to the Grill and hear me play?

TROY. I ain't going down there. I'm too old to be sitting around in them clubs.

BONO. You got to be good to play down at the Grill.

LYONS. Come on, Pop . . .

TROY. I got to get up in the morning.

LYONS. You ain't got to stay long.

TROY. Naw, I'm gonna get my supper and go on to bed.

LYONS. Well, I got to go. I'll see you again.

TROY. Don't you come around my house on my payday.

ROSE. Pick up the phone and let somebody know you coming. And bring Bonnie with you. You know I'm always glad to see her.

LYONS. Yeah, I'll do that, Rose. You take care now. See you, Pop. See you, Mr. Bono. See you, Uncle Gabe.

GABRIEL. Lyons! King of the Jungle!

(LYONS *exits.*)

TROY. Is supper ready, woman? Me and you got some business to take care of. I'm gonna tear it up too.

ROSE. Troy, I done told you now!

TROY. (*Puts his arm around* BONO). Aw hell, woman . . . this is Bono. Bono like family. I done known this nigger since . . . how long I done know you?

BONO. It's been a long time.

TROY. I done known this nigger since Skippy was a pup. Me and him done been through some times.

608

BONO. You sure right about that.

TROY. Hell, I done know him longer than I known you. And we still standing shoulder to shoulder. Hey, look here, Bono . . . a man can't ask for no more than that.

(Drinks to him.)

I love you, nigger.

BONO. Hell, I love you too . . . but I got to get home see my woman. You got yours in hand. I got to go get mine.

*(*BONO *starts to exit as* CORY *enters the yard, dressed in his football uniform. He gives* TROY *a hard, uncompromising look.)*

CORY. What you do that for, Pop?

(He throws his helmet down in the direction of TROY.*)*

ROSE. What's the matter? Cory . . . what's the matter?

CORY. Papa done went up to the school and told Coach Zellman I can't play football no more. Wouldn't even let me play the game. Told him to tell the recruiter not to come.

ROSE. Troy . . .

TROY. What you Troying me for. Yeah, I did it. And the boy know why I did it.

CORY. Why you wanna do that to me? That was the one chance I had.

ROSE. Ain't nothing wrong with Cory playing football, Troy.

TROY. The boy lied to me. I told the nigger if he wanna play football . . . to keep up his chores and hold down that job at the A&P. That was the conditions. Stopped down there to see Mr. Stawicki . . .

CORY. I can't work after school during the football season, Pop! I tried to tell you that Mr. Stawicki's holding my job for me. You don't never want to listen to nobody. And then you wanna go and do this to me!

TROY. I ain't done nothing to you. You done it to yourself.

CORY. Just cause you didn't have a chance! You just scared I'm gonna be better than you, that's all.

TROY. Come here.

ROSE. Troy . . .

*(*CORY *reluctantly crosses over to* TROY.*)*

TROY. Alright! See. You done made a mistake.

CORY. I didn't even do nothing!

TROY. I'm gonna tell you what your mistake was. See . . . you swung at the ball and didn't hit it. That's strike one. See, you in the batter's box now. You swung and you missed. That's strike one. Don't you strike out!

(Lights fade to black.)

ACT II

SCENE ONE

The following morning. CORY *is at the tree hitting the ball with the bat. He tries to mimic* TROY, *but his swing is awkward, less sure.* ROSE *enters from the house.*

ROSE. Cory, I want you to help me with this cupboard.

CORY. I ain't quitting the team. I don't care what Poppa say.

ROSE. I'll talk to him when he gets back. He had to go see about your Uncle Gabe. The police done arrested him. Say he was disturbing the peace. He'll be back directly. Come on in here and help me clean out the top of this cupboard.

(CORY *exits into the house.* ROSE *sees* TROY *and* BONO *coming down the alley.*)

Troy . . . what they say down there?

TROY. Ain't said nothing. I give them fifty dollars and they let him go. I'll talk to you about it. Where's Cory?

ROSE. He's in there helping me clean out these cupboards.

TROY. Tell him to get his butt out here.

(TROY *and* BONO *go over to the pile of wood.* BONO *picks up the saw and begins sawing.*)

TROY (*To* BONO). All they want is the money. That makes six or seven times I done went down there and got him. See me coming they stick out their *hands.*

BONO. Yeah. I know what you mean. That's all they care about . . . that money. They don't care about what's right.

(*Pause.*)

Nigger, why you got to go and get some hard wood? You ain't doing nothing but building a little old fence. Get you some soft pine wood. That's all you need.

TROY. I know what I'm doing. This is outside wood. You put pine wood inside the house. Pine wood is inside wood. This here is outside wood. Now you tell me where the fence is gonna be?

BONO. You don't need this wood. You can put it up with pine wood and it'll stand as long as you gonna be here looking at it.

TROY. How you know how long I'm gonna be here, nigger? Hell, I might just live forever. Live longer than old man Horsely.

BONO. That's what Magee used to say.

TROY. Magee's a damn fool. Now you tell me who you ever heard of gonna pull their own teeth with a pair of rusty pliers.

BONO. The old folks . . . my granddaddy used to pull his teeth with pliers. They ain't had no dentists for the colored folks back then.

TROY. Get clean pliers! You understand? Clean pliers! Sterilize them! Besides we ain't living back then. All Magee had to do was walk over to Doc Goldblums.

BONO. I see where you and that Tallahassee gal . . . that Alberta . . . I see where you all done got tight.

TROY. What you mean "got tight"?

BONO. I see where you be laughing and joking with her all the time.

TROY. I laughs and jokes with all of them, Bono. You know me.

BONO. That ain't the kind of laughing and joking I'm talking about.

(CORY *enters from the house.*)

CORY. How you doing, Mr. Bono?

TROY. Cory? Get that saw from Bono and cut some wood. He talking about the wood's too hard to cut. Stand back there, Jim, and let that young boy show you how it's done.

BONO. He's sure welcome to it.

(CORY *takes the saw and begins to cut the wood.*)

Whew-e-e! Look at that. Big old strong boy. Look like Joe Louis.[1] Hell, must be getting old the way I'm watching that boy whip through that wood.

CORY. I don't see why Mama want a fence around the yard noways.

TROY. Damn if I know either. What the hell she keeping out with it? She ain't got nothing nobody want.

BONO. Some people build fences to keep people out . . . and other people build fences to keep people in. Rose wants to hold on to you all. She loves you.

TROY. Hell, nigger, I don't need nobody to tell me my wife loves me, Cory . . . go on in the house and see if you can find that other saw.

CORY. Where's it at?

TROY. I said find it! Look for it till you find it!

(CORY *exits into the house.*)

What's that supposed to mean? Wanna keep us in?

BONO. Troy . . . I done known you seem like damn near my whole life. You and Rose both. I done know both of you all for a long time. I remember when you met Rose. When you was hitting them baseball out the park. A lot of them old gals was after you then. You had the pick of the litter. When you picked Rose, I was happy for you. That was the first time I knew you had any sense. I said . . . My man Troy knows what he's doing . . . I'm gonna follow this nigger . . . he might take me somewhere. I been following you too. I done learned a whole heap of things about life watching you. I done learned how to tell where the shit lies. How to tell it from the alfalfa. You done learned me a lot of things. You showed me how to not make the same

---

[1] Joe Louis: popular African-American boxer

mistakes . . . to take life as it comes along and keep putting one foot in front of the other.

(Pause.)

Rose a good woman, Troy.

TROY. Hell, nigger, I know she a good woman. I been married to her for eighteen years. What you got on your mind, Bono?

BONO. I just say she a good woman. Just like I say anything. I ain't got to have nothing on my mind.

TROY. You just gonna say she a good woman and leave it hanging out there like that? Why you telling me she a good woman?

BONO. She loves you, Troy. Rose loves you.

TROY. You saying I don't measure up. That's what you trying to say. I don't measure up cause I'm seeing this other gal. I know what you trying to say.

BONO. I know what Rose means to you, Troy. I'm just trying to say I don't want to see you mess up.

TROY. Yeah, I appreciate that, Bono. If you was messing around on Lucille I'd be telling you the same thing.

BONO. Well, that's all I got to say. I just say that because I love you both.

TROY. Hell, you know me . . . I wasn't out there looking for nothing. You can't find a better woman than Rose. I know that. But seems like this woman just stuck onto me where I can't shake her loose. I done wrestled with it, tried to throw her off me . . . but she just stuck on tighter. Now she's stuck on for good.

BONO. You's in control . . . that's what you tell me all the time. You responsible for what you do.

TROY. I ain't ducking the responsibility of it. As long as it sets right in my heart . . . then I'm okay. Cause that's all I listen to. It'll tell me right from wrong every time. And I ain't talking about doing Rose no bad turn. I love Rose. She done carried me a long ways and I love and respect her for that.

BONO. I know you do. That's why I don't want to see you hurt her. But what you gonna do when she find out? What you got then? If you try and juggle both of them . . . sooner or later you gonna drop one of them. That's common sense.

TROY. Yeah, I hear what you saying, Bono. I been trying to figure a way to work it out.

BONO. Work it out right, Troy. I don't want to be getting all up between you and Rose's business . . . but work it so it come out right.

TROY. Aw hell, I get all up between you and Lucille's business. When you gonna get that woman that refrigerator she been wanting? Don't tell me you ain't got no money now. I know who your banker is. Mellon[2] don't need that money bad as Lucille want that refrigerator. I'll tell you that.

---

[2] Melon: Andrew Mellon, famous banker and multi-millonaire

BONO. Tell you what I'll do . . . when you finish building this fence for Rose . . .
I'll buy Lucille that refrigerator.

TROY. You done stuck your foot in your mouth now!

(TROY *grabs up a board and begins to saw.* BONO *starts to walk out the yard.*)

Hey, nigger . . . where you going?

BONO. I'm going home. I know you don't expect me to help you now. I'm pro-
tecting my money. I wanna see you put that fence up by yourself. That's
what I want to see. You'll be here another six months without me.

TROY. Nigger, you ain't right.

BONO. When it comes to my money . . . I'm right as fire-works on the Fourth
of July.

TROY. Alright, we gonna see now. You better get out your bankbook.

(BONO *exits, and* TROY *continues to work.* ROSE *enters from the house.*)

ROSE. What they say down there? What's happening with Gabe?

TROY. I went down there and got him out. Cost me fifty dollars. Say he was
disturbing the peace. Judge set up a hearing for him in three weeks. Say to
show cause why he shouldn't be re-committed.

ROSE. What was he doing that cause them to arrest him?

TROY. Some kids was teasing him and he run them off home. Say he was howling and carrying on. Some folks seen him and called the police. That's all
it was.

ROSE. Well, what's you say? What'd you tell the judge?

TROY. Told him I'd look after him. It didn't make no sense to recommit the
man. He stuck out his big greasy palm and told me to give him fifty dollars and take him on home.

ROSE. Where's he at now? Where'd he go off to?

TROY. He's gone on about his business. He don't need nobody to hold his hand.

ROSE. Well, I don't know. Seem like that would be the best place for him if they
did put him into the hospital. I know what you're gonna say. But that's
what I think would be best.

TROY. The man done had his life ruined fighting for what? And they wanna
take and lock him up. Let him be free. He don't bother nobody.

ROSE. Well, everybody got their own way of looking at it I guess. Come on
and get your lunch. I got a bowl of lima beans and some cornbread in the
oven. Come on get something to eat. Ain't no sense you fretting over Gabe.
(ROSE *turns to go into the house.*)

TROY. Rose . . . got something to tell you.

ROSE. Well, come on . . . wait till I get this food on the table.

TROY. Rose!

(She stops and turns around.)

I don't know how to say this.

(Pause.)

I can't explain it none. It just sort of grows on you till it gets out of hand. It starts out like a little bush . . . and the next think you know it's a whole forest.

ROSE. Troy . . . what is you talking about?

TROY. I'm talking, woman, let me talk. I'm trying to find a way to tell you . . . I'm gonna be a daddy. I'm gonna be somebody's daddy.

ROSE. Troy . . . you're not telling me this? You're gonna be . . . what?

TROY. Rose . . . now . . . see . . .

ROSE. You telling me you gonna be somebody's daddy? You telling your *wife* this?

(GABRIEL enters from the street. He carries a rose in his hand.)

GABRIEL. Hey, Troy! Hey, Rose!

ROSE. I have to wait eighteen years to hear something like this.

GABRIEL. Hey, Rose . . . I got a flower for you.

(He hands it to her.)

That's a rose. Same rose like you is.

ROSE. Thanks, Gabe.

GABRIEL. Troy, you ain't mad at me is you? Them bad mens come and put me away. You ain't mad at me is you?

TROY. Naw, Gabe, I ain't mad at you.

ROSE. Eighteen years and you wanna come with this.

GABRIEL *(Takes a quarter out of his pocket)*. See what I got? Got a brand new quarter.

TROY. Rose . . . it's just . . .

ROSE. Ain't nothing you can say, Troy. Ain't no way of explaining that.

GABRIEL. Fellow that give me this quarter had a whole mess of them. I'm gonna keep this quarter till it stop shining.

ROSE. Gabe, go on in the house there. I got some watermelon in the frigidaire. Go on and get you a piece.

GABRIEL. Say, Rose . . . you know I was chasing hellhounds and them bad mens come and get me and take me away. Troy helped me. He come down there and told them they better let me go before he beat them up. Yeah, he did!

ROSE. You go on and get you a piece of watermelon, Gabe. Them bad mens is gone now.

GABRIEL. Okay, Rose . . . gonna get me some watermelon. The kind with the stripes on it.

(GABRIEL exits into the house.)

ROSE. Why, Troy? Why? After all these years to come dragging this in to me now. It don't make no sense at your age. I could have expected this ten or fifteen years ago, but not now.

TROY. Age ain't got nothing to do with it, Rose.

ROSE. I done tried to be everything a wife should be. Everything a wife could be. Been married eighteen years and I got to live to see the day you tell me you been seeing another woman and done fathered a child by her. And you know I ain't never wanted no half nothing in my family. My whole family is half. Everybody got different fathers and mothers . . . my two sisters and my brother. Can't hardly tell who's who. Can't never sit down and talk about Papa and Mama. It's your papa and your mama and my papa and my mama . . .

TROY. Rose . . . stop it now.

ROSE. I ain't never wanted that for none of my children. And now you wanna drag your behind in here and tell me something like this.

TROY. You ought to know. It's time for you to know.

ROSE. Well, I don't want to know, goddamn it!

TROY. I can't just make it go away. It's done now. I can't wish the circumstance of the thing away.

ROSE. And you don't want to either. Maybe you want to wish me and my boy away. Maybe that's what you want? Well, you can't wish us away. I've got eighteen years of my life invested in you. You ought to have stayed upstairs in my bed where you belong.

TROY. Rose . . . now listen to me . . . we can get a handle on this thing. We can talk this out . . . come to an understanding.

ROSE. All of a sudden it's "we." Where was "we" at when you was down there rolling around with some godforsaken woman? "We" should have come to an understanding before you started making a damn fool of yourself. You're a day late and a dollar short when it comes to an understanding with me.

TROY. It's just . . . She gives me a different idea . . . a different understanding about myself. I can step out of this house and get away from the pressures and problems . . . be a different man. I ain't got to wonder how I'm gonna pay the bills or get the roof fixed. I can just be a part of myself that I ain't never been.

ROSE. What I want to know . . . is do you plan to continue seeing her. That's all you can say to me.

TROY. I can sit up in her house and laugh. Do you understand what I'm saying. I can laugh out loud . . . and it feels good. It reaches all the way down to the bottom of my shoes.

(Pause.)

Rose, I can't give that up.

ROSE. Maybe you ought to go on and stay down there with her . . . if she a better woman than me.

TROY. It ain't about nobody being a better woman or nothing. Rose, you ain't the blame. A man couldn't ask for no woman to be a better wife than you've been. I'm responsible for it. I done locked myself into a pattern trying to take care of you all that I forgot about myself.

ROSE. What the hell was I there for? That was my job, not somebody else's.

TROY. Rose, I done tried all my life to live decent . . . to live a clean . . . hard . . . useful life. I tried to be a good husband to you. In every way I knew how. Maybe I come into the world backwards, I don't know. But . . . you born with two strikes on you before you come to the plate. You got to guard it closely . . . always looking for the curve-ball on the inside corner. You can't afford to let none get past you. You can't afford a call strike. If you going down . . . you going down swinging. Everything lined up against you. What you gonna do. I fooled them, Rose. I bunted. When I found you and Cory and a halfway decent job . . . I was safe. Couldn't nothing touch me. I wasn't gonna strike out no more. I wasn't going back to the penitentiary. I wasn't gonna lay in the streets with a bottle of wine. I was safe. I had me a family. A job. I wasn't gonna get that last strike. I was on first looking for one of them boys to knock me in. To get me home.

ROSE. You should have stayed in my bed, Troy.

TROY. Then when I saw that gal . . . she firmed up my backbone. And I got to thinking that if I tried . . . I just might be able to steal second. Do you understand after eighteen years I wanted to steal second.

ROSE. You should have held me tight. You should have grabbed me and held on.

TROY. I stood on first base for eighteen years and I thought . . . well, goddamn it . . . go on for it!

ROSE. We're not talking about baseball! We're talking about you going off to lay in bed with another woman . . . and then bring it home to me. That's what we're talking about. We ain't talking about no baseball.

TROY. Rose, you're not listening to me. I'm trying the best I can to explain it to you. It's not easy for me to admit that I been standing in the same place for eighteen years.

ROSE. I been standing with you! I been right here with you, Troy. I got a life too. I gave eighteen years of my life to stand in the same spot with you. Don't you think I ever wanted other things? Don't you think I had dreams and hopes? What about my life? What about me. Don't you think it ever crossed my mind to want to know other men? That I wanted to lay up somewhere and forget about my responsibilities? That I wanted someone to make me laugh so I could feel good? You not the only one who's got wants and needs. But I held on to you, Troy. I took all my feelings, my wants and needs, my dreams . . . and I buried them inside you. I planted a seed and watched and prayed over it. I planted myself inside you and waited to bloom. And it didn't take me no eighteen years to find out the soil was hard and rocky and it wasn't never gonna bloom.

But I held on to you, Troy. I held you tighter. You was my husband. I owed you everything I had. Every part of me I could find to give you. And upstairs in that room . . . with the darkness falling in on me . . . I gave everything I had to try and erase the doubt that you wasn't the finest man in the world. And wherever you was going . . . I wanted to be there with you. Cause you was my husband. Cause that's the only way I was gonna survive as your wife. You always talking about what you give . . . and what you don't have to give. But you take too. You take . . . and don't even know nobody's giving!

(ROSE *turns to exit into the house;* TROY *grabs her arm.*)

TROY. You say I take and don't give!
ROSE. Troy! You're hurting me!
TROY. You say I take and don't give.
ROSE. Troy . . . you're hurting my arm! Let go!
TROY. I done give you everything I got. Don't you tell that lie on me.
ROSE. Troy!
TROY. Don't you tell that lie on me!

(CORY *enters from the house.*)

CORY. Mama!
ROSE. Troy. You're hurting me.
TROY. Don't you tell me about no taking and giving.

(CORY *comes up behind* TROY *and grabs him.* TROY, *surprised, is thrown off balance just as* CORY *throws a glancing blow that catches him on the chest and knocks him down.* TROY *is stunned, as is* CORY.)

ROSE. Troy. Troy. No!
(TROY *gets to his feet and starts at* CORY.)
   Troy . . . no. Please! Troy!

(ROSE *pulls on* TROY *to hold him back.* TROY *stops himself.*)

TROY (*To* CORY). Alright. That's strike two. You stay away from around me, boy. Don't you strike out. You living with a full count. Don't you strike out.

(TROY *exits out the yard as the lights go down.*)

SCENE TWO

It is six months later, early afternoon. TROY *enters from the house and starts to exit the yard.* ROSE *enters from the house.*

ROSE. Troy, I want to talk to you.

TROY. All of a sudden, after all this time, you want to talk to me, huh? You ain't wanted to talk to me for months. You ain't wanted to talk to me last night. You ain't wanted no part of me then. What you wanna talk to me about now?

ROSE. Tomorrow's Friday.

TROY. I know what day tomorrow is. You think I don't know tomorrow's Friday? My whole life I ain't done nothing but look to see Friday coming and you got to tell me it's Friday.

ROSE. I want to know if you're coming home.

TROY. I always come home, Rose. You know that. There ain't never been a night I ain't come home.

ROSE. That ain't what I mean . . . and you know it. I want to know if you're coming straight home after work.

TROY. I figure I'd cash my check . . . hang out at Taylors' with the boys . . . maybe play a game of checkers . . .

ROSE. Troy, I can't live like this. I won't live like this. You livin' on borrowed time with me. It's been going on six months now you ain't been coming home.

TROY. I be here every night. Every night of the year. That's 365 days.

ROSE. I want you to come home tomorrow after work.

TROY. Rose . . . I don't mess up my pay. You know that now. I take my pay and I give it to you. I don't have no money but what you give me back. I just want to have a little time to myself . . . a little time to enjoy life.

ROSE. What about me? When's my time to enjoy life?

TROY. I don't know what to tell you, Rose. I'm doing the best I can.

ROSE. You ain't been home from work but time enough to change your clothes and run out . . . and you wanna call that the best you can do?

TROY. I'm going over to the hospital to see Alberta. She went into the hospital this afternoon. Look like she might have the baby early. I won't be gone long.

ROSE. Well, you ought to know. They went over to Miss Pearl's and got Gabe today. She said you told them to go ahead and lock him up.

TROY. I ain't said no such thing. Whoever told you that is telling a lie. Pearl ain't doing nothing but telling a big fat lie.

ROSE. She ain't had to tell me. I read it on the papers.

TROY. I ain't told them nothing of the kind.

ROSE. I saw it right there on the papers.

TROY. What it say, huh?

ROSE. It said you told them to take him.

TROY. Then they screwed that up, just the way they screw up everything. I ain't worried about what they got on the paper.

ROSE. Say the government send part of his check to the hospital and the other part to you.

TROY. I ain't got nothing to do with that if that's the way it works. I ain't made up the rules about how it work.

ROSE. You did Gabe just like you did Cory. You wouldn't sign the paper for Cory . . . but you signed for Gabe. You signed that paper.

(*The telephone is heard ringing inside the house.*)

TROY. I told you I ain't signed nothing, woman! The only thing I signed was the release form. Hell, I can't read, I don't know what they had on that paper! I ain't signed nothing about sending Gabe away.

ROSE. I said send him to the hospital . . . you said let him be free . . . now you done went down there and signed him to the hospital for half his money. You went back on yourself, Troy. You gonna have to answer for that.

TROY. See now . . . you been over there talking to Miss Pearl. She done got mad cause she ain't getting Gabe's rent money. That's all it is. She's liable to say anything.

ROSE. Troy, I seen where you signed the paper.

TROY. You ain't seen nothing I signed. What she doing got papers on my brother anyway? Miss Pearl telling a big fat lie. And I'm gonna tell her about it too! You ain't seen nothing I signed. Say . . . you ain't seen nothing I signed.

(ROSE *exits into the house to answer the telephone. Presently she returns.*)

ROSE. Troy . . . that was the hospital. Alberta had the baby.

TROY. What she have? What is it?

ROSE. It's a girl.

TROY. I better get on down to the hospital to see her.

ROSE. Troy . . .

TROY. Rose . . . I got to go see her now. That's only right . . . what's the matter . . . the baby's alright, ain't it?

ROSE. Alberta died having the baby.

TROY. Died . . . you say she's dead? Alberta's dead?

ROSE. They said they done all they could. They couldn't do nothing for her.

TROY. The baby? How's the baby?

ROSE. They say it's healthy. I wonder who's gonna bury her.

TROY. She had family, Rose. She wasn't living in the world by herself.

ROSE. I know she wasn't living in the world by herself.

TROY. Next thing you gonna want to know if she had any insurance.

ROSE. Troy, you ain't got to talk like that.

TROY. That's the first thing that jumped out your mouth.

"Who's gonna bury her?" Like I'm fixing to take on that task for myself.

ROSE. I am your wife. Don't push me away.

TROY. I ain't pushing nobody away. Just give me some space. That's all. Just give me some room to breathe.

(ROSE *exits into the house.* TROY *walks about the yard.*)

TROY (*With a quiet rage that threatens to consume him*). Alright . . . Mr. Death. See now . . . I'm gonna tell you what I'm gonna do. I'm gonna take and build me a fence around this yard. See? I'm gonna build me a fence around what belongs to me. And then I want you to stay on the other side. See? You stay over there until you're ready for me. Then you come on. Bring your army. Bring your sickle. Bring your wrestling clothes. I ain't gonna fall down on my vigilance this time. You ain't gonna sneak up on me no more. When you ready for me . . . when the top of your list say Troy Maxson . . . that's when you come around here. You come up and knock on the front door. Ain't nobody else got nothing to do with this. This is between you and me. Man to man. You stay on the other side of that fence until you ready for me. Then you come up and knock on the front door. Anytime you want. I'll be ready for you.

(*The lights go down to black.*)

SCENE THREE

The lights come up on the porch. It is late evening three days later. ROSE *sits listening to the ball game waiting for* TROY. *The final out of the game is made and* ROSE *switches off the radio.* TROY *enters the yard carrying an infant wrapped in blankets. He stands back from the house and calls.*

(ROSE *enters and stands on the porch. There is a long, awkward silence, the weight of which grows heavier with each passing second.*)

TROY. Rose . . . I'm standing here with my daughter in my arms. She ain't but a wee bittie little old thing. She don't know nothing about grownups' business. She innocent . . . and she ain't got no mama.

ROSE. What you telling me for, Troy? (*She turns and exits into the house.*)

TROY. Well . . . I guess we'll just sit out here on the porch.

(*He sits down on the porch. There is an awkward indelicateness about the way he handles the baby. His largeness engulfs and seems to swallow it. He speaks loud enough for* ROSE *to hear.*)

A man's got to do what's right for him. I ain't sorry for nothing I done. It felt right in my heart.

(*To the baby.*)

What you smiling at? Your daddy's a big man. Got these great big old hands. But sometimes he's scared. And right now your daddy's scared cause we sitting out here and ain't got no home. Oh, I been homeless before. I ain't had no little baby with me. But I been homeless. You just be out on the road by your lonesome and you see one of them trains coming and you just kinda go like this . . .

(*He sings as a lullaby.*)

Please, Mr. Engineer let a man ride the line
Please, Mr. Engineer let a man ride the line
I ain't got no ticket please let me ride the blinds

(ROSE *enters from the house.* TROY *hearing her steps behind him, stands and faces her.*)

She's my daughter, Rose. My own flesh and blood. I can't deny her no more than I can deny them boys.

(*Pause.*)

You and them boys is my family. You and them and this child is all I got in the world. So I guess what I'm saying is . . . I'd appreciate it if you'd help me take care of her.

ROSE. Okay, Troy . . . you're right. I'll take care of your baby for you . . . cause . . . like you say . . . she's innocent . . . and you can't visit the sins of the father upon the child. A motherless child has got a hard time.

(*She takes the baby from him.*)

From right now . . . this child got a mother. But you a womanless man.

(ROSE *turns and exits into the house with the baby. Lights go down to black.*)

SCENE FOUR

It is two months later. LYONS *enters from the street. He knocks on the door and calls.*

LYONS. Hey, Rose! (*Pause.*) Rose!

ROSE (*From inside the house*). Stop that yelling. You gonna wake up Raynell. I just got her to sleep.

LYONS. I just stopped by to pay Papa this twenty dollars I owe him. Where's Papa at?

ROSE. He should be here in a minute. I'm getting ready to go down to the church. Sit down and wait on him.

LYONS. I got to go pick up Bonnie over her mother's house.

ROSE. Well, sit it down there on the table. He'll get it.

LYONS (*Enters the house and sets the money on the table*). Tell Papa I said thanks. I'll see you again.

ROSE. Alright, Lyons. We'll see you.

(LYONS *starts to exit as* CORY *enters*)

CORY. Hey, Lyons.

LYONS. What's happening, Cory. Say man, I'm sorry I missed your graduation. You know I had a gig and couldn't get away. Otherwise, I would have been there, man. So what you doing?

CORY. I'm trying to find a job.

LYONS. Yeah I know how that go, man. It's rough out here. Jobs are scarce.

CORY. Yeah, I know.

LYONS. Look here, I got to run. Talk to Papa . . . he know some people. He'll be able to help get you a job. Talk to him . . . see what he say.

CORY. Yeah . . . alright, Lyons.

LYONS. You take care. I'll talk to you soon. We'll find some time to talk.

(LYONS *exits the yard.* CORY, *wanders over to the tree, picks up the bat and assumes a batting stance. He studies an imaginary pitcher and swings. Dissatisfied with the result, he tries again.* TROY *enters. They eye each other for a beat.* CORY *puts the bat down and exits the yard.* TROY *starts into the house as* ROSE *exits with* RAYNELL. *She is carrying a cake.*)

TROY. I'm coming in and everybody's going out.

ROSE. I'm taking this cake down to the church for the bakesale. Lyons was by to see you. He stopped by to pay you your twenty dollars. It's laying in there on the table.

TROY (*Going into his pocket*). Well . . . here go this money.

ROSE. Put it in there on the table, Troy. I'll get it.

TROY. What time you coming back?

ROSE. Ain't no use in you studying me. It don't matter what time I come back.

TROY. I just asked you a question, woman. What's the matter . . . can't I ask you a question?

ROSE. Troy, I don't want to go into it. Your dinner's in there on the stove. All you got to do is heat it up. And don't you be eating the rest of them cakes in there. I'm coming back for them. We having a bakesale at the church tomorrow.

(ROSE *exits the yard.* TROY *sits down on the steps, takes a pint bottle from his pocket, opens it and drinks. He begins to sing.*)

TROY.

> Hear it ring! Hear it ring!
> Had an old dog his name was Blue
> You know Blue was mighty true
> You know Blue as a good old dog
> Blue trees a possum in a hollow log
> You know from that he was a good old dog

(BONO *enters the yard.*)

BONO. Hey, Troy.

TROY. Hey, what's happening, Bono?

BONO. I just thought I'd stop by to see you.

TROY. What you stop by and see me for? You ain't stopped by in a month of Sundays. Hell, I must owe you money or something.

BONO. Since you got your promotion I can't keep up with you. Used to see you everyday. Now I don't even know what route you working.

TROY. They keep switching me around. Got me out in Greentree now . . . hauling white folks' garbage.

BONO. Greentree, huh? You lucky, at least you ain't got to be lifting them barrels. Damn if they ain't getting heavier. I'm gonna put in my two years and call it quits.

TROY. I'm thinking about retiring myself.

BONO. You got it easy. You can *drive* for another five years.

TROY. It ain't the same, Bono. It ain't like working the back of the truck. Ain't got nobody to talk to . . . feel like you working by yourself. Naw, I'm thinking about retiring. How's Lucille?

BONO. She alright. Her arthritis get to acting up on her sometime. Saw Rose on my way in. She going down to the church, huh?

TROY. Yeah, she took up going down there. All them preachers looking for somebody to fatten their pockets.

(*Pause.*)

> Got some gin here.

BONO. Naw, thanks. I just stopped by to say hello.

TROY. Hell, nigger . . . you can take a drink. I ain't never known you to say no to a drink. You ain't got to work tomorrow.

BONO. I just stopped by. I'm fixing to go over to Skinner's. We got us a domino game going over his house every Friday.

TROY. Nigger, you can't play no dominoes. I used to whup you four games out of five.

BONO. Well, that learned me. I'm getting better.

TROY. Yeah? Well, that's alright.

BONO. Look here . . . I got to be getting on. Stop by sometime, huh?

TROY. Yeah, I'll do that, Bono. Lucille told Rose you bought her a new refrigerator.
BONO. Yeah, Rose told Lucille you had finally built your fence . . . so I figured we'd call it even.
TROY. I knew you would.
BONO. Yeah . . . okay. I'll be talking to you.
TROY. Yeah, take care, Bono. Good to see you. I'm gonna stop over.
BONO. Yeah. Okay, Troy.

(BONO *exits.* TROY *drinks from the bottle.*)

TROY.
    Old Blue died and I dig his grave
    Let him down with a golden chain
    Every night when I hear old Blue bark
    I know Blue treed a possum in Noah's Ark.
    Hear it ring! Hear it ring!

(CORY *enters the yard. They eye each other for a beat.* TROY *is sitting in the middle of the steps.* CORY *walks over.*)

CORY. I got to get by.
TROY. Say what? What's you say?
CORY You in my way. I got to get by.
TROY. You got to get by where? This is my house. Bought and paid for. In full. Took me fifteen years. And if you wanna go in my house and I'm sitting on the steps . . . you say excuse me. Like your mama taught you.
CORY. Come on, Pop . . . I got to get by.

(CORY *starts to maneuver his way past* TROY. TROY *grabs his leg and shoves him back.*)

TROY. You just gonna walk over top of me?
CORY. I live here too!
TROY (*Advancing toward him*). You just gonna walk over top of me in my own house?
CORY. I ain't scared of you.
TROY. I ain't asked if you was scared of me. I asked you if you was fixing to walk over top of me in my own house? That's the question. You ain't gonna say excuse me? You just gonna walk over top of me?
CORY. If you wanna put it like that.
TROY. How else am I gonna put it?
CORY. I was walking by you to go into the house cause you sitting on the steps drunk, singing to yourself. You can put it like that.
TROY. Without saying excuse me???

(CORY *doesn't respond.*)

    I asked you a question. Without saying excuse me???

CORY. I ain't got to say excuse me to you. *You don't count around here no more.*

TROY. Oh, I see . . . I don't count around here no more. You ain't got to say excuse me to your daddy. All of a sudden you done got so grown that your daddy don't count around here no more . . . Around here in his own house and yard that he done paid for with the sweat of his brow. You done got so grown to where you gonna take over. You gonna take over my house. Is that right?

You gonna wear my pants. You gonna go in there and stretch out on my bed. You ain't got to say excuse me cause I don't count around here no more. Is that right?

CORY. That's right. You always talking this dumb stuff. Now, why don't you just get out my way.

TROY. I guess you got someplace to sleep and something to put in your belly. You got that, huh? You got that? That's what you need. You got that, huh?

CORY. You don't know what I got. You ain't got to worry about what I got.

TROY. You right! You one hundred percent right! I done spent the last seventeen years worrying about what you got. Now it's your turn, see? I'll tell you what to do. You grown . . . we done established that. You a man. Now, let's see you act like one. Turn your behind around and walk out this yard. And when you get out there in the alley . . . you can forget about this house. See? Cause this is my house. You go on and be a man and get your own house. You can forget about this. 'Cause this is mine. You go on and get yours cause I'm through with doing for you.

CORY. You talking about what you did for me . . . what'd you ever give me?

TROY. Them feet and bones! That pumping heart, nigger! I give you more than anybody else is ever gonna give you.

CORY. You ain't never gave me nothing! You ain't never done nothing but hold me back. Afraid I was gonna be better than you. All you ever did was try and make me scared of you. I used to tremble every time you called my name. Every time I heard your footsteps in the house. Wondering all the time . . . what's Papa gonna say if I do this? . . . What's he gonna say if I do that? . . . What's Papa gonna say if I turn on the radio? And Mama, too . . . she tries . . . but she's scared of you.

TROY. You leave your mama out of this. She ain't got nothing to do with this.

CORY. I don't know how she stand you . . . after what you did to her.

TROY. I told you to leave your mama out of this! (*He advances toward* CORY.)

CORY. What you gonna do . . . give me a whupping? You can't whup me no more. You're too old. You just an old man.

TROY (*Shoves him on his shoulder*). Nigger! That's what you are. You just another nigger on the street to me!

CORY. You crazy! You know that?

TROY. Go on now! You got the devil in you. Get on away from me!

CORY. You just a crazy old man . . . talking about I got the devil in me.

TROY. Yeah, I'm crazy! If you don't get on the other side of that yard . . . I'm gonna show you how crazy I am! Go on . . . get the hell out of my yard.

CORY. It ain't your yard. You took Uncle Gabe's money he got from the army to buy this house and then you put him out.

TROY (TROY *advances on* CORY). Get your black ass out of my yard!

(TROY's *advance backs* CORY *up against the tree.* CORY *grabs up the bat.*)

CORY. I ain't going nowhere! Come on . . . put me out! I ain't scared of you.

TROY. That's my bat!

CORY. Come on!

TROY. Put my bat down!

CORY. Come on, put me out.

(CORY *swings at* TROY, *who backs across the yard.*)

What's the matter? You so bad . . . put me out!

(TROY *advances toward* CORY.)

CORY (*Backing up*). Come on! Come on!

TROY. You're gonna have to use it! You wanna draw that bat back on me . . . you're gonna have to use it.

CORY. Come on! . . . Come on!

(CORY *swings the bat at* TROY *a second time. He misses.* TROY *continues to advance toward him.*)

TROY. You're gonna have to kill me! You wanna draw that bat back on me. You're gonna have to kill me.

(CORY, *backed up against the tree, can go no farther.* TROY *taunts him. He sticks out his head and offers him a target.*)

Come on! Come on!

(CORY *is unable to swing the bat.* TROY *grabs it.*)

TROY. Then I'll show you.

(CORY *and* TROY *struggle over the bat. The struggle is fierce and fully engaged.* TROY *ultimately is the stronger, and takes the bat from* CORY *and stands over him ready to swing. He stops himself.*)

Go on and get away from around my house.

(CORY, *stung by his defeat, picks himself up, walks slowly out of the yard and up the alley.*)

CORY. Tell Mama I'll be back for my things.

TROY. They'll be on the other side of that fence.

(CORY *exits.*)

TROY. I can't taste nothing. Helluljah! I can't taste nothing no more. (TROY *assumes a batting posture and begins to taunt Death, the fastball in the outside corner.*) Come on! It's between you and me now! Come on! Anytime you want! Come on! I be ready for you . . . but I ain't gonna be easy.

(*The lights go down on the scene.*)

ACT II

SCENE FIVE

The time is 1965. The lights come up in the yard. It is the morning of TROY's *funeral. A funeral plaque with a light hangs beside the door. There is a small garden plot off to the side. There is noise and activity in the house as* ROSE, GABRIEL *and* BONO *have gathered. The door opens and* RAYNELL, *seven years old, enters dressed in a flannel nightgown. She crosses to the garden and pokes around with a stick.* ROSE *calls from the house.*

ROSE. Raynell!
RAYNELL. Mam?
ROSE. What you doing out there?
RAYNELL. Nothing.

(ROSE *comes to the door.*)

ROSE. Girl, get in here and get dressed. What you doing?
RAYNELL. Seeing if my garden growed.
ROSE. I told you it ain't gonna grow overnight. You got to wait.
RAYNELL. It don't look like it never gonna grow. Dag!
ROSE. I told you a watched pot never boils. Get in here and get dressed.
RAYNELL. This ain't even no pot, Mama.
ROSE. You just have to give it a chance. It'll grow. Now you come on and do what I told you. We got to be getting ready. This ain't no morning to be playing around. You hear me?
RAYNELL. Yes, mam.

(ROSE *exits into the house.* RAYNELL *continues to poke at her garden with a stick.* CORY *enters. He is dressed in a Marine corporal's uniform, and carries a duffel bag. His posture is that of a military man, and his speech has a clipped sternness.*)

CORY (*To* RAYNELL). Hi.

(*Pause.*)

I bet your name is Raynell.

RAYNELL. Uh huh.

CORY. Is your mama home?

(RAYNELL *runs up on the porch and calls through the screendoor.*)

RAYNELL. Mama . . . there's some man out here. Mama?

(ROSE *comes to the door.*)

ROSE. Cory? Lord have mercy! Look here, you all!

(ROSE *and* CORY *embrace in a tearful reunion as* BONO *and* LYONS *enter from the house dressed in funeral clothes.*)

BONO. Aw, looka here . . .

ROSE. Done got all grown up!

CORY. Don't cry, Mama. What you crying about?

ROSE. I'm just so glad you made it.

CORY. Hey Lyons. How you doing, Mr. Bono.

(LYONS *goes to embrace* CORY.)

LYONS. Look at you, man. Look at you. Don't he look good, Rose. Got them Corporal stripes.

ROSE. What took you so long.

CORY. You know how the Marines are, Mama. They got to get all their paperwork straight before they let you do anything.

ROSE. Well, I'm sure glad you made it. They let Lyons come. Your Uncle Gabe's still in the hospital. They don't know if they gonna let him out or not. I just talked to them a little while ago.

LYONS. A Corporal in the United States Marines.

BONO. Your daddy knew you had it in you. He used to tell me all the time.

LYONS. Don't he look good, Mr. Bono?

BONO. Yeah, he remind me of Troy when I first met him.

(*Pause.*)

Say, Rose, Lucille's down at the church with the choir. I'm gonna go down and get the pallbearers lined up. I'll be back to get you all.

ROSE. Thanks, Jim.

CORY. See you, Mr. Bono.

LYONS (*With his arm around* RAYNELL). Cory . . . look at Raynell. Ain't she precious? She gonna break a whole lot of hearts.

ROSE. Raynell, come and say hello to your brother. This is your brother, Cory. You remember Cory.

RAYNELL. No, Mam.

CORY. She don't remember me, Mama.

ROSE. Well, we talk about you. She heard us talk about you.

(*To* RAYNELL.) This is your brother, Cory. Come on and say hello.

RAYNELL. Hi.

CORY. Hi. So you're Raynell. Mama told me a lot about you.

ROSE. You all come on into the house and let me fix you some breakfast. Keep up your strength.

CORY. I ain't hungry, Mama.

LYONS. You can fix me something, Rose. I'll be in there in a minute.

ROSE. Cory, you sure you don't want nothing. I know they ain't feeding you right.

CORY. No, Mama . . . thanks. I don't feel like eating. I'll get something later.

ROSE. Raynell . . . get on upstairs and get that dress on like I told you.

(ROSE *and* RAYNELL *exit into the house.*)

LYONS. So . . . I hear you thinking about getting married.

CORY. Yeah, I done found the right one, Lyons. It's about time.

LYONS. Me and Bonnie been split up about four years now. About the time Papa retired. I guess she just got tired of all them changes I was putting her through. (*Pause.*)
I always knew you was gonna make something out yourself. Your head was always in the right direction. So . . . you gonna stay in . . . make it a career . . . put in your twenty years?

CORY. I don't know. I got six already, I think that's enough.

LYONS. Stick with Uncle Sam and retire early. Ain't nothing out here. I guess Rose told you what happened with me. They got me down the workhouse. I thought I was being slick cashing other people's checks.

CORY. How much time you doing?

LYONS. They give me three years. I got that beat now. I ain't got but nine more months. It ain't so bad. You learn to deal with it like anything else. You got to take the crookeds with the straights. That's what Papa used to say. He used to say that when he struck out. I seen him strike out three times in a row . . . and the next time up he hit the ball over the grandstand. Right out there in Homestead Field. He wasn't satisfied hitting in the seats . . . he want to hit it over everything! After the game he had two hundred people standing around waiting to shake his hand. You got to take the crookeds with the straights. Yeah, Papa was something else.

CORY. You still playing?

LYONS. Cory . . . you know I'm gonna do that. There's some fellows down there we got us a band . . . we gonna try and stay together when we get out . . . but yeah, I'm still playing. It still helps me to get out of bed in the morning. As long as it do that I'm gonna be right there playing and trying to make some sense out of it.

ROSE (*Calling*). Lyons, I got these eggs in the pan.

LYONS. Let me go on and get these eggs, man. Get ready to go bury Papa.

(*Pause.*)

How you doing? You doing alright?

(CORY *nods.* LYONS *touches him on the shoulder and they share a moment of silent grief.* LYONS *exits into the house.* CORY *wanders about the yard.* RAYNELL *enters.*)

RAYNELL. Hi.

CORY. Hi.

RAYNELL. Did you used to sleep in my room?

CORY. Yeah . . . that used to be my room.

RAYNELL. That's what Papa call it "Cory's room." It got your football in the closet.

(ROSE *comes to the door.*)

ROSE. Raynell, get in there and get them good shoes on.

RAYNELL. Mama, can't I wear these? Them other one hurt my feet.

ROSE. Well, they just gonna have to hurt your feet for a while. You ain't said they hurt your feet when you went down to the store and got them.

RAYNELL. They didn't hurt then. My feet done got bigger.

ROSE. Don't you give me no backtalk now. You get in there and get them shoes on.

(RAYNELL *exits into the house.*)

Ain't too much changed. He still got that piece of rag tied to that tree. He was out here swinging that bat. I was just ready to go back in the house. He swung that bat and bat and then he just fell over. Seem like he swung it and stood there with this grin on his face . . . and then he just fell over. They carried him on down to the hospital, but I knew there wasn't no need . . . why don't you come on in the house?

CORY. Mama . . . I got something to tell you. I don't know how to tell you this . . . but I've got to tell you . . . I'm not going to Papa's funeral.

ROSE. Boy, hush your mouth. That's your daddy you talking about. I don't want hear that kind of talk this morning. I done raised you to come to this? You standing there all healthy and grown talking about you ain't going to your daddy's funeral?

CORY. Mama . . . listen . . .

ROSE. I don't want to hear it, Cory. You just get that thought out of your head.

CORY. I can't drag Papa with me everywhere I go. I've got to say no to him. One time in my life I've got to say no.

ROSE. Don't nobody have to listen to nothing like that. I know you and your daddy ain't seen eye to eye, but I ain't got to listen to that kind of talk this morning. Whatever was between you and your daddy . . . the time has come to put it aside. Just take it and set it over there on the shelf and forget about it. Disrespecting your daddy ain't gonna make you a man, Cory. You got to find a way to come to that on your own. Not going to your daddy's funeral ain't gonna make you a man.

CORY. The whole time I was growing up . . . living in his house . . . Papa was like a shadow that followed you everywhere. It weighed on you and sunk into your flesh.

It would wrap around you and lay there until you couldn't tell which one was you anymore. That shadow digging in your flesh. Trying to crawl in. Trying to live through you. Everywhere I looked, Troy Maxson was staring back at me . . . hiding under the bed . . . in the closet. I'm just saying I've got to find a way to get rid of that shadow, Mama.

ROSE. You just like him. You got him in you good.

CORY. Don't tell me that, Mama.

ROSE. You Troy Maxson all over again.

CORY. I don't want to be Troy Maxson. I want to be me.

ROSE. You can't be nobody but who you are, Cory. That shadow wasn't nothing but you growing into yourself. You either got to grow into it or cut it down to fit you. But that's all you got to make life with. That's all you got to measure yourself against that world out there. Your daddy wanted you to be everything he wasn't . . . and at the same time he tried to make you into everything he was. I don't know if he was right or wrong . . . but I do know he meant to do more good than he meant to do harm. He wasn't always right. Sometimes when he touched he bruised. And sometimes when he took me in his arms he cut.

When I first met your daddy I thought . . . Here is a man I can lay down with and make a baby. That's the first thing I thought when I seen him. I was thirty years old and had done seen my share of men. But when he walked up to me and said, "I can dance a waltz that'll make you dizzy," I thought, Rose Lee, here is a man that you can open yourself up to and be filled to bursting. Here is a man that can fill all them empty spaces you been tipping around the edges of. One of them empty spaces was being somebody's mother.

I married your daddy and settled down to cooking his supper and keeping clean sheets on the bed. When your daddy walked through the house he was so big he filled it up. That was my first mistake. Not to make him leave some room for me. For my part in the matter. But at that time I wanted that. I wanted a house that I could sing in. And that's what your daddy gave me. I didn't know to keep up his strength I had to give up little pieces of mine. I did that. I took on his life as mine and mixed up the pieces so that you couldn't hardly tell which was which anymore. It was my choice. It was my life and I didn't have to live it like that. But that's what life offered me in the way of being a woman and I took it. I grabbed hold of it with both hands. By the time Raynell came into the house, me and your daddy had done lost touch with one another. I didn't want to make my blessing off of nobody's misfortune . . . but I took on to Raynell like she was all them babies I had wanted and never had.

(*The phone rings.*)

Like I'd been blessed to relive a part of my life. And if the Lord see fit to keep up my strength . . . I'm gonna do her just like your daddy did you . . . *I'm gonna give her the best of what's in me.*

RAYNELL (*Entering, still with her old shoes*). Mama . . . Reverend Tollivier on the phone.

(ROSE *exits into the house.*)

RAYNELL. Hi.
CORY. Hi.
RAYNELL. You in the Army or the Marines?
CORY. Marines.
RAYNELL. Papa said it was the Army. Did you know Blue?
CORY. Blue? Who's Blue?
RAYNELL. Papa's dog what he sing about all the time.
CORY (*Singing*). Hear it ring! Hear it ring!
    I had a dog his name was Blue
    You know Blue was mighty true
    You know Blue was a good old dog
    Blue treed a possum in a hollow log
    You know from that he was a good old dog.
    Hear it ring! Hear it ring!

(RAYNELL *joins in singing.*)

CORY and RAYNELL. Blue treed a possum out on a limb
    Blue looked at me and I looked at him
    Grabbed that possum and put him in a sack
    Blue stayed there till I came back

Old Blue's feets was big and round
Never allowed a possum to touch the ground.

Old Blue died and I dug his grave
I dug his grave with a silver spade
Let him down with a golden chain
And every night I call his name
Go on Blue, you good dog you
Go on Blue, you good dog you

RAYNELL. Blue laid down and died like a man
    Blue laid down and died . . .
BOTH. Blue laid down and died like a man
    Now he's treeing possums in the Promised Land
    I'm gonna tell you this to let you know
    Blue's gone where the good dogs go
    When I hear old Blue bark
    When I hear old Blue bark
    Blue treed a possum in Noah's Ark
    Blue treed a possum in Noah's Ark.

(ROSE *comes to the screen door.*)

ROSE. Cory, we gonna be ready to go in a minute.
CORY (*To* RAYNELL). You go on in the house and change them shoes like Mama
    told you so we can go to Papa's funeral.
RAYNELL. Okay, I'll be back.

(RAYNELL *exits into the house.* CORY *gets up and crosses over to the tree.* ROSE
stands in the screen door watching him. GABRIEL *enters from the alley.*)

GABRIEL (*Calling*). Hey, Rose!
ROSE. Gabe?
GABRIEL. I'm here, Rose. Hey Rose, I'm here!

(ROSE *enters from the house.*)

ROSE. Lord . . . Look here, Lyons!
LYONS. See, I told you, Rose . . . I told you they'd let him come.
CORY. How you doing, Uncle Gabe?
LYONS. How you doing, Uncle Gabe?
GABRIEL. Hey, Rose. It's time. It's time to tell St. Peter to open the gates. Troy,
    you ready? You ready, Troy. I'm gonna tell St. Peter to open the gates. You
    get ready now.

(GABRIEL, *with great fanfare, braces himself to blow. The trumpet is without a mouthpiece. He puts the end of it into his mouth and blows with great force, like a man who has been waiting some twenty-odd years for this single moment. No sound comes out of the trumpet. He braces himself and blows again with the same result. A third time he blows. There is a weight of impossible description that falls away and leaves him bare and exposed to a frightful realization. It is a trauma that a sane and normal mind would be unable to withstand. He begins to dance. A slow, strange dance, eerie and lifegiving. A dance of atavistic signature and ritual.* LYONS *attempts to embrace him.* GABRIEL *pushes* LYONS *away. He begins to howl in what is an attempt at song, or perhaps a song turning back into itself in an attempt at speech. He finishes his dance and the gates of heaven stand open as wide as God's closet.*)

That's the way that go!

(*BLACKOUT.*)

[1986]

QUESTIONS

1. How does the introduction to *Fences* define the American Dream? How does the pursuit of that dream differ for European immigrants and for the descendents of African slaves?

2. In the first line of the play, Bono exclaims, "Troy, you ought to stop that lying!" What expectations does this line establish regarding Troy's character? What lies does Troy tell throughout the play? Why does he tell them?

3. What does the story that Troy narrates in this opening scene tell us about his character?

4. Describe the friendship between Troy and Bono. What role does "men talk" play in their relationship? Why do they eventually drift apart?

5. Why doesn't Troy want to lend Lyons money? Why doesn't he want Cory to play football? Do you think Troy is a good father to his sons? Why or why not? Is he a good father to his daughter, Raynell?

6. What values and lessons did Troy learn from his sharecropper father? How do those values inform and shape Troy's life?

7. How does Troy attempt to justify his infidelity to Rose? What are the literal meanings of the baseball metaphors he employs to explain his behavior? Why does Rose refuse those metaphors?

8. Look closely at the play's conclusion and explain what function music plays in *Fences*.

9. Fences play an important symbolic role in this play. Locate and explain the different types of fences, both literal and metaphorical, that appear in this drama.

10. August Wilson has written plays about the African-American experience based in each decade of the twentieth century. *Fences* takes place in 1957. Write a paper discussing how Wilson represents 1950s America in *Fences*. Look closely at the setting (time, place, atmosphere) that the playwright has chosen, as well as at other elements of drama including character, plot, tone, and theme.

11. Write a short essay explaining the function of work and labor in *Fences*. What jobs do the characters value? What jobs do they actually hold? In Troy's mind, what jobs count as legitimate work and what jobs do not? What does his attitude about work reflect about his personal history, his understanding of gender, his relationship to his sons, his generation?

Introduction to *Everyman* [c. 1485]

The author of Everyman *(c. 1485) is unknown, though the play's attention to Christian theology suggests to some that the author perhaps was a priest. Similarities to* Everyman *can be found in a diverse array of earlier writings, such as the parables of Buddha and the Flemish play* Elckerlijk *(c. 495) from which* Everyman *might have been translated. The play's attention to the inevitability of death and the quest for salvation clearly spoke to late medieval audiences; it was frequently produced in the fifteenth and early sixteenth centuries.*

Rich with examples of moral instruction, Everyman *provides a useful example of medieval drama. During the Middle Ages, theater was frequently used to teach audiences important theological lessons. Mystery plays were one form of medieval theater. These plays, such as the* Second Shepherd's Play, *offered audiences dramatized scripture in which characters acted out Biblical stories. Similarly Christian in theme, another type of medieval drama—the morality play—presented dramatized allegory. An allegory can be read simultaneously on a literal level, in which characters and events can be easily recognized, and on an allegorical level, in which characters and events represent more abstract moral, political, philosophical, and religious concepts.*

Everyman *is a morality play. In this short play, the best surviving example of a morality play, the complacent Everyman is summoned by Death, but he can persuade none of his friends, including Beauty, Kindred, and Worldly Goods, to accompany him on his journey. Only Good Deeds agrees to attend him. Similar to other morality plays,* Everyman *employs a central figure who represents all of humanity, and the plot encompasses the span of one human life. It examines what is necessary for salvation—in particular, salvation according to Catholic doctrine.*

𝔊 𝔊 𝔊

Everyman

ANONYMOUS
MODERNIZED BY KATE FRANKS

CHARACTERS

MESSENGER	KNOWLEDGE
GOD	CONFESSION
DEATH	BEAUTY
EVERYMAN	STRENGTH
FELLOWSHIP	DISCRETION
KINDRED	FIVE WITS
COUSIN	ANGEL
GOODS	DOCTOR
GOOD DEEDS	

(Here beginneth a treatise how the High Father of Heaven sendeth Death to summon every creature to come and give account of their lives in this world, and is in manner of a moral play.)

(Enter MESSENGER.*)*

MESSENGER. I pray you all give your audience
    And hear this matter with reverence,
    By figure[1] a moral play:
    The Summoning of Everyman called it is,
    That of our lives and ending shows   5
    How transitory we be all day.
    This matter is wondrous precious,
    But the intent of it is more gracious[2]
    And sweet to bear away.
    The story saith: Man, in the beginning   10
    Look well, and take good heed to the ending,
    Be you never so gay!

---

[1]In form

[2]Devout

This play may have originated in northern Europe; a Flemish play *Elckerlijk* ("Everyman") dates from c. 1495, and it is uncertain whether the English version came before or after.

Ye think sin in the beginning full sweet,
Which in the end causeth the soul to weep,
When the body lieth in clay.   *15*
Here shall you see how Fellowship and Jollity
Both, Strength, Pleasure and Beauty
Will fade from thee as flower in May;
For ye shall hear how our Heaven's King
Calleth Everyman to a general reckoning.   *20*
Give audience, and hear what he doth say.

(*Exit* MESSENGER.)

(GOD *speaks.*)

GOD. I perceive, here in my majesty,
How that all creatures be to me unkind,
Living without dread in worldly prosperity.
Of ghostly sight³ the people be so blind,   *25*
Drowned in sin, they know me not for their God.
In worldly riches is all their mind;
They fear not my righteousness, the sharp rod.
My law that I showed when I for them died
They forget clean, and shedding of my blood red.   *30*
I hanged between two thieves, it cannot be denied;
To get them life I suffered to be dead;
I healed their feet, with thorns hurt was my head.
I could do no more than I did, truly;
And now I see the people do clean forsake me.   *35*
They use the seven deadly sins⁴ damnable,
As pride, covetise,⁵ wrath, and lechery
Now in the world be made commendable;
And thus they leave of angels the heavenly company.
Every man liveth so after his own pleasure,   *40*
And yet of their life they be nothing sure.
I see the more that I them forbear
The worse they be from year to year.

---

³Knowledge of God, spiritual vision.

⁴Seven deadly sins are the list of offences (pride, gluttony, lust, envy, anger, greed, sloth), advanced
during the Middle Ages by church hierarchy.

⁵Covetousness

All that liveth appaireth[6] fast;
Therefore I will, in all the haste,   *45*
Have a reckoning of every man's person;
For, if I leave the people thus alone
In their life and wicked tempests,
Verily they will become much worse than beasts;
For now one would by envy another up eat;   *50*
Charity they do all clean forget.
I hoped well that every man
In my glory should make his mansion,
And thereto I had them all elect;
But now I see, like traitors deject,   *55*
They thank me not for the pleasure that I to them meant,
Nor yet for their being that I them have lent.
I proffered the people great multitude of mercy,
And few there be that asketh it heartily.   *60*
They be so cumbered with worldly riches
That needs on them I must do justice,
On every man living without fear.
Where art thou, Death, thou mighty messenger?

(Enter DEATH.*)*

DEATH. Almighty God, I am here at your will,
    Your commandment to fulfill.   *65*
GOD. Go thou to Everyman
    And show him, in my name,
    A pilgrimage he must on him take,
    Which he in no wise may escape;
    And that he bring with him a sure reckoning   *70*
    Without delay or any tarrying.
DEATH. Lord, I will in the world go run over all
    And cruelly search out both great and small.
    Every man will I beset that liveth beastly
    Out of God's laws, and dreadeth not folly.   *75*
    He that loveth riches I will strike with my dart,
    His sight to blind, and from Heaven to depart—
    Except that alms be his good friend—
    In hell for to dwell, world without end.

---

[6]Deteriorates

(Enter EVERYMAN.*)*

Lo, yonder I see Everyman walking.   *80*
Full little he thinketh on my coming;
His mind is on fleshly lusts and his treasure,
And great pain it shall cause him to endure
Before the Lord, Heaven's King.
Everyman, stand still! Whither art thou going   *85*
Thus gaily? Hast thou thy Maker forgot?
EVERYMAN. Why askest thou?
    Wouldest thou know?
DEATH. Yea, sir. I will you show:
    In great haste I am sent to thee   *90*
    From God out of his majesty.
EVERYMAN. What, sent to me?
DEATH. Yea, certainly.
    Though thou have forgot him here,
    He thinketh on thee in the heavenly sphere,   *95*
    As, ere we depart, thou shalt know.
EVERYMAN. What desireth God of me?
DEATH. That I shall show to thee:
    A reckoning he will needs have
    Without any longer respite.   *100*
EVERYMAN. To give a reckoning longer leisure I crave;
    This blind[7] matter troubleth my wit.
DEATH. On thee thou must take a long journey;
    Therefore thy book of account with thee thou bring.
    For turn again thou cannot, by no way.   *105*
    And look thou be sure of thy reckoning,
    For before God thou shalt answer and show
    Thy many bad deeds, and good, but a few;
    How thou hast spent thy life, and in what wise,
    Before the Chief Lord of Paradise.   *110*
    Have ado that thou were in that way,
    For know thou well, thou shalt make no attorney.[8]
EVERYMAN. Full unready I am, such reckoning to give.
    I know thee not. What messenger art thou?

---

[7]Obscure

[8]Unable to plead own cause.

DEATH. I am Death that no man dreadeth,[9]   *115*
    For every man I rest and no man spareth;
    For it is God's commandment
    That all to me should be obedient.
EVERYMAN. O Death, thou comest when I had thee least in mind!
    In thy power it lieth me to save;   *120*
    Yet of my goods will I give thee, if thou will be kind—
    Yea, a thousand pound shalt thou have!—
    And defer this matter till another day.
DEATH. Everyman, it may not be, by no way.
    I set not by gold, silver, nor riches,   *125*
    Nor by pope, emperor, king, duke, nor princes;
    For, if I would receive gifts great,
    All the world I might get;
    But my custom is clean contrary:
    I give thee no respite. Come hence, and not tarry!   *130*
EVERYMAN. Alas, shall I have no longer respite?
    I may say Death giveth no warning!
    To think on thee, it maketh my heart sick,
    For all unready is my book of reckoning.
    But twelve years if I might have abiding,   *135*
    My accounting book I would make so clear
    That my reckoning I should not need to fear.
    Wherefore, Death, I pray thee, for God's mercy,
    Spare me till I be provided of remedy.
DEATH. Thee availeth not to cry, weep and pray;   *140*
    But haste thee lightly[10] that thou were gone that journey,
    And prove thy friends if thou can.
    For know thou well the tide[11] abideth no man,
    And in the world each living creature
    For Adam's sin must die of nature.   *145*
EVERYMAN. Death, if I should this pilgrimage take
    And my reckoning surely make,
    Show me, for sainted charity,
    Should I not come again shortly?
DEATH. No, Everyman. If thou be once there   *150*

---

[9]Who fears no man.

[10]Quickly

[11]Time

Thou mayst never more come here,
  Trust me verily.
EVERYMAN. O gracious God in the high seat celestial,
  Have mercy on me in this most need!
  Shall I have no company from this vale terrestrial   *155*
  Of mine acquaintance, that way me to lead?
DEATH. Yea, if any be so hardy
  That would go with thee and bear thee company.
  Hie[12] thee that thou were gone to God's magnificence,
  Thy reckoning to give before his presence.   *160*
  What, thinkest thou thy life is given thee
  And thy worldly goods also?
EVERYMAN. I had thought so, verily.
DEATH. Nay, nay, it was but lent thee;
  For as soon as thou art gone,   *165*
  Another a while shall have it and then go therefrom,
  Even as thou hast done.
  Everyman, thou art mad! Thou hast thy wits five[13]
  And here on earth will not amend thy life;
  For suddenly I do come.   *170*
EVERYMAN. O wretchéd caitiff,[14] whither shall I flee,
  That I might escape this endless sorrow?
  Now, gentle Death, spare me till tomorrow,
  That I may amend me
  With good advisement.   *175*
DEATH. Nay, thereto I will not consent,
  Nor no man will I respite;
  But to the heart suddenly I shall smite
  Without any advisement.
  And now out of thy sight I will me hie.   *180*
  See thou make thee ready shortly;
  For thou mayst say this is the day
  That no man living may escape away.

(Exit DEATH.*)*

EVERYMAN. Alas, I may well weep with sighs deep!

---

[12]Strive or hasten.

[13]The five senses.

[14]Captive

Now have I no manner of company 185
To help me in my journey and me to keep;
And also my writing is full unready.
How shall I do now for to excuse me?
I would to God I had never been begot!
To my soul a full great profit it had been; 190
For now I fear pains huge and great.
The time passeth. Lord, help, that all wrought!
For though I mourn it availeth naught.
The day passeth and is almost ago;
I know not well what for to do. 195
To whom were I best my complaint to make?
What if I to Fellowship thereof spake
And showed him of this sudden chance?
For in him is all mine affiance,[15]
We have in the world so many a day 200
Been good friends in sport and play.

(Enter FELLOWSHIP.*)*

I see him yonder, certainly.
I trust that he will bear me company;
Therefore to him will I speak to ease my sorrow.
Well met, good Fellowship, and good morrow! 205
FELLOWSHIP. Everyman, good morrow, by this day!
Sir, why lookest thou so piteously?
If anything be amiss, I pray thee me say,
That I may help to remedy.
EVERYMAN. Yea, good Fellowship, yea, 210
I am in great jeopardy.
FELLOWSHIP. My true friend, show to me your mind.
I will not forsake thee to my life's end
In the way of good company.
EVERYMAN. That was well spoken and lovingly. 215
FELLOWSHIP. Sir, I must needs know your heaviness;
I have pity to see you in any distress.
If any have you wronged, ye shall revenged be,
Though I on the ground be slain for thee,
Though that I know before that I should die. 220

---

[15]Trust

EVERYMAN. Verily, Fellowship, gramercy.[16]
FELLOWSHIP. Tush! By thy thanks I set not a straw.
  Show me your grief, and say no more.
EVERYMAN. If I my heart should to you break,
  And then you to turn your mind from me   225
  And would not me comfort when ye hear me speak,
  Then should I ten times sorrier be.
FELLOWSHIP. Sir, I say as I will do in deed.
EVERYMAN. Then be you a good friend in need.
  I have found you true herebefore.   230
FELLOWSHIP. And so ye shall evermore;
  For, in faith, if thou go to hell,
  I will not forsake thee by the way.
EVERYMAN. Ye speak like a good friend; I believe you well.
  I shall deserve[17] it, if I may.   235
FELLOWSHIP. I speak of no deserving, by this day!
  For he that will say and nothing do
  Is not worthy with good company to go;
  Therefore show me the grief of your mind,
  As to your friend most loving and kind.   240
EVERYMAN. I shall show you how it is:
  Commanded I am to go a journey,
  A long way hard and dangerous,
  And give a straight account without delay
  Before the high judge, Adonai.[18]   245
  Wherefore I pray you, bear me company,
  As ye have promised, in this journey.
FELLOWSHIP. That is matter indeed! Promise is duty;
  But if I should take such a voyage on me,
  I know it well, it should be to my pain;   250
  Also it maketh me afeared, certain.
  But let us take counsel here as well as we can,
  For your words would fear a strong man.
EVERYMAN. Why, ye said if I had need
  Ye would me never forsake, quick nor dead,   255
  Though it were to hell, truly.

---

[16]Thanks

[17]Repay

[18]Hebrew name for God.

FELLOWSHIP. So I said, certainly,
 But such pleasures be set aside, the sooth to say;
 And also, if we took such a journey
 When should we again come?   *260*
EVERYMAN. Nay, never again till the day of doom.
FELLOWSHIP. In faith, then will not I come there!
 Who hath you these tidings brought?
EVERYMAN. Indeed, Death was with me here.
FELLOWSHIP. Now, by God that all hath bought,   *265*
 If death were the messenger,
 For no man that is living today
 I will not go that loath journey—
 Not for the father that begat me!
EVERYMAN. Ye promised otherwise, pardie.[19]   *270*
FELLOWSHIP. I know well I said so, truly;
 And yet, if thou wilt eat and drink and make good cheer,
 Or haunt to women the lusty company
 I would not forsake you while the day is clear,
 Trust me verily.   *275*
EVERYMAN. Yea, thereto ye would be ready!
 To go to mirth, solace and play
 Your mind will sooner apply
 Than to bear me company in my long journey.
FELLOWSHIP. Now, in good faith, I will not that way; *280*
 But if thou will murder or any man kill,
 In that I will help thee with a good will.
EVERYMAN. O, that is a simple advice indeed.
 Gentle fellow, help me in my necessity!
 We have loved long, and now I need;   *285*
 And now, gentle Fellowship, remember me.
FELLOWSHIP. Whether ye have loved me or no,
 By Saint John, I will not with thee go!
EVERYMAN. Yet, I pray thee, take the labor and do so much for me
 To bring me forward, for sainted charity,   *290*
 And comfort me till I come within the town.
FELLOWSHIP. Nay, if thou would give me a new gown,
 I will not a foot with thee go;
 But if thou had tarried, I would not have left thee so.

---

[19]By God

And as now, God speed thee in thy journey,   *295*
For from thee I will depart as fast as I may.
EVERYMAN. Wither away, Fellowship? Will thou forsake me?
FELLOWSHIP. Yea, by my faith! To God I betake[20] thee.
EVERYMAN. Farewell, good Fellowship! For thee my heart is sore.
Adieu forever! I shall see thee no more.   *300*
FELLOWSHIP. In faith, Everyman, farewell now at the ending!
For you I will remember that parting is mourning.

(*Exit* FELLOWSHIP.)

EVERYMAN. Alack, shall we thus depart indeed—
Ah, Lady, help!—without any more comfort?
Lo, Fellowship forsaketh me in my most need.   *305*
For help in this world whither shall I resort?
Fellowship herebefore with me would merry make,
And now little sorrow for me doth he take.
It is said, "In prosperity men friends may find,
Which in adversity be full unkind."   *310*
Now whither for succor shall I flee,
Since that Fellowship hath forsaken me?
To my kinsmen I will, truly,
Praying them to help me in my necessity.
I believe that they will do so,   *315*
For kind[21] will creep where it may not go.

(*Enter* KINDRED *and* COUSIN.)

I will go say, for yonder I see them.
Where be ye now, my friends and kinsmen?
KINDRED. Here be we now at your commandment.
Cousin, I pray you show us your intent   *320*
In any wise and not spare.
COUSIN. Yea, Everyman, and to us declare
If ye be disposed to go anywhither;
For know you well, we will live and die together.
KINDRED. In wealth and woe we will with you hold,   *325*
For over his kin a man may be bold.
EVERYMAN. Gramercy, my friends and kinsmen kind.
Now shall I show you the grief of my mind:

---

[20]Entrust

[21]Kin

I was commanded by a messenger,
That is a high king's chief officer;   *330*
He bade me go a pilgrimage, to my pain,
And I know well I shall never come again.
Also I must give a reckoning strait,
For I have a great enemy[22] that hath me in wait,
Which intendeth me for to hinder.   *335*
KINDRED. What account is that which ye must render?
That would I know.
EVERYMAN. Of all my works I must show
How I have lived and my days spent;
Also of ill deeds that I have used   *340*
In my time, since life was me lent;
And of all virtues that I have refused.
Therefore, I pray you, go thither with me
To help to make mine account, for saint charity.
COUSIN. What, to go thither? Is that the matter?   *345*
Nay, Everyman, I had liefer[23] fast bread and water
All this five years and more.
EVERYMAN. Alas, that ever I was born!
For now shall I never be merry
If that you forsake me.   *350*
KINDRED. Ah, sir, but ye be a merry man!
Take good heart to you, and make no moan.
But one thing I warn you, by Saint Anne—
As for me, ye shall go alone.
EVERYMAN. My Cousin, will you not with me go?   *355*
COUSIN. No, by our Lady! I have the cramp in my toe.
Trust not to me; for, so God me speed,
I will deceive you in your most need.
KINDRED. It availeth not us to entice.
Ye shall have my maid with all my heart;   *360*
She loveth to go to feasts, there to be nice,
And to dance and abroad to start.
I will give her leave to help you in that journey,
If that you and she may agree.
EVERYMAN. Now show me the very effect of your mind: *365*
Will you go with me, or abide behind?

---

[22]The Devil

[23]Rather

KINDRED. Abide behind? Yea, that will I, if I may!
    Therefore farewell till another day.

(*Exit* KINDRED.)

EVERYMAN. How should I be merry or glad?
    For fair promises men to me make,   *370*
    But when I have most need they me forsake.
    I am deceived; that maketh me sad.
COUSIN. Cousin Everyman, farewell now,
    For verily I will not go with you.
    Also of mine own an unready reckoning   *375*
    I have to account; therefore I make tarrying.[24]
    Now God keep thee, for now I go.

(*Exit* COUSIN.)

EVERYMAN. Ah, Jesus, is all come hereto?
    Lo, fair words maketh fools fain;
    They promise and nothing will do, certain.   *380*
    My kinsmen promised me faithfully
    For to abide with me steadfastly,
    And now fast away do they flee,
    Even so Fellowship promised me.
    What friend were best me of to provide?   *385*
    I lose my time here longer to abide.
    Yet in my mind a thing there is:
    All my life I have loved riches;
    If that my Goods now help me might,
    He would make my heart full light.   *390*
    I will speak to him in this distress.
    Where art thou, my Goods and riches?

(GOODS *revealed in a corner.*)

GOODS. Who calleth me? Everyman? What, hast thou haste?
    I lie here in corners, trussed and piled so high,
    And in chests I am locked so fast,   *395*
    Also sacked in bags. Thou mayst see with thine eye
    I cannot stir, in packs, low I lie.
    What would ye have? Lightly me say.

---

[24]Delay

EVERYMAN. Come hither, Goods, in all the haste thou may,
    For of counsel I must desire thee.   400
GOODS. Sir, if ye in the world have sorrow or adversity,
    That can I help you to remedy shortly.
EVERYMAN. It is another disease that grieveth me;
    In this world it is not, I tell thee so.
    I am sent for, another way to go,   405
    To give a strait account general
    Before the highest Jupiter of all;[25]
    And all my life I have had joy and pleasure in thee.
    Therefore, I pray thee, go with me;
    For, peradventure, thou mayst before God Almighty   410
    My reckoning help to clean and purify;
    For it is said ever among
    That "money maketh all right that is wrong."
GOODS. Nay, Everyman, I sing another song.
    I follow no man in such voyages;   415
    For if I went with thee,
    Thou shouldst fare much the worse for me.
    For because on me thou did set thy mind,
    Thy reckoning I have made blotted and blind,
    That thine account thou cannot make truly—   420
    And that hast thou for the love of me!
EVERYMAN. That would grieve me full sore,
    When I should come to that fearful answer.
    Up, let us go thither together.
GOODS. Nay, not so! I am too brittle, I may not endure.   425
    I will follow no man one foot, be ye sure.
EVERYMAN. Alas, I have thee loved, and had great pleasure
    All my life-days in goods and treasure.
GOODS. That is to thy damnation, without lying,
    For my love is contrary to the love everlasting.   430
    But if thou had loved me moderately during,
    As to the poor given part of me,
    Then shouldst thou not in this dolor be,
    Nor in this great sorrow and care.
EVERYMAN. Lo, now was I deceived ere I was aware,   435
    And all I may lay to my spending of time.
GOODS. What, thinkest thou that I am thine?

---

[25]God

EVERYMAN. I had thought so.
GOODS. Nay, Everyman, I say no.
    As for a while I was lent thee;   *440*
    A season thou hast had me in prosperity.
    My condition is a man's soul to kill;
    If I save one, a thousand I do spill.
    Thinkest thou that I will follow thee?
    Nay, from this world not, verily.   *445*
EVERYMAN. I had thought otherwise.
GOODS. Therefore to thy soul Goods is a thief;
    For when thou art dead, this is my guise—
    Another to deceive in this same wise
    As I have done thee, and all to his soul's reprief.[26]   *450*
EVERYMAN. O false Goods, cursed thou be,
    Thou traitor to God, that hast deceived me
    And caught me in thy snare!
GOODS. Marry, thou brought thyself in care,
    Whereof I am glad.   *455*
    I must needs laugh; I cannot be sad.
EVERYMAN. Ah, Goods, thou hast had long my hearty love;
    I gave thee that which should be the Lord's above.
    But wilt thou not go with me indeed?
    I pray thee truth to say.   *460*
GOODS. No, so God me speed!
    Therefore farewell, and have good day.

(Exit GOODS.*)*

EVERYMAN. O, to whom shall I make my moan
    For to go with me in that heavy journey?
    First Fellowship said he would with me go;   *465*
    His words were very pleasant and gay,
    But afterward he left me alone.
    Then spake I to my kinsmen, all in despair,
    And also they gave me words fair;
    They lacked no fair speaking,   *470*
    But all forsook me in the ending.
    Then went I to my Goods that I loved best,
    In hope to have comfort; but there had I least,

---

[26]Harm or shame.

For my Goods sharply did me tell
That he bringeth many into Hell.   475
Then of myself I was ashamed,
And so I am worthy to be blamed;
Thus may I well myself hate.
Of whom shall I now counsel take?
I think that I shall never speed   480
Till that I go to my Good Deeds.
But, alas, she is so weak
That she can neither go nor speak;
Yet will I venture on her now.
My Good Deeds, where be you?   485

(GOOD DEEDS *revealed on the ground.*)

GOOD DEEDS. Here I lie, cold in the ground.
    Thy sins hath me so sore bound
    That I cannot stir.
EVERYMAN. O Good Deeds, I stand in fear!
    I must you pray of counsel,   490
    For help now should come right well.
GOOD DEEDS. Everyman, I have understanding
    That ye be summoned account to make
    Before Messiah, of Jerusalem King;
    If you do by me, that journey with you will I take.   495
EVERYMAN. Therefore I come to you my moan to make.
    I pray you that ye will go with me.
GOOD DEEDS. I would full fain,[27] but I cannot stand, verily.
EVERYMAN. Why, is there anything on you fallen?
GOOD DEEDS. Yea, sir, I may thank you of all.   500
    If ye had perfectly cheered me,
    Your book of account full ready would be.
    Look, the books of your works and deeds eke,[28]
    As how they lie under the feet
    To your soul's heaviness.   505
EVERYMAN. Our Lord Jesus help me!
    For one letter here I cannot see.
GOOD DEEDS. There is a blind reckoning in time of distress.

---

[27]Glad

[28]Also

EVERYMAN. Good Deeds, I pray you help me in this need,
    Or else I am forever damned indeed;   510
    Therefore help me to make reckoning
    Before the Redeemer of all things,
    That King is, and was, and ever shall.
GOOD DEEDS. Everyman, I am sorry of your fall,
    And fain would I help you if I were able.   515
EVERYMAN. Good Deeds, your counsel I pray you give me.
GOOD DEEDS. That shall I do verily.
    Though that on my feet I may not go,
    I have a sister that shall with you also,
    Called Knowledge,[29] which shall with you abide   520
    To help you to make that dreadful reckoning.

(Enter KNOWLEDGE.*)*

KNOWLEDGE. Everyman, I will go with thee and be thy guide,
    In thy most need to go by thy side.
EVERYMAN. In good condition I am now in everything
    And am wholly content with this good thing;   525
    Thanked be God my Creator.
GOOD DEEDS. And when she hath brought you there,
    Where thou shalt heal thee of thy smart,
    Then go you with your reckoning and your Good Deeds together
    For to make you joyful at heart   530
    Before the Blessèd Trinity.
EVERYMAN. My Good Deeds, gramercy!
    I am well content, certainly,
    With your words sweet.

*(*EVERYMAN *and* KNOWLEDGE *leave* GOOD DEEDS.*)*

KNOWLEDGE. Now go we together lovingly   535
    To Confession, that cleansing river.
EVERYMAN. For joy I weep; I would we were there!
    But, I pray you, give me cognition
    Where dwelleth that holy man, Confession.
KNOWLEDGE. In the house of salvation;[30]   540
    We shall find him in that place
    That shall us comfort, by God's grace.

---

[29]Recognition of sins.

[30]A church

(KNOWLEDGE *leads* EVERYMAN *to* CONFESSION.)

Lo, this is Confession. Kneel down and ask mercy,
For he is in good esteem with God Almighty.
EVERYMAN. O glorious fountain, that all uncleanness doth clarify,   *545*
Wash from me the spots of vice unclean,
That on me no sin may be seen.
I come with Knowledge for my redemption,
Redempt with hearty and full contrition;
For I am commanded a pilgrimage to take   *550*
And great accounts before God to make.
Now I pray you, Shrift,[31] mother of salvation,
Help my Good Deeds for my piteous exclamation.
CONFESSION. I know your sorrow well, Everyman.
Because with Knowledge ye come to me,   *555*
I will you comfort as well as I can,
And a precious jewel I will give thee,
Called penance, voider of adversity;
Therewith shall your body chastised be,
With abstinence and perseverance in God's serviture.   *560*
Here shall you receive that scourge of me
Which is penance strong that ye must endure,
To remember thy Saviour was scourged for thee
With sharp scourges and suffered it patiently;
So must thou, ere thou escape that painful pilgrimage.   *565*

(CONFESSION *gives scourge to* KNOWLEDGE.)

Knowledge, keep him in this voyage,
And by that time Good Deeds will be with thee.
But in any wise be sure of mercy,
For your time draweth fast; if ye will saved be,
Ask God mercy, and he will grant truly.   *570*
When with the scourge of penance man doth him bind,
The oil of forgiveness then shall he find.

(EVERYMAN *and* KNOWLEDGE *leave* CONFESSION.)

EVERYMAN. Thanked be God for his gracious work!
For now I will my penance begin.
This hath rejoiced and lighted my heart,   *575*

---

[31]Confession

Though the knots be painful and hard within.
KNOWLEDGE. Everyman, look your penance that ye fulfill,
 What pain that ever it to you be;
 And Knowledge shall give you counsel at will
 How your account ye shall make clearly. 580
EVERYMAN. O eternal God, O heavenly figure,
 O way of righteousness, O goodly vision,
 Which descended down in a virgin pure
 Because he would every man redeem,
 Which Adam forfeited by his disobedience; 585
 O blessèd Godhead, elect and high divine,
 Forgive me my grievous offence!
 Here I cry thee mercy in this presence.
 O ghostly treasure, O ransomer and redeemer,
 Of all the world hope and conductor, 590
 Mirror of joy, foundation of mercy,
 Which illumineth Heaven and earth thereby,
 Hear my clamorous complaint though it late be;
 Receive my prayers unworthy in this heavy life!
 Though I be a sinner most abominable, 595
 Yet let my name be written in Moses' table.
 O Mary, pray to the Maker of all things,
 Me for to help at my ending;
 And save me from the power of my enemy,
 For Death assaileth me strongly. 600
 And, Lady, that I may by means of thy prayer
 Of your Son's glory to be partner,
 By the means of his passion, I it crave;
 I beseech you, help my soul to save.
 Knowledge, give me the scourge of penance; 605
 My flesh therewith shall give acquittance.
 I will now begin if God give me grace.

(KNOWLEDGE *gives scourge to* EVERYMAN.)

KNOWLEDGE. Everyman, God give you time and space!
 Thus I bequeath you in the hands of our Saviour;
 Now may you make your reckoning sure. 610
EVERYMAN. In the name of the Holy Trinity,
 My body sore punishèd shall be:
 Take this, body, for the sins of the flesh!
 Also thou delightest to go gay and fresh,

And in the way of damnation thou did me bring;   *615*
Therefore suffer now strokes of punishing.
Now of penance I will wade the water clear
To save me from Purgatory, that sharp fire.

(GOOD DEEDS *rises from the ground.*)

GOOD DEEDS. I thank God, now I can walk and go
     And am delivered of my sickness and woe.   *620*
     Therefore with Everyman I will go and not spare;
     His good works I will help him to declare.
KNOWLEDGE. Now, Everyman, be merry and glad!
     Your Good Deeds cometh now; ye may not be sad
     Now is your Good Deeds whole and sound,   *625*
     Going upright upon the ground.
EVERYMAN. My heart is light and shall be evermore;
     Now will I smite[32] faster than I did before.
GOOD DEEDS. Everyman, pilgrim, my special friend,
     Blessed be thou without end!   *630*
     For thee is prepared the eternal glory.
     Ye have me made whole and sound,
     Therefore I will bide by thee in every stound.[33]
EVERYMAN. Welcome, my Good Deeds! Now I hear thy voice
     I weep for very sweetness of love.   *635*
KNOWLEDGE. Be no more sad, but ever rejoice;
     God seeth thy living in his throne above.

(KNOWLEDGE *gives* EVERYMAN *the garment of contrition.*)

     Put on this garment to thy behove,[34]
     Which is wet with your tears,
     Or else before God you may it miss   *640*
     When you to your journey's end come shall.
EVERYMAN. Gentle Knowledge, what do ye it call?
KNOWLEDGE. It is the garment of sorrow;
     From pain it will you borrow.
     Contrition it is   *645*

---

[32]Strike

[33]Hard time

[34]Benefit

That getteth forgiveness;
It pleaseth God passing well.
GOOD DEEDS. Everyman, will you wear it for your heal?[35]

(EVERYMAN *puts on the garment of contrition.*)

EVERYMAN. Now bléssed be Jesu, Mary's Son,
    For now have I on true contrition;   650
    And let us go now without tarrying.
    Good Deeds, have we clear our reckoning?
GOOD DEEDS. Yea, indeed, I have it here.
EVERYMAN. Then I trust we need not fear.
    Now, friends, let us not part in twain.   655
KNOWLEDGE. Nay, Everyman, that will we not, certain.
GOOD DEEDS. Yet must thou lead with thee
    Three persons of great might.
EVERYMAN. Who should they be?
GOOD DEEDS. Discretion and Strength they hight[36]   660
    And thy Beauty may not abide behind.
KNOWLEDGE. Also ye must call to mind
    Your Five Wits as for your counsellors.
GOOD DEEDS. You must have them ready at all hours.
EVERYMAN. How shall I get them hither?   665
KNOWLEDGE. You must call them all together,
    And they will hear you incontinent.[37]
EVERYMAN. My friends, come hither and be present:
    Discretion, Strength, my Five Wits, and Beauty.

(*Enter* DISCRETION, STRENGTH, FIVE WITS, *and* BEAUTY.)

BEAUTY. Here at your will we be all ready.   670
    What would ye that we should do?
GOOD DEEDS. That ye would with Everyman go
    And help him in his pilgrimage.
    Advise you, will ye with him or not in that voyage?
STRENGTH. We will bring him all thither   675
    To his help and comfort, ye may believe me.
DISCRETION. So will we go with him all together.

---

[35]Salvation

[36]Are called

[37]At once

EVERYMAN. Almighty God, loved may thou be!
    I give thee laud that I have hither brought
    Strength, Discretion, Beauty and Five Wits. Lack I naught;   *680*
    And my Good Deeds, with Knowledge clear,
    All be in company at my will here.
    I desire no more to my business.
STRENGTH. And I, Strength, will by you stand in distress,
    Though thou would in battle fight on the ground.   *685*
FIVE WITS. And though it were through the world round,
    We will not depart for sweet nor sour.
BEAUTY. No more will I unto death's hour,
    Whatsoever thereof befall.
DISCRETION. Everyman, advise you first of all;   *690*
    Go with a good advisement and deliberation.
    We all give you virtuous monition[38]
    That all shall be well.
EVERYMAN. My friends, hearken what I will tell:
    I pray God reward you in his heavenly sphere.   *695*
    Now hearken, all that be here,
    For I will make my testament
    Here before you all present:
    In alms, half of my goods I will give with my hands twain
    In the way of charity with good intent,   *700*
    And the other half still shall remain
    In queth,[39] to be returned where it ought to be.
    This I do in despite of the fiend of hell,
    To go quite out of his peril
    Ever after and this day.   *705*
KNOWLEDGE. Everyman, hearken what I say:
    Go to Priesthood, I you advise,
    And receive of him in any wise
    The holy sacrament and ointment together;
    Then shortly see ye turn again hither.   *710*
    We will all abide you here.
FIVE WITS. Yea, Everyman, hie you that ye ready were.[40]
    There is no emperor, king, duke, nor baron

---

[38]Forewarning

[39]As a bequest.

[40]Hurry and prepare yourself.

That of God hath commission
As hath the least priest in the world being;   *715*
For of the blesséd sacraments pure and benign,
He beareth the keys, and thereof hath the cure
For man's redemption—it is ever sure—
Which God for our soul's medicine
Gave us out of his heart with great pine.[41]   *720*
Here in this transitory life, for thee and me,
The blessed sacraments seven there be:
Baptism, confirmation with priesthood good,
And the sacrament of God's precious flesh and blood,
Marriage, the holy extreme unction, and penance.   *725*
These seven be good to have in remembrance,
Gracious sacraments of high divinity.
EVERYMAN. Fain would I receive that holy body,[42]
And meekly to my ghostly father I will go.
FIVE WITS. Everyman, that is the best that ye can do.   *730*
God will you to salvation bring,
For priesthood exceedeth all other things:
To us holy scripture they do teach
And converteth man from sin, Heaven to reach;
God hath to them more power given   *735*
Than to any angel that is in Heaven.
With five words[43] he may consecrate,
God's body in flesh and blood to make,
And handleth his Maker between his hands.
The priest bindeth and unbindeth all bands,   *740*
Both in earth and in Heaven.
Thou ministers all the sacraments seven;
Though we kissed thy feet, thou were worthy.
Thou art surgeon that cureth sin deadly;
No remedy we find under God   *745*
But all only priesthood.
Everyman, God gave priests that dignity
And setteth them in his stead among us to be;
Thus be they above angels in degree.

---

[41]Anguish, suffering.

[42]Sacrament of Holy Communion.

[43]"For this is my body"; in Catholicism, the phrase that consecrates and converts bread into the body of Christ during Holy Communion.

(Exit EVERYMAN.*)*

KNOWLEDGE. If priests be good, it is so, surely.   750
    But when Jesu hanged on the cross with great smart,
    There he gave, out of his blesséd heart,
    The seven sacraments in great torment;
    He sold them not to us, that Lord omnipotent;
    Therefore Saint Peter the apostle doth say   755
    That Jesu's curse hath all they
    Which God their Saviour do buy or sell,
    Or they for any money do take or tell.[44]
    Sinful priests giveth the sinners example bad;
    Their children sitteth by other men's fires, I have heard;   760
    And some haunteth women's company
    With unclean life, as lusts of lechery;
    These be with sin made blind.
FIVE WITS. I trust to God no such may we find;
    Therefore let us priesthood honor   765
    And follow their doctrine for our souls' succour.
    We be their sheep, and they shepherds be
    By whom we all be kept in surety.
    Peace! For yonder I see Everyman come,
    Which hath made true satisfaction.   770
GOOD DEEDS. Methinks it is he indeed.

(Re-enter EVERYMAN.*)*

EVERYMAN. Now Jesu be your alder speed![45]
    I have received the sacrament for my redemption
    And then mine extreme unction.[46]
    Blesséd be all they that counselled me to take it!   775
    And now, friends, let us go without longer respite.
    I thank God that ye have tarried so long.
    Now set each of you on this rood[47] your hand
    And shortly follow me.
    I go before where I would be. God be our guide!   780

---

[44]Count out, a reference to simony.

[45]Help to all of you.

[46]Sacrament to give spiritual comfort and/or to restore bodily health.

[47]Cross

(They go toward the grave.)

STRENGTH. Everyman, we will not from you go
    Till ye have done this voyage long.
DISCRETION. I, Discretion, will bide by you also.
KNOWLEDGE. And though this pilgrimage be never so strong,
    I will never part you from.   *785*
STRENGTH. Everyman, I will be as sure by thee
    As ever I did by Judas Maccabee.[48]

(They arrive at the grave.)

EVERYMAN. Alas, I am so faint I may not stand;
    My limbs under me do fold.
    Friends, let us not turn again to this land,   *790*
    Not for all the world's gold;
    For into this cave must I creep
    And turn to earth, and thereto sleep.
BEAUTY. What, into this grave? Alas!
EVERYMAN. Yea, there shall ye consume,[49] more and less.   *795*
BEAUTY. And what, should I smother here?
EVERYMAN. Yea, by my faith, and never more appear.
    In this world live no more we shall,
    But in Heaven before the highest Lord of all.
BEAUTY. I cross out all this. Adieu, by Saint John!   *800*
    I take my tap[50] in my lap and am gone.
EVERYMAN. What, Beauty, whither will ye?
BEAUTY. Peace! I am deaf. I look not behind me,
    Not if thou wouldest give me all the gold in thy chest.

(Exit BEAUTY.*)*

EVERYMAN. Alas, whereto may I trust?   *805*
    Beauty goeth fast away from me.
    She promised with me to live and die.
STRENGTH. Everyman, I will thee also forsake and deny;
    Thy game liketh me not at all.
EVERYMAN. Why, then, ye will forsake me all?   *810*
    Sweet Strength, tarry a little space.

---

[48]Judas Maccabee: Jewish leader renowned for bravery (I Macc. iii).

[49]Shall all of you decay; be consumed.

[50]Unspun wool

STRENGTH. Nay, sir, by the rood of grace!
   I will hie me from thee fast,
   Though thou weep till thy heart to-brast.[51]
EVERYMAN. Ye would ever bide by me, ye said.   *815*
STRENGTH. Yea, I have you far enough conveyed.
   Ye be old enough, I understand,
   Your pilgrimage to take in hand.
   I repent me that I hither came.
EVERYMAN. Strength, you to displease I am to blame;   *820*
   Yet promise is debt, this ye well wot.[52]
STRENGTH. In faith, I care not.
   Thou art but a fool to complain;
   You spend your speech and waste your brain.
   Go thrust thee into the ground!   *825*

(Exit STRENGTH.*)*

EVERYMAN. I had thought surer I should you have found.
   He that trusteth in his Strength,
   She him deceiveth at length.
   Both Strength and Beauty forsaketh me;
   Yet they promised me fair and lovingly.   *830*
DISCRETION. Everyman, I will after Strength be gone.
   As for me, I will leave you alone.
EVERYMAN. Why, Discretion, will ye forsake me?
DISCRETION. Yea, in faith, I will go from thee;
   For when Strength goeth before,   *835*
   I follow after evermore.
EVERYMAN. Yet, I pray thee, for the love of the Trinity,
   Look in my grave once piteously.
DISCRETION. Nay, so nigh will I not come.
   Farewell, everyone!   *840*

(Exit DISCRETION.*)*

EVERYMAN. O, all things faileth, save God alone—
   Beauty, Strength and Discretion;
   For when Death bloweth his blast,
   They all run from me full fast.

---

[51]Burst in two.

[52]Know

FIVE WITS. Everyman, my leave now of thee I take.   *845*
   I will follow the others, for here I thee forsake.
EVERYMAN. Alas, then may I wail and weep,
   For I took you for my best friend.
FIVE WITS. I will no longer thee keep.
   Now farewell, and there an end.   *850*

(*Exit* FIVE WITS.)

EVERYMAN. O Jesu, help! All hath forsaken me.
GOOD DEEDS. Nay, Everyman, I will bide with thee.
   I will not forsake thee in deed;
   Thou shalt find me a good friend in need.
EVERYMAN. Gramercy, Good Deeds! Now may I true friends see.   *855*
   They have forsaken me, every one;
   I loved them better than my Good Deeds alone.
   Knowledge, will ye forsake me also?
KNOWLEDGE. Yea, Everyman, when ye to Death shall go;
   But not yet, for no manner of danger.   *860*
EVERYMAN. Gramercy, Knowledge, with all my heart.
KNOWLEDGE. Nay, yet I will not from hence depart
   Till I see where ye shall be come.
EVERYMAN. Methinks, alas, that I must be gone
   To make my reckoning and my debts pay,   *865*
   For I see my time is nigh spent away.
   Take example, all ye that this do hear or see,
   How they that I loved best do forsake me,
   Except my Good Deeds that bideth truly.
GOOD DEEDS. All earthly things is but vanity: *870*
   Beauty, Strength and Discretion do man forsake,
   Foolish friends and kinsmen that fair spake—
   All fleeth save Good Deeds, and that am I.
EVERYMAN. Have mercy on me, God most mighty,
   And stand by me, thou mother and maid, Holy Mary!   *875*
GOOD DEEDS. Fear not, I will speak for thee.
EVERYMAN. Here I cry God mercy.
GOOD DEEDS. Shorten our end, and diminish our pain;
   Let us go and never come again.

(GOOD DEEDS *leads* EVERYMAN *into grave.*)

EVERYMAN. Into thy hands, Lord, my soul I commend;   *880*
   Receive it, Lord, that it be not lost.

As thou me boughtest, so me defend
And save me from the fiend's boast,
That I may appear with that blessèd host
That shall be saved at the day of doom.   885
In manus tuas, of might most
Forever, *commendo spiritum meum.*[53]

(Exeunt EVERYMAN *and* GOOD DEEDS.*)*

KNOWLEDGE. Now hath he suffered that we all shall endure;
The Good Deeds shall make all sure.
Now hath he made ending;   890
Methinks that I hear angels sing
And make great joy and melody
Where Everyman's soul received shall be.

(Enter ANGEL.*)*

THE ANGEL. Come, excellent elect spouse,[54] to Jesu!
Here above thou shalt go   895
Because of thy singular virtue.
Now thy soul is taken thy body from,
Thy reckoning is crystal clear.
Now shalt thou into the heavenly sphere,
Unto the which all ye shall come   900
That liveth well before the day of doom.

(Exeunt ANGEL *and* KNOWLEDGE.*)*

(Enter DOCTOR.*)*

DOCTOR. This moral men may have in mind.
Ye hearers, take it of worth, old and young,
And forsake Pride, for he deceiveth you in the end;
And remember Beauty, Five Wits, Strength, and Discretion, 905
They all at the last do Everyman forsake,
Save his Good Deeds there doth he take.
But beware, for if they be small,
Before God he hath no help at all:
No excuse may be there for Everyman.   910
Alas, how shall he do then?

---

[53]In manus tuas . . . commendo spiritum meum: Into thy hands, I commend my spirit.

[54]Bride of Jesus, a common medieval metaphor to convey union of soul with God.

For after death amends may no man make,
For them mercy and pity doth him forsake.
If his reckoning be not clear when he doth come,
God will say, "*Ite, maledicti, in ignem eternum.*"⁵⁵   *915*
And he that hath his account whole and sound,
High in Heaven he shall be crowned;
Unto which place God bring us all thither,
That we may live body and soul together.
Thereto help the Trinity!   *920*
Amen, say ye, for saint charity.

(Exit DOCTOR.*)*

(Thus endeth this moral play of Everyman.)

[C. 1485]

---

⁵⁵Ite . . . eternum: Go, sinners, into eternal fire (Matt. xxv.41).

QUESTIONS

ANONYMOUS, *Everyman*

1. *Everyman* opens with the Messenger's direct address, which is spoken to the audience watching the play. He asks these spectators to "all give your audience." What does this question literally mean? Look up the word "audience" in the *Oxford English Dictionary* or another dictionary that provides the original meaning of this word.

2. *Everyman* can be read simultaneously on a literal level, in which characters and events can be easily recognized, and on an allegorical level, in which characters and events represent more abstract moral, political, philosophical, and religious concepts. Select two characters from *Everyman* and explain their literal and allegorical significance.

3. What are the four requests that Everyman makes of Death? Which request does Death agree to meet, and what conditions does he set for Everyman?

4. Who is the only character that follows Everyman to his grave? Why?

5. Everyman is portrayed as a man, while Good Deeds and Knowledge are women. Why? Why do you think Confession is portrayed as a man?

6. In this morality play, what is redemption based on? Do any of the characters in the play change during the course of the dramatic action?

7. What is the theme of *Everyman*?

8. *Everyman* is rich with references to speed or haste. Find as many of these references as you can throughout the play. When are they invoked? Given the play's focus on a pilgrimage and its insistent concern with mortality, why do these references occur so frequently?

9. During the Middle Ages, morality plays were condoned by the Christian church and by civil authorities to teach values in an entertaining, and therefore widely engaging, format. Discuss the social and moral values advanced by *Everyman*. What does it teach readers and audiences about the human condition?

10. Imagine you are a director who will stage this medieval morality play for a contemporary audience, but you are instructed not to present the play in a typical theater. Where would stage this play? Why? Discuss this and other possibilities for a staging of *Everyman* that would make the play come alive for contemporary audiences.

A Midsummer Night's Dream

WILLIAM SHAKESPEARE

DRAMATIS PERSONAE

THESEUS,   Duke of Athens

HIPPOLYTA,   Queen of the Amazons, betrothed to
Theseus
PHILOSTRATE,   Master of the Revels
EGEUS,   father of Hermia

HERMIA,   daughter of Egeus, in love with Lysander
LYSANDER,   in love with Hermia
DEMETRIUS,   in love with Hermia and favored by Egeus
HELENA,   in love with Demetrius

OBERON,   King of the Fairies
TITANIA,   Queen of the Fairies
PUCK,
or ROBIN GOODFELLOW

PEASEBLOSSOM,
COBWEB,   } fairies attending Titania
MOTE,
MUSTARDSEED,
Other FAIRIES attending

		representing
PETER QUINCE,	a carpenter,	PROLOGUE
NICK BOTTOM,	a weaver,	PYRAMUS
FRANCIS FLUTE,	a bellows mender,	THISBE
TOM SNOUT,	a tinker,	WALL
SNUG,	a joiner,	LION
ROBIN STARVELING,	a tailor,	MOONSHINE

LORDS AND ATTENDANTS ON THESEUS AND HIPPOLYTA
SCENE:

Athens, and a wood near it

Reprinted by permission from *The Complete Works of Shakespeare*, edited by David Bevington. Copyright © 1997 Pearson Education.

1.1

Enter Theseus, Hippolyta, (and Philostrate,) with others.

THESEUS. Now, fair Hippolyta, our nuptial hour
    Draws on apace. Four happy days bring in
    Another moon; but, oh, methinks, how slow
    This old moon wanes! She lingers my desires,   4
    Like to a stepdame or a dowager   5
    Long withering out a young man's revenue.   6
HIPPOLYTA. Four days will quickly steep themselves in night;   7
    Four nights will quickly dream away the time;
    And then the moon, like to a silver bow
    New bent in heaven, shall behold the night
    Of our solemnities.
THESEUS.   Go, Philostrate,   11
    Stir up the Athenian youth to merriments.
    Awake the pert and nimble spirit of mirth.
    Turn melancholy forth to funerals;
    The pale companion is not for our pomp.   15

                    (Exit Philostrate.)

    Hippolyta, I wooed thee with my sword   16
    And won thy love doing thee injuries;
    But I will wed thee in another key,
    With pomp, with triumph, and with reveling.   19

*(Enter Egeus and his daughter Hermia, and Lysander, and
Demetrius.)*

EGEUS. Happy be Theseus, our renownèd duke!
THESEUS. Thanks, good Egeus. What's the news with thee?
EGEUS. Full of vexation come I, with complaint
    Against my child, my daughter Hermia.—
    Stand forth, Demetrius.—My noble lord,
    This man hath my consent to marry her.—

1.1. Location: Athens. Theseus's court.
4 **lingers** frustrates   5 **stepdame** stepmother.   **a dowager** i.e., a widow (whose right of inheritance from her dead husband is eating into her son's estate)   6 **withering out** causing to dwindle   7 **Four . . . night** (The image is of the day sinking into the ocean as night comes on.)   11 **solemnities** festive ceremonies of marriage.   15 **companion** fellow. (A pale complexion is linked to melancholy.) **pomp** ceremonial magnificence.   16 **with my sword** i.e., in a military engagement against the Amazons, when Hippolyta was taken captive   19 **triumph** public festivity

Stand forth, Lysander.—And, my gracious Duke,
This man hath bewitched the bosom of my child.—
Thou, thou Lysander, thou hast given her rhymes
And interchanged love tokens with my child.
Thou hast by moonlight at her window sung
With feigning voice verses of feigning love,   *31*
And stol'n the impression of her fantasy   *32*
With bracelets of thy hair, rings, gauds, conceits,   *33*
Knacks, trifles, nosegays, sweetmeats—messengers   *34*
Of strong prevailment in unhardened youth.   *35*
With cunning hast thou filched my daughter's heart,
Turned her obedience, which is due to me,
To stubborn harshness. And, my gracious Duke,
Be it so she will not here before Your Grace   *39*
Consent to marry with Demetrius,
I beg the ancient privilege of Athens:
As she is mine, I may dispose of her,
Which shall be either to this gentleman
Or to her death, according to our law
Immediately provided in that case.   *45*
THESEUS. What say you, Hermia? Be advised, fair maid.
To you your father should be as a god—
One that composed your beauties, yea, and one
To whom you are but as a form in wax
By him imprinted, and within his power
To leave the figure or disfigure it.   *51*
Demetrius is a worthy gentleman.
HERMIA. So is Lysander.
THESEUS.   In himself he is;
But in this kind, wanting your father's voice,   *54*
The other must be held the worthier.
HERMIA. I would my father looked but with my eyes.
THESEUS. Rather your eyes must with his judgment look.
HERMIA. I do entreat Your Grace to pardon me.
I know not by what power I am made bold,
Nor how it may concern my modesty

---

31 feigning (1) counterfeiting (2) faining, desirous **32 And ... fantasy** and made her fall in love
with you (imprinting your image on her imagination) by stealthy and dishonest means **33 gauds,
conceits** playthings, fanciful trifles **34 Knacks ... sweetmeats** knicknacks, trinkets, bouquets, can-
dies **35 prevailment in** influence on **39 Be it so** if **45 Immediately** directly, with nothing intervening **51 leave** i.e., leave unaltered **54 kind** respect. **wanting** lacking. **voice** approval

In such a presence here to plead my thoughts;
But I beseech Your Grace that I may know
The worst that may befall me in this case
If I refuse to wed Demetrius.

THESEUS. Either to die the death or to abjure   65
Forever the society of men.
Therefore, fair Hermia, question your desires,
Know of your youth, examine well your blood,   68
Whether, if you yield not to your father's choice,
You can endure the livery of a nun,   70
For aye to be in shady cloister mewed,   71
To live a barren sister all your life,
Chanting faint hymns to the cold fruitless moon.
Thrice blessèd they that master so their blood
To undergo such maiden pilgrimage;
But earthlier happy is the rose distilled   76
Than that which, withering on the virgin thorn,
Grows, lives, and dies in single blessedness.

HERMIA. So will I grow, so live, so die, my lord,
Ere I will yield my virgin patent up   80
Unto His Lordship, whose unwishèd yoke
My soul consents not to give sovereignty.

THESEUS. Take time to pause, and by the next new moon—
The sealing day betwixt my love and me
For everlasting bond of fellowship—
Upon that day either prepare to die
For disobedience to your father's will,
Or else to wed Demetrius, as he would,
Or on Diana's altar to protest   89
For aye austerity and single life.

DEMETRIUS. Relent, sweet Hermia, and, Lysander, yield
Thy crazèd title to my certain right.   92

LYSANDER. You have her father's love, Demetrius;
Let me have Hermia's. Do you marry him.

EGEUS. Scornful Lysander! True, he hath my love,
And what is mine my love shall render him.

---

65 die the death be executed by legal process   **68 blood** passions   **70 livery** habit, costume
71 aye ever.   **mewed** shut in. (Said of a hawk, poultry, etc.)   **76 earthlier happy** happier as respects
this world.   **distilled** i.e., to make perfume   **80 patent** privilege   **89 protest** vow   **92 crazèd**
cracked, unsound

And she is mine, and all my right of her
I do estate unto Demetrius.   *98*
LYSANDER. I am, my lord, as well derived as he,   *99*
As well possessed; my love is more than his;   *100*
My fortunes every way as fairly ranked,   *101*
If not with vantage, as Demetrius';   *102*
And, which is more than all these boasts can be,
I am beloved of beauteous Hermia.
Why should not I then prosecute my right?
Demetrius, I'll avouch it to his head,   *106*
Made love to Nedar's daughter, Helena,
And won her soul; and she, sweet lady, dotes,
Devoutly dotes, dotes in idolatry
Upon this spotted and inconstant man.   *110*
THESEUS. I must confess that I have heard so much,
And with Demetrius thought to have spoke thereof;
But, being overfull of self-affairs,   *113*
My mind did lose it. But, Demetrius, come,
And come, Egeus, you shall go with me;
I have some private schooling for you both.   *116*
For you, fair Hermia, look you arm yourself   *117*
To fit your fancies to your father's will,   *118*
Or else the law of Athens yields you up—
Which by no means we may extenuate—   *120*
To death or to a vow of single life.
Come, my Hippolyta. What cheer, my love?
Demetrius and Egeus, go along.   *123*
I must employ you in some business
Against our nuptial, and confer with you   *125*
Of something nearly that concerns yourselves.   *126*
EGEUS. With duty and desire we follow you.

(*Exeunt [all but Lysander and Hermia].*)

LYSANDER. How now, my love, why is your cheek so pale?
How chance the roses there do fade so fast?

---

98 estate unto settle or bestow upon   **99 as well derived** as well born and descended   **100 possessed** endowed with wealth   **101 fairly** handsomely   **102 vantage** superiority   **106 head** i.e., face   **110 spotted** i.e., morally stained   **113 self-affairs** my own concerns   **116 schooling** admonition   **117 look you arm** take care you prepare   **118 fancies** likings, thoughts of love   **120 extenuate** mitigate, relax   **123 go** i.e., come   **125 Against** in preparation for   **126 nearly that** that closely

HERMIA. Belike for want of rain, which I could well   *130*
   Beteem them from the tempest of my eyes.   *131*
LYSANDER. Ay me! For aught that I could ever read,
   Could ever hear by tale or history,
   The course of true love never did run smooth;
   But either it was different in blood—   *135*
HERMIA. Oh, cross! Too high to be enthralled to low.   *136*
LYSANDER. Or else misgrafted in respect of years—   *137*
HERMIA. Oh, spite! Too old to be engaged to young.
LYSANDER. Or else it stood upon the choice of friends—   *139*
HERMIA. Oh, hell, to choose love by another's eyes!
LYSANDER. Or if there were a sympathy in choice,   *141*
   War, death, or sickness did lay siege to it,
   Making it momentany as a sound,   *143*
   Swift as a shadow, short as any dream,
   Brief as the lightning in the collied night   *145*
   That in a spleen unfolds both heaven and earth,   *146*
   And ere a man hath power to say "Behold!"
   The jaws of darkness do devour it up.
   So quick bright things come to confusion.   *149*
HERMIA. If then true lovers have been ever crossed,   *150*
   It stands as an edict in destiny.
   Then let us teach our trial patience,   *152*
   Because it is a customary cross,
   As due to love as thoughts, and dreams, and sighs,
   Wishes, and tears, poor fancy's followers.   *155*
LYSANDER. A good persuasion. Therefore, hear me, Hermia: *156*
   I have a widow aunt, a dowager
   Of great revenue, and she hath no child.
   From Athens is her house remote seven leagues;   *159*
   And she respects me as her only son.   *160*
   There, gentle Hermia, may I marry thee,
   And to that place the sharp Athenian law
   Cannot pursue us. If thou lovest me, then,
   Steal forth thy father's house tomorrow night;

---

130 Belike Very likely   **131 Beteem** grant, afford   **135 blood** hereditary rank   **136 cross** vexation.
137 misgrafted ill grafted, badly matched   **139 friends** relatives   **141 sympathy** agreement
143 momentany lasting but a moment   **145 collied** blackened (as with coal dust), darkened
146 in a spleen in a swift impulse, in a violent flash.   **unfolds** reveals   **149 confusion** ruin.
150 ever crossed always thwarted   **152 teach . . . patience** i.e., teach ourselves patience in this trial
155 fancy's amorous passion's   **156 persuasion** doctrine.   **159 seven leagues** about 21 miles
160 respects regards

And in the wood, a league without the town,   165
Where I did meet thee once with Helena
To do observance to a morn of May,   167
There will I stay for thee.
HERMIA.   My good Lysander!
I swear to thee, by Cupid's strongest bow,
By his best arrow with the golden head,   170
By the simplicity of Venus' doves,   171
By that which knitteth souls and prospers loves,
And by that fire which burned the Carthage queen   173
When the false Trojan under sail was seen,   174
By all the vows that ever men have broke,
In number more than ever women spoke,
In that same place thou hast appointed me
Tomorrow truly will I meet with thee.
LYSANDER. Keep promise, love. Look, here comes Helena.

(*Enter Helena.*)

HERMIA. God speed, fair Helena! Whither away?   180
HELENA. Call you me fair? That "fair" again unsay.
Demetrius loves your fair. Oh, happy fair!   182
Your eyes are lodestars, and your tongue's sweet air   183
More tunable than lark to shepherd's ear   184
When wheat is green, when hawthorn buds appear.
Sickness is catching. Oh, were favor so,   186
Yours would I catch, fair Hermia, ere I go;
My ear should catch your voice, my eye your eye,
My tongue should catch your tongue's sweet melody.
Were the world mine, Demetrius being bated,   190
The rest I'd give to be to you translated.   191
Oh, teach me how you look and with what art
You sway the motion of Demetrius' heart.   193
HERMIA. I frown upon him, yet he loves me still.

---

165 without outside   **167 To do . . . May** to perform the ceremonies of May Day   **170 best arrow**
(Cupid's best gold-pointed arrows were supposed to induce love; his blunt leaden arrows, aversion.)
171 simplicity innocence.   **doves** i.e., those that drew Venus's chariot   **173, 174 Carthage queen,
false Trojan** (Dido, Queen of Carthage, immolated herself on a funeral pyre after having been
deserted by the Trojan hero Aeneas.)   **180 fair** fair-complexioned. (Generally regarded by the
Elizabethans as more beautiful than a dark complexion.)   **182 your fair** your beauty (even though
Hermia is dark complexioned).   **happy fair** lucky fair one.   **183 lodestars** guiding stars.   **air** music
184 tunable tuneful, melodious   **186 favor** appearance, looks   **190 bated** excepted   **191 translated**
transformed.   **193 sway the motion** control the impulses

HELENA. Oh, that your frowns would teach my smiles such skill!

HERMIA. I give him curses, yet he gives me love.

HELENA. Oh, that my prayers could such affection move!   *197*

HERMIA. The more I hate, the more he follows me.

HELENA. The more I love, the more he hateth me.

HERMIA. His folly, Helena, is no fault of mine.

HELENA. None, but your beauty. Would that fault were mine!

HERMIA. Take comfort. He no more shall see my face.
> Lysander and myself will fly this place.
> Before the time I did Lysander see   *204*
> Seemed Athens as a paradise to me.   *205*
> Oh, then, what graces in my love do dwell,
> That he hath turned a heaven unto a hell?

LYSANDER. Helen, to you our minds we will unfold.
> Tomorrow night, when Phoebe doth behold   *209*
> Her silver visage in the watery glass,   *210*
> Decking with liquid pearl the bladed grass,   *211*
> A time that lovers' flights doth still conceal,   *212*
> Through Athens' gates have we devised to steal.

HERMIA. And in the wood, where often you and I
> Upon faint primrose beds were wont to lie,   *215*
> Emptying our bosoms of their counsel sweet,   *216*
> There my Lysander and myself shall meet,
> And thence from Athens turn away our eyes
> To seek new friends and stranger companies.   *219*
> Farewell, sweet playfellow. Pray thou for us,
> And good luck grant thee thy Demetrius!
> Keep word, Lysander. We must starve our sight
> From lovers' food till morrow deep midnight.

LYSANDER. I will, my Hermia.   (*Exit Hermia.*)
>   Helena, adieu!
> As you on him, Demetrius dote on you!

     (*Exit Lysander.*)

HELENA. How happy some o'er other some can be!   *226*
> Through Athens I am thought as fair as she.

---

197 Oh, that . . . move! Would that my prayers could arouse such desire! **204–5 Before . . . to me** (Love has led to complications and jealousies, making Athens hell for Hermia.) **209 Phoebe** Diana, the moon **210 glass** reflecting surface (of a lake, etc.) **211 liquid pearl** i.e., dew **212 still** always **215 faint** pale **216 counsel** secret thought **219 stranger companies** the company of strangers. **226 o'er . . . can be** can be in comparison to some others.

But what of that? Demetrius thinks not so;
He will not know what all but he do know.
And as he errs, doting on Hermia's eyes,
So I, admiring of his qualities.
Things base and vile, holding no quantity,   *232*
Love can transpose to form and dignity.
Love looks not with the eyes, but with the mind,
And therefore is winged Cupid painted blind.
Nor hath Love's mind of any judgment taste;   *236*
Wings and no eyes figure unheedy haste.   *237*
And therefore is Love said to be a child,
Because in choice he is so oft beguiled.   *239*
As waggish boys in game themselves forswear,   *240*
So the boy Love is perjured everywhere.
For ere Demetrius looked on Hermia's eyne,   *242*
He hailed down oaths that he was only mine;
And when this hail some heat from Hermia felt,
So he dissolved, and showers of oaths did melt.
I will go tell him of fair Hermia's flight.
Then to the wood will he tomorrow night
Pursue her; and for this intelligence   *248*
If I have thanks, it is a dear expense.   *249*
But herein mean I to enrich my pain,
To have his sight thither and back again.   (*Exit.*)

1.2

Enter Quince the carpenter, and Snug the joiner, and Bottom the weaver, and Flute the bellows mender, and Snout the tinker, and Starveling the tailor.

QUINCE. Is all our company here?
BOTTOM. You were best to call them generally, man by   *2*
    man, according to the scrip.   *3*
QUINCE. Here is the scroll of every man's name which

---

232 **holding no quantity** i.e., unsubstantial, unshapely 236 **Nor ... taste** i.e., Nor has Love, which dwells in the fancy or imagination, any least bit of judgment or reason 237 **figure** signify 239 **in choice** in choosing. **beguiled** self-deluded, making unaccountable choices. 240 **waggish** playful, mischievous. **game** sport, jest 242 **eyne** eyes. (Old form of plural.) 248 **intelligence** information 249 **a dear expense** i.e., a trouble worth taking on my part.
1.2. **Location: Athens.**
2 **generally** (Bottom's blunder for "individually.") 3 **scrip** script.

is thought fit, through all Athens, to play in our inter-   *5*
lude before the Duke and the Duchess on his wedding   *6*
day at night.

BOTTOM. First, good Peter Quince, say what the play treats
on, then read the names of the actors, and so grow to a   *9*
point.

QUINCE. Marry, our play is "The most lamentable comedy   *11*
and most cruel death of Pyramus and Thisbe."

BOTTOM. A very good piece of work, I assure you, and a
merry. Now, good Peter Quince, call forth your actors
by the scroll. Masters, spread yourselves.

QUINCE. Answer as I call you. Nick Bottom, the weaver.   *16*

BOTTOM. Ready. Name what part I am for, and proceed.

QUINCE. You, Nick Bottom, are set down for Pyramus.

BOTTOM. What is Pyramus? A lover or a tyrant?

QUINCE. A lover, that kills himself most gallant for love.

BOTTOM. That will ask some tears in the true performing of
it. If I do it, let the audience look to their eyes. I will move
storms; I will condole in some measure. To the rest—yet   *23*
my chief humor is for a tyrant. I could play Ercles rarely,   *24*
or a part to tear a cat in, to make all split.

> "The raging rocks
> And shivering shocks
> Shall break the locks
>> Of prison gates;
> And Phibbus' car   *30*
> Shall shine from far
> And make and mar
>> The foolish Fates."

This was lofty! Now name the rest of the players. This is
Ercles' vein, a tyrant's vein. A lover is more condoling.

QUINCE. Francis Flute, the bellows mender.

FLUTE. Here, Peter Quince.

QUINCE. Flute, you must take Thisbe on you.

FLUTE. What is Thisbe? A wandering knight?

QUINCE. It is the lady that Pyramus must love.

5–6 interlude play   **9 grow to** come to   **11 Marry** (A mild oath; originally the name of the Virgin Mary.)   **16 Bottom** (As a weaver's term, a *bottom* was an object around which thread was wound.) **23 condole** lament, arouse pity   **24 humor** inclination   **Ercles** Hercules. (The tradition of ranting came from Seneca's *Hercules Furens.*)   **tear a cat** i.e., rant.   **make all split** i.e., cause a stir, bring the house down.   **30 Phibbus' car** Phoebus's, the sun god's chariot

FLUTE. Nay, faith, let not me play a woman. I have a beard
coming.

QUINCE. That's all one. You shall play it in a mask, and you   *43*
may speak as small as you will.   *44*

BOTTOM. An I may hide my face, let me play Thisbe too.   *45*
I'll speak in a monstrous little voice: "Thisne, Thisne!"
"Ah, Pyramus, my lover dear! Thy Thisbe dear, and
lady dear!"

QUINCE. No, no, you must play Pyramus, and Flute, you
Thisbe.

BOTTOM. Well, proceed.

QUINCE. Robin Starveling, the tailor.

STARVELING. Here, Peter Quince.

QUINCE. Robin Starveling, you must play Thisbe's mother.
Tom Snout, the tinker.

SNOUT. Here, Peter Quince.

QUINCE. You, Pyramus' father; myself, Thisbe's father;
Snug, the joiner, you, the lion's part; and I hope here is
a play fitted.

SNUG. Have you the lion's part written? Pray you, if it be,
give it me, for I am slow of study.

QUINCE. You may do it extempore, for it is nothing but
roaring.

BOTTOM. Let me play the lion too. I will roar that I will do
any man's heart good to hear me. I will roar that I will
make the Duke say, "Let him roar again, let him roar
again."

QUINCE. An you should do it too terribly, you would fright
the Duchess and the ladies, that they would shriek; and
that were enough to hang us all.

ALL. That would hang us, every mother's son.

BOTTOM. I grant you, friends, if you should fright the
ladies out of their wits, they would have no more dis-
cretion but to hang us; but I will aggravate my voice so   *74*
that I will roar you as gently as any sucking dove; I will   *75*
roar you an 'twere any nightingale.   *76*

QUINCE. You can play no part but Pyramus; for Pyramus

---

43 That's all one It makes no difference.   **44 small** high-pitched   **45 An** If. (Also at line 68.)
74 aggravate (Bottom's blunder for "moderate.")   **75 roar you** i.e., roar for you. **sucking dove**
(Bottom conflates *sitting dove* and *sucking lamb,* two proverbial images of innocence.)
76 an 'twere as if it were

is a sweet-faced man, a proper man as one shall see in   *78*
a summer's day, a most lovely gentlemanlike man.
Therefore you must needs play Pyramus.
BOTTOM. Well, I will undertake it. What beard were I
best to play it in?
QUINCE. Why, what you will.
BOTTOM. I will discharge it in either your straw-color   *84*
beard, your orange-tawny beard, your purple-in-grain   *85*
beard, or your French-crown-color beard, your perfect   *86*
yellow.
QUINCE. Some of your French crowns have no hair at all,   *88*
and then you will play barefaced. But, masters, here are
your parts. (*He distributes parts.*) And I am to entreat
you, request you, and desire you to con them by   *91*
tomorrow night, and meet me in the palace wood, a
mile without the town, by moonlight. There will we
rehearse; for if we meet in the city, we shall be dogged
with company, and our devices known. In the mean-   *95*
time I will draw a bill of properties, such as our play   *96*
wants. I pray you, fail me not.
BOTTOM. We will meet, and there we may rehearse most
obscenely and courageously. Take pains, be perfect.   *99*
Adieu.
QUINCE. At the Duke's oak we meet.
BOTTOM. Enough. Hold, or cut bowstrings.   (*Exeunt.*)   *102*

2.1

*Enter a Fairy at one door, and Robin Goodfellow (Puck) at
another.*

PUCK. How now, spirit, whither wander you?
FAIRY. Over hill, over dale,
    Thorough bush, thorough brier,   *3*

---

78 proper handsome   **84 discharge** perform.   **your** i.e., you know the kind I mean   **85 purple-in-grain** dyed a very deep red. (From *grain,* the name applied to the dried insect used to make the dye.)   **86 French-crown-color** i.e., color of a French crown, a gold coin   **88 crowns** heads bald from syphilis, the "French disease"   **91 con** memorize   **95 devices** plans   **96 draw a bill** draw up a list   **99 obscenely** (An unintentionally funny blunder, whatever Bottom meant to say.)   **perfect** i.e., letter-perfect in memorizing your parts.   **102 Hold ... bowstrings** (An archers' expression, not definitely explained, but probably meaning here "keep your promises, or give up the play.")
2.1. Location: A wood near Athens.
3 Thorough through

Over park, over pale, 4
    Thorough flood, thorough fire,
I do wander everywhere,
Swifter than the moon's sphere; 7
And I serve the Fairy Queen,
To dew her orbs upon the green. 9
The cowslips tall her pensioners be. 10
In their gold coats spots you see;
    Those be rubies, fairy favors; 12
    In those freckles live their savors. 13
I must go seek some dewdrops here
And hang a pearl in every cowslip's ear.
Farewell, thou lob of spirits; I'll be gone. 16
Our Queen and all her elves come here anon. 17
PUCK. The King doth keep his revels here tonight.
Take heed the Queen come not within his sight.
For Oberon is passing fell and wrath, 20
Because that she as her attendant hath
A lovely boy, stolen from an Indian king;
She never had so sweet a changeling. 23
And jealous Oberon would have the child
Knight of his train, to trace the forests wild. 25
But she perforce withholds the lovèd boy, 26
Crowns him with flowers, and makes him all her joy.
And now they never meet in grove or green,
By fountain clear, or spangled starlight sheen, 29
But they do square, that all their elves for fear 30
Creep into acorn cups and hide them there.
FAIRY. Either I mistake your shape and making quite,
Or else you are that shrewd and knavish sprite 33
Called Robin Goodfellow. Are not you he
That frights the maidens of the villagery, 35
Skim milk, and sometimes labor in the quern, 36

---

4 pale enclosure **7 sphere** orbit **9 dew** sprinkle with dew. **orbs** circles, i.e., fairy rings (circular bands of grass, darker than the surrounding area, caused by fungi enriching the soil) **10 pensioners** retainers, members of the royal bodyguard **12 favors** love tokens **13 savors** sweet smells. **16 lob** country bumpkin **17 anon** at once. **20 passing fell** exceedingly angry. **wrath** wrathful **23 changeling** child exchanged for another by the fairies. **25 trace** range through **26 perforce** forcibly **29 fountain** spring. **starlight sheen** shining starlight **30 square** quarrel **33 shrewd** mischievous. **sprite** spirit **35 villagery** village population **36 Skim milk** i.e., steal the cream. **quern** hand mill (where Puck presumably hampers the grinding of grain)

And bootless make the breathless huswife churn,   *37*
And sometimes make the drink to bear no barm,   *38*
Mislead night wanderers, laughing at their harm?   *39*
Those that "Hobgoblin" call you, and "Sweet Puck,"   *40*
You do their work, and they shall have good luck.
Are you not he?
PUCK.   Thou speakest aright;
I am that merry wanderer of the night.
I jest to Oberon and make him smile
When I a fat and bean-fed horse beguile,   *45*
Neighing in likeness of a filly foal;   *46*
And sometimes lurk I in a gossip's bowl   *47*
In very likeness of a roasted crab,   *48*
And when she drinks, against her lips I bob
And on her withered dewlap pour the ale.   *50*
The wisest aunt, telling the saddest tale,   *51*
Sometime for three-foot stool mistaketh me;
Then slip I from her bum, down topples she,
And "Tailor" cries, and falls into a cough;   *54*
And then the whole choir hold their hips and laugh,   *55*
And waxen in their mirth, and neeze, and swear   *56*
A merrier hour was never wasted there.   *57*
But, room, fairy! Here comes Oberon.   *58*
FAIRY. And here my mistress. Would that he were gone!

(*Enter [Oberon] the King of Fairies at one door, with his train, and [Titania] the Queen at another, with hers.*)

OBERON. Ill met by moonlight, proud Titania.
TITANIA. What, jealous Oberon? Fairies, skip hence.
I have forsworn his bed and company.
OBERON. Tarry, rash wanton. Am not I thy lord?   *63*
TITANIA. Then I must be thy lady; but I know
When thou hast stolen away from Fairyland

---

37 bootless in vain. (Puck prevents the cream from turning to butter.)   **huswife** housewife
38 barm head on the ale. (Puck prevents the barm or yeast from producing fermentation.)
39 Mislead night wanderers i.e., mislead with false fire those who walk abroad at night (hence earning Puck his other names of Jack o' Lantern and Will o' the Wisp)   **40 Those ... Puck** i.e., Those who call you by the names you favor rather than those denoting the mischief you do   **45 bean-fed** full of beans   **46 a filly foal** a mare (in heat)   **47 gossip's** old woman's   **48 crab** crab apple   **50 dewlap** loose skin on neck   **51 aunt** old woman.   **saddest** most serious   **54 "Tailor"** (Seemingly a cry of distress or embarrassment.)   **55 choir** company   **56 waxen** increase.   **neeze** sneeze   **57 wasted** spent   **58 room** stand aside, make room   **63 wanton** headstrong creature.

And in the shape of Corin sat all day,	*66*
Playing on pipes of corn and versing love	*67*
To amorous Phillida. Why art thou here	*68*
Come from the farthest step of India,	*69*
But that, forsooth, the bouncing Amazon,	
Your buskined mistress and your warrior love,	*71*
To Theseus must be wedded, and you come	
To give their bed joy and prosperity.	

OBERON. How canst thou thus for shame, Titania,
    Glance at my credit with Hippolyta,   *75*
    Knowing I know thy love to Theseus?
    Didst not thou lead him through the glimmering night
    From Perigenia, whom he ravishèd?   *78*
    And make him with fair Aegles break his faith,   *79*
    With Ariadne and Antiopa?   *80*

TITANIA. These are the forgeries of jealousy;
    And never, since the middle summer's spring,   *82*
    Met we on hill, in dale, forest, or mead,   *83*
    By pavèd fountain or by rushy brook,   *84*
    Or in the beachèd margent of the sea,   *85*
    To dance our ringlets to the whistling wind,   *86*
    But with thy brawls thou hast disturbed our sport.
    Therefore the winds, piping to us in vain,
    As in revenge, have sucked up from the sea
    Contagious fogs which, falling in the land,   *90*
    Hath every pelting river made so proud   *91*
    That they have overborne their continents.   *92*
    The ox hath therefore stretched his yoke in vain,   *93*
    The plowman lost his sweat, and the green corn   *94*

66, 68 Corin, Phillida (Conventional names of pastoral lovers.)   **67 corn** (Here, oat stalks.) **versing love** writing love verses   **69 step** farthest limit of travel, or, perhaps, *steep*, "mountain range"   **71 buskined** wearing half-boots called buskins   **75 Glance ... Hippolyta** make insinuations about my favored relationship with Hippolyta   **78 Perigenia** i.e., Perigouna, one of Theseus's conquests. (This and the following women are named in Thomas North's translation of Plutarch's "Life of Theseus.")   **79 Aegles** i.e., Aegle, for whom Theseus deserted Ariadne according to some accounts   **80 Ariadne** the daughter of Minos, King of Crete, who helped Theseus to escape the labyrinth after killing the Minotaur; later she was abandoned by Theseus.   **Antiopa** Queen of the Amazons and wife of Theseus; elsewhere identified with Hippolyta, but here thought of as a separate woman.   **82 middle summer's spring** beginning of midsummer   **83 mead** meadow   **84 pavèd** with pebbled bottom. **rushy** bordered with rushes   **85 in** on.   **margent** edge, border   **86 ringlets** dances in a ring. (See *orbs* in line 9.) **to** to the sound of   **90 Contagious** noxious   **91 pelting** paltry   **92 continents** banks that contain them.   **93 stretched his yoke** i.e., pulled at his yoke in plowing   **94 corn** grain of any kind

Hath rotted ere his youth attained a beard;
The fold stands empty in the drownèd field,   *96*
And crows are fatted with the murrain flock;   *97*
The nine-men's morris is filled up with mud,   *98*
And the quaint mazes in the wanton green   *99*
For lack of tread are undistinguishable.
The human mortals want their winter here;   *101*
No night is now with hymn or carol blessed.
Therefore the moon, the governess of floods,   *103*
Pale in her anger, washes all the air,   *104*
That rheumatic diseases do abound.   *105*
And thorough this distemperature we see   *106*
The seasons alter: hoary-headed frosts
Fall in the fresh lap of the crimson rose,
And on old Hiems' thin and icy crown   *109*
An odorous chaplet of sweet summer buds
Is, as in mockery, set. The spring, the summer,
The childing autumn, angry winter, change   *112*
Their wonted liveries, and the mazèd world   *113*
By their increase now knows not which is which.   *114*
And this same progeny of evils comes
From our debate, from our dissension.   *116*
We are their parents and original.   *117*
OBERON. Do you amend it, then. It lies in you.
Why should Titania cross her Oberon?
I do but beg a little changeling boy
To be my henchman.   *120*
TITANIA.   Set your heart at rest.
The fairy land buys not the child of me.
His mother was a vot'ress of my order,   *123*
And in the spicèd Indian air by night
Full often hath she gossiped by my side

---

96 **fold** pen for sheep or cattle   97 **murrain** having died of the plague   98 **nine-men's morris** i.e.,
portion of the village green marked out in a square for a game played with nine pebbles or pegs
99 **quaint mazes** i.e., intricate paths marked out on the village green to be followed rapidly on foot
as a kind of contest.   **wanton** luxuriant   101 **want** lack.   **winter** i.e., regular winter season; or,
proper observances of winter, such as the *hymn* or *carol* in the next line (?)   103 **Therefore** i.e., As a
result of our quarrel   104 **washes** saturates with moisture   105 **rheumatic diseases** colds, flu, and
other respiratory infections   106 **distemperature** disturbance in nature   109 **Hiems'** the winter
god's   112 **childing** fruitful, pregnant   113 **wonted liveries** usual apparel.   **mazèd** bewildered
114 **their increase** the increasing pace of change; or, their produce   116 **debate** quarrel   117 **origi-nal** origin.   120 **henchman** attendant, page.   123 **was . . . order** had taken a vow to serve me

And sat with me on Neptune's yellow sands,
Marking th'embarkèd traders on the flood, 127
When we have laughed to see the sails conceive
And grow big-bellied with the wanton wind; 129
Which she, with pretty and with swimming gait, 130
Following—her womb then rich with my young
    squire—
Would imitate, and sail upon the land
To fetch me trifles, and return again
As from a voyage, rich with merchandise.
But she, being mortal, of that boy did die;
And for her sake do I rear up her boy,
And for her sake I will not part with him.
OBERON. How long within this wood intend you stay?
TITANIA. Perchance till after Theseus' wedding day.
    If you will patiently dance in our round 140
    And see our moonlight revels, go with us;
    If not, shun me, and I will spare your haunts. 142
OBERON. Give me that boy, and I will go with thee.
TITANIA. Not for thy fairy kingdom. Fairies, away!
    We shall chide downright, if I longer stay.

        (*Exeunt* [*Titania with her train*].)

OBERON. Well, go thy way. Thou shalt not from this grove 146
    Till I torment thee for this injury.
    My gentle Puck, come hither. Thou rememb'rest
    Since once I sat upon a promontory, 149
    And heard a mermaid on a dolphin's back
    Uttering such dulcet and harmonious breath 151
    That the rude sea grew civil at her song, 152
    And certain stars shot madly from their spheres
    To hear the sea-maid's music?
PUCK.   I remember.
OBERON. That very time I saw, but thou couldst not,
    Flying between the cold moon and the earth
    Cupid, all armed. A certain aim he took 157

---

127 **traders** trading vessels. **flood** flood tide 129 **wanton** (1) playful (2) amorous 130 **swimming** smooth, gliding 140 **round** circular dance 142 **spare** shun 146 **from** go from 149 **Since** when 151 **dulcet** sweet. **breath** voice, song 152 **rude** rough 157 **all** fully. **certain** sure

At a fair vestal thronèd by the west,   158
And loosed his love shaft smartly from his bow   159
As it should pierce a hundred thousand hearts;   160
But I might see young Cupid's fiery shaft   161
Quenched in the chaste beams of the wat'ry moon,
And the imperial vot'ress passèd on,
In maiden meditation, fancy-free.   164
Yet marked I where the bolt of Cupid fell: 165
It fell upon a little western flower,
Before milk-white, now purple with love's wound,
And maidens call it love-in-idleness.   168
Fetch me that flower; the herb I showed thee once.
The juice of it on sleeping eyelids laid
Will make or man or woman madly dote   171
Upon the next live creature that it sees.
Fetch me this herb, and be thou here again
Ere the leviathan can swim a league.   174
PUCK. I'll put a girdle round about the earth
In forty minutes.   *(Exit.)*
OBERON.   Having once this juice,
I'll watch Titania when she is asleep
And drop the liquor of it in her eyes.
The next thing then she waking looks upon,
Be it on lion, bear, or wolf, or bull,
On meddling monkey, or on busy ape,
She shall pursue it with the soul of love.
And ere I take this charm from off her sight,
As I can take it with another herb,
I'll make her render up her page to me.
But who comes here? I am invisible,
And I will overhear their conference.

(He stands aside.)

(Enter Demetrius, Helena following him.)

DEMETRIUS. I love thee not; therefore pursue me not.
Where is Lysander and fair Hermia?

---

158 **vestal** vestal virgin. (Contains a complimentary allusion to Queen Elizabeth as a votaress of Diana and probably refers to an actual entertainment in her honor at Elvetham in 1591.) **by** in the region of   159 **loosed** released   160 **As** as if   161 **might** could   164 **fancy-free** free of love's spell. 165 **bolt** arrow   168 **love-in-idleness** pansy, heartsease.   171 **or man** either man   174 **leviathan** sea monster, whale

The one I'll slay; the other slayeth me.
Thou toldst me they were stol'n unto this wood;
And here am I, and wood within this wood   *192*
Because I cannot meet my Hermia.
Hence, get thee gone, and follow me no more.
HELENA. You draw me, you hardhearted adamant!   *195*
But yet you draw not iron, for my heart
Is true as steel. Leave you your power to draw,   *197*
And I shall have no power to follow you.
DEMETRIUS. Do I entice you? Do I speak you fair?   *199*
Or rather do I not in plainest truth
Tell you I do not nor I cannot love you?
HELENA. And even for that do I love you the more.
I am your spaniel; and, Demetrius,
The more you beat me I will fawn on you.
Use me but as your spaniel, spurn me, strike me,
Neglect me, lose me; only give me leave,
Unworthy as I am, to follow you.
What worser place can I beg in your love—
And yet a place of high respect with me—
Than to be usèd as you use your dog?
DEMETRIUS. Tempt not too much the hatred of my spirit,
For I am sick when I do look on thee.
HELENA. And I am sick when I look not on you.
DEMETRIUS. You do impeach your modesty too much   *214*
To leave the city and commit yourself   *215*
Into the hands of one that loves you not,
To trust the opportunity of night
And the ill counsel of a desert place   *218*
With the rich worth of your virginity.
HELENA. Your virtue is my privilege. For that   *220*
It is not night when I do see your face,
Therefore I think I am not in the night;
Nor doth this wood lack worlds of company,
For you, in my respect, are all the world.   *224*

---

192 wood mad, frantic. (With an obvious wordplay on *wood,* meaning "woods.")   **195 adamant** lodestone, magnet. (With pun on *hardhearted,* since adamant was also thought to be the hardest of all stones and was confused with the diamond.)   **197 Leave you** Give up   **199 speak you fair** speak courteously to you.   **214 impeach** call into question   **215 To leave** by leaving   **218 desert** deserted   **220 privilege** safeguard, warrant.   **For that** Because   **224 in my respect** as far as I am concerned, in my esteem

Then how can it be said I am alone
When all the world is here to look on me?
DEMETRIUS. I'll run from thee and hide me in the brakes,   227
And leave thee to the mercy of wild beasts.
HELENA. The wildest hath not such a heart as you.
Run when you will. The story shall be changed:
Apollo flies and Daphne holds the chase,   231
The dove pursues the griffin, the mild hind   232
Makes speed to catch the tiger—bootless speed,   233
When cowardice pursues and valor flies!
DEMETRIUS. I will not stay thy questions. Let me go!   235
Or if thou follow me, do not believe
But I shall do thee mischief in the wood.
HELENA. Ay, in the temple, in the town, the field,
You do me mischief. Fie, Demetrius!
Your wrongs do set a scandal on my sex.   240
We cannot fight for love, as men may do;
We should be wooed and were not made to woo.

(*Exit Demetrius.*)

I'll follow thee and make a heaven of hell,
To die upon the hand I love so well.   (*Exit.*)   244
OBERON. Fare thee well, nymph. Ere he do leave this grove
Thou shalt fly him, and he shall seek thy love.

(*Enter Puck.*)

Hast thou the flower there? Welcome, wanderer.
PUCK. Ay, there it is.   (*He offers the flower.*)
OBERON.   I pray thee, give it me.
I know a bank where the wild thyme blows,   249
Where oxlips and the nodding violet grows,   250
Quite overcanopied with luscious woodbine,   251
With sweet muskroses and with eglantine.   252
There sleeps Titania sometime of the night,   253

---

227 brakes thickets   **231 Apollo . . . chase** (In the ancient myth, Daphne fled from Apollo and was saved from rape by being transformed into a laurel tree; here it is the female who *holds the chase*, or pursues, instead of the male.)   **232 griffin** a fabulous monster with the head and wings of an eagle and the body of a lion.   **hind** female deer   **233 bootless** fruitless   **235 stay** wait for, put up with. **questions** talk or argument.   **240 Your . . . sex** i.e., The wrongs that you do me cause me to act in a manner that disgraces my sex.   **244 upon** by   **249 blows** blooms   **250 oxlips** flowers resembling cowslip and primrose   **251 woodbine** honeysuckle   **252 muskroses** a kind of large, sweet-scented rose.   **eglantine** sweetbrier, another kind of rose.   **253 sometime of** for part of

Lulled in these flowers with dances and delight;
And there the snake throws her enameled skin,   *255*
Weed wide enough to wrap a fairy in.   *256*
And with the juice of this I'll streak her eyes   *257*
And make her full of hateful fantasies.
Take thou some of it, and seek through this grove.

(He gives some love juice.)

A sweet Athenian lady is in love
With a disdainful youth. Anoint his eyes,
But do it when the next thing he espies
May be the lady. Thou shalt know the man
By the Athenian garments he hath on.
Effect it with some care, that he may prove
More fond on her than she upon her love;   *266*
And look thou meet me ere the first cock crow.
PUCK. Fear not, my lord, your servant shall do so.

(Exeunt [separately].)

2.2

Enter Titania, Queen of Fairies, with her train.

TITANIA. Come, now a roundel and a fairy song;   *1*
Then, for the third part of a minute, hence—
Some to kill cankers in the muskrose buds,   *3*
Some war with reremice for their leathern wings   *4*
To make my small elves coats, and some keep back
The clamorous owl, that nightly hoots and wonders
At our quaint spirits. Sing me now asleep.   *7*
Then to your offices, and let me rest.

(Fairies sing.)

FIRST FAIRY. You spotted snakes with double tongue,   *9*
    Thorny hedgehogs, be not seen;
    Newts and blindworms, do no wrong;   *11*

---

255 throws sloughs off, sheds   **256 Weed** garment   **257 streak** anoint, touch gently   **266 fond on** doting on
2.2. Location: The wood.
1 roundel dance in a ring   **3 cankers** cankerworms (i.e., caterpillars or grubs)   **4 reremice** bats
7 quaint dainty   **9 double** forked   **11 Newts** water lizards. (Considered poisonous, as were *blindworms*—small snakes with tiny eyes—and spiders.)

Come not near our Fairy Queen.
CHORUS. *(dancing)*.
    Philomel, with melody   13
    Sing in our sweet lullaby;
Lulla, lulla, lullaby, lulla, lulla, lullaby.
    Never harm
    Nor spell nor charm
Come our lovely lady nigh.
So good night, with lullaby.
FIRST FAIRY. Weaving spiders, come not here;
    Hence, you long-legged spinners, hence!
Beetles black, approach not near;
    Worm nor snail, do no offense.   23
CHORUS *(dancing)*.
    Philomel, with melody
    Sing in our sweet lullaby;
Lulla, lulla, lullaby, lulla, lulla, lullaby.
    Never harm
    Nor spell nor charm
Come our lovely lady nigh.
So good night, with lullaby.   *(Titania sleeps.)*
SECOND FAIRY.
    Hence, away! Now all is well.
    One aloof stand sentinel.   32

(Exeunt Fairies, leaving one sentinel.)

(Enter Oberon [and squeezes the flower on Titania's eyelids].)

OBERON. What thou see'st when thou dost wake,
    Do it for thy true love take;
    Love and languish for his sake.
    Be it ounce, or cat, or bear,   36
    Pard, or boar with bristled hair,   37
    In thy eye that shall appear
    When thou wak'st, it is thy dear.
    Wake when some vile thing is near.   *(Exit.)*

(Enter Lysander and Hermia.)

---

13 **Philomel** the nightingale. (Philomela, daughter of King Pandion, was transformed into a nightingale, according to Ovid's *Metamorphoses* 6, after she had been raped by her sister Procne's husband, Tereus.) **23 offense** harm. **32 sentinel** (Presumably Oberon is able to outwit or intimidate this guard.) **36 ounce** lynx   **37 Pard** leopard

LYSANDER. Fair love, you faint with wand'ring in the wood;
    And to speak truth, I have forgot our way.
    We'll rest us, Hermia, if you think it good,
    And tarry for the comfort of the day.
HERMIA. Be it so, Lysander. Find you out a bed,
    For I upon this bank will rest my head.
LYSANDER. One turf shall serve as pillow for us both;
    One heart, one bed, two bosoms, and one troth.   *48*
HERMIA. Nay, good Lysander, for my sake, my dear,
    Lie further off yet. Do not lie so near.
LYSANDER. Oh, take the sense, sweet, of my innocence!   *51*
    Love takes the meaning in love's conference.   *52*
    I mean that my heart unto yours is knit,
    So that but one heart we can make of it;
    Two bosoms interchainèd with an oath—
    So then two bosoms and a single troth.
    Then by your side no bed-room me deny,
    For lying so, Hermia, I do not lie.   *58*
HERMIA. Lysander riddles very prettily.
    Now much beshrew my manners and my pride   *60*
    If Hermia meant to say Lysander lied.
    But, gentle friend, for love and courtesy
    Lie further off, in human modesty.
    Such separation as may well be said
    Becomes a virtuous bachelor and a maid,
    So far be distant; and, good night, sweet friend.
    Thy love ne'er alter till thy sweet life end!
LYSANDER. Amen, amen, to that fair prayer, say I,
    And then end life when I end loyalty!
    Here is my bed. Sleep give thee all his rest!
HERMIA. With half that wish the wisher's eyes be pressed!   *71*

               (*They sleep, separated by a short distance.*)

(*Enter Puck.*)

PUCK. Through the forest have I gone,
    But Athenian found I none

---

48 troth faith, trothplight.   **51–2 take . . . conference** take my meaning in an innocent sense, with generosity and sympathy! True lovers do so when they converse.   **58 lie** tell a falsehood. (With a riddling pun on *lie,* "recline.")   **60 beshrew** (A mild oath.)   **71 With . . . pressed!** i.e., I return half that wish, so that you, the wisher, may sleep well too (instead of Sleep giving all his rest to me)!

On whose eyes I might approve   *74*
This flower's force in stirring love.
Night and silence.—Who is here?
Weeds of Athens he doth wear.
This is he, my master said,
Despisèd the Athenian maid;
And here the maiden, sleeping sound,
On the dank and dirty ground.
Pretty soul, she durst not lie
Near this lack-love, this kill-courtesy.
Churl, upon thy eyes I throw
All the power this charm doth owe.   *85*

(*He applies the love juice.*)

When thou wak'st, let love forbid   *86*
Sleep his seat on thy eyelid.   *87*
So awake when I am gone,
For I must now to Oberon.   (*Exit.*)

(*Enter Demetrius and Helena, running.*)

HELENA. Stay, though thou kill me, sweet Demetrius!
DEMETRIUS. I charge thee, hence, and do not haunt me thus.
HELENA. Oh, wilt thou darkling leave me? Do not so.   *92*
DEMETRIUS. Stay, on thy peril! I alone will go.   (*Exit.*)   *93*
HELENA. Oh, I am out of breath in this fond chase!   *94*
The more my prayer, the lesser is my grace.   *95*
Happy is Hermia, wheresoe'er she lies,   *96*
For she hath blessèd and attractive eyes.
How came her eyes so bright? Not with salt tears;
If so, my eyes are oft'ner washed than hers.
No, no, I am as ugly as a bear,
For beasts that meet me run away for fear.
Therefore no marvel though Demetrius   *102*
Do, as a monster, fly my presence thus.   *103*
What wicked and dissembling glass of mine   *104*
Made me compare with Hermia's sphery eyne?   *105*

---

74 approve test   **85 owe** own.   **86–7 let . . . eyelid** may love, heretofore denied, be enthroned in your
eyes.   **92 darkling** in the dark   **93 on thy peril** i.e., on pain of reprisal if you don't obey me and
stay.   **94 fond** doting   **95 my grace** the favor I obtain.   **96 lies** dwells   **102–3 no marvel . . . thus**
i.e., no wonder that Demetrius flies from me as from a monster.   **104 glass** mirror   **105 compare**
compare myself.   **sphery eyne** eyes as bright as stars in their spheres.

But who is here? Lysander, on the ground?
Dead, or asleep? I see no blood, no wound.
Lysander, if you live, good sir, awake.
LYSANDER. (*awaking*)
And run through fire I will for thy sweet sake.
Transparent Helena! Nature shows art,   *110*
That through thy bosom makes me see thy heart.
Where is Demetrius? Oh, how fit a word
Is that vile name to perish on my sword!
HELENA. Do not say so, Lysander; say not so.
What though he love your Hermia? Lord, what though?
Yet Hermia still loves you. Then be content.
LYSANDER. Content with Hermia? No! I do repent
The tedious minutes I with her have spent.
Not Hermia but Helena I love.
Who will not change a raven for a dove?
The will of man is by his reason swayed,   *121*
And reason says you are the worthier maid.
Things growing are not ripe until their season;
So I, being young, till now ripe not to reason.   *124*
And, touching now the point of human skill,   *125*
Reason becomes the marshal to my will
And leads me to your eyes, where I o'erlook   *127*
Love's stories written in love's richest book.
HELENA. Wherefore was I to this keen mockery born?   *129*
When at your hands did I deserve this scorn?
Is't not enough, is't not enough, young man,
That I did never—no, nor never can—
Deserve a sweet look from Demetrius' eye,
But you must flout my insufficiency?
Good troth, you do me wrong, good sooth, you do,   *135*
In such disdainful manner me to woo.
But fare you well. Perforce I must confess
I thought you lord of more true gentleness.   *138*
Oh, that a lady, of one man refused,   *139*
Should of another therefore be abused!   (*Exit.*)   *140*
LYSANDER. She sees not Hermia. Hermia, sleep thou there,

---

110 Transparent Radiant, pure. **art** skill, magic power   **121 will** desire   **124 ripe not** have not
ripened   **125 touching . . . skill** reaching now the age of mature judgment   **127 o'erlook** read over
129 Wherefore Why   **135 Good troth, good sooth** i.e., Indeed, truly   **138 lord of** i.e., possessor of.
gentleness courtesy.   **139 of** by   **140 abused** ill treated.

And never mayst thou come Lysander near!
For as a surfeit of the sweetest things
The deepest loathing to the stomach brings,
Or as the heresies that men do leave   145
Are hated most of those they did deceive,   146
So thou, my surfeit and my heresy,
Of all be hated, but the most of me!   148
And, all my powers, address your love and might   149
To honor Helen and to be her knight!   (*Exit.*)
HELENA. (*awaking*)
Help me, Lysander, help me! Do thy best
To pluck this crawling serpent from my breast!
Ay me, for pity! What a dream was here!
Lysander, look how I do quake with fear.
Methought a serpent ate my heart away,
And you sat smiling at his cruel prey.   156
Lysander! What, removed? Lysander! Lord!
What, out of hearing? Gone? No sound, no word?
Alack, where are you? Speak, an if you hear;   159
Speak, of all loves! I swoon almost with fear.   160
No? Then I well perceive you are not nigh.
Either death, or you, I'll find immediately.

(*Exit. [The sleeping Titania remains.]*)

3.1

Enter the clowns (Quince, Snug, Bottom, Flute, Snout, and Starveling).

BOTTOM. Are we all met?
QUINCE. Pat, pat; and here's a marvelous convenient place   2
  for our rehearsal. This green plot shall be our stage,
  this hawthorn brake our tiring-house, and we will do it   4
  in action as we will do it before the Duke.
BOTTOM. Peter Quince?
QUINCE. What sayest thou, bully Bottom?   7

145–6 **as . . . deceive** as renounced heresies are hated most by those persons who formerly were
deceived by them 148 **Of . . . of** by . . . by 149 **address** direct, apply 156 **prey** act of preying.
159 **an if** if 160 **of all loves** for love's sake.
3.1. **Location: The action is continuous.**
0.1 **clowns** rustics 2 **Pat** On the dot, punctually 4 **brake** thicket. **tiring-house** attiring area, hence
backstage 7 **bully** i.e., worthy, jolly, fine fellow

BOTTOM. There are things in this comedy of Pyramus and
Thisbe that will never please. First, Pyramus must draw
a sword to kill himself, which the ladies cannot abide.
How answer you that?

SNOUT. By'r lakin, a parlous fear. 12

STARVELING. I believe we must leave the killing out, when
all is done. 14

BOTTOM. Not a whit. I have a device to make all well.
Write me a prologue, and let the prologue seem to say, 16
we will do no harm with our swords, and that Pyramus
is not killed indeed; and for the more better assurance,
tell them that I, Pyramus, am not Pyramus but Bottom
the weaver. This will put them out of fear.

QUINCE. Well, we will have such a prologue, and it shall be
written in eight and six. 22

BOTTOM. No, make it two more: let it be written in eight
and eight.

SNOUT. Will not the ladies be afeard of the lion?

STARVELING. I fear it, I promise you.

BOTTOM. Masters, you ought to consider with yourself, to
bring in—God shield us!—a lion among ladies is a most 28
dreadful thing. For there is not a more fearful wildfowl 29
than your lion living, and we ought to look to 't.

SNOUT. Therefore another prologue must tell he is not a
lion.

BOTTOM. Nay, you must name his name, and half his face
must be seen through the lion's neck, and he himself
must speak through, saying thus or to the same defect: 36
"Ladies," or "Fair ladies, I would wish you," or "I would
request you," or "I would entreat you, not to fear, not to
tremble; my life for yours. If you think I come hither as a 39
lion, it were pity of my life. No, I am no such thing; I am 40

---

12 **By'r lakin** By our ladykin, i.e., the Virgin Mary. **parlous** perilous, alarming   14 **when all is done**
i.e., when all is said and done.   16 **Write me** i.e., Write at my suggestion. (*Me* is used colloquially.)
22 **eight and six** alternate lines of eight and six syllables, a common ballad measure.   28 **lion among
ladies** (A contemporary pamphlet tells how, at the christening in 1594 of Prince Henry, eldest son of
King James VI of Scotland, later James I of England, a "blackamoor" instead of a lion drew the tri-
umphal chariot, since the lion's presence might have "brought some fear to the nearest.")   29 **fearful**
fear-inspiring   36 **defect** (Bottom's blunder for "effect.")   39 **my life for yours** i.e., I pledge my life
to make your lives safe.   40 **it were ... life** i.e., I should be sorry, by my life; or, my life would be
endangered.

a man as other men are." And there indeed let him name his name, and tell them plainly he is Snug the joiner.

QUINCE. Well, it shall be so. But there is two hard things: that is, to bring the moonlight into a chamber; for, you know, Pyramus and Thisbe meet by moonlight.

SNOUT. Doth the moon shine that night we play our play?

BOTTOM. A calendar, a calendar! Look in the almanac. Find out moonshine, find out moonshine.

(*They consult an almanac.*)

QUINCE. Yes, it doth shine that night.

BOTTOM. Why then may you leave a casement of the great chamber window where we play open, and the moon may shine in at the casement.

QUINCE. Ay; or else one must come in with a bush of thorns and a lantern and say he comes to disfigure, or to present, the person of Moonshine. Then there is another thing: we must have a wall in the great chamber; for Pyramus and Thisbe, says the story, did talk through the chink of a wall.

SNOUT. You can never bring in a wall. What say you, Bottom?

BOTTOM. Some man or other must present Wall. And let him have some plaster, or some loam, or some roughcast about him, to signify wall; or let him hold his fingers thus, and through that cranny shall Pyramus and Thisbe whisper.

QUINCE. If that may be, then all is well. Come, sit down, every mother's son, and rehearse your parts. Pyramus, you begin. When you have spoken your speech, enter into that brake, and so everyone according to his cue.

(*Enter Robin [Puck].*)

PUCK (*aside*). What hempen homespuns have we swaggering here So near the cradle of the Fairy Queen? What, a play toward? I'll be an auditor;

55
56

64
65

72
73
74

55–6 **bush of thorns** bundle of thornbush fagots. (Part of the accoutrements of the man in the moon, according to the popular notions of the time, along with his lantern and his dog.) 56 **disfigure** (Quince's blunder for "figure," "represent.") 64–5 **roughcast** a mixture of lime and gravel used to plaster the outside of buildings 72 **hempen homespuns** i.e., rustics dressed in homespun fabric made from hemp 73 **cradle** i.e., Titania's bower 74 **toward** about to take place.

An actor, too, perhaps, if I see cause.

QUINCE. Speak, Pyramus. Thisbe, stand forth.

BOTTOM (*as Pyramus*).

"Thisbe, the flowers of odious savors sweet—"

QUINCE. Odors, odors.

BOTTOM. "—Odors savors sweet;

    So hath thy breath, my dearest Thisbe dear.

But hark, a voice! Stay thou but here awhile,

    And by and by I will to thee appear."   (*Exit.*)

PUCK. A stranger Pyramus than e'er played here.   (*Exit.*)   83

FLUTE. Must I speak now?

QUINCE. Ay, marry, must you; for you must understand

he goes but to see a noise that he heard, and is to come

again.

FLUTE (*as Thisbe*).

"Most radiant Pyramus, most lily-white of hue,

    Of color like the red rose on triumphant brier,   89

Most brisky juvenal and eke most lovely Jew,   90

    As true as truest horse that yet would never tire.

I'll meet thee, Pyramus, at Ninny's tomb."

QUINCE. "Ninus' tomb," man. Why, you must not speak   93

that yet. That you answer to Pyramus. You speak all

your part at once, cues and all. Pyramus, enter. Your   95

cue is past; it is "never tire."

FLUTE. Oh—"As true as truest horse that yet would never tire."

(*Enter Puck, and Bottom as Pyramus with the ass head.*)   97

BOTTOM. "If I were fair, Thisbe, I were only thine."   98

QUINCE. Oh, monstrous! Oh, strange! We are haunted.

Pray, masters! Fly, masters! Help!

(*Exeunt Quince, Snug, Flute, Snout, and Starveling.*)

PUCK. I'll follow you: I'll lead you about a round,   101

---

83 **A stranger ... here** The strangest Pyramus you ever saw.   89 **triumphant** magnificent
90 **brisky juvenal** lively youth. **eke** also. **Jew** (A desperate attempt to rhyme with *hue*, inspired
perhaps by the first syllable of *juvenal*.) 93 **Ninus** mythical founder of Nineveh (whose wife,
Semiramis, was supposed to have built the walls of Babylon where the story of Pyramus and Thisbe
takes place) 95 **part** (An actor's *part* was a script consisting only of his speeches and their cues.)
97.1–2 **with the ass head** (This stage direction, taken from the Folio, presumably refers to a standard
stage property.) 98 **If** Even if. **fair** handsome. **were** would be 101 **about a round** roundabout

Through bog, through bush, through brake,
　　through brier.
Sometimes a horse I'll be, sometimes a hound,
　　A hog, a headless bear, sometimes a fire;　　　　*104*
And neigh, and bark, and grunt, and roar, and burn,
Like horse, hound, hog, bear, fire, at every turn. *(Exit.)*
BOTTOM. Why do they run away? This is a knavery of
　　them to make me afeard.

(Enter Snout.)

SNOUT. Oh, Bottom, thou art changed! What do I see on
　　thee?
BOTTOM. What do you see? You see an ass head of your
　　own, do you?　　　　　　　　　　　　*(Exit Snout.)*

(Enter Quince.)

QUINCE. Bless thee, Bottom, bless thee! Thou art trans-　*113*
　　lated.　　　　　　　　　　　　　　　*(Exit.)*　　*114*
BOTTOM. I see their knavery. This is to make an ass of me,
　　to fright me, if they could. But I will not stir from this
　　place, do what they can. I will walk up and down here,
　　and I will sing, that they shall hear I am not
　　afraid.　　　　　　　　　　　　　*(He sings.)*
　　　The ouzel cock so black of hue,　　　　　　*120*
　　　　With orange-tawny bill,
　　　The throstle with his note so true,　　　　　*122*
　　　The wren with little quill—　　　　　　　*123*
TITANIA. *(awaking).* What angel wakes me from my
　　flow'ry bed?
BOTTOM *(sings).* The finch, the sparrow, and the lark,
　　　The plainsong cuckoo gray,　　　　　　　*126*
　　Whose note full many a man doth mark,
　　　And dares not answer nay—　　　　　　　*128*
For indeed, who would set his wit to so foolish a bird?　*129*
Who would give a bird the lie, though he cry "cuckoo"　*130*
never so?　　　　　　　　　　　　　　　　*131*

---

104 **fire** will-o'-the-wisp　113–14 **translated** transformed.　120 **ouzel cock** male blackbird
122 **throstle** song thrush　123 **with little quill** with small pipe, i.e., high-pitched note; or else with
small feathers　126 **plainsong** singing a melody without variations　128 **dares . . . nay** i.e., cannot
deny that he is a cuckold　129 **set his wit to** employ his intelligence to answer　130 **give . . . lie** call
the bird a liar　131 **never so** ever so much.

TITANIA. I pray thee, gentle mortal, sing again.
Mine ear is much enamored of thy note;
So is mine eye enthrallèd to thy shape;
And thy fair virtue's force perforce doth move me 135
On the first view to say, to swear, I love thee.
BOTTOM. Methinks, mistress, you should have little reason
for that. And yet, to say the truth, reason and love keep
little company together nowadays—the more the pity
that some honest neighbors will not make them
friends. Nay, I can gleek upon occasion. 141
TITANIA. Thou art as wise as thou art beautiful.
BOTTOM. Not so, neither. But if I had wit enough to get
out of this wood, I have enough to serve mine own 144
turn. 145
TITANIA. Out of this wood do not desire to go.
Thou shalt remain here, whether thou wilt or no.
I am a spirit of no common rate. 148
The summer still doth tend upon my state, 149
And I do love thee. Therefore, go with me.
I'll give thee fairies to attend on thee,
And they shall fetch thee jewels from the deep,
And sing while thou on pressèd flowers dost sleep.
And I will purge thy mortal grossness so
That thou shalt like an airy spirit go.—
Peaseblossom, Cobweb, Mote, and Mustardseed! 156

*(Enter four Fairies [Peaseblossom, Cobweb, Mote, and
Mustardseed].)*

PEASEBLOSSOM. Ready.
COBWEB. And I.
MOTE. And I.
MUSTARDSEED. And I.
ALL.   Where shall we go?
TITANIA. Be kind and courteous to this gentleman.
Hop in his walks and gambol in his eyes; 160
Feed him with apricots and dewberries, 161

---

135 **thy . . . force** the power of your unblemished excellence   141 **gleek** jest   **144–5 serve . . . turn**
answer my purpose.   148 **rate** rank, value.   149 **still . . . state** always waits upon me as a part of my
royal retinue   156 **Mote** i.e., speck. (The two words *moth* and *mote* were pronounced alike, and
both meanings may be present.)   160 **in his eyes** in his sight (i.e., before him)   161 **dewberries**
blackberries

With purple grapes, green figs, and mulberries;
The honey bags steal from the humble-bees,
And for night tapers crop their waxen thighs, 164
And light them at the fiery glowworms' eyes, 165
To have my love to bed and to arise;
And pluck the wings from painted butterflies
To fan the moonbeams from his sleeping eyes.
Nod to him, elves, and do him courtesies.

PEASEBLOSSOM. Hail, mortal!

COBWEB. Hail!

MOTE. Hail!

MUSTARDSEED. Hail!

BOTTOM. I cry Your Worships mercy, heartily. I beseech 174
Your Worship's name.

COBWEB. Cobweb.

BOTTOM. I shall desire you of more acquaintance, good 177
Master Cobweb. If I cut my finger, I shall make bold 178
with you.—Your name, honest gentleman? 179

PEASEBLOSSOM. Peaseblossom.

BOTTOM. I pray you, commend me to Mistress Squash, 181
your mother, and to Master Peascod, your father. Good 182
Master Peaseblossom, I shall desire you of more
acquaintance too.—Your name, I beseech you, sir?

MUSTARDSEED. Mustardseed.

BOTTOM. Good Master Mustardseed, I know your 186
patience well. That same cowardly, giantlike ox-beef 187
hath devoured many a gentleman of your house. I
promise you, your kindred hath made my eyes water 189
ere now. I desire you of more acquaintance, good
Master Mustardseed.

TITANIA. Come wait upon him; lead him to my bower.
The moon methinks looks with a wat'ry eye;
And when she weeps, weeps every little flower, 194

---

164 night ... thighs (The waxen thighs of the bumble-bee are to be fashioned into wax candles to light Bottom's way in the dark.) **165 eyes** (In fact, the light is emitted by the abdomen. *Eyes* may be metaphorical.) **174 I cry ... mercy** I beg pardon of Your Worships (for presuming to ask a question) **177 I ... acquaintance** I crave to be better acquainted with you **178–9 If ... you** (Cobwebs were used to stanch bleeding.) **181 Squash** unripe pea pod **182 Peascod** ripe pea pod **186–7 your patience** what you have endured. (Mustard is eaten with beef.) **189 water** (1) weep for sympathy (2) smart, sting **194 And ... flower** (Dew was thought to fall from the heavens in greater proportion as the moon shown fully.)

Lamenting some enforcèd chastity.   195
Tie up my lover's tongue; bring him silently.   196

(Exeunt.)

3.2

Enter [Oberon,] King of Fairies.

OBERON. I wonder if Titania be awaked;
Then, what it was that next came in her eye,
Which she must dote on in extremity.

([Enter]) Robin Goodfellow [Puck].)

Here comes my messenger. How now, mad spirit?
What night-rule now about this haunted grove?   5
PUCK. My mistress with a monster is in love.
Near to her close and consecrated bower,   7
While she was in her dull and sleeping hour,   8
A crew of patches, rude mechanicals,   9
That work for bread upon Athenian stalls,   10
Were met together to rehearse a play
Intended for great Theseus' nuptial day.
The shallowest thickskin of that barren sort,   13
Who Pyramus presented, in their sport   14
Forsook his scene and entered in a brake.   15
When I did him at this advantage take,
An ass's noll I fixèd on his head.   17
Anon his Thisbe must be answerèd,
And forth my mimic comes. When they him spy,   19
As wild geese that the creeping fowler eye,   20
Or russet-pated choughs, many in sort,   21
Rising and cawing at the gun's report,
Sever themselves and madly sweep the sky,   23
So, at his sight, away his fellows fly;

---

195 enforcèd violated. (The moon is associated throughout the play with the goddess Diana and chastity.) **196 Tie . . . tongue** (Presumably Bottom is braying like an ass.)
3.2. Location: The wood.
5 night-rule diversion or misrule for the night **7 close** secret **8 dull** drowsy **9 patches** clowns, fools. **rude mechanicals** ignorant artisans **10 stalls** market booths **13 barren sort** stupid company or crew **14 presented** acted **15 scene** playing area **17 noll** noddle, head **19 mimic** actor **20 fowler** hunter of game birds **21 russet-pated choughs** reddish brown or gray-headed jackdaws. **in sort** in a flock **23 Sever themselves** i.e., scatter

And, at our stamp, here o'er and o'er one falls;
He "Murder!" cries and help from Athens calls.
Their sense thus weak, lost with their fears thus strong,   27
Made senseless things begin to do them wrong,   28
For briers and thorns at their apparel snatch;
Some, sleeves—some, hats; from yielders all things catch.   30
I led them on in this distracted fear
And left sweet Pyramus translated there,
When in that moment, so it came to pass,
Titania waked and straightway loved an ass.
OBERON. This falls out better than I could devise.
But hast thou yet latched the Athenian's eyes   36
With the love juice, as I did bid thee do?
PUCK. I took him sleeping—that is finished too—
And the Athenian woman by his side,
That, when he waked, of force she must be eyed.   40

(*Enter Demetrius and Hermia.*)

OBERON. Stand close. This is the same Athenian.
PUCK. This is the woman, but not this the man.

(*They stand aside.*)

DEMETRIUS. Oh, why rebuke you him that loves you so?
Lay breath so bitter on your bitter foe.
HERMIA. Now I but chide; but I should use thee worse,
For thou, I fear, hast given me cause to curse.
If thou hast slain Lysander in his sleep,
Being o'er shoes in blood, plunge in the deep,   48
And kill me too.
The sun was not so true unto the day
As he to me. Would he have stolen away
From sleeping Hermia? I'll believe as soon
This whole earth may be bored, and that the moon   53
May through the center creep, and so displease
Her brother's noontide with th'Antipodes.   55

27–8 Their . . . wrong Their weakened physical senses, disabled by their strong fears, made it seem to them as though inanimate things in the forest were attacking them   **30 from . . . catch** the forest snatches away everything from those who yield to it.   **36 latched** snared, taken prisoner   **40 of force** perforce   **48 Being o'er shoes** having waded in so far   **53 whole** solid   **55 Her . . . Antipodes** i.e., the sun's noontime on the opposite side of the earth, among the people who live there, the Antipodes.

It cannot be but thou hast murdered him;
So should a murderer look, so dead, so grim.   57
DEMETRIUS. So should the murdered look, and so should I,
Pierced through the heart with your stern cruelty.
Yet you, the murderer, look as bright, as clear
As yonder Venus in her glimmering sphere.
HERMIA. What's this to my Lysander? Where is he?   62
Ah, good Demetrius, wilt thou give him me?
DEMETRIUS. I had rather give his carcass to my hounds.
HERMIA. Out, dog! Out, cur! Thou driv'st me past the bounds
Of maiden's patience. Hast thou slain him, then?
Henceforth be never numbered among men.
Oh, once tell true, tell true, even for my sake: 68
Durst thou have looked upon him being awake?   69
And hast thou killed him sleeping? Oh, brave touch!   70
Could not a worm, an adder, do so much?   71
An adder did it; for with doubler tongue   72
Than thine, thou serpent, never adder stung.
DEMETRIUS. You spend your passion on a misprised mood.   74
I am not guilty of Lysander's blood,
Nor is he dead, for aught that I can tell.
HERMIA. I pray thee, tell me then that he is well.
DEMETRIUS. And if I could, what should I get therefor?   78
HERMIA. A privilege never to see me more.
And from thy hated presence part I so.
See me no more, whether he be dead or no.   (*Exit.*)
DEMETRIUS. There is no following her in this fierce vein.
Here therefore for a while I will remain.
So sorrow's heaviness doth heavier grow   84
For debt that bankrupt sleep doth sorrow owe,   85
Which now in some slight measure it will pay,   86
If for his tender here I make some stay.   87

(*[He] lie[s] down [and sleeps].*)

OBERON. What hast thou done? Thou hast mistaken quite

---

57 dead deadly, or deathly pale   **62 to** to do with   **68 once** once and for all   **69 being awake** when
he was awake.   **70 brave touch!** fine stroke! (Said ironically.)   **71 worm** serpent   **72 doubler** (1)
more forked (2) more deceitful   **74 You . . . mood** Your anger is misdirected.   **78 therefor** in return
for that.   **84–7 So . . . stay** The heaviness of sorrow grows still heavier when sleepiness adds to the
weariness caused by sorrow, which debt to sleepiness I will now repay in part if I can stop here and
accept what sleep has to offer.

And laid the love juice on some true love's sight.
Of thy misprision must perforce ensue   90
Some true love turned, and not a false turned true.
PUCK. Then fate o'errules, that, one man holding troth,   92
A million fail, confounding oath on oath.   93
OBERON. About the wood go swifter than the wind,
And Helena of Athens look thou find.
All fancy-sick she is and pale of cheer   96
With sighs of love, that cost the fresh blood dear.   97
By some illusion see thou bring her here.
I'll charm his eyes against she do appear.   99
PUCK. I go, I go, look how I go,
Swifter than arrow from the Tartar's bow.   *(Exit.)*   101
OBERON *(applying love juice to Demetrius's eyes).*
Flower of this purple dye,
Hit with Cupid's archery,
Sink in apple of his eye.
When his love he doth espy,   104
Let her shine as gloriously
As the Venus of the sky.
When thou wak'st, if she be by,
Beg of her for remedy.

(Enter Puck.)

PUCK. Captain of our fairy band,
Helena is here at hand,
And the youth, mistook by me,
Pleading for a lover's fee.   113
Shall we their fond pageant see?   114
Lord, what fools these mortals be!
OBERON. Stand aside. The noise they make
Will cause Demetrius to awake.
PUCK. Then will two at once woo one;
That must needs be sport alone.
And those things do best please me   119

---

90 misprision mistake   **92–3 Then...oath** If so, then fate prevails; for each male who is able to keep true faith in love, a million will fail, breaking oath on oath.   **96 fancy-sick** lovesick.   **cheer** face   **97 sighs...dear** (Each sigh was supposed to cost the heart a drop of blood.)   **99 against...appear** in anticipation of her coming.   **101 Tartar's bow** (Tartars were famed for their skill with the bow.)   **104 apple** pupil   **113 fee** privilege, reward.   **114 fond pageant** foolish spectacle   **119 alone** unequaled.

That befall preposterously.   *121*

(*They stand aside.*)

(*Enter Lysander and Helena.*)

LYSANDER. Why should you think that I should woo in
  scorn?
      Scorn and derision never come in tears.
      Look when I vow, I weep; and vows so born,   *124*
        In their nativity all truth appears.   *125*
      How can these things in me seem scorn to you,
      Bearing the badge of faith to prove them true?
HELENA. You do advance your cunning more and more.   *128*
      When truth kills truth, oh, devilish-holy fray!   *129*
      These vows are Hermia's. Will you give her o'er?
        Weigh oath with oath, and you will nothing weigh;
      Your vows to her and me, put in two scales,
      Will even weigh, and both as light as tales.
LYSANDER. I had no judgment when to her I swore.
HELENA. Nor none, in my mind, now you give her o'er.
LYSANDER. Demetrius loves her, and he loves not you.
DEMETRIUS (*awaking*).
      O Helen, goddess, nymph, perfect, divine!
      To what, my love, shall I compare thine eyne?
      Crystal is muddy. Oh, how ripe in show   *139*
      Thy lips, those kissing cherries, tempting grow!
      That pure congealèd white, high Taurus' snow,   *141*
      Fanned with the eastern wind, turns to a crow   *142*
      When thou hold'st up thy hand. Oh, let me kiss
      This princess of pure white, this seal of bliss! *144*
HELENA. Oh, spite! Oh, hell! I see you all are bent
      To set against me for your merriment.   *146*
      If you were civil and knew courtesy,
      You would not do me thus much injury.
      Can you not hate me, as I know you do,
      But you must join in souls to mock me too?   *150*

---

121 **preposterously** out of the natural order.   124 **Look when** Whenever   124–5 **vows . . . appears**
i.e., vows made by one who is weeping give evidence thereby of their sincerity.   128 **advance** carry
forward, display   129 **When . . . truth** i.e., When one of your vows cancels the other   133 **tales** lies.
139 **show** appearance   141 **Taurus** a lofty mountain range in Asia Minor   142 **turns to a crow** i.e.,
seems black by contrast   144 **seal** pledge   146 **set against** attack   150 **in souls** i.e., heart and soul

If you were men, as men you are in show,
You would not use a gentle lady so—
To vow, and swear, and superpraise my parts,   153
When I am sure you hate me with your hearts.
You both are rivals, and love Hermia,
And now both rivals to mock Helena.
A trim exploit, a manly enterprise,   157
To conjure tears up in a poor maid's eyes
With your derision! None of noble sort   159
Would so offend a virgin and extort   160
A poor soul's patience, all to make you sport.
LYSANDER. You are unkind, Demetrius. Be not so.
For you love Hermia; this you know I know.
And here, with all good will, with all my heart,
In Hermia's love I yield you up my part;
And yours of Helena to me bequeath,
Whom I do love, and will do till my death.
HELENA. Never did mockers waste more idle breath.
DEMETRIUS. Lysander, keep thy Hermia; I will none.   169
If e'er I loved her, all that love is gone.
My heart to her but as guestwise sojourned,   171
And now to Helen is it home returned,
There to remain.
LYSANDER. Helen, it is not so.
DEMETRIUS. Disparage not the faith thou dost not know,
Lest, to thy peril, thou aby it dear.   175
Look where thy love comes; yonder is thy dear.

(*Enter Hermia.*)

HERMIA. Dark night, that from the eye his function takes,   177
The ear more quick of apprehension makes;
Wherein it doth impair the seeing sense,
It pays the hearing double recompense.
Thou art not by mine eye, Lysander, found;
Mine ear, I thank it, brought me to thy sound.
But why unkindly didst thou leave me so?
LYSANDER. Why should he stay, whom love doth press to go?
HERMIA. What love could press Lysander from my side?

---

153 **superpraise** overpraise. **parts** qualities   157 **trim** pretty, fine. (Said ironically.)
159 **sort** character, quality   160 **extort** twist, torture   169 **will none** i.e., want no part of her
171 **to ... sojourned** only visited with her.   175 **aby** pay for   177 **his** its

LYSANDER. Lysander's love, that would not let him bide—
Fair Helena, who more engilds the night
Than all yon fiery oes and eyes of light.   *188*
Why seek'st thou me? Could not this make thee know
The hate I bear thee made me leave thee so?
HERMIA. You speak not as you think. It cannot be.
HELENA. Lo, she is one of this confederacy!
Now I perceive they have conjoined all three
To fashion this false sport, in spite of me.   *194*
Injurious Hermia, most ungrateful maid!
Have you conspired, have you with these contrived
To bait me with this foul derision?   *197*
Is all the counsel that we two have shared—   *198*
The sisters' vows, the hours that we have spent
When we have chid the hasty-footed time
For parting us—oh, is all forgot?
All schooldays' friendship, childhood innocence?
We, Hermia, like two artificial gods   *203*
Have with our needles created both one flower,
Both on one sampler, sitting on one cushion,
Both warbling of one song, both in one key,
As if our hands, our sides, voices, and minds
Had been incorporate. So we grew together,   *208*
Like to a double cherry, seeming parted,
But yet an union in partition,
Two lovely berries molded on one stem;
So, with two seeming bodies but one heart,
Two of the first, like coats in heraldry,   *213*
Due but to one and crownèd with one crest.   *214*
And will you rend our ancient love asunder,
To join with men in scorning your poor friend?
It is not friendly, 'tis not maidenly.
Our sex, as well as I, may chide you for it,
Though I alone do feel the injury.
HERMIA. I am amazèd at your passionate words.
I scorn you not. It seems that you scorn me.
HELENA. Have you not set Lysander, as in scorn,

---

188 oes spangles (here, stars)   **194 in spite of me** to vex me.   **197 bait** torment, as one sets on dogs to bait a bear   **198 counsel** confidential talk   **203 artificial** skilled in art or creation **208 incorporate** of one body.   **213–14 Two . . . crest** i.e., we have two separate bodies, just as a coat of arms in heraldry can be represented twice on a shield but surmounted by a single crest.

To follow me and praise my eyes and face?
And made your other love, Demetrius,
Who even but now did spurn me with his foot,
To call me goddess, nymph, divine, and rare,
Precious, celestial? Wherefore speaks he this
To her he hates? And wherefore doth Lysander
Deny your love, so rich within his soul,
And tender me, forsooth, affection,   230
But by your setting on, by your consent?
What though I be not so in grace as you,   232
So hung upon with love, so fortunate,
But miserable most, to love unloved?
This you should pity rather than despise.
HERMIA. I understand not what you mean by this.
HELENA. Ay, do! Persever, counterfeit sad looks,   237
  Make mouths upon me when I turn my back,   238
  Wink each at other, hold the sweet jest up.   239
  This sport, well carried, shall be chronicled.   240
  If you have any pity, grace, or manners,
  You would not make me such an argument.   242
  But fare ye well. 'Tis partly my own fault,
  Which death, or absence, soon shall remedy.
LYSANDER. Stay, gentle Helena; hear my excuse,
  My love, my life, my soul, fair Helena!
HELENA. Oh, excellent!
HERMIA (*to Lysander*). Sweet, do not scorn her so.
DEMETRIUS (*to Lysander*). If she cannot entreat, I can compel.   248
LYSANDER. Thou canst compel no more than she entreat.
  Thy threats have no more strength than her weak
      prayers.—
  Helen, I love thee, by my life, I do!
  I swear by that which I will lose for thee,
  To prove him false that says I love thee not.
DEMETRIUS (*to Helena*). I say I love thee more than he can do.
LYSANDER. If thou say so, withdraw, and prove it too.   255
DEMETRIUS. Quick, come!

---

230 tender offer   **232 grace** favor   **237 sad** grave, serious   **238 mouths** i.e., mows, faces, grimaces.
upon at   **239 hold ... up** keep up the joke.   **240 carried** carried out, brought off   **242 argument**
subject for a jest.   **248 entreat** i.e., succeed by entreaty   **255 withdraw ... too** i.e., withdraw with
me and prove your claim in a duel. (The two gentlemen are armed.)

HERMIA.   Lysander, whereto tends all this?
LYSANDER. Away, you Ethiope!

          (*He tries to break away from Hermia.*)

DEMETRIUS.   No, no; he'll   257
  Seem to break loose; take on as you would follow,   258
  But yet come not. You are a tame man. Go!
LYSANDER (*to Hermia*). Hang off, thou cat, thou burr!
  Vile thing, let loose,   260
  Or I will shake thee from me like a serpent!
HERMIA. Why are you grown so rude? What change is this,
  Sweet love?
LYSANDER.   Thy love? Out, tawny Tartar, out!
  Out, loathèd med'cine! O hated potion, hence!   264
HERMIA. Do you not jest?
HELENA.   Yes, sooth, and so do you.   265
LYSANDER. Demetrius, I will keep my word with thee.
DEMETRIUS. I would I had your bond, for I perceive
  A weak bond holds you. I'll not trust your word.   268
LYSANDER. What, should I hurt her, strike her, kill her dead?
  Although I hate her, I'll not harm her so.
HERMIA. What, can you do me greater harm than hate?
  Hate me? Wherefore? Oh, me, what news, my love?   272
  Am not I Hermia? Are not you Lysander?
  I am as fair now as I was erewhile.   274
  Since night you loved me; yet since night you left me.
  Why, then you left me—oh, the gods forbid!—
  In earnest, shall I say?
LYSANDER.   Ay, by my life!
  And never did desire to see thee more.
  Therefore be out of hope, of question, of doubt;
  Be certain, nothing truer. 'Tis no jest
  That I do hate thee and love Helena.
HERMIA (*to Helena*).Oh, me! You juggler! You cankerblossom!   282
  You thief of love! What, have you come by night
  And stol'n my love's heart from him?

---

257 Ethiope (Referring to Hermia's relatively dark hair and complexion; see also *tawny Tartar* six lines later.) **258 take on as** act as if, make a fuss as if **260 Hang off** Let go **264 med'cine** i.e., poison **265 sooth** truly **268 weak bond** i.e., Hermia's arm. (With a pun on *bond,* "oath," in the previous line.) **272 what news** what is the matter **274 erewhile** just now. **282 cankerblossom** worm that destroys the flower bud, or wild rose.

HELENA.   Fine, i'faith!
Have you no modesty, no maiden shame,
No touch of bashfulness? What, will you tear
Impatient answers from my gentle tongue?
Fie, fie! You counterfeit, you puppet, you!   288
HERMIA. "Puppet"? Why, so! Ay, that way goes the game.
Now I perceive that she hath made compare
Between our statures; she hath urged her height,
And with her personage, her tall personage,
Her height, forsooth, she hath prevailed with him.
And are you grown so high in his esteem
Because I am so dwarfish and so low?
How low am I, thou painted maypole? Speak!
How low am I? I am not yet so low
But that my nails can reach unto thine eyes.

(She flails at Helena but is restrained.)

HELENA. I pray you, though you mock me, gentlemen,
Let her not hurt me. I was never curst;   300
I have no gift at all in shrewishness;
I am a right maid for my cowardice.   302
Let her not strike me. You perhaps may think,
Because she is something lower than myself,   304
That I can match her.
HERMIA.   Lower? Hark, again!
HELENA. Good Hermia, do not be so bitter with me.
I evermore did love you, Hermia,
Did ever keep your counsels, never wronged you,
Save that, in love unto Demetrius,
I told him of your stealth unto this wood.   310
He followed you; for love I followed him.
But he hath chid me hence and threatened me   312
To strike me, spurn me, nay, to kill me too.   313
And now, so you will let me quiet go,   314
To Athens will I bear my folly back
And follow you no further. Let me go.
You see how simple and how fond I am.   317
HERMIA. Why, get you gone. Who is't that hinders you?

---

288 puppet (1) counterfeit (2) dwarfish woman (in reference to Hermia's smaller stature)
300 curst shrewish   **302 right** true   **304 something** somewhat   **310 stealth** stealing away
312 chid me hence driven me away with his scolding   **313 spurn** kick   **314 so** if only
317 fond foolish

HELENA. A foolish heart, that I leave here behind.
HERMIA. What, with Lysander?
HELENA.   With Demetrius.
LYSANDER. Be not afraid; she shall not harm thee, Helena.
DEMETRIUS. No, sir, she shall not, though you take her part.
HELENA. Oh, when she is angry, she is keen and shrewd.   *323*
  She was a vixen when she went to school;
  And though she be but little, she is fierce.
HERMIA. "Little" again? Nothing but "low" and "little"?—
  Why will you suffer her to flout me thus?
  Let me come to her.
LYSANDER.   Get you gone, you dwarf!
  You minimus, of hind'ring knotgrass made!   *329*
  You bead, you acorn!
DEMETRIUS.   You are too officious
  In her behalf that scorns your services.
  Let her alone. Speak not of Helena;
  Take not her part. For, if thou dost intend   *333*
  Never so little show of love to her,
  Thou shalt aby it.
LYSANDER.   Now she holds me not.   *335*
  Now follow, if thou dar'st, to try whose right,
  Of thine or mine, is most in Helena.   (*Exit.*)
DEMETRIUS. Follow? Nay, I'll go with thee, cheek by jowl.   *338*

                (*Exit, following Lysander.*)

HERMIA. You, mistress, all this coil is 'long of you.   *339*
  Nay, go not back.
HELENA.   I will not trust you, I,   *340*
  Nor longer stay in your curst company.
  Your hands than mine are quicker for a fray;
  My legs are longer, though, to run away.   (*Exit.*)
HERMIA. I am amazed and know not what to say.   (*Exit.*)

(*Oberon and Puck come forward.*)

OBERON. This is thy negligence. Still thou mistak'st,
  Or else commit'st thy knaveries willfully.

---

323 keen and shrewd fierce and shrewish. **329 minimus** diminutive creature. **knotgrass** a weed, an infusion of which was thought to stunt the growth **333 intend** give sign of **335 aby** pay for **338 cheek by jowl** i.e., side by side. **339 coil** turmoil, dissension. **'long of** on account of **340 go not back** i.e., don't retreat. (Hermia is again proposing a fight.)

PUCK. Believe me, king of shadows, I mistook.
Did not you tell me I should know the man
By the Athenian garments he had on?
And so far blameless proves my enterprise
That I have 'nointed an Athenian's eyes;
And so far am I glad it so did sort,   352
As this their jangling I esteem a sport.   353
OBERON. Thou see'st these lovers seek a place to fight.
Hie therefore, Robin, overcast the night;   355
The starry welkin cover thou anon   356
With drooping fog as black as Acheron,   357
And lead these testy rivals so astray
As one come not within another's way.   359
Like to Lysander sometimes frame thy tongue,   360
Then stir Demetrius up with bitter wrong;   361
And sometimes rail thou like Demetrius.
And from each other look thou lead them thus,
Till o'er their brows death-counterfeiting sleep
With leaden legs and batty wings doth creep.   365
Then crush this herb into Lysander's eye,   366

(giving herb)

Whose liquor hath this virtuous property,   367
To take from thence all error with his might   368
And make his eyeballs roll with wonted sight.   369
When they next wake, all this derision   370
Shall seem a dream and fruitless vision,
And back to Athens shall the lovers wend
With league whose date till death shall never end.   373
Whiles I in this affair do thee employ,
I'll to my queen and beg her Indian boy;
And then I will her charmèd eye release
From monster's view, and all things shall be peace.
PUCK. My fairy lord, this must be done with haste,
For night's swift dragons cut the clouds full fast,   379

---

352 **so far** at least to this extent. **sort** turn out   353 **As** in that   355 **Hie** Hasten   356 **welkin** sky
357 **Acheron** river of Hades (here representing Hades itself)   359 **As** that   360 **frame thy tongue**
fashion your speech   361 **wrong** insults   365 **batty** batlike   366 **this herb** i.e., the antidote (mentioned in 2.1.184) to love-in-idleness   367 **virtuous** efficacious   368 **his** its   369 **wonted** accustomed   370 **derision** laughable business   373 **date** term of existence   379 **dragons** (Supposed here
to be yoked to the car of the goddess of night or the moon.)

And yonder shines Aurora's harbinger,   *380*
At whose approach ghosts, wand'ring here and there,
Troop home to churchyards. Damnèd spirits all,
That in crossways and floods have burial,   *383*
Already to their wormy beds are gone.
For fear lest day should look their shames upon,
They willfully themselves exile from light
And must for aye consort with black-browed night.   *387*
OBERON. But we are spirits of another sort.
   I with the Morning's love have oft made sport,   *389*
   And, like a forester, the groves may tread   *390*
   Even till the eastern gate, all fiery red,
   Opening on Neptune with fair blessèd beams,
   Turns into yellow gold his salt green streams.
   But notwithstanding, haste, make no delay.
   We may effect this business yet ere day.   *(Exit.)*
PUCK. Up and down, up and down,
   I will lead them up and down.
   I am feared in field and town.
   Goblin, lead them up and down.   *399*
   Here comes one.

(Enter Lysander.)

LYSANDER. Where art thou, proud Demetrius? Speak thou
   now.
PUCK *(mimicking Demetrius)*.
   Here, villain, drawn and ready. Where art thou?   *402*
LYSANDER. I will be with thee straight.
PUCK.   Follow me, then,   *403*
   To plainer ground.

(Lysander wanders about, following the voice.)

---

380 Aurora's harbinger the morning star, precursor of dawn **383 crossways ... burial** (Those who had committed suicide were buried at crossways, with a stake driven through them; those who intentionally or accidentally drowned (in *floods* or deep water) would be condemned to wander disconsolately for lack of burial rites.) **387 for aye** forever **389 the Morning's love** Cephalus, a beautiful youth beloved by Aurora; or perhaps the goddess of the dawn herself **390 forester** keeper of a royal forest **399 Goblin** Hobgoblin. (Puck refers to himself.) **402 drawn** with drawn sword **403 straight** immediately.

(*Enter Demetrius.*)

DEMETRIUS.   Lysander! Speak again!   404
  Thou runaway, thou coward, art thou fled?
  Speak! In some bush? Where dost thou hide thy head?
PUCK (*mimicking Lysander*).
  Thou coward, art thou bragging to the stars,
  Telling the bushes that thou look'st for wars,
  And wilt not come? Come, recreant; come, thou child,   409
  I'll whip thee with a rod. He is defiled
  That draws a sword on thee.
DEMETRIUS.   Yea, art thou there?
PUCK. Follow my voice. We'll try no manhood here.   412

                                              (*Exeunt.*)

(*Lysander returns.*)

LYSANDER. He goes before me and still dares me on.
  When I come where he calls, then he is gone.
  The villain is much lighter-heeled than I.
  I followed fast, but faster he did fly,
  That fallen am I in dark uneven way,
  And here will rest me. (*He lies down.*) Come, thou
    gentle day!
  For if but once thou show me thy gray light,
  I'll find Demetrius and revenge this spite. (*He sleeps.*)

([*Enter*] *Robin* [*Puck*] *and Demetrius.*)

PUCK. Ho, ho, ho! Coward, why com'st thou not?
DEMETRIUS. Abide me, if thou dar'st; for well I wot   422
  Thou runn'st before me, shifting every place,
  And dar'st not stand nor look me in the face.
  Where art thou now?
PUCK.   Come hither. I am here.
DEMETRIUS. Nay, then, thou mock'st me. Thou shalt buy
    this dear,
  If ever I thy face by daylight see.
  Now go thy way. Faintness constraineth me

---

404 plainer more open. **s.d. Lysander wanders about** (Lysander may exit here, but perhaps not;
neither exit nor reentrance is indicated in the early texts.) **409 recreant** cowardly wretch
412 try test **422 Abide** Confront, face. **wot** know **426 buy this dear** pay for this dearly

To measure out my length on this cold bed.
By day's approach look to be visited.

(He lies down and sleeps.)

(Enter Helena.)

HELENA. O weary night, O long and tedious night,
 Abate thy hours! Shine comforts from the east,   *432*
That I may back to Athens by daylight
 From these that my poor company detest;
And sleep, that sometimes shuts up sorrow's eye,
Steal me awhile from mine own company!

([She lies down and] sleep[s].)

PUCK. Yet but three? Come one more;
 Two of both kinds makes up four.
Here she comes, curst and sad.   *439*
Cupid is a knavish lad,
Thus to make poor females mad.

(Enter Hermia.)

HERMIA. Never so weary, never so in woe,
 Bedabbled with the dew and torn with briers,
I can no further crawl, no further go;
 My legs can keep no pace with my desires.
Here will I rest me till the break of day.
Heavens shield Lysander, if they mean a fray!

(She lies down and sleeps.)

PUCK. On the ground
 Sleep sound.
 I'll apply
 To your eye,
Gentle lover, remedy.

(He squeezes the juice on Lysander's eyes.)

When thou wak'st,
Thou tak'st
True delight
In the sight

---

432 **Abate** lessen, shorten 439 **curst** ill-tempered

Of thy former lady's eye;
And the country proverb known,
That every man should take his own,
In your waking shall be shown:
    Jack shall have Jill;   *461*
    Naught shall go ill;
The man shall have his mare again, and all shall
be well.   *(Exit. The four sleeping lovers remain.)*

4.1

*Enter (Titania,) Queen of Fairies, and (Bottom the) clown,
and Fairies; and (Oberon,) the King, behind them.*

TITANIA. Come, sit thee down upon this flow'ry bed,
    While I thy amiable cheeks do coy,   2
And stick muskroses in thy sleek smooth head,
    And kiss thy fair large ears, my gentle joy.

                          (They recline.)

BOTTOM. Where's Peaseblossom?

PEASEBLOSSOM. Ready.

BOTTOM. Scratch my head, Peaseblossom. Where's
    Monsieur Cobweb?

COBWEB. Ready.

BOTTOM. Monsieur Cobweb, good monsieur, get you your
    weapons in your hand, and kill me a red-hipped
    humble-bee on the top of a thistle; and, good mon-
    sieur, bring me the honey bag. Do not fret yourself too
    much in the action, monsieur; and, good monsieur,
    have a care the honey bag break not. I would be loath
    to have you overflown with a honey bag, signor.

                          (Exit Cobweb.)

    Where's Monsieur Mustardseed?

MUSTARDSEED. Ready.

BOTTOM. Give me your neaf, Monsieur Mustardseed.   *19*

---

461 **Jack shall have Jill** (Proverbial for "boy gets girl.")
4.1. Location: The action is continuous. The four lovers are still asleep onstage. (Compare with
the Folio stage direction: *"They sleep all the act."*)
2 **amiable** lovely. **coy** caress   19 **neaf** fist

Pray you, leave your courtesy, good monsieur.   20
MUSTARDSEED. What's your will?
BOTTOM. Nothing, good monsieur, but to help Cavalery   22
  Cobweb to scratch. I must to the barber's, monsieur,   23
  for methinks I am marvelous hairy about the face; and
  I am such a tender ass, if my hair do but tickle me I
  must scratch.
TITANIA. What, wilt thou hear some music, my sweet love?
BOTTOM. I have a reasonable good ear in music. Let's have
  the tongs and the bones.   29

                    (*Music: tongs, rural music.*)

TITANIA. Or say, sweet love, what thou desirest to eat.
BOTTOM. Truly, a peck of provender. I could munch your   31
  good dry oats. Methinks I have a great desire to a bot-
  tle of hay. Good hay, sweet hay, hath no fellow.   33
TITANIA. I have a venturous fairy that shall seek
  The squirrel's hoard, and fetch thee new nuts.
BOTTOM. I had rather have a handful or two of dried peas.
  But, I pray you, let none of your people stir me. I have an   37
  exposition of sleep come upon me.   38
TITANIA. Sleep thou, and I will wind thee in my arms.—
  Fairies, begone, and be all ways away.   40

                    (*Exeunt Fairies.*)

So doth the woodbine the sweet honeysuckle   41
Gently entwist; the female ivy so
Enrings the barky fingers of the elm.
Oh, how I love thee! How I dote on thee!

                    (*They sleep.*)

(*Enter Robin Goodfellow* [*Puck*].)

OBERON (*coming forward*). Welcome, good Robin. See'st
  thou this sweet sight?

---

20 leave your courtesy i.e., stop bowing, or put on your hat   **22 Cavalery** Cavalier. (Form of address for a gentleman.)   **23 Cobweb** (Seemingly an error, since Cobweb has been sent to bring honey, while Peaseblossom has been asked to scratch.)   **29 tongs ... bones** instruments for rustic music. (The tongs were played like a triangle, whereas the bones were held between the fingers and used as clappers.)   **29.1 Music ... music** (This stage direction is added from the Folio.) **31 peck of provender** one-quarter bushel of grain.   **33 bottle** bundle. **fellow** equal.   **37 stir** disturb   **38 exposition of** (Bottom's phrase for "disposition to.")   **40 all ways** in all directions **41 woodbine** bindweed, a climbing plant

Her dotage now I do begin to pity.
For, meeting her of late behind the wood
Seeking sweet favors for this hateful fool,   48
I did upbraid her and fall out with her.
For she his hairy temples then had rounded
With coronet of fresh and fragrant flowers;
And that same dew, which 'sometime on the buds   52
Was wont to swell like round and orient pearls,   53
Stood now within the pretty flowerets' eyes
Like tears that did their own disgrace bewail.
When I had at my pleasure taunted her,
And she in mild terms begged my patience,
I then did ask of her her changeling child,
Which straight she gave me, and her fairy sent
To bear him to my bower in Fairyland.
And, now I have the boy, I will undo
This hateful imperfection of her eyes.
And, gentle Puck, take this transformèd scalp
From off the head of this Athenian swain,
That he, awaking when the other do,   65
May all to Athens back again repair,   66
And think no more of this night's accidents
But as the fierce vexation of a dream.
But first I will release the Fairy Queen.

(*He squeezes an herb on her eyes.*)

Be as thou wast wont to be;
See as thou wast wont to see.
Dian's bud o'er Cupid's flower   72
Hath such force and blessèd power.
Now, my Titania, wake you, my sweet queen.
TITANIA (*awaking*).
My Oberon! What visions have I seen!
Methought I was enamored of an ass.
OBERON. There lies your love.
TITANIA   How came these things to pass?
Oh, how mine eyes do loathe his visage now!

---

48 favors i.e., gifts of flowers   **52 sometime** formerly   **53 orient** lustrous   **65 other** others
66 repair return   **72 Dian's bud** (Perhaps the flower of the *agnus castus* or chaste-tree, supposed to preserve chastity; or perhaps referring simply to Oberon's herb by which he can undo the effects of "Cupid's flower," the love-in-idleness of 2.1.166–8.)

OBERON. Silence awhile. Robin, take off this head.
    Titania, music call, and strike more dead
    Than common sleep of all these five the sense.   *81*
TITANIA. Music, ho! Music, such as charmeth sleep! (*Music.*)   *82*
PUCK (*removing the ass head*).
    Now, when thou wak'st, with thine own fool's eyes peep.
OBERON. Sound, music! Come, my queen, take hands with
    me,
And rock the ground whereon these sleepers be.

                           (*They dance.*)

    Now thou and I are new in amity,
    And will tomorrow midnight solemnly   *87*
    Dance in Duke Theseus' house triumphantly,
    And bless it to all fair prosperity.
    There shall the pairs of faithful lovers be
    Wedded, with Theseus, all in jollity.
PUCK. Fairy King, attend, and mark:
    I do hear the morning lark.
OBERON. Then, my queen, in silence sad,   *94*
    Trip we after night's shade.
    We the globe can compass soon,
    Swifter than the wand'ring moon.
TITANIA. Come, my lord, and in our flight
    Tell me how it came this night
    That I sleeping here was found
    With these mortals on the ground.

            (*Exeunt [Oberon, Titania, and Puck].*)

                (*Wind horn [within].*)

(*Enter Theseus and all his train; [Hippolyta, Egeus].*)

THESEUS. Go, one of you, find out the forester,
    For now our observation is performed;   *103*
    And since we have the vaward of the day,   *104*
    My love shall hear the music of my hounds.
    Uncouple in the western valley; let them go.   *106*

---

81 these five i.e., the four lovers and Bottom   **82 charmeth** brings about, as though by a charm
87 solemnly ceremoniously   **94 sad** solemn   **103 observation** i.e., observance to a morn of May
(1.1.167)   **104 vaward** vanguard, i.e., earliest part   **106 Uncouple** Set free for the hunt

Dispatch, I say, and find the forester.

(*Exit an Attendant.*)

We will, fair queen, up to the mountain's top
And mark the musical confusion
Of hounds and echo in conjunction.

HIPPOLYTA. I was with Hercules and Cadmus once   111
   When in a wood of Crete they bayed the bear   112
   With hounds of Sparta. Never did I hear   113
   Such gallant chiding; for, besides the groves,   114
   The skies, the fountains, every region near
   Seemed all one mutual cry. I never heard
   So musical a discord, such sweet thunder.

THESEUS. My hounds are bred out of the Spartan kind,   118
   So flewed, so sanded; and their heads are hung   119
   With ears that sweep away the morning dew;
   Crook-kneed, and dewlapped like Thessalian bulls;   121
   Slow in pursuit, but matched in mouth like bells,   122
   Each under each. A cry more tunable   123
   Was never holloed to nor cheered with horn   124
   In Crete, in Sparta, nor in Thessaly.
   Judge when you hear. (*He sees the sleepers.*) But soft!
   What nymphs are these?   126

EGEUS. My lord, this is my daughter here asleep,
   And this Lysander; this Demetrius is;
   This Helena, old Nedar's Helena.
   I wonder of their being here together.   130

THESEUS. No doubt they rose up early to observe
   The rite of May, and hearing our intent,
   Came here in grace of our solemnity.   133
   But speak, Egeus. Is not this the day
   That Hermia should give answer of her choice?

EGEUS. It is, my lord.

THESEUS. Go bid the huntsmen wake them with their horns.

---

111 **Cadmus** mythical founder of Thebes. (This story about him is unknown.)   112 **bayed** brought
to bay   113 **hounds of Sparta** (A breed famous in antiquity for their hunting skill.)   114 **chiding**
i.e., yelping   118 **kind** strain, breed   119 **So flewed** similarly having large hanging chaps or fleshy
covering of the jaw.   **sanded** of sandy color   121 **dewlapped** having pendulous folds of skin under
the neck.   **Thessalian** from Thessaly, in Greece   122–3 **matched . . . each** i.e., harmoniously
matched in their various cries like a set of bells, from treble down to bass.   123 **cry** pack of hounds.
tunable well tuned, melodious   124 **cheered** encouraged   126 **soft** i.e., gently, wait a minute.
130 **of** at   133 **in . . . solemnity** in honor of our wedding ceremony.

(*Exit an Attendant.*)

(*Shout within. Wind horns. They all start up.*)

Good morrow, friends. Saint Valentine is past.   *138*
Begin these woodbirds but to couple now?
LYSANDER. Pardon, my lord.   (*They kneel.*)
THESEUS.   I pray you all, stand up.

(*They stand.*)

I know you two are rival enemies;
How comes this gentle concord in the world,
That hatred is so far from jealousy
To sleep by hate and fear no enmity?
LYSANDER. My lord, I shall reply amazedly,
    Half sleep, half waking; but as yet, I swear,
    I cannot truly say how I came here.
    But, as I think—for truly would I speak,
    And now I do bethink me, so it is—
    I came with Hermia hither. Our intent
    Was to be gone from Athens, where we might,
    Without the peril of the Athenian law—
EGEUS. Enough, enough, my lord; you have enough.
    I beg the law, the law, upon his head.
    They would have stol'n away; they would, Demetrius,
    Thereby to have defeated you and me,
    You of your wife and me of my consent,
    Of my consent that she should be your wife.
DEMETRIUS. My lord, fair Helen told me of their stealth,
    Of this their purpose hither to this wood,
    And I in fury hither followed them,
    Fair Helena in fancy following me.   *162*
    But, my good lord, I wot not by what power—
    But by some power it is—my love to Hermia,
    Melted as the snow, seems to me now
    As the remembrance of an idle gaud   *166*
    Which in my childhood I did dote upon;
    And all the faith, the virtue of my heart,
    The object and the pleasure of mine eye,

---

138 Saint Valentine (Birds were supposed to choose their mates on Saint Valentine's Day.)
162 in fancy driven by love   **166 idle gaud** worthless trinket

Is only Helena. To her, my lord,
Was I betrothed ere I saw Hermia,
But like a sickness did I loathe this food;
But, as in health, come to my natural taste,
Now I do wish it, love it, long for it,
And will forevermore be true to it.
THESEUS. Fair lovers, you are fortunately met.
Of this discourse we more will hear anon.
Egeus, I will overbear your will;
For in the temple, by and by, with us
These couples shall eternally be knit.
And, for the morning now is something worn,   181
Our purposed hunting shall be set aside.
Away with us to Athens. Three and three,
We'll hold a feast in great solemnity.   184
Come, Hippolyta.

(Exeunt Theseus, Hippolyta, Egeus, and train.)

DEMETRIUS. These things seem small and undistinguishable,
Like far-off mountains turnèd into clouds.
HERMIA. Methinks I see these things with parted eye,   188
When everything seems double.
HELENA.   So methinks;
And I have found Demetrius like a jewel,   190
Mine own, and not mine own.
DEMETRIUS.   Are you sure   191
That we are awake? It seems to me
That yet we sleep, we dream. Do not you think
The Duke was here, and bid us follow him?
HERMIA. Yea, and my father.
HELENA.   And Hippolyta.
LYSANDER. And he did bid us follow to the temple.
DEMETRIUS. Why, then, we are awake. Let's follow him,
And by the way let us recount our dreams.

(Exeunt the lovers.)

BOTTOM *(awaking)*. When my cue comes, call me, and I
will answer. My next is "Most fair Pyramus." Heigh-ho!

---

181 for since. **something** somewhat   **184 in great solemnity** with great ceremony.
188 parted i.e., improperly focused   **190–1 like ... own** i.e., something precious that seems mine
and yet so mysteriously found that I can hardly believe it is mine.

Peter Quince! Flute, the bellows mender! Snout, the
tinker! Starveling! God's my life, stolen hence and left   *202*
me asleep! I have had a most rare vision. I have had a
dream, past the wit of man to say what dream it was.
Man is but an ass if he go about to expound this   *205*
dream. Methought I was—there is no man can tell
what. Methought I was—and methought I had—but
man is but a patched fool if he will offer to say what   *208*
methought I had. The eye of man hath not heard, the   *209*
ear of man hath not seen, man's hand is not able to   *210*
taste, his tongue to conceive, nor his heart to report,   *211*
what my dream was. I will get Peter Quince to write a
ballad of this dream. It shall be called "Bottom's   *213*
Dream," because it hath no bottom; and I will sing it in   *214*
the latter end of a play, before the Duke. Peradventure,
to make it the more gracious, I shall sing it at her   *216*
death.   (*Exit.*)

4.2

Enter Quince, Flute, (Snout, and Starveling).

QUINCE. Have you sent to Bottom's house? Is he come
home yet?

STARVELING. He cannot be heard of. Out of doubt he is
transported.   *4*

FLUTE. If he come not, then the play is marred. It goes not
forward. Doth it?

QUINCE. It is not possible. You have not a man in all
Athens able to discharge Pyramus but he.   *8*

FLUTE. No, he hath simply the best wit of any handicraft   *9*
man in Athens.

QUINCE. Yea, and the best person too, and he is a very   *11*
paramour for a sweet voice.

FLUTE. You must say "paragon." A paramour is, God bless
us, a thing of naught.   *14*

---

202 **God's** May God save   205 **go about** attempt   208 **patched** wearing motley, i.e., a dress of
various colors.   **offer** venture   209–11 **The eye ... report** (Bottom garbles 1 Corinthians 2:9.)
213 **ballad** (The proper medium for relating sensational stories and preposterous events.)
214 **hath no bottom** is unfathomable   216 **her** Thisbe's (?)
4.2. Location: Athens.
4 **transported** carried off by fairies; or, transformed.   8 **discharge** perform   9 **wit** intellect
11 **person** appearance   14 **a ... naught** a shameful thing

(*Enter Snug the joiner.*)

SNUG. Masters, the Duke is coming from the temple, and
there is two or three lords and ladies more married. If
our sport had gone forward, we had all been made   17
men.   18
FLUTE. Oh, sweet bully Bottom! Thus hath he lost sixpence
a day during his life; he could not have scaped sixpence   20
a day. An the Duke had not given him sixpence a day
for playing Pyramus, I'll be hanged. He would have
deserved it. Sixpence a day in Pyramus, or nothing.

(*Enter Bottom.*)

BOTTOM. Where are these lads? Where are these hearts?   25
QUINCE. Bottom! Oh, most courageous day! Oh, most
happy hour!
BOTTOM. Masters, I am to discourse wonders. But ask me   28
not what; for if I tell you, I am no true Athenian. I will
tell you everything, right as it fell out.
QUINCE. Let us hear, sweet Bottom.
BOTTOM. Not a word of me. All that I will tell you is that 32
the Duke hath dined. Get your apparel together,
good strings to your beards, new ribbons to your   34
pumps; meet presently at the palace; every man look   35
o'er his part; for the short and the long is, our play is
preferred. In any case, let Thisbe have clean linen; and   37
let not him that plays the lion pare his nails, for they
shall hang out for the lion's claws. And, most dear actors, eat no onions nor garlic, for we are to utter sweet
breath; and I do not doubt but to hear them say it is a
sweet comedy. No more words. Away! Go, away!

(*Exeunt.*)

5.1

*Enter Theseus, Hippolyta, and Philostrate, (lords, and
attendants).*

17–18 we ... men i.e., we would have had our fortunes made.   **20 sixpence a day** i.e., as a royal
pension   **25 hearts** good fellows.   **28 am ... wonders** have wonders to relate.   **32 of** out of
34 strings (to attach the beards)   **35 pumps** light shoes or slippers   **37 preferred** selected for
consideration.

HIPPOLYTA. 'Tis strange, my Theseus, that these lovers speak of.   *1*
THESEUS. More strange than true. I never may believe   *2*
  These antique fables nor these fairy toys.   *3*
  Lovers and madmen have such seething brains,
  Such shaping fantasies, that apprehend   *5*
  More than cool reason ever comprehends.   *6*
  The lunatic, the lover, and the poet
  Are of imagination all compact.   *8*
  One sees more devils than vast hell can hold;
  That is the madman. The lover, all as frantic,
  Sees Helen's beauty in a brow of Egypt.   *11*
  The poet's eye, in a fine frenzy rolling,
  Doth glance from heaven to earth, from earth to
    heaven;
  And as imagination bodies forth
  The forms of things unknown, the poet's pen
  Turns them to shapes and gives to airy nothing
  A local habitation and a name.
  Such tricks hath strong imagination
  That, if it would but apprehend some joy,
  It comprehends some bringer of that joy;   *20*
  Or in the night, imagining some fear,   *21*
  How easy is a bush supposed a bear!
HIPPOLYTA. But all the story of the night told over,
  And all their minds transfigured so together,
  More witnesseth than fancy's images   *25*
  And grows to something of great constancy;   *26*
  But, howsoever, strange and admirable.   *27*

(*Enter lovers: Lysander, Demetrius, Hermia, and Helena.*)

THESEUS. Here come the lovers, full of joy and mirth.
  Joy, gentle friends! Joy and fresh days of love
  Accompany your hearts!

5.1. Location: Athens. The palace of Theseus.
1 **that** that which 2 **may** can 3 **antique** old-fashioned. (Punning, too, on *antic*, "strange," "grotesque.") **fairy toys** trifling stories about fairies. 5 **fantasies** imaginations. **apprehend** conceive, imagine 6 **comprehends** understands. 8 **compact** formed, composed. 11 **Helen's** i.e., of Helen of Troy, pattern of beauty. **brow of Egypt** i.e., face of a gypsy. 20 **bringer** i.e., source 21 **fear** object of fear 25 **More . . . images** testifies to something more substantial than mere imaginings 26 **constancy** certainty 27 **howsoever** in any case. **admirable** a source of wonder.

LYSANDER.   More than to us
    Wait in your royal walks, your board, your bed!
THESEUS. Come now, what masques, what dances shall we
      have,   32
    To wear away this long age of three hours
    Between our after-supper and bedtime?
    Where is our usual manager of mirth?
    What revels are in hand? Is there no play
    To ease the anguish of a torturing hour?
    Call Philostrate.
PHILOSTRATE.   Here, mighty Theseus.
THESEUS. Say, what abridgment have you for this evening?   39
    What masque? What music? How shall we beguile
    The lazy time, if not with some delight?
PHILOSTRATE (*giving him a paper*).
    There is a brief how many sports are ripe.   42
    Make choice of which Your Highness will see first.
THESEUS (*reads*). "The battle with the Centaurs, to be sung   44
    By an Athenian eunuch to the harp"?
    We'll none of that. That have I told my love,
    In glory of my kinsman Hercules.   47
    (*He reads.*) "The riot of the tipsy Bacchanals,   48
    Tearing the Thracian singer in their rage"?   49
    That is an old device; and it was played   50
    When I from Thebes came last a conqueror.
    (*He reads.*) "The thrice three Muses mourning for the
      death   52
    Of Learning, late deceased in beggary"?   53
    That is some satire, keen and critical,
    Not sorting with a nuptial ceremony.   55
    (*He reads.*) "A tedious brief scene of young Pyramus
    And his love Thisbe; very tragical mirth"?

---

32 masques courtly entertainments   **39 abridgment** pastime (to abridge or shorten the evening)
42 brief summary   **44 battle . . . Centaurs** (Probably refers to the battle of the Centaurs and the
Lapithae, when the Centaurs attempted to carry off Hippodamia, bride of Theseus's friend
Pirothous. The story is told in Ovid's *Metamorphoses* 12.)   **47 kinsman** (Plutarch's "Life of
Theseus" states that Hercules and Theseus were near kinsmen. Theseus is referring to a version of
the battle of the Centaurs in which Hercules was said to be present.)   **48–9 The riot . . . rage** (This
was the story of the death of Orpheus, as told in *Metamorphoses* 11.)   **50 device** show, performance
52–3 The thrice . . . beggary (Possibly an allusion to Spenser's *Teares of the Muses*, 1591, though
"satires" deploring the neglect of learning and the creative arts were commonplace.)   **55 sorting
with** befitting

Merry and tragical? Tedious and brief?
That is, hot ice and wondrous strange snow.   *59*
How shall we find the concord of this discord?
PHILOSTRATE. A play there is, my lord, some ten words long,
Which is as brief as I have known a play;
But by ten words, my lord, it is too long,
Which makes it tedious. For in all the play
There is not one word apt, one player fitted.
And tragical, my noble lord, it is,
For Pyramus therein doth kill himself.
Which, when I saw rehearsed, I must confess,
Made mine eyes water; but more merry tears
The passion of loud laughter never shed.
THESEUS. What are they that do play it?
PHILOSTRATE. Hardhanded men that work in Athens here,
Which never labored in their minds till now,
And now have toiled their unbreathed memories   *74*
With this same play, against your nuptial.   *75*
THESEUS. And we will hear it.
PHILOSTRATE.   No, my noble lord,
It is not for you. I have heard it over,
And it is nothing, nothing in the world;
Unless you can find sport in their intents,
Extremely stretched and conned with cruel pain   *80*
To do you service.
THESEUS.   I will hear that play;
For never anything can be amiss
When simpleness and duty tender it.
Go, bring them in; and take your places, ladies.

(*Philostrate goes to summon the players.*)

HIPPOLYTA. I love not to see wretchedness o'ercharged,   *85*
    And duty in his service perishing.   *86*
THESEUS. Why, gentle sweet, you shall see no such thing.
HIPPOLYTA. He says they can do nothing in this kind.   *88*
THESEUS. The kinder we, to give them thanks for nothing.

---

59 strange (Sometimes emended to an adjective that would contrast with *snow*, just as *hot* contrasts
with *ice*.)   **74 toiled** taxed.   **unbreathed** unexercised   **75 against** in preparation for   **80 conned**
memorized   **85 wretchedness o'ercharged** social or intellectual inferiority overburdened
86 his service its attempt to serve   **88 kind** kind of thing.

Our sport shall be to take what they mistake;
And what poor duty cannot do, noble respect   *91*
Takes it in might, not merit.   *92*
Where I have come, great clerks have purposèd   *93*
To greet me with premeditated welcomes;
Where I have seen them shiver and look pale,
Make periods in the midst of sentences,
Throttle their practiced accent in their fears,   *97*
And in conclusion dumbly have broke off,
Not paying me a welcome. Trust me, sweet,
Out of this silence yet I picked a welcome;
And in the modesty of fearful duty
I read as much as from the rattling tongue
Of saucy and audacious eloquence.
Love, therefore, and tongue-tied simplicity
In least speak most, to my capacity.   *105*

(*Philostrate returns.*)

PHILOSTRATE. So please Your Grace, the Prologue is addressed.   *106*
THESEUS. Let him approach.   (*A flourish of trumpets.*)

(*Enter the Prologue [Quince].*)

PROLOGUE. If we offend, it is with our good will.
     That you should think, we come not to offend,
But with good will. To show our simple skill,
     That is the true beginning of our end.
Consider, then, we come but in despite.
     We do not come, as minding to content you,   *113*
Our true intent is. All for your delight
     We are not here. That you should here repent you,
The actors are at hand; and, by their show,
You shall know all that you are like to know.
THESEUS. This fellow doth not stand upon points.   *118*

91–2 noble . . . merit noble consideration values it for the effort made rather than for the actual worth.   **93 clerks** learned men   **97 practiced accent** i.e., rehearsed speech; or, usual way of speaking   **105 least** i.e., saying least.   **to my capacity** in my judgment and understanding. **106 Prologue** speaker of the prologue.   **addressed** ready.   **113 minding** intending   **118 stand upon points** (1) heed niceties or small points (2) pay attention to punctuation in his reading. (The humor of Quince's speech is in the blunders of its punctuation.)

LYSANDER. He hath rid his prologue like a rough colt; he   *119*
knows not the stop. A good moral, my lord: it is not enough   *120*
to speak, but to speak true.
HIPPOLYTA. Indeed, he hath played on his prologue like a
child on a recorder: a sound, but not in government.   *123*
THESEUS. His speech was like a tangled chain: nothing   *124*
impaired, but all disordered. Who is next?

(Enter Pyramus [Bottom], and Thisbe [Flute], and Wall
[Snout], and Moonshine [Starveling], and Lion [Snug].)

PROLOGUE. Gentles, perchance you wonder at this show;
    But wonder on, till truth make all things plain.
This man is Pyramus, if you would know;
    This beauteous lady Thisbe is, certain.
This man with lime and roughcast doth present
    Wall, that vile wall which did these lovers sunder;
And through Wall's chink, poor souls, they are content
    To whisper. At the which let no man wonder.
This man, with lantern, dog, and bush of thorn,
    Presenteth Moonshine; for, if you will know,
By moonshine did these lovers think no scorn   *136*
    To meet at Ninus' tomb, there, there to woo.
This grisly beast, which Lion hight by name,   *138*
The trusty Thisbe coming first by night
    Did scare away, or rather did affright;
And as she fled, her mantle she did fall,   *141*
    Which Lion vile with bloody mouth did stain.
Anon comes Pyramus, sweet youth and tall,   *143*
    And finds his trusty Thisbe's mantle slain;
Whereat, with blade, with bloody, blameful blade,
    He bravely broached his boiling bloody breast.   *146*
And Thisbe, tarrying in mulberry shade,
    His dagger drew, and died. For all the rest,
Let Lion, Moonshine, Wall, and lovers twain
At large discourse, while here they do remain.   *150*

(Exeunt Lion, Thisbe, and Moonshine.)

---

119 rid ridden.   **rough** unbroken   **120 stop** (1) stopping of a colt by reining it in (2) punctuation
mark.   **123 recorder** wind instrument like a flute.   **government** control.   **124 nothing** not at all
136 think no scorn think it no disgraceful matter   **138 hight** is called   **141 fall** let fall
143 tall courageous   **146 broached** stabbed   **150 At large** in full, at length

THESEUS. I wonder if the lion be to speak.

DEMETRIUS. No wonder, my lord. One lion may, when many asses do.

WALL. In this same interlude it doth befall   *154*
That I, one Snout by name, present a wall;
And such a wall as I would have you think
That had in it a crannied hole or chink,
Through which the lovers, Pyramus and Thisbe,
Did whisper often, very secretly.
This loam, this roughcast, and this stone doth show
That I am that same wall; the truth is so.
And this the cranny is, right and sinister,   *162*
Through which the fearful lovers are to whisper.

THESEUS. Would you desire lime and hair to speak better?

DEMETRIUS. It is the wittiest partition that ever I heard discourse, my lord.

(*Pyramus comes forward.*)

THESEUS. Pyramus draws near the wall. Silence!

PYRAMUS. O grim-looked night! O night with hue so black! *169*
 O night, which ever art when day is not!
O night, O night! Alack, alack, alack,
 I fear my Thisbe's promise is forgot.
And thou, O wall, O sweet, O lovely wall,
 That stand'st between her father's ground and mine,
Thou wall, O wall, O sweet and lovely wall,
 Show me thy chink, to blink through with mine
  eyne. (*Wall makes a chink with his fingers.*)
Thanks, courteous wall. Jove shield thee well for this.
But what see I? No Thisbe do I see.
O wicked wall, through whom I see no bliss!
Cursed be thy stones for thus deceiving me!

THESEUS. The wall, methinks, being sensible, should curse *181*
again. *182*

---

154 **interlude** play 162 **right and sinister** from right to left 166 **partition** (1) wall (2) section of a learned treatise or oration 169 **grim-looked** grim-looking 181 **sensible** capable of feeling 182 **again** in return.

PYRAMUS. No, in truth, sir, he should not. "Deceiving me"
  is Thisbe's cue: she is to enter now, and I am to spy her
  through the wall. You shall see, it will fall pat as I told
  you. Yonder she comes.

(*Enter Thisbe.*)

THISBE. O wall, full often hast thou heard my moans
  For parting my fair Pyramus and me.
  My cherry lips have often kissed thy stones,
  Thy stones with lime and hair knit up in thee.
PYRAMUS. I see a voice. Now will I to the chink,
  To spy an I can hear my Thisbe's face.   *192*
  Thisbe!
THISBE.   My love! Thou art my love, I think.
PYRAMUS. Think what thou wilt, I am thy lover's grace,   *194*
  And like Limander am I trusty still.   *195*
THISBE. And I like Helen, till the Fates me kill.   *196*
PYRAMUS. Not Shafalus to Procrus was so true.   *197*
THISBE. As Shafalus to Procrus, I to you.
PYRAMUS. Oh, kiss me through the hole of this vile wall!
THISBE. I kiss the wall's hole, not your lips at all.
PYRAMUS. Wilt thou at Ninny's tomb meet me straight-
  way?
THISBE. 'Tide life, 'tide death, I come without delay.   *202*

(*Exeunt Pyramus and Thisbe.*)

WALL. Thus have I, Wall, my part dischargèd so;
  And, being done, thus Wall away doth go.   (*Exit.*)
THESEUS. Now is the mural down between the two neigh-
  bors.
DEMETRIUS. No remedy, my lord, when walls are so willful
  to hear without warning.   *208*
HIPPOLYTA. This is the silliest stuff that ever I heard.
THESEUS. The best in this kind are but shadows; and the   *210*
  worst are no worse, if imagination amend them.
HIPPOLYTA. It must be your imagination then, and not theirs.

---

185 pat exactly   **192 an** if   **194 lover's grace** i.e., gracious lover   **195, 196 Limander, Helen** (Blunders for "Leander" and "Hero.")   **197 Shafalus, Procrus** (Blunders for "Cephalus" and "Procris," also famous lovers.)   **202 'Tide** Betide, come   **208 willful** willing. **without warning** i.e., without warning the parents. (Demetrius makes a joke on the proverb "Walls have ears.")   **210 in this kind** of this sort. **shadows** likenesses, representations

THESEUS. If we imagine no worse of them than they of themselves, they may pass for excellent men. Here come two noble beasts in, a man and a lion.

(*Enter Lion and Moonshine.*)

LION. You, ladies, you, whose gentle hearts do fear
    The smallest monstrous mouse that creeps on floor,
May now perchance both quake and tremble here,
    When lion rough in wildest rage doth roar.
Then know that I, as Snug the joiner, am   *221*
A lion fell, nor else no lion's dam;   *222*
For, if I should as lion come in strife
Into this place, 'twere pity on my life.
THESEUS. A very gentle beast, and of a good conscience.
DEMETRIUS. The very best at a beast, my lord, that e'er I saw.
LYSANDER. This lion is a very fox for his valor.   *228*
THESEUS. True; and a goose for his discretion.   *229*
DEMETRIUS. Not so, my lord, for his valor cannot carry his discretion, and the fox carries the goose.
THESEUS. His discretion, I am sure, cannot carry his valor; for the goose carries not the fox. It is well. Leave it to his discretion, and let us listen to the moon.
MOON. This lanthorn doth the hornèd moon present—   *235*
DEMETRIUS. He should have worn the horns on his head.   *236*
THESEUS. He is no crescent, and his horns are invisible   *237*
within the circumference.   *238*
MOON. This lanthorn doth the hornèd moon present;
Myself the man i'th' moon do seem to be.
THESEUS. This is the greatest error of all the rest. The man should be put into the lanthorn. How is it else the man i'th' moon?
DEMETRIUS. He dares not come there for the candle, for   *245*
you see it is already in snuff.   *246*

221–2 am ... dam enact the part of a fierce lion, but otherwise am not really a lion. (*Dam* means "mother"; in Shakespeare's source the beast is a lioness.) **228 is ... valor** i.e., his valor consists of craftiness and discretion. **229 a goose ... discretion** i.e., as discreet as a goose, that is, more foolish than discreet. **235 lanthorn** (This original spelling, "lanthorne," may suggest a play on the *horn* of which lanterns were made and also on a cuckold's horns; however, the spelling "lanthorne" is not used consistently for comic effect in this play or elsewhere. At 5.1.134, for example, the word is "lanterne" in the original.) **236 on his head** (As a sign of cuckoldry.) **237 crescent** a waxing moon **245 for** because of, for fear of **246 in snuff** (1) offended (2) in need of snuffing or trimming.

HIPPOLYTA. I am aweary of this moon. Would he would change!

THESEUS. It appears, by his small light of discretion, that he is in the wane; but yet, in courtesy, in all reason, we must stay the time.

LYSANDER. Proceed, Moon.

MOON. All that I have to say is to tell you that the lanthorn is the moon, I, the man i'th' moon, this thornbush my thornbush, and this dog my dog.

DEMETRIUS. Why, all these should be in the lanthorn, for all these are in the moon. But silence! Here comes Thisbe.

(Enter Thisbe.)

THISBE. This is old Ninny's tomb. Where is my love?

LION *(roaring)*. Oh!

DEMETRIUS. Well roared, Lion.

(Thisbe runs off, dropping her mantle.)

THESEUS. Well run, Thisbe.

HIPPOLYTA. Well shone, Moon. Truly, the moon shines with a good grace.

(The Lion worries Thisbe's mantle.)

THESEUS. Well moused, Lion.   265

(Enter Pyramus.)   *(Exit Lion.)*

DEMETRIUS. And then came Pyramus.

LYSANDER. And so the lion vanished.

PYRAMUS. Sweet Moon, I thank thee for thy sunny beams;
   I thank thee, Moon, for shining now so bright;
For, by thy gracious, golden, glittering gleams,
   I trust to take of truest Thisbe sight.
     But stay, oh, spite!
     But mark, poor knight,
What dreadful dole is here?   274
     Eyes, do you see?
     How can it be?
Oh, dainty duck! Oh, dear!
     Thy mantle good,
     What, stained with blood?

---

265 moused shaken, torn, bitten   **274 dole** grievous event

Approach, ye Furies fell! 280
   O Fates, come, come, 281
   Cut thread and thrum; 282
Quail, crush, conclude, and quell! 283
THESEUS. This passion, and the death of a dear friend, 284
   would go near to make a man look sad. 285
HIPPOLYTA. Beshrew my heart, but I pity the man. 286
PYRAMUS. Oh, wherefore, Nature, didst thou lions frame? 287
   Since lion vile hath here deflowered my dear,
   Which is—no, no, which was—the fairest dame
   That lived, that loved, that liked, that looked with
   cheer. 290
      Come, tears, confound,
      Out, sword, and wound
   The pap of Pyramus; 293
      Ay, that left pap,
      Where heart doth hop.   (*He stabs himself.*)
   Thus die I, thus, thus, thus.
      Now am I dead,
      Now am I fled;
   My soul is in the sky.
      Tongue, lose thy light;
      Moon, take thy flight.   (*Exit Moonshine.*)
   Now die, die, die, die, die.   (*Pyramus dies.*)
DEMETRIUS. No die, but an ace, for him; for he is but one. 303
LYSANDER. Less than an ace, man; for he is dead, he is
   nothing.
THESEUS. With the help of a surgeon he might yet recover,
   and yet prove an ass. 308
HIPPOLYTA. How chance Moonshine is gone before Thisbe
   comes back and finds her lover?
THESEUS. She will find him by starlight.

---

280 Furies fell fierce avenging goddesses of Greek myth.   **281 Fates** the three goddesses (Clotho, Lachesis, Atropos) of Greek myth who spun, drew, and cut the thread of human life   **282 thread and thrum** i.e., everything—the good and bad alike; literally, the warp in weaving and the loose end of the warp   **283 Quail** overpower. **quell** kill, destroy.   **284–5 This ... sad** i.e., If one had other reason to grieve, one might be sad, but not from this absurd portrayal of passion. **286 Beshrew** Curse. (A mild curse.)   **287 frame** create.   **290 cheer** countenance.   **293 pap** breast   **303 ace** the side of the die featuring the single pip, or spot. (The pun is on *die* as a singular of *dice*; Bottom's performance is not worth a whole *die* but rather one single face of it, one small portion.) **one** (1) an individual person (2) unique.   **308 ass** (With a pun on *ace*.)

(*Enter Thisbe.*)

Here she comes; and her passion ends the play.

HIPPOLYTA. Methinks she should not use a long one for
such a Pyramus. I hope she will be brief.

DEMETRIUS. A mote will turn the balance, which Pyramus   315
which Thisbe, is the better: he for a man, God warrant   316
us; she for a woman, God bless us.

LYSANDER. She hath spied him already with those sweet
eyes.

DEMETRIUS. And thus she means, videlicet: 320

THISBE. Asleep, my love?
    What, dead, my dove?
O Pyramus, arise!
    Speak, speak. Quite dumb?
    Dead, dead? A tomb
Must cover thy sweet eyes.
    These lily lips,
    This cherry nose,
These yellow cowslip cheeks,
    Are gone, are gone!
    Lovers, make moan.
His eyes were green as leeks.
    O Sisters Three,   333
    Come, come to me,
With hands as pale as milk;
    Lay them in gore,
    Since you have shore   337
With shears his thread of silk.
    Tongue, not a word.
    Come, trusty sword,
Come, blade, my breast imbrue!   341

            (*She stabs herself.*)

    And farewell, friends.
    Thus Thisbe ends.
Adieu, adieu, adieu.   (*She dies.*)

---

315 mote small particle   **315–16 which ... which** whether ... or   **320 means** moans, laments.
(With a pun on the meaning, "lodge a formal complaint.")   **videlicet** to wit   **333 Sisters Three** the
Fates   **337 shore** shorn   **341 imbrue** stain with blood.

THESEUS. Moonshine and Lion are left to bury the dead.
DEMETRIUS. Ay, and Wall too.
BOTTOM (*starting up, as Flute does also*). No, I assure
you, the wall is down that parted their fathers. Will it
please you to see the epilogue, or to hear a Bergomask
dance between two of our company?

349

(*The other players enter.*)

THESEUS. No epilogue, I pray you; for your play needs no
excuse. Never excuse; for when the players are all dead,
there need none to be blamed. Marry, if he that writ it
had played Pyramus and hanged himself in Thisbe's
garter, it would have been a fine tragedy; and so it is,
truly, and very notably discharged. But, come, your
Bergomask. Let your epilogue alone. (*A dance.*)
The iron tongue of midnight hath told twelve.
Lovers, to bed, 'tis almost fairy time.
I fear we shall outsleep the coming morn
As much as we this night have overwatched.
This palpable-gross play hath well beguiled
The heavy gait of night. Sweet friends, to bed.
A fortnight hold we this solemnity,
In nightly revels and new jollity.   (*Exeunt.*)

358

361
362
363

(*Enter Puck [carrying a broom].*)

PUCK. Now the hungry lion roars,
      And the wolf behowls the moon,
   Whilst the heavy plowman snores,
      All with weary task fordone.
   Now the wasted brands do glow,
      Whilst the screech owl, screeching loud,
   Puts the wretch that lies in woe
      In remembrance of a shroud.
   Now it is the time of night
      That the graves, all gaping wide,
   Every one lets forth his sprite,

368
369
370

376

---

349 **Bergomask dance** a rustic dance named from Bergamo, a province in the state of Venice
358 **iron tongue** i.e., of a bell.   **told** counted, struck ("tolled")   361 **overwatched** stayed up too late.
362 **palpable-gross** palpably gross, obviously crude   363 **heavy** drowsy, dull   368 **heavy** tired
369 **fordone** exhausted.   370 **wasted brands** burned-out logs   376 **Every . . . sprite** every grave lets
forth its ghost

In the churchway paths to glide.
And we fairies, that do run
    By the triple Hecate's team.   *379*
From the presence of the sun,
    Following darkness like a dream,
Now are frolic. Not a mouse   *382*
    Shall disturb this hallowed house.
I am sent with broom before,
To sweep the dust behind the door.   *385*

(*Enter [Oberon and Titania,] King and Queen of Fairies,
with all their train.*)

OBERON. Through the house give glimmering light,
    By the dead and drowsy fire;
Every elf and fairy sprite
    Hop as light as bird from brier;
And this ditty, after me,
Sing, and dance it trippingly.
TITANIA. First, rehearse your song by rote,   *392*
To each word a warbling note.
Hand in hand, with fairy grace,
Will we sing, and bless this place.

                    (*Song and dance.*)

OBERON. Now, until the break of day,
Through this house each fairy stray.
To the best bride-bed will we,
Which by us shall blessèd be;
And the issue there create   *400*
Ever shall be fortunate.
So shall all the couples three
Ever true in loving be;
And the blots of Nature's hand
Shall not in their issue stand;
Never mole, harelip, nor scar,
Nor mark prodigious, such as are   *407*

---

379 triple Hecate's (Hecate ruled in three capacities: as Luna or Cynthia in heaven, as Diana on earth, and as Proserpina in hell.)   **382 frolic** merry.   **385 behind** from behind, or else like sweeping the dirt under the carpet. (Robin Goodfellow was a household spirit who helped good housemaids and punished lazy ones, but he could, of course, be mischievous.)   **392 rehearse** recite **400 issue** offspring.   **create** created   **407 prodigious** monstrous, unnatural

Despisèd in nativity,
Shall upon their children be.
With this field dew consecrate,   410
Every fairy take his gait,   411
And each several chamber bless,   412
Through this palace, with sweet peace;
And the owner of it blest
Ever shall in safety rest.
Trip away; make no stay;
Meet me all by break of day.

(*Exeunt [Oberon, Titania, and train].*)

PUCK (*to the audience*).
If we shadows have offended,
Think but this, and all is mended,
That you have but slumbered here   420
While these visions did appear.
And this weak and idle theme,
No more yielding but a dream,   423
Gentles, do not reprehend.
If you pardon, we will mend.   425
And, as I am an honest Puck,
If we have unearnèd luck
Now to scape the serpent's tongue,   428
We will make amends ere long;
Else the Puck a liar call.
So, good night unto you all.
Give me your hands, if we be friends,   432
And Robin shall restore amends.   (*Exit.*)   433

[1594–1596]

---

410 **consecrate** consecrated   411 **take his gait** go his way   412 **several** separate   420 **That ... here** i.e., that it is a "midsummer night's dream"   423 **No ... but** yielding no more than   425 **mend** improve.   428 **serpent's tongue** i.e., hissing   432 **Give ... hands** Applaud   433 **restore amends** give satisfaction in return.

QUESTIONS

WILLIAM SHAKESPEARE, *A Midsummer Night's Dream*

1. Playwrights knew that there were such things as "the Classical Unities of time, place, and plot." Yet in *A Midsummer Night's Dream*, Shakespeare creates four separate plots. How does this reflect themes central to this play? How does Bottom the Weaver ultimately unify these plots?

2. If this play had a "governing planet," it would probably be the moon. Locate at least five references to the moon and consider why Shakespeare chose this heavenly body as an important symbol.

3. Why did Shakespeare choose Athens as the location?

4. Though the woods seem a place of tremendous freedom, it also shows the shaping hand of hierarchy. Show at least one instance in which fairy "lawlessness" leads to confusion for humans. Comment on the poetic devices and character types that establish order in chaos.

5. What motivates Oberon's desire to remove the young Indian boy from Titania's company? Oberon "wins" the boy, but does Titania freely turn the boy over to him? What is the role of free will in this play?

6. The "play within the play" tells the tragic story of Pyramus and Thisbe, but the amateurs who put on the play unintentionally make it comical. How? What does that transformation say about "the art of playing"? What does this very extended metaphor say about other transformations in the play?

7. At Oberon's instruction, Puck removes the spell from Lysander's eyes so that the young man can returns to his "true love," Hermia. The mischievous fairy leaves the spell on Demetrius's eyes. Is his love for Helena true?

8. Who speaks to us in the Epilogue: Puck or the actor who plays Puck?

9. Our dreams are "real" (we really have them), but function according to their own strange illogic. Discuss how the young lovers' and Bottom's time in the woods resembles the nature of human dreams. Consider what the play might be saying about the limitations of logic.

10. This play is very much concerned with how humans perceive and misperceive reality. After you locate significant references to the various human senses, discuss how the play uses sensory images to comment on the difference between "knowing" and "believing."

Glossary of Literary Terms

ACCENT. The emphasis placed on syllables in the rhythm of a line of poetry.

ACCENTUAL METER. Accentual meter measures the rhythms in poetic verse based on the number of speech stresses per line. Different accents create different meanings, e.g., "government *by* the people, *for* the people, as opposed to government by the *people*, for the *people* . . . ."

ACT. The major division in the action of a play. Smaller divisions within acts are called *scenes*.

AFTERWORD. A final passage or scene following the conclusion of a story or play, also called an *epilogue*. The afterword often presents the narrator's assessment of the overall meaning of the story.

ALIENATION EFFECT. An effect, such as a mask or a surreal setting, designed to prevent audiences from becoming emotionally involved in a play. This technique was used by the German dramatist Bertolt Brecht to move audiences to political action.

ALLEGORY. A narrative in which the characters, action, and dialogue work to represent an abstract concept. The fable of the ant and the grasshopper, for example, is an allegory advocating industriousness.

ALLITERATION. The repetition of a sound, usually the initial sound, in a sequence of words, such as "Full many a flower is born to blush unseen" (Thomas Gray, "Elegy Written in a Country Churchyard").

ALLUSION. A reference, often to a historical figure, myth, or artwork, that exists outside the literary work. Allusions to the *Bible* are common in Western literature.

AMBIGUITY. A deliberate use of language to suggest multiple meanings. For example, Young Goodman Brown's adventure in Nathaniel Hawthorne's story of the same name may have been a dream, or may have actually occurred.

AMPITHEATER. Originating in classical Greece, a theater designed with a stage surrounded by tiers of seats arranged in a semicircle.

ANALOGY. A comparison between two apparently unlike things that share some common features; a reference to the familiar in order to help readers understand the unfamiliar.

ANAPEST. A metrical foot comprised of two short syllables and one long syllable, e.g., like a child, like a ghost.

ANECDOTE. A brief episode within a longer work, designed to make a point or illustrate an idea.

ANTAGONIST. The character who opposes the lead character, or protagonist. Occasionally, when the conflict is internal, the antagonist is actually another side of the protagonist's own personality.

ANTICLIMAX. A failure to achieve the anticipated high point in a narrative, usually resulting in disappointed expectations.

ANTIHERO. A main character who does not possess the normal positive qualities of a hero; antiheroes appear primarily in modern works.

ANTISTROPHE. With *strophe* and *epode,* a stanza in a Greek Ode. The antistrophe represents the reverse of the strophe.

ANTITHESIS. The balancing of one word or expression against a contrasting word or expression, as in "It was the best of times, it was the worst of times" (Charles Dickens, *A Tale of Two Cities*).

APOSTROPHE. An address either to a person who is dead or not present, to an inanimate object, or to an abstract concept, designed in part to provide insight into a character's thoughts.

APPROXIMATE RHYME. Also referred to as slant or near rhyme, these rhymes share sound qualities or sounds within words. An example of such a rhyme is the feminine or half rhyme. Approximate rhymes are often repeated strategically within a perfect rhyme scheme in order to achieve a particular affect, e.g., told, woe.

APRON STAGE. Popularized by Elizabethan theater, a stage that extends toward the audience, beyond the arch of the stage.

ARCHETYPE. A character, place, or event that represents a universal truth, often of mythic proportions. The archetype appeals to what psychologist Carl Jung referred to as the "collective unconscious," or the sublimated memories of an entire race.

ARENA STAGE. A stage that is surrounded on every side by the audience, with actors entering and exiting through the aisles.

ARGUMENT. An introductory statement to a longer work of prose or poetry that summarizes the main point of the work.

ASIDE. In drama, a monologue spoken by an actor directly to the audience, outside the hearing of other characters onstage. The aside was relatively common in Elizabethan drama, used to express a character's inner thoughts; in modern drama, it is sometimes used for humorous effect.

ASSONANCE. A pattern of identical or similar vowel sounds, usually in stressed syllables of words with different end sounds. For example, the "o" sound is repeated five times in this line from George Gordon, Lord Byron's "Childe Harold": "Roll on, thou deep and dark-blue ocean, roll!"

ATMOSPHERE. The general feeling evoked through setting or dialogue. In Charlotte Perkins Gilman's "The Yellow Wall-Paper," for example, the early description of the narrator's house creates a sense of foreboding and unease in the reader.

AUBADE. A lyric poem in which two lovers express their regret over the coming of the dawn.

AUDITORY IMAGE. A mental perception that recalls a particular sound, specifically a word or words that refer to something heard.

AUGUSTAN AGE. The period of English literature encompassing the first half of the eighteenth century, featuring such writers as Jonathan Swift and Alexander Pope, who emulated the work of figures in ancient Rome such as Virgil and Horace.

AUTHORIAL VOICE. An idealized projection of the author, or someone to whom the reader must give approval, that is the beliefs, attitude, and tone of the author, as opposed to the narrator or any other character in a work.

AVANT GARDE. Any form of writing that deliberately rejects tradition, instead employing thoroughly innovative style or subject matter.

BACCHIC. In classical Latin poetry, a foot consisting of a short syllable followed by two longs or a weak syllable followed by two strong syllables.

BALLAD. A song or poem that tells a story and often features a repeated refrain. Because the ballad was originally an oral rather than written form, a single ballad may appear in a number of different versions.

BEAST FABLE. A short tale illustrating a moral truth, featuring animals as the main characters. Aesop's tales, such as the tortoise and the hare or the fox and the grapes, are the most widely known beast fables.

BEAT. The pattern of stress in a poem.

BEGINNING RHYME. The rhyme located in the first syllables of a poem, e.g., Why should I have returned?

BILDUNGSROMAN. A novel, often autobiographical, that recounts the development of a character from childhood to maturity, for example, Ralph Ellison's *Invisible Man*.

BIOGRAPHY. A full account of a person's life written by another. Biography moves beyond mere facts to create a portrait of the subject. *Autobiography* refers to such an account of the writer's own life.

BLANK VERSE. Unrhymed verse written in iambic pentameter. Considered to be the poetic form closest to normal speech patterns, blank verse is featured in Shakespeare's plays and in narrative poems such as John Milton's *Paradise Lost*.

BLOCKING. The positioning of actors on a stage, including their movements and physical interaction. The director is responsible for blocking.

BOX SET. A stage designed to represent a room realistically, with three walls and an invisible fourth wall facing the audience.

BROADSIDE BALLADS. Popular in sixteenth-century England, cheaply printed ballads, speeches, and diatribes.

BURLESQUE. A comedy presented in the style of a lofty, serious work but featuring gross exaggeration and distortion.

CACOPHONY. A series of discordant or harsh sounds used to jar the senses of the audience, as in Thomas Hardy's antiwar poem "The Man He Killed": "You shoot a fellow down / You'd treat if met where any bar is."

CAESURA. Any pause in a line of poetry, often in the middle of a line, sometimes used to create rhythmic effect, e.g., "Had we but world enough, and time."

CANON. Originally referring to the authenticated books of the Bible, now used to indicate those works considered by scholars to represent the best writing in a literary tradition, the masterpieces. Since the 1960s, many scholars have questioned more traditional interpretations of the canon because of the absence of works by women and writers from other marginalized groups. Canon may also refer to a comprehensive list of works by a specific author (e.g., the canon of Shakespeare).

CARPE DIEM. Latin for "Seize the day," a common theme in lyric poetry emphasizing the need to pursue sensual pleasure because life is short. The theme was prevalent in English love poems written during the sixteenth and seventeenth centuries.

CASTING. The selection of actors to play specific roles in drama.

CATASTROPHE. The conclusion of a tragic drama, in which the protagonist often dies. Based on Gustav Freytag's analysis of typical five-act plays, catastrophe follows introduction, rising action, climax, and falling action.

CATHARSIS. According to Aristotle, the purging of emotions at the end of a tragedy. During the play, audiences experience pity and fear as they identify with the tragic hero; a successful tragedy ends by reaffirming traditional human values, allowing the audience to experience catharsis.

CHARACTER. A person presented in either fiction or drama, whose behavior contributes to the plot and whose personality lends meaning to the narrative.

CHARACTERIZATION. The methods by which a writer brings a character to life, usually through the character's own words and actions, the responses of other characters, and the narrator's commentary.

CHORUS. In classical Greek drama, a group of actors set apart from the main action of the play, who commented regularly on the implications of the action. The chorus often wore masks and performed ritualized dance movements as they chanted.

CHRONOLOGY. The arrangement of time in a work. Some works follow a *linear* chronology, relating a story from beginning to end, while some begin *in medias res*, or in the middle, and move back and forth in time.

CLASSICISM. A value system based on the culture of ancient Greece and Rome, focusing on such features as balance, simplicity, clarity, order, and reason.

CLICHÉ. A figurative expression that has become trite from overuse, such as "raging inferno" or "ship of state." In drama and fiction, a character or setting can be a cliché, such as the prostitute with a heart of gold or the dark and stormy night.

CLIMAX. The high point, or point of greatest tension, in the plot. Climax is sometimes referred to as the turning point.

CLOSED COUPLET. A couplet consisting of two rhymed lines of poetry expressing a complete thought, e.g.,

> A dog starved at his Master's Gate
> Predicts the ruin of the State

CLOSED FORM. Closed form refers to any poem that conforms to established conventions for rhyme, meter, or stanza form, such as a sonnet or haiku.

CLOSET DRAMA. A play written primarily to be read rather than performed onstage.

COLLOQUIAL DICTION. Language representative of ordinary people speaking informally, often using slang, such as the language in Bobbie Ann Mason's "Shiloh."

COMEDY. Drama featuring a happy ending, designed to amuse the audience.

COMEDY OF MANNERS. Popular in late seventeenth-century England, drama that satirizes the behavior of sophisticated, high-society characters.

COMEDY OF THE ABSURD. A type of twentieth-century drama rooted in existentialism, portraying humans as isolated creatures living a meaningless existence. Such plays dismiss conventional plot, setting, and characterization.

COMIC RELIEF. A humorous character or scene, usually introduced in a serious play, whose jokes and buffoonery are intended as a brief break from the tension created by the main narrative. A character introduced for comic relief will often comment directly upon the absurdity of the protagonist's dilemma. Examples of such characters include the drunken porter in Shakespeare's *Macbeth*.

COMING-OF-AGE STORY. A narrative which takes as its subject the central character's emergence from childhood into some form of maturity; this emergence is often produced by a traumatic experience of the adult world. Examples of the coming-of-age story include Sharon Olds' "Rites of Passage" and Julia Alvarez's "Trespass."

COMMEDIA DELL'ARTE. A form of improvised drama that developed in Italy during the fourteenth century, and that flourished in the sixteenth and seventeenth centuries. Commedia dell'arte (or "comedy of the profession," pointing to its creation by professional performers) used stock characters and scenarios, usually farcical in nature, but required actors to embellish and develop their roles in order to maintain the attention of the audience.

COMPLICATION. In the Aristotelian model of a narrative's action, a complication occurs after the onset of the narrative's problem, interfering with the protagonist's attempts to restore the status quo or a state of equilibrium. Complications generally function to push the plot along and to heighten the audience's tension.

CONCEIT. An extended metaphor, often using an unusual image to show the resemblances between otherwise unlike things. Common conceits in Elizabethan poetry include the frequent comparison of the beloved to a flower or a garden. The "metaphysical" poets extended the conceit in ways that were often startling and provocative, such as John Donne's comparison between a flea bite and a sexual encounter in "The Flea."

CONCRETE DICTION. Language that describes qualities that can be perceived with the five senses. Concrete diction is defined in opposition to abstract language, which cannot be so perceived; an adjective such as "good" is thus abstract, while "sweet" is concrete.

CONCRETE POETRY. Poetry that is shaped on the page, often to resemble the object it describes. For example, George Herbert's "Easter Wings" creates those wings both typographically and through its imagery.

CONFESSIONAL POEM. A poem which focuses on its narrator's state of mind, often describing that state of mind in less-than-flattering terms. The chaos or trauma of the narrator's internal life is often intended as a metaphor for the world at large. Confessional poets include Anne Sexton, Sylvia Plath, and Robert Lowell.

CONFLICT. A struggle between two forces that drives a narrative's plot. The two forces in conflict can be two characters, a character and his or her environment or society, or two large social groups. Conflict can also be wholly internal to a character, as in narratives in which a character struggles with his or her psychological issues or conflicting desires.

CONNOTATION. The implied or figurative meaning that a word or image carries, as distinct from its literal or explicit meaning. Connotation often includes contextual or culturally specific overtones. For instance, "home" literally means the place one lives, but it often carries the connotations of safety and security. See denotation.

CONSONANCE. A pleasant combination of sounds; also, the repetition of consonants or groups of consonants, particularly at the ends of words. See also alliteration, assonance.

CONVENTIONS. Structures, devices, or other features that are traditional or expected within particular literary genres. For instance, an English sonnet's rhyme scheme is a convention; similarly, the *femme fatale* is a convention of hardboiled detective novels.

COSMIC IRONY. Irony related to a deterministic or fatalistic view of the world, usually implying that fate or some other cosmic force is toying with human lives.

COUPLET. Two successive lines of poetry of the same metrical length, usually rhyming, that form a complete unit.

COZY. A light English mystery novel, filled with suspense but typically avoiding gruesome bloodshed or terror. The detective in a cozy is generally an amateur sleuth, and often a sweet elderly lady likely not to seem a threat to a criminal. Agatha Christie's Miss Marple novels are typical of the genre.

CRISIS. The peak of a narrative's tension; the critical turning point of a narrative's action that usually leads to or produces its climax.

CRITICISM. The interpretive or analytical work performed by a serious reader of a text, in which the reader evaluates the textual evidence in order to more fully comprehend a text's meaning. Criticism is so named not because it is of necessity "negative," but rather because the critic asks difficult questions in performing such analysis.

CYBERPUNK. A sub-genre of science fiction, growing out of the work of writers including William Gibson and Bruce Sterling, often focused on a dystopian, heavily computerized near-future world. Cyberpunk combines the nihilism of the punk movement with an interest in the ways new technologies shape the future of human societies.

DACTYL. A three-syllable metrical foot composed of one stressed and two unstressed syllables. Examples include "strawberry" and "horrible."

DECORUM. Literary and dramatic appropriateness, particularly in terms of the use of appropriate language and form. Decorum is a key principle of classical rhetoric.

DENOTATION. The literal or explicit meaning that a word or image carries, as distinct from its implied or figurative meaning. Denotation usually disregards the cultural or contextual overtones of a term. Dictionary definitions are generally denotative. See connotation.

DENOUEMENT. The outcome or resolution of a narrative's action. "Denouement" derives from a French term meaning "unknotting" or "unwinding," and thus refers to the period after a narrative's climax, during which the status quo or equilibrium is restored.

DETECTIVE STORY. A branch of mystery stories focusing on the investigation of a crime. The genre of the detective story was established in Sir Arthur Conan Doyle's tales of Sherlock Holmes, and was later revolutionized by the work of Dashiell Hammett and Raymond Chandler. The detective story frequently focuses as much on the psychology of the detective him- or herself as on the puzzle he or she is charged with solving.

DEUS EX MACHINA. Literally, "god from the machine," the device often used to resolve Greek drama, whereby a god would be lowered onto the stage in order to bring a divine end to the play's conflict. The term has come to be used to describe any improbable or unrealistic solution to a narrative's plot.

DIALECT. The language of a particular class, ethnic group, or region, as represented in literature. Dialect is a method of characterization that uses spelling, grammar, and word choice to represent the sounds of that character's speech, often with the intent of distinguishing the character from others in the narrative. A famous example of the use of dialect can be found in Mark Twain's *The Adventures of Huckleberry Finn*.

DIALOGUE. The lines spoken by a character in a work of fiction or drama, and particularly a conversation between two characters.

DICTION. The particular word choices made by an author. Diction may be formal or informal, concrete or abstract; diction is a major contributor to an author's style.

DIDACTIC POETRY. Poetry that is instructive in aim, seeking to teach its reader a lesson, or otherwise convince its reader of a particular argument.

DIMETER. A poetic line consisting of two metrical feet.

DISCOURSE. Traditionally, a formal verbal expression or exchange, taking place in either speech or writing. "Discourse" has been adopted as a key term in recent critical theory to describe the ways in which meaning, and particularly ideology, is disseminated within a culture through its uses of language.

DOCUMENTARY THEATER. A recent mode of theatrical production that brings together ethnographic research with performance, creating a play which is both factual and dramatic. The term usually implies that the dialogue has been taken verbatim from interviews. Documentary theater has roots in the Depression-era Federal Theater Project and the German "theater of fact" of the 1960s. Examples of documentary theater include Anna Deveare Smith's *Fires in the Mirror* and the Tectonic Theater Project's *The Laramie Project*.

DOGGEREL. Comic verse composed in a loose, irregular measure. "Doggerel" is today most often used in a derogatory fashion, to refer to crudely written or otherwise bad poetry.

DOUBLE ENTENDRE. A French term for "double meaning." A double entendre is a deliberately ambiguous phrase, usually conveying a secondary meaning of a humorously sexual nature.

DOUBLE PLOT. Two interwoven plots contained in one narrative. Often one plot is treated more centrally than the other, producing a main plot and a subplot. An example of such a double plot is contained in Shakespeare's *King Lear*, one with Lear at its center and the other revolving around Gloucester.

DRAMA. A genre of literary work, written in either prose or verse, in which characters enact a narrative through dialogue and pantomime. Most drama is written to be performed on the stage, though "closet" drama is intended to be read rather than performed.

DRAMATIC IRONY. A dramatic device in which the reader or spectator knows something about a situation that a character does not, with the result that the character either behaves inappropriately or expects an outcome that is opposed to that which the reader knows is forthcoming. Dramatic irony runs rampant in Sophocles's *Oedipus Rex*, as Oedipus repeatedly curses the murderer of Laius, not knowing that he is in fact that murderer.

DRAMATIC MONOLOGUE. A poem narrated by an individual speaker who addresses either the reader or an implied listener. The poetry of Robert Browning includes many dramatic monologues, including "My Last Duchess."

DRAMATIC POETRY. Drama written in verse. Also, poetry that presents a character speaking directly to the reader or audience without additional authorial devices.

DYNAMIC CHARACTER. Also known as a round character; a complex character depicted as having psychological depth, particularly one who develops and changes over the course of a narrative. See flat character.

DYSTOPIA. Literally, "bad place." As opposed to a utopia (a good place, an idealized imaginary world), a dystopia is a nightmarish fictional future world, in which characters lead dehumanized, fear-filled lives. Dystopian narratives often focus on totalitarian regimes, and are often satiric commentaries on our own society. Examples of dystopian narratives include George Orwell's *1984* and Margaret Atwood's *The Handmaid's Tale*.

ECHO VERSE. A kind of literary resonance, in which a sound, or word, or image in a text recalls a similar effect in another text. As a poetic form dating back to late classical Greek poetry, the final syllables of the lines repeat in reply or commentary.

ELEGY. In classical literature, "elegy" referred only to poems written in strict elegiac meter, with alternating lines of hexameter and pentameter. Since the Renaissance, however, "elegy" has been used to describe any poem that conducts a sustained and formal lamentation, usually over the death of a particular person. The poem, usually longer than a lyric but not so long as an epic, generally contains a speaker and is delivered in the first person, often uses classical allusions and motifs, and frequently traces the speaker's path from grief through acceptance to joy.

ELISION. The omission of a letter or syllable, often combining two words into one, for metrical effect.

END RHYME. Rhyme occurring in the final words or syllables of two or more lines of poetry, as opposed to internal rhyme, which occurs within a line.

END-STOPPED LINE. One of two major types of line breaks in poetry. End-stopped lines generally end in conjunction with the end of a phrase or a sentence. Contrast with enjambment.

ENGLISH SONNET. Also known as a Shakespearean sonnet. The English sonnet typically contains three quatrains and a couplet, with an abab/cdcd/efef/gg rhyme scheme.

ENJAMBMENT. One of two major types of line breaks in poetry. Enjambed lines break in mid-phrase, and thus do not contain a sustained pause at the end of a line. Contrast with end-stopped line.

ENVIRONMENTAL THEATER. A form of political theater, related to performance art, in which the performance moves out of the restricted space of the theater and into the public arenas of streets or parks, intentionally blurring the lines between performance and audience, and between reality and illusion.

ENVOY. Also spelled "envoi," a brief postscript to a poem or a piece of prose writing, which often dedicates the poem to its patron or sends it on its way into the world. "Envoy" is also a term for the short concluding stanza of a ballad or sestina.

EPIC THEATER. Commonly associated with Bertolt Brecht, a form of theater in which the style of acting, the inclusion of multimedia effects such as film and electronic sounds, and the presentation of rational argument are used to create a shock of realization in the audience. Epic theater operates through what Brecht called the "alienation effect," which works to distance the viewer from the play's characters, maintaining a constant awareness of the spectacle's unreality. By preventing the audience from identifying with the play's characters, Brecht hoped to engage them intellectually in thinking about the play's issues.

EPIGRAM. Originally, an inscription in verse on a building, monument, or coin. "Epigram" is now used to refer to short, often witty verse, usually with a surprising turn at the end.

EPIGRAPH. A quotation or verse taken from another poem, used to introduce a literary text.

EPIPHANY. The sudden revelation or dawning insight that a character frequently reaches at the climax of a short story, usually sparked by ordinary circumstances but of such power that it is understood to be life-changing.

The term was most notably used by James Joyce to describe the experiences of characters such as Gabriel, the young central figure in "The Dead."

EPISTLE. A poem that imitates the form of a personal letter. An example is Alexander Pope's "Epistle to Dr. Arbuthnot."

EPITAPH. Literally, an inscription on a gravestone. "Epitaph" is also used to describe a brief poem in memory of a dead person, as well as the final words spoken by a character before his or her death.

ESSAY. An interpretive or analytical piece of literary writing. Essays can be personal or critical in focus; the essay nearly always treats its subject from the limited point of view of the author.

EUPHEMISM. The substitution of a more pleasant or agreeable word or phrase for one that might be considered rude or offensive. For example, "passed away" is a euphemism for "dead."

EUPHONY. A grouping of words that produces a pleasant, soothing sound, as opposed to the harsh sounds of cacophony.

EXACT RHYME. Also known as "perfect rhyme," a rhyme in which the final vowel and consonant sounds are the same, as in "rhyme" and "crime." Homophones (such as "die" and "dye") are sometimes included in discussions of exact rhyme. Contrast with inexact or imperfect rhyme, eye rhyme, half rhyme, or slant rhyme.

EXODUS. The last piece of a Greek tragedy, including or following the final choral ode.

EXPLICATION. A detailed analysis of a piece of prose or poetry, one which attempts to account for the meaning and function of all of the elements of the text.

EXPOSITION. The early portion of a play or story's narrative structure in which the characters and situations are introduced. Exposition is also used to refer to any parts of a narrative that provide background information necessary to understanding the story.

EXPRESSIONISM. A style of art or literature, particularly associated with early twentieth-century Europe, in which the artist or writer focuses upon the expression of his or her internal feelings and emotions. Expressionist literature emphasizes the psychological and emotional aspects of the text.

EXTENDED METAPHOR. A sustained metaphor that is elaborated over the course of an entire stanza or poem.

EXTENDED SIMILE. A sustained comparison between two things, using "like" or "as" to draw the connection.

EYE RHYME. Words that give the appearance of rhyming when in print, but that are pronounced slightly differently, as in "bury" and "fury." Contrast with exact rhyme.

FABLE. A legendary tale usually including animals as characters, who display and represent human foibles, and often having a moral or instructional aspect to the telling. Fables are often humorous, and the animals often take on stylized traits—the tricky fox and the clever rabbit.

FAIRY TALE. A tale that constructs a world of the imagination often with ancient settings and/or characters of either royal or peasant background interacting. Many of the old fairy tales were transmitted orally before they were collected and written down. These stories usually contain magical elements, including supernatural creatures, and suggest a world where anything but the ordinary is likely to happen.

FALLING ACTION. In the plot of a narrative the action rises to a particular point (a climax) and then begins to fall to the inevitable conclusion. (Also referred to as the fourth part of plot structure.)

FALLING METER. Poetry includes regular beats that are divided into feet which include accented and unaccented syllables. Falling meter occurs in trochaic and dactylic meters when a foot ends with an unaccented syllable or two unaccented syllables. Trochaic: fearsome. Dactylic: tragedy.

FANTASY. A fantasy must have magic and magical characters, and these characters must find themselves in amazing and imaginative situations. The stories often unfold in worlds far away or long ago, and the characters often find themselves doing and experiencing things quite impossible in the ordinary world.

FARCE. A play that includes the boisterous and even crude types of action that happen when characters indulge in horseplay and sexual humor. Characters usually speak in colloquial terms and may even knock one another about and tumble down with and upon one another.

FEMININE RHYME. In poetic metrical feet, a foot that ends in an unaccented syllable is said to have feminine meter. Feminine rhyme occurs when two lines with feminine meter rhyme: Today comedy, tonight tragedy.

FICTION. A narrative shaped or made (from the Latin *ficio*, to shape or make) from the author's imagination. Parts of a fictional story, novel, or drama may refer to factual reality, but the story and characters arise from the musings of the creator.

FIGURATIVE. Referring to the use of figures of speech, that is, language that explains through metaphors or similes, comparing one thing to another in order to enhance or underscore the meaning.

FIGURES OF SPEECH. An image that relies on the comparative imagination of the reader or listener, e.g., cold as ice, mad as a hornet.

FIRST PERSON NARRATIVE. Literary works appear in a variety of voices. The speaker may be a master narrator who tells the story from outside of the characters' worlds, or the speaker may know about the characters' thoughts but still not be in the story him or herself. Finally, the first person narrative speaks from the point of view of one character in the narrative. That person has complete control of the line of the narrative. Readers are dependent on the point of view of that narrator and must either trust or suspect the speaker throughout the narrative.

FIXED FORM. Poetic form may be either open or fixed. Fixed forms are those in which the poet decides to follow a particular form both for the effect on the reader and for the challenge of expressing the meaning through a controlled rhythm and rhyme scheme.

FLASHBACK. An interruption in the line of the narrative which occurs when a character suddenly remembers a past event so vividly that it takes over the line of action for a time. Flashbacks are used in both novels and film to enhance the story line or to add information that is necessary to the plot of the work. Often in stories of war or conflict, the character will suddenly find him or herself out of time and into an episode of memory. This memory may explain something in the current action or something in the motivation of the character.

FLAT CHARACTER. A character who usually carries the action of a narrative without adding emotional insight or plot development. E. M. Forster coined the term to describe a character with few traits. The parlor maid in a play or the sheriff in a cowboy movie may be a flat character if she or he is there merely to facilitate the scene.

FLEXIBLE THEATER. Also called experimental theater and sometimes referred to as a black box. The theater is small, often with space for 100–200 persons in the audience, often providing flexible seating and space, allowing for theater in the round, a proscenium arch or fourth wall, thrust staging, or other innovative designs.

FLY-ON-THE-WALL NARRATOR. A narrator who does not enjoy knowledge of the thoughts or feelings of the characters but tells what is seen from a distance. The narrator does not intrude in the action but also does not give emotional insight into the characters except through observation of action. This form of narration demands that the reader follow the narrator in the inferences that are made from the observations, though perhaps the reader may also be encouraged to guess at more than the narrator is revealing.

FOIL. A character that sets off or contrasts with another character maybe serving as a foil or opposite.

FOLK BALLADS. Ballads that were sung by minstrels for hundreds of years before being written down. They are usually in a set ballad form with set rhyme and often with a repeated chorus that begins to draw and hold the listener in the story. Often, ballads exist in several forms since they changed as they were sung and passed on from minstrel to minstrel.

FOLK EPIC. An oral tradition that tells the story of a nation's heroes, the folk epic may have a variety of versions, as do the great Norse and Celtic legends, or the epic may have been recorded so long ago that one author claims the tale as in Homer's *Iliad* and *Odyssey*.

FOLKTALE. A tale that has been passed down by oral tradition, usually not having found a set form in the manner of a fairy tale.

FOOT. In poetry, the means of measuring meter. A foot has either two or three syllables with varying accents.

FORESHADOWING. In a narrative work, events are constructed so that early events will suggest later events in the development of the plot; thus a gun in the first act of a play suggests that someone will be shot in a later act. Without foreshadowing, the reader or audience might not be prepared for the outcome of the narrative.

FORM. Humans want to see order in the world, and authors and their readers or viewers are no exception. Thus a work of art will have some kind of form, whether that be a traditional plot or a more experimental shape. Poetry especially can be constructed in prescribed forms or can take more inventive shapes, but finally the form must be there as an essential part of the telling and understanding.

FORMULA LITERATURE. Literary works fall into genres that have more or less predictable forms. When the form controls the literary work to the extent that the outcome may be predictable or even obvious, the narrative work is considered to be formulaic, e.g., romance novels or westerns or action movies. The formula does not necessarily mean that the work is of less value, but when the formula so dominates the work that the creative element bends to the expected form or shape, then the work may not please the reader.

FOUND POEM. The poet may notice words in an ad or in a conversation, write them down, and then rearrange them into a pleasing and meaningful pattern, thus, a found poem.

FOURTH WALL. A proscenium "wall" located between the curtain and the orchestra used in modern experimental theater to create space outside the stage itself for movement and action.

FRAME NARRATIVE. In a story within a story, the outside story is the frame narrative or the story that enfolds the second narrative. Shakespeare's *Midsummer Night's Dream* tells the story of a group of characters, some of whom in turn are working on their own story, the acting out of the old tale of star-crossed lovers who meet at a wall. In this play the frame is the main narrative, and the internal narrative is entertaining and also linked to the main plot. In other narratives, such as *Heart of Darkness*, the narrator tells his own story and then that of another trip to the same dark place, the second tale being the main narrative of the story.

FREE VERSE. Free verse has no prescribed form or meter, but free verse does have form, often a form found by the poet while composing. Meter and rhythm vary according to the needs and demands of the poem itself.

FREYTAG'S PYRAMID. In 1863 Gustav Freytag (Technique of the Drama) suggested that the five parts of classical drama suggest a pyramid, the rising action peaking at the climax and leading to the falling action; the five are exposition, complication (conflicting elements), climax, catastrophe, and resolution.

GENRE. The literary form that an author chooses to follow, assuming that the reader or viewer will enter into the agreed upon pattern. Thus if a work begins with a rhymed couplet and continues with more couplets, the reader quickly knows that the genre is poetry and reads accordingly. If a playgoer sees a very silly master of ceremonies appear before the curtain, the viewer will assume that the genre is dramatic comedy.

GOTHIC FICTION. The genre of fiction suggesting terror and suspense, often with the use of heavy medieval architecture (also referred to as Gothic). Horace Walpole is credited with the first Gothic novel, *The Castle of Otranto*, in 1764, but the Bronte's and Poe have given the form is true shape.

HAIKU. An unrhymed form derived from Japan, requiring seventeen syllables in a set five, seven, five form and using imagery from nature; the poem often resolves into an observation about nature and meaning in the last line.

HALF-RHYME. In poetic form, the middle of the line and the end of the line rhyme.

HAMARTIA. The Greek word for error, but in drama the word has come to mean something more drastic. For example, Hamlet is too hesitant to think clearly about the political situation in which he finds himself. His hesitance is his fatal error that will lead to his death. This error is not one that the character intends to make but is rather a part of the personality that cannot be evaded or avoided but that will inevitably lead to disaster for all involved.

HARD-BOILED FICTION. The hard-boiled detective of either gender works in a dangerous world where criminals are vicious, deaths are violent, and only a tough character can survive and solve the crime. This world of fiction has evolved in the twentieth century as detective fiction moved from the polite mysteries of the drawing room and the tea parlor to the mysteries of the streets where everyone carries a weapon, and the criminals are most certainly not gentlemen or gentlewomen.

HEAVY-STRESS RHYME. A poetic rhyme involving a spondee (two accented syllables together) or a free-verse form that uses internal emphatic rhyme.

HEPTAMETER. A line of poetry that has seven feet, including seven primary stresses.

HERMENEUTICS. Originally meaning the close study and interpretation of the *Bible,* but in modern criticism it means the principles and systems used to interpret meaning in any text.

HERO/HEROINE. In Greek epics, the leading warriors were called by the term from which hero is derived (heros). The term came to mean the lead character in a narrative or drama, the character who saves the day or who triumphs over adversity. Heroine was used as a feminine term, but current usage applies hero to both genders.

HEROIC COUPLET. A couplet written in iambic pentameter, that is five feet per line, each foot being an iamb, or two beat syllable with the stress on the second syllable. The heroic couplet is a closed couplet, a form that sums up an idea in two lines, but the heroic couplet must follow the metric form as well. Heroic couplets often appear at the end of scenes in Shakespeare's plays to sum up the action of the scene and to send the actor off stage with an exact and effective closing line.

HEURISTIC. From the Greek word for the modern word *eureka* (*heureka*, meaning "I found it"), any method or technique that helps a writer or speaker come up with ideas for a topic or for developing a topic.

HEXAMTER. Poetic lines with six rhythmic feet are said to be written in hexameter.

HIGH COMEDY/VERBAL COMEDY. Comedy that derives its humor from witty and satirical conversations on the parts of the players. The comic wit is often at the expense of human foibles, especially in the Restoration form known as the comedy of manners in which romantic alliances among upper-class partners are played out through witty exchanges between the characters.

HUBRIS. From Greek drama, the term used to describe a character who is laid low by his pride and arrogance, inasmuch as these qualities make anyone unable to see his or her own weaknesses.

HUMOR. Occurs in literature in at least two distinct ways, one being the farcical action where actors or characters buffet one another about and speak in crude and colloquial language. The other form of humor occurs when more observant and reflective characters satirize the foibles of human nature.

HYMN. A song of praise, best shown by the psalms in the Judeo-Christian scriptures or by other poetic songs written in praise.

HYPERBOLE. An overstatement used to stress a point.

IAMB. A poetic foot consisting of at least two syllables. An iamb is a foot with one accented and one unaccented set of syllables: beside or demand are words which demonstrate an iamb. This meter is common in English poetry, for it reflects the form of many English words.

IDENTICAL RHYME. Occurs when the same word is used for a rhyme in a poem.

IDEOLOGY. A system of beliefs and values belonging to an individual or to a group.

IDIOM. A particular means of expression used in a particular language. In American English one stands "in line," but in British English one stands "on line."

IMAGE/IMAGERY. In poetic writing the stress may be expressly on the image that is being described or envisioned. Imagery is also used in fiction to create a particular mood or impression. It is important to keep in mind that these images appeal to the senses, giving an evocative picture of that which is being described.

IMAGISM. This movement in American twentieth century poetry stressed the image above all, leaving behind the poetic forms that emphasized meter and rhyme. The imagists such as Ezra Pound owed much to the Japanese haiku form that stresses one vivid picture.

IMPERFECT FOOT. In poetic meter, a foot is usually one stressed and one unstressed syllable, or one unstressed and one stressed, two unstressed and one stressed, one stressed and two unstressed, or two stressed syllables. Any variation from these five patterns is considered an imperfect foot.

IMPERFECT RHYME. Imperfect rhyme, including slant rhyme, presents a rhyme that is almost a rhyme but not quite so: love/leave.

IMPRESSIONISM. In fiction, impressionism stresses the impact of the external world on the internal world of a character. Flannery O'Connor's intellectual characters often muse over the possible meanings of the various incidents that happen in rural southern Georgia.

IN MEDIAS RES. Literally translated from Latin to mean "in the middle of the circle." It is used to refer to an epic tale that begins in the middle of the story and then reveals the previous incidents. *Star Wars* was a movie series that began in medias res.

INCREMENTAL REPETITION. This poetic term refers to phrases or lines that occur regularly at particular points in a poem as do the choruses in ballads or the repeated lines in some set poetic forms such as a villanelle which repeats lines from the first stanza in set form throughout the poem.

INEXACT RHYME. Like imperfect rhyme, inexact rhyme refers to a poetic variation on the expected rhyme: heart/hearth; laugh/wrath.

INITIATION STORY. A story that provides the first experience of a person, usu- ally young, who faces a great life experience for the first time, especially death, sex, or religious doubt and faith. James Joyce's collection of stories, *Dubliners*, includes these three types of initiation stories.

INTERIOR MONOLOGUE. In fiction, the place where a character muses over a problem or issue internally. This musing is written out in the voice of the character but is not spoken to another character.

INTERNAL ALLITERATION. Within the lines of a poem, vowels or consonants will be repeated so that the internal alliteration will strike the reader's or listener's ear almost unaware: the slippery snake hissed softly.

INTERNAL RHYME. Within the line of a poem, words will rhyme, affecting the ear more than the rhythm, as does a rhyme at the end of a line: with laugh the gaff was gone.

INTERTEXTUALITY. Texts constantly refer back to other texts, even when one text does not quote another. Speech and writing are full of references to well known stories or to the Bible or Shakespeare. Writers like the poet T. S. Eliot use intertextuality purposefully to emphasize meaning; at the end of his poem "Little Gidding" he quotes Dame Julian of Norwitch, "And all shall be well and/All manner of things shall be well," but he does not reference the quote, assuming that his intended reader will know and understand the reference. Cited references demonstrate intertextuality as well, showing the relationship between the text being written and earlier writers on the subject.

IRONY. Occurs in a literary work when the text operates on at least two levels of meaning. Dramatic or tragic irony occurs when the audience has information that the characters do not, as in *Romeo and Juliet* when the audience knows that Juliet is not dead but Romeo thinks she is. Situa- tional irony occurs when the story turns out to be the opposite of the expected as in *The Open Window* in which the woman telling the story to the visitor has created a false story that will shock the visitor when the truth is known. Cosmic irony occurs when the character can do nothing to change the fate that is prepared, and verbal irony occurs when the words spoken are the opposite of the meaning intended.

ITALIAN SONNET. The Italian or Petrarchen sonnet consists of an octet (eight lines) of iambic pentameter (five feet of unaccented and accented sylla- bles) which presents the argument or dilemma and a sextet (six lines) that answer the argument or sorts out the dilemma. The lines are rhymed aaba/aaba and cdecde or cdcdcd.

KINETIC IMAGERY. Imagery in motion; thus a poem or story will show a vivid image in action.

LIMERICK. A short form of poetry including five anapestic lines (two unaccented and one accented syllables) rhymed aabba. Lines one, two, and five have three feet, and lines three and four have two feet.

LINE. In drama, refers to words spoken by a particular character. In poetry, a line is one specific line of poetry that can be either metric or set off in free verse for emphasis.

LITERARY BALLAD. A narrative poem written in calculated imitation of the form and style of traditional, anonymous ballads. Unlike traditional ballads, a literary ballad is not sung; it is written for sophisticated readers.

LITERARY EPIC. A careful, conscious emulation in writing by an individual author of earlier oral folk epic. Literary epics, such as Virgil's *Aeneid* or Milton's *Paradise Lost*, frequently compare the present to the glorious past

LITOTES. An indirect affirmation, usually understated, made by the denial of its opposite, such as "I was not a little hungry" to mean "I was very hungry."

LOCAL COLOR. The use in fiction of distinctive though typically superficial regional material intended to provide realistic background. Regional particularities can be expressed in specific types of setting, dialect, dress, custom or habit.

LOW COMEDY/PHYSICAL COMEDY. Characterized by boisterous activity or clownish behavior without intellectual appeal. Low comedy attempts to incite laughter by employment of jokes, gags, or slapstick humor.

LYRIC. A short, emotionally expressive poem by a single speaker. Commonly written in the first person, lyric poetry is frequently emotional, highlighting personal moods, thoughts, feelings, perceptions, and states of mind. Lyric typically evokes a songlike or musical quality. In ancient Greece, "lyric" was sung to the accompaniment of a lyre.

MADRIGAL. Short, secular song, typically dedicated to love or pastoral themes, arranged in counterpoint for several voices without accompaniment. The madrigal originated in Italy during the fourteenth century and triumphed in England during the Elizabethan period.

MAGIC REALISM. Contemporary narrative that combines mundane events and descriptive details with fantastic and magical elements in a realistic framework. Though usually associated with Latin American fiction, magic realism has blossomed into an international trend.

MALAPROPISM. The mistaken, comic use of a word in place of another with which it shares a close resemblance. The inaccurate, inappropriate word choice derives from confusion between the two words. The term derives from the character Mrs. Malaprop in *The Rivals* (1775) by Richard Brinsley Sheridan.

MASCULINE RHYME. Rhyme consisting of single stressed syllables or of stressed final syllables in polysyllabic words.

MEDITATION. A contemplative essay or sermon.

MELODRAMA. A popular form of theater that features stereotyped characters, such as villains, heroes, and young lovers, engaged in sensational events, intrigue, and action. Melodrama presents suspenseful plots centered on exaggerated conflicts between good and evil. The term is often employed pejoratively to connote a lack of psychological depth and an excess of emotional excitement.

METAFICTION. A type of fiction that renounces the illusion of verisimilitude to explore or comment on, in a self-conscious and self-referential manner, its own fictional nature. Repudiating realism, metafiction concentrates on the role of author and reader in the creation and reception of fiction.

METAPHOR. A figure of speech, not meant to be factually true, in which one thing is compared or substituted for something else. Although the two things are not identical, they are associated in language to emphasize a similarity between them.

METER. A regular, recurring rhythm, or pattern of stresses and pauses, in lines of verse.

METONYMY. A figure of speech which substitutes the name of one thing with that of another with which it is closely associated in common experience. The use of the "White House" or "Oval Office" to refer to the United States presidency is a familiar example.

MIME. A non-literary performance that involves acting with movement and gesture, but without any words.

MIMESIS. Imitation or mimicry intended to represent or reproduce reality.

MINIMALISM. A form of contemporary fiction written in an austere style with a severe restriction of content and setting, such as the work of Raymond Carver.

MISE EN SCÈNE. French term referring to the elements of a dramatic production including costume, scenery, lighting, etc. In cinema, the term refers more specifically to the arrangement of action in front of the camera.

MONOLOGUE. A long speech by one person. In drama, the monologue provides the spoken thoughts of a single character. In fiction, an interior monologue can similarly represent the thoughts, not the actual spoken words, of a character.

MONOMETER. A verse line with one metrical foot.

MONOSYLLABIC FOOT. A unit of meter with a single syllable.

MOOD. The atmosphere or tone of a literary work, conveyed through diction, characterization, and setting.

MORALITY PLAY. A form of religious drama popular in Europe during the fifteenth and sixteenth centuries consisting of moralized allegories. Featuring a variety of personifications, morality plays showcase the struggle for the Christian soul and communicate simple messages of salvation.

MOTIF. Any element that is repeated and developed throughout a narrative. Motif also refers to an element that recurs in many different literary works. Motifs encompass a wide variety of possible elements such as image, idea, situation, action, incident, or theme.

MOTIVATION. The explicit or implicit reason provided for the actions of a character. In drama or fiction, motivation defines what a character desires.

MULTICULTURALISM. In literary studies, the attention to work produced by or about cultural "minorities."

MYSTERY PLAY. A popular, religious medieval play on biblical themes.

MYTH. Traditional, anonymous story derived from oral tradition usually involving supernatural or heroic figures. Adopting a cosmic perspective, myths offer accounts of origins of human, social, and natural phenomena in boldly imaginative terms. It is believed that the fictional narratives of myth embody the popular ideas, values, and belief systems of cultures that create them.

MYTHOPOEIC. A term employed to describe writing that uses myth as a source or that bears a strong resemblance to myth especially in subject matter.

NARRATIVE. The ordered account of a true or fictitious event, or of connected events. Narrative selects and arranges the recounting of these events in a particular sequence.

NARRATIVE BALLAD. A common form of narrative poetry.

NARRATIVE POEM. A class of poem that tells a story.

NARRATIVE STRUCTURE. See "plot."

NARRATOR. The voice or character who relates the story of the narrative. The narrator is different than the author. The degree of participation, perspective, and personality of the narrator varies greatly though the narrator generally provides information and commentary on other characters and events.

NATURALISM. An extreme, deliberate form of realism in fiction or drama in which human characters are inevitable products or passive victims of the natural or social environment or of a particular genetic inheritance. Writers promoting naturalism strove for precise, objective recording of reality capable of demonstrating laws of causality, and aspired to scientific status for their researched, detailed accounts of behavior.

NEAR RHYME. See "slant rhyme."

NEOCLASSICAL COUPLET. Due to its popularity during the Neoclassical Period (a.k.a. the Augustan Age), the neoclassical couplet is another name for a heroic couplet (two successive rhyming lines of iambic pentameter).

NEOCLASSICAL PERIOD. See "Augustan Age."

NEW COMEDY. In ancient Greece, a form of comedy developed between 400–300 B. C. E. New comedy, frequently associated with Menander, is witty and offers unexpected plot twists.

NOVEL. Extended fictional prose narrative of book length. As a genre, the novel is enormously open and flexible, admitting innumerable exceptions. The novel is distinguished from the short story by its greater number of characters, variety of scenes, and span of time covered.

NOVELLA. Novel or narrative story of intermediate length, longer than a short story but less complex than a novel.

OBJECTIVE CORRELATIVE. The external expression of an interior mood or feeling by the deliberate use of a specific object, scene, or event to evoke a particular emotion.

OBJECTIVE POINT OF VIEW. The dramatic third person point of view, when the narrator reports on events and speech, but does not comment on the thoughts of other characters.

OCCASIONAL POEM. A poem expressly written for or inspired by a specific, typically significant, event.

OCTAMETER. A verse line with eight metrical feet.

OCTAVE. An eight line stanza. Octave indicates the first eight verse line section of sonnets.

OCTOSYLLABIC COUPLET. A type of couplet with eight syllables per line.

ODE. A formal, elaborate lyric poem of exalted style and serious, elevated tone.

OEDIPUS COMPLEX. Term used to describe child's attraction to the parent of the opposite sex; applied most frequently to the attraction of male children to a mother figure, often including overtones of jealousy directed at the father.

OFF RHYME. See "Inexact rhyme."

ONE-ACT PLAY. A shorter dramatic work, most one-act plays take place in a single location, focus on a limited number of characters, and depict a single, powerful incident. Like a short story or a poem, the characterization, setting, and themes must be presented efficiently and, consequently, one-acts sometimes seem less subtle than longer plays.

ONOMATOPOEIA. The attempt to label a thing by forming a word from sounds associated with it.

OPEN FORM. Free verse without any formal scheme including meter, rhyme, or stanza pattern.

ORCHESTRA. In classical Greek drama, the orchestra was the space separating the audience and the players on the stage. The chorus would perform in this space.

ORGANIC FORM. A concept that equates literature to living organisms in so far as both, it is believed, are created by a natural growth process. Value is placed on the entire literary work itself, whereby the "whole" exceeds the "sum" of its parts.

ORGANIC UNITY. Belief in the indissoluble synthesis of form and content in a literary work.

OXYMORON. A condensed paradox combining two contradictory terms, such as bittersweet.

PANTOMIME. Dramatic entertainment employing gesture, posture, and facial expression without speech to convey meaning, mimic action, and express feeling.

PARABLE. Brief, usually allegorical, tale intended to teach a moral or lesson. Typically the moral is only implied and consequently open to different interpretations.

PARADOS. In classical Greek drama, the section of the play that allowed the chorus to enter and comment on the events described in the prologue.

PARADOX. A statement or expression playing on words that initially seems self-contradictory, but which provokes reflection on ways or contexts in which it might seem valid. Also called an "oxymoron."

PARALLELISM. Arrangement of words, phrases or similarly constructed clauses or sentences in sequence or in a similar grammatical or structural way that suggests a recognizable correspondence between them.

PARAPHRASE. Restatement of the meaning or sense of a passage in different words often with the intention of clarification.

PARODY. Mocking or exaggerated imitation of distinctive features of a literary work, author, or style for comic, humorous effect.

PARTICIPATORY DRAMA. A form of drama in which audience members are encouraged to join in the action taking place around them, such as the popular *Tony and Tina's Wedding*.

PASTORAL. Derived from the Latin word for "shepherd," the pastoral is a literary mode that celebrates the virtues of rural, agrarian life and love. Also called "idylls."

PATHOS. This Greek word for passions has come to designate any element of a text that evokes sympathetic feelings in the reader or audience.

PENTAMETER. A line of poetic verse that consists of five metrical feet.

PERFECT RHYME. A rhyme in which the rhymed sounds precisely correspond, as in cat/hat, master/plaster, or dedicate/medicate.

PERIPETEIA. As defined by Aristotle in *Poetics* (350 B.C.E.), peripeteia or "peripety" denotes a sudden, often tragic, reversal in the fortunes of a protagonist.

PERSONA. Derived from the Latin word for the mask, the term "persona" refers to any speaker or narrator of a literary text.

PERSONIFICATION. Also known as "anthropomorphism," personification is the attribution of human characteristics to an inanimate object or phenomenon.

PETRARCHAN SONNET. Named after the Italian poet Francesco Petrarca, also known as Petrarch (1304–1374), the Petrarchan or Italian sonnet is a poem that consists of fourteen lines divided into two sections—the eight line octave and the six line sestet. The octave rhymes abbaabba and presents some kind of problem or conflict that is conventionally resolved in the sestet (rhymed cdecde). Also see "Italian sonnet."

PHONETIC. This term applies to transcriptions of words or letters that reflect the sound of spoken language.

PICARESQUE. Originating in fifteenth-century Europe, this literary genre concerns the escapades and misadventures of a wandering rascal ("picaro" is the Spanish word for rogue). Picaresque narratives are generally satiric, episodic, and involve minimal character development. Prominent examples include Le Sage's Gil Blas (1715), Henry Fieldings's Tom Jones (1749), and Voltaire's Candide (1759).

PICTURE POEM. As its name implies, a poem with its lines arranged in the form of a visual image.

PIDGIN. Derived from a Chinese pronunciation of the English word "business," a pidgin is a language heuristically developed by speakers of mutually unintelligible languages for purposes such as commerce and trade.

PLAY. A literary text intended for dramatic performance.

PLOT. The series of events unfolded throughout the course of a narrative. A conventional plot is organized in terms of conflict, climax, resolution, and denouement.

POETIC DICTION. The highly elevated and formalized language that rejects everyday speech in favor of literary devices such as archaism (outmoded words and expressions), epithets (personalized adjectival phrases, as in Alexander the Great), and circumlocution (roundabout or indirect description).

POINT OF VIEW. The perspective from which a story is told. Third-person omniscient and first-person narration are the most common points of view.

PREFACE. A short introduction that explains the purpose or intent of a given literary text.

PROLOGUE. Originally applied to the introductory speech of a Greek tragedy, this term has come to signify the preface of any literary text.

PROPAGANDA. Any literature written with the intention of recruiting its readers to a given social, political, or religious cause.

PROPS. A shortened form of the word "properties," the physical objects used to create the setting or "mise en scène" of a stage drama.

PROSE POEM. A poetic text written in prose form.

PROSODY. The collective formal techniques of poetry, including rhythm and meter, versification, and diction.

PROTAGONIST. The main character—whether hero or anti-hero—of any given literary text.

PSALMS. Worship songs, most particularly the collection of 150 sacred songs of praise collected in the Biblical Book of Psalms.

PULP FICTION. The collective name for sensational crime, adventure, and science-fiction stories printed on cheap "pulp" paper and published in popular magazines of the 1920s, 30s, and 40s.

PUN. A kind of word-play that depends upon identical or similar sounds among words with different meanings.

PYRRHIC. Within the context of poetic technique, a metrical unit with two consecutive unstressed syllables.

QUANTITATIVE METER. A type of meter based on the interplay between "long" and "short" syllables rather than stressed and unstressed syllables. Common to Greek and Latin poetry, quantitative meter concerns the duration of the spoken word.

QUATRAIN. A verse paragraph that consists of four lines.

RAP. This sub-genre of Rhythm and Blues music involves heavily vernacular lyrics spoken with the accompaniment of music. Also known as hip-hop, rap music was developed by African-American artists throughout the 1970s, 80s, and 90s.

REALISM. Originating in eighteenth-century Europe, this literary mode promotes faithful representation of human life and experience. Realist texts reject idealistic and fantastic subject matter in favor of detailed, accurate description and frank treatment of pessimistic themes.

RED HERRING. A distraction meant to divert the reader from a central point or issue. This tactic is particularly relevant for mystery fiction, in which the writer often frustrates the reader's attempt to arrive at a solution.

REFRAIN. Sometimes called the chorus, the refrain is a recurring line or set of lines in a poem or song.

REGIONALISM. Attention to the ways in which geographical location influences or emerges from a given literary text or set of texts. Also see "Local color."

RESOLUTION. The outcome or conclusion of a narrative conflict. A literary work that withholds clear resolution may be termed an "open-ended" narrative.

RESTORATION PERIOD. The interval between 1660–1700, following restoration of the British monarchy. In 1649, Oliver Cromwell successfully led a revolution against King Charles I; these strict Puritan rebels banned theatrical performance, which they considered worldly and decadent. When the monarchy was restored in 1699, King Charles II reopened England's theaters, giving rise to the bawdy "Restoration Comedy."

REVENGE TRAGEDY. Originating in England during the Elizabethan and Jacobean periods, revenge tragedy is a dramatic genre that concerns the protagonist's self-destructive attempts to avenge the death of a loved one. Notable examples include Thomas Kyd's *The Spanish Tragedy*, William Shakespeare's *Hamlet*, and John Webster's *The Duchess of Malfi*.

REVERSAL. A radical change in the situation of a literary character. See also "peripeteia."

RHETORIC. A term used to describe the collective techniques of persuasive writing.

RHYME. Concurrence of similar or identical sounds within different words.

RHYME ROYALE. Invented by Chaucer in the fourteenth century, the rhyme or "rime" royale is a type of poetic stanza which adheres to iambic pentameter and a fixed rhyme scheme of ababccdd.

RHYME SCHEME. The pattern of repeated words-sounds throughout the course of an entire poem or stanza.

RHYTHM. With respect to any literary text, rhythm refers to the sound-patterns created by organization of stressed and unstressed or long and short syllables.

RISING ACTION. With respect to conventional narrative structure, the term rising action describes the series of events that build tension and lead to a climax.

RISING METER. A metrical foot—such as an iamb or anapest—that concludes with a stressed syllable.

RISING RHYME. Also known as a "masculine rhyme," a rising rhyme concludes with a stressed syllable.

ROMANCE. Originally applied to medieval narratives of courtly love, the term has come to designate any adventure story that concerns fantastic situations and exotic settings.

ROMANTICISM. A nineteenth-century European artistic movement that stresses individualism, personal spiritual development, and human interactions with nature. Often favoring lyric poetry, Romantic writers favor intimate autobiographical themes and radical formal innovations.

RONDEL. Related to the rondeau, a rondel is a fourteen line poem that holds only two rhyming sounds. In this type of poem, the same two lines are repeated at the beginning, middle, and end of the poem.

ROUND CHARACTERS. Realistic literary characters distinguished by depth, psychological complexity, and even self-contradiction.

RUN-ON LINE. A line of verse that concludes without a natural pause or "caesura." This disjunction between syntax and versification often creates a feeling of anxiety or discomfort.

SATIRE. A literary text that uses comedy toward the end of derision.

SCANSION. The process of determining a poem's rhythmic pattern through recognition of stressed and unstressed syllables.

SCENE. Either the physical set of a play or one of the discrete narrative units that comprises an act in a play.

SELECTIVE OMNISCIENCE. Applies to a narrator that reveals only the perspective of a single character.

SELF-REFLEXIVITY. Most pronounced in metafiction, the quality of self-awareness in a literary text. A self-reflexive text underscores and celebrates its own status as a work of fiction.

SENTIMENTALITY. A style of writing that appeals to human sympathy and emotion rather than reason. This literary mode originated in eighteenth-century England; notable examples include Oliver Goldsmith's *The Vicar of Wakefield*, Susanna Rowson's *Charlotte Temple*, and Harriet Beecher Stowe's *Uncle Tom's Cabin*.

SESTET. The last six lines of an Italian sonnet. This conclusive stanza conventionally offers a resolution or response to the problem posed by the poem's first eight lines, which are known as the octave.

SESTINA. A thirty-six line poem that consists of three stanzas: six sestets and a final three-line "envoy." The sestina form also requires that the six words found at the end of the first sestet's lines variously recur at the end of the following sestet's lines and in the envoy.

SET. The physical elements that represent the setting of a dramatic production.

SETTING. The time and place in which a narrative takes place.

SHAKESPEAREAN SONNET. The Shakespearean or English sonnet consists of three quatrains and a conclusive couplet; its most common rhyme scheme is abab/cdcd/efef/gg. In contrast to the octave/sestet structure of the Italian, the Shakespearean form posits a thematic break between the twelfth and thirteenth lines of the poem. Also see "English Sonnet."

SHAPED VERSE. A poem printed in such a way that its visual shape reflects its content.

SHORT STORY. A work of prose-fiction that consists of 15,000–20,000 words.

SIGNIFYIN'(G). Within various African-American communities, "signifyin'(g)" represents the practice of appropriating, parodying, and otherwise transforming cultural elements of the dominant or mainstream group. African-American slaves, in particular, found signifyin'(g) a valuable form of resistance culture.

SIMILE. In poetry, a figure of speech whereby two unlike objects are compared to each other with the word *like* or *as*, e.g., "My mistress' eyes are nothing like the sun."

SITUATIONAL IRONY. A type of irony in which an action differs markedly from audience expectations, resulting in surprise and sometimes discomfort. Herman Melville uses situational irony in *Benito Cereno*, for example, as readers discover at the end of the novella that the reality of the situation is the complete opposite of their (and the protagonist's) perceptions.

SKENE. A wooden structure used by actors in fifth century B.C.E. Greek dramas, it typically represented a palace or temple. The skene was located in the back of the stage, allowing the actors to switch costumes when changing roles.

SLANT RHYME. Also referred to as near rhyme, in slant rhyme the sound of the words is nearly alike. This is because such rhymes share the same vowel sound but have different consonant sounds, e.g., scored and word.

SOLILOQUY. A speech given by a character in a play revealing the character's state of mind or motivation.

SONNET. Meaning little sound or song, one of the most popular poetic forms, particularly for poems dealing with love. It is comprised of fourteen lines written in iambic pentameter. Also see "Italian Sonnet" and "English Sonnet."

SPEAKER. In poetry, the speaker refers to the voice of the poem, the self or persona created by the author.

SPECTACLE. In drama, a scene often included for its spectacular effect.

SPENSERIAN STANZA. A form created by Edmund Spenser for *The Faerie Queen*, comprised of nine lines, the first eight written in iambic pentameter, and the ninth written in iambic hexameter.

SPONDEE. The spondee in poetry is composed of a metric foot of two accented syllables, often created for emphasis, e.g., "oh joy!"

STAGE BUSINESS. In drama, refers to any nonverbal action intended to capture the audience's attention and reveal the feelings of a character.

STAGE DIRECTIONS. In the text of a play, the directions that represent the playwright's view of the positions of the actors on the stage and their physical expressions.

STANZA. The basic unit of a poem typically comprised of two or more lines. A stanza operates much as the paragraph does in prose.

STATIC CHARACTER. A character who does not grow or change throughout a narrative.

STEREOTYPE. An unrealistic character based on assumptions about common traits of a certain group (e.g., women, homosexuals, Asians). Tom in Harriet Beecher Stowe's *Uncle Tom's Cabin*, for example, is a stereotype of the long-suffering, docile African slave.

STOCK CHARACTER. A kind of character, usually one-dimensional, appearing regularly in certain types of literature: the wicked stepmother in fairy tales, for example.

STREAM-OF-CONSCIOUSNESS TECHNIQUE. A technique in modern fiction designed to approximate the uncensored, disorganized flow of thought running through the mind of a character. Two of the most notable examples of the technique are James Joyce's *Ulysses* and William Faulkner's *The Sound and the Fury*.

STRESS. In poetry, the emphasis given a syllable often for metrical, or musical, purposes, e.g., *pro*ject and pro*ject* are different words depending on the stress and part of speech.

STROPHE. In poetry, strophe often refers to a stanza that does not have a regular metrical or rhythmic pattern.

STRUCTURE. Pertaining to any genre, the structure of a work refers to the arrangement of its elements.

STYLE. The term used to capture an author's way of expressing. Style is conveyed through the author's use of language, such as diction, syntax, metaphor and other figurative language.

SUBJECT. Refers to what a literary work is about, as distinct from its meaning.

SUBPLOT. A secondary plot within a larger story, normally related to and often reflective of the main plot.

SUMMARY. The summary of a work captures its main idea and the subtopics that develop the idea. Summaries come in various forms and lengths.

SURREALISM. The movement in literature and art founded by the poet Andre Breton in the early twentieth century. This movement attempted to capture the deepest recesses of the unconscious and dream-life through imagery that explored, as described by Arthur Rimbaud, "the reasoned disorder of the senses." For example: "Chicago/The trams make a noise like doughnut batter/dropped in oil."

SUSPENSE. The tension and anticipation that develops in the audience with regard to the plot, usually focusing on what will happen to the main character.

SYLLABIC VERSE. Poetry in which an established number of syllables in a line is repeated in subsequent lines, e.g., "Do not go gentle into that good night . . . Though wise men at their end know dark is right."

SYMBOL. A symbol in a work of art is an element that stands for something beyond its literal meaning in the text. It embodies an idea, such as the way in which the white whale in *Moby-Dick* is invested with meaning.

SYMBOLIST MOVEMENT. A literary movement that began in France during the late nineteenth century with writers such as Charles Baudelaire and Paul Verlaine, focusing on the mysteriousness of life, and relying on suggestion and symbol rather than explicitness and description.

SYNECDOCHE. A synecdoche is a figure of speech in which a part signifies the whole or the whole signifies the part, e.g., in the phrase "All hands on deck," hands stand for people.

SYNESTHESIA. From the Greek, a term meaning "perceiving together." The experience of two or more senses stimulated simultaneously when only one of them is being addressed; for example, "seeing" a color while hearing an actual sound (visualizing the color blue while hearing the Blues played on instruments).

SYNESTHESIS. In literature, refers to the description of one kind of sense in terms of another, such as "sweet as moonlight."

SYNOPSIS. A summary of the main points of an artistic work. In a short story, novel, or play, it relates the main plot line.

SYNTAX. Syntax refers to the way words are put together in sentences. The syntax of a sentence can make significant contributions to an author's style, e.g., "Ask not what your country can do for you . . . ."

TERCET. In poetry, a three line stanza, each line ending in the same rhyme. For example:
> Whenas in silks my Julia goes,
> Then, then, methinks, how sweetly flows
> That liquefaction of her clothes.

TERMINAL REFRAIN. A terminal refrain is that which appears at the end of each stanza of a poem, such as the "Nevermore" refrain in Poe's "The Raven."

TERZA RIMA. A three-line stanza in which one rhyme is used in the first and third lines and the rhyme in the second line is used in the first and third lines of the next stanza. It is also referred to as an overlapping or interlocking rhyme scheme, e.g.,
> I have been one acquainted with the night.
> I have walked out in rain—and back in rain.
> I have outwalked the furthest city light.
> I have looked down the saddest city lane,
> I have passed by the watchman on his beat
> And dropped my eyes, unwilling to explain.

TETRAMETER. In poetry, a meter consisting of four metrical feet, e.g., "Had we but world enough, and time,/This coyness, lady, were no crime . . . ."

THEME. In poetry, fiction, or drama, the theme is the dominating idea in a work. For example, one might say that the theme of *Romeo and Juliet* is the problem of star-crossed love.

THESIS. Associated mainly with the essay, the thesis represents the writer's main idea or attitude toward the subject of the writing.

THRUST STAGE. In theatre, a thrust stage is a stage where the audience is seated on three sides of the acting area.

TONE. Tone signifies the mood of a work of literature. The mood may be ironic, sad, joyful, or pensive.

TRAGEDY. A drama in which the main characters suffer a catastrophic end for the purpose of arousing pity on the part of the audience. Often a tragedy involves the downfall of a person of great significance.

TRAGIC FLAW. In tragedies, the tragic flaw represents the defect in the hero that is the cause of his downfall.

TRAGIC IRONY. A tragic irony is that which conspires against the hero in spite of his best efforts to avoid his fate.

TRAGICOMEDY. A play that uses the elements of a tragedy, but ends happily, such as in Shakespeare's *The Merchant of Venice.*

TRILOGY. A trilogy is a long literary work in three parts, each part standing on its own. William Faulkner's *The Hamlet, The Town,* and *The Mansion* are referred to as The Snopes Trilogy.

TRIMETER. In poetry, a meter consisting of three metrical feet. For example:

> The idle life I lead
>
> Is like a pleasant sleep,
>
> Wherein I rest and heed
>
> The dreams that by me sweep.

TRIOLET. A French poetic form of eight lines and using only two rhymes. The first two lines are repeated as the last two lines. Here is a playful example of this lyric form:

> Easy is the triolet,
>
> If you really learn to make it!
>
> Once a neat refrain you get,
>
> Easy is the triolet.
>
> As you see!—I pay my debt
>
> With another rhyme. Deuce take it,
>
> Easy is the triolet,
>
> If you really learn to make it!

TRIPLE RHYME. A triple rhyme occurs when the rhyming stressed syllable is followed by two unstressed syllables, e.g., "meticulous" and "ridiculous."

TROCHEE. A foot comprised of a stressed syllable followed by an unstressed syllable. Here is an example of an unrhymed trochaic:

> There they are, my fifty men and women
>
> Naming me the fifty poems finished!
>
> Take them, Love, the book and me together:
>
> Where the heart lies, let the brain lie also.

UNDERSTATEMENT. A figure of speech making something appear less important or true than it really is. Understatement is used to intensify meaning of a statement, as well as for the purposes of irony, sarcasm, or humor. It is the opposite of hyperbole., e.g, "Nor are thy lips ungraceful, Sire of men, / Nor tongue ineloquent."

UNITIES. The unities refer to the qualities of good plots, which possess unity of action, time, and place. Unity of action adheres to a sense of cause and effect inevitability. Unity of time adheres to the natural cycle of twenty-four hours. Unity of place adheres to consistency of location.

UNIVERSAL SYMBOL. The notion that a literary work may have some organizing principle, by virtue of its symbolism, to which all parts are related.

UNRELIABLE NARRATOR. A narrator whose judgment cannot be trusted by the reader, either because of the narrator's naivete, prejudices, emotional state, or mental age. In Eudora Welty's "Why I Live at the P.O.," for example, Sister's emotional instability, coupled with her hatred of her family, makes her an unreliable narrator.

UTOPIA. From the Greek word meaning "no place," a type of fiction that describes an ideal—or utopian—world.

VERBAL IRONY. A figure of speech in which the implied meaning of something differs from the literal meaning, such as in a sarcastic remark.

VERISIMILITUDE. Pertains to the qualities that make a work of fiction true to life. A work achieves verisimilitude when events, characters, situations, and places are plausible to the reader.

VERS LIBRE. A Latin term meaning free verse, or poetry without any consistent, fixed form or pattern.

VERSE PARAGRAPH. A verse paragraph appears in a poem lacking stanzaic form, that is, the lines are not grouped together within a regular, recurring pattern.

VILLANELLE. A nineteen-line poetic form in six stanzas. It uses only two rhymes and repeats two of its lines according to a set pattern.

VOICE. Refers to the attitude of the author as conveyed through the style or tone of the speaker in a work of literature.

WELL-MADE PLAY. A term that applies to the logical inevitability within so-called problem plays, farces, or comedies of manners.

A Thumbnail Sketch of Western Theater History

THE HISTORY OF DRAMA is rich and complex, and scholars continue to provide us with new insights into dramatic texts, theatrical performances, theaters themselves, and even changing audiences. This thumbnail sketch of theater history seeks only to introduce key events and terms necessary for your introduction to Western drama.

Ancient Greek and Roman Drama

According to the Greek philosopher Aristotle, drama arose from the rituals honoring Dionysus, the god of wine and agriculture, who served as the patron god of the Greek stage. Ancient Greek playwrights such as Aeschylus, Sophocles, and Euripides wrote their plays to be performed and judged at yearly festivals in honor of Dionysus. Audiences in the thousands would watch these tragedies and comedies in open-air theaters that look much like today's outdoor sports stadiums. The audience looked down on the **orchestra**, which was the space between the audience and the players on stage. In the orchestra, the **chorus** of about ten to fifteen members would perform. The chorus members, all men, would comment through highly stylized **odes** on the actions performed on stage by the actors. The productions in ancient Greece were not lifelike: there were likely no realistic props or scenery, there were only two or three actors performing all of the roles. Each of the actors was male, even if playing a female role; all wore large masks that identified their roles. Most Greek drama was divided into parts: the **prologue** provided the background of events that would unfold on stage; the **parados** allowed the chorus to enter and comment on the events described in the prologue; the **episodes** developed the central conflict of the play, and the accompanying choral odes allowed the chorus to again comment on the action taking place; and the **exodos** concluded the play by resolving the conflict and allowing the actors to leave the stage. The choral odes, moreover, were recited or sung by the chorus as they moved across the orchestra in one direction (in the **strophe**) and then back across the stage (in the **antistrophe**).

The Romans adopted many of the devices of Greek drama, including the generic divisions of **tragedy** and **comedy**. Though Roman drama is rarely performed today, work by the tragic playwright Seneca and the comic playwrights Plautus and Terence had a profound influence on future playwrights such as Shakespeare.

The Middle Ages

During the Middle Ages, drama centered on religious spectacles performed at local pageants, in the courtyard or on the steps of churches, or by traveling companies who performed from their pageant wagons. This type of theater was frequently staged as an endeavor to teach audiences important theological lessons. **Mystery plays** were one form of medieval theater. These plays, such as the *Second Shepherd's Play*, offered audiences dramatized scripture in which characters acted out Biblical stories. Similarly Christian in theme, another type of medieval drama—the **morality play**—presented dramatized **allegory**. An allegory can be read simultaneously on a literal level, in which characters and events can be easily recognized, and on an allegorical level, in which characters and events represent more abstract moral, political, philosophical, and religious concepts. Rich with examples of moral instruction and church teachings about the sacraments, especially penance, *Everyman* in its depiction of one man's journey toward death provides the most famous example of a morality play.

The Renaissance

The Renaissance in Europe engendered many changes in drama and dramatic performance, changes that influence theater even today. The broad allegories of medieval mystery and morality plays declined in popularity as many classical tragedies and dramas were rediscovered; these classical comedies and tragedies allowed playwrights a new model from which to draw inspiration. Material changes in theatrical production followed the rise in interest in drama during the Renaissance: for instance, buildings were now created specifically for theatrical performance, and professional theater companies arose throughout Europe. Audience members were still called to use their imaginations because in England, for example, all of the acting roles were performed by men, with young boys often playing the female roles; few sets and props were used; and theaters open to the elements had no artificial lighting. While William Shakespeare remains the most famous of the English Renaissance playwrights, other figures such as Thomas Kyd, Ben Jonson, and Christopher Marlowe also produced important and influential work during this period. In Italy, the **commedia dell'arte** prospered. This zany comedy, rich with familiar and predictable **stock characters**, would be adopted by other countries as well.

Seventeenth- and Eighteenth-Century Theater

During the seventeenth and eighteenth centuries, Europe was rich with playwrights writing **satire**, a type of humorous drama that mocks social institutions and individual human foible. In France, Molière mocked the pretensions of the upper-classes, and English audiences enjoyed the comedies of the female playwright Aphra Behn. In theaters, women now began more regularly to perform female roles, and a host of technological innovations slowly altered the way that audiences watched plays. Drama was now performed in indoor theaters with covered roofs, and productions were illuminated by candlelight so audiences could see not only the action on the stage, but also their fellow audience members. These enclosed theaters placed audiences closer to the stage; consequently, playgoers could respond to a performer's more subtle gestures and expressions. Many productions in these theaters were framed by a **proscenium**, the arch that runs across the front of the stage. Actors also performed for the first time among more realistic scenery, including painted backdrops, stage makeup, elaborate costumes, and relevant props.

Nineteenth-Century Theater

During the nineteenth century, audiences enjoyed the **melodrama**, a popular dramatic form that offered suspenseful plots in which the good hero always triumphed over the evil villain. Melodrama offered audiences plenty of visual **spectacle**—it was not unheard of to see a melodrama with actual horses or a real train placed on stage to enthrall audiences. Meanwhile, writers such as Henrik Ibsen and Anton Chekhov were writing plays informed by **realism**, the first of many innovative dramatic movements that arose during this century. These dramas focused on contemporary life and depicted the everyday struggles of average men and women; they also explicitly engaged with social problems. Realism had a profound effect not only on dramatic form, but also on stage craft. Because it focused so frequently on domestic life, realism sought to reproduce a world on stage that resembled the interior of a middle-class home. Consequently, many productions of realist drama offered audiences a **box set** composed of three flat panels forming connected walls; the **fourth wall** refers to the imaginary fourth wall separating the audience from the action on stage. Like realism, **naturalism** sought to depict the reality of life on stage, but it focused on the darker aspects of humanity; as evident in the work of August Strindberg, these plays advanced the notion that humans were largely powerless in the face of heredity and environment. And as in centuries previous, playwrights such as George Bernard Shaw and Oscar Wilde employed the **comedy of manners** to critique social conventions. Meanwhile, the still popular Gilbert and Sullivan developed the form we now know as **light opera**.

Twentieth- and Twenty-First-Century Theatre

With the advent of the twentieth century, innovations in both dramatic form and theatrical production continued apace. Playwrights began aggressively to dismantle the conventions of the **well made play**, a nineteenth-century dramatic form that relied on clever plotting rather than realistic character development. Architectural improvements also influenced the ways plays were staged, and audiences in the twentieth century were introduced to new seating arrangements and watching plays. These innovations included the **thrust stage**, which projects into the audience, and the **arena stage**, which is placed in the middle of the theater and is surrounded by the audience. Drama began to focus more on the psychology of the characters. As a consequence of technological advances, actors could now convey their feelings through more subtle gestures and expressions. Electric footlights and spotlights, as well as microphones, transformed acting styles. These advances also allowed for innovative special effects. **Expressionism**, for instance, used light and shadow to depict the distortions of a character's interior psychology. This attention to psychology, and its depiction on stage through creative uses of stagecraft, allowed playwrights such as Arthur Miller and Tennessee Williams to add more interiority to their realist dramas.

Drama also began to move aggressively away from realism's quest to mimic real life. Inspired by the philosophical movement of existentialism, **absurdist theater**, represented by playwrights such as Eugène Ionesco, Samuel Beckett, and Edward Albee, offered audiences aggressively non-realistic productions to depict the absurd aspects of human life. Antonin Artaud's **theater of cruelty** deliberately worked to shock its audiences into an awareness of human cruelty and destruction through its aggressive use of light, noise, and spectacle. The German playwright Bertold Brecht also wrote anti-realist drama that he hoped might inspire audiences to think critically about the real world and structures of power. His **epic theater** focused on political and historical themes, but it refused audiences the ability to empathize with the characters on stage. Brecht sought to create an **alienation effect** to prevent audiences from losing themselves in the performance. To keep his audiences thinking critically throughout the play, Brecht provided short scenes with a detached tone. He also exposed the "behind the scenes" artifice of theatrical productions by placing the lighting devices and orchestra in view of the audience.

Innovations offered by absurdist theater, the theater of cruelty, and epic drama have had a profound influence on subsequent twentieth- and twenty-first-century drama. **Documentary theater** employs actual historical documents to weave together a narrative, one frequently performed by a large cast; it has been produced by companies affiliated with the 1930s Federal Theater

Project in depression-era America, as well as by the contemporary playwright and director Moisés Kaufman and his Tectonic Theater Project. The personal **monologues** authored by playwrights such as Eve Ensler, whose *Vagina Monologues* is frequently performed on college campuses, also seek to inspire critical thought among audiences. As well, artists such as Anna Deavere Smith, Laurie Anderson, and Richard Foreman have created work described as **performance art**. This live performance weaves together music, film, spoken word performance, dance and other media.

Since ancient times, drama has worked not only to generate aesthetic pleasure, but also to inspire critical thought among its audiences. But contemporary audiences can sometimes experience the formal innovations of modern political theater couched in the easy pleasures of melodrama. For instance, the popular *Tony and Tina's Wedding* is a form of **participatory drama** in which audience members are encouraged to join in the action taking place around them. This entertainment was ironically inspired in part by **environmental theater**, a form of aggressively political drama which takes place among audience members and sometimes encouraged them to participate in the performance.

Documentation in the Humanities: MLA Style

DOCUMENTATION IS LIKE TRAFFIC SIGNS AND SIGNALS. Everyone in a culture agrees to use them in a certain way so that nobody gets hurt. Communities of readers and writers do the same thing: They agree to identify their sources according to a given set of rules. There are several forms of documentation for particular areas of study and specific journals.

The Modern Language Association of America (MLA) is an international organization of teachers and researchers dedicated to the study and teaching of language and literature. Many humanities departments in schools and colleges as well as a host of journals and magazines require that writers use the MLA style when presenting a manuscript. The details of MLA style are presented in two books: the *MLA Handbook for Writers of Research Papers 7/e* (2009), used mostly by high school and undergraduate college students; and the *MLA Style Manual and Guide to Scholarly Publishing 3/e* (May 2008), used by graduate students, scholars, and professional writers.

MLA Manuscript Format

In addition to the many specifics of preparing a manuscript in MLA style, the following general rules apply.

Page layout:
- Use standard 8-1/2 by 11 paper and standard typeface. Avoid odd typefaces or other unusual variations available with word processing.
- Place name, date, and course information in the upper left-hand corner of the first page; double-space before the centered title.
- Double-space between lines.
- Leave at least one-inch margins.
- Place page numbers in the upper right-hand corner, one half inch from the top of the paper; include your last name before the number for identification.

In the body of the paper:
- Cite sources in the text, not in footnotes or endnotes.
- Don't use punctuation between the author's name and the page number in a citation.
- Cite the page number(s) of direct quotations in in-text citations.

- Indent the first line of each paragraph five spaces.
- Indent quotations more than four typed lines ten spaces; omit the quotation marks.
- Leave one space after all punctuation; MLA allows either a single or a double space after periods or question and exclamation marks.
- Form a dash with two hyphens, using no spaces.

In the list of sources:
- Center the words "Works Cited" on the top of the page.
- List sources alphabetically by author's last name. If there is no author, alphabetize by book or selection title.
- Use hanging indentation (first line flush left against the margin, second and subsequent lines indented five spaces).
- Separate items in a citation (author, title, place and date of publication) with periods.
- If the city of publication is not easily recognizable, add a two-letter abbreviation for the state.

In-Text Citation

The purpose of in-text citations is to tell the reader exactly where to look for the reference being made. The details of the reference will be listed in a Works Cited list at the end of the paper. These in-text citations are to be as simple and clear as possible, giving the reader only what is necessary to know that the information came from another source. If the source is mentioned in the text, only the page number is given. If the source is not mentioned in the text, then the name of the author is mentioned in the citation; if that author is referenced for more than one work, the work in question is identified in the citation or text.

1. AUTHOR NAMED IN TEXT
   If the author is named in the text, only page numbers are given.

   Stephen Jay Gould discusses the power of scientific drawings (18).

2. AUTHOR NOT NAMED IN TEXT
   When the author is not named in the text, the name appears in the notation.

   Deep time appears as a new concept in Lavoisier (Gould 22).

3. TWO OR THREE AUTHORS
   Use only the last names of the authors.

   Scharton and Neuleib claim that professors change when they work with writing centers (65).

4. FOUR OR MORE AUTHORS

All four authors may be named, or author number one and "et al." (Latin for "et alia" which means "and others") may be referenced in the text or in parentheses.

> Duin, Lammers, Mason, and Graves suggest that mentors with much teaching experience will give more help than mentors who have taught little (143).

> Mentors with much teaching experience will give more help than mentors who have taught little (Duin et al. 143).

5. UNKNOWN AUTHOR

The title substitutes for the author's name in the text or in parentheses.

> "The Twin Corbies" is a poem about two crows (119).

6. CORPORATE AUTHOR

A corporate author can be named in either the text or in the parentheses.

> Illinois State University notes that it employs 264 professors (1).

7. TWO OR MORE WORKS BY THE SAME AUTHOR

When two or more works by one author appear on the Works Cited page, either name the work in the text, or include a short form of the title in the parentheses.

> In "The Gift of Insight," Neuleib and Scharton explain the complexities of type preference (197).

If author and shortened form both appear in parentheses, use this form:

> (Neuleib and Scharton, "Insight" 197).

8. A SOURCE QUOTED IN ANOTHER SOURCE

To show that one author is quoting another, use the abbreviation "qtd. in."

> Flower notes that "research in composition shows an alternative picture of how knowledge can be developed" (qtd. in Neuleib and Scharton 54).

9. NOVEL, PLAY, OR POEM

Give the title if not mentioned in text when the work is first referred to, then follow with specific information as listed below.

NOVEL: part or chapter.

> Ged said, "I fear what follows behind me" (*A Wizard of Earthsea* 117: ch. 6).

PLAY: act and scene and line numbers in Arabic numerals.

> "He waxes desperate with imagination," cries Horatio (*Hamlet* 1.4.87).

POEM: refer to the part (if applicable) and line numbers.

"Surely some revelation is at hand," muses Yeats' "The Second Coming" (10).

10. WORK IN AN ANTHOLOGY

Cite the author's name, not the editor's name.

In his essay "On Stories," Lewis observes that "No book is really worth reading at the age of ten that is not equally worth reading at the age of fifty" (100).

11. ENTIRE WORK

Name the author in the text or note in parentheses.

Freire was introduced to North American scholars in *Freire for the Classroom* (Shor).

Works Cited

The new 2008 style manual introduces significant changes in documentation style for college-level and professional publications. Thus Works Cited formats will be considerably different than those used in the past.

The important changes from earlier editions of the manual represented here in this guide include the following:

- The *medium of publication* appears in every works-cited list.
- A simplified on-line source citation format (no URL)
- Volume and issue numbers included for journal citation
- Titles in italics rather than underlined.

Please consult the MLA Web site (www.mla.org) for additional information.

Changes to Works Cited Entries

MLA guidelines divide sources into three types: print, Web, and other common sources. Two new general rules apply to all entries:

1. Include the medium of publication (place where entry was found) in each entry.
   - A book would be *Print*, but an online book would be categorized as *Web*. Publications also appear on *CD*, *Laser disc*, *Performance*, etc.
   - Any citation found online (whatever the original place of publication) is listed as *Web*.
   - The medium of publication is the last item in the citation, but when *Web* is the medium, the last item is the date of publication.

2. Titles of all independently published works are in italics rather than underlined. These include books, plays, CDs, Web sites, television and radio broadcasts, works of art, performances, and recordings. Use regular type and quotations marks for short works such as stories, articles, poems, and chapters or shorter works from larger publications.

Books

1. ONE AUTHOR

   LeGuin, Ursula K. *A Wizard of Earthsea*. New York: Ace, 1968. Print.

2. TWO OR THREE AUTHORS

   Scharton, Maurice, and Janice Neuleib. *Inside/Out: A Guide to Writing*. Needham Heights, MA: Allyn & Bacon, 1992. Print.

3. MORE THAN THREE AUTHORS OR EDITORS

   Lawson, Bruce, et al., eds. *Encountering Student Texts*. Urbana: NCTE, 1989. Print.

4. EDITOR

   Hooper, Walter, ed. *The Letters of C. S. Lewis*. New York: Macmillan, 1979. Print.

5. AUTHOR WITH EDITOR

   Tolkien, J.R.R. *The Tolkien Reader*. Ed. Christopher Tolkien. New York: Ballantine, 1966. Print.

6. UNKNOWN AUTHOR

   Primary Colors. New York: Random House, 1996. Print.

7. CORPORATE AUTHOR

   Illinois State University. *Facts 2008–9*. Normal, IL: Illinois State UP, 2009. Print.

8. TWO OR MORE WORKS BY THE SAME AUTHOR

   Lewis, C. S. *The Lion, the Witch, and the Wardrobe*. New York: Macmillan, 1950. Print.

   ——. *The Magician's Nephew*. New York: Macmillan, 1955. Print.

9. TRANSLATION

   Tolstoy, L. N. *Anna Karenina*. Trans. Rosemary Edmunds. New York: Viking, 1954. Print.

10. WORK IN AN ANTHOLOGY

> Walsh, Chad. "The Reeducation of the Fearful Pilgrim." *The Longing for a Form.* Ed. Peter J. Schakel. Kent, OH: Kent State UP, 1977. 64–72. Print.

Periodicals

11. NEWSPAPER ARTICLE
(signed)

> Wagner, Daniel. "Bank Stress Tests Show Some Banks Need More Funds." *Daily Pantagraph* 7 May 2009: A5. Print. [See below for Web version.]

(unsigned)

> "Honda Motor Recalls Several Models to Fix Ball-Joint Assembly." *Wall Street Journal* 13 May 1999: B14. Print.

12. MAGAZINE ARTICLE
(signed)

> Gould, Stephen Jay. "Capturing the Center." *Natural History* Dec. 1998: 14+. Print.

(unsigned)

> "College Can Give You Grief." *Psychology Today* Oct. 1998: 20. Print.

13. JOURNAL ARTICLE
(with continuous page numbering from issue to issue within a year)

> Fleckenstein, Kristie. "Writing Bodies." *College English* 61 (1999): 281–306. Print.

(with each issue paged separately)

> Becker, Becky K. "Women Who Choose: The Theme of Mothering in Selected Dramas." *American Drama* 6.2 (1997): 43+. Print.
> [note that "6.2" means vol. 6, issue #2]

Other Sources

14. THE BIBLE

> *The New International Bible.* Colorado Springs: International Bible Society, 1972. Print.

(The King James Bible need not be named or italicized. You need only note chapter and verse in parentheses in the text (Matt: 12.1–3). Translations of the Bible other than King James should be identified and italicized.)

15. LETTER TO THE EDITOR

White, Curt. Letter. *The Vidette*. 18 Feb. 1999: 6. Print.

16. PERSONAL OR TELEPHONE INTERVIEW

Kay, Martha. Personal interview. 10 Mar. 1999.

17. RECORD, TAPE, OR CD

Dravs, Markus, Brian Eno, John Hopkins, and Rik Simpson.
Coldplay. *Viva la Vida*. Rec. June 2007-April 2008. Prod.
Parlophone, 17 June 2008. CD.

18. DVD

Twilight. Catherine Hardwicke. Perf. Kristen Stewart and Robert
Pattinson. Summit Entertainment, 21 November 2008. DVD.

Online Sources

These sources include a variety of types of communication: personal e-mail
between persons or among private group members, listservs among several
individuals with common work or interests, or news groups that serve associations or subscribers. The World Wide Web connects the individual to a wider
community, including businesses and other commercial groups. Former citation methods have required more information that is needed to retrieve information. The newest citation format provides adequate information for
retrieving the material. The standard publication information does not
include a URL unless the writer feels it is needed to locate the source.

Standard publication information for all online sources:

1. Name of author, compiler, director, performer, editor, or producer. For
   more than one author or for anonymous works, follow print source
   guidelines. If no author is given, begin the entry with the title.
2. Title of the work. Italicize the title unless it is part of a larger work; in
   that case, enclose it in quotation marks.
3. Title of the overall Web site (in italics) if distinct from item 2.
4. Version or edition of the site, if relevant.
5. Publisher or sponsor of the site. Look for this information at the bottom
   of the Web page. If not available, use *N.P.* (for no publisher).
6. Date of publication (day, month, and year). If no date, use *n.d.*
7. Medium for publication. For all online sources, Web.
8. Date of access (day, month, year).

Format for URL when given:
- Place a period and space after the date of access: the URL is the last item in the entry.
- Enclose the URL in angle brackets, followed by a period.
- Give the complete URL, including the access-mode identifier (*http, ftp,* etc.) Copy and paste the URL for accuracy.
- Break the URL only **after** a slash.
- Do not allow your word processor to insert a hyphen in a URL.

Here is an example of the newspaper article listed above as it would appear if taken from the web. The example also shows how to break the URL if it is used for citation.

> Wagner, Daniel. "Bank Stress Tests Show Some Banks Need More Funds." *Daily Pantagraph.* Pantagraph Publishing Company, 7 May 2009. Web. 9 May 2009. <http://hosted.ap.org/dynamic/stories/U/ US_BANKS_STRESS_TESTS?SITE=ILBLO&SECTION=HOME&T EMPLATE=DEFAULT>.

Sources Found Through Web Sites

19. PROFESSIONAL SITE

(entire online site)

> *The National Writing Project.* The National Writing Project 2008. Web. 4 Mar. 2008.

(part of a site)

> Art Peterson, "The Importance of Resiliency in Reading and Writing." *The National Writing Project.* The National Writing Project, 2009 Web. 29 April 2009.

20. A PERSONAL SITE

> Neuleib, Janice Witherspoon. Home page. Illinois State University, 1 Feb. 2009. Web. 26 Feb. 2009.

21. A BOOK

> Crane, Stephen. *The Red Badge of Courage.* Project Guttenberg. May 2009. Argonne National Laboratory. Web. 5 May 2009.

22. A POEM

> Dickinson, Emily. "A Narrow Fellow in the Grass," *Poetry Archive,* eMule.com, 1 Feb. 2008. Web. 10 March 2009.

23. AN ARTICLE IN A REFERENCE DATABASE

"Word Formation." *American Heritage Book of English Usage.*
Houghton Mifflin, 1996. Web. 5 Mar. 2009.

24. AN ARTICLE IN A SCHOLARLY JOURNAL

Applebee, Arthur N., and Judith A. Langer. "Discussion-Based
Approaches to Student Understanding: Classroom Instruction in
the Middle School Classroom." *American Education Research Journal*
40:3 (2003). American Education Research Association, January
2003. Web. 2 Mar. 2009.

25. AN ARTICLE IN A MAGAZINE

Yeager, Ashley. "Recipe for an Avalanche." *Science News.* Society for
Science and the Public, 2 August 2008. Web. 16 Feb. 2009.

26. A REVIEW

Traister, Rebecca. "Is 'The Sopranos' a Chick Flick?" Rev. of *The
Sopranos TV Series. Salon.* Salon Media Group, 6 Mar. 2004. Web. 8
Mar. 2009.

27. WIKI

"Mona Lisa." *Wikipedia.* Wikipedia Foundation, 2009. Web. 28 April
2009.

28. BLOG

Pinker, Steven. "The Moral Instinct." *The American Journal of
Bioethics.* Bioethics.net, 16 May 2008. Web. 23 April 2009.

29. PODCAST

"Off the Clock Podcast." *NPR.* National Public Radio, 1 Apr. 2009.
Web. 7 May 2009.

30. ONLINE AUDIO OR VIDEO

"Shocking Climate Change Video." *YouTube.* YouTube, 30 March
2009. Web. 26 April 2009.

31. WORK OF ART ACCESSED ONLINE

de Zubaran, Francisco. St. Francis. 2008. Art Links. *Artcyclopedia.*
Web. 4 April 2008.

32. FILM ACCESSED ONLINE

Triumph of the Will. Dir. Leni Riefenstahl. Internet Archive, 1935.
Archive.org. Public Domain. Web. 3 April 2009.